MOON

CAMINO DE SANTIAGO

SACRED SITES, HISTORIC VILLAGES, LOCAL FOOD & WINE

BEEBE BAHRAMI

EUROPA COMPOSTELA
2010

CAMINO DE SANTIAGO

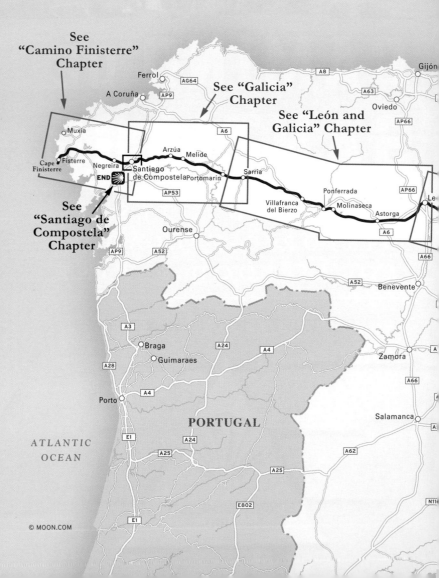

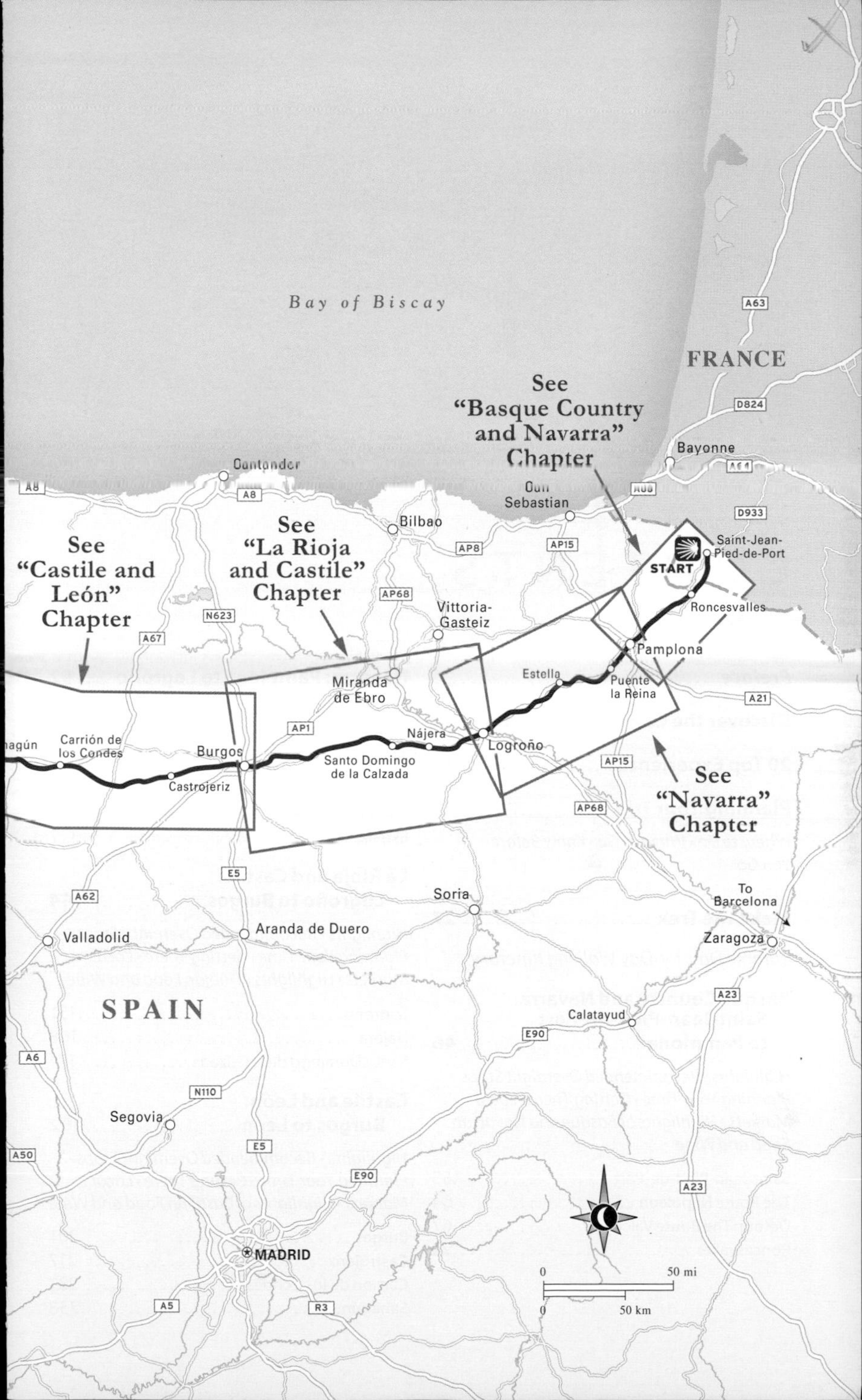

Bay of Biscay

FRANCE

See "Basque Country and Navarra" Chapter

Bayonne

Santander

Bilbao

San Sebastián

Saint-Jean-Pied-de-Port

START

See "La Rioja and Castile" Chapter

Roncesvalles

See "Castile and León" Chapter

Vittoria-Gasteiz

Pamplona

Estella

Puente la Reina

Miranda de Ebro

Sahagún

Carrión de los Condes

Burgos

Nájera

Logroño

Santo Domingo de la Calzada

Castrojeriz

See "Navarra" Chapter

To Barcelona

Soria

Zaragoza

Valladolid

Aranda de Duero

SPAIN

Calatayud

Segovia

MADRID

0   50 mi

0   50 km

CONTENTS

Preface 6

Discover the Camino de Santiago 8

20 Top Experiences 10

Planning Your Trip 22

Where to Go • When to Go • Know Before You Go

Make the Trek 27

Sample Day-by-Day Walking Itinerary

**Basque Country and Navarra:
    Saint-Jean-Pied-de-Port
    to Pamplona** 46

Highlights • Recommended Overnight Stops • Planning Your Time • Getting There • Local Markets • Highlights of Basque and Navarran Food and Wine

Saint-Jean-Pied-de-Port 55
The Route Napoleon 64
Detour: The Route Valcarlos 67
Roncesvalles 74

Navarra: Pamplona to Logroño 92

Highlights • Recommended Overnight Stops • Planning Your Time • Getting There • Local Markets

Pamplona 98
Puente la Reina 121
Estella 127

**La Rioja and Castile:
    Logroño to Burgos** 144

Highlights • Recommended Overnight Stops • Planning Your Time • Getting There • Local Markets • Highlights of Riojan Food and Wine

Logroño 151
Nájera 168
Santo Domingo de la Calzada 174

**Castile and León:
    Burgos to León** 192

Highlights • Recommended Overnight Stops • Planning Your Time • Getting There • Local Markets • Highlights of Castilian Food and Wine

Burgos 201
Castrojeriz 217
Carrión de los Condes 231
Sahagún 238

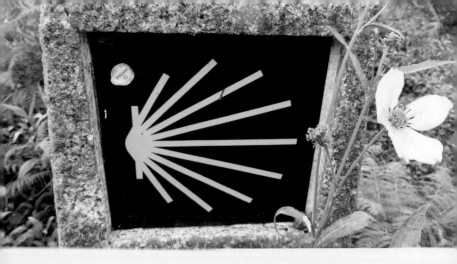

León and Galicia: León to Sarria 252

Highlights • Recommended Overnight Stops • Planning Your Time • Getting There • Local Markets • Highlights of León's Food and Wine

León 260
Astorga................................. 284
Molinaseca 305
Ponferrada............................. 307
Villafranca del Bierzo 322
O Cebreiro 333

Galicia: Sarria to Santiago de Compostela...................350

Highlights • Recommended Overnight Stops • Planning Your Time • Getting There • Local Markets • Highlights of Galician Food and Wine

Sarria 357
Portomarín 369
Melide 382

Santiago de Compostela...........396

Highlights • Planning Your Time • Getting There • Local Markets

Santiago de Compostela................. 398
Day Trip to Padrón 425

Camino Finisterre: Finisterre and Muxía 428

Highlights • Recommended Overnight Stops • Planning Your Time • Getting There • Local Markets

Hospital 439
Finisterre 443
Muxía 457

History 464

Early History • Medieval Era • Early Modern to Modern Era • The Modern Camino

Essentials 475

Before You Go 476
Getting There and Around 477
Packing Checklist 478
20-Day Driving Itinerary 483
The Camino By Bike 484
On the Camino 485
Health and Safety...................... 491
Festivals and Events................... 493
Practical Details 496
Travel Advice.......................... 498
Resources............................. 500
Glossary 502
Spanish Phrasebook.................... 505

Index 507

PREFACE

In my many returns to the Camino since my first trek in 1995, I heard a common lament from secular and religious pilgrims alike: that they were in such a hurry to find a bed, and reliant on guidebooks that did not point out the significance of what they were walking past, that they missed many of the Camino's most meaningful elements.

I wrote this guide to the Camino Francés—the most popular branch of a vast network that crisscrosses Spain, France, Portugal, and really all of Europe, destined for the holy city of Santiago de Compostela in northwestern Spain—to fulfill this desire for context and connection. I set out to answer not only practical questions (where should I stop for lunch?) but also deeper, cultural ones (why do locals in Basque Country hang bundles of thistle on their doors, and what do the Camino's Black Madonnas represent?).

I also know how much pilgrims enjoy food and wine, topics that are glossed over in other Camino guides. In these pages, I've called out my favorite dishes, from succulent fresh-caught seafood to hearty stews, along with the best local restaurants that serve them.

The result is a book that balances crucial practical details with thoughtful insights and enriching experiences. In each chapter you'll find:

Highlights that point out places and experiences that are not to be missed, such as tasting tapas in León's Barrio Húmedo, waking up for sunrise on O Cebreiro mountain, and making a detour to the enigmatic octagonal church of Eunate.

Starting points, and detailed recommendations for how to reach each one, if you (like many pilgrims) aren't able to complete the entire trek.

Recommended overnight stops, chosen either for their ideal location or for an exceptional experience that adds depth to the pilgrim journey, such as sung prayer with the nuns who run the Albergue de Santa María in Carrión de los Condes, or the delicious farm-to-table

dinner at Albergue Vieira in San Martín del Camino.

Route options that help you decide what to do when the trail forks, whether you prefer to stay on a supported section near a highway, or take a quieter, more remote path with fewer cafes and accommodations. This section also alerts you to worthwhile sights that many travelers miss because they are not well marked or require a short detour off the trail.

Local food and wine callouts that highlight regional specialties and the best places to taste them, and a list of **local markets** so you can easily plan your journey around these festive weekly events.

Folklore callouts that describe the sacred traditions that are distinct in each region of the Camino, with a special focus on pagan rituals that have influenced modern Christian traditions. (Many churches that were built over pre-Christian sites retain elements of the older pagan forms. These are fascinating to behold—if you know where to look—and I make sure to note them so that you do.)

I also fold into these pages another aspect I have learned about pilgrimage: It is not only a sacred engagement but also a great adventure. No matter who you are—secular, spiritual, or religious—walking along the Camino's dirt paths, through medieval villages and beautiful wild landscapes, becomes simultaneously a journey of insight and transformation and an exhilarating physical challenge.

The Camino is in many ways the act of reclaiming a sense of wonder and beauty in one's life. It is a great road of transcendence open to all and barred to none; a walking meditation punctuated by churches, chapels, shrines, streams, hills, mountains, rivers, and valleys. More than anything, the Camino is an experience to be savored, not rushed. This book helps you to slow down the journey, so that you discover the Camino at its best.

—Beebe Bahrami

DISCOVER the
Camino de Santiago

The Camino de Santiago is a great adventure, a sacred pilgrimage in the footsteps of millions of others intertwined with an outdoor trek across northern Spain. Leading from the town of Saint-Jean-Pied-de-Port on the border with France, it travels west for 780 kilometers (485 miles), traversing daunting mountains, lush river valleys, sweeping plains, striated vineyards, and rolling hills swaying with wheat to the purported tomb of Saint James the Greater in Santiago de Compostela. And the path doesn't really stop there: It continues all the way to the rugged shores of the Atlantic.

The Camino is a rare chance in the busy world for solitude and self-reflection, even for self-reinvention, while traveling in the company of pilgrims from more than 140 nations and while encountering engaging and generous locals who have lived on and served the Camino for generations. It is a path of strange trail magic, where

solutions are delivered just as you need them, and where someone walking past spontaneously gives the perfect answer to the very question rolling around in your head.

The Camino is also a paradox. When a person becomes a pilgrim—*pèlerin* in French, *peregrino* in Spanish—and temporarily disconnects from normal life to go for a long walk, he or she enters into a deep experience of presence and connectedness on many levels, with nature, with others, and with him- or herself. Many *peregrinos* marvel that the Camino naturally cultivates such a profound experience, and with it, transformation, just by walking.

Officially a Christian pilgrimage that is over 1,200 years old, the Camino is older than this. Humans have long traversed the lands crossed by the Camino, along southwestern France and northern Spain. They left signs—stone tools, painted caves, rock art, dolmens, hilltop settlements, prehistoric roads—and, only later, medieval towns and chapels. You still feel their footsteps as you step along the trail. Some locals claim that there is a special energy in the land itself, a ley line poetically tracing on the earth the path of the Milky Way seen by pilgrims in the night sky. It is a perfect melding of nature and culture, an outdoor adventure and a historic European grand tour.

20 TOP EXPERIENCES

1 Taking your first step on to the Camino in **Saint-Jean-Pied-de-Port's Rue de la Citadelle,** a cobblestone path worn smooth by thousands of pilgrims over 900 years (page 59).

2 Crossing the Pyrenees on the way to Roncesvalles, with incredible views at the peak of **Col de Lepoeder** (page 67) and **Puerto de Ibañeta** (page 72).

3 Joining the locals for *pintxos* in **Pamplona** (page 110) or on **Calle del Laurel in Logroño** (page 162), where proprietors at each bar specialize in one distinctive tiny bite, or **tapas in León's Barrio Húmedo** (page 271), the "wet quarter," so named because it contains more than 100 bars.

>>>

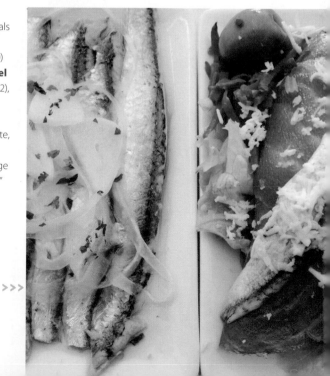

4 Stepping inside the enigmatic, octagonal **Santa María de Eunate,** known as the "Church of 100 Doors," which was constructed as a meditation on numbers held sacred by many ancient faiths (page 117).

<<<

5 Seeing grooves worn by Roman cart wheels as you walk across the **Roman road and bridge** as you leave Cirauqui (page 125).

>>>

6 Filling your scallop shell with local red wine at **Dodegas Irache Wine Fountain,** a relatively new Camino tradition that has quickly become a classic (page 134).

<<<

7 Visiting **Iglesia de San Nicolás de Barí** on the spring and autumn equinox, when a beam of sunlight perfectly illuminates a capital featuring a scene of Mary and her cousin Elizabeth (page 187).

8 Exploring the **Atapuerca Archaeological Site,** where archaeologists have unearthed 1.2-million-year-old human remains (page 208).

<<<

9 Standing inside the hauntingly romantic 12th-century **San Antón Monastery Ruins,** whose crumbling Gothic walls are overgrown with wild foliage (page 217).

>>>

10 Joining the nuns in sacred song at **Albergue de Santa María in Carrión de los Condes** (page 233).

<<<

11 Stepping into a swirl of color filtered through stained-glass windows at **Catedral de Santa María de León** (page 264).

12 Crossing the **Puente del Paso Honroso,** the 19-arched medieval bridge, made famous by a medieval jousting tournament, that leads to the village of Hospital de Órbigo (page 280).

13 Laying a stone at **Cruz de Ferro** on Monte Irago, the Camino's highest point, as you silently enact a ritual of gratitude, forgiveness, or letting go (page 300).

14 Transporting to the era of knights, pilgrims, and passionate causes as you cross the drawbridge of the **Castillo de los Templarios,** a 12th- and 13th-century castle with thick, high walls and toothy ramparts (page 308).

>>>

15 watching the sunset and sunrise from **O Cebreiro,** a charming Galician village that marks the Camino's third-highest point (page 334).

>>>

16 Exploring the **Castro de Castromaior,** a partially excavated hilltop fortress surrounded by concentric rings of protective walls (page 374).

>>>

17 Partaking in the **ritual drinking of *queimada,*** a heated concoction of spirits, sugar, coffee beans, and orange and lemon peels that's said to *quemar* (burn) out all bad karma and energy and to prepare you to approach Santiago with a clean slate (page 387).

<<<

18 Arriving (at last!) at the **Catedral de Santiago de Compostela,** where you can deliver a traditional hug to the statue of Saint James before collecting your Compostela (page 404).

>>>

19 Taking a final pilgrimage to the coast, where you can gaze out on infinite sea and sky at the **lighthouse at Cabo Finisterre** (page 448) or **Virxe da Barca Sanctuary in Muxía** (page 458).

20 Looking up at **the Milky Way** as you ponder the fact that the route of the Camino traces this celestial galaxy (page 160).

<<<

PLANNING YOUR TRIP

Where to Go

Basque Country and Navarra: Saint-Jean-Pied-de-Port to Pamplona

The Camino de Santiago today officially begins at **Saint-Jean-Pied-de-Port,** a stunning threshold at the **Pyrenees** and the border with France and Spain. You have two traditional options here: the popular **Route Napoleon** or the **Route Valcarlos,** which is used in winter and bad weather. Both ascend green-gray mountain peaks capped with snow and speckled with grazing sheep, leading to breathtaking views before descending to the huddled monastic hamlet of **Roncesvalles.** Throughout you are immersed in ancient **Basque and Navarran culture,** its hospitality, and its celebrated, colorful **cuisine.** This initial stretch is one of the **most challenging** on the Camino and includes the second-highest peak of the entire way. Especially from fall through spring, the **weather** can be prohibitive.

Navarra: Pamplona to Logroño

Beginning in **Pamplona,** Hemingway's famed stomping ground, the Camino climbs and descends between open plains, high ridges, and steep ravines into wild and dynamic landscapes where early humans built dolmens and medieval masons created **enigmatic and beautiful churches** reflecting a mix of influences (pagan, Jewish, Christian, and Muslim), including Eunate, Torres del Rio, Cirauqui, Puente la Reina, and Estella. The Camino also traverses an **ancient Roman road** and takes you into wheat and wine country, including a surprise at the monastery of **Irache:** a **fountain flowing with wine.**

La Rioja and Castile: Logroño to Burgos

Defined by radiating **vineyards** and billowing **wheat fields** awash with red poppies in spring, the Camino treads along dark, rust-red earth that, toward Castile, turns gold. Here, you enter into **remote pine forests** rich with song birds and pass some of the path's **most spiritual monasteries,** at Nájera, San Millan de la Cogolla, and San Juan de la Ortega.

Castile and León: Burgos to León

Deep into **Spain's breadbasket,** the Camino gradually climbs and enters the famous *meseta*—high plateau—of north-central Spain, with infinite swaying wheat fields where shepherds have tended their flocks for millennia. Land of hefty **hilltop castles** and **frontier towns,** this is El Cid country, saturated with epic poems of chivalrous (and roguish) knights. It is characterized by **endless sky** and **wide horizons,** which brings a different cadence to the walk. The food reflects this sturdiness with hearty farmer fare and strong wine. At an *albergue* in Carrión de los Condes, **singing nuns** invite you to listen to or join in sacred song. Burgos, at the begining of this route, is home to a world-class **human evolution museum** and also the gateway city to the **Atapuerca archeological site,** inhabited by humans 1.2 million years ago.

León and Galicia: León to Sarría

Mountainous terrain makes this one of the more **challenging** sections of the Camino. Slowly leaving the open *meseta,* the Camino passes into the multicolored mountains of León, so rich with minerals that ancient peoples, including Romans, built extensive roads here. After summiting **Monte Irago,** the **Camino's highest point,** pilgrims can **leave a ritual stone** at the foot of the **Cruz de Ferro** iron cross—for many, one of the most meaningful experiences on the journey. You next trek into a vast

If You're Looking For...

Though a multifaceted feast all the way across, some sections of the Camino offer more immediate and concentrated experiences, some focused on the physical, and others on the social or spiritual.

- **A physical challenge:** Saint-Jean-Pied-de-Port to Pamplona, Leon to Sarria, and the Camino Finisterre offer mountainous terrain, and the stretch from Burgos to León offers open exposed high plateau *meseta* terrain.

- **An easier walk:** Sarria to Santiago de Compostela.

- **Churches:** Pamplona to Logroño (most unusual); Logroño to Burgos (for miracle-based and Camino Saint-built churches); Burgos to León (classic Romanesque, Gothic, and Mudéjar churches built for some of the most miracle-working Marys); and Sarria to Santiago de Compostela (small village churches).

- **Wine:** The middle of the route, from Pamplona to Sarria, offers distinctive wines. Logroño to Burgos, in particular, is known for world-class La Rioja wines.

- **Nightlife:** Choose a route that hits one of the following towns: Pamplona, Logroño, León, or Santiago de Compostela.

- **Solitude:** Start anywhere before Sarria, and walk any time but summer. In general, the center of the route (after Pamplona and before Sarria) tends to be less crowded than the beginning and end sections.

- **Camaraderie:** Found everywhere in high doses (especially if you stay in *albergues*), but especially potent at the beginning, from Saint-Jean-Pied-de-Port to Pamplona, and at the end, from Sarria to Santiago de Compostela.

- **A Compostela:** You must walk the last 100 kilometers (62 miles) of the Camino (200 km/124 mi if you're cycling) to earn a Compostela. Sarria is the most popular staring point for walkers wishing to do this. You can also earn official certificates by walking from Santiago de Compostela to Muxía and Finisterre.

valley and garden paradise of fruit orchards, vegetable gardens, and unique **El Bierzo wines.** The trail then enters narrow mountain valleys dotted with riverside villages, making a steep ascent into Galicia's mountains at the ancient mountaintop village of **O Cebreiro.**

Galicia: Sarría to Santiago de Compostela

As one of the most convenient places to begin the final 100 kilometers (62 miles) of the Camino (required to earn a pilgrim's certificate, the **Compostela**), Sarría is **one of the most popular starting points.** From here, the Camino leads through a green and mysterious realm defined by deeply folding river valleys and mountains covered in **ancient oak**

and chestnut forest, some of the oldest in Iberia. Listen to locals tell stories of *meigas* (white witches) who cast healing cures, try **queimada,** a heated elixir of well-being offered to pilgrims, and sample celebrated **cheeses** from local cows (who are often more present on the trail than humans). You can also get a taste of the nearby sea in cafés serving Galicia's famous spicy octopus, **pulpo á feira.**

Santiago de Compostela

The Camino ends here in this mythic medieval city, at the **Catedral de Santiago de Compostela,** where the body of Saint James is entombed. Pilgrims head straight to the cathedral to **hug the statue of Santiago** on the high altar. Afterward, wander arcaded **cobblestone streets** lined with granite churches, monasteries, museums, shops, and galleries built of gray granite, or visit the **Mercado de Abastos,** one of northern Spain's most colorful and dynamic daily markets. The **restaurants and cafés** surrounding the cathedral showcase Galicia's most tantalizing dishes from ocean, field, river, and mountain. One in particular, **Casa Manolo,** has been a **popular pilgrim meeting spot** for more than three decades.

Camino Finisterre: Finisterre and Muxía

The Camino doesn't have to end at Saint James's tomb in Santiago de Compostela: More and more pilgrims are trekking farther west toward the **Atlantic coast towns** of Finisterre and Muxía. At first, the journey through dense forest, undulating hills, and **challenging small mountains** feels deceptive: You can smell the ocean, but you can't see it until you are almost upon it. At last, you meet *finis terrae,* earth's end: a narrow finger of land with endless sky above, crashing waves below, and infinite watery horizon ahead. The coastline known as the Costa da Morte ("coast of death") is rugged and dangerous, but that just adds to the filmic ending of a long walk across northern Spain. End-of-journey rituals include collecting a **scallop shell** from the beach or taking a purifying **swim in the Atlantic.**

When to Go

Whenever you decide to begin your Camino, remember that **rain**—and need for rain gear, at minimum a rain poncho—is a year-round prospect. Also consider that the last 114 kilometers (71 miles), from Sarria to Santiago de Compostela, is the **busiest section** and you will feel a significant surge in numbers here. You may want to plan the timing of your Camino by thinking about when in your walk you will reach this benchmark.

The Credential and the Compostela

A pilgrim's credential—*credencial del peregrino* in Spanish and *carnet de pélerin* in French, also known as your pilgrim passport—is what allows you to stay in *albergues* along the Camino. They typically cost **€2,** and you can order one online from a pilgrim association before leaving, or pick one up at a number of places along the way, including at the pilgrims' office in Saint-Jean-Pied-de-Port. Getting your passport stamped at *albergues,* churches, and other landmarks is an important part of walking the Camino: You need a minimum of **two stamps per day** from the **last 100 kilometers/62 miles** (or the last 200 kilometers/124 miles if you're traveling by bicycle) to collect your **Compostela** (the certificate completing the pilgrimage) in Santiago de Compostela.

When you arrive in Santiago de Compostela, take your credential to the pilgrim reception office to receive your Compostela. It's a jubilant moment.

High Season: May-September

Some 85 percent of annual trekkers walk the Camino from mid-May to mid-September. This is a time when you can carry the least amount of gear, but you do need to **carry more water,** watch for dehydration, and **protect yourself from sun exposure.** You'll also have to deal with the **crowds** who can inundate the trail as well as the accommodations. But if you like warm weather, the company of other pilgrims, want to travel light, and are ready either to deal with the "bed race" or to **book ahead,** then this may be your season.

Low Season: November-March

If you desire **solitude,** late November to early March can be ideal. You will need to carry more gear for warmth and also

Scallop Shells

The scallop shell has been a symbol of the pilgrimage to Santiago de Compostela since medieval times. You'll see it on many architectural decorations and on sculptures of Saint James on the Camino. Many modern pilgrims like to bring or find a scallop shell early, to tie to their pack to join the symbolic tribe of *peregrinos* (pilgrims). If you want to sport a scallop shell, you can bring one from home. (If you live near the ocean, this is easy; if you don't, you can buy one in a culinary supply store, where they are often sold to use in the famous French dish, *coquilles Saint Jacques*, baked scallops in their shells, a delicacy inspired by the pilgrimage). But the majority of *peregrinos* like to pick one up on the Camino, such as in **Saint-Jean-Pied-de-Port** for a *donativo* (donation) in the Pilgrims' Welcome Office, or in one of the many shops all along the Camino selling them; some wait until they reach the ocean at Finisterre or

Muxía to find one and carry home, which was a tradition in the Middle Ages. It's a new Camino tradition to drink wine from your scallop shell at **Irache's wine fountain,** so you may want to be sure you have one by that point.

Leaving a stone at the Cruz de Ferro is another rite of passage for Camino pilgrims. You can pick up a stone from anywhere on the Camino, but many pilgrims like to carry a stone all the way from home that has some personal and symbolic meaning attached to it for what they hope to release or offer once they reach the Cruz de Ferro.

be prepared for around **60 percent of the** *albergues* **to be closed,** usually from October until the week before Easter Sunday. This may demand that you stay in hotels, or walk farther to reach open *albergues*, but there is no bed race whatsoever. You may also need to carry more food, as some **cafés and restaurants also close in winter.**

Shoulder Season: March-May and September-November

For a balance between socializing and solitude, spring or autumn are ideal, and are also the most **pleasant, moderate** seasons to walk. Most seasonal *albergues* and cafés open around late March to early May, and stay open until around late September to mid-November. The bed race is also less intense. You will need more layers of clothing than in summer, but not as much as in winter.

Know Before You Go

Packing

The Camino is well supported so you can keep your pack weight light, ideally carrying no more than **10-15 percent of your body weight.** Be sure your pack's final weight includes the **2-3 pounds of water and food you need to carry each day.** Of all the gear that you'll bring, the three most important items are **trekking shoes,** such as light hiking shoes or sturdy cross trainers, that you've broken in and that fit you perfectly; **socks** designed for blister prevention; and a good, light moderate-sized **pack.** The Camino is pretty much a **cash economy,** and it's a good strategy to have an average of **€200** in your pocket, replenishing at ATMs along the way in cities, towns, and some large villages. You'll find a **packing checklist** in the Essentials chapter.

How Far to Walk

How far to go is a personal matter based not only on how many days you have, but also on how far you want to walk each day. Plan shorter days at the beginning, so that your body can adjust to the terrain and to carrying a pack for 6-8 hours a day and also to prevent injuries—the early stages are when pilgrims are most likely to get hurt by pushing too hard too soon. As you walk, you'll find your own rhythm and can add more kilometers a day or find your sweet spot. Some trekkers love going slow to take in the natural beauty and the small churches along the way, and may average 12-18 kilometers (7.5-11 miles) a day. Others get their high from rushing it, and cover 25-35 kilometers (15.5-22 miles) a day. The vast majority fall somewhere in between, averaging **21-25 kilometers (13-15.5 miles) per day.**

Note also that while **there are no public restrooms on the Camino,** restrooms are available at bars and restaurants along the trail, where you can purchase a drink or snack to use their facilities; this is a good practice to keep the trail clean, take periodic breaks, and stay hydrated and fueled. Long stretches where there are few services are noted throughout this book.

Advance Reservations

Part of the Camino's magic is letting each day unfold unplanned and savoring the chance to travel without making reservations. However, some people may prefer to avoid racing for a bed at the end of a day of walking, especially during the peak months of May-September. You can either make reservations in advance or as you go. Good times to reserve ahead: to stay in the historic state-run paradors in León (Parador San Marcos) and Santiago de Compostela (Hostal de los Reyes Católicos); to break the Pyrenees crossing on the Route Napoleon into two days, book a night in Refuge Orisson; to offer ease on arrival, for your first night on the Camino; and to arrive in Santiago de Compostela, especially around July 25, Saint James' feast day.

walking toward León's mountains and Rabanal del Camino

MAKE THE TREK

It can take anywhere from **31 to 45 days** to walk the entire Camino from the French border at the Pyrenees to Santiago de Compostela, plus up to **7 days** more to continue onward to the Atlantic coast. For many, this is impractical and intimidating. It need not be. Take a tip from the Spanish and French, who together make up 50 percent of the people who walk the Camino annually: Many often walk the trail in sections, returning a year or more later to pick up where they left off. Many others walk only that one portion and feel that it fulfilled their desire for sacred adventure. Even a three-day walk on the Camino is profound and transformative, and there are no right or wrong ways to walk it.

Most days you really won't need to pack a lunch. Unless otherwise noted, stops for food are frequent along the trail, and many cafés offer options for good sandwiches, omelets, and salads. Most pilgrims feel more like having the larger meal at dinner anyway, and may rely on trail snacks such as dried fruit and nuts for their midday meal. Always carry plenty of water.

Basque Country and Navarra: Saint-Jean-Pied-de-Port to Pamplona

Day 1
ARRIVE IN SAINT-JEAN-PIED-DE-PORT
Settle in to your *refuge* (*albergue*, pilgrims' hostel) or hotel and then head to the **Pilgrims' Welcome Office** to pick up your pilgrim's **credential**, elevation map, *albergue* listings, and good advice on trail conditions. Climb to the **citadel** for a first view of the mountains, visit the **Eglise de Notre Dame** and the **pilgrims' bridge**, and then dine on the banks of the river Nive or enjoy a first ritual communal meal with fellow pilgrims at your *refuge*.

Day 2
SAINT-JEAN-PIED-DE-PORT TO RONCESVALLES
31.1 km/19.3 mi
Begin your walk today! Ascend the **Pyrenees** via the **Route Napoleon** for endless views of mountain peaks spotted with black and white sheep. Stop in **Orisson** (7.6 km/4.8 mi after Saint-Jean) for lunch and to refill your water bottle (or even to spend the night if you're tired). You'll surmount **Col de Lepoeder,** the second-highest climb of the entire Camino, 12.8 kilometers (8 miles) after Orisson. (In bad weather and winter, use the **Route Valcarlos** instead, stopping in **Valcarlos,** 11.7 kilometers/7.2 mi after Saint-Jean, for lunch and a water-bottle refill or an overnight.)

The two routes rejoin near **Roncesvalles.** Descending into primordial beech forests, you'll glimpse your first view of Spain and this town's cream-colored and slate-roofed monastery. Celebrate the first and hardest day over dinner with fellow *peregrinos* in **Roncesvalles'** *albergue* and the **pilgrims' mass** in the 13th-century **Iglesia de la Colegiata de Santa María.** Alternatively, continue another 3 kilometers (1.9 miles) to the village of **Burguete** to stay in **Hostal Burguete**, where Hemingway stayed to go trout fishing in the Pyrenees.

Day 3
RONCESVALLES TO ZUBIRI
21.4 km/13.3 mi
Pass through rolling hills carpeted with wildflowers and fields inhabited by sturdy chestnut horses, then descend into a **forest path** of oak and beech to the Basque-Navarran village of **Espinal** and then **Biskarreta,** 11.6 kilometers (7.2 miles) after Roncesvalles. The latter offers a great terrace-side rest stop at **Bar**

Clockwise from top: wheat fields and Cantabrian mountains in mist near Torres del Rio; ironwork on Obanos' Iglesia de San Juan Bautista; green hills and forest on the way to Espinal; stork family nesting on Plaza de San Juan in Burgos.

Dena Ona, where you should stop for a mid-morning snack or an early lunch.

After lunch, descend again into oak and pine forest along rising and falling rocky footpaths, then climb to views of the Pyrenees foothills at the **Alto de Erro** before arriving in the medieval riverside village of **Zubiri**.

Day 4
ZUBIRI TO PAMPLONA
21 km/13 mi

Shimmy along intimate footpaths that follow the foothills to the ridge guarding Pamplona. You will pass through the hamlet of **Zuriain,** 9.5 kilometers (6 miles) after Zubiri, where you can enjoy rest and pilgrim cheer at the riverside café of **La Parada de Zuriain.**

Follow the Arga river past small rural homestead gardens, fields of miniature horses or geese, and forest enter to the 13th-century hilltop church of **San Esteban** in **Zabaldika,** 3.5 kilometers (2.2 miles) after Zuriain. Climb its bell tower before taking the final footpath through wild flowers to Pamplona. Enter the city through its ancient towering **fortress walls,** soak up medieval Pamplona's Gothic **Catedral de Santa María,** and step into **Hemingway's Pamplona** at **Café Iruña** for a drink (and dinner) on the stately **Plaza del Castillo.**

Navarra: Pamplona to Logroño

Day 5
PAMPLONA TO OBANOS
24.4 km/15.2 mi

Leave Pamplona, passing the university, and enter open hills flowing with wheat fields, rising to the steep climb at **Alto del Perdón,** 13.2 kilometers (8.2 miles) after Pamplona, where ceaseless wind animates the hilltop windmills. Then descend steeply into the ravine that leads toward the enigmatic round church of **Santa María de Eunate**, one of the most beautiful churches of the Camino. Pause here for half an hour or longer before climbing to the ridge-top town of **Obanos,** where you can enjoy the warm welcome and stay in the village center at **Hostal Mamerto.**

Day 6
OBANOS TO ESTELLA
24.2 km/15 mi

Kitchen gardens line the path to the town of **Puente la Reina,** 2.3 kilometers (1.5 miles) after Obanos. Here, the Camino joins the town's central street, passing two unusual medieval churches—**Iglesia del Crucifijo,** with its goose-foot-shaped cross, and **Iglesia de Santiago,** with its Islamic-style doorway—before leaving the town over the arching medieval bridge that gives the town its name. After Puente la Reina, for about 8 kilometers (5 miles), you'll dip into ravines and ridges, past wheat fields and almond groves, and though the hilltop village of **Cirauqui**. Leaving Cirauqui, you'll actually be walking on surviving ancient **Roman roads** as you approach the village of Lorca.

After Lorca, you'll pass the serene and poetic **Ermita de San Miguel,** worth a few minutes to visit. The path then leads uphill to Estella. Enter **Estella** as thousands have done before, passing the **Iglesia de Santo Sepulcro**, where Saint James smiles at you from the left of the central arch.

Day 7
EXPLORING ESTELLA

Estella is a good place for a rest day, especially if you arrive in time for the **Thursday weekly market** on the town's two medieval squares. Highlights of Estella are the Romanesque churches of **San Pedro de la Rúa** (also possessing Islamic influences) and **San Miguel**, on one of the highest hills with expressive human sculptures. Visit the old mills on the riverbank, stop at a traditional **woodworker's shop** right on the

Best Food and Wine Festivals

- **Logroño: Fiestas de San Mateo**, which is also the **Fiesta de Vendimia**, the wine harvest festival with processions, food and flowing wine (mid-Sept.), and **Festividad de San Bernabó**, in honor of Logroño's patron saint, which includes a communal feast (June 11).

- **Nájera: Fiesta del Pimiento Riojano**, Rioja pepper festival (late Oct.).

- **Santo Domingo de la Calzada: Fiestas del Santo**, the feast days in honor of the town's saint, Santo Domingo, involve a 15-day food festival (late Apr. – early May), and **Ferias de la Concepción**, including **Mercado Medieval** and **Mercado del Camino**, medieval and Camino markets, that highlight millennia-old arts, crafts, foods, music, dance, and theater (mid-Dec.).

- **Castrojeríz: Fiesta de Ajo**, garlic festival (mid-Jul.).

- **Sahagún: Romería de la Virgen del Puente**, a local bread and cheese pilgrimage, unofficially called the *romeria del pan y queso*, a celebration of the produce of the land, and of spring (Apr. 25).

- **Sarria: Fiesta del Cocido del Porco Celta**, Celtic pork festival celebrating products and dishes made from the native black and pink pigs of Galicia (late Jan.).

- **Portomarín: Festival del Aguardiente**, *orujo* (eau de vie) festival, with traditional dances, music, and tasting of the locally produced firewater, as a part of the *queimada* (Easter weekend).

- **Palas de Rei: Feira do Queixo**, celebrating the region's cheese, known as *queso de Ulloa* (late Apr.).

- **Melide: Fiesta de Melindres**, pastry festival (mid-May).

- **Arzúa: Fiesta de Queso**, annual cheese fair (3 days in early Mar.).

- **Corcubión: Fiesta de la Almeja**, clam festival with various types of clams and diverse dishes (first Sat. in Aug.).

- **Finisterre: Festa da Praia**, beach festival, with food, song, and festivities throughout town (late July). Also, the third weekend in August is the **Fiesta del Fin del Camino**, the end of the Camino festival that is also an anchovy festival (late Aug.).

Camino, and enjoy a good meal on the main square, **Plaza de los Fueros**.

Day 8
ESTELLA TO LOS ARCOS
21.4 km/13.3 mi
Leave Estella through 3 kilometers (1.9 miles) of rolling hills and native pine forest to reach the vineyards surrounding the **Monasterio de Irache** and the **Bodegas Irache wine fountain**, where you are invited to fill your scallop shell or bottle with a glass of local red wine.

(Note that the fountain isn't turned on until 9am). Continue through four more kilometers of pine forest to the hamlet of **Azqueta,** then continue on the gently weaving footpath past the medieval pointed arched cistern, **Fuente de los Moros**, to the vineyards and village of **Villamayor de Monjardín**. A climb to the fortified ruins of the **Castillo de Monjardín**, a medieval castle over earlier Roman fortifications, gives a remarkable view of the peak and valley landscape.

Continue through vineyards, pine forest, wheat fields, and olive groves on a softly descending path to **Los Arcos**, home of one of the powerful **Black Madonnas** of Spain in the 12th-century **Iglesia de Santa María**. Take 15 minutes to visit this church and see her on the high altar.

Day 9
LOS ARCOS TO LOGROÑO
27.6 km/17.1 mi
Enter a more exposed path of open wheat fields and pastureland dotted with grazing sheep on your way to the hilltop settlement of **Torres del Río**, 7.7 kilometers (4.8 miles) from Los Arcos. Allow a few minutes to visit the interior of the **Iglesia del Santo Sepulcro** and its octagonal dome designed after the mosque of Cordoba.

Leaving Torres del Rio, you'll see vineyards from here to **Viana** and then cross into La Rioja and the region's capital of **Logroño**. Stop for water, figs (when in season), and a passport stamp at **Casa Felisia** just before crossing the **Puente de Piedra** to enter the city.

La Rioja and Castile: Logroño to Burgos

Day 10
EXPLORE LOGROÑO
From Logroño, you can take a day-long wine tour to surrounding vineyards with **Rioja Like a Native**, or make a day trip to the picturesque hilltop wine town of **Laguardia** to taste wine and explore **dolmens**—prehistoric standing stones—in the vineyards.

If you stay in Logroño, start your day exploring Logroño's riverside center, which retains its medieval shape. Walk the labyrinth and inlaid mosaic squares of the **Game of the Goose** on the **Plaza de Santiago** and discover how each square is connected to a place on the Camino.

Then sign up for a **city walking tour** that includes visits to underground urban *bodegas* (wine cellars).

Kick off the evening sampling mouthwatering *pinchos* and celebrated La Rioja wines in over 50 bars on the historic streets around **Calle del Laurel**.

Day 11
LOGROÑO TO NÁJERA
29.8 km/18.5 mi
For the next 5 kilometers (3.1 miles), Logroño's industrial outskirts are unappealing; you can skip them by taking a bus to the hilltop town of **Navarrete**, where you can stamp your credential at **Iglesia de la Asunción**. Leaving Navarrete, take a small detour to the hamlet of **Ventosa**. On your way into town, stop at **Bar Virgen Blanca** for a snack or lunch and to try the local vintage.

Two kilometers (1.2 miles) after Ventosa, climb to breathtaking views of vines and the steep red cliffs of the **Alto de San Antón**. Next is a long and industrialized walk into **Nájera**, where you'll be rewarded with tree-covered parks running along both banks of the refreshing Río Najerilla. Cross the bridge to enter the **Monasterio de Santa María la Real**, built into the red cliffs. Inside, the miraculous medieval statue of Mary is reached through a tunnel into the rock.

Day 12
NÁJERA TO SANTO DOMINGO DE LA CALZADA
20.8 km/13 mi
This is a fairly low-impact day. First, climb over Nájera's ridge into more wheat fields and vineyards, past the pilgrim support villages of **Azofra** and **Cirueña**, the latter with a golf course right before entry. Continue to **Santo Domingo** and allow an hour to see the town's cathedral, **Santo Domingo de la Calzada**, which contains the tomb of the great engineer saint, along with the living descendants of the miracle rooster-and-hen pair who,

centuries ago, saved an innocent pilgrim's life.

Day 13
SANTO DOMINGO DE LA CALZADA TO VILLAFRANCA MONTES DE OCA
34.8 km/21.6 mi

This is a long but reasonably level trail day. Leave Santo Domingo crossing the Rio Oja, which gives its name to the autonomous community of La Rioja, and gently climb to the corn, wheat, and herding community of **Grañon**. Pass more sweeping wheat fields and oak forest, where you cross from La Rioja into Castile and enter the village of **Redecilla del Camino** (11.2 km/7 mi after Santo Domingo), whose **Iglesia de la Virgen de la Calle** is noted for its finely carved Romanesque **baptismal font** of the celestial city of heaven and is worth a quick five-minute stop.

To break up the day into two, stop at **Hostal El Chocolatero** (which offers excellent pilgrim menus) in Castildelgado, 12.8 kilometers (8 miles) after Santo Domingo. Otherwise, press on for 22 more kilometers (13.7 miles) to **Villafranca Montes de Oca**, where you can stay in **San Antón Abad**, the restored 14th-century pilgrims' hospital on the edge of a large native pine forest.

Day 14
VILLAFRANCA MONTES DE OCA TO ATAPUERCA
18.1 km/11.2 mi

Before you leave, note that this first stretch of this day, from Villafranca Montes de Oca to San Juan de la Ortega, is a long 12.1 kilometers (7.5 miles) with **no support services.**

Climb the Camino directly out of Villafranca and into pine forest, to a 1,100-meter-high (3,609 feet) lookout point. Then descend into pine and fern forest and into the valley, where you will find one of the Camino's great gems, the monastery and church of **Iglesia de San Nicolás de Barí,** in the town of **San Juan de la Ortega.** Take a half-hour to visit the church and enjoy the Zen-style meditation niche, and then stop for lunch at the cheery **Bar Marcela.**

Continue to **Atapuerca,** crossing a landscape that's been inhabited by humans for up to 1.2 million years. Stay at **Casa Rural Papasol,** a French-style country inn, and splurge on dinner at the innovative nouveau Castilian cuisine restaurant, **Comosapiens.**

Day 15
ATAPUERCA TO BURGOS
20.6 km/12.8 mi

Leave Atapuerca before dawn so you can take in a beautiful **sunrise** on the **Matagrande** ridge of the Sierra de Atapuerca. This ridge is your last climb before a slow descent toward **Burgos**, passing into more urban development as you go. You have three choices for routes, the shortest being the least attractive, and the longest (the one along the river) the prettiest and most pleasant.

Castile and León: Burgos to León

Day 16
EXPLORING BURGOS

In the morning, arrange a bus trip from Burgos's **Human Evolution Museum** to the **Atapuerca Archaeological Site**.

Alternatively, explore Burgos's **medieval town center.** Visit the Gothic **Catedral de Santa María,** where El Cid is buried, and the surrounding churches and squares within the walled medieval town.

In the afternoon, climb up the hill behind the cathedral to Burgos's castle, **Castillo de Burgos,** for stunning views of the city and countryside. Walk along the river Arga through the center of the city, stopping at the **Cartuja de Miraflores** and the royal **Las Huelgas** monasteries on the way.

Top: on the road to Obanos from Santa María de Eunate; **Bottom:** on trail on the *meseta* to Carrión de los Condes.

Best Parties On The Camino

These parties, often festivals, involve some form of religious procession, folk songs, music, or dance, and a lot of good food and wine, as well as rambunctious, unfettered merrymaking. In addition, all year round, weekends in the cafés and bars of the historic centers of **Pamplona, Viana, Logroño, Burgos, León,** and **Santiago de Compostela** become festive *pincho* and tapas parties, with friends going from one place to the next to visit and nosh deep into the night.

- **Pamplona: Los San Fermines,** the running of the bulls (July 6-14).

- **Obanos:** The festival of **El Misterio de Obanos,** a medieval festival, re-enacting the village's medieval history (late Aug.).

- **Castrojeriz: Fiesta de San Juan** (June 24) and **Fiesta de Sejo,** celebrating the town's patroness, Nuestra Señora del Manzano (mid-Sept.).

- **Sahagún: Fiesta de la Virgen de la Peregrina**, with folkloric groups, processions, bonfires, food, and wine (July 2), and **Fiesta de San Juan de Sahagún,** a celebration of the town's patron saint (June 12-13).

- **León: Semana Santa**, holy week leading up to and including Easter.

- **Hospital de Órbigo: Medieval festival**, with food, drink, and fanfare when the town re-enacts the tale of the jousting 15th-century knight, Don Suero de Quiñones, along its long bridge (early June).

- **Castrillo de los Polvazares: Fiesta de la Magdalena**, with the village dressed in traditional Maragato attire, making processions of music, song, dance, and festive foods (July 22).

- **Camponaraya: Fiesta de la Soledad**, celebrating the village patroness and wine harvest (third weekend in Sept).

- **Sarria: Fiesta de San Xoán** (Galician for John), with music, dance, folkloric and religious processions, and bullfights (June 21-25).

- **Santiago de Compostela**: **Saint James's feast day**, every July 25, which becomes a even bigger party when this day falls on a Sunday (making it a holy year).

- **Muxía:** A region-wide *romería*, small pilgrimage, and festival honoring the **Virxe da Barca** (Sept. 9-15), and **Fiesta del Carmen**, with decked-out fishing boats sailing across the estuary to the village of Camariñas (last Sun. in July).

End the day with tapas and *pinchos* on **Plaza Mayor,** followed by live music at Burgos's 1921 literary café, **Café España**.

Day 17
BURGOS TO HORNILLOS DEL CAMINO
21.1 km/13.1 mi

Follow the Camino west out of Burgos through the old city's fortified wall at the medieval gate of **San Martin**. Ten kilometers (6.2 miles) outside Burgos, stop for a hearty egg sandwich at **Tardajos** village's **Café Bar Ruiz**. A couple kilometers (a mile or so) later, in **Rabé de las Calzadas**, stop in for a stamp at the 13th-century **Iglesia de Santa Marina.**

Next up is the village of **Hornillos del Camino**, a Celtiberian town that has been welcoming pilgrims since the 12th century. Stop here to enjoy the fresh and flavorful *menú del peregrino* at the **Bar Casa Manolo,** and stay for the night. Alternatively, for a more rustic experience (no plumbing or electricity), continue another 5.7 kilometers (3.6 miles) further to **Arroyo de Sanbol** to slumber in a beehive-shaped *albergue* with unforgettable views of the Milky Way.

Day 18
HORNILLOS DEL CAMINO TO SAN NICOLAS
27.3 km/17 mi
Rippling exposed hills, some rather steep, define this day. Leave Hornillos del Camino toward **Arroyo de Sanbol,** pausing to dip your feet in the **healing spring** a few meters south of the Camino. Then climb about 5 kilometers (3.1 miles) more toward **Hontanas,** from where you'll descend about 4 kilometers (2.5 miles) to the isolated ruins of **Monasterio de San Antón**. Take a few moments to leave a note in the stone niche of the ruined monastery before continuing to the Celtiberian hilltop town of **Castrojeriz.**

In Castrojeriz, stop a few minutes in the Iglesia del Manzano at the town entrance to see the Camino's second most miracle-working Mary, **Nuestra Señora del Manzano**, on the altar. Proceed through Castrojeriz toward the steepest climb of the day, and best views, to the **Alto de Mostelares**, then descend to the solitary **Ermita de San Nicolás**, 7.5 kilometers (4.7 miles) from Castrojeriz on the bank of the Pisuerga river. Stay here in the one-room medieval hermitage-turned-*albergue* that sleeps up to 12 in its chapel, with evening prayer, a good **communal meal by candlelight,** and views of the Milky Way. If it is full, continue 3.3 kilometer (2 miles) to the agreeable agricultural village of **Itero de la Vega** on the other side of the river.

Day 19
SAN NICOLAS TO FRÓMISTA
17.3 km/10.7 mi
You'll press deeper into this wide-open country of the *meseta*. Entering **Boadilla del Camino** after 11.6 kilometers (7.2 miles), pause a moment at its square to see the ornate 15th-century pillar of justice, **Rollo de Boarilla**, where laws and sentences were issued, then continue 5.7 kilometers (3.5 miles) to the farming town of **Frómista** and take at least a half-hour to explore the **Iglesia de San Martín**, considered the purest French-style Romanesque church in Spain.

Day 20
FRÓMISTA TO CARRIÓN DE LOS CONDES
19.8 km/12.3 mi
Continue on a straight, 14.2-kilometer (8.8-mile) path to **Villalcázar de Sirga**, a village centered around the immense red stone 13th-century **Iglesia de Santa María la Blanca**, which houses the most miraculous and celebrated Mary on the Camino. Stay at **Hostal Las Cantigas** and enjoy a medieval-style dinner in **Mesón de los Templarios** (a destination for people across the region), or press on 5.6 more kilometers (3.5 miles) to **Carrión de los Condes** and join the nuns for their evening sing-along and communal dinner at the **Albergue de Santa María**.

Day 21
CARRIÓN DE LOS CONDES TO TERRADILLOS DE LOS TEMPLARIOS
26.4 km/16.3 mi
If you're walking during warm weather, get an early start to get some walking done before the hot afternoon. Otherwise, take a half-hour to visit the two **medieval churches** in Carrión de los Condes, and slow down to take in the immensity of the medieval monastery of **San Zoilo,** once the second most powerful in Castile.

Stock up with water and food for the day before leaving Carrion: There are no support services for the next 17 kilometers (10.6 miles). When you reach **Calzadilla de la Cueza,** pause at the village bar for refreshment and food. I don't recommend staying here, though. Instead, continue 9.5 more kilometers (6 miles) to **Terradillos de los Templarios**, a Roman town connected to Templars in the Middle Ages. Stop here for the night at the **Albergue Jacques de Molay.** Alternatively, continue 3.2 more kilometers (2 miles) to **Moratinos,** where you can dine in an underground wine bodega at **Castello de Moratinos** and sleep at the basic, Italian-run **Albergue San Bruno.**

Day 22
TERRADILLOS TO SAHAGÚN
13.3 km/8.3 miles

This short day of walking allows a half-day to explore Sahagún and pick up your halfway certificate. Leave Moratinos and in 2.6 kilometers (1.6 miles) enter the gregarious hamlet of **San Nicolás del Camino Real,** where you can pause for a good breakfast at the two excellent village cafés, **Casa Barrunta** and **Albergue Laganares.** Follow the dirt tract from there toward the **Ermita de la Virgen del Puente,** a Mudéjar (Islamic-style) hermitage dedicated to Mary.

From the hermitage, continue 2.4 kilometers (1.5 miles) to **Sahagún,** once the center of the most powerful monastery in Spain. Enjoy lunch and the vibrant social life on the **Plaza Mayor.** Pick up your **halfway certificate** at the **Santuario de la Peregrina,** one of several beautiful Mudéjar brickwork-and-stucco sacred sights that is worth taking an hour to see. Take another hour to walk around town and see the other Mudéjar churches of **San Lorenzo** and **San Tirso.**

Day 23
SAHAGÚN TO EL BURGO RANERO
17.9 km/11.1 mi

Four kilometers (2.5 miles) after leaving Sahagún, the path forks. Take the left fork to stay on the historic Camino Real, which leads to the **Ermita de Nuestra Señora de Perales,** just before the village of **Bercianos del Real Camino.** Cheerful local caretakers at the hermitage enjoy greeting pilgrims and stamping credentials.

At 7.3 kilometers (4.5 miles) after Bercianos del Real Camino is the decent-sized village of **El Burgo Ranero,** which offers several choices for lodging. Play

cards with locals at the bars of the side-by-side **Hostal El Peregrino** and **Hostal Piedra Blanca,** and enjoy an organic, local, and homemade dinner at **La Costa del Adobe.**

Day 24
EL BURGO RANERO TO
MANSILLA DE LA MULAS
19.2 km/12 mi

From El Burgo Ranero, it's nearly 13 kilometers (8 miles) to the former Roman villa of **Reliegos,** which is today a pilgrim and farming town. Upon entering town, keep an eye out for **bodegas,** private family wine cellars built into the ground.

The town of **Mansilla de las Mulas,** 6.3 kilometers (3.9 miles) after Reliegos, is surrounded by 10-foot-thick walls built on Roman foundations. Pass into the walled center of the small town and meander along its many small squares. Visit the **Museo Etnográfico Provincial de León,** the town's ethnographic museum highlighting regional cultures, especially the **Maragatos,** the traditional muleteers of León. Consider hiring a taxi with other pilgrims for an hour-long round-trip excursion (including the time to explore) from Mansilla de las Mulas to the 10th-century Visigothic and Mozarabic church of **San Miguel de Escalada.**

Day 25
MANSILLA DE LA MULAS TO LEÓN
18.4 km/11.4 mi

At 3.2 kilometers (2 miles) after Mansilla de la Mulas, a 1-kilometer (0.6-mile) detour to the right leads you to one of the best **Roman remains** on the Camino: The archaeological site of **Lancía,** which was occupied by Romans 2,000 years ago. Take 30 minutes to explore the site (visits are usually possible in the morning Mon.-Fri.).

The approach to León is through heavily industrialized urban terrain. To skip this long, unpleasant stretch, walk another 2 kilometers (1.2 miles) to the settlement of **Puente Villarente**, where you can catch the local bus into León.

León and Galicia: León to Sarria

Day 26
EXPLORING LEÓN

Spend the morning exploring Spain's purest and most French Gothic cathedral, **Catedral de Santa María**, with an astounding number of stained-glass windows; also see Spain's best-preserved medieval frescoes in the royal pantheon of the **Basilica de San Isidoro**.

Next, walk along the walls of the original Roman town, where you can still see the **Roman walls** enclosing the old city center. Pause for a glass of León's best wines at **Vinos Grifo** on the city's oldest and most atmospheric square, the **Plaza del Grano**.

In the evening, treat yourself to the luxury quarters of the restored medieval monastery **Parador San Marcos**, and join the locals for a tapas crawl in the **Barrio Húmedo**, where each venue prides itself in creating innovative little dishes to serve with your order of wine or beer.

Day 27
LEÓN TO SAN MARTÍN DEL CAMINO
25.4 km/15.8 mi

The stretch leaving León is almost as ugly as the stretch entering the city. Fortunately, it's easy to catch a **bus** to the shrine of **La Virgen del Camino**, 7.7 kilometers (4.8 miles) away. Spend a half-hour taking in the living mysticism of this modern but appealing temple dedicated to the vision and presence of Mary. Then refresh yourself with a good egg sandwich, orange juice, and coffee at the bar across the street, **El Peregrino.**

From here, the Camino resumes on flat terrain. In 17.7 kilometers (11 miles), you'll reach one of the most welcoming *albergues* on the Camino, **La Vieira** in **San Martín del Camino,** where you can get a bed for the night and a generous communal dinner made with produce from the owner's daughter's farm.

Day 28
SAN MARTÍN DEL CAMINO TO ASTORGA
24.1 km/15 mi

This is your last full day on the *meseta.* Around 7 kilometers (4.3 miles) after leaving San Martín del Camino, you arrive at the **Puente del Paso Honroso,** the medieval 19-arched bridge that's known for a legendary jousting tournament. Cross it, then walk through the village of **Hospital de Órbigo.**

Passing through a few other villages, you'll enter **Astorga,** one of Roman Spain's most important cities, through its high Roman walls. Dig into the town's Roman roots at the **Museo Romano,** from where you can also depart for an hour-long **archaeological walking tour** of the town. Follow up with a half-hour in local chocolate history, with samples, at the **Museo de Chocolate.** Finally, spend an hour taking in taking in the sacred art in the 15th-century **Catedral de Santa María** and the **Museo de Catedral.**

Day 29
ASTORGA TO RABANAL DEL CAMINO
19.8 km/12.3 mi

Today you leave the *meseta* and enter León's mountains. As you depart Astorga, pause at the restful and poignant pilgrim memorial garden at **Ermita de Ecce Homo** hermitage, then continue toward the traditional Maragato village of **Castrillo de los Polvazares.** (If you have the time, stopping for a day or more at the powerful and creative sacred art retreat of **Flores del Camino** is strongly recommended.)

Continue to **El Ganso,** 13 kilometers (8 miles) from your starting point in Astorga, and pause for refreshment at the **Mesón Cowboy,** a Wild-West-themed bar. Then continue along increasingly rocky terrain into the gateway of the mountains at **Rabanal del Camino.** Eat and sleep at the rural B&B, **The Stone Boat,** and conclude the evening with **chanted Gregorian prayer** led by the Benedictines in Rabanal's **Iglesia de la Asunción** daily at 7pm and 9pm.

Day 30
RABANAL DEL CAMINO TO MOLINASECA
24.6 km/15.3 mi

Today you will climb deeply and, at times, steeply into Leon's mountains along a rugged trail toward **Foncebadón** (5.5 km/3.4 mi after Rabanal del Camino), a perfect place to rest and refuel before climbing the last few kilometers to the Camino's highest altitude point: the **Cruz de Ferro** on **Monte Irago.** When you arrive at Cruz de Ferro, you have the chance to perform the Camino's most potent ritual, **leaving a stone** at the base of the towering iron-and-oak cross.

Next, continue to the modern Templar hamlet of **Manjarín,** where you can stop for a stamp from modern-day Templar Knight, Tomás Martinez de la Paz, before continuing to the pretty stone villages of **El Acebo** and **Riego de Ambros**. A final stretch of gorgeous alpine terrain leads into the refreshing riverside town of **Molinaseca,** where you leave the mountains behind and enter the fertile garden valley of El Bierzo. Stop at **El Capricho de Josana** for a room and a passionately prepared meal with El Bierzo and Italian flourishes. Alternately, continue to Ponferrada and stay in **La Virgen de la Encina** *hostal,* joining the evening tapas and dinner scene at **Taberna La Obrera.**

Day 31
MOLINASECA TO CACABELOS
24.5 km/15.2 mi

From Molinaseca, it is an easy 8-kilometer (5-mile) walk to **Ponferrada.** Allow 1-2 hours to explore the town's attractions: **Castillo de los Templarios,** the large Templar castle on the riverbank; **Basilica de Nuestra Señora de la Encina,** a church with pagan and possibly Templar roots, and the extraordinary 10th-century pre-Romanesque church, **Santo Tomás de las Ollas,** a 1-kilometer (0.6-mile) detour north of the town center.

After your sightseeing, stop for refreshment or lunch at Ponferrada's **Bar Virgen de la Encina.** Then cross the Sil river and pass several medieval hamlets, with olive groves and apple and pear orchards, on the way to **Cacabelos,** where you enter an important wine region since Roman times.

Day 32
CACABELOS TO TRABADELO
17.8 km/11 mi

As you leave Cacabelos you enter the hamlet of **Pieros,** and the edge of a **Celtic castro** that defines the original settlement. Continue through the gorgeous, vineyard-covered hills that produce the unique **El Bierzo wines**.

Arrive in **Villafranca del Bierzo** (8.5 km/5.3 mi from where you started in Cacabelos) in time for lunch on the **Plaza Mayor (Restaurante Compostela** is a favorite). But first, pause at the town's most iconic monument, **Iglesia de Santiago** with its ornate **Puerta del Perdón** (gate of pardon), where medieval pilgrims who not could make it to Santiago de Compostela sought pardon. (It's rarely open, but touch the door for luck nevertheless!)

Continue across the river and deeper into the mountain pass toward **Pereje,** and then the Valcarce river and valley toward **Trabadelo.** One kilometer (0.6 miles) before Trabadelo, slow down and savor the **ancient chestnut forest** whose branches arch overhead like a natural cathedral canopy. Stay in Trabadelo at **Hostal-Albergue Crispeta** and dine in the establishment's bar-restaurant. (Ask for the homemade quince jam to pair with a dessert of local cheese or the homemade yogurt-like custard, *cuajada.*)

Clockwise from top: fields of wheat and red poppies on the way to Frómista; a falcon in León; Santuario da Virxe da Barca in Muxía; a traditional granary, *horreo,* in Galicia.

Day 33
TRABADELO TO O CEBREIRO
18.5 km/11.5 mi

Pass more deeply into the green, narrow mountain terrain, through the heart of several tiny river-valley hamlets with pretty gray granite chapels that offer good food, drink, and rest. As you pass through Ambasmestas, 5.3 kilometers (3.3 miles) after Trabadelo, duck into **Quesería Veigadarte** to purchase some local goat cheese for a trailside picnic lunch. (It goes great with apples and fresh bread.) Consider setting aside an hour to climb to the 9th-century castle, **Castillo de Sarracín,** from the village of Vega de Valcarce, and pause in the next village of **Ruitelan** to refresh and refuel at **Bar Omega** or the climb ahead.

Las Herrerías is the last valley settlement before the ascent to **O Cebreiro**, the third-highest peak on the Camino. Take it slow, and pace yourself on the sheer incline. At the mountain-hugging village of **La Faba**, you can rest at the enjoyable village café, and then push up into the final ascent.

When you arrive at **O Cebrerio,** wander the small village, taking in its traditional round stone- and thatch-roofed *pallozas.* Pause at **Mesón Antón** for a drink to watch the **sunset**, or attend **evening pilgrims' mass** in the **Iglesia de Santa María**.

Day 34
O CEBREIRO TO TRIACASTELA
21 km/13 mi

Take in the **sunrise** over the eastern mountains before leaving O Cebreiro. From here, the terrain gets greener and greener as it weaves in and out of several mountain villages that offer food, drink, and lodging. Good places to stop for a bite are the high lookout point of **Alto do Poio**, 8.7 kilometers (5.4 miles) after O Cebreiro, where the **Bar Puerto** serves a tasty *caldo Gallego,* or **Fonfría,** 3.4 kilometers (2.1 miles) later, with an *albergue* bar and a lady who sells crepes in front of her village house.

Next, descend deeply into the rich river valley and village of **Triacastela**, where you can stay in two joined refurbished farmhouses at **Albergue Atrio**, attend an inspiring early **evening pilgrims' mass** in the 12th-century church, **Iglesia de Santiago**, and enjoy good pilgrim's fare at **Restaurante Complexo Xacobeo**.

Day 35
TRIACASTELA TO SARRIA
17.8 km/11 mi

You have two choices to get to Sarria. Either detour to the Benedictine **Monasterio de Samos** (which will add 6.4 km/4 mi to your trek), where you can stay and attend a monastic retreat, or continue on the more **traditional Camino**, where you will pass through **exquisite old chestnut woods** and several villages with tiny chapels that offer support. The paths rejoin in Aguiada and near **Sarria**.

Sarria is not terribly pretty, but is very welcoming and has all the amenities. Its 13th-century **Iglesia de San Salvador** has an appealingly primitive engraving of Christ over the entrance, which is worth pausing to see. Stay in the Pensión or Albergue **Don Álvaro** where you can enjoy an after-dinner homemade *orujo, eau de vie*, with fellow pilgrims after taking a delicious Italian dinner at **Matias Locanda Italiana**.

Galicia: Sarria to Santiago de Compostela

Day 36
SARRIA TO PORTOMARÍN
22.1 km/13.7 mi

Leaving Sarria, you'll pass its **castle ruins** and cross the medieval **Ponte Áspera** over the Celeiro river, traversing ancient oak forest until you reach the village of **Barbadelo,** 4 kilometers (2.5 miles) away. Here, be sure to take the 50-meter (164-foot) detour to the left to see the **Iglesia**

Best Views

- **La Citadelle:** The highest point in Saint-Jean-Pied-de-Port (Km 779.9) offers breathtaking views of the surrounding hills and mountains and into the town where the modern Camino officially begins.

- **Col de Lepoeder** (Km 759.5): The second-highest summit on the entire Camino, with panoramic views of the Pyrenees in France and Spain.

- **Puerto de Ibañeta** (Km 757.4): It was fabled among medieval pilgrims that they could touch heaven from this pinnacle (the high point on the Route Valcarlos), which overlooks multicolored heather- and fern-covered mountains.

- **Alto del Perdón** (Km 698.3): It's said that the wind on this high ridge (whose name means "height of forgiveness") has the power to carry away one's burdens and sorrows. Views overlook the sweeping slopes and rocky fields of the Cantabrian mountains.

- **Cuesta de Matamulos:** On this hill, just before Hornillos del Camino (Km 468.6), the road suddenly opens to a glorious vista of fields that in the spring are specked with red poppies.

- **Alto de Mostelares** (approx. Km 445.3): A final steep climb before the vast *meseta*, this high hilltop reveals infinite, open blue sky and endless green and gold patchwork wheat fields far below your feet.

- **Monte Irago and Alto Altar Mayor:** After enacting one of the Camino's most potent rituals—laying a stone at the base of the Cruz de Ferro monument (Km 231.9)—you'll encounter the path's true highest summit, just past the hamlet of Manjarín. Take in a view of the surrounding mountains and, soon after, the approaching village of El Acebo at your feet below

and of the large town of Ponferrada in the distance, nestled in the bowl of a mountain valley.

- **Mountaintop view from La Faba** (Km 159.2): As you leave La Faba, turn around for an idyllic view of Iglesia de San Andrés nestled below the village, with multicolored mountains rolling out beyond the bell tower.

- **O Cebreiro** (Km 154.3): Sunrise and sunset are stunning from the Camino's third-highest point.

- **Monte del Gozo** (Km 4.9): A couple kilometers after this historic hill, you'll catch your first glimpse of the cathedral spires in Santiago de Compostela. You've almost arrived!

- **Cabo Finisterre:** From this jutting peninsula of *finis terrae* (literally, the end of the world), look out over the cliffs where infinite sky meets the infinite Atlantic Ocean.

- **Santuario da Virxe da Barca:** This picturesque monument on Muxia's small peninsula, a bottleneck of land between ocean and bay, offers incredible views of sunrise and sunset.

Alto de Mostelares just after Castrojeriz

de Santiago, with its unusual and primitive engravings of Christ. Continue to **Ferreiros** and its tiny but expressive Romanesque **Iglesia de Santa María**.

Climb to the plateau overlooking Portomarín's river valley, then descend, crossing the river at the high, vertigo-inducing modern bridge into **Portomarín.** Take half an hour to visit Portomarín's two Romanesque churches, **San Nicolás** and **San Pedro**. Then enjoy a good meal along the central **arcaded passageways** in the town center (a favorite is **Posada del Camino,** seated on the terrace overlooking Iglesia de San Nicolás).

Day 37
PORTOMARÍN TO EIREXE
17.8 km/11 mi
Leave Portomarín, crossing a small tributary of the Belesar dam. Pass through oak and chestnut forest on the climb to the farm village of **Gonzar** (7.8 km/4.8 mi from Portomarín), where you can rest on the outdoor terrace at **Casa García.** Continue a couple more kilometers (a little over a mile) to **Castromaior,** a small village with an excellent bar making homemade treats, including fresh yogurt.

Allow a half-hour to take the 200-meter (656-foot) detour left off the Camino after Castromairo to the 2,400-year-old castro site of **Castro de Castromaior.** Follow the path from there through fields and forest to the deeply symbolic **Cruceiro de Lameiros** near **Ligonde,** another pretty farming village. Finally, stop for the night in **Eirexe** at the cozy **Pensión Eirexe,** taking a pilgrim's dinner across the street at the cheerful village restaurant, **Restaurante Ligonde.**

Day 38
EIREXE TO MELIDE
22.6 km/14 mi
From Eirexe, the Camino meanders 7.6 kilometers (4.7 miles) to **Palas de Rei,** a serious working farm town centered

on the **Iglesia de San Tirso**. From here, continue to **San Xulián do Camino** with its well-preserved 12th-century Romanesque church. After several other hamlets, enter **Leboreiro**, whose village church, **Iglesia de Santa María**, is dedicated to Mary, who is said to have appeared in a nearby fountain one night, combing her hair. Take a few moments to study the church entrance, an unusual tympanum of appealingly primitive design.

On your way to **Melide** (5.7 km/3.5 mi from Leboreiro), you'll cross over two pretty stone medieval bridges, in Leboreiro and in Furelos. Melide is where you can get your first best taste of Galicia's famous dish, *pulpo á feria,* paprika-spiced octopus. To sample the dish, you have your pick of three excellent places.

Day 39
MELIDE TO ARZÚA
13.9 km/8.6 mi
One kilometer (0.6 miles) from the center of Melide, pause for perhaps 15-30 minutes at a crown jewel of the Camino: the **Iglesia de Santa Maria de Melide,** a 12th-century church with expressive animal sculptures and well-preserved frescoes, all overseen by a modern-day Templar knight. Then follow the tree-covered lanes and forest paths to the 13th-century bridge that leads into **Ribadiso da Baixo,** a hamlet of nine people where they are restoring the medieval pilgrims' **Hospital de San Antón.**

Continue along country roads and a slight ascent until you reach the substantial town of **Arzúa,** an upbeat place famous for locally produced cow's milk **cheeses** (and a great place to try them). Stay the night in the family-run **Pensión Casa Frade,** and dine at **Restaurante Casa Nene,** where the dessert cheese plate will let you sample the best of Arzua's cheeses.

Day 40
ARZÚA TO O PEDROUZO
19.1 km/11.9 mi

From Arzúa, the Camino continues through bucolic countryside and tiny settlements. Make a point of being in **O Empalme** (15.3 km/9.5 mi from Arzúa) in time for lunch at **O Ceadoiro,** a delightful roadside café with locally harvested and home-cooked meals popular with locals.

A kilometer (half a mile) after O Empalme, pass through the hamlet of Santa Irene and soon after a short detour leads to an array of food and accommodations options in **O Pedrouzo.** Alternately, continue straight on to the hamlet of **Amenal** where the only show in town is the **Hotel Amenal,** an excellent option for accommodations, drinks, and dinner.

Day 41
O PEDROUZO TO
SANTIAGO DE COMPOSTELA
20 km/12.4 mi

Your last day starts in fragrant eucalyptus forest and proceeds to the historic village of **Lavacolla** (10 km/6.2 mi after O Pedrouzo, and 6.6 km/4.1 mi after Amenal), where you will pass over the village stream where medieval pilgrims washed themselves in preparation for arriving in Santiago. Continue through a neighborhood on the outskirts of Santiago and climb toward **Monte del Gozo,** the traditional spot where medieval pilgrims first saw the spires of **Santiago de Compostela**'s cathedral. The tree cover now hides the view, so you'll have to wait another kilometer to see the spires (but you can still jump for joy here anyway).

Follow the descending path along the side of the road and into the neighborhood of **San Lázaro,** where waymarkers along the streets lead you into the medieval center of the city and straight to the cathedral square, **Plaza de Obradoiro,** which faces the western entrance of the cathedral, **Catedral de Santiago de Compostela,** where Saint James is said to be entombed. Do as pilgrims have done over the past millennia: Enter the cathedral and deliver a long-awaited hug to Santiago on the high altar. Congratulations! You did it!

nighttime in Santiago de Compostela

Santiago de Compostela

Day 42
EXPLORE SANTIAGO DE COMPOSTELA

If you did not yet do it, head first to the cathedral to hug Santiago on the high altar and soak in the splendor of the Romanesque church, then head to the **pilgrims' reception office** to receive your Compostela.

Stop for a celebratory lunch at **Casa Manolo** (near the cathedral), or purchase picnic foods at the vibrant daily market **Mercado de Abastos**. After lunch, spend an hour in the pilgrimage museum, **Museo de Peregrinaciones,** then spend another hour walking to the outer edge of the old town to see either the surviving 3,000-year-old petroglyph, **Castriño de Conxo,** or the Romanesque **Iglesia del Sar.**

Return to the cathedral for evening pilgrims' mass at 7:30pm daily. (If you're lucky, you will get to see the massive incense burner, *botafumeiro,* in use.) Then kick off the evening sampling the tapas, *pinchos,* and regional wines at the bars lining on the streets of **Rúas Franco, Nova, Vilar,** and **Raiña.** Finish the evening at **Costa Vella**'s starry garden café or over a flaming cup of *queimada* at **Cafe Casino.**

Camino Finisterre: Finisterre and Muxía

Day 43
SANTIAGO DE COMPOSTELA TO NEGREIRA
21 km/13 mi

Prepare for a day of constant up-and-down climbing, some of it fairly steep. Leave Santiago de Compostela via pleasant city streets and forest paths into green countryside. Arrive in **Pontemaceira** (17 kilometers/10.6 miles from Santiago de Compostela) and pause at the **Restaurante Ponte Maceira** for a late lunch. In 4 more kilometers (2.5 miles), cross the medieval bridge to **Negreira,** an agreeable small town with stately *pazos* (country mansions), along with several options to eat and sleep well.

Day 44
NEGREIRA TO SANTA MARIÑA
21.5 km/13.4 mi

Continue through rural green terrain, dotted with distinctive Galician *horreos* (traditional granaries mounted on stone stilts), that rises and falls less dramatically than yesterday's section. Options for food and drink are hit or miss, so stock up before leaving Negreira. In the tiny village of **Santa Mariña,** the upbeat **Albergue Casa Pepa** offers good lodging in a traditional country home as well as delicious dinners. Alternately, you can press on for 11.9 kilometers (7.4 miles) to **Olveiroa,** a similarly sized village with options for accommodations and food.

Day 45
SANTA MARIÑA TO CEE AND CORCUBIÓN
31.4 km/19.5 mi

Get an early start and continue for 17 kilometers (10.6 miles) on a gentle ascent through **Olveiroa, Logoso,** and **Hospital.** Be sure to stock up on food and water in one of these villages; there is no support on the final 14.4-kilometer (9-mile) stretch from Hospital to Cee. After Hospital, the trail forks; go left for Finisterre. The trail here is a dirt path through verdant forests and fields. It passes a regionally celebrated shrine, **Capela de Nosa Señora das Neves,** that's worth a few minutes' pause to see the sculpture of the chapel's namesake in the covered porch outside; it's also worth it to stop at the traditional **healing well.**

Soon after you leave the chapel you will catch your **first glimpse of the bay and ocean** beyond. The trail then descends steeply to the picturesque fishing towns of **Cee** and **Corcubión.** Both have ample options for food and accommodations. Be sure to take a few minutes in Cee to visit the **Iglesia de Santa Maria de Xunquiera**, and in Corcubión to visit the **Iglesia de San Marcos**.

Day 46
CEE TO FINISTERRE
15.4 km/9.6 mi

From Cee and Corcubión, the trail follows along the rocky coast to the sweeping sandy beach of **Praia da Langosteira**, less than 2 kilometers (1.2 miles) before Finisterre. Stop at this beach to join other pilgrims in a ritual **dive into the ocean,** and search for a **scallop shell** to take home.

When you reach **Finisterre,** make the final climb to kilometer 0 at the "Earth's end," the tip of land where the **lighthouse** stands at **Cabo Finisterre**. Take the road from the lighthouse up to the top of Monte Facho to see the **Piedras Sagradas** (sacred stones), then follow the branching trail to the hermitage of **Ermita de San Guillerme.** Both are possible locations of the ancient **Ara Solis**, pagan sun altar.

Watching the **sunset from Cabo Finisterre** is an ancient pilgrim's ritual. To view it, some pilgrims like to return to the lighthouse and carefully climb to the rocks below its base, take a seat, and dangle their feet over the edge tumbling down to the waves.

Day 47
FINISTERRE TO MUXÍA
29.3 km/18.2 mi

This trek along the coast, deep in maritime hills and river valleys, may be the prettiest and wildest of all the stretches of the Camino. The only village offering food and accommodations is midway at **Lires,** 13.6 kilometers (8.5 miles) north of Finisterre. In 9.1 kilometers (5.7 miles) after Lires, the climb to **Monte Facho de Lourido** (269 m/883 ft) is the steepest on this route.

As you near Muxía, take in views of the sparkling blue ocean and massive stones that make up the coast. A festive meal of crisp local white wine and grilled scallops or steamed gooseneck barnacles is in order at **Bar A Marina** on the harbor. Before sunset, walk the 900 meters (0.6 mile) from the settlement to Muxía's seaside church at the village's tip of land, the **Santuario da Virxe da Barca**, and settle in along the large polished rocks to watch the **sunset** over the ocean.

Day 48
MUXÍA TO SANTIAGO DE COMPOSTELA

Two direct buses from Muxía (one in the morning and one in the afternoon) will get you back to Santiago de Compostela (1.5 hours), your nearest transportation hub from which to make train, bus, or flight connections to return home.

Basque Country and Navarra

Saint-Jean-Pied-de-Port to Pamplona

Km: 779.9–711.5
Total Distance: 68.4 km (42.5 miles)
Days: 3–4

Basque Country and Navarra

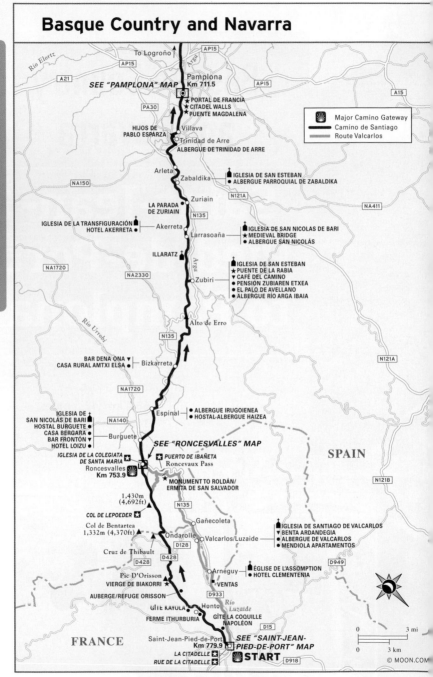

To Logroño

Pamplona
Km 711.5
★ PORTAL DE FRANCIA
★ CITADEL WALLS
★ PUENTE MAGDALENA

SEE "PAMPLONA" MAP

HIJOS DE
PABLO ESPARZA ○ Villava
○ Trinidad de Arre
ALBERGUE DE TRINIDAD DE ARRE

Arleta ─
○ Zabaldika ▌ IGLESIA DE SAN ESTEBAN
● ALBERGUE PARROQUIAL DE ZABALDIKA

Zuriain

LA PARADA
DE ZURIAIN

IGLESIA DE LA TRANSFIGURACIÓN ▌
HOTEL AKERRETA ● ─ Akerreta

Larrasoaña ─ ▌ IGLESIA DE SAN NICOLÁS DE BARI
★ MEDIEVAL BRIDGE
● ALBERGUE SAN NICOLÁS

ILLARATZ ▌

○ Zubiri ▌ IGLESIA DE SAN ESTEBAN
★ PUENTE DE LA RABIA
▼ CAFÉ DEL CAMINO
● PENSION ZUBIAREN ETXEA
● EL PALO DE AVELLANO
● ALBERGUE RÍO ARGA IBAIA

Alto de Erro

BAR DENA ONA ▼ ─
CASA RURAL AMTXI ELSA ● ─ Bizkarreta

Espinal ─ ● ALBERGUE IRUGOIENEA
● HOSTAL-ALBERGUE HAIZEA

IGLESIA DE ↑
SAN NICOLÁS DE BARI
HOSTAL BURGUETE ●
CASA BERGARA ●
BAR FRONTÓN ▼
HOTEL LOIZU ▲ ─ Burguete

SEE "RONCESVALLES" MAP

SPAIN

IGLESIA DE LA COLEGIATA
DE SANTA MARÍA
Roncesvalles
Km 753.9   ✚ PUERTO DE IBAÑETA
Roncevaux Pass

★ MONUMENT TO ROLDÁN/
ERMITA DE SAN SALVADOR

1,430m
(4,692ft)

COL DE LEPOEDER ✚

Col de Bentartea
1,332m (4,370ft) ▲

Gañecoleta
○ Ondarolle   ▌ IGLESIA DE SANTIAGO DE VALCARLOS
○ Valcarlos/Luzaide ▼ BENTA ARDANDEGIA
● ALBERGUE DE VALCARLOS
● MENDIOLA APARTAMENTOS

Cruz de Thibault

Pic D'Orisson
VIERGE DE BIAKORRI ★

AUBERGE/REFUGE ORISSON ▲

○ Arnéguy ▌ ÉGLISE DE L'ASSOMPTION
● HOTEL CLEMENTENIA

■ VENTAS

GÎTE KAYOLA ○ Honto
FERME ITHURBURIA   Río
Luzaide

FRANCE

Saint-Jean-Pied-de-Port
Km 779.9

*SEE "SAINT-JEAN-
PIED-DE-PORT" MAP*

🐚 **START**

LA CITADELLE ✚
RUE DE LA CITADELLE ✚

🐚 Major Camino Gateway
━━━ Camino de Santiago
▬▬▬ Route Valcarlos

0 ─────── 3 mi
0 ─────── 3 km

© MOON.COM

Highlights

★ **La Citadelle:** The highest point in Saint-Jean-Pied-de-Port offers breathtaking views of the surrounding hills and mountains. The climb to get up there—along a narrow footpath skirting the high walls—is a part of the adventure (page 57).

★ **Rue de la Citadelle:** It is an electric feeling to take your first step onto the Camino on the smooth cobblestones of this steep and sloping medieval street that cuts through old Saint-Jean-Pied-de-Port (page 59).

★ **Col de Lepoeder:** At 1,430 meters (4,692 feet), this second-highest summit on the entire Camino affords full panoramic views of the Pyrenees in France and Spain (page 67).

★ **Puerto de Ibañeta:** The high point on the Route Valcarlos offers vistas of heather and fern-covered mountains fanning out in ripples. It was fabled among medieval pilgrims that they could touch heaven from this pinnacle (page 72).

★ **Iglesia de la Colegiata de Santa María:** A spacious yet intimate Gothic church dedicated to the Mary of Roncesvalles, a powerful Madonna of the Pyrenees, this *iglesia* is tucked into the base of the mountains just after you cross into Spain from France (page 76).

Few places on the Camino capture the exhilaration of the journey ahead as this threshold at the foot of the Pyrenees. Saint-Jean-Pied-de-Port has been a pilgrims' staging place for over 900 years. Many knew that going forward from here was the final commitment: once they crossed the mountains, there was no turning back. The deeply worn cobblestones of Saint-Jean-Pied-de-Port echo the electricity and the anticipation of hundreds of Camino travelers arriving each day to begin their adventure. Here, and in Roncesvalles on the other side of the mountains, is where many form the beginnings of their "Camino family" with people who share the same *albergue* (hostel) on the first night of their journey. Your "family" is part of the magic of the Camino. They will serendipitously appear on and off for the rest of the trek, becoming a part of a network of reliance and comfort *peregrinos* (pilgrims) offer each other throughout.

This stretch of the Camino passes through some of the prettiest natural landscapes of the entire route. The Valcarlos Pass over the Pyrenees offers stunning views from one of the three highest altitudes of the Camino (the other two are in León and Galicia, at Monte Irago and O Cebreiro respectively). The trail through the forests from Roncesvalles to Zubiri is enchanted with beech, oak, and pine trees, and native wildflower and birdlife. This section of the Camino also weaves together several overlapping cultures and languages—Basque, Navarrese, Gascogne, Occitan, French, and Spanish. It also traverses the territory where Ernest Hemingway liked to go trout fishing in the Pyrenees (in Burguete, just after Roncesvalles), a passion captured viscerally in his novel *The Sun Also Rises*. The rivers here are still plentiful with excellent trout, which make their way onto many local menus, fried with cured ham and red peppers, and served with local wines—from the effervescent white txakoli to the coveted Irouléguy and Navarrese rosés.

Recommended Overnight Stops

Saint-Jean-Pied-de-Port
(Km 779.9, page 55)

Roncesvalles (Km 753.9, page 74)
or **Burguete** (Km 750.9, page 80)

Zubiri (Km 732.5, page 85)

In spring, the hills erupt with multicolored wildflowers even as morning frost still frames the leaves and grasses with shimmering edges. In autumn, the African pigeon makes a massive migration south, turning this part of the Pyrenees into pigeon-hunting madness for the succulent bird. This is a territory rich in fertile mountains and river valleys, in culinary traditions, and in some of Europe's oldest cultural practices and outlooks. Quite a threshold indeed to begin the Camino, with a first day set to surmount one of the trail's toughest legs.

Planning Your Time

If you are arriving in Saint-Jean-Pied-de-Port directly from a far-flung international destination, consider allowing yourself two days here to recover from jetlag and to have time to soak up the pilgrim town, your only French town before crossing the Pyrenees on the Camino. Allow 3-4 days for walking this 68.4-kilometer (42.5-mile) stretch, when averaging 20-25 kilometers (12.5-15.5 miles) a day. You may also want to build flexibility into your start to allow for changes of weather any time of year, especially from early autumn to early summer, that might delay crossing the Pyrenees.

Note that not all accommodations, especially the pilgrims' *albergues* in Saint-Jean, have **wifi** (though you can get it at the Pilgrims' Office in town). When you cross the Pyrenees on the way to Roncesvalles, wifi is all but nonexistent.

Route Options

Right off the bat, you have two choices for routes leaving Saint-Jean-Pied-de-Port. The **Route Napoleon** (open Apr.-Oct. and at its best mid-June to mid-Sept.) is the most popular route, celebrated for its high vistas that are some of the Camino's most beautiful views. The **Route Valcarlos,** the winter route, is open all year, but is also to be taken only if weather permits, as it too has treacherous sections not advised in heavy rain or snow.

Because the Route Valcarlos is considered the "safer" route, there is a misconception that the Route Napoleon is harder, and therefore "better." The Route Valcarlos is not necessarily easier: the path ascends slowly at first, then climbs up and down on narrow footpaths, some along the edge of the mountain highway and some skirting the steep mountainsides. It also has one dramatically steep and persistent 7.6-kilometer (4.7-mile) climb from Gañecoleta to Puerto de Ibañeta. The Route Napoleon makes a higher elevation climb than the Route Valcarlos, peaking at **Col de Lepoeder** (1,430 m/4,692 ft), where it then makes a steep descent to Roncesvalles. From the Col de Lepoeder, you have two possible paths: The steepest is straight ahead (4 km/2.5 mi long and only advised when the trail is dry), while a path to the right leads to Puerto de Ibañeta, where it joins the Route Valcarlos to continue into Roncesvalles (a total of 5.6 km/3.5 mi).

The two routes are almost the same length: Route Napoleon is 24.7 kilometers (15.3 miles) long (or 26.3 km/16.3 mi, if you take the final path to the right to Puerto de Ibañeta), and the Route Valcarlos is 24 kilometers (15 miles)

From top to bottom: a citril finch in Navarra; pilgrims on the path to Espinal; trail marker after Zubiri.

Highlights of Basque and Navarran Food and Wine

Among the celebrated cuisines of Europe, Basque and Navarran cuisine is colorful, fresh, and full of diverse ingredients. This is thanks to year-round kitchen gardens, the nearness of fresh catch from the Atlantic, the many rivers full of trout that run down from the Pyrenees, and wild ingredients such as mushrooms and berries.

Cheese

Sheep graze everywhere here, eating the wild herbs and grass of the hillsides, giving the local Saint-Jean-Pied-de-Port **Ossau-Iraty** *fromage de brebis* its special herby and nutty flavor. You will find this cheese for sale in town, and it is well worth trying and taking a 200-300 gram (7-10.6 oz) chunk with you on the trail.

Trout

Grilled trout, especially stuffed and cooked with slices of cured ham, *jamón Serrano* or *jambon de Bayonne,* is available everywhere from Saint-Jean-Pied-de-Port to Pamplona (and beyond, in Navarra and Rioja), where streams thriving with trout abound. The mountain pub and restaurant **Benta Ardandegia** in Valcarlos prepares it perfectly, using fresh-caught fish from the Arga river. You'll also find it on the menu at Burguete's **Hotel Loizu**.

Vegetable Dishes

Celebrated local vegetables include red peppers, asparagus, artichokes, and green beans. Of these, the red peppers reign supreme, and Basque Country and Navarra are known across Europe for their special pepper varieties as well as their dishes, such as **piquillos,** roasted red peppers stuffed with cod, tuna, crab, wild mushrooms, or anything else the chef imagines. Other popular vegetable dishes are *menestre de verduras,* a great mix of vegetables sautéed together in oil and garlic, and *omelette de pipérade,* omelets made with peppers and cured ham. Wild mushrooms foraged from local forests are also celebrated and enhance regional dishes.

Wild Game

Wild boar, venison, rabbit, pigeon, and quail are all hunted in this territory. Traditionally, pigeon hunting is also a rite of passage for boys, especially in autumn, when they head off to the forests around

long. Both route options are well marked (with red and white parallel stripes in France, and yellow and blue scallop shells and yellow arrows in Spain), except for a 2-kilometer (1.2-mile) section in the final 10 kilometers (6.2 miles) of the Route Valcarlos.

Geography and Terrain

Regardless of which route you choose, pilgrims who decide to begin at Saint-Jean-Pied-de-Port set before them one of the **hardest days of trekking on the Camino.** This is one of the Camino's steepest and longest ascents—and it is on the first day, when pilgrims, even those who trained in advance, are not yet acclimated. Remember to take it slow and steady. Even if you have trained for this, the Camino's lesson (and its challenge) is endurance and perseverance, not speed. A good idea is to break the first day, the Pyrenean crossing from Saint-Jean-Pied-de-Port to Roncesvalles, into two days, spending one night midway up into the mountains, either in Orisson (7.6 km/4.7 mi. after Saint-Jean) if taking the Route Napoleon, or in Valcarlos (if taking the Route Valcarlos).

On the Route Napoleon, you cross from France into Spain at Col de Bentartea. If you take the Route Valcarlos, you'll cross from France into Spain after Arnéguy (Km 771.5). Because both France and Spain are members of

fresh salad with *piquillos* and asparagus

Saint-Jean-Pied-de-Port and Roncesvalles to capture as many of the migrating wood pigeons flying south as possible, using tree-top lookouts and nets laid out on the forest floor. This is also duck and goose country, and a place to sample grilled duck breast and foie gras.

Wine, Cider, and Patxaran

Both Basque Country and Navarra make excellent wines unique to these parts of France and Spain, a tradition that goes back some 2,000 years and that was perfected by monks, such as those in Roncesvalles in the 11th century, who cultivated vineyards to provide wine for their monastery and for pilgrims to Compostela. Look for **txakoli**, a sparkling dry white wine, and for the wines from the **Irouléguy area** near Saint-Jean-Pied-de-Port that produces white (crisp and dry), rosé (drier than most rosés and light), and red (medium-bodied and mineral-forward) wines. You will find these in pretty much every bar and café. (The red Irouléguy is divine with the local sheep's milk cheeses.) And Hemingway had a point that remains valid today: **Navarra** makes excellent and inexpensive **rosé,** dry and mineral forward, with just the right amount of fruit.

Basque **sidra** (cider) is pleasingly tart, with strong apple tastes that tend to be slightly drier and less sweet than counterparts in North America, France, or the UK. Navarrans also make a regional elixir called **patxaran,** an after-dinner digestive liquor, medium red in color, and made from sloe (*Prunus spinosa*), similar to plums. It tastes very much like a plum liquor, sweet but tart at once. You can sample it at **Bar Dena Ona** in Biskarreta.

---

the western European Schengen Area, there are no passport border controls; you will simply walk across the border.

On the Route Napoleon, after you leave Orisson, there is no support until Roncesvalles, over 18 kilometers (11.2 miles) away. On the Route Valcarlos, after the town of Valcarlos there are no support structures until Roncesvalles, over 15 kilometers (9.3 miles) away. Stock up in Orisson or Valcarlos on both water and food.

After the two routes rejoin in Roncesvalles, the Camino enters rolling foothills and dense forests, weaving its way to Pamplona. Near Zubiri, the forested trail gets very rocky. This is a point at which many pilgrims are tired, nearing Zubiri as their final destination for the day, so it is a good time to slow down and step carefully.

Weather

Average temperatures in Saint-Jean-Pied-de-Port are in the range of 3°C (37°F) in winter to 27°C (80°F) in summer. But weather in this foothill town is not an indication of weather on the high mountaintops: The higher-altitude portions of the climb over the Pyrenees can plummet to below freezing nearly any time of year, and at times in the summer can exceed 30°C (86°F). The Route Napoleon can get freezing rains, dense fog that blocks visibility, and, in the late spring, even snow. Take the weather seriously, and inquire with locals at the Pilgrims' Welcome Office before leaving Saint-Jean-Pied-de-Port. Pilgrims have been injured, and have even died, by pushing ahead on the higher route in inclement weather.

The Route Valcarlos is used in winter and during bad weather, but even that route warrants caution. Heed local advice. If the weather is bad and you can't wait for it to clear up, be prepared to take a taxi to Roncesvalles, which you can share with other pilgrims to defray the cost (around €55 for the 45-minute drive).

Getting There

Starting Points

An average of 12 percent of pilgrims begin in **Saint-Jean-Pied-de-Port,** the contemporary Camino's official starting point. **Roncesvalles** is another common starting point, and allows you to skip the rigorous mountain crossing from Saint-Jean-Pied-de-Port, which can be treacherous in bad weather.

Both Saint-Jean and Roncesvalles

Local Markets

Saint-Jean-Pied-de-Port has a colorful **weekly market** of produce, regional food products, and crafts. It sets up every Monday 8am-1pm. This is also generally a slower day as far as pilgrims, trekkers, and tourists pouring into town, so it's a good chance to take things slow with the locals.

have transport networks via train, bus, shuttle, and taxi—expressly for getting pilgrims to their desired starting point—despite the fact that both places are far from urban hubs and nestled in rugged foothills.

Car

If driving the Camino from Saint-Jean-Pied-de-Port or Roncesvalles, the best airports to fly into and rent a car are Bilbao, San Sebastian, and Biarritz.

Saint-Jean-Pied-de-Port connects to Roncesvalles via the mountain road **D933** in France, which becomes the **N-135** after

Rue de la Citadelle, Saint-Jean-Pied-de-Port

you cross into Spain. (You will rarely find any passport control stopping you at the border of France and Spain, and the only indications you've crossed the border will be a road sign welcoming you to Spain and the change in the naming of the road you are on.) The D933 in France/N-135 in Spain passes over the Pyrenees and runs parallel with the Route Valcarlos. After Roncesvalles, continue on the **N-135**, driving southwest, which follows and parallels the Camino de Santiago all the way to Pamplona.

Air

The most common international entry points to reach the Camino are **Paris**—at both **Charles De Gaulle Airport (CDG)** and **Orly Airport (ORY)**—**Madrid Barajas Airport (MAD)**, and **Barcelona El Prat International Airport (BCN)**, with connecting flights to **Bilbao Airport (BIO)**, **Pamplona Nóain Airport (PNA)**, and **Biarritz Parme Airport (BIQ)**, the nearest airports to Roncesvalles and Saint-Jean-Pied-de-Port.

Express Bourricot (661-960-476, www.expressbourricot.com, €19-220, based on distance and number of passengers) runs shuttles from the Biarritz, Bilbao, and Pamplona airports to Saint-Jean-Pied-de-Port and Roncesvalles.

Train

SCNF (892-353-535, www.oui.sncf) efficiently connects trains from Paris to Saint-Jean-Pied-de-Port, with changes in Bordeaux and Bayonne. From Madrid and Barcelona, **RENFE** (902-240-505, www.renfe.com) goes as far as Pamplona, where a bus, shuttle, or taxi can deliver you to Roncesvalles or Saint-Jean-Pied-de-Port.

Bus

ALSA (902-422-242, www.alsa.com) connects Madrid and Barcelona to Pamplona, and Pamplona to Roncesvalles and Saint-Jean-Pied-de-Port. **Autocares Artieda** (www.autocaresartieda.com) runs buses between Pamplona and Roncesvalles.

Taxi

Taxi Urolategui (948-790-218 or 636-191-423, €55-100) is based in Valcarlos, with service between Pamplona, Roncesvalles, and Saint-Jean-Pied-de-Port.

Saint-Jean-Pied-de-Port Km 779.9

After 1177, the year Richard the Lionheart (1157-1199) destroyed the older pilgrim town of Saint-Jean-le-Vieux, locals rebuilt here, nearer the foot of the Pyrenees—hence the name, *pied de port*, foot of the pass. It was a strategic move, a more protected place and higher up where they could see marauders before they were at the town walls.

The new Saint-Jean (called Donibane Garazi in Basque, pop. 1,600) has splendid enclosing walls built of earth-red schist, like all of the town's buildings. They wrap around the medieval town and mark it out well for arriving pilgrims, creating a physical container that is rich with spiritual energy. Just walking along its ancient passageways and climbing up to its citadel, which overlooks and protects the town, naturally transports you to the Middle Ages—but with all the modern advantages of great food and hot showers.

When pilgrims coming from destinations across France and Europe passed here on their way toward the Pyrenees and Spain, it would have been an emotional moment: Many had been on the path for days and weeks already, but the mountains they were about to climb were famous for making or breaking a pilgrim. If they made the passage, they had a good chance of getting to Compostela. If they did not, no gate of pardon would free them of their mortal burdens.

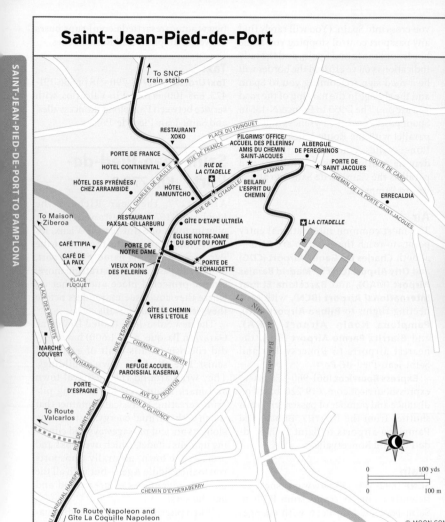

Saint-Jean-Pied-de-Port

To SNCF train station

RESTAURANT XOKO

PLACE DU TRINQUET

PORTE DE FRANCE

RUE DE FRANCE

HOTEL CONTINENTAL

PILGRIMS' OFFICE/ ACCUEIL DES PÈLERINS/ AMIS DU CHEMIN SAINT-JACQUES

ALBERGUE DE PEREGRINOS

ROUTE DE CARO

RUE DE LA CITADELLE

PORTE DE SAINT JACQUES

HÔTEL DES PYRÉNÉES/ CHEZ ARRAMBIDE

CAMINO

CHEMIN DE LA PORTE SAINT-JACQUES

HÔTEL RAMUNTCHO

BEILARI/ L'ESPRIT DU CHEMIN

ERRECALDIA

PL CHARLES DE GAULLE

RUE DE LA CITADELLE

To Maison Ziberoa

RESTAURANT PAXSAL OILLARBURU

GÎTE D'ÉTAPE ULTREÏA

LA CITADELLE

CAFÉ TTIPIA

ÉGLISE NOTRE-DAME DU BOUT DU PONT

CAFÉ DE LA PAIX

PORTE DE NOTRE DAME

VIEUX PONT DES PELERINS

PORTE DE L'ECHAUGETTE

PLACE FLOQUET

La Nive

de

Béherobie

PLACE DES REMPARTS

GÎTE LE CHEMIN VERS L'ETOILE

RUE D'ESPAGNE

MARCHÉ COUVERT

CHEMIN DE LA LIBERTE

RUE ZUHARPETA

REFUGE ACCUEIL PAROISSIAL KASERNA

PORTE D'ESPAGNE

AVE DU FRONTON

To Route Valcarlos

CHEMIN D'OLHONCE

RUE DE SAINT-MICHEL

R DU MARICHAL HARISPE

CHEMIN D'EYHERABERRY

0   100 yds

0   100 m

To Route Napoleon and Gîte La Coquille Napoleon

© MOON.COM

Sights

Over the centuries, this small French town has received millions of pilgrims arriving on foot, and its layout is built for pedestrians. These medieval pilgrims would have passed by the older settlement of Saint-Jean-le-Vieux, and then entered Saint-Jean-Pied-de-Port via the Porte de Saint Jacques. This then leads straight onto the Rue de la Citadelle, the

road on which millions, and by now billions, of feet have passed, for over 900 years—all sharing the same purpose as you now, to walk the Camino over the Pyrenees and into Spain.

Modern pilgrims coming from roads in France still take this same approach. The vast majority arrive by train, and from the station, it's an easy 10-minute walk through the modern town to the

Amular and the Flowering Thistle

Basque and Navarran folklore holds that the supreme creator divinity, Amular, created the earth, the water, the sun, moon, and stars, and all life on earth. When early humans were afraid of living in the dark, she created the moon. When it was not enough light, she created the sun. When the two were too cyclical and not offering permanent light and we still were afraid, she listened to us again, and created a sun-like flowering thistle called *eguzkilore* in Basque.

The dwarf thistle *(Carlina acaulis)* is a perennial in the Pyrenees. Look for dried bundles of it (and rosemary and laurel leaves, as well) fixed to many people's doors here in Saint-Jean and along the Camino through villages and towns in Basque Country and Navarra (and into Rioja as well). You'll find them in Pamplona, too; no city is too big here not to keep the old ways intact. These bundles serve as protection and good luck.

Amular's flower on a doorway in Navarra

Here in Saint-Jean, as you're looking at the homes pressed shoulder to shoulder into a rising hill, notice also their heavy wooden doors framed in stone. Engravings on the lintels indicate the home's age. Some are 500 years old and still standing strong.

Porte de France, which accesses the medieval walled town from a side gate on the lower end. Inside, you will readily find the Rue de la Citadelle—it defines the central spine of the walled settlement—and discover the church straight ahead, the bridge to your right, and the rest uphill and to your left and right. If you're arriving in Saint-Jean-Pied-de-Port by taxi, ask your driver to drop you off in town at the top road of the citadel to experience the town as pilgrims of yore did.

★ La Citadelle

More recent than the walled town below it, **La Citadelle** (559-370-092, www.saintjeanpieddeport-paysbasque-tourisme.com/citadelle) was built for defense in 1628 and rebuilt by military engineers in 1680. The Citadelle building itself is closed to the public—it is now a school—but the extensive surrounding grounds are free to access and an open-air sight that's open all day (dawn to dusk) but gated off at night. The highest point in Saint-Jean, the site offers impressive views, not only of the town below, but also of the deep folds of foothills and river valley and of the steep sloping vineyards on the other end of Saint-Jean. For the best views, climb to the lookout platform located at the high point of the citadel walls. Someone has fastened a dream catcher to the railing there, a lovely reminder that many who come here are riding on hopes and dreams.

Access to explore the outer walls of the citadel has two paths. One is uphill, on the Rue de la Citadelle, near the Porte-St-Jacques. I prefer the other because it aligns you to descend from the citadel and enter Saint-Jean the way medieval pilgrims did, passing through the Porte de Saint Jacques. This path is accessed via the footpath along the river Nive. Go past the **Église de Notre-Dame du Bout du Pont**, through the arched gate, and approach the bridge, but don't

First Stop: Pilgrims' Office

The **Pilgrim Office of Le Amis du Chemin Saint Jacques** (39 Rue de la Citadelle; open year-round 7-9am, 11am-12:30pm, 3:30-9:30pm), is your single most important stop in Saint-Jean-Pied-de-Port. It is run by the **Amis du Chemin Saint-Jacques,** the French association of friends of the Camino, all volunteers and locals who have walked the Camino, most of them many times. This is where all your questions can be answered, problems solved, rooms/beds found, plans made, and nerves calmed, with a good dose of mirth.

In addition to great advice, a warm welcome, and enthusiasm for the rite of passage before you, the experienced volunteers will also give you an altitude map and a three-page document listing all the *albergues* on the Camino, from here to Santiago de Compostela, in tiny print. Here you can also get your pilgrim's passport, the credential, for €2 and get your first stamp in it from this vibrant moment: You are now officially a pilgrim.

Here also you can pick up a scallop shell to hang on your pack, the medieval and modern symbol identifying pilgrims on the Camino. Choose one from a basket that the voluneteers keep filled with scallop shells of various shapes and sizes. They ask for a small donation (€1-2 is

pilgrims' welcome office in Saint-Jean-Pied-de-Port

good). This also sets you up for a ritual up ahead, of drinking red wine from your scallop shell when you reach the wine fountain at Bodegas de Irache (Km 659.8) just after leaving Estella (Km 662.9).

The Amis can also help you find a place to stay, including calling to confirm a place for you in one of the town's auberges/*albergues* or hotels. There is almost always an English-speaking volunteer at the office. When the town is booked full, they can help troubleshoot and find you a place nearby. They also have wifi, with the passcode posted inside.

cross. Instead, make a left and go about 20 meters (66 feet) along the river, where to the left you'll see an iron gate, called the **Porte de l'Echaugette**, that leads to steep steps going up. Climb these steps to the path that traces the upper wall of the old town. From here, you'll see the Église de Notre Dame below you, a great perspective on the back side of this red stone Gothic church. Continue on the path toward the top of the citadel walls. The path then wraps around the walled citadel grounds and exits at the top of Rue de la Citadelle, next to the Porte de Saint Jacques. The full circuit will take about 20 minutes to complete.

Porte de Saint Jacques

Porte de Saint Jacques (Saint James's Gate), a delightful arched passage of dark red stone, enters Saint-Jean-Pied-de-Port from the east, bringing in pilgrims from three of the four main roads in France that merge a few kilometers before here to cross the Pyrenees at the Cize/Valcarlos pass ahead. This feels like a natural threshold, stepping through this gate and into the footsteps of medieval pilgrims arriving from across France. It also sets you at the top of the steep Rue de la Citadelle, the street that cuts through the medieval town, with great views of the old town below.

Top Experience

★ Rue de la Citadelle

When you step onto this road, you are officially stepping onto the Camino as it enters and passes through the first half of medieval Saint-Jean-Pied-de-Port. Here, it may be that for the first time you will feel the reality that you are now following in the footsteps of countless thousands of other pilgrims who have come to this town over hundreds of years to walk the Camino. Seeing and feeling the timeworn cobblestones underfoot can be emotional: it is as if pilgrims have left energetic postcards between the stone cracks to cheer you forward on this amazing adventure. Slow down and really savor it.

The Rue de la Citadelle is also the road along which the vast majority of pilgrim *albergues* (*auberges* or *gîtes* in French) in Saint-Jean-Pied-de-Port are arrayed, as is the all-important office, **Accueil des Peleríns** (Pilgrims' Welcome Office) of the Amis du Chemin Saint Jacques, where you can get your credential (€2), as well as all the advice and enthusiasm you need.

Église de Notre Dame du Bout du Pont

Rue de la Citadelle naturally descends down the hill toward the ancient church of Notre-Dame du Bout du Pont, the dark red schist stone church of Our Lady. This is the spot of the original church building that was constructed soon after 1177, though this particular structure dates to the 13th and 14th centuries. It has a strong Gothic style but with quirky details, such as especially expressive carving in the entrance door's pillar capitals (look for the two women who look like best buddies and seem to watch your every move). The inside feels more intimate, maybe because of the warm red stone. The church can get busy, with tourists popping in during the late morning and early afternoon, but returns to its role as a quiet sanctuary in the early evening and early morning. During those times, it is a pleasure to come here and perhaps light a candle to shed light and blessings upon your forthcoming pilgrimage over the Pyrenees. Daily **mass** is typically offered at 10:30am.

Vieux Pont des Peleríns

Vieux Pont des Peleríns (Old Pilgrims' Bridge) is the picturesque and often photographed bridge over the river Nive that all pilgrims pass over. As you approach it from the Rue de la Citadelle, with the church of Notre-Dame du Bout du Pont to your left, look up over the gate, called the **Porte de Notre Dame,** to see a sculpture of Saint-Jean's namesake, Saint John the Baptist. After you pass under it and cross the river, stop and turn around to see the other side, this time, of a wooden sculpture of Mary, Notre Dame du Bout du Pont, in the overhead niche.

Many pilgrims take turns taking pictures of each other crossing this bridge, a ritual moment of stepping foot into the great transformative journey ahead.

Porte d'Espagne

The old pilgrims' bridge leads to another momentous threshold, Porte d'Espagne. This gate at the far end of the medieval town is your exit from Saint-Jean-Pied-de-Port and your entry onto the full Camino before you: It is 779.9 kilometers (484.6 miles) from here to Santiago de Compostela. Not as elaborate as the Porte de Saint Jacques, the passage is marked by two thick square pillars. But just before passing through, you step over a black-and-white stone inlay of a massive scallop shell, the symbol of the Camino.

While there is no true official starting point of the Camino—traditionally, it is from your front door when you set off on the Camino—this *feels* like the official threshold. Once you step off from here, you are entering your destiny on the Way of Saint James, an ancient route taken by hunters and gatherers, herders, Romans, Charlemagne and Roland, Napoleon's troops, and countless millions of pilgrims for over one thousand years.

Food

This pilgrim town is full of great little restaurants, some that are more oriented toward the river and hidden from the street. Wander around and follow what pulls you in. Be sure to try the local cheese, the creamy but firm sheep's milk Ossau-Iraty AOC (*appellation d'origine contrôlée,* protected name of origin), and the wine unique to this little region, Irouléguy AOC, which is produced in white (10%), rosé (20%), and red (70%) varieties.

★ **Café Ttipia** (2 Place Floquet; 559-371-196; www.cafettipia.com; €15-20) is a classic French brasserie elevated with the fresh and colorful flavors of southwestern French and classic Basque cuisine, such as spring greens salad with almonds and port-poached foie gras, grilled lamb with red peppers and salad, and the *gabure maison* (the house-made, rich vegetable stew of this part of the Pyrenees).

Dining is at long wooden communal tables, assuring you'll fold in to local life and cheer. Local Irouléguy wines and Ossau-Iraty cheeses are on hand to try.

★ **Restaurant Paxsal Oillarburu** (8 Rue Eglise; 559-370-644; €15) is the place to come for trout, grilled and seasoned with *Espelette*, the special red pepper grown in the region and named after the central town of Espelette, 37 kilometers (23 miles) northwest of Saint-Jean. Also try the *piquillos,* the *confit de canard* (duck confit), and the grilled squid with peppers. A warming fire roars in the fireplace on cold nights, and outdoor café tables splay on the terraced sidewalk on warm days.

Restaurant Xoko (1 Place du Trinquet; 559-373-935; €12.50-15) has morning-to-evening good eats, from full meals to just coffee or a glass of wine. Try the *café gourmand,* the gourmet coffee, that comes with an array of small tastes of various desserts with an espresso. The menu includes a selection of salads, grilled plates and charcuterie, and omelets, with specific offerings changing each day based on market finds.

Restaurant Xoko and the town center of Saint-Jean-Pied-de-Port

Café de la Paix (4 Place Foquet; 559-370-099) has well-priced offerings with a solid daily menu (€12.50) that includes local specialties such as red pepper-spiced sausages, hot goat cheese salad, and thin-crust pizzas. Locals come here as much as visitors, and each time I've been here, the service has been impeccable and amicable.

Accommodations

Saint-Jean-Pied-de-Port has a lot of accommodations, most of them very good—and not all of it just for pilgrims, as this is also a popular holiday destination for Spanish and French trekkers as well as food and wine lovers. Most of the pilgrim *albergue*-style accommodations are in the old walled city, and the hotels are all around town outside the medieval walls.

If you land here without a place to stay, head first to the Pilgrims' Welcome Office of the Amis de Chemin Saint-Jacques (39 Rue de la Citadelle), where they will help you find a bed. I've seen them work miracles over and over, dealing with "no rooms at the inn" and other situations that seemed unsolvable, and landing everyone a good place to stay. Here are some favorites, popular with many—and so it's a good idea to book ahead.

Errecaldia (5 Chemin de la Porte St-Jacques; 559-491-702; www.errecaldia.com; €55-75), right across from the upper street passing the Citadelle and just outside the medieval walls above the Porte de Saint-Jacques, is a traditional home from 1673 that two local transplants from England, Tim and Louisa, have turned into a splendid B&B with three rooms with ensuite bath and a delicious breakfast including local breads, cheese, and ham.

The municipal **Albergue de Peregrinos** (55 Rue de la Citadelle; 617-103-189; open all year; 32 beds in three dorm rooms, €10 including breakfast) takes no reservations—just show up and see if there is a bed in this traditional stone, stucco, and wood-beam town home with solid wood bunks.

★ **Beilari**, also known as **L'Esprit du Chemin** (40 rue de la Citadelle; www.beilari.info; 559-372-468; open Mar.-Oct.; 18 beds in three dorm rooms; €33 for a bed, dinner and breakfast) is right across from the Pilgrims' Office. Josef and Jakline, who speak English, offer the sincere welcome of those who honor the deep spirit of the pilgrimage and you as an honored guest. Reservations are recommended and can be easily done online via email. A name card (if you reserved ahead) and a candy rest on the stack of clean sheets, blanket, and pillow of your assigned bunk. After the generous vegetarian dinner, the hosts guide guests through a moving ritual that frames and celebrates the pilgrimage ahead. You can arrange a packed lunch for the next day (€5).

Gîte d'Etape Ultreia (8 Rue de la Citadelle; 680-884-622; www.ultreia64.fr), which opened in 2009, is run by an experienced and passionate hiker who wants others to experience living in a well-restored traditional home as if it were their own. Available are two dorm rooms with both bunk and single beds (11 beds total; €16-17) and two private rooms (€44-48). Breakfast is €5, and there is also a communal kitchen for guests' use. Proprietor speaks English.

The **Refuge Accueil Paroissial Kaserna** (43 Rue d'Espagne; 559-376-517; 14 beds in two bunkhouses) is a parochial *albergue,* run by the Diocese of Bayonne, a simple, basic, and clean place that is open Apr.-Oct. A donation of €15-20, which includes the very good communal dinner and breakfast, is suggested for those who can afford to pay. You'll find this *albergue* to the left on the Rue d'Espagne as the Camino makes its way out of the old city and toward the Cize Pass.

A few steps outside of Saint-Jean-Pied-de-Port on the Route Napoleon (to your right after you pass the Porte d'Espagne), you can find the **Gîte La Coquille**

Napoleon (Route Napoleon; 662-259-940; www.lacoquillenapoleon.simplesite.com; 10 beds in one bunkhouse for €20 and two private rooms, each for €48), a pretty white-and-red-trim country house with a very warm welcome. Communal dinner is €12, and breakfast is €4. Bunk beds are built into the wall, each with its own window, a luxury dorm bed on the Camino. A backyard porch with a long dining table makes for an enchanted gathering place.

Gîte le Chemin vers l'Etoile (21 Rue d'Espagne; 559-372-071; www.pelerinage-saint-jacques-compostelle.com; 46 beds in five dormitories; €17-20) has a winding staircase with mezzanine view to the ground floor in this traditional home from 1580 that was turned into an auberge in 2009. Shared rooms range from having several beds to as few as two or three beds. For €12, you can dine in for the evening meal. Ask also for their packed lunch to take with you onto the trail, for an additional €5-7. Proprietors speak English.

Looking out on the outer walls of the old city, **Hotel des Pyrénées** (19 Place Charles de Gaulle; €180) is a high-end luxury hotel worthy of a honeymoon, with engaging and attentive staff who speak English. The traditional building harbors elegant contemporary rooms and a private back-garden pool. The hotel restaurant **Chez Arrambide** creates dishes that are as beautiful as they are tasty, with the vibrant colors and flavors of local produce, made with both modern and postmodern techniques (including foams)—but, like the hotel, they are truly not for the budget minded: A tasting menu begins at €110.

Hotel Ramuntcho (1 Rue de France; 559-370-391; www.hotel-ramuntcho.com; 16 rooms; €75-100) is the place for central location and comfort. It is a traditional Basque building with modern comforts and amenities, a private courtyard garden, view of the rooftops and mountains, and central location on the Rue de la Citadelle. The staff engagement is less personal and more like what you would find in an international chain hotel, compared to the more personable pilgrim gîtes and *albergues* on the street. They run a good restaurant, with a streetside terrace café that is a delight to sit in and watch the old town.

A few paces from the western outskirts of the old city is the delightful **Maison Ziberoa** (3 Route d'Arneguy; 661-235-944; www.ziberoa.com; four rooms; €65-80; dinner, €24), with crisp bed linens and plush beds, large windows opening onto the countryside, and rooms painted in soft but saturated colors, like the interior of a classic French country farmhouse. The large walled garden has a stand of wisteria that acts as a natural parasol over reclining chairs. Guests get to dine in with home cooking, including *piquillos,* French lentil and carrot casserole, and roasted white asparagus. Proprietors speak English.

The **Hotel Continental** (3 Avenue Renaud; 559-370-025; €65) has to be mentioned, for this is where Tom (Martin Sheen) stayed in the 2010 movie *The Way*. But it is not a luxury hotel: It is in need of a make-over, but still charming (for its enthusiastic, rugby-loving owner). In fact, it is in every way what it appeared in the movie: old-fashioned, basic, and informal. I mention this here for those nostalgic *peregrinos* dedicated to visiting sites found in the movie.

Getting There

Saint-Jean-Pied-de-Port is best reached by train via Bayonne, where the trains from Paris, via Bordeaux, connect to Saint-Jean. If you want to fly to the nearest airport and arrange a shuttle, Biarritz is the nearest airport in southwestern France. You can also take a shuttle, bus, or shared taxi from Pamplona.

Air

One of the most direct ways to get to Saint-Jean-Pied-de-Port is to fly into Paris with a connecting flight to **Biarritz** (www.biarritz.aeroport.fr). The shuttle service **Express Bourricot** (31 Rue de la Citadelle; 661-960-476; www.express-bourricot.com; cash only) picks passengers up at Biarritz's airport and takes them directly to the Pilgrims' Office in Saint-Jean-Pied-de-Port (about 1 hour, €19-84, depending on number of passengers in the shuttle). You can arrange a similar pickup from **Bilbao** and **Pamplona**'s airports and train stations via Express Bourricot to Saint-Jean-Pied-de-Port and Roncesvalles (around 2.5 hours from Bilbao and 1.5 hours from Pamplona, €20-220). The prices of these shuttles vary based on distance and how many passengers are in a shuttle. As such, it is a good idea to inquire ahead about the price and schedule via the contact page on the website, where you can also book your ride.

Car

Rent-A-Car has an agency in Saint-Jean-Pied-de-Port (Route de Bayonne, Garage DTH; 559-507-060; www.renta-car.fr), with other offices in Biarritz and Bayonne.

From **Santander** (291 km/181 mi; 3.5 hours), where ferry passengers arrive, take the **S-10** south and **A-8** to **AP-8**, past Bilbao, east to the border at Irun and Hendaye, and continue on the **A-63** south of Anglet; exit onto **D-932 southeast** and follow **D-918** to Saint-Jean-Pied-de-Port.

Similarly, from **Bilbao** (192 km/120 mi; 2.5 hours), take **AP-8** east to the border at Irun and Hendaye, then **A-63** south of Anglet; exit onto **D-932** southeast and follow **D-918** to Saint-Jean-Pied-de-Port.

From **Pamplona** (75 km/47 mi; 1.5 hours), take the **N-135** north to Roncesvalles and continue to Saint-Jean-Pied-de-Port via Valcarlos. The N-135 becomes the **N-933** in France.

From **Bordeaux** (235 km/146 mi; 3 hours), exit south to Bayonne on the **A-63;** after Bayonne, take the **D-932** and **D-918** to Saint-Jean-Pied-de-Port.

From the airport in **Biarritz** (53 km/33 mi; 1 hr.), take **D-810** southwest to **D-932** and **D-918** to Saint-Jean-Pied-de-Port.

Train

SNCF (892-353-535; www.oui.scnf) runs trains from Bayonne (five trains daily; 1.5 hours; €11) to Saint-Jean-Pied-de-Port, which is the train line's last stop. From Paris, you can buy your ticket for the whole journey; you will change trains in Bordeaux and in Bayonne to reach Saint-Jean. Note that Paris's Charles De Gaulle Airport (CDG) has its own SNCF train station and has one daily departure directly for Bordeaux, so if you get on one of these, you won't have to go into Paris. The whole trip, from CDG to Saint-Jean-Pied-de-Port (€180-200), will take around 8 hours, including the time to change trains in Bordeaux and Bayonne. All other trains depart Paris's Montparnasse Station, also with train changes in Bordeaux and Bayonne (three daily; 6.5-7 hours total, including train changes; €124-180).

RENFE (902-240-505; www.renfe.com) runs nine daily direct trains from Madrid to Pamplona (3-4 hours; €46-60), from where you will need to catch a bus, taxi, or Express Bourricot shuttle to Saint-Jean-Pied-de-Port.

If you take the train from Bayonne, the most common way pilgrims get to Saint-Jean-Pied-de-Port, the ride is a part of the magic—not only for the landscape, but also for the camaraderie of other pilgrims, as well as locals (this is a commuter line). By the time you disembark, you may already have found members of your "Camino family." The train will deposit you at the town's train station, a 5-10-minute walk from the north side of town into the center to the **Porte de France,** the gate into the medieval walled town. Signs from the station will direct you to the historic center, where most of the accommodations are.

Bus

ALSA (www.alsa.com) connects Pamplona to Saint-Jean-Pied-de-Port (3-4 buses daily; 2 hours; €22) with a stop in Roncesvalles. ALSA also runs from Roncesvalles to Saint-Jean-Pied-de-Port (three buses daily; 45 min.; €5).

Taxi

A taxi from Pamplona to Saint-Jean-Pied-de-Port (1.5 hours) costs around €110-120. **Taxi Goenaga** (559-370-500) and **Taxi Maïtia** (683-946-932) are both based in Saint-Jean-Pied-de-Port.

Leaving Saint-Jean-Pied-de-Port

Before you leave, check with the pilgrims' office about the weather conditions and which path—the more popular Route Napoleon up the mountain, or the Route Valcarlos, used during bad weather and in winter—they recommend that day. Both routes are accessed after you leave the walled town through the Porte d'Espagne. Soon after passing this gate, signs will direct you ahead on the **Route Napoleon** (24.7 km/15.3 mi) and to the right toward the **Route Valcarlos** (24 km/15 mi).

Be sure also to stock up on food and water before leaving Saint-Jean-Pied-de-Port, whichever route you decide to take. On the Route Napoleon your last place for food and water before reaching Roncesvalles is in Orisson, 7.6 kilometers (4.7 miles) after Saint-Jean. On the Route Valcarlos, there are only two places to refuel on the 11.7-kilometer (7.3-mile) stretch between Saint-Jean and Valcarlos: a shopping complex called Ventas (7.4 km/4.6 mi. after Saint-Jean) and the town of Arnéguy (8.4 km/5.2 mi after Saint-Jean); and Valcarlos is the last place

to stock up on food and water before reaching Roncesvalles (a 12.3-km/7.6-mi stretch).

Both routes have historic roots and pass through the **Cize Pass,** the easiest pass to traverse on the western side of the Pyrenees. In Roman times this was a part of the **Via Traiana,** the road that began in Bordeaux (Roman Burdegala) and went over the mountains, continuing across the north of Spain to connect to the mines at Astorga. The Romans preferred the higher, mountaintop Route Napoleon, which allowed them to see all around and which reduced the risk of being ambushed by marauders. (Down in the valley, the Route Valcarlos had many places where bandits hid, preying upon vulnerable pilgrims, as the Camino grew in popularity in later centuries. Today, the only safety concerns on the Route Valcarlos are the stretches where you have to walk on the mountain road—watch for cars!) Historically, the valley route had the advantage of better access to water and food, and was the path Charlemagne (Charles the Great) took to return to France in AD 778; this is why Valcarlos—Carlos's Valley—is named after him.

The Route Napoleon

Considered the recommended route in good weather, and only open April-October, this path is largely recommended for its departure from major roads and its breathtaking mountaintop views. If you embark on the Route Napoleon on a sunny day, you will be rewarded with those promised views of the Pyrenees mountains stretching in layers to the ends of the horizon, hawks and griffins circling the sky, and white and black sheep dotting the green slopes. But if you embark on an overcast day, chances are good that once you ascend to the first high point, at the

Pic D'Orisson and **Vierge de Biakorri,** you will have your head quite physically in the clouds and will see nothing but the trail just a few feet before you. In this case, keep vigilant to stay on the trail and look for way-markers. Your best view will be from the highest point, the second highest on the whole Camino, at **Col de Lepoeder,** and then 4 kilometers (2.5 miles) later, arriving at **Roncesvalles,** the monastery complex promising warmth and food.

A good strategy for this ascent, if the weather is iffy or if you want to break up the trek into two days, is to reserve ahead at one of the two auberges (*albergues*) on the mountain, in **Honto** or in **Orisson** (the larger and more popular of the two). Both lodging options are pretty much all that there is, but they offer gorgeous views of the mountains.

The path will veer slightly left as you depart Saint-Jean-Pied-de-Port and follow the D428 uphill to Honto.

Honto   Km 774.7
In Honto (also spelled Huntto) you have views of both the town of Saint-Jean nestled at the foot of the mountains below, and of the mountains before you yet to traverse. Honto essentially consists of one traditional farm house, which is open for lodging (and for dinner and breakfast, for those staying there).

Accommodations and Food
Ferme Ithurburia (on D-428 through Honto; 559-371-117; www.gite64.com/ferme), a farmhouse to the left of the road in Honto, offers private rooms in its **Chambre d'Hôtes** (€55) for up to 14 people, and beds for up to 22 people (€16) in its **Gîte.** The evening meal is €20. Proprietors speak English.

From top to bottom: climbing to La Citadelle in Saint-Jean-Pied-de-Port; Refuge Orisson; the view from Honto.

Leaving Honto

A dirt path just after Honto will lead you left off the D428 for 1 kilometer (0.6 miles) and then will return to the D428 just before entering Orisson.

Orisson   Km 772.3

Orisson consists of the refuge serving pilgrims, and it is your last settement before reaching Roncesvalles.

Accommodations and Food

Jean-Jacques Etchandy runs both the **Refuge Orisson** and the **Gîte Kayola** (559-491-303; www.refuge-orisson.com; both open Apr.-mid-Oct.), the only structures in Orisson. Both are on the Camino's path, which continues on the D428. The Gîte Kayola appears first, to the left of the road. Kayola is intended for pilgrims desiring just a bed (15 beds in one dorm room; some beds are single beds; €15), not dinner or breakfast, in a small country abode with a shared kitchen where you can prepare your own dinner and breakfast. It also has a rustic common room with dining table and fireplace, but you can opt to use the bar-restaurant attached to the Auberge Orisson for drinks, snacks, and meals (at extra cost). Just let Jean-Jacques know you will be there for dinner so he can add a plate.

Eight hundred meters (0.5 miles) onward after Kayola is the **Refuge Orisson,** which straddles both sides of the road, and is for those seeking dinner and breakfast as a part of their accommodations. The rate (€36) includes your dorm bed, communal dinner, and breakfast the next day. For another €4-5 (make sure to request it the day before), you can secure a packed lunch to take on the trail—a good idea if you have not brought your own provisions, as after Orisson, there are no places for food until Roncesvalles. You check in upon arriving at the Refuge Orisson restaurant, the building on the right as you hike in, where you will be assigned your bed and where you can order lunch for the next day. The pilgrim dorms are on the other side of the road and trail, on your left as you enter Orisson, hugging the steep slope of the mountainside. Some of the Refuge Orisson dorm rooms are a bit tight, with too many bunks packed in, but still it is a spotless place with decent bathrooms. The location and the communal dinner are the highlights. Enjoy locally procured produce and products and classic Basque French home cooking—the *coq au vin* is a specialty.

Leaving Orisson

Before leaving Orisson, be sure you fill your water bottles and stock up on food for lunch: There are no other guaranteed places for food until Roncesvalles, over 18 kilometers (11.2 miles) ahead. For water, you will have the option to refill bottles at the pilgrims' fountain, Fontaine de Roland (Roland's Fountain), 9 kilometers (5.6 miles) past Orisson near the French-Spanish border at Col de Bentartea peak.

From Orisson, continue walking on the small D428 mountain road for another 8.8 kilometers (5.5 miles). In 3.8 kilometers (2.4 miles), you will reach the Pic d'Orisson.

Pic D'Orisson   Km 768.5

Pic D'Orisson (1,095 meters/3,593 feet), the first summit after Orisson, is most famous for its ceramic Mary statue, called the **Vierge de Biakorri** (Biakorri Virgin) or Vierge d'Orisson, that is mounted on the top of a pile of rocks at the highest point. She stands just to the left of the trail, and if a fog descends, it will be easy to miss her. Two decades ago, the stand of stones on which she rests was split in half by lightning, but the statue held firm and was unharmed. The stones and the statue of the Vierge de Biakorri make for a picturesque outdoor shrine, with flower offerings from locals tucked near her feet. She is known as the Vierge de Bergers (Shepherds' Virgin), an important patroness and protector of shepherds and their sheep, as well as of all who pass here on this climactic mountaintop.

If you happen to be here on the Sunday after August 15, you will see locals dedicated to Mary's grace making a pilgrimage to this point to attend a **mass** that is held here once a year. A local priest began the tradition in 1995 after lamenting that shepherds in his parish could rarely make it down the mountain to attend mass. The date of the pilgrimage in August commemorates Mary's Assumption (her body and soul ascending to heaven).

Leaving Pic D'Orisson

At 3.6 kilometers (2.2 miles) after Pic D'Orisson, a *crucero* (standing crossroads crucifix) known as **Cruz de Thibault** marks where the path veers to the right and off the D428 road onto a rocky dirt path. From this fork, in another 1.6 kilometers (1 mile) and on the left side of the trail, you will pass the **Fontaine de Roland** (Roland's Fountain), named in honor of Charlemagne's officer who, according to legend, died in these mountains. If you need water, fill up here: It's another 8 kilometers (5 miles) to Roncesvalles. In a few meters, at the peak of **Col de Bentartea** (1,332 meters/4,370 feet, Km 763.3), you will cross the French-Spanish border. The next 3.8 kilometers (2.7 miles) from the Col de Bentartea to Col de Lepoeder are a steep but final climb.

■■■■■ **Top Experience** ■■■■■

★ Col de Lepoeder   Km 759.5

At 1,430 meters (4,692 feet), this is the highest peak of this crossing and the second highest peak of the whole Camino (the highest is Monte Irago, in Leon, at 1,515 meters/4,970 feet). The views afforded here are expansive and revealing of the geology of the Pyrenees mountains. It is exhilarating to see all of Spain sweeping before you and France behind you, the steep jutting green-gray-blue mountain peaks capped with snow or dotted

with herds of cream-colored sheep, and griffon vultures with nine-foot (274-cm) wingspans riding air currents overhead. Equally exhilarating may be the fact that you can see the huddled rooftops of Roncesvalles, signaling that you are almost there.

Leaving Col de Lepoeder

Although you've reached the apex, the hardest part of the hike is to come: the steep descent. Thankfully, here you have a choice of two possible trails, both marked. If you wish, you can continue straight ahead on the Route Napoleon down a sharply steep hillside, a task that should only be undertaken with strong knees, no rain, and a dry trail. It is this one descent that causes the bulk of injuries for pilgrims, all too early on their Camino. If you take this path, another 4 kilometers (2.5 miles) remain to reach Roncesvalles.

Alternatively, you can follow the signposted trail to the right from Col de Lepoeder for a 4.3-kilometer (2.7-mile) trek on a gentler, paved path to **Puerto de Ibañeta,** the pass where Charlemagne's military guard led by Roland was defeated; here, the trail joins the **Route Valcarlos** for the rest of the 1.5 kilometers (1 mile) to Roncesvalles. This route adds 1.8 kilometers (1.1 miles) more to the walk, a total of 5.8 kilometers (3.6 miles) from Col de Lepoeder to Roncesvalles. This is a recommended path, not only for the softer slope down, but also the chance to see the views from Ibañeta pass.

👉 Detour: The Route Valcarlos

This sublimely beautiful 24-kilometer (15-mile) route is dense with native beech, chestnut, oak, and pine forest, and intimate valley passages along steep cliffs carved out by the Nive river. The Camino follows the river toward Valcarlos and Roncesvalles. It parallels in many places the mountain road D933, as it is called in France, and the N-135, as the same road is called after you cross into Spain—but more often you will be on smaller country lanes or dedicted foot paths. In two places you will have to walk directly on the N-135, as there is no bank: On the 2.5 kilometers (1.6 miles) before Gañecoleta (Km 765), and a 2-kilometer (1.2-mile) stretch that begins 1 kilometer (0.6 miles) past Gañecoleta. Be cautious of cars, and step carefully to avoid slipping down the steep slope to the river below.

The trail from Saint-Jean-Pied-de-Port via Valcarlos to Roncesvalles is marked with the French-style red and white stripes, along with yellow signs indicating place names and distances. It is well marked, except for the 2-kilometer (1.2-mile) stretch after Valcarlos, overlapping with the first of two sections where the path has no bank and is on the N-135.

One kilometer (0.6 miles) before the village of Arnéguy, plunked in the midst of wild terrain, you will pass through a somewhat incongruently modern luxury goods shopping complex, **Ventas** (Km 772.5), a good place nonetheless to do some food shopping at the grocery store, to refill water bottles, or to grab a bite at the café.

Arnéguy   Km 771.5

Your last settlement in France—truly the last, as it sits right on the border between France and Spain—Arnéguy (pop. 232) is an international zone where you still feel the strong French culture as well as that of the Basques, the Navarrese, the Spanish, and most profoundly, the special mountain mood of people from the heart of the Pyrenees. Many locals speak all three languages—Basque, French, and Spanish—and enjoy welcoming pilgrims to their mountain spot on the pretty banks of the Nive d'Arnéguy river. Neat rows of kitchen gardens and hanging terraces line the water's edge. Arnéguy's 17th-century church, **Église de l'Assomption,** is on the central high spot of the village and is easy to find.

Accommodations
Enjoy the terraces and country inn rooms at the riverside **Hotel Clementenia** (on the left on the D933 through Arnéguy; 524-341-006; www.hotelclementenia.com; €45-70), which offers nine spotless and cozy rooms. The restaurant serves home-cooked meals, including on-the-spot special requests for vegetarian dishes. Some rooms look out on the river. Proprietors speak English.

Leaving Arnéguy
Note that the **D933** becomes the **N-135** as you cross into Spain. (There are no passport or border controls, so you may not even notice the crossing.) The Camino continues to parallel the N-135 after Arnéguy, but you have an alternate option to take a smaller country road just a few meters to the left off the N-135, toward the hamlet of **Ondarolle** (Km 768.9), less than 1 kilometer (0.6 miles) before Valcarlos. Take this option; it is beautiful and calm, with little traffic, and adds no significant extra distance.

The final 400-meter climb into Valcarlos goes from the river up to the mountainside to the town and is steep and paved. It is surrounded by chestnut trees that drop nuts, making it easy to slip; step carefully to avoid turning an ankle.

Valcarlos   Km 768.2

Called Luzaide in Basque, Valcarlos (pop. 387) is named for the valley where Charlemagne is thought to have camped in 778, as he and his army retreated back to France after a war campaign in Spain. Valcarlos today is a neat, tiny mountain town steeped in ancient Pyrenees traditions, despite being a thoroughfare from France to Spain. It is also a place where people passionate for hiking, immersion in nature, and trout fishing come for holidays. The narrow Nive River valley offers respite and retreat all around you.

Top: Valcarlos. **Bottom:** Monument to Roldan at Puerto de Ibañeta

In the Middle Ages, Valcarlos was a pilgrim town with a medieval hospital and church, neither of which have survived. The modern town church, **Iglesia de Santiago,** stands on the highest point on the road that cuts centrally through town. You will most likely find it locked, but you can ask for the key from the town hall (Ayuntamiento de Luzaide; Calle Elizaldea s/n; 948-790-117; www.luzaide-valcarlos.net), across the street from the church. An interesting modern **mural** a few paces from the church, on the same side of the street, depicts traditional aspects of Basque culture. In the mural's foreground, a man in a traditional Basque red-and-white shirt and trousers walks toward a pilgrim with a staff, with the hilly green countryside and Valcarlos's church sweeping down behind him. Most intriguingly, in front of the painted church are three women and a dancing bullheaded creature, all of them circling a large bonfire. This image is similar to one by the famous 18th-century Spanish painter, Francisco de Goya, who is known for for his paintings on *brujería* (witchcraft). Both Goya and this muralist drew inspiration from the older source of local folklore, which held that witchcraft was not a dark force but a positive healing force. This mural feels like a celebration.

Food

The rivers of the Pyrenees are full of trout, but it was the streams crossed by the Camino that drew Hemingway. Many restaurants in the area feature the fish, but few capture the panache of Valcarlos's pub, restaurant, and grocery store, ★ **Benta Ardandegia** (Calle Elizaldea, 15; 948-796-002; www.ardandegia.com), a one-stop shop for all food needs. Come here for a three-course *menú* (€10, including local trout and Ossau-Iraty

From top to bottom: the village of Arnéguy; sheep on the cliffside in the village of Gañecoleta; stone honoring Our Lady Roncesvalles at Ermita de San Salvador.

sheep's milk cheese), a drink with fellow pilgrims and locals, or to do your grocery shopping: just-picked produce, regional food products, or a freshly baked loaf. The staff is determined to make their customers happy and the chef is a master, turning an ordinary daily menu into a gastronomic adventure, including thick grilled steaks, vibrant fresh garden salads, and homemade desserts—including the classic yogurt-like custard, *cuajada,* served with local honey. But it is her trout, caught fresh and fried with cured ham, that tops the list. The grocery store stays open as long as the bar and restaurant are open, and this can be late into the night. Come here for the trout, stay for the society.

Accommodations
The municipal **Albergue de Valcarlos** (Plaza de Santiago; 948-790-117; turismo@luzaide-valcarlos.net; 24 beds in two dorm rooms; €10), which opened in 2008, is excellent. Located next to the school, this *albergue* is small and efficient, with new facilities including a washing machine, kitchen equipment, and sturdy metal bunks—plus a view overlooking the gardens of the river valley you just climbed up from. You will either have to cook for yourself or enjoy the bars and restaurants in town, all of which are an easy saunter up the small hill to the main road.

Mendiola Apartamentos (Calle Elizaldea, 113; 609-755-105; www.turismomendiola.com) consists of six rural apartments in a mountain chalet structure with white walls and dark slate tiles and roof. The owner makes these available for one night and offers *peregrinos* the chance to cook in a private kitchen in their own space at remarkable prices: While they run around €75, which can be shared with several people, you may be able to get an apartment for €25 in the low season. A bouquet of fresh mountain flowers and herbs on the counter adds a splash of love to the place.

Leaving Valcarlos
On the 12.3 kilometers (7.6 miles) from Valcarlos to Roncesvalles, there are no places for food, water, or lodging. Be sure to fill water bottles and carry enough food for lunch and snacks. The Camino continues to be marked with a mix of yellow arrows, red-and-white-striped trail markers, and pillars with the blue-and-yellow scallop shell. It leaves Valcarlos following the N-135 south (the sun will rise to your left). Carefully stick to the bank of the road, watching for blind turns and oncoming traffic. About 1 kilometer (0.6 mile) after leaving Valcarlos, trail markers disappear for the next 2-3 kilometers (1.2-1.9 miles), and so does the road bank—you will need to walk on the road itself. Markers will appear more frequently again thereafter, and thankfully will also lead you to the left, off the road and onto a peaceful country path toward the village of Gañecoleta.

Gañecoleta   Km 765
Huddled in a narrow dale of the Nive d'Arneguy river, this hamlet (pop. <10) is forgotten by time, with sheep grazing along its steep sides and foot bridges crossing bucolically from one side of the settlement to the other. The path passes through groves, gardens, and dense undergrowth; sunlight barely reaches here, a few hours a day at most, because it is so narrow and steep. Chestnut trees grow densely all around. The dirt trail is narrow in many spots, sometimes with a steep edge. Step carefully. It will often be damp and covered with leaves. More and more, yellow arrows and blue-and-yellow scallop-shell markers will guide you on the trail.

Leaving Gañecoleta
At 1.5 kilometers (1 mile) beyond Gañecoleta, the Camino will return to the N-135 for 2.4 kilometers (1.5 miles): Be very careful on this stretch, as there is little bank and you will be walking on the road itself. The Camino then veers

off the road to the left and departs the N-135 for good, to pass on dirt footpaths through wild beech forests. This passage, from here all the way to Roncesvalles, is resplendent with some of the most beautiful chestnut and beech forests anywhere in the north, competing with the forests of Galicia. The entire 7.6-kilometer (4.7-mile) stretch, from here to Puerto de Ibañeta, is also an upward climb; the last 4 kilometers (2.5 miles) are especially steep and relentless

▬▬ Top Experience ▬▬

★ Puerto de Ibañeta   Km 757.4

At 1,057 meters (3,468 feet), this is the highest point on the Route Valcarlos, affording a bird's eye view of the multicolored heather- and fern-covered mountains facing France, as well as the rolling forest terrain facing Spain and leveling out toward Roncesvalles. Of this site, Aimery Picaud, the purported author of the *Codex Calixtinus* (the 12th-century pilgrim guide), wrote that it "is so high it appears to touch the sky; those who make the ascent believe they can touch

the heavens" (courtesy of T.A. Layton's translation that appears in his book, *The Way of Saint James,* 1976).

This is also where some believe Charlemagne's officer Roland fell during his defeat in 778, when the local Basques defended their territory against Charlemagne's expansionist designs on the region.

Sights
Monument to Roland
This historic marker, an upright rough-cut gray standing stone, is engraved simply with the name Roland, the date of his death (778), and the date the stone was erected, 1967. It makes a good fixed point in the foreground for the magnificent backdrop of mountains facing back toward France.

Ermita de San Salvador
Down the hill from the monument is the **Ermita de San Salvador** (948-790-301; www.roncesvalles.es; usually closed), a small A-frame chapel of red schist and black slate, built in 1964. It marks the site of the earlier chapel of

the Route Valcarlos trail through chestnut and beech forest after Gañecoleta

Basque and Navarran Folklore

In traditional Basque and Navarran folklore, nature is full of wild and powerful spirits. As you walk through the rugged mountains, lush valleys, and dense forests of the Pyrenees, you may find it's easy to imagine them yourself. These are some of the most significant:

Mari

Mari, the great mother of the natural world, dwells in caves, mountains, and water sources, and is associated with the moon and lightning. She may have bird's feet, and can be seen sitting at a cave opening, spinning her signature spool or running a golden comb through her long hair. Mari can also shape-shift into a male ram, a horse, a cow, a tree, a gust of wind, a cloud, a rainbow, or fire. Though the name Mari predates the name Mary and comes from an independent history, one easily slipped into the other as Christianity made its way into this region. Mari is still revered here and is experiencing a resurgence as perhaps the most important being in Basque sacred culture. Many places in Basque Country, such as hilltops and caves, are named in her honor.

Maju

Maju (also called Sugaar) is Mari's male partner; his main form is a great snake. Together they are a formidable pair as patrons of the earth and defenders of nature, seeking justice when humans harm the natural world or when they are dishonest and mean with one another. Maju can also be seen in the sky with bolts of lightning. Basque gender studies scholar Margaret Bullen theorizes that, long before the arrival of Christianity, Maju was actually a part of Mary, her masculine side. The two were later separated, to align with the Christian view of Mother Mary (syncretic with Mari) as separate from the snake that she stands upon and "tames."

a Romanesque depiction of Mari on a church in the French Pyrenees

Lamiñak

Lamiñak are fairies of water sources and caves, who often have duck-like feet. They do Mari's bidding and, like her, can be found sitting at stream mouths and cave openings, combing their hair with golden combs. Many names of wells and caves in Basque Country include a variation of their name.

Other Creatures

Ancient Basque culture included a host of other beings. **Maide,** male fairies, are said to have built the stone circles that are found along remote parts of the western Pyrenees. **Basajaun** and **Basandere,** a mythic wild man and wild woman, protect the forests and the wild beasts. The **Maindi,** the spirits of peoples' ancestors, visit old ancestral homes and churches at night and then return to their spirit homes by day. And lastly, **Hartza,** the great bear of an old Basque cult, is considered the ancestor of the Basques.

Charlemagne, where it is believed he fell to his knees and prayed to Santiago. (For Charlemagne did return, many times, according to legends. In fact, after his death Charlemagne was made one of the Camino's leading champions; like Saint James, he leapt from far places to arrive in the nick of time for the church.)

More interesting than the 1964 chapel are some of the stones from the original walls of the medieval monastery that rest just in front of the modern chapel, tracing an outline of the wall foundations. Next to these scant remains is a pretty, modern standing stone engraved with the image of **Our Lady of Roncesvalles,** where you are invited to stand and utter a silent prayer. The outlines of the older ruin may date to the 11th century. This was the original chapel that sounded a bell at night and in fog to guide pilgrims to Roncesvalles. That bell is now said to be the one set in the Capilla de Santiago in Roncesvalles.

Leaving Puerto de Ibañeta

From here, Roncesvalles is a gentle, 1.5-kilometer (1 mile) downhill walk through more lovely beech and oak forest. You will soon see the blessed view of Roncesvalles's monastery slipping above the trees and enter the hamlet through a passage along the back wall, near the *albergue*, monastery hotel, and collegiate church. Sometimes horses graze the forest here. Don't be surprised if they meet you on the path.

Roncesvalles   Km 753.9

The present monastery complex that defines the village of Roncesvalles (known as Orreaga in Basque) dates to the 12th century, but people have been traversing this territory for millennia. Given its importance as a pilgrim stop, it may come as a shock to discover the year-round population is only 21 people. The cream-white stone and black-slate-roofed hamlet is huddled around itself, with the monastery and abbey church at the center.

Nuestra Señora de Roncesvalles

A miraculous story said to have occurred during the 9th century gives Roncesvalles its own Mary. One night, on a hillside somewhere around here, two shepherds looking over their flock saw a stag approach them and indicate that they should follow it. The stag led them to a hidden area in the mountain and began to scratch the earth with its hoof. As the dirt fell away, it revealed an ancient dolmen—standing stones from the Neolithic—buried by time. Inside it sat an image of Mary. That Mary became not only **Nuestra Señora de Roncesvalles,** but also **La Reina de los Pirineos,** the Queen of the Pyrenees. She has a following that goes beyond this tiny hamlet and even beyond all the pilgrims who pass through. Among many peoples of the Pyrenees, she possesses as revered and potent spiritual power as does Our Lady of Lourdes—perhaps even more, since she has had more centuries to build up a following.

The legend seems to have clear parallels to that of Mari, the Basque earth goddess who lives in subterranean places, such as dolmens, caves, and the openings of underground streams. In **Burguete**, the next village over, **Bar Frontón** displays the village's coat of arms, which includes an image of the stag. According to locals, the story of Mary and the stag has as many tellings and interpretations as there are people who live here—including ancient pagan versions.

Roncesvalles

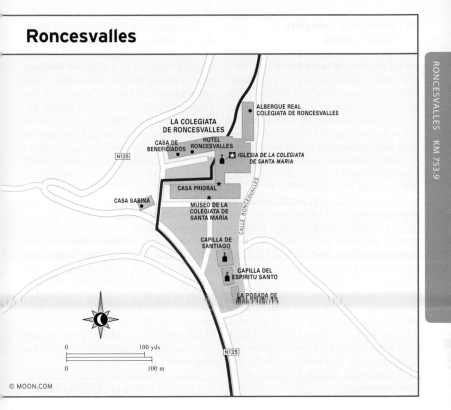

Map labels:

- ALBERGUE REAL COLEGIATA DE RONCESVALLES
- LA COLEGIATA DE RONCESVALLES
- CASA DE BENEFICIADOS
- HOTEL RONCESVALLES
- N135
- IGLESIA DE LA COLEGIATA DE SANTA MARIA
- CASA PRIORAL
- CASA SABINA
- MUSEO DE LA COLEGIATA DE SANTA MARÍA
- CALLE RONCESVALLES
- CAPILLA DE SANTIAGO
- CAPILLA DEL ESPIRITU SANTO
- LA POSADA DE
- 0   100 yds
- 0   100 m
- N135
- © MOON.COM

Forest, more hills, and fertile fields surround the whole.

Sights

Roncesvalles is essentially a hamlet founded for, and defined by, its large 12th-century monastery complex of interlocking white and gray buildings. Collectively it is called **La Colegiata de Roncesvalles,** and to confuse matters, its most illustrious part, the monastery church of Santa Maria, is often simply called La Colegiata as well. The full extent of the Colegiata monastery complex includes (in the order you will encounter them as you step into Roncesvalles on the Camino): the pilgrims' Albergue Real Colegiata de Roncesvalles, where most *peregrinos* stay in Roncesvalles; Hotel Roncesvalles (on

your right after a short arched passageway), a modern hotel located inside a historic pilgrims' hospital called Casa de los Beneficiados; the Iglesia de la Colegiata de Santa Maria (on your left); and finally, the rest of the monastery complex, immediately in front of you from the church. The cloister shares a wall with the church and is located just past the church on the left (closed from view and behind the wall). Straight ahead, the long Casa Prioral (Priory House) houses the monastery's museum. Museum admission will give you access to the cloister, the exhibits, and the priory house, as well as a guided tour to the two other historic buildings of Roncesvalles, the Capilla de Santiago and the Capilla del Espíritu Santo, which otherwise remain closed.

★ Iglesia de la Colegiata de Santa María

The abbey or collegiate church, **Iglesia de la Colegiata de Santa Maria** (948-790-480; www.roncesvalles.es; daily, 8am-9pm) was consecrated in 1219 and is the monastery complex's greatest highlight, an early Gothic building with beautiful stained-glass windows depicting both sacred and profane (but royal) personages.

At the center is a silver-wrought canopy sheltering the altar and the church's most sacred possession: the 13th-century Gothic statue of **Nuestra Señora de Roncesvalles,** Our Lady of Roncesvalles. It is possible that a devout pilgrim brought the statue from Toulouse, where it was most likely made. I find the best-spent time in Roncesvalles to be in the church itself, enjoying the stained glass and the sweeping stone walls that form a structure that is more square than rectangular, embracing you on all sides. This is Spain's earliest Gothic church and a great place to contemplate the Queen of the Pyrenees, as Our Lady of Roncesvalles is called all across the mountain range.

You can enjoy celebrations of Mary during **mass,** a formal and celebratory observation for pilgrims and locals, which is followed by a **pilgrims' blessing** every evening at 8pm. This is one of the more formal and potent masses on the Camino, even for secular pilgrims, because it is a colorful ritual enacted at the beginning of a charged journey on the Camino. The power here also comes from the great sense of accomplishment at meeting the challenge of climbing over the Pyrenees.

Museo de la Colegiata de Santa María

The highlight of the Museo (948-790-480; www.roncesvalles.es; daily 10am-2pm and 3:30-7pm; €5, €4 for pilgrims) is the guided tour (English possible), included in the price of admission, which takes you through the small square monastery cloister and the other historic buildings of Roncesvalles, Capilla de Santiago and the Capilla del Espíritu Santo, that are otherwise closed to the public.

The museum itself is also interesting for two pieces of religious history

the Capilla de Santiago and Capilla del Espíritu Santo in Roncesvalles

associated with the village's Camino history. First, there is an **oliphant,** an ancient horn made from an elephant tusk that can make quite a blasting sound; it may be the one that Roland blew on Puerto de Ibañeta when he was seeking Charlemagne's aid. (The other possible candidate is held in a basilica in Bordeaux.) Then there is the so-called **Charlemagne's chessboard,** a pretty inlaid black-and-white chessboard pattern found not on a board, but on a reliquary box from the 14th century. Though it's neither a chessboard nor personally associated with Charlemagne, who lived in the 8th and early 9th centuries, it is a fine example of fine medieval craftsmanship. The museum occupies the space of the long, two-storied **Casa Prioral** (Priory House), which connects perpendicularly to the collegiate church and cloister.

Capilla de Santiago

Once you pass the large monastery complex, to your left you will see the Capilla de Santiago and the Capilla del Espíritu Santo standing side to side. The diminutive Capilla de Santiago (access by guided tour is included with admission to the Museo de la Colegiata) is a 13th-century Gothic building, and since that century its bell has been rung at night to help delayed or lost pilgrims make their way to Roncesvalles in the dark. In Christianity, the bell symbolizes the voice of God calling the faithful to him. It is possible this is the same bell that once belonged to the 11th-century chapel of San Salvador at Puerto de Ibañeta. Inside, it is a simple stone single-aisle nave chapel with a solitary sculpture of Saint James on the altar.

Capilla del Espíritu Santo

Right next to the Iglesia de Santiago

From top to bottom: Iglesia de la Colegiata de Santa Maria; detail on the Iglesia de la Colegiata de Santa María; the pilgrims' albergue in Roncesvalles.

Pintxos Primer

Pinchos (spelled *pintxos* here, the Basque spelling of things with a "ch" sound) are creative bite-sized appetizers from Basque Country and Navarra that are meant to accompany a glass of wine or short glass of beer (*un corto*) as a part of the tradition of the culinary pub crawl. The more elaborate *pintxos* you see arrayed on counters are the ones you order and pay for (usually €2-3). But if you just order beer or wine at a bar, it's tradition for the bartender to give you a small, simple bite to eat with it, free of charge. (This tradition comes from a law passed by Alfonso X, the 13th-century king of Castile and León, who declared that tavern keepers must serve food with alcoholic drinks to benefit people's health and prevent drunkenness.)

The more elaborate tradition of €2-3 *pintxos* is especially prevalent in Pamplona and is increasingly common thereafter on the Camino. In this area, you'll find the tradition in play on a smaller scale, at places such as **Casa Sabina** in Roncesvalles, **Bar Frontón** in Burguete, and **Café del Camino** in Zubiri.

you'll find the broad, square, 12th-century Capilla del Espíritu Santo. The chapel is built over a crypt holding the bones of pilgrims who died during the Valcarlos crossing; it is a somber reminder of the fleeting nature of life. The chapel was built first in memory of Charlemagne and Roland; some believe that the bones of Roland and some of his men were buried here, too. The structure is rarely open, except for on a tour arranged via the museum, but it's always visible through the iron gate and open arcaded windows.

Events

Along with Lourdes, Roncesvalles is one of the most important Marian sanctuaries in the Pyrenees. Region-wide festivities in Mary's honor take place in September, to celebrate her birth on September 8.

Every Sunday in May and early June, there are small pilgrimages made to Roncesvalles from the surrounding villages—beautiful, cheerful, and reverent processions that are all dedicated to the Mary of Roncesvalles. To see which village makes its pilgrimage on which Sunday, visit www.roncesvalles.es. I especially enjoyed being part of one from Burguete, right on the Camino, making a reverse walk back to Roncesvalles.

Food and Accommodations

Roncesvalles is a tiny hamlet, despite the large and famous monastery, and you will find everything easily by standing in the middle of the settlement and simply looking around. All the accommodations are next to each other.

The largest and most traditional, in operation since 1127, is now housed in the modern and fully renovated sections of Roncesvalles's monastery, the **Albergue Real Colegiata** (open all year; 948-760-000; www.alberguederoncesvalles.com; 218 beds; €12). The *albergue* is managed by Dutch *hospitaleros* and is clean, with very comfortable facilities, hot showers, and semi-private cubicle accommodations (four beds per compartment). The communal meal is fortifying, basic but good.

Next door, also on church grounds, the priests' quarters known as the **Casa de Beneficiados**, built in 1724, have been renovated and converted into the **Hotel Roncesvalles** (Calle Nuestra Señora de Roncesvalles, 14; 948-760-105; www.hotelroncesvalles.com; €55-135), with 25 luxury apartments or rooms. You can step in to see the space, though it looks more like a modern luxury hotel on the inside; the outside remains unchanged and shows continuity with the pilgrims' *albergue* that you just passed.

Getting to Roncesvalles from Saint-Jean-Pied-de-Port

If you arrive in Saint-Jean and need to skip the first part of the journey due to inclement weather, here are your options:

- **ALSA** (www.alsa.com) buses connect Saint-Jean-Pied-de-Port to Roncesvalles (three buses daily; 45 min.; €5).

- **Express Bourricot** (31 Rue de la Citadelle; 661-960-476; www.express-bourricot.com; €12-40 per person, depending on time of day) shuttles pilgrims from Saint-Jean-Pied-de-Port to Roncesvalles (40-45 mintues).

- A **taxi** from Saint-Jean costs around €55 one way and takes around 45 minutes. To save costs, share with other passengers. Call **Taxi Urolategui** (948-790-218 or 636-191-423), **Taxi Goenaga** (559-370-500), or **Taxi Maïtia** (683-946-932).

The accommodations here are impeccable, but the atmosphere and reception is somewhat neutral and far less interested in you as a pilgrim than other local accommodations. There is a decent hotel restaurant, but try to get a table at Casa Sabina for a more engaging and memorable meal.

Casa Sabina (N135, s/n, Roncesvalles; 948-760-012; www.casasabina.roncesvalles.es; rooms are €45-55; breakfast €3.50, lunch and dinner €13-20) is both a cute country-style inn with rooms on the upper floors and a popular ★ **café-restaurant** on the entry level. Given that this is a small place, and massive amounts of people pour over the mountains on any given day, sometimes the place is too packed and busy and can't cater to everyone. Try to get in, though, for the creative appetizers on their *picoteo* (*pintxo*) menu, but also for the entrees, including homemade ravioli and *empanadas* (savory pies).

The entryway of **La Posada** (N135, s/n, Roncesvalles; 948-790-322; www.laposada.roncesvalles.es; open Mar.-Dec.; 19 rooms; €55-75) will look familiar if you love the movie *The Way*: This is where the character Tom (Martin Sheen) stayed his first night on the Camino. In the movie, La Posada is cast as a basic *albergue*, but in reality, it is a comfy country inn with a bar on the entry floor and, for €10, a quality *plato del peregrino*

(pilgrim's plate) for guests. (Everyone, however, can enjoy the bar.) Also contrary to the movie, the owner is energetic and excited about welcoming *peregrinos*, not tired and washed out. He'll even help you find alternative accommodations if the town is fully booked.

Getting There

Roncesvalles has shuttle, bus, and taxi services that connect it to larger urban hubs, including Pamplona (the closest), Biarritz, and Bilbao.

The best way to reach Roncesvalles is from Pamplona, which is connected to the international hubs of Barcelona and Madrid by train. From Pamplona, you can take a bus with **ALSA** (www.alsa.com) or a more costly but efficient pre-arranged shuttle with **Express Bourricot** (www.expressbourricot.com) to Roncesvalles. You can also fly into Bilbao and arrange this same shuttle to take you to Roncesvalles.

Car

From **Saint-Jean-Pied-de-Port** (27.5 km/17 mi; 40 min.): Take the **D933** in France south to Arnéguy, where it crosses the border (no border controls) and remains the same road but is called the **N-135** in Spain.

From **Santander** via **Bilbao** (300 km/186 mi; 4 hours): Take the **A-8** east and exit onto the **AP-68** south at Bilbao. Continue on the **AP-68/N-622** to Vitoria-Gasteiz and exit onto the **A-1 and A-10.** Take exit 97 onto the **AP-15** to Pamplona. Take the **PA-30** to **N-135** (Carretera de Francia) that goes to Roncesvalles.

From **Pamplona** (47 km/29 mi; 1 hour): Take the **N-135** north from Pamplona to Roncesvalles.

From **Madrid** (440 km/273 mi; 5.5 hours): Leave the city on the **A-2/E-90** northeast toward Medinaceli; take the **N-111** after Soria; next get on the **N-232/A-12/LO-20** at Logroño. Continue on the **A-12** south of Pamplona and take the exit to the **A-21**, then exit onto the **N-234.** Take **NA-1720** at Urrozo and take it to the **N-135** and Roncesvalles.

From **Barcelona** (535 km/332 mi; 6 hours): Exit west on **E-90** to **AP7**, then **AP-2** to Zaragoza; exit to **AP-68/E-805** to **AP-15** past Tudela and to Pamplona; take the **AP-15** to **PA-30** and exit north onto **N-135** to Roncesvalles.

Shuttle

Express Bourricot (www.expressbourricot.com) runs shuttles from the airports and train stations in Pamplona (1 hour) and Bilbao (2.5 hours) to Roncesvalles (€84-220).

Train

RENFE (www.renfe.com) connects Madrid (seven trains daily; 3-4 hours; €42-78) and Barcelona (seven trains daily; 4-5 hours; €33-61) to Pamplona, where buses, taxis, and shuttle connect to Roncesvalles.

Bus

Autocares Artieda (www.autocares-sartieda.com; 1.5 hours; €7) runs one bus between Pamplona and Roncesvalles, Monday through Saturday; no buses on Sunday.

Leaving Roncesvalles

Nothing could be easier: Look for the road sign that says "Santiago de Compostela 790 km" (491 mi—that's the distance a car drives, but the numbers are a bit different for thru-hikers). The Camino runs to the right of the sign and road.

The forest between Roncesvalles and Burguete grows dense and intimate, thick with beech and oak growing in animated shapes and postures. It feels physically enchanted. Though the road is not far to the left, here it can get very quiet and still, as if nature spirits are watching. It was believed that in this forest, up until their persecution in the 16th century, witches—white witches, *curanderas*—would meet to hold their healing rituals, in private and in the power of a remarkable natural setting. This "coven" was tried under some of the famous witch trials in Spain, where nine from this area were burned at the stake by the Inquisition's authorities, five of them in Burguete.

In 2 kilometers (1.2 miles)—1 kilometer (0.6 miles) before Burguete, on the left of the forest path—stands **La Cruz Blanca** ("the white cross"), also called Roland's Cross, erected here in the 17th century to protect the path between Roncesvalles and Burguete. As the commemorative plaque states, the cross is a "symbol of divine protection," and it could have been intended for the healers as much as for anyone else. These matters, now in hindsight, are being recast with a more balanced view, as the information board associated with the cross here attests. A similar information board, also on the local witchcraft tradition, can be found in front of the village church in Burguete.

Burguete   Km 750.9

Best known as Hemingway's village in the Pyrenees, Burguete (pop. 244) is where the writer would come and stay, in the Hostal Burguete, to go trout fishing with friends nearby. More than Roncesvalles, Burguete gives the feel of a Navarran-Basque village removed from the demands of city life and tourist pressure, and of the two villages I prefer to spend the night here. Whitewashed stone homes with thick, shuttered windows and heavy stone doorways engraved with coats of arms line the village's single street. Here, too, you'll find several good places to eat and stay.

Sights
Iglesia de San Nicolás de Bari
The interior of this church (Plaza del Ayuntamiento; 948-760-032; www.burguete.es) is a highlight of Burguete, but unfortunately it is open only at select hours for Sunday **mass** and on festival days. Inside, the story of the stag and the Lady of Roncesvalles takes on Mistress of Animals and Mother Forest proportions: Observe the large, beautiful stained-glass window of Our Lady of Roncesvalles seated in a forest, very likely the one you just walked through, appearing like a gracious healer surrounded by leaves, trees, and flowers.

In front of the church is a small billboard with information about the history of witchcraft in the village and surrounding region; it identifies this as the site where five "witches" (traditional healers) were persecuted and some burned at the stake in the 16th century.

Food and Accommodations
Sturdy stone walls and green shutters identify the ★ **Hostal Burguete** (Calle San Nicolás, 71; 948-760-005; www.hotelburguete.com; 20 private rooms; €30-59) on the right entering town. Inside, wooden floors, white walls, and heavy hand-carved furniture greet the visitor, much as they did Ernest Hemingway when he came here to go trout fishing in the Pyrenees. With its private rooms and

From top to bottom: la Cruz Blanca in the forest between Roncesvalles and Burguete; Bar Frontón in Burguete; the Hostal de Burguete where Hemingway stayed to go trout fishing.

large window views of the Pyrenees, this is an ideal respite from the crowds lining up for bunk beds 3 kilometers (1.9 miles) farther back in Roncesvalles. The attached **village bar and restaurant** makes *mojitos* and also serves excellent local wines and good, rustic, home-cooked meals. Room 23 is the fabled room where Hemingway stayed and wrote.

Casa Bergara (Calle San Nicolás, 44; 948-760-044; four rooms; €30-40) is a family home—a mansion, really—with simple but comfortable guest rooms on the upper floor, all with private bath and old-fashioned beds with carved wood frames. Some bedside stands hold Eastern Orthodox painted icons of Mary and Jesus, just for a little bit of extra grace. The matron of the house is low key, but kind and concerned for her guests' comfort.

A great café for drinks, snacks, and casual meals is the ★ **Bar Frontón** (Calle San Nicolás, 58; 948-790-406; €3-11) on the village's main square, on your left just before passing the church. Often a large friendly husky lies at your feet, happy to ignore you. Check out the coat of arms over the door as you leave. See the stag? It's a reference to the legend about the discovery of Our Lady of Roncesvalles by two shepherds who followed a deer, possibly a stag. Try the *empanandas* (savory pies), especially the one filled with garlicky spinach and eggs (€3-6).

At **Hotel Loizu** (Calle San Nicolás, 13; 948-760-008; www.loizu.com; rooms at €55-80), you'll find a consistently good *menú del peregrino* (€10, including locally caught trout, steak, various pasta dishes, and salads) plus more choices on the à la carte menu (€15-20), as well as standard hotel rooms (used by a lot of tour groups) that are neat, fresh, and restful. Best of all, the staff are always positive, energetic, and welcoming.

Leaving Burguete

The Camino continues to follow the road through the center of town, and then, about mid-way, makes a sharp right off the road, right before passing the bank building of Banco Santander, and through a farmstead, where you may share the path with caramel-colored cows. This marks the point where you are no longer walking south but have now turned more toward the west; you will remain westward bound for the rest of the Camino, however far it takes you.

Forest Path to Espinal

Approximately 1.5 kilometers (1 mile) after leaving Burguete, you enter rolling hills and dale, forests of oak and beech, an area rich with bird life—from hawks, falcons, and eagles to titmice, robins, and gold finches. This beautiful 3-kilometer (1.9-mile) stretch flourishes with columbines in spring and October crocuses in autumn. The forest and hills open up on the final approach to Espinal village, with its sturdy stone farmhouses elegantly tucked at the foot of the slope.

Espinal   Km 747.2

Known as Aurizberri in Basque, Espinal (pop. 239) is a quintessential Basque-Navarran village of stucco stone and timber homes painted white with red stone doorways and thick wood windows and shutters. Look for the ever-present herb- and thistle-flower bundles on many of the doors in the village. Espinal was founded in 1269 to support and protect pilgrims on their passage through Navarra. Today it remains a pilgrim-friendly place with food and lodging options.

Food and Accommodations

Albergue Irugoienea (Calle Oihanilun, 2; 649-412-487; www.irugoienea.com; open from Easter to Oct.) has 21 beds in two dorm rooms (€12) and three private rooms (€37-52), all spotless and homey, plus a communal dinner and breakfast (€11, €4) with a great little covered porch and garden. You'll find it in the last building on the left down the main road.

In the same direction, before Albergue Irugoienea, you'll pass the ★ **Hostal-Albergue Haizea** (www.hostalhaizea.com; 948-760-379), featuring a great café for stopping for refreshments (breakfast is popular, €4-5), full meals (€12), or a night's sleep (28 beds in three dorms, €12; 12 private rooms, €45-60). With a rustic wood dining area with a warming fireplace, as well as a sunny terrace overlooking the green hills of Navarra just 100 meters (328 feet) off the edge of the trail, Haizea hits the spot for a mid-morning breakfast or snack to fuel up for the trek to Zubiri. Dorm-room beds are more single-standing than bunks (there are a few of these), and are set in pleasingly angled roof rooms with high wood beams. They are open all year, except the last two weeks of November.

Leaving Espinal

From Espinal to Biskarreta is an idyllic saunter through rolling hills, forests, and grazing pastures. Views of the mountain landscape beyond reveal glimpses of several river valleys and forests you will eventually cross.

Biskarreta   Km 742.3

Biskarreta (pop. 97) is also spelled Viscarreta and is also known by its Basque name, Guerendiain. The village produces *patxaran*, a red-colored brandy-like elixir made from sloe, a locally grown fruit which is similar to small plums. It is a popular digestive drink, typically consumed after a meal, made and drunk in Navarra and Basque Country. You can sample it at Bar Dena Ona, but be warned: Its alcohol content is high!

Food and Accommodations

The best place for food is ★ **Bar Dena Ona** (Calle San Pedro, 2; 669-755-564; €5-10), to the left of the trail before you enter the village proper. (Look for the funky clay-and-metal animal sculptures arrayed across the yard.) While *tortilla Española* is ubiquitous bar food, found everywhere in Spain, I think Dena Ona's may be one of the best examples of this thick, caramelized-onion-and-potato Spanish omelet. Order a bowl of big, plump green olives to go with it, and if you think you can handle it, a foaming cold beer. Heaven. This is also the place to try the locally produced brandy-like elixir called *patxaran*.

Casa Rural Amtxi Elsa (Calle San Pedro, 14; 626-560-675; www.amatxielsa.com; five rooms at €35-60) is to the right of the Camino as you are about to enter into the village. The very kind and warm hosts, Elsa Fábrega and her husband, Jorge, welcome you into a traditional stone and timber Navarran country family home turned into a rural inn. A common room has a corner fireplace and stuffed leather chairs, while an outdoor terrace overlooking the garden is a nice place for breakfast or to enjoy a pre-dinner drink.

Leaving Biskarreta

The Camino passes though Biskarreta and is well marked. Notice the door lintels of the houses you pass; many are engraved with dates and original designs that relate to each household's history. You will walk past backyard gardens, farmsteads, and oak forest.

Around 6 kilometers (3.7 miles) before Zubiri, the path begins to get progressively rockier and more uneven, and the oak forest denser. You'll pass over the lookout point **Alto de Erro** (Km 736) 3.5 kilometers (2.2 miles) before Zubiri. At 810 meters (2,657 feet), this offers one last panoramic view of the mountains before making a gradual descent toward the valley that holds Pamplona.

If you plan to sleep in Zubiri, cross the bridge into town. Otherwise, do not cross the bridge, but instead go left from where the trail enters the edge of Zubiri

Clockwise from top: Zubiri's Puente de la Rabia; trail marker near Alto de Erro; leaving Espinal; Bar Dena Ona in Biskarreta.

and follow the way-markers along the left side of the village; the village and the river Arga will be to your right as you continue.

Zubiri   Km 732.5

Zubiri (pop. 435) has been around at least since 1040, when the monastery in Leyre received the land here to develop. The town name means "town of the bridge," in reference to its most interesting feature, the Puente de la Rabia, which you'll cross to enter town. Zubiri does not live in the past: It is the center of a large magnesite factory that you will pass on your way out of the village.

Enjoy evening **mass** at Zubiri's central **Iglesia de San Esteban** (Plaza de la Iglesia). Hours vary, so ask at your *albergue* or *hostal* or check the church door for posted hours.

Sights
Puenta de la Rabia
Enter Zubiri via the Puente de la Rabia (Rabies Bridge), which is purported to protect animals from rabies. There are several versions of this ritual: Some say you must lead the animals three times across it; and others recommend three times around the middle support pillar of the bridge. Either way, *three* is key.

The bridge's form is Gothic, possibly 13th century, and replaces earlier bridges here that may have been in operation by the 11th century. Animals certainly love it: I've seen happy donkeys and goats grazing on the lush growth beneath it, on the riverbanks of the Río Arga.

Food
Some accommodations in town include the option for communal meals. For those that do not, head to ★ **Café del Camino** (Calle Puente de la Rabia, 2; 948-304-003; www.cafedelcamino.com; €5-12), a hangout among Zubiri's locals of all ages (including teenagers), all enjoying the good food and atmosphere, with contemporary art on the walls as well as on the plate. Try the beef stew, cheese plate (with local sheep's milk cheeses), fresh salads, white bean and pork soup, meatballs in tomato sauce, and *piquillos* (cod or tuna stuffed red peppers). The café also offers a daily menu (€10).

Accommodations
Several places to stay are arrayed on or near the Puente de la Rabia. Greeting you right as you arrive in Zubiri, **Pensión Zubiaren Etxea** (Calle Camino de Santiago, 2, on the left of the bridge before you cross it; 948-304-293; four rooms; €30-50), meaning "house on the bridge" in Basque, is a village house of the same stone as the bridge, with a vegetable garden on the back side and sheep grazing in the field next door. The neat, modern rooms come with private or shared bath, and a common dining area with wicker chairs, television, and an adjoining kitchen offers a place to unwind and cook if you prefer. A substantial breakfast of toast, fruit, cheese, ham, yogurt, juice, and tea /coffee is €4.

The popular "hazel branch," ★ **El Palo de Avellano** (Avenida Roncesvalles, 16; 666-499-175; www.elpalodeavellano; open May-Nov.; 59 beds in five dorm rooms €16-18 incl. breakfast; three private rooms, €46-84) is famous not only for the relaxed and spotless accommodations (with cheery skylights in the dorms and some beds that are single standing), but also excellent dinners with local and seasonal foods and a *menú del peregrino* (€13) that can include vegetarian and gluten-free choices. Dorm rooms are unusually spacious, with firm and sturdy bunks. Proprietors speak English.

Albergue Río Arga Ibaia (Calle Puente de la Rabia, 7; 948-304-243; www.alberguerioarga.com; open all year; eight beds in two dorm rooms, €15 incl. breakfast; two private rooms, €40) opened in 2014 in another traditional stone home right on the bridge, with terraces and views of the river and surrounding garden and valley. It offers solid wooden bunks with firm mattresses, and natural light flooding in through picture windows.

Leaving Zubiri

Backtrack to the other side of the bridge to pick up the Camino again. Take a right from the bridge, with Zubiri and the Río Arga to your right; the Camino now runs parallel to the river. Four kilometers (2.5 miles) after leaving Zubiri, you will pass through the tiny settlement of **Illaratz**, with its solitary, somewhat wing-tipped 12th-century church on the right side of the Camino. The church is now private property and verboten to enter, but you can enjoy its appealing trapezoidal form from the trail.

Larrasoaña   Km 726.9

Mentioned in the *Codex Calixtinus*, Larrasoaña (pop. 143) had an Augustinian monastery by the 11th century and major support services for pilgrims by the 12th century. Most of this

is no longer here, but the simple 13th-century village church, **Iglesia de San Nicolás de Barí** (Calle San Nicolás, 33; usually closed, inquire at the *albergue*), still stands, as does the double-arched **medieval bridge** on the way out of this village. The sturdy and affluent mansions, with coats of arms engraved in their keystones, date to the 15th and 16th centuries.

Accommodations

If you wish to alight here for the night, try the ★ **Albergue San Nicolás** (Calle Sorandi, 5-7; 619-559-225; www.alberguesannicolas.com; open Mar.-Oct.; 40 beds in eight dorm rooms, €12; dinner, €11), a large village home with fresh, luminous, and generously arranged dorm rooms, with no more than four to six beds per room (and eight bathrooms!). The dinners are home cooked, different each night, and based on local and seasonal ingredients. The best part is hanging out on the covered terrace of the *albergue* and sharing stories, drinks, and the setting sun with other fellow journeyers. There is also a small general store next door.

the hamlet of Akerreta

Akerreta   Km 725.9

At the time of writing, Akerreta (pop. 10) was restoring the village church, **Iglesia de la Transfiguración**, the foundations of which date to the 12th century. It is a slow process, but perhaps there will be more to see in Akerreta when you arrive. Meanwhile, this is a delightful place with a great view of the surrounding valley and hills; it's a sleepy little village with a whole different vibe from Zubiri or Larrasoaña.

Accommodations

Nothing embodies Akerreta's lovely vibe better than ★ **Hotel Akerreta** (Calle Transfiguración; 948-304-572; www.hotelakerreta.com, €60 for a private double), to your right on the Camino in the center of the village and below the church. For most Camino budgets, it is a total splurge to stay here—but so worth it to sleep in firm beds in this 18th-century Basque farmhouse. In the evenings, enjoy the three-course dinner (€20) picked from the organic garden outside and procured from local producers. A bit of film trivia: This is also where Martin Sheen stayed when he was filming *The Way* (the hotel itself was refashioned into a more simple pilgrims' *albergue* for the movie). That scene with the host who pretends to be a bullfighter with a red tablecloth—that was shot on the patio here.

Hotel Akerreta is also the first of the 22 hotels in an association called **Posadas del Camino** (www.posadasdelcamino.com) that highlights select inns along the whole route. After you stay in one, you can get a 10 percent discount at all the others. If this is your first Posada del Camino, ask the owner for a card that

From top to bottom: Hotel Akerreta where a part of *The Way* was filmed; miniature spotted ponies outside Akerreta; a sign in the hamlet of Zabaldika.

will set you up for the 10 percent discount on your next posada stay.

Leaving Akerreta

The Camino continues to be well marked through the intimate paths that weave between river valleys and pass into the heart of tiny villages and along country roads. Soon after leaving Akerreta, you will also pass a field on the left sheltering an adorable herd of cream-, grey-, and black-spotted miniature ponies. Be prepared to squeal with delight should they be out and about; they seem to like us pilgrims.

Less than 3 kilometers (1.9 miles) after leaving Akerreta, discover the riverside café and *albergue* in **Zuriain** (Km 723), ★ **La Parada de Zuriain** (Calle Landa, 8; 699-556-741; laparadadezuriain@yahoo.es; seven beds in two dorm rooms, €10, €13 with breakfast; three private rooms, €30-50; dinner, €9), where the always-warm hosts serve up good snacks as well as pilgrim camaraderie. It is a popular riverside bar for breakfast, and an informal *albergue* for relaxing along the sprawling green lawn, with chickens and cats underfoot (they get along with one another, and collectively mooch for scraps and attention). The location on the Arga river is a big part of the charm, as is the upbeat and casual atmosphere and solid Spanish comfort food (sandwiches, omelets, salads). You can also stock up on food for the trail from the small shop at the bar.

Zabaldika   Km 719.7

Zabaldika (pop. 38) is a cluster of some nine sturdy, straw-colored stone homesteads and farm buildings set at the base of the small hill, next to a large sweeping field irrigated by the Río Arga (which passes to the left of the Camino trail here). The Iglesia de San Esteban stands on the peak of that low hill and looks protectively down onto the hamlet.

Sights
Iglesia de San Esteban
I recommend you take the small 300-meter (984-foot) detour northwest from the center of Zabaldika to climb up to the 13th century church, **Iglesia de**

Zabaldika's Iglesia de San Estaban

San Esteban (Barrio de San Esteban de Arriba, 3; usually open during the day, inquire at the Albergue Parroquial de Zabaldika if closed), with its heavily fortified walls and rounded arches that were rebuilt in the 16th and 17th centuries. The way to the church from Zabaldika is well marked, and from the village center you can see both the church and the path to it.

Inside, one of the **Hermanas del Sagrado Corazón** (Sisters of the Sacred Heart) who oversee the church and *albergue* next door (along with volunteers from Spain's national pilgrim association) may invite you to leave a sticky note of gratitude, grace, petition, or blessing on the wall, next to the life-sized Jesus on the Crucifix. You could also climb the bell tower, or pick up a flyer—translated into well over a dozen languages—that includes "The Beatitudes of the Pilgrim" ("Blessed are you, pilgrim, if you discover that the *camino* opens your eyes to what is not seen") as well as a meditation on the transformative spiritual powers of the Camino. One of the sisters is almost always here during the day; you can also find the sisters and the Spanish *hospitaleros* next door in the parish *albergue*.

To get back to the village and the Camino, you don't have to climb back down the way you came. Instead, follow around the left of the church, and pick up the way-marked trial leading you along the ridge; it shortly rejoins the main route of the Camino.

Accommodations

If you enjoy the welcoming spiritual vibe in the church, you'll like the same upbeat energy in the parish *albergue* next door, run by the sisters and the volunteer Spanish *hospitaleros:* The impeccable ★ **Albergue Parroquial de Zabaldika** (948-330-918; www.malele11.wixsite.com; mid-Apr.-mid-Oct.; 18 beds in three rooms; donation) has a garden and sitting room, and quiet space to meditate and relax. The sisters offer very good communal dinner and breakfast, and can provide meaningful spiritual support. At sunset they hold a daily prayer celebration.

nearing Pamplona

Top to bottom: crossing the medieval Romanesque bridge into Trinidad de Arre; approaching the fortified walls of old Pamplona; the Puente de la Magdalena bridge before reaching Pamplona's medieval city walls.

Approaching Pamplona

From Zabaldika, it is a straight shot toward Pamplona. The path takes you along the Arga river valley, past the compelling, ramshackle Romanesque church of **Santa Marina** and the settlement of **Arleta** (Km 718.3). The homestead and the small church (now private property) together frame a farmyard where geese run about with glee.

The approach leads through layers of settlements. It's not unpleasant, compared to the approach of other cities on the Camino, but it makes the entry feel longer than it is. The way-markers begin to appear in different forms, to conform to the urban landscape—from painted arrows, to scallop shells inlaid in the pavement, to signs posted on buildings, poles, and sidewalks. You'll know you're almost there when you cross the five-arched Romanesque bridge over the Ulzama river into what was once the village of **Trinidad de Arre** (Km 716.1), now a neighborhood of outer Pamplona.

On the other side of the bridge is a medieval monastery and hospice, **Albergue de Trinidad de Arre** (Calle Puente del Peregrino, 2; 948-332-941; 34 beds in four dorm rooms, €8), that serves as a modern-day *albergue* but has served pilgrims continuously since the 11th century. Now privately run by José Luis Miral Durán and his family, the *albergue* shelters those in great need for free with donations made by others. There's a donation box at the entrance, which anyone can contribute to. Most evenings they hold an evening prayer service at 7:30pm, and mass every morning at 8am, in the old monastery's church.

Next, you will pass through layer after layer of suburban Pamplona, each neighborhood retaining a personality of its own. When you pick up the enticing scent of anise, you will be near the liquor distillery, **Hijos de Pablo Esparza** (Km 713.5) on the left, where you can step in and purchase a bottle of anise liquor or of *patxaran*. From here, there is a little less than 2 kilometers (1.2 miles) to go before you reach the medieval center.

After you pass through the modern periphery, the Camino will take you through a forested park and over the 12th-century **Puente Magdalena** (Km 712.3), crossing the Arga river. On the other side of the Arga, the Camino proceeds toward the right side of the towering 16th-century **citadel walls.** Though only 500 years old, they demarcate the territory where the earlier Roman Pamplona and early medieval Pamplona were both concentrated.

As a final dramatic gesture of arrival, you climb a ramp up the side of the outer wall, and make a left through the heavy stone gate known as **Portal de Francia.** Here you enter the walled and oldest part of town, where the cobbled streets, the colorful cafés, and the cathedral entice you to step deeper inside.

Navarra

Pamplona
to Logroño

Km:	711.5-613.9
Total Distance:	97.6 km (60.6 miles)
Days:	4-5

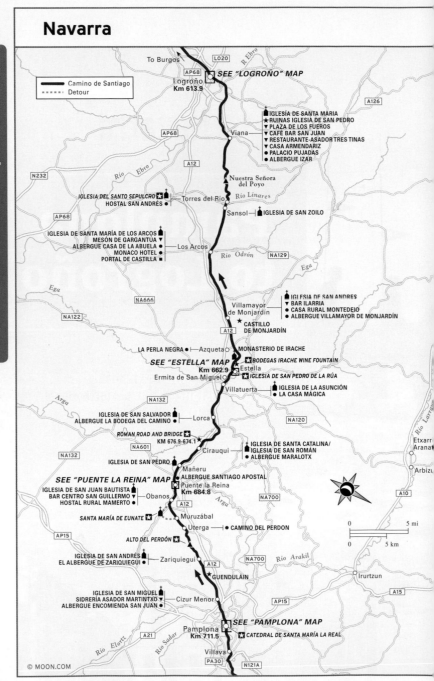

Navarra

— Camino de Santiago
····· Detour

To Burgos
L020
AP68
SEE "LOGROÑO" MAP
Logroño
Km 613.9
R Ebro
A126

Viana
- IGLESIA DE SANTA MARIA
★ RUINAS IGLESIA DE SAN PEDRO
▼ PLAZA DE LOS FUEROS
▼ CAFÉ BAR SAN JUAN
▼ RESTAURANTE-ASADOR TRES TINAS
▼ CASA ARMENDARIZ
● PALACIO PUJADAS
● ALBERGUE IZAR

AP68
A12
Río Ebro
N232

▲ Nuestra Señora del Poyo
Río Linares

IGLESIA DEL SANTO SEPULCRO
HOSTAL SAN ANDRÉS ● — Torres del Río
AP68
Sansol — ● IGLESIA DE SAN ZOILO

IGLESIA DE SANTA MARÍA DE LOS ARCOS
MESÓN DE GARGANTÚA ▼
ALBERGUE CASA DE LA ABUELA ● — Los Arcos
MONACO HOTEL ●
PORTAL DE CASTILLA ■
Río Odrón
NA129

Ega
NA666
NA122
Ega

Villamayor de Monjardín
- IGLESIA DE SAN ANDRES
▼ BAR ILARRIA
● CASA RURAL MONTEDEIO
● ALBERGUE VILLAMAYOR DE MONJARDÍN
A12
★ CASTILLO DE MONJARDÍN

LA PERLA NEGRA ● — Azqueta — MONASTERIO DE IRACHE
SEE "ESTELLA" MAP
Km 662.9
Ermita de San Miguel
BODEGAS IRACHE WINE FOUNTAIN
Estella
IGLESIA DE SAN PEDRO DE LA RÚA
Villatuerta
IGLESIA DE LA ASUNCIÓN
LA CASA MÁGICA

Arga
NA132

IGLESIA DE SAN SALVADOR
ALBERGUE LA BODEGA DEL CAMINO ● — Lorca
NA120

ROMAN ROAD AND BRIDGE
Km 676.9-674.1
NA601
Ciraqui
IGLESIA DE SANTA CATALINA/
IGLESIA DE SAN ROMÁN
● ALBERGUE MARALOTX

NA132
IGLESIA DE SAN PEDRO
Mañeru
● ALBERGUE SANTIAGO APOSTAL
SEE "PUENTE LA REINA" MAP
Puente la Reina
Km 684.8
IGLESIA DE SAN JUAN BAUTISTA
BAR CENTRO SAN GUILLERMO ▼ — Obanos
HOSTAL RURAL MAMERTO ●
A12
Arga
NA700

SANTA MARÍA DE EUNATE — Muruzábal
AP15
Uterga — ● CAMINO DEL PERDON

ALTO DEL PERDÓN
IGLESIA DE SAN ANDRÉS
EL ALBERGUE DE ZARIQUIEGUI ● — Zariquiegui
NA700
Río Arakil

IGLESIA DE SAN MIGUEL
SIDRERÍA ASADOR MARTINTXO ▼ — Cizur Menor
ALBERGUE ENCOMIENDA SAN JUAN ●
★ GUENDULÁIN

A21
Pamplona
Km 711.5
SEE "PAMPLONA" MAP
CATEDRAL DE SANTA MARÍA LA REAL
Villava
PA30
N121A

A10
Arbizu
Etxarr Arana
Río Larra
Irurtzun
A15

0 — 5 mi
0 — 5 km

© MOON.COM

Highlights

★ **Catedral de Santa María la Real:** Pamplona's luminous and colorful Gothic cathedral features unusual courtly frescos painted on the soaring ceiling (page 100).

★ **Alto del Perdón:** Get a birds-eye view of the Camino on this ridge, where the way of the wind and the way of the stars meet—a natural high after climbing the steep slope from Zariquiegui (page 116).

★ **Santa María de Eunate:** No chapel on the Camino is as unusual or harmonious as this octagonal "chapel of 100 doors" set within rolling hills (page 117).

★ **Roman Road and Bridge:** Leaving Cirauqui, you'll walk on an actual Roman road. Feel the echoes of ancient feet, and look for grooves that Roman carts wore into the stone 2,000 years ago (page 125).

★ **Iglesia de San Pedro de la Rúa:** A church built by masons from many faiths, San Pedro stands high on a hill in Estella with sinuous stone stairs, stones engraved with quirky and esoteric designs, and a breathtaking location (page 130).

★ **Bodegas Irache Wine Fountain:** One of the ultimate highlights of the Camino is to drink a glass from this fountain with two spigots, one for wine and one for water (page 134).

★ **Iglesia del Santo Sepulcro:** The third round church of Navarra, this one in Torres del Rio may be the most potent, a towering dome inspired by the mosque at Cordoba (page 139).

With a sense of great accomplishment after crossing the Pyrenees, pilgrims continue from the high protective bluff of the vibrant city of Pamplona and head deeper into rolling hills covered in the grapevines, wildflowers, and wheat fields of Navarra. An adventure waits around every bend, from high wind-blown ridges twirling with windmills, to hidden and enigmatic round churches in remote settings, castle ruins overlooking medieval villages, and monasteries engulfed by endless vineyards—one containing a fountain flowing with wine, inviting the pilgrim to drink the local vintage.

With a coveted geographic location at the intersection of mountains, rivers, hills, plains, and the nearby ocean, Pamplona was the center of numerous imperialistic battles waged by leaders like Pompey, Charlemagne, Napoleon, and Franco. Today, Pamplona is better known for great food, the running of the bulls, and Hemingway. Reaching Pamplona is exhilarating: the tight pass through the mountains gives way to this city on the bluff, with a view all around of rippling fields and hills. The Camino leaves Pamplona toward this expansive vista, plunging into rising and falling waves of dark brown and red hills covered with wheat fields, vineyards, and gardens rich with red peppers and climbing tomatoes tied on tall spikes. It goes through almond groves and pine forests, over still-paved Roman roads, past hilltop fortresses with crumbling castles, and to some of the Camino's most unusual and beautiful churches, built by masons from different faith backgrounds. The three octagonal churches of Eunate, Torres del Rio, and San Pedro in Estella hold a curious trinity with each other, at equal intervals, like beads on a string, speaking of a deeper heritage than meets the eye. Caretakers at all of these chapels are happy to share their historical and mystical dimensions if you chance upon

Recommended Overnight Stops

Pamplona (Km 711.5, page 98)

Obanos (Km 687.1, page 117)

Estella (Km 662.9, page 127)

Los Arcos (Km 641.5, page 138)

them and linger. Then stop for that glass of wine at the Bodegas Irache's wine fountain, just outside of Estella, where water and wine flow side by side, recalling Jesus's first miracle at the Wedding of Cana.

Planning Your Time

Allow 4-5 days for walking the 97.6 kilometers (60.6 miles) from Pamplona to Logroño when averaging 20-25 kilometers (12.5-15.5 miles) a day, and consider taking 1 day for a rest day for a total of 5-6 days.

Pamplona is a great place for a rest day, especially if you crossed the Pyrenees from Saint-Jean-Pied-de-Port. Another good rest day could happen in **Estella** if you want to take in the town's four churches, three perched on their own hill, or in **Villamayor de Monjardín,** if you want to climb up to the castle ruins on the steep hill for impressive views of mountains, forests, and vineyards.

Route Options

There is a small **detour,** picking up from either Villatuerta or Irache via Luquin, that I have not noted because it passes through similar terrain, and the gain is minor in comparison to what you will miss, particularly Estella (a small town with fascinating churches and wonderful public market and squares).

The Camino has another small detour

to the round chapel of Santa María de Eunate (Km 689.6) that adds 3 kilometers (1.9 miles) to the walk; this is one of the top highlights of the whole Camino and is not to be missed.

Geography and Terrain

The trail is well way-marked from Pamplona to Logroño, with cafés, shops, and accommodations strung along at fairly regular intervals, except for three sections: from **Villamayor de Monjardín** to **Los Arcos** (12.2 km/7.6 mi); from **Torres del Rio** to **Viana** (10.6 km/6.6 mi); and from **Viana** to **Logroño** (9.3 km/5.8 mi).

The hardest stretch will be climbing up to and down from the **Alto del Perdón** (770 meters/2,526 feet; Km 698.3) after Pamplona. The descent is steeper than the climb, and many find this the harder part. After this, the terrain rolls into ripples between smaller hills covered with kitchen gardens, wheat fields, and striped, rolling vineyards. Note that when you leave **Los Arcos** (Km 641.5) via the Portal de Castilla, you cross into more open and exposed terrain, and in the warm months you will need to drink more water and protect yourself from the sun with a hat and sunscreen.

The whole of this section of the Camino, from Pamplona to Logroño, is appealing; there are no unappealing stretches, and nearly all of it is on dirt footpaths. The only real roadside walking occurs as you leave Pamplona, a pleasant departure through city parks and into countryside, and on entering Logroño, a reasonably pleasant urban approach and entry, near to—and then crossing—the Ebro river.

Weather

Navarra's foothills experience temperate weather conditions most of the year. Extreme cold and heat are rare, though you may experience some hot days in late spring and summer that will be more trying along the stretch from Arcos to Logroño, where there is less tree cover. Spring and autumn may bring more rain, but largely this is not a major issue here.

a typical street in Pamplona's Casco Antiguo

Getting There

Starting Points

The gateway to this region is **Pamplona**, easily reached via an efficient network of buses and trains from other Spanish cities. All other destinations from here to **Logroño,** such as **Estella, Los Arcos,** and **Viana,** are accessed via Pamplona by bus.

Car

For quick access to major hubs—Pamplona, Estella, and Logroño—the **A-12** highway runs parallel to the Camino all the way and is even called the **Autovía Camino de Santiago.** But for a more leisurely and pretty drive, the recommended path is along the smaller highway—**N-1110/N-111A**—that also parallels the Camino but with better access to all the sights, including the smallest places. From Pamplona to Puente Reina, follow the N-111A (which becomes the N-1110 after Puente la Reina) to Estella and onward to Irache, Los Arcos, Sansol, and Torres del Rio to Viana. After Viana, it becomes the N-111A again, taking you into Logroño on the north side of the city.

Air

The nearest airport is **Pamplona (PNA),** followed by **Bilbao (BIO)** and **Biarritz (BIQ),** and then **Madrid (MAD)** and **Barcelona (BCN).** Madrid's Barajas airport has direct flights to Pamplona. From Barcelona, flights to Pamplona go via Madrid; you may find the train a faster option.

The Saint-Jean-Pied-de-Port-based shuttle company **Express Bourricot** (www.expressbourricot.com) can take passengers from Biarritz's airport, and from Bilbao's airport and train station, to Pamplona (as well as running shuttles to and from Roncesvalles and Saint-Jean-Pied-de-Port).

Local Markets

- **Pamplona:** Covered market, open daily (page 101).

- **Puente la Reina:** Food and goods market every Saturday (page 121).

- **Estella:** Food and general goods market every Thursday (page 128).

- **Los Arcos:** A food and general goods market sets up every Tuesday and Saturday (page 138).

- **Viana:** Weekly market every Friday (page 141).

Train

RENFE (www.renfe.com) connects directly to Pamplona from Madrid and Barcelona. Other destinations in this section of the Camino are connected by bus, including if traveling from Pamplona to Logroño.

Bus

ALSA (www.alsa.com) runs buses from both Biarritz and Madrid's airports and from Madrid's Avenida de America bus station to Pamplona.

The Navarran bus company, **La Estellesa** (www.laestellesa.com) connects the whole Camino between Pamplona and Logroño with stops in Puente la Reina, Mañeru, Cirauqui, Lorca, Villatuerta, Estella, Azqueta, Urbiola (200 meters/656 feet to the left of the Camino after Villamayor de Monjardín), Los Arcos, Sansol/Torres del Rio, and Viana.

Pamplona   Km 711.5

When you first arrive in Pamplona (pop. 198,491)—Iruña in Euskera (Basque)—after crossing the Río Arga at the **Puente de la Magdalena,** the Camino continues toward the massive, ancient walls (six to

Pamplona

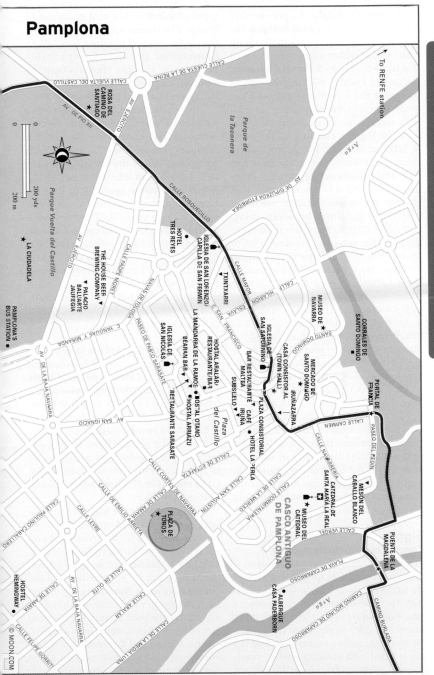

To RENFE station

CALLE CUESTA DE LA REINA

AV. ELERCITO

CALLE VUELTA DEL CASTILLO

ROSA DEL
CAMINO DE
SANTIAGO

AV. DE PIO XII

CALLE BOSQUECILLO

AV. DE GUIPUZCOA ETORBIDEA

Parque de
la Taconera

0
0

200 yds
200 m

Parque Vuelta del Castillo

★ LA CIUDADELA

AV. ELERCITO

PALACIO
BALUARTE
JAUREGIA

THE HOUSE BEEF
BREWING COMPANY

HOTEL
TRES REYES

CALLE PADRE MORET

CALLE MAYOR

HILARION ESLAVA

IGLESIA DE SAN LORENZO/
CAPILLA DE SAN FERMIN

TXINTXARRI

C. SAN FRANCISCO

LA MANDARRA DE LA RAMOS

BEARAN BAR

IGLESIA DE
SAN NICOLAS

PASEO DE PABLO SARASATE

RESTAURANTE SARASATE

NAVAS DE TOLOSA

C. YANGUAS Y MIRANDA

AV. SAN IGNACIO

PAMPLONA'S
BUS STATION ■

AV. DE LA BAJA NAVARRA

MUSEO DE
NAVARRA

SANTO DOMINGO

CORRALES DE
SANTO DOMINGO ■

MERCADO DE
SANTO DOMINGO

CASA CONSISTORIAL
(TOWN HALL)

IGLESIA DE
SAN SATURNINO

BAR RESTAURANTE
MALTEA

SUBSUELO

HOSTAL ARALAR/
RESTAURANTE/BAR

HOSTAL OTANO

HOSTAL ARRIAZU

PLAZA CONSISTORIAL

RUMAZARRA

CAFE
IRUÑA

HOTEL LA PERLA

Plaza
del Castillo

CALLE DE LA MERCED

CALLE SAN AGUSTIN

CALLE DE ESTAFETA

CALLE DE LA MERCED

CALLE DE EMILIO ARRIETA

CALLE CORTES DE NAVARRA

CALLE PAULINO CABALLERO

CALLE LEYRE

PLAZA DE
TOROS

HOSTEL
HEMINGWAY ●

CALLE DE OLITE

AV. DE OLITE

CALLE DE AMAYA

AV. DE LA BAJA NAVARRA

CALLE DE LA MEDIA LUNA

CALLE FELIPE GORRITI

© MOON.COM

PORTAL DE
FRANCIA

CALLE CARMEN

PASEO DEL FEDIN

CALLE NAVARRERIA

CATEDRAL DE
SANTA MARIA LA REAL

MESON DEL
CABALLO BLANCO

MUSEO DEL
CATEDRAL

CALLE VERGEL

CASCO ANTIGUO
DE PAMPLONA

PLAYA DE CAPARROSO

PUENTE DE LA
MAGDALENA

ALBERGUE
CASA PADERBORN

CAMINO MOLINO DE CAPARROSO

CAMINO BURLADA

Area

seven times the height of a person) that define the preserved **Casco Antiguo**, the old part of the city. You then climb up a heavy stone ramp along the outer wall that leads to the thick **Portal de Franca**, the gate of France. Walking through it, you enter the Casco Antiguo, and the modern world slips away.

Pamplona is an exciting city, not only during the running of the bulls in July, but all year. The people—all of them gourmands—are gregarious and chic, and the city is interesting at every turn, surrounded by ancient walls that enclose the walnut-shaped medieval center that is defined by intertwining, maze-like streets. You don't need more than an afternoon and evening to get to know Pamplona, but this is a good spot for a rest day, especially if you're coming from Saint-Jean-Pied-de-Port. (Often this is where your feet, knees, and legs begin to feel it.) If you do make this a rest day, consider a late night out to join Pamplona's nightlife, including the pleasure of *pintxos* (gourmet little bites) served in bars and cafés lining the medieval historical center.

The Camino is well marked in its passage through the Casco Antiguo; it traverses right through the middle of the city, with the modern city of Pamplona radiating out from there. All of the sights and attractions are within or immediately on the outskirts of the small medieval Casco Antiguo, some directly on the Camino and others a short left or right off of the Camino.

Sights
Casco Antiguo de Pamplona
Walking through the Casco Antiguo is an experience of its own. The Catedral de Santa María la Real will be the first historic building you pass, visible down a small side street to your left. Small shops stand shoulder to shoulder along well-worn cobblestone passageways, and the air is filled with enticing smells—roasting red peppers, frying garlic, a dozen

types of salted cod, a hint of anise and honey. The streets naturally pull you to the center, toward the town hall's Plaza Consistorial and Hemingway's favorite, Plaza del Castillo. Like rays from the sun, the maze-like streets of the Casco Antiguo radiate out from both squares.

The walls surrounding the Casco Antiguo were rebuilt many times over the centuries, including after Charlemagne ravaged the city in 778. The Casco Antiguo is where the ancient Vascones first settled, and where Pompey established his Roman town in 75 BCE—a strategic outpost to control peoples and goods coming across the Pyrenees to the northeast and from Astorga to the west. Visigoths, then North Africans, then medieval settlers, merchants, and tradespeople (largely composed of Navarrans, Franks, and Jews) created four main neighborhoods, each a walled and fortified enclave to defend against each other as much as the outside.

★ Catedral de Santa María la Real
Don't let the rather bland Neoclassical façade fool you: **Catedral de Santa María la Real** (www.catedraldepamplona.com; Mon.-Sat., 9-10:30am and 7-8:30pm; Sun. and holidays, 10am-2pm) is another world inside. Built from 1387 to 1525, this is a place of light, soaring pillars, and pure Gothic lines, a masterpiece of space and luminous stone and color. **Daily mass** is at 10:30am and on Sundays at 10am and 2pm.

The highlight is the Mary at the transept, the **Virgen del Sagrario** (Virgin of the Sanctuary), with an ornate gold and silver canopy of Gothic arches overhead. She is a Romanesque sculpture from the 12th century, and she witnessed the crowning of many Navarran kings. Other than the wood of her face and hands—and that of the baby Jesus in her lap—the rest of her body is covered in silver.

The **Museo del Catedral** (www.catedraldepamplona.com/el-museo; Mon-Sat. and holidays, 10:30am-6pm; €5,

€2 for pilgrims), just off the church and cloister, is one of the best church museums on the Camino. Part of the museum takes you through the archaeological excavation under the 12th-century bishop's residence, where archaeologists discovered ancient stones and outlines of prior settlements dating from the 2nd century BCE to the 5th century AD. An interactive display mirrors your image and projects holograms to dress you in different period attire, from Roman to medieval. The museum is set in the cathedral's old refectory and includes one of three surviving Gothic monastic kitchens in all of Europe, a heavily domed, stacked-stone ceiling with four chimneys, one in each corner. It is from 1330 and is a wonder to stand in and look up. Most text panels are in English.

Mercado de Santo Domingo

The colorful daily covered market in the old town center, **Mercado de Santo Domingo** (Calle Mercado, s/n; Mon.-Sat., 8am-2pm) opened in 1876. You'll find 45 food kiosks selling fruits, vegetables, fish, meat, charcuterie, cheeses, breads and pastries, eggs, and flowers.

Plaza Consistorial

This central square in the Casco Antiguo is best known for two things: First, the town hall, **Casa Consistorial**, its most eye-catching building, an ornate three-story Baroque and Neoclassical town hall built in 1951 over the remains of a mid-18th-century building. Second, it's known as the square through which the bulls run on their way to reach the bull ring farther south. This is where the **Sanfermines**—the city's celebration of Pamplona's patron saint, San Fermín, best known as the running of the bulls—kick off each year; every July 6, the mayor appears at noon on the Casa Consistorial's upper balcony and, with the pyrotechnic pop of a small rocket, announces the start of the festival. The Plaza Consistorial is atmospheric year-round, with several cafés that line the small but open square where pilgrims often find each other and gather for a drink.

Iglesia de San Saturnino

The **Iglesia de San Saturnino** (Calle San Saturnino, 3; 948-221-194; www. turismo.navarra.es; Mon.-Sat. 9:15am-12pm and 6:15 7:30pm; Sun. and

Iglesia de San Saturnino seen from Pamplona's Plaza Consistorial

holidays, 10:15am-1:30pm and 6:15-7:30pm; free) is also known as Iglesia de San Cernin for the borough it's located in, and is dedicated to the martyred French saint, Saint Sernin (San Saturnino in Spanish), who was the first bishop of Toulouse. Saint Sernin, along his pupil, San Fermín, have a devout following in Pamplona, a reflection of the strong French presence on the Camino and here in Pamplona in particular. You'll find San Saturnino's image on an altar to the left when you enter the church. A robust bull is painted on the pedestal on which he sits, representing the instrument of his martyrdom. To his right stands a sculpture of Saint James.

When you enter the church, you'll see the extension called **Capilla de la Virgen del Camino** (chapel of the Virgin of the Camino) straight ahead. Legend has it that, around 1487, the statue of the Virgen del Camino—from the Riojan village of Alfaro, 82 kilometers (51 miles) south of Pamplona—kept appearing on the ceiling beam over San Saturnino's altar, no matter how many times people returned her to Alfaro. Alfaro finally gave her to Pamplona, and now she is visible to pilgrims in this chapel.

The current church is Gothic in form, and dates to the 13th century. During Roman times, this same spot probably held a temple devoted to Diana. Outside, at the intersection of three streets—Calles Jarauta, Mayor, and San Saturnino—look for the manhole-like plaque identifying the *pozo* (well) where San Saturnino baptized people, including San Fermín, in the 3rd century. A holy well at a sacred site is a sign that this place most likely has a long spiritual lineage, probably predating the Romans. That Diana was associated with a place of underground water ties in with Basque and other northern Spanish stories of female divinities from prehistory.

Mass is held daily, Mon.-Sat., at 10am, 11am, and 7pm, and on Sun. and holidays at 11am, 12pm, and 7pm.

Museo de Navarra

The **Museo de Navarra** (Calle Santo Domingo, 47; 848-426-492; www.navarra.es; Tues.-Sat., 9:30am-2pm and 5-7pm; Sun. and holidays, 11am-2pm; €2), open since 1956, is housed in the 16th-century pilgrims' hospital of **Nuestra Señora de la Misercordia.** This is Navarra's combined archaeology and fine-arts museum, and it is a delightful place to spend an hour or two, covering over 4,500 years of prehistoric to modern art arrayed on the four floors of the old hospital. English speakers can pick up an informative English flyer on the galleries to augment the panels, which are only in Spanish.

Come here to see Roman remains, medieval relics, and works of art by Spanish painters, including Goya. Highlights include the Roman Mosaics of Theseus, from a villa in Pamplona, that depicts Theseus and the Minotaur; the expressive 12th-century Romanesque capitals salvaged from Pamplona's earlier cathedral; an ivory chest from 1005, with scenes of early 11th-century court life; and a painting by Goya, *El Marqués de San Adrián*, from 1804, depicting a close friend of Goya's who is shown dressed in Napoleonic attire (the Marquis of San Adrián served as the chamberlain of Joseph Bonaparte, Napoleon's older brother, in Spain).

Iglesia de San Lorenzo

Pamplonans built the **Iglesia de San Lorenzo** (Calle Mayor, 74; 948-225-371; www.turismo.navarra.es; Mon.-Sat, 8:30am-12:30pm and 5:30-8pm; Sun. and holidays, 8:30am-1:45pm and 5:30-8pm; free) in the 14th century, and rebuilt it in the 17th and 18th centuries. Located on the western edge of the medieval neighborhood, on the Camino's left on its way out of the Casco Antiguo, the church is known best for its 15th-century wood-and-silver image of famous saint San Fermín, held inside in the **Capilla de San Fermín,** a Neo-Classical chapel within the church. This image is locally

Hemingway's Pamplona

Though the Casco Antiguo, Plaza de Castillo, and Plaza de Toros all existed long before Ernest Hemingway, the writer put Pamplona and these sights on the map for many through his breakout novel, *The Sun Also Rises* (1926). Hemingway loved Pamplona passionately and visited throughout his life. The city loved him back; throughout the city are restaurants and monuments in his honor. Here are some of the writer's favorite haunts:

Plaza del Castillo

Hemingway loved to come to this large, elegant square, with large promenades and gardens crisscrossing the center, to enjoy a drink (okay, many drinks), talk with people, and watch pretty women. When here, Navarran rosé was his favorite drink, and I can think of no better way to enjoy Pamplona than to sit at a table at the Café Iruña on the plaza, Hemingway's old haunt, order a glass of *vino rosado de la casa* (the house rosé), and sit back and watch the world *paseando* by.

Not far from the Café Iruña on the Plaza del Castillo is **La Perla,** a hotel that Hemingway enjoyed on his later visits to the city, and which for this reason now has a suite named after him. Look through the window or go inside the plush 1920s lobby to take a look at a handsome brass bust of Hemingway.

Plaza de Toros

This bullring was built in 1922, and it is where bullfights in Pamplona have been held since. It was a place Hemingway knew well, coming here for the fights during his nine visits (from 1923 to 1959) to

one of Hemingway's favorite cafes, Café Iruña

Pamplona to be a part of the Sanfermines festivities. A statue of the writer—a squarish granite-and-bronze bust—graces the outside entrance to the bullring, with a plaque acknowledging his novel, *Fiesta* (the original name of *The Sun Also Rises*), which did so much to propagate the popularity of Pamplona with visitors around the world.

Hemingway's fascination with bulls, bullfighters, and bullfights stemmed from his lifelong fascination with bravery and death, two themes of all his novels. He admired bullfighters both for their bravery and for their courage to look death in the face, giving more weight to his famous quote, "Nobody ever lives their life all the way up except bullfighters." He really wanted to live his life all the way up, too, and perhaps the Sanfermines gave him that chance.

nicknamed *el morenico,* "the tanned little guy," because of its physical appearance. This is where the cult of San Fermín concentrates, and every July 7 the image of San Fermín is taken out of the church on a procession throughout the Casco Antiguo, an ancient act of blessing and revivifying energy, land, and people.

On the other 364 days of the year, you can visit San Fermín here. Seek out the delightful priest, who loves welcoming pilgrims, offering them a blessing for their Camino, and stamping their pilgrim passports.

Daily **mass** is Mon.-Fri. at 8:30am, 11am, and 7:30pm; Sat, 6pm; and Sun. and holidays, 9am, 11am, 12pm, 1pm, 6pm, and 7pm.

Iglesia de San Nicolás

From the 12th and 13th centuries, the **Iglesia de San Nicolás** (Calle San Miguel, 15; www.parroquiasannicolas.es; Mon.-Sat, 9:30am-12:30pm and 6-8:30pm; Sun. and holidays, 9:30am-1:30pm and 6:30-8:30pm; free) is a transitional church, Romanesque to Gothic. It's unusual in that it remains congruous and intact after so many centuries of battles. (All the other churches in Pamplona, except for the Catedral de Santa María la Real, have been more heavily rebuilt since the 13th century.) You can see from San Nicolás's heavy walls that it too was built to be as much a fortress as a place of worship. Part of the church's appeal is the lack of later Baroque and Renaissance adornments (which are more common in the other churches), allowing you to experience the stark beauty of the dense walls, pillars, and arches.

The church holds a photographic corner in the old city, south of the Camino. In the autumn and winter you'll often find a chestnut roaster near the church's portico exterior on the Plaza de San Nicolás, turning the hot nuts over the fire and selling them in paper cones for €2-3. In the warm season, café tables spread out on the same square, a pleasant way to enjoy the proportions of the church and its pretty arched entrance.

Plaza del Castillo

As you explore the Casco Antiguo, you will eventually land in the center of it, the 14,000-square-meter (150,695-square-foot) Plaza del Castillo, Pamplona's main square, where until 1844 bullfights took place. Surrounded on all four sides by colorful 18th-century town homes huddled shoulder to shoulder, the square itself contains wide walkways, green zones, and a central gazebo for public events. Join the locals here on their daily *paseo* (stroll) in the early evening, when they settle in at a café with friends and family for a refreshment and news. Pamplonans are so gregarious that they may pull you into the conversation if you are seated near them. Showing Pamplonans' kinship with the French, dogs are a big part of the atmosphere, underfoot at many a café table. Look for **Café Iruña** (Plaza del Castillo, 4), Hemingway's old haunt.

Plaza de Toros

A statue of Hemingway graces the entrance to the bullring, the Plaza de Toros, where bullfights have been held since 1922. Outside of the Sanfermines or Semana Santa (Holy Week, the week leading up to Easter), this is a dormant place except for the museum, **Museo de la Plaza de Toros** (Paseo Hemingway, s/n; 948-225-389; www.feriadeltoro.com; €6 including audio guide), which is housed within the perimeter of the bullring.

Opened in 2017, the museum in essence *is* the bull ring, and is a good way to take in the round arena groomed with smooth yellow sand and the immense rings of the spectator stands. You get to enter the bullring and pass into the private outer ring, where *toreadores* prepare, where the bulls are held before being released into the ring, and where the horses and riders wait to enter the game. The museum also gives insight into the bullfighters' training and the traditions surrounding the sport. Handheld audio guide available in English. Open Feb.-mid-Nov. and closed July 17-25 and from mid-Nov.-Jan. Hours: Feb.-Mar.: Sat.-Sun., 10:30am-2:30pm, and from Apr.-Oct., Tues.-Sat., 10:30am-7:30pm, Sun. and holidays, 10:30am-2:30pm. Note: hours can vary during holidays, such as Semana Santa, and in November.

La Ciudadela

La Ciudadela, the citadel, was constructed from 1571 to 1646, with moats, pavilions, and bastions, to defend Pamplona from attack, a new defense within the older city walls all around it. Today, the gray outline of the gray walls largely retains the pentagonal shape of the original defensive complex, which has been mostly flattened and repurposed into walkways that follow the star pattern and which are surrounded by green lawn. The Ciudadela grounds are absorbed into the large, green, and peaceful **Vuelta del Castillo** park, enjoyed daily by students lounging on the lawn, walkers and runners out for exercise, dogs and their humans enjoying the day, and picnickers, including the occasional pilgrim.

La Ciudadela is located outside the Casco Antiguo but on the path of the Camino. The Camino passes the north and west sides of the park on the way out of town, toward Cizur Menor.

Events

Every July 7, the image of San Fermín is removed from its niche in the Iglesia de San Lorenzo and paraded throughout the Casco Antiguo, an ancient act of blessing and revivifying energy, land, and people. While many know this event (called **Fiesta de los Sanfermines**) as the running of the bulls, for Pamplonans the original point of the festivals was to honor their patron saint, San Fermín. It's a massive party.

Pamplonans also hold a smaller, more solemn festival to honor San Fermín, called the **Fiesta de San Fermín Chiquito**, little San Fermín, on September 25, the day he was martyred in AD 303. This is a more religious festival with a much more intimate and local flavor, without bull runs, where you can participate in mass, processions, and more peaceful eating and drinking in surrounding cafés and bars.

Food

All these restaurants are inside the Casco Antiguo. Fans of *The Way* (the 2010 movie) will recognize the appealing stone terrace where Joost enjoyed his first *cordero asado*, roasted leg of lamb, a scene that was filmed at the Pamplonan restaurant, Mesón del Caballo Blanco. While *cordero asado* is (alas) not generally offered there, this traditional Navarran, Riojan, and Castilian dish is present in many places all across the Camino, including periodically as a special at restaurants in Pamplona.

★ **Mesón del Caballo Blanco** (Calle Redin, s/n; 948-211-504; www.caballoblanco.info; €15-26) is located in the oldest corner of old Pamplona, overlooking Pamplona's walls and the river behind the cathedral; it doesn't get more picturesque than this. While *cordero* is not typically on the menu, nearly everything else is, including a varied *pintxos* menu and local sheep's milk cheeses. The fixed-price menus (€22-26) showcase Navarran dishes like *tortilla de bacalao* (Spanish omelet with cod), *gorrín asado* (roasted sucking pig), and *carrilleras de ternera* (stewed beef cheeks). Menus change with the seasons.

Bar Restaurante Maltea (Calle Calceteros, 4; 948-774-801; maltea-pamplona@gmail.com) has a place for all moods; choose either the blissfully peaceful upper floor, with its romantic gray-and-white dining room, or the pulsing street-level bar with outdoor seating, all overlooking the square and baroque Casa Consistorial. Choose from the three-course menu (€15) with vibrant fresh salads, garden vegetable dishes, and traditional entrees such as *cordero estilo chilindrón* (lamb, red and green pepper, paprika, and onion stew), or go for the bar's burgers—beef, salmon, or chicken—served with fries and a drink (€10).

Hemingway's frequent spot on the Plaza del Castillo, ★ **Café Iruña** (Plaza del Castillo, 4; 948-222-064, www.cafeiruna.com; €15-20) doesn't rely on its famous association with the writer to draw customers. The Belle Époque dining room, with high sculpted and painted ceiling, is the initial magnet, but the service, drinks, tapas, and three-course daily menus (€14.50) keep you there. The menu offers starters such as garden-fresh salads or rich soups, entrées such as paella or roasted meats and vegetables, and a selection of desserts (try the

Los Sanfermines and the Running of the Bulls

From July 6 to 14, Pamplona plunges headfirst into Los Sanfermines, a massive party centered on the cult of San Fermín, Pamplona and Navarra's patron saint, who according to local legend was martyred by being dragged by running bulls through the streets—an act that's reflected in the running of the bulls as we know it.

The Cult of San Fermín

San Fermín was the son of an influential Roman family in 3rd-century Pamplona. He became a student of San Saturnino in Toulouse, and later in his life returned to become Pamplona's first bishop. Both he and his teacher were martyred—Saint Saturnino in AD 257 by being dragged by a bull, and San Fermín in AD 303, either by decapitation in northern France or by being dragged by a bull in Pamplona (both legends circulate as possibilities).

These two saints being dragged by bulls is symbolic, a reversal of a more ancient rite popular at the time among Romans. Some Romans were drawn to the ancient Persian worship of Mithra, god of light and truth, and brought their own interpretations of Mithraism to Iberia from the Near East. Their practice of Mithraism included bull sacrifice. Bulls, with their crescent-shaped horns, were seen as a symbol of the moon, which needed to give way in the sky for the sun (light) to return. That Romans may have used bulls to martyr both San Fermín and San Saturnino turned the tables on ancient sacrificial rites involving bulls, and forever connected these two men with the sacrifice of bulls to assure continued light (life).

Running of the Bulls and Los Sanfermines

El encierro—the running of the bulls as we know it today—began much more recently, in the 14th century, with herders who brought the animals into the city for the bullfights centered then on the Plaza del Castillo. Today, the San Fermín festivities (Los Sanfermines) begin in the Plaza Consistorial. At noon on July 6, the mayor of Pamplona stands on the central balcony of the Casa Consistorial, overlooking the plaza, and kicks off the festivities. At this moment, a small rocket/firecracker is set off, and the crowd on the square below gets showered with red wine. The next morning, July 7, marks the first of eight days of bull running, which commences each day at 8am. On this day, around 9:30am, locals also take the statue of San Fermín from San Lorenzo church and carry it around the Casco Antiguo. Many people join this procession, which passes through the streets of the whole old town and then returns to the church, where San Fermín is set back on his altar.

But the bull run, *el encierro,* is what most people know best about Los Sanfermines. It is an unbelievably brief, 850-meter (half-mile) run that passes through the heart of the Casco Antiguo. Every morning from July 7-14, six bulls (each weighing around 1,000 pounds, or 453 kg) are released from the **Corrales de Santo Domingo** on the north end of the Casco Antiguo and directed to the bullring on the edge of the southern end. From the corrals, the bulls run down the **Calle de Santo Domingo,** through the **Plaza Consistorial,** and onto the **Calle de los Mercaderes,** where they hurl into a right turn (often skidding on the cobblestones) onto the **Calle de Estafeta.** From there it is a straight final run into the **Plaza de Toros**. All along the way, daredevils jump off the sidelines to run in front of or alongside the bulls. This whole adrenaline rush takes less than five minutes to complete, but is exceedingly dangerous for the people running. Every year around a dozen people are gored (usually by bulls who are separated from the rest, causing them to feel cornered and angry), and many more are injured in other ways, such as

Pamplona's Casa Consistorial

falling or being kicked under hoof. Since 1924, when they began keeping records, 15 people have died during the bull run.

The party is already well underway by the bull run, as many people have been up all night, eating, drinking, and singing. After the run, the partying continues, and bullfights unfold in the Plaza de Toros. Crowds come from across Spain and around the world to participate in the bull running as well as the full-blown, 24-hour partying. Many Spaniards in attendance wear all white and tie a red scarf around their necks in honor of San Fermín, whose color is red.

Opposition

While some claim that bullfights have an elegance and cultural significance that should be celebrated, animal-rights groups are very vocal about the cruelty of bullfighting. Ultimately, the bull is going to be sacrificed, swiftly but right before your eyes, with a quick thrust of the sword between the shoulder blades and into its heart.

Many activists also oppose the running of the bulls, which exposes the animals to a lot of stress. In recent years, women's-rights groups have also begun to protest the debauchery of the festivals because they have led to some incidents of violence against women. Protestors wear black (as opposed to the traditional white) or sport a purple scarf to identify with victims, in addition to the red one to honor San Fermín. Each year, more and more Spaniards are leaning toward the side of the animal-rights and women's-rights activists.

For those who are ethically opposed to bull-running and bullfighting (and for introverts and teetotalers, too), Pamplona is definitely not the place to be in mid-July. Instead, consider being here on September 25, when locals observe, with processions and *paseos*, a quieter and more reverent festival of San Fermín.

homemade cheesecake with cranberries). I recommend that you order the house rosé (*vino rosado*), Hemingway's favorite drink here.

Connected to the **Hostal Aralar** (Calle San Nicolás, 12; 948-221-116; www.asa-dor-aralar.com) are the **Bar Aralar** (street level) for *pintxos* and the **Restaurante Aralar** (one floor up), popular with Pamplonans for lunch and dinner. The gourmet fixed-price menus (€19.50-30) are creative spins on classic Navarran cuisine, including *asados* (grilled and roasted meats), what the restaurant is best known for. *This* is the place to get a *cordero asado* (wood-oven-roasted lamb). Also consider trying their blueberry-and-quince foie gras mousse, *risotto de hongos* (wild mushroom risotto), or *menestra de verduras* (vegetable stew with *jamón íberico*).

Bearan Bar (Calle San Nicolás, 25; 948-223-428; www.bearanpamplona.com) has daily menus (€15-20), bar food (€4.50-9.50), and breakfasts (€3.5-5) in an appealing zinc, wood, and terracotta bar with high wood bar tables. Some favorites: fish and chips with *pimientos de Padrón* (instead of the classic mushy peas), tuna tartare with avocado, and oxtail stew with a hit of green curry. The breakfast sandwiches can range from the classic ham and cheese omelet piled on top of freshly baked bread to a vegetable and cheese grilled panini.

Restaurante Sarasate (Calle San Nicolas, 19-21; 948-225-727; www.restaurantesarasate.com), located one floor up from street level, has been serving vegetarian cuisine since 1979 and is celebrated for high standards of creative, seasonal, and organic dishes, some vegan and/or gluten-free. They post the changing daily menu on their website. For €11.50, your three-course meal may include such

From top to bottom: Bar Restaurante Maltea; Hotel La Perla; entrance to Café Iruña on the Plaza del Castillo.

dishes as the daily house salad; lasagna with mushrooms and vegetables, creamy seaweed and almond rice, or grilled red pepper and cheese salad with quince coulis; and original desserts such as saffron and orange grilled pineapple and curry apple tart.

Nightlife

Nightlife here is mostly focused on being with friends and making one's way from one great wine and *pintxos* bar to the next, a tradition that is especially vibrant along the **Casco Antiguo**'s streets and on the **Plaza del Castillo**. You can join the locals and meander along these streets all evening, stopping at the places that appeal to you. For live music and dance, nightclubs in the old town open late, typically no earlier than 11pm:

Subsuelo (Plaza del Castillo, 44 Bajo; 689-049-231; www.subsuelo.es), meaning "underground," is a delightful dip down under the plaza level of the Plaza del Castillo into an elegant and classy stone-lined and whitewashed brick-arcaded subterranean venue with a 1900s tin-pressed ceiling, featuring a regular slate of diverse concerts, cocktails, and dancing. Admission to concerts is usually free.

Txintxarri (Calle San Francisco, 26; 679-714-014) is a small, live, eclectic- and world-music venue that proclaims, "At Txintxarri, every day is a fiesta." There are concerts in this tiny, personable space, where people are laid-back, enjoying good but inexpensive drinks (including well-mixed cocktails), and make you feel as if you are a Pamplonan for the night.

Beer lovers in wine country will enjoy **The House Beer Brewing Company** (Calle Rozalejo, 4 Bajo; 848-471-221; www.thehousebeer.es; €5-12), where they also host music and sports evenings. You can dine here, enjoying gourmet hamburgers, or come after dinner to enjoy the society and the long list of beers, including their own three beers—plus 99 from Belgium, 32 from the USA, 30 from Germany, and 24 from England. They close at midnight, early by Pamplonan standards.

For more formal nightlife, Pamplona's auditorium, the **Palacio Baluarte Jauregia** (Plaza del Baluarte; 948-066-066; www.baluarte.com; €8-15), is the venue to take in classical and modern concerts, opera, theater, dance, and musicals, as well as art exhibits, nearly any day of the week. It is one of the biggest conference and concert spaces in Spain, at 63,000 square meters, and you can walk here easily from the Casco Antiguo, where it stands on the western edge.

Accommodations
Albergues and Hostels

The German pilgrim association runs the white- and green-trimmed stone **Albergue Casa Paderborn** (Calle Playa de Caparroso, 6; 948-211-712), outside and right below the towering medieval walls of Pamplona (after you cross the Puente de la Magdalena, to the left of the Camino). Opened in 2007, one of the perks of this impeccable *albergue* is its calm riverside location on the banks of the Arga. The *hospitaleros* (volunteers/staff running the *albergue*) greet you with juice, tea, and cookies, and wake you up with gentle music once breakfast is ready. There are 26 beds in five dorm rooms (€6, €8.50 with breakfast).

The lime-green, violet, ochre-yellow, and rust-red walls of the **Hostel Hemingway** (Calle Amaya, 26, first floor, left side; 948-983-884; www.hostelhemingway.com) are as colorful as the company you'll keep at this mix of youth hostel and pilgrim *albergue,* where a party is always waiting to happen with fellow journeyers and where rooms and common spaces are kept immaculate. There are 30 dorm beds in five dormitories (€13) and two private rooms (€26-44). Open all year except from Dec. 10-Jan. 1. Proprietors speak English.

■■■■■ **Top Experience** ■■■■■

The Art of *Pintxos*

Pintxos (pronounced PEEN-chos), spelled *pinchos* in other parts of Spain, are creative bite-sized appetizers usually consisting of a slice of bread with a tower of ingredients piled on top, but it can also be on a skewer (the more literal meaning of *pintxo/pincho*). Don't confuse *pintxos* with tapas, plates of one item meant to be shared among several people, which are more from Madrid and the south of Spain. *Pintxos* are meant to accompany a glass of wine or a short glass of beer (*un corto*, €1.50-€2) as a part of the tradition of doing a culinary pub crawl. This splendid tradition rules in Pamplona and is common on the Camino.

How to Order

The key is not to be shy: bartenders are masters at taking their cue from eye contact and a smile as you step up to the counter. Whether or not you speak Spanish, just wedge your way between other customers at the bar and point at what you want. The bartender will keep track of your tab. The elaborate *pintxos* that line the counters cost between €1.50-€3, and most glasses of wine or beer between €2-€3. If you just order a drink and no *pintxo*, often the bartender will still give you a simple little bite—perhaps a small toast with ham or cheese, or a bowl of olives—on the house.

Top *Pintxos* in Pamplona

It is easy to tell whether an establishment serves *pintxos:* If the counters are arrayed with colorful dishes from end to end, you've found a *pintxos* bar. In Pamplona, most of the establishments along the historic streets of **San Nicolás, Comedias, San Gregorio, Estafeta, Jarauta, Mercaderes,** and **Navarrería,** plus the additional circuit around the **Plaza del Castillo,** have long bar counters arrayed with copious, colorful, and artful *pintxos*. After rigorous first-hand research into this matter, three places rise to the top for the classic *pintxo* experience:

La Mandarra de la Ramos (Calle San Nicolás, 9; 948212-654; www.lamandarradelosramos.com): The front of this bar is a *pintxo* paradise. Diverse toast-top offerings include hot goat brie with caramelized shallots and tomatoes, sautéed baby eels and shrimp on jamón Ibérico, and fried trout with green peppers. A bodega-style dining room offers more elaborate dining.

Casa Otano (Calle San Nicolás, 5; 948-225-095; www.casaotano.com): Located on the street level of the *hostal* of the same name, Casa Otano has been pulsing with local clientele since 1912. Some signature *pintxos:* seafood-and-cheese-stuffed squash; beef kebabs with mushrooms, peppers and Roquefort cheese; and grilled squid with a garlic mayonnaise.

Iruñazarra (Calle Mercaderes, 15; 948-225-167; www.irunazarra.com; €3-5): A wide-open glass-and-stone entrance leads into this well-lit contemporary bar that's more cutting-edge than the other *pintxo* establishments. *Pintxos* are crafted to look like works of modern art, with colorful vegetables, foams, caramelized encasings, and accordion-folded dough packets containing savory delicacies. The ultimate signature *pintxo* here may be the quinoa-based cracker topped with guacamole, gazpacho, smoked eel, caviar, and multicolored edible algae (€3).

All three of the above also serve excellent three-course and a la carte menus (€10-27) in their more formal dining rooms.

Hotels and *Hostales*

Right on the Plaza del Castillo, 150 meters (492 feet) south of the Camino from the Plaza Consistorial, the shimmering, pearl-toned **Hotel La Perla** (Plaza del Castillo, 1; 948-223-000; www.granhotellaperla.com; €200-350) opened in 1881 and sustains the aura of Hemingway's Pamplona with turn-of-the-century Belle-Epoque décor and sepia photographs from the 1900s. Prices are among the highest on the Camino and vary depending on season; they can exceed €1,000 per night during the Sanfermines. Among the 44 luxury accommodations, four are decorated in the spirit of the famous occupants who stayed there: Hemingway (Suite 201), Pablo Sarasate (Suite 207), Spanish princess Infanta Isabel (Suite 601), and Spanish king Alfonso VIII (Suite 602). These typically run around €750. Proprietors speak English.

★ **Hostal Arriazu** (Calle de las Comedias, 14; 948-210-202; www.hostalarriazu.com; €60-65) is 140 meters (459 feet) to the west from the Plaza del Castilla, and is run by sincere and enthusiastic English speakers who will help with any queries, including helping you find accommodations if all their rooms are booked. But do try to get one: most of the 14 rooms have a balcony, and all have a view. They are attired in the earthy colors of the Casco Antiguo, with early 20th-century furnishings and antique photos of turn-of-the-century Pamplona. On the edge of the old city, it is a little quieter here, but still only a 3-minute walk to the historic town center.

Some 200 meters (656 feet) south of the Plaza Consistorial and 100 meters (328 feet) west of the Plaza del Castillo is **Hostal Aralar** (Calle San Nicolás, 12; 948-221-116; www.asador-aralar.com; €30-40), named after the mountain range to the north, Sierra Aralar. Enter on the steep stairs to the right of the hopping **Bar Aralar** and climb to the next floor to the **Restaurante Aralar**, which will be packed with devoted clients. There, ask for your key. The manager, Alberto Diaz, is a total mensch and will check you into your room between serving lunch and dinner dishes to diners in this popular local joint. Be patient: without too much delay, he'll deliver you to a peaceable kingdom one more floor up, with all-white, spotless, and basic rooms that are surprisingly quiet.

Hostal Otano (Calle San Nicolás, 5; 948-225-095; www.casaotano.com; €40-45), across from Hostal Aralar, is another deal for old Pamplona, with similarly basic, functional, and clean rooms with plush red curtains and stark white linens. It is also located over a good bar and restaurant of the same management and name. As much as a room with a view may appeal, if you are a light sleeper, try to get one set back from the street and bar below. Based on availability, they offer *peregrino* (pilgrim) prices, around €25 for a room with bath, so be sure to ask.

Also on Calle San Nicolás, near Hotel Aralar and Hostal Otano, is the excellent **Bearan Bar & Rooms** (Calle San Nicolás, 25; 948-223-428; www.bearanpamplona.com; €35-45;), a hotel and bar run by an energetic English-speaking staff who welcome you as if you're the first holy pilgrim to step through their doors. Inquire about rooms from the bartender, and pick up the key at the bar. Rooms are simple, comfortable, and immaculate, decorated in greens, browns, and ivories, with wood-grain floors and French windows, possibly feeling more like where Hemingway would have stayed in the 1920s (instead of La Perla) on the slim budget of a young writer. Be sure to eat here, too, especially the breakfast sandwiches that will fortify your return to the trail.

Hotel Tres Reyes (Calle Taconera, 1; 948-226-600; www.hotel3reyes.com; €80-150) is a posh international-style convention hotel on the western edge of the Casco Antiguo, just 50 meters (164 feet) south of the Camino as it leaves the historic town. Not all hotels offer special pilgrim prices, but here they do, at the lower end of the spectrum noted above. (Inquire about these in person, by phone, or email at reserv@hotel3reyes. com, for they don't advertise this offer on their website; the prices vary by season and availability.) The *peregrino* rate includes breakfast, and fruit and water for the trail. You can enjoy the fancy kidney-shaped outdoor pool from June to September and also arrange, for an added fee, a session of massage therapy. Proprietors speak English.

Getting There and Around

Pamplona is well connected by train, bus, shuttle, and air, and also is a hub for car-rental agencies.

Air

Pamplona's airport (PNA, www.aena.es) is 6 kilometers (3.7 miles) south of the city and carries direct flights operated by **Air Nostrum/Iberia Regional** (www.airnostrum.es) from **Madrid** (five flights daily on average). If you fly into **Biarritz**, the bus company **ALSA** (www.alsa.com) runs buses from Biarritz's airport to Pamplona (five buses daily; 3-4 hours; €15).

Taxis (10-15 min.; €15-20) and the airport bus, **Linea A/Line A** (20-30 min.; €1.60), connect Pamplona's airport to the city.

Shuttle

The Saint-Jean-Pied-de-Port-based shuttle company **Express Bourricot** (www. expressbourricot.com) can take passengers from Biarritz's airport and Bilbao's airport and train station to Pamplona. Prices can be anywhere from €20-220, depending on beginning and ending destinations, the availability each day, and how many passengers share a shuttle. Inquire via their contact page to get an estimate.

Car

From **Roncesvalles** (47 km/29 mi; 1 hour): Driving southwest along the N-135, which follows and parallels the Camino de Santiago, will take you all the way to Pamplona.

Driving from **Santander via Bilbao** (255 km/158 mi; 3 hours): Take the **S-10** to **A-8** east toward Bilbao, then the **AP-68** south after Bilbao, connecting to the **N-622** and **A-1/A-10** to Pamplona.

From **Biarritz via San Sebastian** (103 km/64 mi; 1.5 hours): Take the **A-63** southwest to the French-Spanish border at Hendaye and Irun, and continue on the **AP-8/AP-1** skirting the south side of San Sebastian and continue on the **A-1/A-15** south to Pamplona.

From **Barcelona** (435 km/270 mi; 5 hours): Head west toward Lleida on the **A-2;** continue on the **A-22** toward Huesca, then take the **N-240** around the north side of Huesca and exit toward Pamplona on the **A-132** to the **A-21** and continue to Pamplona.

Many car rental companies have offices in Pamplona, including the centrally located **Europcar** (www.europcar. com), near the university, and **Enterprise** (www.enterprise.com) and **Avis** (www. avis.com), next to the train station.

Train

RENFE (www.renfe.com) makes direct connections from Madrid (five trains daily; 3-4 hours; €60-66), Barcelona (seven daily; 4-4.5 hours; €27-68), Burgos (six daily; 2-3.5 hours; €14-23), Leon (two daily; 4.5 hours; €38), and Santiago de Compostela (one daily; 9 hours; €33). There are no direct trains between Logroño from Pamplona; the bus is your most efficient option.

Pamplona's RENFE station (Plaza de las Estacion, 1; 90/232-0320; www.renfe. com) is about 1.5 km (just under 1 mile) north of the bus station and old city. From here, the most efficient way into the historic town and the Camino is to walk south (about 25 minutes), following the Arga river on your right, to the Iglesia de San Lorenzo, your first historic sight on the western edge of the Casco Antiguo

Rose of the Camino

Around 2002, Moisés Ponce de León, a Riojan professor and horticultural specialist based at the University of Rennes in Brittany, and Michel Adam, a florist known for creating award-winning hybrids, joined forces to create a flower dedicated to the Camino. After 10 years of efforts in collaboration with the city of Logroño, Adam arrived at a flower that captured the "color, perfume, and resistance" of the Camino. They unveiled it in 2012 in a rose garden planted near the Ebro river, just before entering Logroño, on the left of the Camino. In 2013, the city of Logroño then gifted the rose to the mayor of Pamplona, who brought it back here to establish the **Rosa del Camino de Santiago** rose garden.

Anyone can acquire the rose and plant it along the Camino as a celebration and

Rosas del Camino hybridized for the Camino, this one on entering Logroño

symbol of the unity of the Way of Saint James. You can even purchase the rose online, directly from the grower: www. roseraie-guerinais.com for around €12.

PAMPLONA KM 711.5

and right on the Camino. You can also catch a taxi (12 min.; €10-15).

Bus

ALSA (www.alsa.com) runs direct buses from Madrid's Barajas Airport, terminal T4 (4-5 daily; 5 hours; €23-47), Madrid's Avenida de América station (10-11 daily; 5-6 hours; €23-47), Barcelona's Estación Nord station (six daily; 7 hours; €32-39), and Santander (six daily; 4-5 hours; €22) to Pamplona.

If you want to skip the Camino, or portions of it, between Saint-Jean-Pied-de-Port and Pamplona, ALSA has two buses daily destined for Pamplona from Saint-Jean-Pied-de-Port (2 hours; €22) with stops in Roncesvalles, Burguete, Espinal, and Zubiri.

Use the very helpful information kiosk, right in front as you go down the stairs into **Estacion de Autobuses de Pamplona** (Avenida de Yanguas y Miranda, 2; 90/202-3651; www.estaciondeautobusesdepamplona.com), the underground bus station, if you need help sorting through the bus companies and their schedules and destinations—or to trouble-shoot, as often there might be more than one route to where you want to go.

Taxi

If you need a cab, call **Teletaxi San Fermín** (948-232-300; www.taxipamplona.com) or **Radiotaxi** (948-221-212).

Bike

To explore Pamplona by bike and take one along the Camino for a few days, stop in or reserve online at **Mundoraintxe** (Calle Nueva, 121 and Calle San Antón, 64; 948-213-033; www.mundoraintxe. com; (starting at €125, a flat rate that covers a rental for 1-6 days; starting at €185 for 7-9 days).

Leaving Pamplona

From Pamplona to the mountains of León, you will have the constant companions of the Cantabrian mountain range

Chi-Rho

Before the cross was used to represent Christ, a symbol known as Chi-Rho served that purpose. *Chi* and *rho* are the names of the first two letters of Christ's name in Greek (Christos); they resemble an X and a P and were overlapped in a circle to show the never-ending nature of Christ. This idea was deepened with the addition of the alpha and omega, the first and last letters of the Greek alphabet, hanging on the upper horizontal arms of the X, symbolizing the beginning and the end.

The Chi-Rho is a form you'll see often on Camino churches, but some places, including and beyond Cizur Menor, such as in Cirauqui, Estella, and León, reverse the placement of the alpha and omega. This may indicate that the stonemasons at work on the Camino were from mixed backgrounds, perhaps schooled in

Reverse Chi-Rho on Cirauqui's Iglesia de San Román

Hebrew and Arabic, where the writing goes from right to left.

in the far horizon running north of you, to your right. These are the mountains that separate the plains of Spain from the ocean. For pilgrims, they are a useful reminder of which way north is.

The Camino follows the Calle Mayor through the west side of Casco Antiguo and passes the Iglesia de San Lorenzo on the left, the last sight on the Camino in the Casco Antiguo. You will then cross Calle Taconera and continue straight on Calle Bosquecillo, which passes through the edge of the **Parque de la Taconera**. Soon after you cross Calle Taconera and enter the park, look to your left to find a small triangular patch of lawn with a small rose garden in the center: This is dedicated to the Camino and identified with a plaque as **Rosa del Camino de Santiago** (rose of the Camino de Santiago). Definitely stop to smell these roses, which were first cultivated in Logroño to commemorate the Camino's joining of diverse people and locales.

Continue southwest, following the way-markers painted on tree trunks, sidewalks, and posted signs. They will

lead you to the northwest side of La Ciudadela (the Citadel) and through the western side of the citadel's large green park; you still have another 3 kilometers (1.9 miles) before fully leaving Pamplona. The urban path is very pleasant and well way-marked, passing through green zones along the university campus and out into the low hills and large fields of the countryside toward Cizur Menor.

Cizur Menor   Km 706.7

As you enter Cizur Minor (pop. 2,433) on the Camino, look to your left to find its most interesting structure, the small, 12th-century, Romanesque Iglesia de San Miguel. Cizur Menor is largely a bedroom community for people who work in Pamplona. Its hub for social life is the small handful of cafés and restaurants here and in the neighboring community of Cizur Mayor, one kilometer (0.6 miles) to your right off the Camino, to the west of Cizur Menor.

Sights
Iglesia de San Miguel

The **Iglesia de San Miguel** (Calle Irunbidea, 6; 948-353-053 or inquire in the *albergue* next door; free) is the sole survivor of a larger San Juan de Jerúsalen monastery founded here in 1135. Used as a grain silo for at least a hundred years, until the 1980s, it was recently restored back to its use as a church. The church is usually locked, but opens for Sunday mass at 6:30pm. The entrance retains its original late-Romanesque arch, from around 1200, though the sculpture on the capitals is all but gone. Still, there is a medallion in the tympanum, a Chi-Rho, that is one of the earlier symbols for Christ, before the cross was used to represent him.

Food

A cider and grill house, **Sidrería Asador Martintxo** (Calle Irunbidea Kalea, 1; 948-180-020; www.sidreriamartintxo. es; €16-25), located on the right side of the Camino 100 meters (328 feet) past the Iglesia de San Miguel, is a popular place for grilled meats—try the *cordero asado* (grilled lamb)—and seafood. Their sautéed artichokes (*alchofas*) are tender and succulent. This is also a great place to sample the local hard cider, *sidra,* contained in massive barrels that are built into some of the walls.

Accommodation

The order of the Knights of Saint John of Malta, who restored Cizur Menor's surviving church of San Miguel, also run a small pilgrims' *albergue* next door to the church, **Albergue Encomienda de San Juan** (616-651-330; open May-Sept.; 27 beds in one bunkhouse; €5). When there are no beds left here, pilgrims are given places to sleep in the church.

Leaving Cizur Menor

Four kilometers (2.5 miles) after Cizur Menor, to your right you will see the ruins, in the distance, of the fortress-like 16th-century church of **Guenduláin** (Km 707.8). Luckily, the best vantage point to view this ruin—which is in a private field and should not be trespassed—is from the Camino, looking out on the sweeping wheat fields, with the chalky gray-and-black Cantabrian mountains in the far horizon.

From Cizur Menor you will feel the Camino begin to climb toward the Alto del Perdón, but the ascent is mild from here until Zariquiegui, when it becomes slightly steeper.

Zariquiegui   Km 700.6

The hamlet of Zariquiegui (pop. 162) sits midway on the slope climbing to the Alto del Perdón ridge. Before reaching the center of village life—its bar and *albergue*—you pass the 13th-century **Iglesia de San Andrés,** which has similar proportions, walls, and arches to Cizur Menor's church, as well as a similar Chi-Rho medallion engraved in its tympanum. San Andrés's church once stood in the center of a prospering settlement that was decimated in 1348 by the plague.

Today, Zariquiegui may strike you as an insignificant spot, missed if you blink, but stop for a moment and discover how welcoming the villagers are. This is an ideal spot to rest before taking on the remaining climb, which is the steepest portion leading to the Alto del Perdón. Aficionados of the movie *The Way* will recognize the church as the spot where the characters Joost and Sarah first meet.

Accommodations and Food

El Albergue de Zariquiegui (Calle San Andrés, 16; 948-334-699 or 670-360-888; open Mar.-Oct.) is a sweet and immaculate place to stay just to the left of the Camino on Calle San Andrés, with 22 beds in three rooms (€10) and a private patio with café tables, as well as an inside bar that opens to the street with outdoor tables. Ana Carricas, the *hospitalera,* serves up a good communal meal (€11). The bar is a fun gathering place at night.

★ Alto del Perdón
Km 698.3

At 770 meters (2,526 feet), the ridge of Alto del Perdón offers a tremendous perspective of sweeping slopes and vast rocky fields, but it also has a spiritual significance, coded in its name, the "height of forgiveness." This locale carries the region's highest winds, and turbine windmills line the spine of the hill. This wind also traditionally plays a role in forgiveness, carrying away one's sorrows and clearing the pilgrim of the burdens he or she carried up here.

"*Perdón*" (pardon) is an old association here: In the Middle Ages, this ridge housed a basilica and a pilgrims' hospital under the name of **Nuestra Señora del Perdón**, Our Lady of Forgiveness. Nothing remains of those structures, but you will see **Monumento al Peregrino** (Monument to the Pilgrim), Vicente Galbete's famous life-size metal sculpture of pilgrims past and present, installed here in 1996. The pilgrims are walking, and some are riding horses (and one, a donkey) a dog at their side, all making their way west. They are surprisingly wonderful company when you make it up this hill, encouraging you to keep going. This dramatic rise over the plains of Navarra toward Puente la Reina is considered the Way of the Wind, and you'll see these words engraved in Galbete's work: *Donde se cruza el camino del viento con el de las estrellas* ("where the way of the wind meets the way of the stars").

Leaving the Alto del Perdón

The climb down is harder than the way up: It is an even steeper slope down a loose, uneven pebble path. It wends through almond groves, Holm oaks, and wheat fields to the village of Uterga. Just before entering Uterga, you will see an **outdoor sanctuary** dedicated to Mary, a pretty marble sculpture of Our Lady set in a shady grove with a bench.

Uterga Km 694.5

Uterga (pop. 164) is a congenial village built along the Camino, which doubles as the town's main street. You'll find a good *albergue* and café here.

Accommodations

The **Camino del Perdón** (Calle Mayor, 61; 948-334-598; www.caminodelperdon.es; open Mar.-Oct.) opened in 2003 and has comfortable beds and rooms, and a fresh, copious, and tasty *menú del peregrino* (€12) in the restaurant for lunch and dinner, and all-day refreshments and sandwiches in the bar. There are four warmly decorated private rooms with bath (€50), and 16 dorm beds, each with their own wood enclosed space, headboard reading light, and electrical outlet, in one bunkhouse (€10). Proprietors speak English.

Leaving Uterga

Continue toward **Muruzábal** (Km 692; pop. 219), where the path diverges. You can either follow the path straight to Obanos in 1.8 kilometers (1.1 miles), or mark the detour to the left, after the village church, to the chapel of **Santa María de Eunate** in 2.4 kilometers (1.5 miles). Eunate is one of the Camino's most stunning churches. It's considered a detour today, but in the Middle Ages Eunate may well have been on the main Camino path: Excavations have uncovered pilgrim graves around Eunate, many containing scallop shells. The detour to Eunate adds an extra 3 kilometers (1.9 miles) to the walk, but I consider it a highlight of the whole Camino, and it truly shouldn't be missed.

▬▬▬ **Top Experience** ▬▬▬

❖ ★ Detour: Santa María de Eunate Km 689.6

Santa María de Eunate (Carretera de Campanas, s/n, Muruzábal; 628-872-835; www.santamariadeeunate.es; Mar 24.-Jun. daily 10:30am-2pm and 3-7pm; Jul.-Aug. daily 10:30am-2pm and 4-8pm; Sept.-Oct. 14 daily 10:30am-2pm, 3-7pm, 3-6pm; Oct. 15-Mar. 23 closed, except Nov.1-4 and Dec. 6-9 10:30am-2pm and 3-6pm; €1.50, €1 for pilgrims) is arguably the loveliest and most enigmatic church of the whole Camino. It was built around 1170, but no one knows by whom. (One theory—that Templars built it to replicate the most important church in Christianity, the similarly octagonal Church of the Holy Sepulcher in Jerusalem—doesn't have enough evidence, though some still believe it, given the strong presence of the Templars all along the Camino.)

The whole building, in sacred numbers—3, 33, 99, 100, and 8—is a meditation on entering heaven/higher consciousness through prayer and meditation. To start with, Eunate is not a typical round church, of which there are several in Spain. Instead, it is surrounded by a 33-arched ring wall around the edifice, perhaps intended as a different style of cloister to the more common form (square and set off on one side of a church). Two bearded figures engraved on an outer portal have spiral beards that coil around three times, possibly implying a 3-times-33 walk around the cloister.

When you step into the chapel entrance, you step into a circle; the nave is the natural path from the door straight to the altar right ahead of you. Look to the right of the altar, a serene space with soft light coming through thin marble windows set in the domed ceiling, to find a capital carved with an angel playing a flute, an unusual image for most medieval churches. Perhaps this echoes the Sufi belief that God created us humans by breathing life into a hollow reed, forming the melody that is the essence of our souls.

Guided visits (948-741-273; visitas@santamariadeeunate.es; €3) in English or Spanish are possible. When the church is closed after mid-October, call to inquire and to see if you can arrange a visit.

The other building on this stretch, next door to the chapel, is the old *albergue* that closed around 2012 and is now called **Casa de Onat** (Carretera de Campanas, s/n, Muruzábal; 628-872-835; www.santamariadeeunate.es/la-casa-de-onat), a quiet place expressly for rest and meditation but not overnight stays. Open during the day, Casa de Onat closes in the late afternoon.

Leaving Santa María de Eunate

From Eunate, the path leads over the small hill opposite the side you arrived from, continuing directly to Obanos, which is on the nearest rise ahead of you and which will be visible before you reach the village in 2.5 kilometers (1.6 miles). This is where the detour from Eunate rejoins the main path of the Camino.

Obanos Km 687.1

Obanos (pop. 903) is built around its large central square and the imposing Iglesia de San Juan Bautista. This appealing village with a noble past goes back to 1234, when Navarran nobles began meeting here to mobilize against the poor treatment they received at the hands of Navarra's kings. But it's even better-known as the place to which Guillermo (William), duke of Aquitaine, retreated after murdering his sister Felicia (or so legend has it). As the story goes, after a pilgrimage, Felicia wanted to enter a hermitage and dedicate her life to God.

Clockwise from top: Santa María de Eunate; Iglesia de San Andrés in Zariquiegui; approaching Obanos; Alto del Perdón.

Sacred Numbers

Santa María de Eunate is a spiritual microcosm of the medieval Camino, and testimony to how diverse and integrated that world was. Stonemasons, in particular, formed their own itinerant society of pagans, Jews, Christians, and Muslims drawn from across Europe, Asia, and the Mediterranean. Their work reflected this blended society, and you can see it in churches across the Camino—many coming up along this stretch, such as the churches in Puente la Reina, Cirauqui, Estella, and Torres del Rio. The stonemasons were influenced by ancient traditions from across the Mediterranean, Middle East, and Europe, which held similar numbers and geometric forms as sacred. The Camino became a natural recipient of these shared ideas, which are encoded onto the road's sacred architecture.

That Santa María de Eunate's edifice contains 33 arches is significant: The number **33** is a sacred number for Christians; it is Jesus's age when he was crucified. Some convents limit the number of nuns to 33 for this reason. Thirty-three is also the number of beads on Muslim prayer beads used for a traditional meditation on the 99 names of God. Three plus three, another expression of 33, is a symbol of the intersecting triangles that represent Solomon's Seal (more popularly known since the 19th century as the Star of David), which itself represents the intersection of heaven and earth, common in sacred symbolism for all three Abrahamic faiths—Judaism, Christianity, and Islam. Three plus three is also basis of the older, pagan seed of life, a six-petaled flower that represents the same alchemy between heaven and earth.

The numbers **99** and **100** are sacred as well. In Sufism (mystical Islam), the meditation on the 99 names of God ends with the passage through the final, 100th door, the act of entering heaven or communion with God: Earth meeting heaven. Here at Eunate (which means "place of one hundred doors" in Basque), the church may be an ecumenical rosary laid out in stone, to be circled three times and entered: the 100th door. That door would be the west chapel entrance, where you will find yourself standing before the Romanesque statue of Santa María de Eunate on the altar.

Lastly, the octagonal shape of Eunate contains the sacred number **8**, which for Christians represents resurrection, redemption, and rebirth. For Muslims, 8 represents the gate of heaven. And in the Kabalistic method of applying numerology to letters of the alphabet, the numeric value of Jesus's Hebrew name (Yeshua) is 888.

Angry at her for renouncing her royal life, Guillermo killed her, but felt remorse the moment the deed was done. He made another pilgrimage to Compostela to purge his soul, but the weight of murdering his own sister did not lift. On his return, he retreated from his royal life and became a hermit near Obanos; by the end of his life he was known as a local holy man, San Guillermo, with miraculous powers to cure and aid others.

Sights
Iglesia de San Juan Bautista

The exterior of **Iglesia de San Juan** (Plaza de Fueros, 1; 948-344-030; open for mass 6pm daily [Vespers], 10am Wed., 12pm Sun. and holidays) retains the church's original, heavily fortified 14th-century Gothic form, but it is actually a reconstruction from 1912 that incorporates the older church's entrance, arches, and tower. The interior is fairly simple, with white plaster walls and neo-Gothic pillars, arches, and pointed ceiling, and a modest gold retable on the altar.

This imposing church holds a reliquary of silver in the form of San Guillermo's head, where the preserved portion of his skull are held within the silver encasing. Most is completely covered, but the back of the head has a glass window set into the silver that allows a person to see a portion of the back of the skull embedded in the silver encasing. It is kept in the church but not on display, and is brought out only on feast days.

Events

Iglesia de San Juan Bautista is the center of sacred life in Obanos. It is a part of an annual festivity called **El Misterio de Obanos** (The Mystery of Obanos), held in late August and involving the whole village as the stage and its inhabitants as the cast, in order to reenact Guillermo and Felicia's stories.

Another event in Iglesia de San Juan Bautista, **San Guillermo's feast day,** occurs on the Thursday before Easter Sunday. On this day, locals stay in the church after mass to partake of the blessings of water and wine. The priest brings out San Guillermo's silver reliquary head, which has a silver funnel fused to the crown. This allows water and wine to be poured from the top, through the hollow head, and to come out at the bottom of the neck, where a large vessel gathers the now-blessed liquid. The priest first holds the reliquary over a vessel, and a parishioner pours water into it. The two then move on to three other vessels, one each for white, then rosé, and then red wine. Everyone is welcome to imbibe the blessing of healing offered by the saint.

Food and Accommodations

Bar Centro San Guillermo (Plaza San Guillermo, 1; 948-344-392; €5-10) is a small village bar tucked on the right side of the Camino when you arrive on the path from Eunate (and down a street and to the left when you come from the direct route from Muruzábal to Obanos). It's a nice place for a meal, snack, or glass of local Navarran vintage and olives, and serves good rustic home cooking, different each day, depending on the fresh harvest from nearby gardens.

★ **Hostal Mamerto** (Calle San Lorenzo, 13-B; 948-344-344; www.hostalmamerto.com; €30-45) is a traditional Basque-Navarran country homestead, where the elderly woman who runs it treats you like a long-lost relative. She has turned this stone house into nine guestrooms with bath and a communal kitchen and salon. With tile floors, thick walls, and wood-beamed ceilings, each room is painted a distinct color—terracotta, pine-green, lavender, rose, and sea-blue. The kitchen is available if you wish to cook.

Leaving Obanos

The Camino passes the church and exits the village under a wonderful pointed Gothic gate. To the left of the path you'll soon see the **Ermita de San Salvador**, a small single-nave chapel from the 16th century. Just past it, right on the Camino, is a modern, rectangular, standing metal **sculpture** with a cutout of shape of a person, inviting you to pass through it. The hermitage and the sculpture both commemorate the site where two major routes of the Camino meet: the Camino Francés, which crosses at the Pyrenees at the Cize/Roncesvalles pass (the one you are on), and the Camino Aragonés, which crosses farther east. The two join here to continue as one road heading to Santiago de Compostela.

This well-marked path to Puente la Reina follows an irrigated gully with fertile kitchen gardens. Lining the path are plots growing red peppers, onions, lettuces, artichokes, collard greens, and tomatoes. Locals, out weeding and tying vines to stakes, enjoy waving to pilgrims and letting you know Puente la Reina is just around the bend.

Puente la Reina
Km 684.8

In a fertile valley between almond tree and grapevine-covered hills, Puente la Reina (Gares in Basque; pop. 2,769) is a town centered on its main street, the Calle Mayor, which is also the Camino. As you walk along it, you can feel the powerful pull of millions of pilgrims' feet, all aiming to make it over the elegantly bowed, six-arched Romanesque bridge at the street's end.

Puente la Reina's **weekly market** (Sat. 9am-1pm) sells food and general goods and sets up along the Calle Cerco Viejo, which runs through town parallel to the Camino, two streets away and on the right.

Sights

For pilgrims, the **Calle Mayor** holds it all: you enter it after passing the Iglesia del Crucifijo on the right, followed by Iglesia de Santiago and Iglesia de San Pedro (which contains a late-Gothic sculpture of Nuestra Señora del Puy, one of Europe's Black Madonnas, but which is unfortunately rarely open). You then leave Puente la Reina over the bridge that gives the town its name.

Iglesia del Crucifijo

The **Iglesia del Crucifijo** (948-341-301; Mon.-Fri., 9am-8pm and Sat.-Sun., 10am-8pm; free) is the first church on the right as the Camino enters Puente la Reina. The name, the Church of the Crucifix, comes from the cross on its altar, an unusual sculpture of the crucified Jesus on a three-pronged cross that looks more like a Y.

The double-nave church began in the 12th century as a Templar church and the older of two naves belongs to that church, along with the icon of Mary on the altar. She is known as **Santa María de las Huertas**, Mary of the gardens/orchards, the name of this church before it

was named after the *crucifijo*. Next to the Romanesque nave, masons built a Gothic second nave in the 14th century, the one with the Y-shaped cross and Jesus on the altar. The cross may have come from Germany as a gift from a German pilgrim around the time masons built the nave. Some more esoterically inclined pilgrims believe that the cross is connected both to the Templars and to the Game of the Goose, and that the shape is that of a goose foot, hinting that this spot holds a key for spiritual wisdom.

The ornate 12th- and 13th-century carvings of animals and plants on the entrance arches and tympanum are distinct, with Byzantine- and Persian-inspired figures, such as the intertwined birds, ornate vines and flowers, and mythical beasts hybridized with parts of different animals' bodies (such as the serpent-tailed and winged lion).

Iglesia de Santiago

Puente la Reina's 11th-century **Iglesia de Santiago** (948-341-301; Mon.-Sun., 10:30am-8pm; free), also on the right side of the Camino as you walk through town, is one of the most remarkable remaining examples of Mudéjar architecture (the style of Iberian Muslims in Christian Spain) mixed with Romanesque. Of the original church, only the doorway survives. The Islamic-styled multi-lobed (scalloped) doorway interweaves Romanesque and Persian characters and symbols on its arches, including images of medieval professions, saints, demons, and gullible humans engaging in follies with temptation and sin. It is likely that the same multi-faith craftsmen who built this church also built the scalloped archway churches in Cirauqui (Km 685.8) and in Estella (Km 671.1).

The rest of the church was rebuilt in the 16th century. The central altar is dedicated to Mary and her appearance to Santiago during his ministry in Iberia. A famous 14th-century Gothic image of Saint James stands on the left

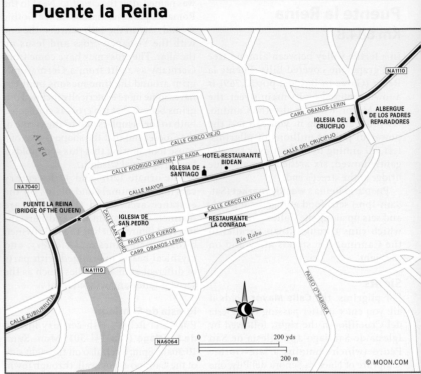

Puente la Reina

aisle's wall, surrounded by scallop shells. This handsome James is popularly called Santiago Beltza, "Black Saint James" in Basque. The name may simply refer to the color of the sculpture, but it may also be symbolic: In older European and circum-Mediterranean traditions, black is the color of fertility and of the sacred Earth, and some connect it to Isis, an ancient Mother Earth figure. Perhaps this is the masculine equivalent to the Black Madonnas of Europe, which represent ancient ideas of female divinity as connected to the Mother Earth? It's one of a handful of possibilities.

Daily **mass** is at 10am and 7:30pm, and at 12pm and 7:30pm on Sundays. You can get a stamp here for your pilgrim's credential.

Puente La Reina

After you pass Iglesia de San Pedro, Puente La Reina ("bridge of the queen"), the bridge that gives the town its name, takes you up and over the Río Arga. The bridge was built in the 11th century, either by Queen Doña Mayor or by the next queen, Estefania. Stop to take a closer look at it: it is the sister to Puente de la Magdalena, which you crossed to enter Pamplona.

The statue of Nuestra Señora del Puy, now contained in the rarely-open Iglesia de San Pedro, used to stand atop a tower on this bridge, and pilgrims would pass under it when leaving town on the Camino. In the mid-19th century, people began to notice a little bird, a *txori* in Basque, who was perpetually around Mary's statue on the tower. Every day the bird would remove spiderwebs from the statue and use its beak to scoop up water from the river to wash Mary's face with its wings. It was such a daily habit for the bird that the statue became known as **La Virgen del Txori**, the Bird's Virgin.

The Carlist Wars in the late 19th century probably destroyed the tower. But when you cross the bridge on your way out of town, look for the bird. Its kin are surely still all around.

Food

★ **Restaurante La Conrada** (Paseo de los Fueros, 17; www.reataurantelaconrada. com; 948-340-052) is best known for its traditional home cooking and seasonal daily menu (€11.50-12.50), including garden-fresh salads, grilled bass and hake, and homemade cheesecake with berry coulis. There is indoor dining in a warm pale-brick dining room, as well as a long bar with open picture windows and outdoor street-side seating. You'll be rubbing shoulders with locals, Pamplonans, and pilgrims, who all are drawn here for the warm service and excellent cuisine. Proprietors speak English.

Accommodations

Hotel-Restaurante Bidean (Calle Mayor, 20; 948-340-457; www.bidean.com; 20 rooms; €40-59) lets you sleep in a 17th-century town home, recognized as a part of the artistic patrimony of Navarra. It has been restored with the original stone, wood, and brick. The street level has a gregarious bar. You can dine there or in the more formal bodega-styled dining room, with its rounded ceiling of stone and brick. The menu (€12-15) offers traditional Navarran dishes, such as asparagus with spinach and shrimp or a green salad topped with red peppers from Puente la Reina, roasted and stuffed with cod and salmon. On weekend evenings, Bidean hosts live music on the terrace.

The first *albergue* in Puente la Reina, to the left as you enter on the Camino, is **Albergue de los Padres Reparadores** (Calle Crucifijo, 1; 948-340-050; economo.puente@esic.es; open year-round; 100 beds in 12 dormitories; €5), run by a German order and connected to the Iglesia del Crucifijo. The monastic building of the *albergue* originates in the 18th-century monastery, but before that, this spot was the site of the 12th-century Templar pilgrims' lodging. It has a huge garden, dorm rooms with simple and clean facilities, and decent showers. The Padres Reparadores hold mass daily in the Iglesia del Crucifijo at 7:30pm.

Albergue Santiago Apostal (Paraje Real de Malinalco, s/n; 948-340-220; www.algerguesantiagoapostal.com; 100 beds in 5 bunkhouses, €10-12) is a large, modern complex set in the countryside on the edge of town, with its own bar, outdoor swimming pool, large garden (a rural field filled with wildflowers), and pool table. The *albergue* is on the other side of Puente la Reina, about 300 meters (984 feet) on the left after crossing the bridge and taking on Calle Camping el Real. A standard pilgrim **menú** (€10) and breakfast (€3.50) are offered. Sleeping quarters and bathrooms are spacious, spotless, and simple, and they also have a few bungalows with bath for 4-6 people (€15/person).

Leaving Puente la Reina

Follow the Puente la Reina over the river and the way-markers out of town. The Camino becomes a dirt tract that snakes along dale and hill, through a little valley and several fields, on the way to **Mañeru** (Km 679.7; pop. 422), with the fortress-like, 18th-century **Iglesia de San Pedro** (Calle Emilio Arrieta, 43; 948-340-007; mass Fri. and holidays 5:30pm; free) on the highest point.

On the way out of Mañeru, you'll pass the village **cemetery** on the Camino's left. If you chance upon this cemetery a few days before or after the end of October, you'll see people cleaning the tombstones and setting fresh flowers on the graves in preparation for *Dia de Todos los Santos*, All Saints Day, on November 1. And on

that day, here and elsewhere where you pass a cemetery, be prepared for color and parties as the living honor and celebrate the dead with graveside gatherings, sometimes involving wine and food, that then turn into larger feasts back at each other's homes.

From here to Cirauqui, you'll walk along a narrow dirt path or road and be surrounded by hills, vines, olive groves, wheat, and wildflowers. It is one of the prettiest and most peaceful stretches of the Camino.

Cirauqui   Km 676.9

It's a climb to get to the village center, but Cirauqui (spelled Zirauki in Basque; pop. 477) is an attractive outpost in a beautiful location, on a hilltop surrounded by prolific vineyards. This is also one of the few places pilgrims can see and walk directly on surviving stones from the 2,000-year-old Roman road that connected the entire north.

The town's ancient Basque name means "nest of vipers," perhaps a reference to the serpents that are said to have lived in the steep crevices nearby. Others theorize that the name referred to the treacherous terrain of hidden nooks and crannies, which hid predatory bandits. Then there is the 12th-century pilgrims' guide, the *Codex Calixtinus*, that reported toxic waters in this area and warned pilgrims not to drink or to let their horses do so. Thankfully none of this holds today, and modern Cirauqui is defined by excellent wine, beauty, and kindness.

Another possibility to the "nest" reference is that underneath you are *bodegas*, subterranean wine cellars. You can enjoy

From top to bottom: bike in front of the Iglesia de Santiago in Puente La Reina; vineyards along the Camino around Cirauqui; Iglesia de San Román in Cirauqui.

a communal dinner inside one if you stop for the night at the Albergue Maralotx.

Sights

In the center of the village are two medieval churches, the 13th-century Iglesia de Santa Catalina, which was largely rebuilt in the 16th century, and the celebrated 12th-century Iglesia de San Román, with its multi-lobed Mudéjar-Romanesque doorway, similar to that on Puenta la Reina's Iglesia de Santiago and Estella's Iglesia de San Pedro de la Rúa. It again calls attention to the mixing of Muslim, Christian, and Jewish craftsmen who were building on the road, commissioned by clergy and kings.

Iglesia de San Román

Originally built in the 12th century, Iglesia de San Román (Calle San Román, 19) was rebuilt in the 17th. The main entrance retains the original church doorway, an interior multi-lobed Mudéjar and Gothic arch surrounded by sacred and decorative carving, such as geometric and floral forms, the hand of God, and most interesting, a Chi-Rho. (This early symbol, comprised of the first two letters of Christ's name in Greek, was used to depict Christ and predates the use of the cross.) Often the letters alpha and omega are hung on the horizontal arms of the Chi-Rho, going left to right, but here, the alpha and omega are placed right to left, as a Hebrew or Arabic writer would engrave them, rather than one schooled in Latin. Along with the multi-lobed arch, this Chi-Rho reinforces the idea that a Muslim or Jewish stonemason worked on this church.

The church is not usually open, but the best of it is right here at the door. Notice the sultry mermaid, reclining on her left side and stroking her hair, on the left capital at the inner arch of the doorway. In medieval art, mermaids often symbolized the world's sensory temptations.

San Román's interior is more modern, from the 16th and 17th centuries,

except for a Roman tombstone that was repurposed as a column on the left side of the nave.

Food and Accommodations

The energetic and welcoming *hospitalera,* Ainhoa Markiegi, makes ★ **Albergue Maralotx** (Calle San Román, 30; 678-635-208; open week before Easter Sunday-mid-Oct.) a great place to stay. The traditional house, right next to the Iglesía San Román, offers 28 solid, wooden bunk beds in one bunkhouse (€11) and two private rooms (€42). Maralotx is best known for its communal dinner served in the *bodega,* an elegant stone-vaulted room set with wooden tables and chairs. The celebrated meal (€11) is often a large, fresh garden salad, spaghetti with garlicky tomato sauce (and for meat eaters, massive tasty meatballs), and, always, excellent wine.

━━━ Top Experience ━━━

★ Roman Road and Bridge
Km 676.9-Km 674.1

Most of the Camino from here to Lorca lies over repurposed Roman roads, but few stretches are as well preserved as this one, especially in the next 3.3 kilometers (2 miles), and especially the first 100 meters (328 feet) just as you exit Cirauqui. Here, you'll climb down, up, and through Roman paving stones that are still in the process of being excavated and restored. Soon after, you'll cross a rare surviving Roman bridge. On the road, notice how the paving stones underfoot have been polished under 2,000 years of feet and hooves, and look for grooves worn by cart wheels.

After you cross the bridge, parts of the Roman road appear right on the surface. From here to Lorca, the terrain is craggy, narrow, wild, and uninhabited, demanding a lot of up and down from the walker. As you go down and climb up the final ravine, look closely for the hidden caves set back on the slopes and covered in undergrowth. By the time you get to Lorca, it will feel like an accomplishment, and the land opens up to a large valley filled with wheat and vineyards.

Lorca   Km 671.3

Lorca (pop. 131) sits on the top of the steep hill you just climbed and faces the open valley toward Estella. The town name comes from the Arabic word *al-'araka*, which means "struggle" or "combat." This defines the experience of much of the territory of Navarra through which the Camino passes, but the Arabic name for this Basque place refers to one conflict in particular: In 920, Muhammad Abenlope, whose name means "son of a wolf" and who was likely of mixed Basque-Muslim descent, thwarted the efforts of Sancho I, the king of Navarra, for control of this strategic spot. Your climb up to Lorca will help understand

how this was a key defensive place, looking out over the pass you just ascended and protecting the valley plains that lead directly to Estella.

Today, this is a delightful location to spend the night if you want a deep slumber in a tiny place. Lorca's only persisting historic feature, the **Iglesia de San Salvador,** located immediately to your right as you enter Lorca on the Camino, was rebuilt in the 18th century. Though you generally cannot enter the church (it is never open except on certain holidays; inquire at the *albergue*), look around the outside corbels of the surviving Romanesque apse that retain a few interesting faces engraved in the stone. Lorca has a great low-key vibe and lives to serve the Camino with two good *albergues,* each with a small café.

Food and Accommodations
Of the two *albergues* in town, my favorite is the **Albergue La Bodega del Camino** (Calle Palceta, 8; 948-541-162; www.albergue-de-lorca-la-bodega-del-camino.es), run by a group of enthusiastic *hospitaleros,* most of whom have walked

stepping onto the Roman road, and over the bridge, just after leaving Cirauqui

and cycled the Camino not just once but several times. La Bodega is open from the week leading up to Easter (Semana Santa, Holy Week) until Oct. They have five private rooms (€20-45), each named after a place on the Camino, in addition to four dormitories with a total of 30 beds (€10). At the entrance is the bodega part of the *albergue,* with a bar and café, and they have a tried-and-true international menu (€10), largely of good pasta dishes and garden-fresh salads. Breakfast is €3.

Villatuerta   Km 666.7

Villatuerta (pop. 1,146) is defined by its old church built on the highest point of the settlement, the 14th-century **Iglesia de la Asunción** (Plaza Iglesia, 11; 948-541-175; usually closed), which also feels like a fortress. The town name means "curved or sinuous village," a good description of its physical setting.

Food and Accommodations

Villatuerta has a unique *albergue,* **La Casa Mágica** (Calle Rebote, 5; 948 536 095; www.alberguevillatuerta.com; open Mar.-Oct.), that channels the calm monastic mood of these hills and is a favorite among pilgrims, with its gorgeous meditation room with vaulted stone ceiling, cotton mats on the wooden floor, and a candle burning in the central niche. In this more than 400-year-old home converted into an *albergue,* there are with 37 beds in five dormitories (€14) and one private room (€60), all immaculate and peaceful. The *albergue* also makes a delicious paella and vegetarian meals, at times followed by a pilgrim ritual.

Ermita de San Miguel   Km 666.2

This small rectangular hermitage is less than 200 meters (656 feet) off the Camino, to the left after you leave Villatuerta, and definitely worth visiting. Standing in the center of olive trees on the highest hill outside of Villatuerta, it is named after the archangel of high places, Saint Michael. It was once connected to a 11th-century monastery that has all but evaporated from this spot.

A certain energy circulates in the air here, especially if you approach the entrance and turn to look out over the olive trees and the purple and dark blue hills toward Estella. The inside is empty, except for the golden glow of its yellow stone and a simple stone platform built into the wall that serves as an altar. It is unadorned except for the notes, flowers, stones, rosaries, and little mementos pilgrims and locals have left on it.

Once I approached the chapel as a group of teenagers arrived with me from the village, and one gave me a handful of pink roses to leave on the altar—a simple but moving ritual. I also listened as people sang, revealing this chapel's ultimate adornment: its acoustics.

Continuing to Estella

From Ermita de San Miguel, you again enter hilly terrain. Right when you think the 3.3 kilometers (2 miles) between here and Estella may never end, you'll turn the bend to find Estella's Iglesia de Santo Sepulcro, then reach the Río Ega that divides the town, which is built on the hills on both sides of the river.

Estella   Km 662.9

Set in a rugged, easy-to-defend crag between four hills straddling the wide Ega river, Estella (pop. 13,707) was inhabited by native Vascones well before the king, Sancho Ramírez I of Navarra and Aragon, moved to make this town a market center on the Camino in 1090. This action enticed merchants from across Europe to settle here, the largest groups being French settlers who spoke Occitan (an old Romance language),

Basque-speaking Navarrans, and Iberian Jews. As in Pamplona, these communities aggregated around their own neighborhoods and fortified temples. At one point, all four of Estella's hills had its own castle, none of which survive.

Thanks to those hills, modern Estella preserves the town's medieval shape, making this an enjoyable place to explore. Consider taking a rest day to visit the four churches and two public squares, and to linger on the banks of the wide and swift-flowing Ega river, where an old tannery used to operate and is now an *albergue*. Estella's Basque name, Lizarra, may come from *lizar,* meaning ash tree, specimens of which grow along the river.

The **weekly market** (Thurs. 9am-2pm), established in 1164, sets up on the two squares, Plaza de Santiago and Plaza de los Fueros. If you decide on a rest day here, try to arrive on or before a Thursday so you don't miss it.

Sights

Sights are on both sides of the river and are listed here in the order that you reach them when entering Estella on foot

via the Camino. (The Camino passes through Estella on the south [left] side of the river.) The best source for practical information on Estella's churches is www.turismo.navarra.es. Estella's **tourist office** (Plaza de San Martín, 4; 948-556-301; www.estellaturismo.com) is located inside the Palacio de los Reyes de Navarra.

Iglesia del Santo Sepulcro

The first church pilgrims encounter on entering Estella, on the left, is the 14th-century Gothic **Iglesia del Santo Sepulcro** (open summers only, Mon.-Fri. 8:30am-8pm and for Sunday mass, 11am). The entrance is the church's most interesting aspect. Dominating the façade are the twelve apostles, six on each side, and the Last Supper on the lower section of the tympanum. (It's a notably animated depiction of the Last Supper, each apostle seeming to be in his own world and thoughts.)

Mixed in with these religious scenes are whimsical little snippets of 14th-century secular life. Look at the capital over the left row of Apostles for the man pulling a pig along with a rope, and also to

a rainbow on the road to Estella

Estella

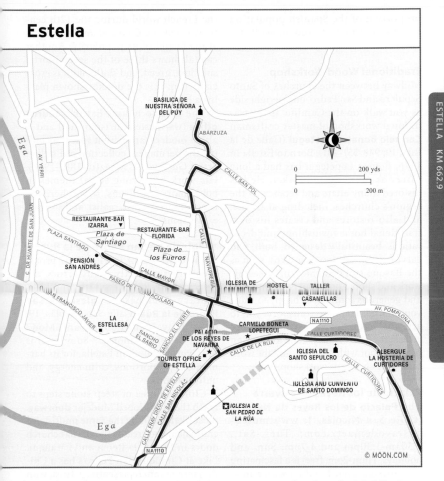

BASÍLICA DE NUESTRA SEÑORA DEL PUY

ABÁRZUZA

CALLE SAN POL

Ega

AV. YERRI

C. DR HUARTE DE SAN JUAN

0   200 yds
0   200 m

RESTAURANTE-BAR IZARRA

PLAZA SANTIAGO

Plaza de Santiago

RESTAURANTE-BAR FLORIDA

Plaza de los Fueros

CALLE NAVARRERÍA

PENSIÓN SAN ANDRÉS

CALLE MAYOR

PASEO DE LA INMACULADA

IGLESIA DE SAN MIGUEL

HOSTEL

TALLER CASANELLAS

JUAN FRANCISCO JAVIER

LA ESTELLESA

SANCHO EL SABIO

SANCHO EL FUERTE

CARMELO BONETA LOPETEGUI

NA1110

AV. POMPLONA

PALACIO DE LOS REYES DE NAVARRA

CALLE DE LA RÚA

IGLESIA DEL SANTO SEPULCRO

CALLE CURTIDORES

ALBERGUE LA HOSTERÍA DE CURTIDORES

TOURIST OFFICE OF ESTELLA

CALLE FRAY DIEGO DE ESTELLA

CALLE SAN NICOLÁS

IGLESIA DE SAN PEDRO DE LA RÚA

IGLESIA AND CONVENTO DE SANTO DOMINGO

Ega

NA1110

© MOON.COM

the inserted square a little right of the pig scene, with two animated medieval citizens chatting with each other as if at market.

Iglesia and Convento de Santo Domingo

Look up the hill behind the Iglesia de Santo Sepulcro to see another massive 13th-century Gothic building, the old Iglesia and Convento de Santo Domingo. Now a private retirement home that's not open to the public, its historic interest to the Camino is that it identifies the area where most of Estella's Jewish

community lived in the Middle Ages. Santo Domingo was also a monastic school that taught many subjects, including Arabic.

A substantial Jewish community in Estella thrived from the 11th century to the late 14th century. During the forced conversions in and around 1492, many chose conversion rather than fleeing their homes. But by 1609, nearly 120 years later, King Phillip III expelled all people deemed *conversos* (Jews who had converted to Catholicism) and *moriscos* (Muslims who had converted to Catholicism), essentially gutting a large proportion of the Spanish population that worked in craft and agricultural labor.

Traditional Wood Workshop

Midway between the churches of Santo Sepulcro and San Pedro, on the right side as you walk on the Camino, is the traditional workshop of master craftsman **Carmelo Boneta Lopetegui** (Calle de la Rúa, 19; 948-551-481). Born in Estella in 1946, Boneta Lopetegui has had a long career as master woodworker. He has restored many altars and retables in the region's churches, including at Irache, and also restores and creates his own traditional home furnishings and decorations, beautifully designed, built, and carved with traditional patterns, such as the Basque sun disk. Stop in to see his work and shop; Lopegegui is an engaging and generous soul who is happy to show you around. His shop transports you to artisanal traditions carried on here since at least the 11th century. Look for the sign over the door with his name and the word *taller*, which means workshop.

Palacio de los Reyes de Navarra

The **Palacio de los Reyes de Navarra** (Calle San Nicolás, 1; www.museo-gustavodemaetz.com; Tues.-Sat., 9:30am-1:30pm and 4-7pm; Sun. and holidays, 11am-2pm; free) is a fascinating Romanesque civic building with a misleading name. (In fact, it probably was never inhabited by Navarra's kings.) The Palacio's fame is that it is a rare work of secular architecture in the Romanesque style, a form almost exclusively used for sacred buildings.

A capital on the building's exterior shows the story of Charlemagne's officer, Roland, fighting Ferragut, a fabled giant who was mostly invincible but for a sort of Achilles heel: a vulnerable area in his stomach. Roland figured out where that was and eventually took the giant down. The presence of this depiction reflects old Estella and Navarra's strong lean toward the French world during the 12th century, when the *Chanson de Roland* was at the height of its popularity. Another capital shows three of the seven mortal sins: lust, greed, and sloth. Sloth is especially fun: It is the donkey shown playing a harp.

The Palacio houses Estella's **tourist office** (www.estellaturismo.com) and is also a modern-art exhibit space, including the permanent collection of Estellan artist Gustavo de Maeztu (1887-1947). His work has strong social themes in bold colors and forms, somewhere between impressionist, realist, and abstract expressions.

★ Iglesia de San Pedro de la Rúa

Located on one of Estella's four prominent hills, directly across from the Palacio de los Reyes, the 12th- and 13th-century Romanesque **Iglesia de San Pedro de la Rúa** (Calle San Nicolás, 19; open daily 10am-1:30pm, and Mon., Tues., Sat., afternoons, 7-8pm; free) is my favorite church in Estella, for its harmonious proportions, calm energy, and quirky details.

Climb up a set of steep stone steps to reach the multi-lobed Mudéjar **doorway**, most likely built by the same multi-faith craftsmen who created the similar church doors in Puente la Reina and Cirauqui. Like at Cirauqui, San Pedro's has a Chi-Rho monogram representing Christ, with the alpha and omega written in reverse, another hint at the mixed backgrounds of its builders. Persian and Byzantine hybrid animal forms, scrolled intricate decorative knots, and floral themes reinforce this diversity.

Inside, the church holds an octagonal shape with three chapels that form the **apse** and **altar.** A 13th-century Romanesque sculpture of Mary is seated in the first chapel to the left, Jesus in the center, and Saint Peter is to the right. Three braided snakes create the pillar on the left of Mary's chapel, their stone tails circling the base, their intertwined bodies forming the center and their heads the crown. They are from 1893, and are the restoration work of Estellan sculptor Cayetano Echauri, a skilled stonemason and specialist in medieval occult symbolism who was commissioned to restore the destroyed church's form and older symbolic content. The serpents represent the three-fold process of wisdom, *la sabiduría*, which is gained through understanding the polarity of good (1) and evil (2) and weaving the two into harmony and correct understanding and action (3). This pillar echoes the twisted triple column in the cloister that dates to the 12th century.

Half of the church's **cloister** is still standing (the other half was destroyed in an explosion in 1572). It's still a pretty place, set into the mountain with a small garden. Along one wall are round tombstones, hybridized forms of the pagan Basque sun disk and the Christian equal-armed cross. Capitals on the west side have Mudéjar-style plants and animals.

Mass is Mon, Tues., and Sat. at 7pm, and Sun. and holidays at 12:30pm.

Iglesia de San Miguel

Iglesia de San Miguel (Plaza de San Miguel; Mon.-Sat., 11am-1pm and 5-8pm; Sun. and holidays, 11am-1pm; free) has a well-preserved, engraved Romanesque doorway on its north side that squirms with different characters all along its arches and walls, looking like the hand of at least a couple different masons. The 5-minute climb to get here, too, is an adventure, feeling like a climb up into a protective castle keep, with steep steps lining the fortress walls. Small surrounding niches shelter venerated olive trees, and there are bird's-eye views of the town and hills all around.

Like nearly all churches dedicated

From top to bottom: Albergue La Bodega del Camino in Lorca; detail in Estella's Iglesia de San Miguel (Elizabeth greeting Mary); Estella's Iglesia del Santo Sepulcro.

to Saint Michael, the archangel of high places, this one was constructed on one of Estella's highest hills. Begun in the late 12th century and altered many times over subsequent centuries, it retains its original north door, dating to around 1170. One left column in the arch shows Elizabeth and Mary, when Elizabeth informs Mary that she too is pregnant, with Saint John the Baptist. That same image and style is similar to the capital in San Juan de la Ortega and may be by the same mason or school.

Another, on a left arch over the door, includes a woman breastfeeding two snakes. This surprising image taps into pre-Christian beliefs that the creator was a female who birthed the earth and all life, nourishing it from her metaphorical breasts. Greeks and Romans sometimes represented Gaia in this fashion. Up until the early 1100s, this image was a positive one, in harmony with the minds and lives of early medieval people who lived and worked in nature as herders and farmers. But near the 1200s, as the male-oriented Catholic church gained power, this image came to represent lust. This one is a bit grim, her contorted face intended to make you rethink your impulses before entering church. The interior is airy and light, a mix of Romanesque and Gothic.

A pilgrim blessing with mass: Wed., Fri., and Sat. (7pm), and Sun. and holidays (11:30am).

Basilica de Nuestra Señora del Puy

Estella's **Basilica del Puy** (Calle Abázuza, 1; daily 8am-8pm, mass Sat. 7:25am, Sun. 1pm; free) stands on what is probably the oldest occupied hill in Estella, with the highest and best views of the town and surrounding hills. Bird life up here is rich, making it worth the 10-minute climb straight up from the middle of town. In local lore, in 1085 shepherds saw stars cascading over this hill in front of the mouth of a cave. They went inside and found an image of Our Lady of Puy, the Black Madonna venerated by French pilgrims and settlers; her original icon is in Le-Puy-en-Velay, in south-central France—the starting point of one of the four major roads in France that are destined to pass here and which continue to Santiago de Compostela. Le Puy's cult dates to the 5th century.

The people of Lizarra built a shrine here to Nuestra Señora del Puy and housed the icon from the cave in it. Ever since, those raining stars—*stella* in Latin and *estrella* in modern Spanish—gave Estella the town's name. The current basilica was built in the 1950s and based on the Mudéjar eight-pointed star pattern; it replaces the older, destroyed church. Estellans chose the design to reflect their town's diverse, multi-faith history.

The icon of Mary is considered the original; some say it is from the Visigothic period (4th to early 8th centuries) and others think it is from the 14th century. It stands to the back and left of the church's nave, where you can get close enough to feel her aura (I swear, joy pours out from all her pores). The altar holds a near-exact replica of her: Like the church, she is all around you. You can buy rosary beads here (€2) if you want a souvenir.

Food

The two main squares, **Plaza de los Fueros** and **Plaza de Santiago,** are home to many cafes and restaurants.

Restaurante-Bar Izarra (Calle Calderería, 20; 948-550-024; €13) holds a corner on the Plaza de Santiago and serves creative and mouth-watering *pintxos*. Each day, the chalkboard announces that day's creation (my favorite: squid wrapped in bacon and grilled, then served with a hot pepper and an herb-garlic dipping sauce). It's also a casual place for a three-course *menú* (€13) with choices such as braised pig cheeks in green salsa, shrimp- and almond-stuffed savory canelones with salsa, and wild mushroom pasta.

★ **Restaurante-Bar Florida** (Plaza de los Fueros, 15; 948-550-015; www.

Black Madonnas of Europe

Black Madonnas have been found throughout Europe, but the highest concentration of them is in France and Spain. These sculptures were created from the 11th to the 15th centuries, peaking during the 12th and 13th centuries. They are mostly carved in wood, and the dark color comes from many sources: aging, soot, an intentional stain, the wood itself. Nearly all the icons have appeared on the scene through a vision, a miracle, and/or an otherworldly discovery.

There are a lot of theories about what they represent:

- That the dark Mother (and the Child who is often depicted with her) represent the influence of the older Egyptian goddess Isis and her son Horus who, like Mary and Jesus, are depicted in ancient Egyptian art as a child sitting on his mother's lap. Some scholars think that this influence entered Europe with the Templar Knights, who brought with them ancient influences from their time in the Near East.

- That medieval Europe's contact with Islam (via Iberia, Sicily, and the Levant) brought in Islamic ideas of Mary, who is the most revered woman in Islam and is the only woman mentioned by name in the Quran (where she has a whole chapter named after and dedicated solely to her). In Islam, black is also the color of wisdom. Some scholars think that medieval Christianity may have absorbed these Islamic perspectives on Mary as the ultimate expression of feminine divinity and wisdom, and created Black Madonnas to convey it.

- That pagan pre-Christian ideas about the fertile, life-giving Earth Mother persisted easily as Black Madonnas, who represent the rich and dark earth. They carry on a continuity with the pagan ideas of the goddess who dwells in natural places, such as dark caves and springs (which is where many later stories about apparitions of Mary also occur). In this third theory, there is an interesting intersection with the pagan female nature beings prevalent across northern Spain, such as the Basque goddess Mari.

There are many Black Madonnas all across Europe, from Poland to Iberia. On the Camino Francés, there are four that date to the Middle Ages: **Puente la Reina** (Iglesia de San Pedro, rarely open), **Estella** (Basílica del Puy), **Los Arcos** (Iglesia de Santa María), and **Ponferrada** (Basílica de la Encina). Additionally, **Frómista's Iglesia de San Martín** holds a 20th-century rendering of a medieval-style Black Madonna that is a beautiful continuation of the medieval tradition.

restaurantebarflorida.com; €16) treats pilgrims with the same warm welcome as the locals who frequent this place for work lunches and family gatherings. The menu centers around classic Navarran cuisine and fresh ingredients. It's a minimalist and modern-art interior with the edible art on the plate, such as juicy thick steaks with grilled peppers, artichokes with cured ham, cream of mushroom and pumpkin soup, and excellent house wines.

Half a kilometer (0.3 miles) east of the Plaza de Fueros, near the Ega river, the **Taller Gastronomico Casanellas** (Calle Espoz y Mina, 3; 638-912-838; www.tallergastronomico.es; €25-30) is both a restaurant and cooking school—so if you love the cuisine, consider taking a rest day in Estella and signing up for a one-day cooking class on *pintxos*, Navarran cuisine, or Basque cuisine (courses are listed on their website and run €35-90). The restaurant serves new Navarran cuisine, with French and Italian influences, and their motto is "our kitchen is local and global." Some specialty dishes are roast lamb with rosemary jam, *gorrín* (roasted suckling pig) with almonds and garlic confit, and grilled cod with apple, tomato and honey.

Accommodations

★ **Pensión San Andrés** (Plaza de Santiago, 58; 948-554-158; 18 rooms; €25-40) is a family-run pension that operates the old-fashioned way—call or show up, as there is no booking online. The wonderful owner has upheld the high standards of this quiet corner in the old town for over two decades. She lives on the premises, treats all guests like family, and has cozy, rustic rooms with ensuite bath (some with a balcony, a few with small refrigerators, and one with a rooftop terrace). All rooms overlook the square below, so if you are here on Thursday morning, you can watch the market unfold (and also store your purchases in the refrigerator). The market starts to set up around 8am and opens by 9am.

Hostel Ágora (Calle Callizo, 3; 948-546-574; www.dormirenestella.com; open Mar.-Nov.; €20; 20 beds in two dorm rooms and three private rooms) is a brand-new *albergue,* opened in 2017, with a retro-1960s style in the lounge area and Japanese-style solid bed units built into the walls, with light-filtering curtains for complete privacy. The kitchen, dining area, and bathrooms are immaculate. There is no communal dinner, but a buffet-style breakfast is included in the price of the bed.

Albergue La Hostería de Curtidores (Calle Curtidores, 43; 948-550-070; www.lahosteriadelcamino.com; 30 beds in five dorm rooms, €15; four private rooms, €40) opened in 2017 in a restored 1796 tannery factory on the riverside, with beautiful views of the Río Ega. It has luxuriously comfortable beds, and even the bunk beds are wood-framed installations, many with their own window. The rooms preserve the historic building's wood beams and warm stone-and-brick walls. Hosts Amaia García and José Antonio Sanz enjoy making guests comfortable and offering ideas for what to do and where to eat in Estella. Buffet breakfast for €5.

Getting There

Frequent bus connections, especially from Pamplona, are the best way to get to and from Estella.

Bus

La Estellesa (www.laestellesa.com) connects Estella to both Pamplona (14 buses daily; 35-60 min.; €4.25) and Logroño (eight daily; 35-60 min.; €5), some with stops in the smaller Camino towns and villages in Navarra. The **bus station** (Plaza de la Coronación) is 450 meters (1,476 feet) to the west of the Camino through Estella (about a 6-minute walk).

Leaving Estella

The Camino passes below and to the right of the Iglesia de San Pedro de la Rúa as it exits Estella, and climbs a small hill toward the Monasterio de Irache, a pleasant path through kitchen gardens and enclosed homesteads—many of the doors and gates are decorated with sculptures of Saint James and scallop shells. Try to time your arrival at the wine fountain for after 9am, when its spigot is turned on for its daily gift of wine.

▬▬▬ **Top Experience** ▬▬▬

★ Bodegas Irache Wine Fountain   Km 659.8

Just before you reach the Monasterio de Irache, you will pass the vineyards of winemaker Bodegas Irache (www. irache.com), founded in 1891—and, to your right, all you need for pilgrim comfort: a fountain that flows with water and wine. Navarrans inaugurated the fountain in 1991, 100 years after the Bodega's founding, and it is well on its way to becoming a fine tradition like the vines and winemaking that surround it.

The vines that supply the fountain grow all around you and have been cultivated since the 12th century, when they produced wines enjoyed by Navarran nobles. The water and wine in the fountain symbolize the first miracle Jesus performed: turning water to wine at the Wedding of Cana. The wine fountain also honors the more local acclaim Estella received from the 12th-century *Codex Calixtinus,* were it was applauded for its excellent food and wine.

You are asked to limit yourself to one glass—and not to become a poster child for gluttony, one of the seven mortal sins. It's tradition to drink from your scallop shell, but you can also use your water bottle. Many pilgrims pass the fountain in the morning. If they arrive after 9am, when the fountain is turned on, many stop for a ritual sip. Check Bodegas Irache's website for the live webcam that lets you watch this ritual from anywhere in the world. (This is also a good way to make sure that people don't abuse the free offering and drink too much.)

Monasterio de Irache   Km 659.7

Less than 100 meters (328 feet) after the wine fountain, the Camino passes to the right of the **Monasterio de Irache** (Monasterio de Irache, Ayegui; 948-554-464; Mon.-Tues., 9am-1:30pm, Wed.-Fri., 9am-1:30pm and 5-9pm; Sat.-Sun., 9am-1:30pm and 4-6pm; free) on the left, standing in its own dale surrounded by vineyards.

Most likely, a monastery has been here since the 7th century, and Benedictines

From top to bottom: the wine spigot of the fountain at Bodegas Irache; Bodegas Irache; Iglesia del Santo Sepulcro, Torres del Río.

founded the Monasterio de Irache in the 10th century. By the early 17th century it was also a Benedictine university that taught medicine, law, philosophy, and theology well into the 19th century. The bulk of the surviving monastery dates to the 16th century, but the church maintains some of its 12th-century Romanesque structure.

There is a peaceful, refreshing energy flowing through the monastic church and cloister that can energize you for the day's walk—and perhaps helps you walk off the buzz from the wine fountain. It is worth wandering along the nave and aisles and looking up at the well-preserved sculptures on the capitals. You'll find a lot of mythic creatures, including mermaids, mermen, centaurs, bird-headed and winged lions, and fabulous dragons.

Part of the calm here is that the walls and passages have been left open and are unadorned with the busy Baroque retables that populate so many churches. Adding to this are the pleasing overall proportions of the church, based in Cistercian design, which give the space excellent acoustics.

From here, the Camino continues onto a dirt path through rolling fields, and into oak forest as it approaches the village of Azqueta.

Azqueta   Km 655.5

Leaving the Monasterio de Irache, the path passes vineyards and wheat fields, and cuts into quiet pine and oak forest; in 4.2 kilometers (2.6 miles), it enters the hamlet of Azqueta (pop. 56). From here, you get great views of the high, pyramid-shaped hill that's topped with the castle ruins of Villamayor de Monjardín up ahead.

Accommodations
Azqueta has a wonderful *albergue*, **La Perla Negra** (Calle Carrera, 18;

627-114-797; €27 includes dinner and breakfast), on the left side of the main street in a restored stone-and-stucco home in the center of the village. It has a comfortable dorm room that sleeps seven in single beds, and a private room for two. A communal dinner made from market-fresh ingredients (harvested by the owner Helena and her helpful *hospitaleros*) and a solid breakfast are served in the common dining room on the same level. A returning pilgrim desiring to serve the Camino, Helena also paints, and La Perla Negra's white walls are covered with her bold, Australian Aboriginal-inspired art.

Leaving Azqueta
The Camino wends toward the peak of Villamayor de Monjardín, in a gradual ascent through red-earth dirt paths passing wheat fields and more vineyards. Just before reaching Villamayor, you will pass the **Fuente de los Moros** (Km 654.1) on the right, a deep cistern full of fresh water (not accessible or for drinking) with a twin-Gothic-arched entrance, possibly an engineering feat of the Muslims who occupied this territory around the 9th century. Below the elegant structure are the grape vines for a white wine produced by the Bodegas de Monjardín and regionally celebrated. Just ask for the house white, *vino blanco de la casa*, when you get to the **Illaria café** in the town of Villamayor de Monjardín.

Villamayor de Monjardín   Km 653.7

This village (pop. 115) is built at the foot of the highest hill in the surrounding area, standing 675 meters (2,215 feet). You can climb that hill to explore the castle ruins that top it and take in a panoramic vista of the surrounding countryside. Consider staying in Villamayor de Monjardín overnight, especially if you decide to explore the castle: The climb is steep, and the next stretch is a long one, over 12 kilometers (7.5 miles), with no services until you reach Los Arcos.

Sights

Iglesia de San Andrés

On entering into the village, you will first pass **Iglesia de San Andrés** (Calle de Santa María, 1; 8am-9pm; free), the medieval church to the left. Stepping into the wide-arched and sunken nave of this medieval church feels like entering a pleasing and expansive bodega. Battling knights and a mermaid inhabit the capitals at the entrance, and a council of wood-carved saints, Mary included, sit in a ring on the inside altar. The red stone of the church makes the whole place feel vital and alive. It was built during the Camino's heyday in the 12th century and is best known for a silver cross, circa 1200, used in processions. (Look up—it is high over the statues in the apse.) One side of the cross depicts the Agnus Dei (lamb of God), and the other depicts the crucifixion. The church's exterior is surrounded by traditional round pagan-Christian Basque sun disk-cross tombstones.

Castillo de Monjardín

The **Castillo de Monjardín** sits on the steepest, most pointed, and most visible hill around, standing at 890 meters (2,920 feet). It was fortified many times: first by Romans, then by the Banu Qasi dynasty (the Sons of Cassius, descendents of Iberian Romans and/or Visigoths who converted to Islam around AD 714), and then by the king of Pamplona, Sancho Garcés, who wrested it from the Banu Qasi in 914. Sancho most likely gave the town its name, Mont Garcés, which morphed over time into Monjardín.

The walls were built on top of a natural outcrop of chunky stones that naturally form the shape of a boat. It is exhilarating to get up there and see the walls continuing up from the base of native rock, and then climbing up into the interior to find a 17th-century hermitage, **Ermita de San Esteban,** plunked into the middle. Builders used the crumbling stones from the castle walls to build the small, rectangular Baroque hermitage. The views up here are breathtaking: steep, sweeping, 360-degree vistas of a patchwork quilt of fields, vineyards, wavy terrain, and the Cantabrian mountain range a distance to the north.

If you decide to climb up here, allow about two hours total for the 4.5-kilometer (2.8-mile) round-trip climb from a dirt road picked up from the highest end of the town (the north side). Before departing, go to Bar Illaria (Calle Mayor, 9), and ask for the key that allows access to the interior of the castle ruin (free, although you will probably be asked to leave some form of identification). From Bar Illaria, walk west on Calle Mayor to Calle el Calvario and make a right. Take Calle el Calvario northeast to the first road on your left. Take it (turn left) and follow it west; it will skirt west then north around the base of the mountain and slowly ascend. In 1.4 kilometers (0.9 mile), the road will switchback 180 degrees where you will follow it, a sharp right, and head briefly south and then east. Continue on it up to the castle, 2.25 kilometers (1.4 miles) from your starting point at Bar Illaria.

Food

The husband-and-wife-run **Bar Illaria** (Calle Mayor, 9; 616-039-893) is great for lunch, dinner, or just to sample the local white or red wine produced by Castillo Monjardín (€1.50). Sit inside, where you may find the whole village gathered in a cheerful space with multicolored walls and a bottle-lined bar, or sit outside on the terrace. The pilgrim's menu is under €10 and features great garden salads, olive-oil-and-garlic-sautéed mixed vegetables with jamón Serrano, and grilled green peppers and hake.

Accommodations

Casa Rural Montedeio (Calle Mayor, 17; 948-551-521 and 676-187-473; www.casaruralmontedeio.com) takes the older name for the hill of the village, Monte Deyo or Deio, before it became Monjardín; it's a good name for the lovingly restored 1832 home. Whether you rent by the night or by the week, the owner makes special discounts for pilgrims, so be sure to let her know you're a legitimate *peregrino/a*. (A €100 room may be discounted to €35-55.) There are only three rooms, so call or email ahead to inquire. If this is full or too pricey, the privately run **Albergue Villamayor de Monjardín** (Calle Mayor, 1; 677-660-586; www.alberguevillamayordemonjardin.com; open Mar.-Oct.) is a good alternative, with 28 beds in two dorm rooms (€15) and one private room (€40); the proprietors speak English.

Leaving Villamayor de Monjardín

Fill up with water before leaving. The next 12.2 kilometers (7.6 miles) run through wheat fields, vineyards, pine forests, and olive groves, and there are no services until Los Arcos. Sometimes **Café Eduard**, a mobile café around 6 kilometers (3.7 miles) after Villamayor, is open for business, but don't count on it.

Los Arcos   Km 641.5

Master archers with their bows (*los arcos*) won this town in the 11th century for the king of Navarra during a three-way battle with the kings of Aragón and Castile, giving the town its name. From here, the landscape opens up and is fed by the Río Odrón. Los Arcos is a small, pleasant, and vibrant modern town with all amenities. It stands on top of an ancient Roman site, and archaeologists have dug up the occasional artifact, including Roman tombs near where the Camino enters the town.

A food and general goods **market** sets up every Tuesday and Saturday (8:30am-2pm) in the central Plaza de Coso (*coso* means arena).

Sights
Iglesia de Santa María de los Arcos

Los Arcos's **Iglesia de Santa María** (Plaza de Santa María; 649-909-514; free) was built in the 12th century and modified in the 16th to 18th centuries. Its sculpture of Mary, Santa Maria de los Arcos, a celebrated 14th-century Black Madonna, holds center stage on the altar. Notice also the swirling designs in the Baroque décor of the church. They aren't simply decorative; they also express the dynamic energy that locals feel in this place. The Gothic **cloister** is small and intimate and has a fragrant, lush rose garden. From May-Sept, the church opens daily, 12-2pm and 5-8pm; during other times of year, the church opens Sat. at noon. You can call to request a visit.

Mass is held daily at 7:30pm and Sun. at 12:30pm. Mass includes a pilgrim blessing.

Food

★ **Mesón de Gargantúa** (Plaza de Santa María; 948-640-915; €10-13) also has a gargantuan heart. The staff serve drinks and dishes with consistent good cheer, and the restaurant has a tremendous view, right on the church square with Santa Maria opposite, where you sit in the sheltered arcade or on the plaza. It's a pilgrim magnet, with several combined dishes and a *menú del peregrino*, including paella, *ensalada mixta* (mixed green salad with asparagus, tomatoes, olives, tuna, and onions), and an array of savory and meaty bean dishes, from split pea and ham to white bean and sausage.

Accommodations

Albergue Casa de la Abuela (Plaza de la Fruta, 8; 630-610-721; www.casadelaabuela.com; open Mar.-Oct., call for other times of year), "Grandmother's

House," is run with pride and precision and has flawless rooms, both shared and private, on several floors. There are painted tile stairways, plenty of space in the communal kitchen, and a traditional, vaulted underground bodega. There are 24 beds in three dorm rooms (€10) and four private rooms (€35 with shared bath and €45 ensuite). Breakfast (€3.50) includes homemade breads and cakes.

★ **Monaco Hotel** (Plaza de Coso, 1; 948-640-000; www.hotelmonaco.es; 14 rooms, €40-70) has simple rooms with cream walls and floral paintings, firm beds, and immaculate baths with hot showers. The standout best features are the rooms with balconies (to request one, ask for *una habitación con balcón*), which look out onto the weekly market square, Plaza de Coso—with added color if you are here on a Tuesday or Saturday for market day. The hotel also has a good **restaurant** serving a *menú del peregrino* (€12) that includes gazpacho, fresh salads, pasta dishes, and grilled meats and fish.

Leaving Los Arcos

Depart Los Arcos through the early 18th-century **Portal de Castilla,** an arched gate that was part of the town's defensive walls. For the pilgrim, Portal de Castilla marks a physical and psychological threshold. Here you enter more open and exposed terrain, and you may need to be sure you have a hat, full water bottles, and sunscreen, especially in the warm months.

Sansol (Km 634.8; pop. 102) is the next settlement with food, water, and refreshments, 6.7 kilometers (4.2 miles) after Los Arcos. Its heavily fortified 18th-century Baroque church is dedicated to **San Zoilo**. You can see Torres del Rio, dramatically situated on the other side of the ravine, 1 kilometer (0.6 miles) away. Just before entering Torres del Río, you'll cross the Río Linares and then begin the steep but short climb into the town.

Torres del Río   Km 633.8

The steep climb and the surrounding vineyards make the approach to Torres del Río, with the church's pretty round tower, all the more stunning. An ancient hilltop with advantageous views and steep slopes for defense, Torres del Rio (pop. 128) has been occupied for millennia and, like Los Arcos and Villamayor de Monjardín, was a Muslim fortress that was conquered by the king of Navarra in the year 914. In 1109, Torres del Río came under the control of the Monasterio de Irache. Some think that it was overseen by Templars soon after, given that its most famous sight, the Iglesia de Santo Sepulcro, is shaped like the Church of the Holy Sepulcher—but, as with the round church of Eunate, there is no evidence for the Templar origin theory. Like Eunate, excavations have unearthed tombs here, making some think that this was a funerary church.

Sights
★ Iglesia del Santo Sepulcro

The **Iglesia del Santo Sepulcro** (Calle Santo Sepulcro, 4), like Santa María de Eunate, reflects a possible connection to the Holy Sepulcher in Jerusalem. Like the church at Eunate, this was built in the 12th century, is Romanesque, and is based on a pure octagonal plan with no other walls or extensions.

This church, just like Eunate's chapel, is among Spain's most unusual, scenic, and celebrated structures, and some think that the two hold a kind of ying-yang relationship with each other. (According to one caretaker, Santo Sepulcro is the yang, a masculine church dedicated to Jesus—an idea reinforced by the only sculpture in the church, a 13th-century crucifix of Jesus on the altar. Eunate, where Mary holds the altar, is the yin. Further, Estella's round church, San Pedro de la Rúa, is right in the middle of these two octagonal churches and may represent a blend of the masculine and feminine energies.)

Inside, the beautifully crafted engravings on the pillars and capitals are filled with fantastic creatures, especially human-devouring monsters with nice sharp teeth. Other capitals are populated with Biblical scenes, animals, and floral designs. But the feature that draws the eye immediately is the star-patterned octagonal ceiling. The technique and pattern of cross-ribbed vaulting was brought from Muslim Spain, most likely inspired by the dome of the prayer niche in Cordoba's mosque in southern Spain. This similarity continues in the smaller details, such as the gutters formed by the two pillars that join at each point of the eight-pointed star. Some locals think this structure was intentionally built to concentrate and channel the flow of energy, which they say is palpable.

The church has no set opening hours, but volunteers open it daily in the morning and afternoon. When it is locked, they post a phone number on the door for you to call for access (or you can ask the staff of a local bar or *albergue* to call for you). It costs €1 to enter.

Food and Accommodations

The ★ **Hostal San Andrés** (948-648-472; www.sanandreshostal.com; 14 rooms; €40-70), right in front of you as you cross the bridge into Torres del Río, is a well-earned treat: each room is outfitted with large, luxuriant beds with crisp white bed linens, and one wall in each white-washed room is covered in a full photographic mural of some aspect of the Camino's natural beauty. French windows open to a view of the valley and river. The **restaurant** serves a good *menú del día* (€12-15) with salads—the lettuce and tomatoes pulse with just-plucked vibrancy—and meat stews, grilled steaks, fish, and excellent local wines. Proprietors speak English.

Leaving Torres del Río

From Torres del Río, it's 10.6 kilometers (6.6 miles) to the town of Viana. The only possible place for food and water might be a trail-side camper/snack stand about 2.5 kilometers (1.6 miles) after departing Torres del Rio, so be sure to fill your water bottles and stock up for the full stretch before leaving.

You'll climb and pass the summit of **Nuestra Señora del Poyo** (Km 631.2; 558 meters/1,831 feet) and still have another 8 kilometers (5 miles) to Viana. The terrain is varied, with hills and open stretches covered in wheat, vines, olive groves, blushes of red poppies in spring, and the occasional stone cairn built by passing pilgrims laying one stone at a time. The last field of grape vines before reaching Viana has rose bushes planted at the end of each row—pale yellow roses for white grapes, and red or pink roses for red grapes. The roses also serve as health indicators: if something is wrong with the soil or environment, the roses will decline before the vines, giving the winemaker time to intervene before it's too late.

Viana   Km 623.2

Viana (pop. 4,078) is a bit crumbling on the edges, but as you approach the town you'll still make out its old walls and strategic history. Navarran king Sancho VII created Viana in the early 13th century out of several villages clustered around this hilltop, enclosing them in a fortified wall to create a defensible fortress town. Much of Viana's history concerns battles between Navarra and Castile. Despite all this, it also became a pilgrim town, at one time having at least four pilgrim hospices.

Viana's citizens today have a passion for food, wine, and *sidra* (locally produced cider), and any time you walk down the main street on the Camino through the old town, you may feel like you are stumbling into a party. On holidays, it amplifies several times. You can fortify well here—which is fortunate, as this is your last opportunity for food and water before the 9.3-kilometer (5.8-mile) trek to Logroño.

Viana has a colorful **weekly market** every Friday, 9:30am-1:30pm, on the Plaza del Coso, to the left of the Camino near the center of town.

Sights
Iglesía de Santa Maria
The Camino takes you right down the center of the old town, passing midway to your right the **Iglesia de Santa María** (948-446-302; Mon.-Sat., 10am-1pm, and a half-hour before daily mass times; free), located in the animated Plaza de los Fueros. This 13th-century church was modified many times over the centuries and comes across as another heavily fortified temple. Its façade is more Renaissance than Gothic. Inside, the Gothic comes out in the towering pillars and pointed arches. The high altar is a towering gold-painted Baroque retable

focused on Mary's life, and especially highlighting her body and soul's ascension to heaven (the Assumption). **Mass** times are Mon.-Fri., 7:30pm; Sat., 8pm, and Sun. 11am and 12:30pm.

Before you head off, look for the simple **tomb of Cesar Borgia** (1475-1507), son of Pope Alexander VI, identified by a memorial plaque on the sidewalk on the south side of the Iglesia de Santa María and to the right of the Camino. Borgia led a complex life and underwent many political incarnations and struggles in his native Italy, which ultimately led to his imprisonment in Spain. But he escaped and made his way to Navarra, where he became a military officer in service of the king. He defended Navarra during a siege against Viana in 1507, which ended his life but connected him thereafter to this place as a local hero.

Ruinas Iglesia de San Pedro
San Pedro gets its name from a nearby 11th-century Benedictine monastery that no longer exists except for its ruins, which consist of a few walls, a Baroque door, and the partially standing arches

approaching Viana

of the interior. The 13th-century Gothic church managed to survive intact all the way into the 19th century, when the Carlist wars destroyed it.

These ruins are located on the left side of the Camino as it departs the old town. It's worth stepping through the Baroque door to take in the crumbling Gothic arches as they meet wide-open blue sky. On the one surviving wall are remarkably well-preserved snippets of medieval frescos, populated with animated courtly characters from troubadours' ballads.

The ruins are free to enter, and the doors are usually open throughout the day. Pilgrims enjoy the shade of the standing wall and the nearby stone bench. Some even rest or picnic here before heading off into the 9.5-kilometer (5.9-mile) stretch to Logroño.

Food and Nightlife

The animated and expansive **Plaza de los Fueros** is where much of local life unfolds and around which most of the bars, cafes, and restaurants are aggregated. All you have to do is walk into the cheer and pick a spot. Among them, sharing the arcaded passageway of the *ayuntamiento* (town hall) next door, **Café Bar San Juan** (Plaza de los Fueros, s/n; 948-645-747) is a popular locals' *cerveceria* (on-tap beer house) with outdoor tables that offer a pleasurable view of the Iglesia de Santa María on the other side of the square (a beer and *pincho* run around €2-3).

Restaurante-Asador Tres Tinas (Calle Serapio Urra, 2; 948-646-039; www.asadortrestinas.com) is an upscale steakhouse, with a huge wood-burning brick grill on one side of the timber-beamed dining room; however, it also excels in risottos. You can go a la carte—and locals gush over the amazing grilled fish—or go for the grill tasting menu (€35) that serves four starters—grilled *txistorrica* (small paprika sausages), romaine-heart salad with anchovies, stuffed red pepper casserole, and cod omelet—followed by a perfectly grilled beef steak and homemade lemon sorbet and cava for dessert. Wine and coffee are included.

★ **Casa Armendariz** (Calle Navarro Villoslada, 15; 948-645-078; www.sidreriacasaarmendariz.es) is a traditional *sidrería* (cider house) with an elaborate fire grill and cider menu (€35), but also a more modest and delicious *menú del día* (€11.50) that doubles as the pilgrim's menu, with a good choice of five starters and five main dishes plus dessert and a drink. The traditional Navarran *bacalao con pimientos* (cod with green peppers and garlic) is a flavorful, vibrant signature dish. Locals and pilgrims alike are treated as cherished guests. Of course, this is also the place to try the local *sidra* (hard cider). For a lighter nosh, try the house cider and a local cheese plate with quince paste.

Accommodations

Palacio de Pujadas (Calle Navarro Villoslada, 30; 948-646-464; www.palaciodepujadas.com; €95) is a boutique hotel in a restored 16th-century mansion, with 24 large rooms and four luxury suites decorated with a harmonious mix of 1940s streamlined furniture, Scandinavian-design wooden bedboards, and cozy, thick-striped bedspread quilts. Some rooms have balconies arrayed with potted geraniums and a view of the Camino in the historic street below. A restaurant and grill house pub are on the premises.

Quite at the other end of luxury and budget, but immaculate and well run with engaging staff, **Albergue Izar** (Calle El Cristo, 6; 948-090-002; www.albergueizar.com) is a privately run *albergue* with 38 beds in four dorms (€10), and two private rooms with shared bath (€30). It is in a modern and well-outfitted building just 200 meters (656 feet) from the center of the historic town. The décor is plain, and the rooms and beds are basic, but the space is open, comfortable, unfussy, and immaculate. Breakfast is €3.

Getting There

Frequent buses from **Pamplona** and **Logroño** connect to **Viana**.

Bus

La Estellesa (www.laestellesa.com) connects Viana to both Pamplona (at least four buses daily; 1.5 hours; €7.90) and Logroño (at least five daily; 15 min.; €1.35), some with stops in the smaller Camino towns and villages in Navarra. Buses typically stop right next to the Camino as it enters the center of Viana.

Approaching Logroño

It is 9.3 kilometers (5.8 miles) from Viana to Logroño, with no support services in between; but the trail is well marked, and it is a pleasant amble through rolling vineyards and even vaster wheat fields than before. Three kilometers (1.9 miles) after leaving Viana, the Camino passes through a wetland created by an artificial lake, known as **Pantano de la Cañas**, a last stretch of full wildlife before nearing Logroño. Birdlife, including bitterns and herons, is plentiful.

You will see the city of Logroño from a distance, growing steadily as you approach. On its outskirts, you'll pass through a small pine forest and then arrive at a sign welcoming you to the autonomous community of Rioja. Here, the asphalt path turns from charcoal-toned to wine-colored, in celebration of Rioja's signature product. Soon after crossing under the sign, a more sobering sight appears to your right: a small **civil war memorial** honoring a mass grave from the 1930s that was discovered while workers were improving the path of the Camino.

When you descend down the final road before reaching the Ebro river, slow down for **Casa Felisa,** the house to the right where, since 1940, Felisa Rodríguez Medel (and now her daughter, María Medel), have welcomed pilgrims to Logroño. You won't miss the house: It is marked with a small billboard saying, *Información y Sellado a Los Peregrinos. Felisa.* ("Information and stamps for pilgrims. Felisa.") The front garden is covered with a shading canopy, and there is a table with the stamp (depicting figs, a scallop shell, and a jug of water) as well as water (and figs, when in season). You'll also see a fig tree offering shade in the garden. Whether or not someone is there to greet you, you are welcome to refresh yourself, rest, take figs and water, and stamp your passport. You can leave a small offering in thanks.

Soon after Casa Felisa, you will reach the Ebro river. Just before crossing it, you will pass a **rose garden.** The garden you passed when you left Pamplona is planted with roses that came from this garden, *las rosas del Camino* (roses of the Camino), part of a wider trend of planting roses on the Camino to honor the road's interconnectedness of people and places. Michel Adam, the botanist who hybridized these roses, made sure the roses had a compelling perfume, variegated colors (a beautiful mix of butter cream, rose, and orange), and a resilience worthy of the Way.

The arrival at the river crossing can feel dramatic. The Ebro is the widest river encountered on the Camino so far, and it is crossed by an elegant, cream-colored, wide-arched stone bridge with the spires of Logroño's medieval churches peeking up behind it.

La Rioja and Castile

Logroño to Burgos

Km: 613.9-489.7
Total Distance: 124 km (77 miles)
Days: 6-9

La Rioja and Castile

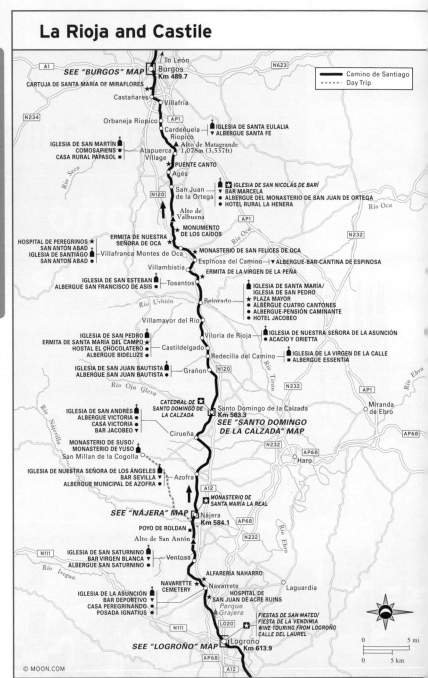

To León
Burgos
Km 489.7

SEE "BURGOS" MAP

CARTUJA DE SANTA MARÍA DE MIRAFLORES

Castañares — Villafría

Orbaneja Riopico

Cardeñuela Riopico

IGLESIA DE SANTA EULALIA
▼ ALBERGUE SANTA FE

IGLESIA DE SAN MARTÍN
COMOSAPIENS ●
CASA RURAL PAPASOL ■

Atapuerca Village

Alto de Matagrande
1,078m (3,537ft)

PUENTE CANTO

Agés

San Juan de la Ortega

IGLESIA DE SAN NICOLÁS DE BARÍ
▼ BAR MARCELA
● ALBERGUE DEL MONASTERIO DE SAN JUAN DE ORTEGA
● HOTEL RURAL LA HENERA

Alto de Valbuena

MONUMENTO DE LOS CAÍDOS

ERMITA DE NUESTRA SEÑORA DE OCA

HOSPITAL DE PEREGRINOS ★
SAN ANTÓN ABAD
IGLESIA DE SANTIAGO ▲
SAN ANTÓN ABAD ●

Villafranca Montes de Oca

MONASTERIO DE SAN FELICES DE OCA

Espinosa del Camino — ▼ ALBERGUE-BAR-CANTINA DE ESPINOSA

Villambistia

ERMITA DE LA VIRGEN DE LA PEÑA

IGLESIA DE SAN ESTEBAN
ALBERGUE SAN FRANCISCO DE ASÍS — Tosantos

Belorado

IGLESIA DE SANTA MARÍA/
IGLESIA DE SAN PEDRO
★ PLAZA MAYOR
● ALBERGUE CUATRO CANTONES
● ALBERGUE-PENSIÓN CAMINANTE
● HOTEL JACOBEO

Villamayor del Río

Viloria de Rioja

IGLESIA DE NUESTRA SEÑORA DE LA ASUNCIÓN
● ACACIO Y ORIETTA

IGLESIA DE SAN PEDRO ▲
ERMITA DE SANTA MARÍA DEL CAMPO
HOSTAL EL CHOCOLATERO ● — Castildelgado
ALBERGUE BIDELUZE ●

Redecilla del Camino

IGLESIA DE LA VIRGEN DE LA CALLE
■ ALBERGUE ESSENTIA

IGLESIA DE SAN JUAN BAUTISTA ▲
ALBERGUE SAN JUAN BAUTISTA ● — Grañón

CATEDRAL DE SANTO DOMINGO DE LA CALZADA

IGLESIA DE SAN ANDRÉS ▲
ALBERGUE VICTORIA ●
CASA VICTORIA ●
BAR JACOBEO ▼

Santo Domingo de la Calzada
Km 563.3

SEE "SANTO DOMINGO DE LA CALZADA" MAP

Cirueña

MONASTERIO DE SUSO/
MONASTERIO DE YUSO

San Millán de la Cogolla

Haro

Miranda de Ebro

IGLESIA DE NUESTRA SEÑORA DE LOS ÁNGELES ▲
BAR SEVILLA ▼
ALBERGUE MUNICIPAL DE AZOFRA ●

Azofra

SEE "NÁJERA" MAP

MONASTERIO DE SANTA MARÍA LA REAL

Nájera
Km 584.1

POYO DE ROLDÁN

Alto de San Antón

IGLESIA DE SAN SATURNINO
BAR VIRGEN BLANCA ▼
ALBERGUE SAN SATURNINO ●

Ventosa

ALFARERÍA NAHARRO

NAVARRETE CEMETERY

Navarrete

Laguardia

IGLESIA DE LA ASUNCIÓN ▲
BAR DEPORTIVO ▼
CASA PEREGRINANDO ●
POSADA IGNATIUS ●

HOSPITAL DE SAN JUAN DE ACRE RUINS

Parque Grajera

FIESTAS DE SAN MATEO/
FIESTA DE LA VENDIMIA
WINE TOURING FROM LOGROÑO
CALLE DEL LAUREL

SEE "LOGROÑO" MAP

Logroño
Km 613.9

Camino de Santiago
Day Trip

Río Seco
Río Oca
Río Urbión
Río Oja Glera
Río Najerilla
Río Tirón
Río Ebro
Río Iregua

0   5 mi
0   5 km

© MOON.COM

Highlights

★ **Fiestas de San Mateo and Fiesta de la Vendimia:** In mid-September, Logroño celebrates the wine harvest with colorful festivities and harvest blessings involving great food, and of course, flowing La Rioja wine (page 158).

★ **Wine Tasting and Touring from Logroño:** Numerous opportunities exist for sampling La Rioja's world-renowned wines. Tour local underground bodegas in the city, or make a day trip to the outlying vines (page 159).

★ **Calle del Laurel:** It's easy to turn a pub crawl on this Logroño street—packed with over 39 bars and 12 restaurants—into a movable meal of creative *pinchos/pintxos* inspired by the nearby market (page 162).

★ **Monasterio de Santa María la Real:** Pass through this monastery and church, built into a red rock face, to access the red-earth cave where the magical Mary, flanked by a dove and a falcon, appeared to King García III of Navarra in 1044 (page 169).

★ **Catedral de Santo Domingo de la Calzada:** This Romanesque and Gothic church is chock-full of beautiful engravings and sacred art. It also houses descendents of the rooster-and-hen pair who saved a pilgrim's neck in the 12th century (page 176).

★ **Iglesia de San Nicolás de Barí:** This church full of rich engravings was built in harmony with the solar equinoxes. It also contains the ancient tomb of San Juan de Ortega, set in a rounded niche with candles (page 187).

The Camino through La Rioja is defined by endless hills of deep red earth striped with green vines. Fields explode with wildflowers in the spring, a striking sight against the chalky backdrop of the Cantabrian mountains and the intense blue sky. This intoxicating, autonomous little community with big wine is named for one of its rivers, the Río Oja. It is also irrigated by one of Iberia's most important rivers, the Ebro, a waterway that divides the northern alpine world of the Pyrenees from the central and southern plateau of Castile and Aragon. It is a place so bountiful and strategic that its history is dominated by stories of invasion and conquest. Today, thankfully, wine is the winner. Walking here allows you to enjoy some of the world's best wines for a pittance (€0.60-2 per glass).

Just past Grañon, the Camino leaves La Rioja's vineyards and enters Castile. Here, the infinite wheat fields are a signal that this place has been Spain's breadbasket since Roman times. This stretch of the Camino, then, is defined by an abundance of wine and bread, as well as by its undulating terrain of high vistas and river-hugging valleys. This territory contains Europe's oldest human remains, at the Sierra de Atapuerca archaeological site.

The Camino here also reveals the heavy influence of the road's two master builders, Santo Domingo de la Calzada and San Juan de Ortega, whose 11th- and 12th-century bridges, roads, hospices, and churches anchored the Camino and made it safe to pass. It also passes through the Montes de Oca ("hills of the goose"), whose name signifies the creature that holds great symbolic value for some pilgrims.

Planning Your Time

Plan to spend a total of **6-9 days** in this region: 6-7 days for walking, and 2 for

Recommended Overnight Stops

Logroño (Km 613.9, page 151)

Nájera (Km 584.1, page 168)

Santo Domingo de la Calzada (Km 563.3, page 174)

Villafranca Montes de Oca (Km 528.5, page 183)

Atapuerca Village (Km 510.3, page 189)

rest days and detours. This stretch covers **124 kilometers** (77 miles), so plan to walk **20-25 kilometers (12.5-15.5 miles) per day.**

Consider a day to explore **Logroño,** especially for the wine tours. Consider another extra day for a day trip to **San Millán de la Cogolla** from Nájera, to explore early Christian sacred history in **La Rioja,** of hermit caves and early monasteries. You can easily spend another day exploring the archaeology of the **Sierra de Atapuerca** via the town of Atapuerca (though travelers find it's more efficient to use Burgos as the access point for this).

Route Options

Many choose to skip the unappealing five kilometers after Logroño by hopping a bus to Navarrete. There is a small 1-kilometer (0.6-mile) **detour** to Ventosa that is becoming more and more popular. It's well worth it, as it leaves the road and lets you amble along a delightful footpath through rows of green vines growing in dark red earth.

After **Cardeñuela Riopico** (Km 504), there are **three route options** for entering **Burgos** (Km 489.7), two of which offer pleasant alternatives to the historic Camino, which follows the most industrial path paralleling the N-1.

Local Markets

Several towns across La Rioja on the Camino have weekly markets, showing this small region's big passion for daily, fresh, and local ingredients. Most weekly markets set up between 8-9am and stay set up until 1-2pm.

* **Logroño:** Flea market and weekly market on Sundays; covered market open Monday-Saturday (page 155).

* **Navarrete:** Weekly market with produce, general goods, and local ceramics every Wednesday (page 166).

* **Najera:** Weekly food and general goods market every Thursday (page 170).

* **Santo Domingo de la Calzada:** Food products and general goods market every Saturday (page 177).

Logroño's covered daily market, Mercado de San Blas

* **Belorado:** General goods and food market every Monday (page 102).

GETTING THERE

Geography and Terrain

There are several stretches here with no support structures: From **Logroño to Navarrete** (12.6 km/7.9 mi); **Ventosa to Nájera** (10.3 km/6.4 mi); **Azofra to Cirueña** (9.1 km/5.7 mi); and **Villafranca Montes de Oca to San Juan de Ortega** (12.1 km/7.5 mi). The 12.5-14.5 kilometers (7.8-9 miles) after **Cardeñuela Riopico** are hit or miss, so it's best to fill water bottles and carry provisions.

This is hill country, with green slopes and rich river valleys. Most ascents and descents are gentle, though there are a few steep climbs, such as the climb up the ridge of the **Sierra de Atapuerca** (1,078 m/3,537 ft) just after **Atapuerca** village (Km 510.3).

The Camino here is mostly on pleasant dirt paths, though you'll parallel the road in a few places. The only truly unpleasant stretch is the industrialized 5 kilometers (3.1 miles) after leaving Logroño. If you want to bypass this, a local bus runs from the center of Logroño to **Navarrete** (Km 601.3), which is 12.6 kilometers (7.8 miles) away and a good place to start walking.

Getting There

Starting Points

Logroño is the best starting point, followed by **Nájera**. Both are best accessed by bus via Logroño, which connects to Nájera, Santo Domingo de la Calzada, Redecilla del Camino, Belorado, and onward to Burgos.

Car

If you plan to drive the Camino from Logroño to Burgos, follow the **N-120,** which follows near and has access to all the stops on the Camino. Both Logroño and Nájera (via Logroño or Burgos) are easily accessible from major cities and highways.

Clockwise from top: in Logroño's Casco Antiguo; Catedral de Santo Domingo de la Calzada; Puente de Piedra, Logroño's stone bridge across the Ebro river; the Camino to San Juan de la Ortega.

Air

The nearest airport is in **Bilbao** (BIO), 149 kilometers from Logroño. From Bilbao, train and bus connections can get you to Logroño, and from there, the bus to Nájera.

Train

Coming from most urban hubs, you will need to change trains to get to Logroño, including from Madrid, via Zaragoza. **RENFE** (www.renfe.es) runs direct lines to Logroño from Bilbao, Barcelona, Zaragoza, and Burgos. No trains connect to Nájera and other places between Logroño and Burgos, only buses.

Bus

ALSA (www.alsa.com) has direct buses to Logroño from Madrid, Barcelona, and Santander. **CuadraBus Linéas** (www.cuadrabuslineas.com) connects Bilbao to Logroño. **La Estellesa** (www.laestellesa.com) connects Pamplona to Logroño. **RiojaCar** (www.riojacar.com) connects Logroño to Nájera.

Logroño Km 613.9

Crossing the 19th-century **Puente de Piedra** into Logroño feels dramatic: the wide expanse of the Erbo river, the long bridge itself, and the backdrop of the city on the other side, punctuated by the steeples of the centuries-old churches. This is La Rioja's administrative and wine capital. Some 152,107 people live here, about half the population of all of La Rioja.

Logroño's history reads as a constant competition for ownership and control by the kings of Aragon, Navarra, and Castile and León. These struggles continued into the early modern era, including with the French in 1521, and later civil wars from the Carlists of the 19th century right up to Franco. La Rioja finally gained the right to self-govern as an autonomous community in 1982.

Logroño occupies an appealing place on the Ebro river, which is navigable by boats and connects to the Mediterranean. The outline of the medieval city remains, with some interesting churches, a few fragments of walls, and a vibrant community that elevates the art of living to its highest expression: not only food and wine, but also the kindness Logroñans like to show to visitors and to each other.

Consider making Logroño a rest day, to sample the *pinchos* on **Calle del Laurel** (also just called Calle Laurel), take in the nearby covered market, **Mercado de San Blas**, and sign up for a wine tour. You may also want to time your arrival here to coincide with one of the two major festivals.

Sights

The Camino passes through the northern edge of the Casco Antiguo, the old medieval city, and all the sights here are within this historic old town. All are south of the Camino's passage, except for the Plaza de Santiago (directly on the Camino) and the Iglesia de Santiago (to your right as you walk).

Though not much of medieval Logroño survives, there is enough left for you to experience some gems. The old medieval city, the Casco Antiguo, is centered on the youngest church, Catedral de Santa Maria de la Redonda, and is bordered by the churches of Santiago, Santa María del Palacio, and San Bartolomé, the oldest. These outline the most colorful parts of old Logroño and are edged on their south side by the city's large public square and park, Parque de Espolón. But the real color and pleasure of the Casco Antiguo unfolds along the many *pincho* bars on Calle del Laurel and the Mercado de San Blas.

Iglesia de Santa María del Palacio

Once a palace donated by Castile's king Alfonso VII (hence its name), the 12th-century **Iglesia de Santa María del Palacio** (Marqués de San Nicolás, 30; 941-249-660; www.lariojaturismo.com; Mon.-Sun. 9am-1:30pm and 6:30-8:30pm; free)

Logroño

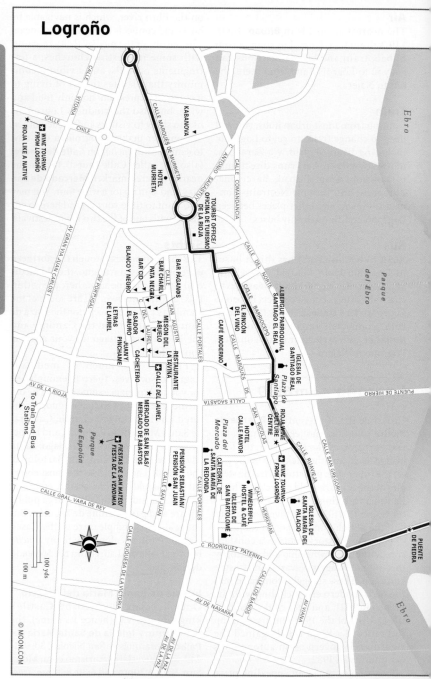

★ WINE TOURING FROM LOGROÑO
★ RIOJA LIKE A NATIVE

KABANOVA

HOTEL MURRIETA

TOURIST OFFICE/
OFICINA DE TURISMO
DE LA RIOJA

BAR PÁGANOS

BAR CHARLY
PATA NEGRA

BLANCO Y NEGRO

BAR CID

MESÓN DEL ABUELO

ASADOR EL MURO

LETRAS DE LAUREL

JUAN Y PINCHAME

CACHETERO

RESTAURANTE LA TAVINA

CALLE DEL LAUREL

EL RINCÓN DEL VINO

CAFÉ MODERNO

ALBERGUE PARROQUIAL SANTIAGO EL REAL

IGLESIA DE SANTIAGO REAL

Plaza de Santiago

RIOJA WINE CULTURE CENTRE

★ WINE TOURING FROM LOGROÑO

MERCADO DE SAN BLAS/
MERCADO DE ABASTOS

★ FIESTAS DE SAN MATEO/
FIESTA DE LA VENDIMIA

To Train and Bus Stations

Parque de Espolón

HOTEL CALLE MAYOR

Plaza del Mercado

PENSIÓN SEBASTIÁN/
PENSIÓN SAN JUAN

CATEDRAL DE SANTA MARÍA DE LA REDONDA

IGLESIA DE SAN BARTOLOMÉ

WINEDERFUL HOSTEL & CAFÉ

IGLESIA DE SANTA MARÍA DEL PALACIO

PUENTE DE HIERRO

PUENTE DE PIEDRA

Parque del Ebro

Ebro

Ebro

CALLE VITORIA
CALLE CHILE
CALLE MARQUÉS DE MURRIETA
CALLE ANTONIO SAGASTI
CALLE COMANDANCIA
CALLE DEL NORTE
CALLE BARRIOCEPO
CALLE MARQUÉS DE
CALLE PORTALES
CALLE SAGASTA
CALLE SAN NICOLÁS
CALLE RUAVIEJA
CALLE SAN GREGORIO
CALLE HERRERÍAS
CALLE PORTALES
CALLE SAN JUAN
C. RODRÍGUEZ PATERNA
CALLE LOS BAÑOS
CALLE DUQUESA DE LA VICTORIA
CALLE GRAL. VARA DE REY
AV DE NAVARRA
AV DE LA PAZ
AV DE LA RIOJA
AV PORTUGAL
AV GRAN VÍA JUAN CARLOS I
AV VIANA
CALLE DEL LAUREL
CALLE SAN AGUSTÍN

0   100 yds
0   100 m

© MOON.COM

contains one of Logroño's most sacred treasures: the 12th- or 13th-century icon of **Nuestra Señora del Ebro,** which was discovered floating down the Ebro river by a washerwoman in the 19th century. Her small chapel, on the left of the nave across from the entrance, is a popular place of local devotion; don't be surprised to see men and women paying their respects and asking for her intervention. It's also a spot to meet neighbors and chitchat in church. The afternoon is especially busy.

The 12th-century church was altered many times from the 13th to 18th centuries. Outside, its sky-piercing tower, locally called *la aguja* ("the needle"), stands 45 meters (148 feet) tall, but the flat, undimensional outside walls may deter you from entering. Please do enter, both to visit Our Lady of the Ebro and her washerwoman magic, as well as to take in the Gothic interior, still visible under the heavy Baroque gold adornments.

Iglesia de San Bartolomé

Iglesia de San Bartolomé (Plaza de San Bartolomé, s/n; 941-252-254; visiting hours are Mon.-Sun., 11:30am-12pm and 12:30-1:15pm; free) is Logroño's oldest surviving church with its original plan still intact. This is the place to come if you seek a peaceful, meditative atmosphere, or just to drink up what medieval Logroño may have felt like.

The church is named for Bartholomew, one of the twelve apostles, who also is known by the name Nathaniel. The Gothic exterior is largely from the 13th century, and the doorway façade has scenes recreating Saint Bartholomew's life and martyrdom. The most harrowing scene is on the left side of the arch, where Bartholomew is being flayed alive and beheaded. His skinning is the reason

From top to bottom: Logroño's Catedral de Santa María de la Redonda at night; Iglesia de San Bartolomé; La Rioja vineyards around Logroño.

Highlights of Riojan Food and Wine

Cuisine in La Rioja works with ingredients' colors and textures as much as their fresh flavors. Like many Iberian cuisines, there are signature dishes with stews, beans, sausages, fresh garden vegetables, orchard fruits, and meats and game. Expect to see fish on the menu, too: trout, hake, sea bream, cod, and mackerel, among others. Popular vegetables here are red and green peppers, white and green asparagus, and artichokes. You are also still in *pinchos* territory, spelled both "*pintxos*" and "*pinchos*," showing both the Castilian and the Basque and Navarran influences.

Camerano Cheese

This cottage cheese is from the herby milk of the goats that graze on the mountainside of the Sierra de los Cameros. It is sublime in pinchos with anchovies, and in desserts, such as with *membrillo* (quince paste). Taste it at the restaurant **Cachetero** in Logroño, which makes a savory *raviolis de calabacín y queso trufado* (zucchini ravioli stuffed with truffled Camerano cheese).

Soups and Stews

La Rioja grows a special variety of red kidney beans, *alubias rojas,* that are earthy and rich in the traditional bean and chorizo stew known as *potaje de alubias rojas con chorizo* or *caparrones,* made with spicy smoked paprika and lots of garlic. *Cocido de callos* is a hefty piquant stew of chickpeas, vegetables, and tripe.

And if you don't like tripe, take note of its name in Spanish—*callos*—as it will appear more on menus as you enter Castile and León.

Meat and Game

Riojans love wood-fire-grilled meats, especially lamb and beef, but also chicken and pork. A favorite game dish is *perdiz estofado* (braised pigeon). La Rioja is also known for its take on *chorizo,* an extra-spicy, dark red sausage seasoned with paprika and garlic. If you like snails, *caracoles a la riojana* are a specialty, sautéed and simmered in a terracotta dish with chorizo, onions, garlic, tomatoes, and *guindillas* (chili peppers).

Other Dishes

Try *la riojana* (meat or poultry sautéed with chorizo, red peppers, and asparagus) or *piquillo,* a spicy little red pepper often stuffed with a pork-and-breadcrumb mixture. Other stuffings may include cod, beef, or mushrooms.

Desserts

A strong French influence shows up in Riojan desserts, especially *milhojas* (mille feuille), layered pastry creations with chocolate and cream. Homemade cheesecakes are also common, as are baked fruit, especially baked peaches or apples in wine. La Rioja also retains a tradition of almond-based desserts (heaven for those seeking gluten-free sweets); the medieval Arab and North African influ-

---

why he is the patron saint of leather workers and tanners. The interior retains the older Romanesque elements, including the semicircular apse. Upper portions of the tower are decorated with Mudéjar (Muslim craftsmen in Christian Spain) geometric brickwork.

Catedral de Santa María de la Redonda

Set on a large and sweeping square, **Plaza del Mercado**, the **Catedral de Santa María**

de la Redonda (Calle Portales, 14; 941-257-611; Mon.-Sat. 8am-1pm and 6:30-8:45pm, Sun. 9am-2pm and 6:30-8:45pm, free) has been rebuilt many times. Its origins go back to a small chapel that stood here in the 12th century. The towers, locally called *las gemelas*, the twins, are pure Riojan Baroque. Nothing of the church retains any aspect of its medieval foundations. Daily **mass** is at 9am, 10am, 11am, and 12pm. This is a popular spot for weddings, so you may see a party,

La Rioja's piquillo red peppers

ence can be seen in the pastries known as *golmajerias*. One of the best known is *mazapanes de Soto*, which are dense, ball-shaped cookies made from almonds, potatoes, lemon zest, and sugar, baked and then dipped in syrup. Look for these in the many bakeries and pastry shops on the Camino through La Rioja.

Wine

La Rioja has three wine-growing regions, each with its own unique soil and climate: Rioja Alava, Rioja Alta, and Rioja Baja. Rioja *vinos tintos*, red wines (mostly made from Tempranillo and Garnacha), make up 85 percent of the region's production. The remaining 15 percent of Rioja wines are medium-bodied, dry *vinos blancos*, white wines (mostly viura, but also tem-

pranillo blanco), and pale-to-fuchsia dry *rosados* (rosés), all also quite good.

Wines are designated by a system based on the aging process and labeled accordingly. Joven wines are young and either never oaked or briefly oaked. Next, Crianza wines are aged two years, with one of those two years in an oak barrel for reds, and six months of barrel aging for whites. Reserva wines are aged three years, with at least one of those years in an oak barrel for reds and six months for whites. And finally, Gran Reserva wines are aged for five years, with at least three of those years in an oak barrel for reds, and six months for whites. Tastings may let you enjoy a flight of these three from a vineyard, beginning with the younger vintages and ending with the older.

white flowers decorating the church, and rose petals and confetti strewn onto the paving stones outside.

Mercado de San Blas

Logroño's daily covered market, the **Mercado de San Blas** (Calle Sagasta, 1; 941-220-430; www.eabastos.com, Mon.-Fri. 7am-2pm and 4-8pm, Sat. 7:30am-2pm, closed Sun.), also known as the Mercado de Abastos, occupies the center of the upper U-shape of the curving street of Calle/Travesía del Laurel. It is a small but spacious and colorful covered market on two levels. Inaugurated in 1930, today the market houses dozens of kiosks selling fresh produce, fish, meats, sausages, cheese, dried herbs and spices, and liquors. It is like a living museum, and worth just walking through to see La Rioja's abundant produce. Large bunches of dried red peppers, artichokes on stalks, and garlic braids are among the most flamboyant displays.

The Game of the Goose

The Game of the Goose, a children's board game, appeared in Spain in 1574 as a diplomatic gift from Francesco de Medici, ambassador of Florence, to the king, Philip II. But it most likely has earlier roots in Greece and Egypt, and is rife with symbolism. Birds, especially waterfowl, represented fertility (through the laying of eggs) and rebirth (through the molting of feathers, as well as disappearance and reappearance through the seasons with migration). Being creatures of both earth and sky, they also intersect different levels of reality (sky, earth, and water).

The Game of the Goose has become a metaphor for the Camino, perhaps because both are games of chance that involve forms of death (dying to the old self) and rebirth (awakening to the new self). Some think the Templars initiated this connection, building into the Camino signs and codes that only spiritual initiates would recognize. It's also thought that the goose footprint was a way for medieval stonemasons, trained in esoteric traditions such as earth energies and sacred geometry, to identify each other. Or perhaps the goose footprint is a symbol of the sacred feminine that went underground with the rise of patriarchal religions. (Folk stories include figures of sacred women with bird features such as geese feet.)

Whatever the case may be, the connection of the game to an esoteric path on the Camino has captured many imaginations. Even today, some pilgrims and scholars see the game as a spiritual tool, and the goose's footprint as a sign that initiates look for on places along the Camino. Believers take note of goose imagery engraved on churches, or towns whose names refer to geese, along the Camino. It's thought that each pilgrim will see and experience the goose on the path in a way that's unique to him or her.

How to Play

Similar to *Snakes and Ladders*, this is a game of chance, played by throwing the dice and moving your game piece forward on a labyrinth-like board divided into 63 squares. Twenty-one of those squares have figures that determine one's fate; 13 are marked with geese, which are considered lucky. Here's how to play:

- Throw the dice, then move your game piece forward on the coiled form of the gameboard.

- If you land on a goose, move forward the same number again.

- If you land on a square occupied by another player's piece, that person has to go back to where you started in that turn.

- If you land on square 6 (The Bridge), move forward 12 spaces.

- If you land on square 19 (The Inn), you miss a turn.

Plaza de Santiago

Midway on the Camino through the Casco Antiguo you will pass into the Plaza de Santiago on your right. The square is often full of kids riding their bikes or playing soccer over a massive inlaid board game in black, charcoal, and pale gray stone that pretty much takes up the whole plaza. The inlaid stone, commissioned in 1991, is the popular European children's game, the Game of the Goose, which has become a popular metaphor for the Camino. The square even has huge stone dice that serve as benches on the game's periphery, and the 63 game squares are laid out with places on the Camino. If you have a pair of dice in your pocket, you could actually play the game, using yourself as the game piece. But it is also a great deal of fun to walk it like a labyrinth, discovering locations on the Camino and following the lucky geese.

The **Iglesia de Santiago** holds the

The Game of the Goose inlaid into Logroño's Plaza de Santiago

- If you land on square 26 or 53 (marked with dice), roll again.

- If you land on square 31 (The Well), you must wait until someone lands on that square and releases you.

- If you land on square 42 (The Maze), go back to square 30.

- If you land on square 52, The Prison, you have to wait for someone to land on that square to release you—like The Well, square 31.

- If you land on square 58 (Death), you have to go all the way back to the beginning.

- The first person to land on the 63rd square wins. (That square often has a 14th goose, one that transforms into a swan, a figure of ultimate spritual elevation.) But you must roll the *exact* number to land on the 63rd square. If you roll too high a number, you must move your piece forward into the 63rd square and then backward, counting the full number that you rolled. If you land on Death, you have to start again, and if you land on a goose, you have to move backward the number on the dice that you rolled.

northwest corner of the Plaza de Santiago. Before you fully leave the square, look to the left, where an old **pilgrims' fountain** survives. Though restored in the 1980s with Neoclassical stone designs, an older fountain of some form has stood here to sustain thirsty pilgrims passing along this very path since the Middle Ages.

Iglesia de Santiago Real

The 15th- or 16th-century Baroque **Iglesia de Santiago** (Calle Barriocepo, 6; 941-209-501; free) is dominated by its 17th-century entrance capped with a sculpture of Santiago swinging a sword from the back of a large horse and decapitating heads all around him. Known as *Santiago Matamoros*, Saint James the Moorslayer, the sculpture is at complete odds with the quieter sculpture, set beneath him in the same façade, of Santiago el Peregrino, Saint James the Pilgrim.

This sculpture is based on a false story about Santiago Matamoros. As the fable goes, in 834, King Ramiro I of Asturias went into battle against the emir of Córdoba at Clavijo, 18 kilometers (11.2 miles) south of Logroño. The odds were stacked against Ramiro, but Saint James miraculously arrived from the sky on a white horse and slaughtered the emir's soldiers. This account gave birth to the idea of Santiago Matamoros. The legend persisted for centuries, but in fact there is no evidence for a battle at Clavijo, and the tale has been discredited by historians. (It turns out that the tale was fabricated in 1150 by the canon of the cathedral of Santiago de Compostela, Pedro Marcio, in an effort to set taxes on wine and cereals from across the northern kingdoms on the Camino, to show gratitude to Santiago for his protection; these taxes were payable to the cathedral in Santiago de Compostela.)

Enter the single nave church to find a 16th-century image of the more agreeable Santiago, *El Peregrino*, on the altar. There, too, you'll see a 13th-century statue, *Nuestra Señora de la Esperanza*, Our Lady of Hope. Together, these two inspire an inner journey of peace and self-mastery.

The church runs the parish *albergue* next door and welcomes pilgrims of all walks as sacred guests. Daily **mass** is at 8:30am, 9am, and 12pm, and visiting hours are 8:15am-1:15pm and 4:30-7pm.

Parque de Espolón

Old Logroño is edged to the south by the city's large public square and park, **Parque de Espolón**. If you desire to people-watch and take a break in the fresh air and dappled sunshine, come here and settle on a bench. In Parque de Espolón's center is a large statue of the 19th-century general, politician, and progressive, Baldomero Espartero, mounted on a well-endowed stallion to symbolize the man's prowess. Espartero helped overthrow the Carlist claim to the throne and defended Isabel II (1830-1904) as the legitimate Spanish ruler. That horse has

as much fame as he. To this day, especially in Logroño and Madrid, a popular expression to describe someone as really daring is *"El/ella tiene más cojones que el caballo de Espartero"* (s/he has more balls than Espartero's horse).

Festivals and Events
★ Fiestas de San Mateo and Fiesta de la Vendimia

The Fiestas de San Mateo is also the Fiesta de la Vendimia, festival of the wine harvest, and takes place the third week of September, centered around **September 21,** with copious food and wine and eruptive cheer interspersed with serious blessings and gratitude expressed to the vines, to wine, to the annual harvest, and to Rioja's patroness, La Virgen de Valvanera. This festival has taken place since the 12th century and unfolds all across La Rioja; it's a region-wide party and prayer for the harvest to yield a good vintage. It is arguably La Rioja's most important festival and a wonderful time to be in Logroño.

Other Events

Every **Sunday** morning to early afternoon there is both a *rastro* (flea market) and the **weekly market.** The *rastro* sets up on Plaza del Mercado, right in front of the cathedral. The weekly market sets up on the Paseo de las Norias with 217 stands and kiosks, and is on the other side of the Ebro river; it is accessed by crossing the bridge, Puente de Piedra, back to the side from which you entered the city on the Camino, then going west toward the Parque las Norias (1.4 km/0.9 mi from the bridge). Logroño also has an elegant 1920s **covered market,** open daily except Sundays.

The **Festividad de San Bernabó** takes place on **June 11** each year in honor of Logroño's patron saint, Bernabó. The festival commemorates Logroño's successful defense against French troops in 1521. According to legend, the town survived the siege by eating fish from the

Ebro river, and so part of the observation includes a feast of bread, fish, and wine. This tradition has evolved into a more elaborate communal feast, where the town leaders prepare meat (instead of fish) stew with bread and wine, for the city's poorest members. The stew is made from prime meat from the bulls slaughtered on the prior day's traditional bullfights. A medieval market, **Mercado Medieval**, selling medieval foods and crafts, sets up near the Iglesia de Santiago.

Though nearly every night on Calle del Laurel is a fiesta, the street hosts **Las Fiestas del Calle del Laurel** in the last week of May, during which each venue features its own *pintxos/pinchos* and wines 1pm-12am. This food festival may explain why this particular street's pub crawl is called *la senda de los elefantes* (the path of the elephants): Watch for overly exuberant drinking and swaying trunks.

★ Wine Tasting and Touring

The opportunities for wine tasting in and around Logroño are nearly infinite, ranging from sampling the wines along Calle del Laurel to arranging your own plunge into wine country with a day trip to the medieval wine village of Laguardia.

Bodega Tours

Logroño, like the surrounding countryside, has underground bodegas where wine is made and stored. You can visit them on a 2-hour **walking tour** (www. azafatasrioja.sacatuentrada.es; 941-214-121; €8) of the Casco Antiguo, ending with a visit to a 16th-century bodega, where you'll learn about the wine-making process and enjoy a complementary glass of Rioja wine and an aperitif. Tours depart from the **tourist office** (Calle Portales, 50; www.lariojaturismo.com) at 6:30pm daily in July and August at 6:30pm and at 5:30pm every Saturday from Sept.-July. Most tours are in Spanish and need a minimum of eight people.

Inquire about English tours at the tourist office.

A shorter tour (1-2 hours; some offered in English; €5) is of Logroño's wine spaces, including underground wine cellars and the museum and wine shop of the **Rioja Wine Culture Centre** (Calle Mercaderes, 9; 941-124-820; www.vinoturismorioja.com; €4-8), which you can also visit on your own. Inquire about this at the tourist office (Calle Portales, 50; 941-291-260; www.lariojaturismo.com) where you can also purchase tour tickets. Tours commence at the San Gregorio cellar (Calle Rúa Vieja, 29) in the old town.

Countryside Wine Tours

For a more extensive and English-speaking plunge into La Rioja's wine world, consider a tour with Rebeca Pérez, founder of **Rioja Like a Native** (Calle de Chile, 7; 629-548-075; www.riojalikeanative.com). Pérez, born in Rioja and educated in the UK, offers a variety of engaging multilingual tours to wineries and historic sights in Rioja. Her passion for La Rioja's food and wine history is infectious, and tours are personal, informative, and fun, ranging from a half-day to a full day. You can select from many themes (underground vineyards, avantgarde winemakers, castles and wine routes, and many more, ranging from €110-150) or go for a general tour, such as Winery & Wine Tasting (€110) or a wine-tasting course or winemaking (€45). At the higher end of the spectrum, a Luxury Wine Tour (€200) accesses some of La Rioja's more exclusive wineries and samples tasting menus from Michelin-star restaurants. You can also sign up for a guided tapas and *pincho* crawl in historic Logroño (€60).

Day Trip to Laguardia

This medieval hilltop town, 18 kilometers (11.2 miles) northwest of Logroño, is surrounded by prime vineyards as well as several Neolithic dolmens from 4,000-5,000 years ago. It also holds over 230

Symbolism on the Camino

Since at least the early Middle Ages, the Camino has been treated as a mythic and mystical road. Many symbols have come to represent an interior, mystical, and deeply spiritual Camino beyond the physical road, strung along with stone churches and other sacred sites.

The center of the Game of the Goose where the goose arrives in Santiago de Compostela

▬ Top Experience ▬

The Milky Way

The road itself is considered the east-west road traced on earth by the path of the stars of the Milky Way—a road that, in many mythologies, can transport souls from here to the hereafter. Any time of year on the Camino, in places free of nighttime light pollution (far from cities and with few street lights), you can see the Milky Way, but the best times are from **April to August**. Good places to see the Milky Way include **Lorca** (Km 671.3), **Ventosa** (Km 594.4), **Tosantos** (Km 535.4), **San Juan de la Ortega** (Km 516.4), **Arroyo de San Bol** (Km 462.9), **Ermita San Nicolás** (Km 441.3), **Castrillo de los Polvazares** (Km 250.7), **Foncebadón** (Km 234.2), and **Manjarín** (Km 230).

Geese

They may have followed the stars at night, but by day, medieval pilgrims fol-lowed the predictable flight pattern of geese and also called the Camino "the way of the wild geese." Geese are faithful and reliable, and excellent navigators. They also represent protection, good luck, strength, and fidelity. Their foot-print may be a symbol of the ancient society of stonemasons, maybe also of the Templars, and perhaps the signature of the mother goddess.

According to this lore, you will find—and experience the energy of—the goose in places on the Camino unique to you. However, some places have left physical depictions, including geese or ducks engraved in Romanesque churches, such as a corbel on Iglesia de San Martín in **Frómista** (Km 424), or actual three-pronged goose-foot signs on walls or in sacred art—such as the shape of the cru-cifix in the Iglesia de Crucifijo in **Puente**

---

ancient (500-year-old) bodegas, two of which are still in operation. The lace-like underground caverns are so fragile that the winemakers must carry in the wine harvest by foot. No vehicles, or even don-keys, are allowed because the vibration might be too much.

Stop at the very helpful **tourist office** (Calle Mayor, 52; 945-600-845; www.la-guardia-alava.com; Mon.-Fri. 10am-2pm and 4-7pm, Sat. 10am-2pm and 5-7pm, Sun. 10:45am-2pm) inside the walled town to inquire about **tasting tours** in the bodegas (starting at €5), guided tours of the town (€2), and a route map to the dol-mens and vines.

It is easy to get to Laguardia from Logroño on the **Line 10** bus with **Alavabus** (www.araba.eus/alavabus; five buses daily each way, 22-30 min.; €1.80). Buses depart from the city bus station, **Estación de Auobuses** (Avenida de España, 1; 941-235-983; www.transpor-teurbano.logro-o.org).

Food

★ **Restaurante La Tavina** (Calle del Laurel, 2; 941-102-300; www.latavina. com) is great both for *pinchos* and full meals focusing on local products and dishes. Try the local cheese tasting plate, the *alubias rojas con chorizo* (red beans la **Reina** (Km 684.8), an engraved goose footprint on the walls of the **Ruinas de San Antón** (Km 452.5) and the church in **Villalcazar de Sirga** (Km 409.8), or the left doorway to the church sacristy in **Vega de Valcarce** (Km 166). Some places also code the goose into their name, such as **Villafranca Montes de Oca** (French town of the goose, at Km 528.5), and **El Ganso** (another Spanish word for goose, at Km 246.5). You will have to search patiently to find any of these, another aspect of the spiritual quest, but the lesson remains: For each person, the experience of the "goose" will be unique in both timing and place.

Tau Cross

Some equate the T-shaped Tau cross, with its upturned tips at the end of the horizonal bar, to the goosefoot in form and symbolism, and consider it to be another way stonemasons or Templars communicated key experiences or sights through hidden symbols. The Tau cross is also a symbol of the healing powers of the Antonine order, its strongest expression on the Camino being found at the **Ruinas de San Antón** (Km 452.5), where the Tau cross is carved into one of the Gothic windows. Soon after, in **Castrojeriz** (Km 448.8), locals have re-inforced this healing symbol with a work of public art, a pillar topped with the Tau cross on the central square as you walk through town on the Camino.

Scallop Shell

The scallop shell, which is the official symbol of the Camino and so visible everywhere, has associations with the pagan creator goddess. (Think of the image of Venus standing in the scallop shell.) Like the goose and goose footprint, it is a symbol of rebirth. Some even say that the goose footprint and the scallop shell carry the same design, radiating lines fanning out from the center. For the pilgrim, this rebirth happens at the ocean's edge in Galicia, where they go to gather a shell after arriving in Compostela. Some modern pilgrims also see the shell as a map of the many roads of the Camino itself, which all join eventually at Santiago de Compostela.

with chorizo stew), or *merluza a la riojana* (hake Riojan style with spicy paprika-stewed peppers and tomatoes). The changing daily menu lets you sample the best of La Rioja's cuisine (€18, includes wine specially selected to pair well). Enjoy the bar-side *pinchos* at street level, or go up one floor to the collection of 500-plus wines, or up another level to the dining room with chalkboard for daily specials.

Since 1916, **Café Moderno** (Plaza Martínez Zaporta, 7; 941-220-042; www.cafemoderno.com; €7-12) has been a popular local gathering place and offers daily menu specials, including *menú del peregrino* (€11), combined plates (such as steak with stuffed red peppers, salad, and fries), and complex salads of produce from local Riojan and Navarran gardens. Choose indoor seating amidst sepia-tone photos of the café and city or the relaxed outdoor terrace on the small square.

El Rincon del Vino (Calle Marqués de San Nicolás, 136; 941-205-392; €25-40) is a romantic spot in the Casco Antiguo, set in an old bodega with a beautifully vaulted brick-work ceiling and warm mustard-toned tablecloths. They specialize in an extensive selection of Rioja wines and grilled meats with a wood fire grill, such as *cordero* (roast lamb) and steaks, as well as stuffed red peppers and a goat cheese terrine.

★ **Cachetero**, right on Calle del Laurel (Calle del Laurel, 3; 941-228-463; www. cachetero.com; €25-35), is another world from the packed *pincho* scene when you step into the calm, white-linen dining room. Dedicated to creative Riojan cuisine, the three-course tasting menu, *menú degustación* (€25, wine not included), offers a chance to sample the chef's best offerings, inspired by that day's finds in the covered market next door. Signature dishes include *caparrones,* a spicy traditional Riojan stew of kidney beans and chorizo, and *raviolis de calabacín y queso trufado* (zucchini ravioli stuffed with truffled Queso Camerano, a protected-denomination-of-origin Riojan goat cheese). Proprietors speak English.

Kabanova (Calle Guardia Civil, 9; 941-212-995; www.grupopasion.com; €18-25) showcases the best of Rioja's experimental and innovative new cuisine, still founded on traditional principles of local and fresh ingredients. The chef cooks with vibrant colors as much as bright flavors, painting beautiful dishes for the plate and palate (such as *lubina llena del mar,* bass "filled with the sea," a rolled bass filet baked with algae in the center and set on a seasoned sea of colorful vegetables). The dining room is jazzy, with walls covered in musical notes and set behind two-by-four beam frames that serve double duty as wine-bottle shelving.

Nightlife

▬▬▬ Top Experience ▬▬▬

★ Calle del Laurel

The best nightlife in Logroño is the nightly scene on **Calle del Laurel** (www. callelaurel.org; website includes a listing of each place's specialty *pinchos*), an exciting feast of *pinchos* in the distinctive cafés, many specializing in one kind of *pintxo/pincho* that is so good, it's all they have to make. It is also the place to

explore La Rioja's wine wealth. There are some 39 bars and 12 restaurants on this street, which is really one of four streets wrapping around the covered market. (The whole block is referred to as Calle del Laurel.)

These wonderful, old tavern-style places line the streets and have a lot of patrons standing outside or crowded around the bar just inside. The best way to enjoy Calle del Laurel is to go from place to place, ordering a *pincho* and glass of wine at each bar. The bartender will keep track of your order, so you can pay when ready. Visit:

- **Asador El Muro** (Travesía del Laurel, s/n) for grilled chorizo and morcilla sausage, and for *pimientos del piquillo rellenos de setas* (roasted red peppers stuffed with wild mushrooms).

- **Bar Cid** (Travesía del Laurel, 1) for 27 years (and counting) of serving up *setas a la plancha con salsita de la abuela* (large grilled oyster mushrooms with Grandma's sauce), perfectly paired with a red Rioja.

- **Blanco y Negro** (Travesía del Laurel and Calle Bretón de los Herreros, 48) for *matrimonio de anchoas con pimientos verde*, a heady "marriage" of marinated fresh anchovies with fried green peppers stuffed into a small loaf of freshly baked bread.

- **Bar Charly** (Travesía del Laurel, 2) for *morritos*, fried pig snouts with sea salt, and *tigres* (mussel shells stuffed with mussel meat, béchamel, red pepper, and onion, coated with bread crumbs and deep fried).

- **Juan y Pinchamé** (Travesía del Laurel, 9) for *brochetas de langostino con piña*, skewers of perfectly grilled langoustine with pineapple using local olive oil.

- **Mesón del Abuelo** (Travesía del Laurel,

12) for *sepia a la plancha con exquisite salsa casera* (grilled squid with the "exquisite" homemade secret sauce . . . I detect herbs and garlic, but can't identify the rest of this savory bite).

- **Letras de Laurel** (Travesía del Laurel, 22) for *piruletas de solomillo con salsa de hongas* (sirloin skewers with mushroom sauce).

- **Bar Páganos** (Travesía del Laurel, 22) for grilled kebabs, especially their most famous, *pincho moruno*, spicy pork kebabs.

- **Pata Negra** (Travesía del Laurel, 24), mini-sandwiches, from oven-warmed jamón Serrano with tomato to vegetarian *bocatitos de queso brie y membrillo* (small brie sandwiches with quince jam on really good artisanal bread rolls).

Accommodations

Evening prayer in the neighboring Iglesia de Santiago and a satisfying communal dinner and breakfast make the ★ **Albergue Parroquial Santiago El Real** (Calle Barriocepo, 8; 941-209-501; info@santiagoelreal.org; donation) popular with pilgrims who are made to feel like sacred guests. The address varies by season: from June-Sept, pilgrims are housed at Calle Barriocepo, 8 (30 beds), and from Oct.-May, they are housed down the street at Calle Barriocepo, 58 (18 beds). It is pretty rustic and basic, with some mattresses on the floor and two toilets and showers, one set for men and the other for women. Proprietors speak English.

★ **Pensión Sebastian** (Calle San Juan, 21; 941-242-800; www.pensionsebastian.com; €20-40) is run by a kind, no-nonsense lady who runs an efficient ship, with immaculate rooms in the traditional Spanish style of simple furnishings, white walls, a splash of color in the fresh quilted bedspreads, pale wooden floors, and sparkling bathrooms. The street below is lined with several casual eating options. Ask for an inner courtyard room that is very quiet; many have windows with views of the rooftops of the old city. Rooms share a bath. However, the **Pensión San Juan**, in the same building as Pensión Sebastian (and with the same contact information), is run by the same lady and offers similar rooms (€30-50) but with private baths. The owner offers special prices for pilgrims for both, so be sure to inquire.

Hotel Murrieta (Calle Marqués de Murrieta, 1; 941-224-150; www.hotel-murrietalogrono.com; €55-70) is at the chic end of the Camino before it leaves the old town, and benefits from a quiet atmosphere at night when the old town is amping up its late-night eating and drinking expeditions. Rooms and lobby have a strong turn-of-the-19th-century flavor.

Hotel Calle Mayor (Calle Marqués de San Nicolás, 71; 941-232-368; www.hotelcallemayor.com; €140) is a traditional 16th-century stone building with a neo-Romanesque arch. While the exterior is sturdy stone and old Logroño, the interior is fresh and contemporary, with boxy firm beds, padded walls, and 1960s style Twiggy chairs. Proprietors speak English.

Winederful Hostel & Café (Calle Herrerias, 2-14; 941-139-618; www.winederful.es; breakfast included) offers Japanese-style enclosed dorm beds (€16-18) as solid independent units built into the wall, each bed with its own storage drawer. There are also private rooms (€55), also outfitted with the urban industrial décor of steel-trim bed frames, slate bedcovers, and walls that accurately reinforce the pristine spaces. Pen-and-ink murals of youthful action-oriented characters make it feel as if you've wandered into an Anime graphic novel, in a fun way. The turquoise-tiled kitchen may eliminate the need for caffeine in the morning. Proprietors speak English.

Getting There and Around

Logroño is not directly connected by train to many major cities except for Bilbao, Zaragoza, Barcelona, and Burgos. All others will require a train change. The easiest and best way to get to and around Logroño is often by bus. The bus and train stations are 700 meters (0.4 mile) away from each other, an 8-10 minute walk.

Car

From **Santander and Bilbao** (235 km/146 mi; 2.5 hours): Take the **S-10** south from Santander, then the **A-8** east to Bilbao, and the **AP-68** south to Logroño.

From **Pamplona** (86 km/53 mi; 55 min.): Take the **A-12** southwest to Logroño.

From **Barcelona and Zaragoza** (477 km/296 mi; 4.5 hours): Take the **A-2/AP-7/E-90** west to Zaragoza, then continue northwest on the **AP-68/E-804** to Logroño.

From **Madrid** (327 km/203 mi; 3.5 hours): Take the **A-2/E-90** northeast past Guadalajara and the **A-15** north to Soria, then the **SO-20** to **N-111** to Logroño.

From **Burgos** (114 km/71 mi; 1.5 hours): Take the **N-120** east to Logroño.

Europcar (www.europcar.com), **Alamo** (www.alamo.com), **Enterprise** (www.enterprise.com), and **Avis** (www.avis.com) all have offices next to each other between the bus and train stations, as do other rental companies nearby.

Train

Logroño's **RENFE/ADIF train station** (Avenida de Colón, 83; www.renfe.com) is not directly on the major train lines, but there are direct trains from Bilbao (two trains daily; 2.5 hours; €9-11.25), Barcelona (five daily; 4-5 hours; €30-45), Zaragoza (nine daily; 2-2.5 hours; €12-22.20), and Burgos (three daily; 2 hours; €11-22). From Madrid (six trains daily; 3.5-4 hours; €36-62), a train change in Zaragosa is necessary.

The Camino is 1.5 kilometers to the north of the train station, an easy 20-minute walk. Exit the station onto Avenida de Colón, facing north, and take it for 400 meters (0.25 mile) to Calle Villamediana and turn left. Take Calle Villamediana for 550 meters (0.35 mile), and turn right onto Avenida de La Rioja for another 550 meters (0.35 mile), where it will intersect with Calle Rúa Vieja, which is the Camino. Turn left and you will pass the Plaza de Santiago on your right.

Bus

ALSA (www.alsa.com) has direct buses to Logroño from Madrid, both from Barajas airport (six buses daily; 3-4 hours; €24.20) and Estacion Avenida América (eight daily; 3-4 hours; €24.20); Barcelona (seven daily; 6-8 hours; €20.50), and Santander (three daily; 3-4 hours; €20-33.40).

CuadraBus (www.cuadrabuslineas.com) connects Bilbao to Logroño (11 daily; 2 hours; €13). **La Estellesa** (www.laestellesa.com) connects Pamplona to Logroño (eight daily; 1.5-2 hours; €9.10).

Logroño's **Estación de Autobuses** (Avenida de España, 1) is just 450 meters (0.28 mile) northwest of the train station. The Camino is 1.1 kilometers to the north of the bus station and an easy 15-minute walk. Leave the station, and go right, onto Avenida de España, and follow it north. At Avenida Pérez Galdós, turn left and then take the next right onto Calle San Antón; take it straight north to Avenida de La Rioja and continue straight north to Calle Rúa Vieja, which is the Camino. Turn left and continue west.

Taxi

A taxi from Logroño to Navarrete (15-minutes) will average around €30-35. Try **Radio Raxi Rioja** (941-222-122) or **Uni-Taxi Rioja** (941-505-050; www.uni-taxirioja.es).

Leaving Logroño

The next stop with guaranteed services in is Navarrete, in 13 kilometers (8 miles), so be sure to fill water bottles and have food or snacks on hand if you'll need to refuel before then.

The first 5 kilometers (3.1 miles) leaving the city is dismal, as you walk past car dealerships and concrete urban outskirts. If you opt to skip this, catch the **M-1 Cenicero-Logroño bus line** (2-3 buses per hour; €2), which has a stop called Beneficencias (near Calle Marqués de Murrieta, 76), the stop nearest to the point at which the Camino exits the historic center heading west. There are many others stops, and locals will gladly help you locate the closest one, based on where you are; just ask them about *el autobus á Navarrete.*

If you opt to walk it, in 6 kilometers (3.7 miles) you'll reach a large park, **Parque Grajera** (Km 607.9) centered on a small artificial lake, **Pantano de la Grajera,** near which you *might* find a stand selling refreshments, **Cabaña Tío Jarvi.** From Alto de la Grajera, 6.6 kilometers (4.1 miles) remain to Navarrete.

Navarrete will appear perched on the high hill ahead of you long before you reach it, its church and bell tower holding the central high point. Some 700 meters (0.4 mile) before entering Navarrete, you will pass the ruins of the **Hospital de San Juan de Acre** (Km 609.3), founded in 1185 to house and heal pilgrims under the order of San Juan de Jerusalén. It had a good long run and stood here until the 19th century, when it was abandoned and left to decay. But in 1887, the architect Luis Barrón salvaged its portal and windows for the construction of the cemetery that you'll find to the left of the Camino on your way out of Navarrete, at the other end of town.

Navarrete   Km 601.3

Navarrete (pop. 2,948) is a classic hilltop town—like so many on the Camino, an ideal site for strategic settlement and fortification. The town is known for wine (as is the entire surrounding region), as well as for terracotta pottery, a craft that's been practiced here since Roman times. Under the hilltop are cavernous, family-owned private bodegas for storing food and wine, a feature you will see often in or around villages in La Rioja and into Castile and León.

The Camino passes through the center of the town, which is centered on its church; the town's roads all wrap around the hill like coils.

Sights
Iglesia de la Asunción
Iglesia de la Asunción (Calle Mayor Baja, 1; open Mon.-Sat., 11am-2pm and 5-8pm, and Sun., 11am-2pm; free) is from the late 16th to early 17th centuries. The church's Baroque retable, the ornate wooden altar piece reaching all the way to the ceiling and dominated by gold, is often hailed as its most outstanding feature, but the church itself also has appealing proportions in its sweeping Gothic arches. Tucked to the side, it also has an expressive stained-glass window of John the Baptist baptizing Jesus in the river Jordan, showing the serene harmony that connects the two of them. You'll also find a small table near the entrance with a stamp for your pilgrim's passport.

Navarrete Cemetery
Soon after you leave Navarrete, to the left is the town cemetery whose gate was rescued and recycled from the Romanesque-Gothic façade of the 12th-century Hospital de San Juan de Acre (which you passed as you entered Navarrete). Among its most attractive features is the six-petaled floral medallion in the center of the pointed arch, but the engraved capitals are also interesting. Among them is Saint George thrusting his sword into the dragon. Another capital shows two medieval hooded faces with human upper bodies and serpent-like lower bodies twisting around each other; the two stand cheek to cheek and seem to enjoy a good

secret. Another friendly-looking dragon has his tongue sticking out, but the scene around him has been eroded by time.

Alfarería Naharro

As you depart Navarrete on the Camino and you pass the town cemetery on your left, directly across the street (the N-120) is the traditional terracotta shop and workshop of craftsman Antonio Naharro Flores, **Alfarería Naharro** (Calle Carretera de Burgos/N-120; 941-440-157; www. alfarerianaharro.com) where you can see (and buy) a good selection of Navarrete's pottery tradition.

Events

Navarrete has a produce and general goods **market** every Wednesday morning that sets up on the **Plaza de Coso** just a few dozen meters south of the church. Local ceramicists also sell their goods here, which is the best chance to see several artisans' works. Every July the town hosts a ceramics fair, **Fería de Alfarería y Cerámica,** where many more artisans bring their wares.

Food and Accommodations

★ **Bar Deportivo** (Plaza las Pilas, 2; 941-441-065), also known as Casa de Comidas de Begoña y Antonio, is a great hangout, with tables under the plain trees on the square and a warm rose-toned interior with checkered tablecloths. The bar serves varieties of *pinchos* and excellent and creative Riojan dishes, such as spinach-and-chickpea soup, stuffed red peppers, and wild mushroom egg scramble. Pilgrims also rejoice in the outgoing and always jovial owner, who gives avuncular hugs and encouragement should you wish it or need it. The *menú del peregrino* is €15.

Navarrete boasts several good *albergues,* but right on the Calle Mayor and on the Camino (midway, left side) is a traditional mansion turned boutique B&B, **Casa Peregrinando** (Calle Mayor Alta, 34; 674-552-545; www.casaperegrinando20.

wixsite.com; €40-70, including breakfast) with six rooms in 19th-century country-manor décor, eclectic modern and global art, French windows, bed canopies, and an interior garden and covered terrace. For breakfast, there are home-baked goods, bread, fresh fruit, and yogurt.

If you wish to see a private underground bodega and tunnels, stay at **Posada Ignatius** (Plaza del Arco, 4; 941-124-094; www.posadaignatius.com; €40-50), a 15th-century building named after its most famous guest, Ignatius of Loyola, who stayed here 1517-1521 when he was a knight fighting for the Duke of Nájera (and before he became a priest and founded the Jesuit Order). The Posada may well be much the same as it was in his time, with stone stairways, river rock mosaic inlay floors, crisp linens, and firm beds. Proprietors speak English.

Leaving Navarrete

Well way-marked and following the central road out of town, in 5.7 kilometers (3.5 miles) the Camino offers a detour to Ventosa through vineyards off the roadside (A-12/N-120). It adds only 1 kilometer (0.6 miles), but is a beautiful stretch and not to be missed. You will climb slightly in altitude until just past Ventosa at **Alto de San Antón** (670 meters/2,200 feet), when the trail begins its descent to the river valley of Nájera.

☞ Detour: Ventosa
Km 594.4

Ventosa (pop. 175) is a sweet hamlet arrayed around its little hill. Founded in the 11th century, it was on the original medieval Camino, a beacon guiding *peregrinos* with its hilltop church. Today it stands in a sea of red earth hills that are striped with radiating green rows of grape vines. The village is worth that extra 1 kilometer (0.6 miles) to arrive here, not only because it allows you to skip the more modern route that parallels the A-12/N-120, but also because of the village's agreeable physical and social atmosphere, small village bar, *albergue,* and church on the hill.

Sights
Iglesia de San Saturnino
The Iglesia de San Saturnino is often overlooked, beyond its pretty perch on the high point of Ventosa's hilltop. It's a heavily fortified landmark, with a pointed bell tower visible to pilgrims wading through the vineyards. But while it seems fairly modern (it dates to the 16th century), its engravings speak of more ancient affiliations, which the stonemasons would have been schooled in, including symbols of earth energy and regeneration, two sinuous serpent-dragons, and my favorite earthly image of all, a pig snarfing down acorns. It is almost never open, but fortunately, all this is going on around the outside arch of the doorway.

Food and Accommodations
★ **Bar Virgen Blanca** (Calle San Roque, 27; 625-896-355, €4-10) sits right at the foot of the hill as you enter Ventosa, and is a thriving village social center and a great place to rest and refuel if you are continuing on to Nájera, or to relax and chill if staying the night. Just order a drink and watch the vines growing all around you. The bar serves wines from the surrounding vineyards, snacks (tortilla Española, sandwiches, cheeses), pizza, paella, and *menú.* Be sure to ask for olives, dark green orbs that taste like the sun.

Albergue San Saturnino (Calle Mayor, 33; 941-441-899; 42 beds in six rooms; €10) is an oasis in a sea of vines, with *hospitaleros* who make every effort for see to your comfort and restful stay. It features large and spotless bathrooms, homey

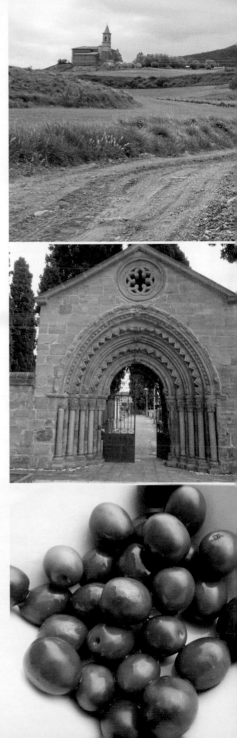

From top to bottom: Ventosa village in the middle of La Rioja vineyards; reused wall of San Juan de Acre's monastery for Navarrete's cemetery; olives in Ventosa.

bunk beds with plaid mattress covers and pillow cases, a beautiful courtyard, and 6am wake-up music of Gregorian chant. A small food store on the premises lets you purchase ingredients to cook dinner in the communal kitchen.

Leaving Ventosa

The path is well marked from Ventosa to Nájera, but the next 10.2 kilometers (6.3 miles) are without support services, so fill your water bottles before heading off.

Two kilometers (1.2 miles) from Ventosa, you will reach the highest point on this 29.8-kilometer (18.5-mile) section from Logroño to Nájera. It's a steady climb to the **Alto de San Antón** (670 meters/2,200 feet), which offers a good view of the surrounding vineyards. Three kilometers (1.9 miles) from Alto de San Anton, after a steady slope downhill, you'll see a beehive-shaped structure on a small hill, **Poyo de Roldán,** named after Charlemagne's officer who is fabled to have fought and defeated the giant Ferragut here. The beehive hut is a traditional shelter for shepherds and farmers. From the Poyo de Roldán, you have

4 kilometers (2.5 miles) more to go, and you can see Nájera arrayed before you.

Nájera   Km 584.1

The unattractive entry into Nájera (pop. 8,088) feels longer than it is as you tromp toward the historic center. But don't miss the welcome on entry, the mural painted on a building in a garden to the right that says, in big bold letters, *Peregrino, en Nájera, Najerino* ("Pilgrim in Najera, you're Najeran"). A warmer welcome cannot be found.

Follow the way-markers into the center of Nájera. You'll find the town inhabiting both sides of the Río Najerillo, the newer town on the side before you cross the bridge and the older medieval town set right against the cliffs and along the river bank.

This bridge over the Najerilla river, a modern replacement of the first bridge (built by San Juan de Ortega in the 11th or 12th century), gives the prettiest perspective on Nájera. As you cross it, take in the saturated orange-red rock face on

Nájera's old town built into the red cliff walls of the Monasterio de Santa María la Real

Nájera

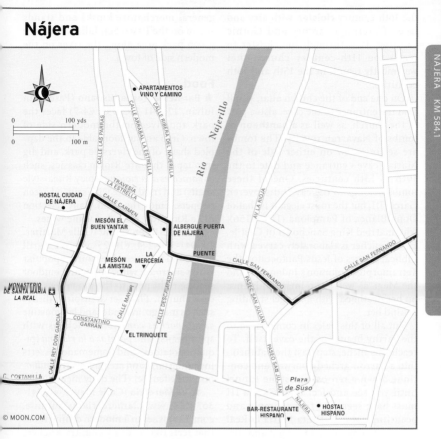

© MOON.COM

the right, set against the green of the riverside park and the cobalt blue of both river and sky. On either side of the bridge are good places to enjoy the cafés and color of this gregarious small town.

Sights

Old Nájera, located after you cross the bridge, is centered on the church and monastery, which is built right into the red cliff wall and caverns.

★ Monasterio de Santa María la Real

The town of Nájera emerged around a miraculous discovery in 1044, when King García III of Navarra was out hunting with his falcon along the Najerilla

river. The bird suddenly flew off after a dove, disappeaing into a thicket of trees. When García went to investigate, he found a hidden cave emitting light. Inside, he found his falcon and the dove peacefully perched on either side of an ancient wooden statue of Mary and the baby Jesus. In front of mother and son was a vase of lilies and a bell. (Bells in Christianity often represent the voice of God; lilies are Mary's flowers, symbols of purity and grace.) García quickly ordered a chapel built, which soon became a church and monastery.

Today, the **Monasterio de Santa María la Real** (Plaza de Santa María; 941-361-083; www.santamarialareal.net; €4) is reached from the doorway leading into the 16th-century **cloister**, with airy and lacey Plateresque arches and Gothic vaulting. Pass through the cloister to reach the 11th-century church that was mostly rebuilt in the 15th and 16th centuries.

On one end of the church altar, you'll find the entrance to the cave, also a part of the church, as well as a **pantheon** of tombs of Navarran royalty. The tombs are set in a row on either side of the Marian cave's entrance and date to the 10th to 13th centuries. One of these tombs belongs to the cave's discoverer, García III, but the most elegant is that of Doña Blanca of Pamplona (1137-1156), who married King Sancho III of Castile. Her sepulcher is elaborately carved with Biblical images of Jesus Pantocrator, the Tetramorphs, Solomon's judgment, and the Magi, as well as an image of Blanca on her deathbed with an angel standing behind her.

But all of this pales in comparison to the earthy beauty of the cave itself. To reach this niche, step past the pantheon into a narrow arched doorway and continue down a red-orange stone tunnel until you see and feel what García III must have seen and felt: a simple and beautiful statue of Santa María la Real illuminated by soft golden light and surrounded by the warmth of the rust red rock and the scent of lilies, which stand in a vase in the center, along with a bell.

The monastery complex is open Tues.-Sat. 10am-1:30pm and 4-7pm (5:30pm in winter), and Sun. and holidays, 10am-1:30pm and 4-7pm (5:30pm in winter).

Events

The **Fiesta del Pimiento Riojano,** celebrating the flavorful piquant little red pepper in Riojan cuisine, is the last Sunday in October. Locals celebrate **Santa María la Real** from September 15-18 with processions, concerts, and food festivities.

At Nájera's **weekly market** (Thurs. around 9am-2:30pm), 100 food and general merchanise kiosks and stands set up on the Paseo San Julián, the large green park area along the river on the modern side of town.

Food

★ **Bar-Restaurante Hispano** (Paseo San Julián, 12; 941-362-957; €4-7) faces the park and river on the modern side of town. Grab an outdoor table in the dappled shade of the riverside park, and dig into tapas that are Riojan classics, such as *caracoles a la riojana* (spicy Rioja-style snails) and fried hake with sautéed green peppers. Enjoy the good, daily selection of La Rioja red, rosé, and white wines.

Mesón El Buen Yantar (Calle Mártires, 19; 941-360-274; €10-25) is both a grill house and traditional restaurant popular with *peregrinos,* with indoor and outdoor seating right next to the monastery and cave church. They serve inspired dishes such as mango, avocado, and langoustine salad, *pochas con almejas* (clams with spicy beans), and *patatas a la riojana* (piquant potatoes), and homemade desserts including tarts and creamy layered *milhojas* (mille feuille). The daily menu is €15.

★ **La Mercería** (Calle Mayor, 41; 941-363-028; www.lamerceriarestaurante.com; €15) is set in a modern dining room that feels like a sunny country kitchen. The *menú del dia* features extensive choices, including *ensalada de piquillos con bonito* (tuna-stuffed red pepper salad), *lentejas con chorizo* (chorizo and lentil stew), and *arroz con boletus* (wild mushroom rice). Bottles of wine are arrayed in large see-through buckets on the bar counter, making it easy to pick and choose. Save room for desserts such as homemade flan. Proprietors speak English.

Mesón La Amistad (Calle la Cruz, 6; 941-362-647; menu for €15) in an unfussy, agreeable, and open dining room that lets the warm service and excellent, colorful food steal the show. Come here for *pinchos* (such as grilled foie with shrimp) or the three-course menu, featuring dishes like *patatas a la riojana* (spicy paprika stew with sausage and potatoes), grilled hake with green salsa and salad, and a series of homemade tarts, from cheesecake to chocolate.

Accommodations

There are lodging options on both sides of the river: modern Nájera (before you cross the river) and the old town (after you cross the bridge), where the pilgrim *albergues* are located.

Modern Nájera

Near the river and set on a narrow block in a boat-shaped oval building, the **Hostal Hispano** (Calle la Cepa, 2; 941-363-615; www.hostalhispanonajera.com; €40-65) offers some rooms facing the river and others facing a charming farmyard cohabited by turkeys, a rooster, a hen, ducks, geese, and a goat who roam and graze together. The lodging itself has a fun energy, welcoming *peregrinos* from around the world with the same warmth and getting everyone efficiently situated in one of the 22 rooms. Each is outfitted with country-home-style printed fabrics and quilts (some feeling like your childhood room), with spotless baths and floor-to-ceiling windows.

Old Nájera

Albergue Puerta de Nájera (Calle Ribera del Najerilla, 1; 941-362-317; www.alberguedenajera.com; open Mar.-Oct.) is both *hostal* and *albergue*, with two private rooms (€30-40) and 35 beds in six dorm rooms (€10-15) in a refurbished traditional house on the other side of the bridge (to the right). French lavender walls and white wooden bunks and beds make for a restful and cheerful experience.

After crossing the bridge, take the second right onto Calle Carmen and continue straight to ★ **Apartamentos Vino y Camino** (Calle Arrabal de la Estrella, 46; 626-017-187; www.vinoycamino.com) for four luxury apartments, some

with kitchens and all with a salon and bath, each decorated with bold stripes, colors, and contemporary furnishings. (And each comes with a courtesy bottle of Rioja wine.) The apartments are named for wine themes: Gran Reserva, Tinto, Blanco, and De Autor. Gran Reserva sleeps up to eight (€110) and the other three apartments sleep 2-4 people (starting at €50-60). The smallest apartment, for two, De Autor, has a rooftop terrace and a fireplace.

Next door, the **Hostal Ciudad de Nájera** (Cuarta Calleja San Miguel, 14; 941-360-660; www.ciudaddenajera.com; eight rooms; €45-60) is a modern rendering of Nájera's red-stone rock face in red bricks of the same color, a contemporary building abutting the cliff where you are assured a quiet night of rest. With marble and tile baths, each impeccable, light-filled room is painted a strong color, with colorful plaid blankets and bedcovers and floor-to-ceiling windows.

Getting There and Around

Nájera has a bus station near the river on the modern side of town, with frequent and efficient connections from Logroño and to Burgos as well as to Santo Domingo de la Calzada and other destinations.

Car

Nájera is 29.8 kilometers (18.5 miles) west of Logroño. The **N-120** and larger **A-12** connect Nájera from Logroño, the most direct way to arrive here.

Bus

Nájera's small but central bus station, **Estación de Autobuses de Nájera** (Calle Paseo San Julián, s/n) is near the bridge and has several bus lines.

Riojacar (www.riojacar.com) connects **Logroño** to **Nájera** (11-18 buses daily; 15 min.; €2-3).

Autobuses Jiménez (902-202-878; www.autobusesjimenez.com) also has 10 buses daily that connect Nájera to

Day Trip to San Millan de la Cogolla

Hermit-turned-saint San Millán de Cogolla (AD 473-574) was born in the nearby village of Berceo. He briefly served as a priest but was drawn to the Cárdenas valley to meditate in a cave now known as La Cueva del Santo ("cave of the saint"). Living on foraged foods, he dedicated his life to God and quiet contemplation. People came to see him for cures and his fame grew. One of his most famous miracles was multiplying loaves of bread for the crowds who gathered to see him. He also cured incurable ailments and exorcised demons. His fame also drew other hermits here to pray, each in his own cave. Periodically, the hermits gathered for communal prayer in a lower cave, which eventually became the Monasterio de Suso.

By the time of the peak of the medieval Camino, the monastery of San Millan de la Cogolla was already a pilgrim destination and a common deviation from the main path. Today, Nájera is a great base from which to visit the monasteries of Suso and Yuso, which are connected to the miracles of San Millán. If you have time to visit only one monastery, make it Suso: Its pre-Romanesque and Romanesque atmosphere is unique and can be appreciated whether you speak Spanish or not. (Both monastery visits are conducted in Spanish.)

Monasterio de Suso
Monasterio de Suso (941-373-082; www.monasteriodesanmillan.com) is set on the hillside overlooking the present village of San Millán (pop. 203). This is where the hermits that San Millán de Cogolla attracted to the region gathered for communal prayer. San Millán died here in the 6th century, and some believe he is still buried here (but no one is certain where his body is). The monastery has Visigothic, Mozarabic, and Romanesque aspects, and is a one-of-a-kind monument in Spain. Its rounded and high horseshoe arches are exquisite, as is the reddish-yellow warmth of the natural stone. Truth be told, you can still feel the serene presence of San Millán the hermit here.

Suso became a monastery by the 6th century and continued to function as one until the early 11th century. Over those five centuries, the monastery developed into a more organized and monastic community, rather than the loosely organized hermitic community of San Millán's era.

To visit, you need to schedule a **guided tour** (€4, 40 minutes), available Tues.-Sun. at 9:30am-1:30pm and 3:30pm-6:30pm (outside of summer months, the last tour starts at 5:30pm). Get tickets from the tourist office inside the entrance to Monasterio de Yuso. A bus (5 min., included) transports visitors from in front of the Monasterio de Yuso to the monastery from the village.

Monasterio de Yuso
By 1069, monks were established in the newly built monastery of Yuso to support the growing numbers of monks

Santo Domingo de la Calzada (25 min.; €1.50), Belorado (1.5 hours), and Burgos (2 hours; €6).

Azofra   Km 578.4

Set in a sweeping open plain with a backdrop of mountains, Azofra's church will stand out for kilometers before you reach this village of 204 people. In the 12th century there was a hospice here, but little of the medieval settlement survives. The town has Arab and North African origins and its name may be from Arabic or Hebrew, meaning "tribute" or "beauty," respectively. The town offers a delightful reminder of the mixed, coexisting world of Iberia's many peoples.

The tall, heavily built, and mostly 16th-century **Iglesia de Nuestra Señora de los Ángeles** (Calle Antonio Perez, 13; 941 117 067, www.azofra.org; if closed, inquire in the albergue; free) holds a good

San Millan de la Cogolla's Monasterio de Yuso, built in the village center

at Suso. **Monasterio de Yuso** (Calle Prestiño s/n; 941-373-049; www.monasteriodesanmillan.com; €7) is situated down the hill from Suso, in the heart of the village. Nothing of the 11th-century structure survives; today, it is more of a 16th-century complex. From the monastery, you can look up the hill to see the older Suso peeking down through the trees.

Where Suso is focused on quiet contemplation, the large and ornate Yuso exudes a strong church officialdom. Highlights are the ivory-carved and jewel-encrusted 11th-century Mozarabic reliquaries, one dedicated to San Millán and the other to his teacher, San Felices.

Advance reservations aren't necessary to visit Yuso: just purchase admission at the entrance during opening hours. Hours from Easter week to Sept. are Tues.-Sun., 10am-1:30pm and 4-6:30pm; in August the monastery also opens on Mondays. Hours from Oct. to Easter week are 10am-1pm and 3:30-5:30pm. All visits are guided and last about 50 minutes.

Getting There

San Millán de la Cogolla is 18 kilometers (11.2 miles) southwest of Nájera. **Autobuses Jiménez** (902-202-878; www.autobusesjimenez.com) runs two buses daily between Nájera to San Millán on weekdays, and one daily on weekends (€1.70; 20 minutes). If the return schedule is limiting, you can get a taxi back (€25-30); try **Taxi Nájera** (608-677-328; www.taxinajera.es).

sculpture of Santiago as pilgrim and was a place of burial for medieval pilgrims. The parish holds a daily pilgrims' **mass** here at 7pm.

Food and Accommodations

The **Bar Sevilla** (Calle Mayor 17, 941-379-239; €10) serves meals and snacks and a decent *menú del peregrino*; the English-speaking owner is gregarious with the many crowds of *peregrinos* who come in each day. The décor is Andalusian, with blue- and white-painted tiles lining the walls. The dishes can be meat- and starch-heavy, but a multilingual menu posted at the door lets you study the options.

Albergue Municipal de Azofra (Calle La Parras, 7; 941-379-325; 60 beds in 30 rooms; open Apr.-Oct; 60 beds; October; €7) is unusual for municipal pilgrim dorms in that all the beds are arranged in double bedrooms, with shared bathrooms down the halls. It also has a courtyard with a fountain that is popular for relaxing and conversing with others. The *albergue* is open year-round, but in winter moves to a small building with 16 places.

Leaving Azofra

There are 9.7 kilometers (6 miles) without support services, and the slope increases as you approach Cirueña (755 meters/2,477 feet), climbing 200 meters (656 feet) in altitude from Azofra. Just before arriving, you'll pass by the golf course of the Rioja Alta Golf Club.

Cirueña   Km 569.3

This village of 101 people has a rustic but pretty little brick-and-stucco church, **Iglesia de San Andrés** (Calle Iglesia, 4), named after a 10th-century monastery, now long gone, which Queen Urraca and her brother Ramiro gave to this village in 972. The current church rests on what was once a 10th-century pre-Romanesque temple, but locals built this one in 1965. Now the village is more a temple to golf and to tired pilgrims desiring a place to eat, rehydrate, and possibly lodge if the 4.5 kilometers (2.8 miles) to Santo Domingo de la Calzada seems too far off (although it is an easy downhill saunter from here).

Food and Accommodations

Albergue Victoria (Calle San Andres, 10; 941-426-105; albergue@casavictoria.com) is in a new (2014) building with shared or private rooms: 10 beds in two dorm rooms (€10) and two private rooms (€25-40). A shared communal meal at the long table in the kitchen adds more intimacy to this small and flawless, if basic place. The same owner runs a rural hotel, **Casa Victoria** (Plaza del Horno, 8; www.casavictoriarural.com; five rooms, €25-55), in another modern building; it has hefty wood ceiling beams, romantic 19th-century carved bedboards, and

throw carpets, and offers an alternative to dorm life.

The village bar and grill house, **Bar Jacobeo** (Plaza del Horno, 12; 941-426-072; €10), has a standard *menú del peregrino* as well as choices of platters, tapas, and special roasted dishes (the garlic roasted pork is succulent). Also worth trying are the grilled fish (often accompanied with a colorful salad), *morcilla* (blood sausage) and paprika spiced chickpea stew, and the *cocido* stew rich in pork, cabbage, potatoes, and carrots.

Santo Domingo de la Calzada   Km 563.3

It seems poetic that Santo Domingo de la Calzada—home of the most important engineer from the 11th and 12th centuries, who built Camino bridges, roads, churches, and hospices, and this town, among other things—is where you will cross the Rio Oja, the river that gives its name to the autonomous community of La Rioja. Santo Domingo (1019-1109) was born in Viloria de Rioja (Km 555.1) and chose the life of a hermit over that of a monk. As a young man, he retreated to the solitude of the wild territory around the Rio Oja and dedicated himself to prayer and a life devoted to God. A dream guided him to become a builder on the Camino and of service to pilgrims, and he spent his days thereafter making this territory safer and easier to traverse. *Calzada* means road, and Santo Domingo built many, often utilizing and extending defunct Roman roads. He picked this spot for his town because it was such a hard place for pilgrims to pass. It also is imbued with a special energy that comes from the fertile land and substantial river. Agriculture remains important here. Every September the town holds a festival of gratitude for the harvest, centered on **Nuestra Señora de la Plaza**.

Santo Domingo de la Calzada

AV BURGOS

CALLE RIO PALOMAREJOS

CALLE MAYOR

CATEDRAL DE SANTO DOMINGO DE LA CALZADA

RESTAURANTE LOS CABALLEROS

ALBERGUE DE LA COFRADÍA DEL SANTO

LA GALLINA QUE CANTÓ

AV CALAHORRA

AV DE LA RIOJA

C ISIDORO SALAS

Plaza del Santo

CATEDRAL BELL TOWER

ERMITA DE NUESTRA SEÑORA DE LA PLAZA

CALLE MAYOR

ABADÍA CISTERCIENSE

CALLE PINAR

HOSPEDERÍA CISTERCIENSE

PARADOR DE SANTO DOMINGO

AV JUAN CARLOS I

CASA AMPARO

CALLE SAN ROQUE

0   100 yds
0   100 m

© MOON.COM

Sights

The old town retains its medieval shape, and on arrival you are pulled magnetically to the solitary cathedral's bell tower in the **Plaza del Santo,** the small square just before the cathedral. On the way, shops selling little pastries baked into the shape of hens and roosters remind *peregrinos* of Santo Domingo's most famous miracle, recounted in the *Codex Calixtinus.* Slow down to take in the Plaza del Santo, the 12th-century bell tower (with 132 stairs that you can climb for the views), and the small Ermita de Nuestra Señora de la Plaza. Santo Domingo may have built the settlement's first chapel here, and before that, this square may have held an outdoor altar.

The adjacent square, reached by passing through arched passageways, holds the cathedral, a place of intricate beauty as well as the home to the famous miracle rooster and hen who saved a pilgrim's neck in the 12th century. Explore also the streets surrounding the cathedral

and notice the balconies hung with large bundles of drying red pepper.

Ermita de Nuestra Señora de la Plaza

Ermita de Nuestra Señora de la Plaza (Plaza del Santo, 5; 941-340-033; free) stands on the small square just before passing through the arcades passage to the cathedral. This small, Gothic-style hermitage chapel from the 15th and 16th centuries is a counterpoint to the cathedral's more grandiose statement about the importance of Santo Domingo, but it is no less spiritual. It possesses a single nave and beautiful stained-glass windows. One, left center from the nave, is simple and traditional, in blue and white glass depicting nothing other than the *seed of life* design (a six-petaled flower, a sacred geometric form that represents harmony and balance and the meeting of heaven and earth). The other, to the right of the altar, is a modern mix of Cubist and Realist styles, depicting a joyous and

Santo Domingo's Birds

The 12th-century *Codex Calixtinus* recounts the story a German family passing through Santo Domingo when their son was falsely accused of stealing silver from an innkeeper. The town hung him on the spot, but Santo Domingo intervened, lifting the boy up so that he would not die from the noose. The boy's parents then begged the judge, who was about to sit down to a delectable meal of roasted hen and rooster, to release their innocent son. He said he would do so as soon as the two birds on his plate sat up and sang. Santo Domingo again came to the rescue: That is just what the cooked fowl did, and the judge released the young man. The two birds you see today in the **Catedral de Santo Domingo de la Calzada** are among several pairs of the original birds (according to locals and legend) who take turns hanging out in the coop. The pairs are rotated often so as not to get too tired of being caged in such an unnatural setting. You can lodge with the other chickens if you stay at the **Casa de la Cofradía del Santo**.

Pilgrims have two rituals connected to visiting these two birds. In the days when they could reach them, they used to feed the birds bread; if the birds took the offering, *peregrinos* felt they were assured safe passage to Compostela. The other ritual was to gather fallen feathers to carry like a talisman of safety and good luck. This power of birds is old magic, one connected not only to Santo Domingo, but also to Mary (recall the falcon and dove in Nájera) and before her, Mari, the mother goddess and creator in Basque and Navarran folklore. In all cases, birds have acted as messengers of divine will. You can see this very association reinforced in the many bird images carved into capitals in churches all across the Camino, as well as in the Catedral de Santo Domingo de la Calzada.

very pregnant Mary, honoring both the Mother Mary in the Christian tradition and her older manifestation as the goddess of fertility and plenty dedicated to the health of the harvest.

In fact, the altar also holds a sculpture of Our Lady of the Plaza, who is the town's patroness of the harvest. She is a 16th-century replica of the earlier 14th-century Gothic Madonna and Child.

★ Catedral de Santo Domingo de la Calzada

The most famous surviving Camino structure in this town is the 13th-century **Catedral de Santo Domingo de la Calzada** (Calle El Cristo, s/n; 941-340-033; www.catedralsantodomingo.com; €5, €3 for pilgrims), site of the saint's tomb. It also contains living descendents of his miracle pair of fowl and an excellent collection of sacred art in the cloister; it preserves the lovely architectural and stone sculptural transitional style of the

13th century. This place is worth taking at least an hour to enjoy.

Around the **apse and altar**, you find the older Romanesque parts of the cathedral elegantly layered with Gothic features along the nave and side chapels. Capitals are intricately engraved with animated characters from the Bible and other sources.

The 14th- and 15th-century **cloister** exhibits one of the best collections in Spain of Romanesque and Gothic painted wood sculptures of Mary and Jesus, each with their own personalities set by each artisan who made them. One, **Nuestra Señora de la Leche,** from 1520, pragmatically holds out a bare breast full of milk to nurse her child. It is an image natural to early peoples and holds continuity with images of Greek and Roman depictions of the Mother Earth, whose breasts offer rich sustenance for all of creation.

The cathedral is open Mon.-Fri.,

9am-8:40pm (8pm, last entry allowed), Sat., 9am-7:20pm (7pm, last entry), and Sun. 9am-12:20pm and 2-8:40pm (8pm, last entry). Audio guides (€1) are available in English.

Santo Domingo's **tomb** is on the right side of the nave (in a sepulcher made by himself, according to legend), surrounded by grills and decorative embellishments largely from the 15th to the 18th centuries. The most moving part is his reclining image on the tomb, a hearty wild man with thick beard and kind countenance.

Near his mausoleum is what may be the fanciest **chicken coop** in all the Western world, housing the descendents of the original hen and rooster who saved an innocent pilgrim's life.

Festivals and Events

Every Saturday a **market** sets up on the Plaza Jacobea, a few blocks south of the cathedral, with 70 stands selling food products and general goods.

From late April to mid-May are the annual and extended celebrations, **Fiestas del Santo**, the feast days of patron saint Santo Domingo de la Calzada. If you pass through town during this time, you'll be in for a lot of eating and evening processions throughout town.

Santo Domingo de la Calzada's patroness is Our Lady of the Plaza, also known as the Lady of the Harvest, and she is revered in her small church, Ermita de la Plaza. She has two feast days, one to celebrate **Mary's assumption** (Aug. 15) into heaven, and the **Fiesta de Gracias** (Sept. 18), the harvest festival of thanks, when her image is carried in procession through town along with Santo Domingo's.

In December, typically around the 6th to the 9th, the town celebrates the

From top to bottom: entrance to Najera's Monasterio de Santa María la Real; a shop window in Santo Domingo de la Calzada; leaving Grañón.

Ferias de la Concepción (www.santo-domingodelacalzada.org), and also sets up the atmospheric **Mercado Medieval** and **Mercado del Camino**, medieval and Camino markets, that highlight thousand-year-old arts, crafts, foods, music, dance, and theater. There is also a small market selling organic foods.

Food

★ **Restaurante Los Caballeros** (Calle Mayor, 58; 941-342-789; www.restauranteloscaballeros.com; €30) is right on the Camino and serves the best of local produce, from acorn-fed *jamón de Bellota* to seasonal vegetable dishes based on local harvest. Try Riojan classics here, such as *pimientos rellenos de bacalao y gambas* (red peppers stuffed with cod and shrimp), *puerros a la vinagreta* (marinated leek), and *queso* (cheese) de Cameros, plus innovative delights such as octopus carpaccio with pistachios and aioli, seared cod on leek puree with pan-fried spinach and almonds, and orange flan with Calvados cream. It's worth the splurge.

Casa Amparo (Calle San Roque, 17; 941-342-125) is a local's traditional eatery with a semiformal dining room; it specializes in salads (including Caesar and Roquefort) as well as varied traditional dishes, such as *cordero al chilindrón* (stewed lamb with peppers, tomatoes, and onion) and grilled steak with roasted peppers. The extensive *menú del dia* (€14-15) can include crepes filled with spinach and ham, fresh artichokes sautéed with ham, and a colorful mixed *ensalada ilustrada*.

Of course, a stop in **La Gallina Que Cantó** (Calle Mayor, 32; 941-341-316; menu in English) may be *de rigueur* given its name, "the hen who sang." The good €12 *menú del dia* specializes in roasted meats (some cooked tableside on a charcoal brazier) and fresh vegetable dishes as well as *pinchos*, the signature one being fried shrimp skewered on top of a croquette made to look like a rooster. A long bar and casual dining area, with black-and-white-checkered floors and cozy tables, pack in locals as well as *peregrinos*.

Accommodations

Nuestra Señora de la Anunciación Abadía Cisterciense (Calle Mayor, 31; 941-340-700; www.cister-lacalzada.com; open May-Sept.; 32 beds in four dorm rooms; €6), is a delightful place run by Cistercian nuns in an 18th-century building, with spotless basic facilities and a moving Vespers service each evening (6:30pm). The same order also runs the **Hospedería Cisterciense** (Calle Pinar, 2; same phone and web; 78 rooms) with the same high standards, but for those desiring homey private rooms (€39-78). Both are in the same complex, but the entrances are from different sides of the building and different streets.

Located near the cathedral, the ★ **Albergue de la Cofradía del Santo** (Calle Mayor, 38-42; 941-343-390; www.alberguecofradiadelsanto.com; open all year; 217 beds in 11 dorm rooms; €7) is dedicated to Santo Domingo's original mission to serve pilgrims, and is a splendid place to stay for the traditional experience of pilgrim hospitality. Recently it underwent a large expansion and restoration; the whole complex reopened in 2009 with a massive number of beds in an equally massive and spacious setting, with beautiful wood and stone rooms and common spaces. Some call it a five-star *albergue*. Proprietors speak English.

Parador Santo Domingo (Plaza del San Francisco, 1; 941-340-300; www.parador.es; €95-150) is one of a group of state-run luxury hotels in refurbished and restored historic buildings; this one is a 12th-century pilgrims' hospital built by Santo Domingo near the cathedral, with Gothic arches and open spaces now occupied by medieval-inspired lounges. The large, opulent, historic rooms have terracotta tile floors, stone walls, wood-coffered ceilings, medieval-style tapestries, and plush-velvet-upholstered furnishings. On the premises is a restaurant highlighting Riojan cuisine.

Leaving Santo Domingo de la Calzada

Follow the way-markers out of Santo Domingo and cross the Río Oja onward toward Grañon. From here to Belorado, the Camino often passes parallel to and near the N-120 road, but the path is pleasant and sprinkled with several small settlements for breaks and refreshments. You remain in hilly country but rarely feel it, except for the surrounding beauty of rolling landscapes covered in fields of wheat and corn.

Grañon   Km 556.4

The pace of life in Grañon (pop. 255) is an experience in and of itself. This is a place that still lives by natural rhythms, from the beret-wearing grandfather sitting in his garage waving kindly to passing pilgrims, to the hawks flying overhead, frogs singing in the waterways, and the shepherd with his red, black, and cream sheep ambling up the slope. Grañon's hilltop view toward the west is also part of the appeal.

The town was a key spot since Celtiberian times, confirmed by archaeological discoveries of over 2,000-year-old burials here. Later, Romans lived here and called it "Libia." In the Middle Ages it was on the frontier between north and south, and by the time of the peak of the Camino in the 12th century, it was a diverse town of commerce and support with mixed populations of people, including a large Jewish community.

In the 1500s, this seemingly remote hilltop housed around 1,300 people. Today, Grañon is largely a practical and pragmatic town by design. You will soon find that the warmth of the locals extends from that grandfather through the rest of the town.

Grañon is known for two culinary specialties: its *sopa de ajo,* garlic soup (made with copious amounts of garlic, smoky paprika, onions, bread, and olive oil) and the local *morcilla,* blood sausage. But the main destination is the Iglesia de San Juan Bautista, which functions as a parish *albergue.*

Food and Accommodations

A great place to gather around pilgrim cheer, warm locals, and (at times) impromptu live music on guitars and piano, is at the brick and timber bar, **My Way** (Plaza de la Iglesia, 4; 656-605-272; €10) across from the Iglesia de San Juan Bautista. The bar offers excellent snacks, combined platters, and a *menú del peregrino* that may at times include a *sopa de ajo* or dish with *morcilla* (so be sure to ask); the selection of beers here is also larger than the usual Spanish bar, especially in wine country, and includes a good dark stout.

Right on the left side of the Camino as you enter Grañon is the **Iglesia de San Juan Bautista** (Calle Mayor, 1; open daily; free), which belonged to a 14th-century monastery that has since disappeared. A lot of the church is from four centuries of rebuilding with strong Baroque aesthetics. One piece, the baptismal font, with four faces peering out at you from the pedestal, dates to 1099 and is the sole survivor of the earlier monastery.

Iglesia de San Juan Bautista also funtions as the ★ **Albergue San Juan Bautista** (Calle Mayor, 1; 941-420-684; open all year; 40 beds in 2 dorm rooms; donation), offering sleeping places on mats on the floor in the attic and tower of the Romanesque church of San Juan. A stay here, while basic and rustic, is like no other in terms of atmosphere. The *hospitaleros* specialize in service and kindness, including an evening ritual of washing pilgrims' feet. They also hold evening prayer in the church after dinner, which is a delicious and copious communal meal (also by donation).

Leaving Grañon

The Camino departs Grañon from a point overlooking sweeping green rolling fields, akin to Middle Earth Shire country. By now, corn and wheat have long replaced vines. As you depart Grañon, keep your eyes open for the yellow trail markers directing you onto a trail to the right. (It is easy to keep going straight on the dirt road and miss this turnoff.)

On the way to Redecilla del Camino you'll pass a monument telling you that you've just left La Rioja. Welcome to the autonomous community of Castilla y León (Castile and León)!

Redecilla del Camino
Km 552.1

The main highlight in this hamlet of 112 is the Iglesia de la Virgen de la Calle, the Church of the Virgin of the Street.

Sights
Iglesia de la Virgen de la Calle

Strongly Baroque and 18th century, the original church (Calle Mayor, 19; 947-588-078; open daily; free) was built in the 12th century but has been heavily renovated. Its crown jewel is the surviving original Mozarabic baptismal font. It has elaborate engravings all around its bowl and stem depicting the idealized Celestial City, the heavenly version of Jerusalem. The pillar holding the font is stylized into eight pillars that support the city on high. This is no accident: eight is the Christian symbol of redemption, resurrection, and rebirth. In keeping with the continuity of Abrahamic faiths (and the font's makers, Christians from Islamic Spain), eight is the Islamic number of the gates of paradise, pretty much the same idea as redemption and resurrection as the means of entering heaven.

Food and Accommodations

Opened in 2016, **Albergue Essentia** (Calle Mayor, 34; 606-046-298; manuramirez6@ hotmail.com; open all year; 10 beds in two dorm rooms; €10) features brand new beds and rose-painted walls, with fluffy fleece blankets on each bed, making Redecilla a tempting place to stop for the night. The *albergue* is run with engagement and dedication by *hospitalero* José Manuel, who aspires to make a positive difference; he creates a gregarious atmosphere and serves up an excellent home-cooked communal dinner (€10) and breakfast (€3). His sweet dog Pintxo adds to the charm.

Leaving Redecilla del Camino

From here to San Juan Ortega, you are in the legendary territory of the **Montes de Oca,** hills of the goose, derived from the ancient Roman name Auca, which means "goose" (possibly named after the native geese that flock here and migrate through this area, but no one really knows for sure). Once dangerous terrain, where bandits hid in the hills and robbed vulnerable pilgrims, today it is a beautiful and safe place, allowing the feet and mind to wander. The river Oca runs through here, and the area gets its name from the Roman settlement along the riverbank known as Auca. Iberians and Celtiberians lived here before that, around 2,700 years ago. The name of the goose also links this place in more esoteric lore to the Game of the Goose.

Castildelgado
Km 550.5

The tiny hamlet of Castildelgado (pop. 40) has a 16th-century church, the most prominent feature on the horizon as you approach and leave, dedicated to **San Pedro**. A few paces away is the 14th-century **Ermita de Santa María del Campo**. Both are locked most of the time. Right on the side of the N-120, Castildelgado has a roadside *hostal* popular with both pilgrims and truckers.

Food and Accommodations

★ **Hostal El Chocolatero** (N-120/ Carretera Burgos-Logroño, 14; 947-588-063; www.elchocolatero.es; 37 rooms; €25-53) is like walking onto the set of the film *Bagdad Cafe,* with German, Dutch, American, and Spanish pilgrims, locals, and truckers stopping for social life and food, all managed by energetic and cheerful staff who will as easily check you into a room as serve you lunch. Rooms are small, basic, and spotless. Lunch and dinner *menús del dia* are fresh and delicious and can include garden-fresh salads and chorizo and tomato spaghetti, homemade chicken noodle soup, and grilled local trout with *jamon Serrano.*

Opened in 2016 in an old refurbished village house, **Albergue Bideluze** (Calle Mayor, 8; 616-647-115; www.albergue-bideluze.com; open Mar.-Oct) offers budget alternatives in this tiny place with brand-new, clean dorm rooms (two rooms with 16 beds, €10), one private room (€35), and a good evening meal (€11).

Viloria de Rioja
Km 548.6

Viloria de Rioja (pop. 45) was the birthplace of Santo Domingo de la Calzada in 1019. Little of the medieval village remains, but the homes are elegant, built of traditional wood beams, stone, and plaster, and painted in warm ochre and mustard tones. In homage to Santo Domingo, you'll see river-rock inlay mosaics of a rooster and hen on the central village's pavement.

Sights
Iglesia de Nuestra Señora de la Asunción
Viloria's heavily fortified, rebuilt, and now largely 17th-century Iglesia de Nuestra Señora de la Asunción originated as an earlier Romanesque church. In the center of its nave stands the original baptismal font used to baptize Santo Domingo de la Calzada (it is infused with a strong mana). It is a solid bowl carved from stone in the 11th century, with engraved images around the rim that are now too faded to identify. The village tradition is to return here, no matter where a person is now living, to baptize one's children from the same font as Santo Domingo's. The church is rarely open; inquire in the *albergue* about options to visit inside.

Food and Accommodations
Viloria de la Rioja is home of the popular *albergue,* ★ **Acácio y Orietta** (Calle Nueva, 6; 947 585-220; www.acacioyorietta.com; open all year but contact ahead in winter; 10 beds; €6). Its modern fame comes both from the sincere kindness of its *hospitaleros,* Acácio da Paz from Brazil and Orietta Prendin from Italy, and from the support Brazilian spiritual author Paulo Coelho (*The Pilgrimage*) has given the *albergue.* Acácio and Orietta are dedicated to serving the Camino and *peregrinos* with generosity, warmth, and a strong ecumenical and spiritual focus. The single dorm room with both bunk and single beds, the ample bathrooms, and the book-filled salon are impeccable and outfitted in traditional stone, stucco, and wood beams. The communal dinner and breakfast are by donation.

Leaving Viloria de Rioja
The Camino continues to **Villamayor del Río** (Km 545.3, pop. 35), crossing the Río Villamayor, and onward to Belorado, where you first begin to feel the ascent deeper into the Montes de Oca.

Belorado   Km 540.3

Built into hills along the Rio Tirón, Belorado (pop. 1,724) harbors caves once occupied by early Christian and medieval hermits. The town is topped with a castle ruin, which you can make out as a stacked brown-red earth form on the hilltop to the right of the Camino as you walk into town. Every Monday, the general goods and food **market** sets up in the Plaza Mayor.

By the 10th century, Belorado was firmly in Christian hands but continued to shelter Muslim and Jewish communities. Belorado became a market town by 1116, and as the Camino grew more popular, many others settled here, and several neighborhoods developed diverse populations of Christians (mostly Castilian), Iberian Jews, Muslims, and settlers from France.

Sights

Little of the castle remains, but a church, **Iglesia de Santa María** (Calle Mayor; www.belorado.es), still stands at the foot of the castle. Its most distinctive feature is the slightly horseshoe-arched entrance that hints at a possible Islamic influence. The interior, rebuilt in the 16th century, is mostly late Gothic. A 17th-century retable shows both Santiago Peregrino and Santiago Matamoros. A beautiful, time-worn 13th-century Romanesque carving of Mary anchors the center.

After passing the church and the organic warmth of the hillside and old stone, entering the modern town has a contrasting functional and pragmatic feel, but the new town also features a large and inviting main square, the **Plaza Mayor**. On one corner of the square, the **Iglesia de San Pedro** shows off a neo-Mudéjar tower done in the 17th century, replicating the geometric brick work style associated with Iberia's medieval Muslims. San Pedro is mostly 18th century but originated as a 13th-century temple.

Food and Accommodations

The **Albergue Cuatro Cantones** (Calle Hipólito López Bernal, 10; 947-580-591; Mar.-Oct.; 65 beds in six dorm rooms beds; €8-12), with hanging potted flowers on its balconies, is distinguished for its sturdy wooden bunks and its designated room for snorers, leaving the other five rooms for peaceful uninterrupted slumber. The refuge also has a swimming pool and a small garden. The four *hospitaleros* (the "four cantons") manage the place with a relaxed and friendly atmosphere. A good **restaurant** serves up dinner (€11.50) and a breakfast buffet (€4). Be sure to stand at the top of the stairs and look down to see the colorful tiles inlaid in each step. Proprietors speak English.

Albergue-Pensión Caminante (Calle Mayor, 36; 947-580-231; g.caminante@ hotmail.com; 22 beds in one bunkhouse, €6; eight private rooms, €25-45) feels like an appealing mix of a hunting lodge (elk antlers mounted between two wonderful fireplaces) and a family home (cozy lounge and sleeping areas and a private courtyard garden). There is a communal meal (€10) and breakfast (€3). Open from Mar.-Oct.

Hotel Jacobeo (Avenida de Burgos, 3; 947-580-010; www.hoteljacobeo.net; 16 rooms; €45-65) is a roadside hotel built in 1850 and serving as an inn since 1888. Rooms are pristine, with ceiling beams and firm beds with crisp linens in bold stripes. The hotel **bar** serves daily inspired *pinchos* and tapas, such as skewers of shrimp and mushroom, anchovies and olives, and other creative bites. Proprietors speak English.

Leaving Belorado

The Camino weaves around the Plaza Mayor and then departs the town. It crosses over the N-120 and then, via a wooden footbridge, passes over the Río Tirón, where it veers left and follows a footpath to Tosantos. Arriving at Tosantos takes you higher up onto a raised plateau, with excellent views of the honeycomb-colored cliffs jutting out from the ridge to the right, the most dramatic rock face, which houses a cave now enclosed by Tosanto's Ermita de la Virgen de la Peña.

Tosantos   Km 535.4

As the village of Tosantos (pop. 56) proudly proclaims, "here is a tiny place with enormous beauty." It's an unusual beauty: stark, arid, textured, and dramatic, with chickpea-colored cliffs that jut into the settlement, and a chapel overhead that is built of the same stone: the Ermita Virgen de la Peña.

Sights
Ermita Virgen de la Peña
The Ermita Virgen de la Peña was built to honor a discovery of the image of the child Jesus, which, legend has it, was found on this site in 712. (The timeline doesn't mesh, as the sculpture is from the 12th century, but it's still a lovely place and a lovely story.) Chances to visit the cave-like interior are limited to June 15-Sept 30 (9-11am and 5-7pm; free), after which it remains closed for the rest of the year. In summer, the image is held in **Iglesia de San Esteban**, and pilgrims can view it there. It then passes the rest of the year in retreat in the cave of the hermitage and is not visible to visitors.

Iglesia de San Esteban
Iglesia de San Esteban, the lower church in the village center, is where the image of Jesus found at Ermita Virgen de la Peña is held in summer. As sacred to the village is the hundred-year-old **chestnut tree** in San Esteban's church yard. You'll see it on your right in front of the church as you pass on the Camino. Next to Iglesia de San Esteban there once stood a pilgrims' hospital.

Food and Accommodations
Mats on the floor and a communal dinner and breakfast reflect the traditional medieval Camino spirit of simplicity and service at the **Albergue San Francisco de Asís** (947-580-371; open Apr.-Oct. to October; 30 places; donation). All 30 places are mattresses on the floor, and the communal dinner and breakfast are by donation. There is an evening ceremony for pilgrims.

Leaving Tosantos
As you leave Tosantos, be sure to look back toward the cliffs for some of the best views of the hermitage. The terrain opens up, so it feels as if you are rising onto a plateau. You are making your way up into the lower slopes of Montes de Oca, and you will pass two hamlets along the way, both with services: **Villambistia** (Km 539.9) and **Espinosa** (Km 538.3), where the excellent ★ **Albergue-Bar-Cantina de Espinosa** (Calle Baruelo, 17; 947-614-323; €5-9) turns out made-to-order omelets, salads, and sandwiches. It's the perfect fuel for the upcoming trek into thick pine forest. (The *albergue* is on Calle Barruelo, 23, 630-104-925, with 10 beds, €5. Open year round, but closed Tues.)

Soon after Espinosa, on the right of the Camino, a beehive structure appears. This small ruin is all that remains of the **Monasterio de San Felices de Oca** (Km 535.6), and a vast field of wheat all but erases an influential 9th-century Mozarabic monastery in northern Spain.

Villafranca Montes de Oca   Km 528.5

Cross a small, tree-shaded bridge over the Oca river and in a few meters you'll arrive in Villafranca Montes de Oca (pop. 110), the heart of all things *oca* (goose). To remind you of this, a sign for the village grocery store depicts a goose dressed as a pilgrim.

Villafranca Montes de Oca is a small but pretty village set on the edge of a forested hill, a respite from the open exposure you endured to get here. This area was occupied by Celtiberians over 2,700 years ago, followed by Romans, and the village's name, *villa franca* ("French town"), speaks of a significant Frankish population that existed here in the Middle Ages.

⊕ Detour: Ermita de Nuestra Señora de Oca

Nowhere on the Camino is the connection between the goose and mother goddess more explicit than the village of **Villafranca de Oca** (www.villafrancamontesdeoca.es), whose patroness, **Nuestra Señora de Oca**, is known locally as "nuestra madre la oca" ("our mother the goose"). This is a full reference to the deepest connections the Game of the Goose makes, both to the Camino and to the earth goddess reborn as Mary.

The stone and terracotta hermitage of Nuestra Señora de Oca dates to the 12th and 13th centuries, and her icon on the altar to the 12th; both are in the Romanesque style. Local lore has it that the **hermitage** was built on an older Celtiberian shrine dedicated to the earth goddess and her symbol, the goose. Other earth goddesses in northern Spain are congruous with this: They usually reside in caves or watery places, and many also have bird feet. This shrine is said to have been associated with the Celtic goose, a sacred animal who served an ancient goddess by protecting her people from harm. The site is also referred to as *el pozo de Indalecio,* the well of Indalecio; legend recounts that he performed

miracles here and that locals buried him here in the 1st century.

The chapel you see today is set near the edge of the Oca river and has a wide bell tower and an open arched and covered porch entrance. It's closed except for feast days, but the magic here is outside anyway. On the north apse side of the chapel, you'll find a triple cascading stone fountain, the **Fuentes de Oca**, San Indalecio's "well." Some Spanish writers think this is the well that is represented on the square of "The Well" in the Game of the Goose.

Villafranca de Oca is also the site of annual local pilgrimage, every June 11, commemorating San Indalecio's feast day.

The hermitage of Nuestra Señora de Oca is a 2-kilometer (1.2-miles) detour south of the Camino (a 25-minute walk each way). To get there, head due south following the N-120 from the Iglesia de Santiago in Villafranca Montes de Oca, essentially walking parallel to the Río Oca to your left. In about 700 meters (0.4 mile), you'll see signs for the hermitage that will lead you to veer left off the N-120 and onto a smaller road that continues south to the hermitage. Allow an hour to make the round-trip.

The village's main surviving historic sight is the **Hospital de la Reina**, also known as **Hospital de Peregrinos San Antón Abad**, a pilgrims' hospital built in 1377 to care for the poor and passing *peregrinos*. A local, inspired by walking the Camino, returned to restore the hospital and opened it in 2009 as **San Antón Abad** to once again serve pilgrims. The Camino passes it on the right, with the **Iglesia de Santiago** (a reconstruction from 1800) on the left.

Food and Accommodations

The historic Hospital de la Reina has been beautifully restored and now contains the ★ **San Antón Abad** (Calle del Hospital, 4; www.hotelsanantonabad.com; 947-582-150; open mid-Mar.-mid-Nov.; 49 dorm beds, three private *albergue* rooms, 14

hotel rooms). All budgets are welcome at this establishment, which contains both a luxury three-star hotel and a more modest *albergue*. You have two choices, the private and luxurious hotel rooms (€60-71 for a room with bath) or the dormitory option in the *albergue* (€9-10 for a bed, €30-45 for a private room), both in the same grand 14th-century pilgrims' hospital. Both *albergue* and hotel share the elegant dining room and flamboyant black-and-white-striped breakfast room. A good pilgrims' menu offers salads, pastas, grilled meats, and fish for €10.

Leaving Villafranca Montes de Oca

On the 12 kilometers (7.5 miles) from here to San Juan de la Ortega, there are no support services (other than a lady who

Clockwise from top: horseshoe arched entrance of Belorado's Iglesia de Santa María; Refugio Acacio y Orietta in Viloria de Rioja; Ermita Virgen de la Peña in Tosantos; hotel and *albergue* San Antón Abad; sign in Villafranca Montes de Oca.

sometimes offers refreshments from the back of her car midway, but that's an unpredictable offering). Stock up on food and water before leaving.

The Camino leaves Villafranca Montes de Oca by passing San Antón Abad on the right and the Iglesia de Santiago on the left. Way-markers lead you up a slope in the village and then turn right, taking you off the paved path and onto a narrow dirt trail heading straight up the hill and into the forest. The forests you are about to enter have tested many pilgrims; it's easy to see why this once made a good bandit hideout. (Thankfully, the Camino is well marked now, so you won't get lost if you observe the markers.) Once you clear the trees (in 1.8 km/1.1 mi), the view of the Montes de Oca and the Sierra de la Demanda is beautiful, from 1,100 meters (3,609 feet) high. The path will descend into pine and fern forest. In another 1.9 kilometers (1.2 miles), you'll reach the the **Monumento de los Caídos** (Km 524.8), a Civil War monument marking a tragic mass grave. It's a startling and sobering sight.

The path continues downhill, then climbs to the **Alto de Valbuena** (Km 521.9; 1,162 meters/3,812 feet) in 3 kilometers (1.9 miles). It will climb again and oscillate like this once more, but less dramatically, continuing through pine forest, until you make a full descent into the valley and village of San Juan de Ortega. If you are lucky, at about the midway point, the lady playing Joaquin Sabina (the Bob Dylan of Spain) will be there on the forest's edge with a table and umbrella, selling water, juice, and snacks from the trunk of her car. The forest is full of acrobatic blue and yellow titmice and the pretty song of the European robin.

San Juan de la Ortega   Km 516.4

Born Juan Velázquez, San Juan de Ortega (1080-1163) was Santo Domingo de la Calzada's student and joined him in building roads, bridges, churches, and hospices on the Camino in service to pilgrims, making the Camino safer. Like Santo Domingo, he preferred a solitary, hermitic life and the physical labor of taming the wilds. Ortega comes

hamlet, monastery, and church in San Juan de la Ortega

An Ancient Solar Alignment

Iglesia de San Nicolás de Barí orients to an important solar alignment on the spring and autumn equinoxes, every **March 20/21** and **September 20/21**. Around 5pm on the equinox, when the sun marks the exact midpoint of the day where night and day are equal, a ray of light enters the left-side back window of the nave, which faces west and the lowering sun, and beams perfectly onto the engraved capital of the pillar on the left of the altar, lighting up the scene of Mary and her cousin Elizabeth embracing in celebration at Elizabeth's news that she too is pregnant. (Six months after Mary gave birth to Jesus, Elizabeth gave birth to Saint John the Baptist.) There is more to this Biblical tale than meets the eye: in early Christianity, Jesus and John represented the dance of light in the cycle of the year and the promise of light's return. Their birthdays are exactly six months apart. Christmas is the winter solstice, the ancient pagan association with the rebirth of light on the shortest day of the year. Saint John the Baptist was born on the summer solstice, the longest day of the year, a promise that light will return even as the days grow shorter. That engraving, of Mary and Elizabeth, is exquisite in its emotions and detail. The equinoxes illuminating them also tells us that the church builders held the two lights as equally important for the process of life and spiritual illumination.

from *ortiga,* which means "nettle," and it is here that he cleared a particularly inhospitable valley—full of nettles and bandits—and made it a more agreeable place to pass.

The whole village of 20 people is centered on the joined building complex of monastery and church. Every June 2, surrounding villages make a local pilgrimage, a *romería,* to San Juan de la Ortega.

■■■ Top Experience ■■■

★ Iglesia de San Nicolás de Barí

This church (947-560-438 and 947-277-751; daily spring-autumn 10am-7pm; free) is dedicated to San Nicolás de Barí, who saved San Juan's life when the saint was returning from his pilgrimage to the Holy Land and his boat hit treacherous waters. In thanks, San Juan vowed to build a church in San Nicolás's honor. The church is pleasingly wide and square, with a central altar flanked on each side by smaller niches.

San Juan not only initiated and helped build this Romanesque church; he also died here, and his simple and appealing tomb, from the 12th century, is set in the niche to the left of the altar, which is usually illuminated with dozens of candles set on the floor around his sepulcher. Legend recounts that when people opened the tomb, white honeybees were discovered inside, and the scent of roses filled the air. (Rose perfume is the scent of heaven, and honeybees are an ancient symbol of rebirth—even reincarnation—as well as prosperity, fertility, and unborn souls waiting for their right time to incarnate.) San Juan is seen as a protector of children, one reason why women desiring children visited his tomb.

The right side of the church is a Zen-inspired meditation space, with colorful cushions on the floor and several long candles lit and set in a stone bowl filled with sand. The parish invites visitors to sit in quiet contemplation. A more ornate late Gothic stone arched canopy in the church center surrounds and covers an alabaster tomb dedicated to San Juan that was engraved with scenes from his life by Gil de Siloé in 1474; however, the older 12th-century tomb, noted above, is where San Juan really is, allowing a more personal veneration of this gentle saint. The Romanesque elements of the church are some of the best engravings of the whole Camino, from the detailed and expressive forms in the capitals around the altar to the simplicity of San Juan's original tomb.

The church is most impressive on the spring and autumn equinox, when a beam of sunlight perfectly illuminates a capital featuring a scene of Mary and her cousin Elizabeth.

The church is open daily in spring to autumn (another hat tip to the equinoxes); if you find it closed, call or ask at the *albergue* or the bar. Entry is free, inviting you to really savor the church as an ecumenical place of meditation, prayer, and peace. Daily **mass** and pilgrims' blessing are at 6pm.

Food and Accommodations

Just beyond the monastery quarters of the parish *albergue* is the ★ **Bar Marcela** (Calle Igelsia, 3; 947-560-092 or 606-198-734; open throughout the day, €5-10), in the same complex as the monastery/*albergue* and open from spring to early autumn. It is a positively congenial place, and a magnet for pilgrims. I seem to meet more people from all walks of life here than anywhere else, perhaps because it is the only eatery in the Lilliputian village. The staff are savvy and upbeat, and the chef churns out tasty made-to-order omelets, salads, sandwiches, and more.

Past the church, and attached to it, is the church *albergue* in the old monastery, **Albergue del Monasterio de San Juan de Ortega** (Calle de la Iglesia, 1; 947-560-438; www.alberguesanjuandeortega.es; open Mar.-Oct.; 60 beds in three dorm rooms; €10). It is famous for its garlic soup, a tradition begun by Father José María Marroquin (d.2008), who was assigned to oversee San Juan de Ortega in the 1980s when the Camino began growing in popularity. This is a legendary place to stay on the modern camino for its old-style *peregrino* hospitality and amazing garlic soup as a part

of the communal meal (€9). It isn't for everyone; many have complained about the worn beds, bath, and kitchen. But that's not the point of this place: people love the spiritual experience.

An alternative exists: on the left as you enter and just before you pass the church, you will see the very comfortable rural inn, **Hotel Rural La Henera** (Calle de la Iglesia, 4; 606-198-734; www.sanjuanortega.es; 10 rooms; €44-55).

Leaving San Juan de la Ortega

After San Juan de la Ortega, the path briefly enters a pine forest, then emerges into the open rolling terrain leading to the Sierra de Atapuerca and the oldest site of humanity in Europe. As you walk, consider that the earth underfoot hides ancient passageways slowly carved by the flow of subterranean water. Every now and then, one of those tunnels or caverns opened to the surface, offering shelter to ancient people and animals. Over time, they were covered up again or collapsed, preserving ancient remains underground.

The path begins to descend as it nears the village of **Agès** (Km 512.8; pop. 59), which in the 11th century belonged to the Monasterio de Santa María la Real in Nájera. Soon after, you'll see the single-arch **Puente Canto,** another bridge built by San Juan de Ortega, bridging a creek on your left. One kilometer (0.6 miles) before reaching Atapuerca village, on your right, is a road leading to the **Atapuerca Visitor Reception Center** (www.museoevolucionhumana.com; Tues.-Fri., 3:45pm, Sat., 11am and 3:45pm, and Sun., 11am), where you can arrange a visit to the Atapuerca archeological site (€6) and the didactic archaeological park (€5). It's also possible to arrange a visit from the **Museum of Human Evolution** in **Burgos** (Km 489.7). The actual archaeological site is in the rise of mountains to your left and ahead of you.

Atapuerca Village
Km 510.3

The approach into Atapuerca (pop. 124) is dramatic: a big billboard dominates the horizon, with an artist's sketch of an ancient Atapuercan who lived here some 1.2 million years ago, looking over his shoulder at you and grinning. Behind the billboard are the pretty terracotta rooftops of the village of Atapuerca, clustered together at the foot of the rising Sierra de Atapuerca mountains, a limestone range full of porous sinkholes and subterranean caves covered with low-growing, scrubby bushes and wheat fields. Consider stopping here for the night to feel this ancient land work on you: it has provided shelter, food, and drink to humans for more than a million years. The Milky Way is pretty here at night, too.

As a village, Atapuerca has existed since around 750, when it was a small Christian settlement. In the 12th century, the Hospitallers San Juan de Jerusalén controlled the settlement and used it as a frontier town in conquests against the south, as well as a place to shelter pilgrims. Its present church, **Iglesia de San Martín**, is from the 15th century.

Food and Accommodations
★ **Comosapiens** (Calle Camino de Santiago, 24 y 26; 947-430-501; www.comospaiens.com; €25) already shows its fun in the wordplay (*como* can mean *like* and also *I eat*), and the English-speaking staff extend this cheer in their upbeat service and exquisite food. The dining room, a restored 19th-century barn of warm golden stone and a high wood-beam ceiling, would please our ancestors who hunted and gathered here. The contemporary Castilian cuisine features carefully procured ingredients: pan-fried morcilla with rainbow-colored garden vegetables, organic ginger-pumpkin soup, chickpea-quinoa salad, and eggplant carpaccio.

A wonderful English-speaking Castilian-Aquitanian family with a passion for prehistory as well as hospitality runs ★ **Casa Rural Papasol** (Calle de la Iglesia, 31; 947-430-320; www.burgosturismorural.com; €45-65). A classic country inn with contemporary rooms with solid beds and turn-of-the-century armoires, Papasol is also one of the favorite watering holes for the archaeologists who excavate at Atapuerca. The inn features a private garden with views all around, and a magnetic bar, dining area, and wood-burning fireplace lounge on the ground floor. The **restaurant** offers a la carte options and three set menus: *del dia, vegetarian,* and *especial* (€12, €12, and €18).

Leaving Atapuerca
Right out of the village, the trail makes a steep ascent then a descent over the Sierra de Atapuerca at ridge of the **Alto de Matagrande** (1,078 meters/3,537 feet), then continues as a small incline downhill through the village of Cardeñuela Riopico.

Cardeñuela Riopico
Km 504

A village of 90 on Burgos's outskirts, Cardeñuela Riopico is the first settlement you'll see with services after traversing the Sierra de Atapuerca. Its landmark is the **Iglesia de Santa Eulalia**, a more modern church with Renaissance aesthetics and a Renaissance image of Saint Eulalia, protector of the vulnerable (and also against bad weather).

Accommodations
Hospitalera Miryam Janeth Santa Fernández, who loves interacting with *peregrinos,* runs a great rest stop and accommodations just before Burgos that vegetarians will enjoy. **Albergue Santa Fe** (Calle Huertos, 2; 626-352-269; www.baralberguesantafe.com; open year-round) is known for its excellent

Top to bottom: approaching the Sierra de Atapuerca after San Juan de la Ortega; village café in Agés; near Atapuerca village and archaeological site.

vegetarian communal meal options (€8). Opened in 2014, this is a clean, warm, and modern oasis on the banks of the Río Pico. There is a relaxing terrace and bar-restaurant that is more elegant than most, with white tablecloths and chandeliers. The *albergue* has 15 beds in two dorm rooms (€8-10) and also two private rooms (€25-35). Breakfast is €2.

Leaving Cardeñuela Riopico

The approach to Burgos gets complicated. There are three paths, two of which were recently devised to bypass the traditional Camino's last 7 kilometers (4.3 miles) through industrial and unpleasant outer Burgos before hitting the city center. Whatever path you choose, Burgos is 12.5-14.5 kilometers (7.8-9 miles) away, and services are limited.

The traditional path is the shortest in distance, but the longest psychologically. It's also the best marked, so if you are concerned with time and ease, stay on it and follow it to **Villafria** (Km 505.6). It is the northernmost route and enters the city from the northeast.

Two **alternate paths** weave closer to the Río Arlanzón, the river that runs right through the heart of historic Burgos. The paths begin as one, then split at the settlement of Castañares. To take one of these paths, 1 kilometer (0.6 miles) after **Orbaneja Riopico**, instead of following the traditional path straight ahead to Villafria, look for markers directing you to go left on a southwest route to **Castañares,** following the right side of the Río Pico. In Castañares, the two paths split. One directs you to make a right and heads due west into Burgos, staying on the north side of the river Arlanzón (but you won't be able to see the river). The other path in Castañares continues straight and south, then veers right after the town, crosses the river Arlanzón, and turns sharply to the right to follow the south bank of the river into Burgos. This is the longest but by far the most pleasant path, leading through the city's riverside park and also passing the still-active 15th-century monastery, **Cartuja de Santa Maria de Miraflores**, set in its own rarified patch of riverside pine forest.

Castile and León

Burgos to León

Km: 489.7-309
Total Distance: 181 km (112 miles)
Days: 7-9

Burgos to Carrión de los Condes

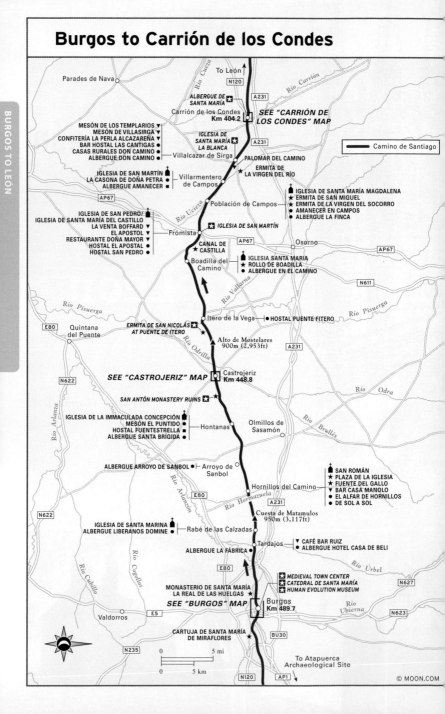

Parades de Nava

To León
N120

Río Cueza

Río Carrión

A231

ALBERGUE DE
SANTA MARÍA

Carrión de los Condes
Km 404.2

SEE "CARRIÓN DE
LOS CONDES" MAP

MESÓN DE LOS TEMPLARIOS ▼
MESÓN DE VILLASIRGA ▼
CONFITERÍA LA PERLA ALCAZAREÑA ▼
BAR HOSTAL LAS CANTIGAS ▼
CASAS RURALES DON CAMINO ●
ALBERGUE DON CAMINO ■

Villalcazar de Sirga

IGLESIA DE
SANTA MARÍA
LA BLANCA

A231

Camino de Santiago

PALOMAR DEL CAMINO

ERMITA DE
LA VIRGEN DEL RÍO

IGLESIA DE SAN MARTÍN ▲
LA CASONA DE DOÑA PETRA ●
ALBERGUE AMANECER ■

Villarmentero
de Campos

AP67

Río Ucieza

Población de Campos

IGLESIA DE SANTA MARÍA MAGDALENA ▲
ERMITA DE SAN MIGUEL ★
ERMITA DE LA VIRGEN DEL SOCORRO ★
AMANECER EN CAMPOS ●
ALBERGUE LA FINCA ■

IGLESIA DE SAN PEDRO/
IGLESIA DE SANTA MARÍA DEL CASTILLO ▲
LA VENTA BOFFARD ▼
EL APOSTOL ▼
RESTAURANTE DOÑA MAYOR ▼
HOSTAL EL APOSTAL ●
HOSTAL SAN PEDRO ●

Frómista

IGLESIA DE SAN MARTÍN

CANAL DE
CASTILLA

AP67

Osorno

AP67

Boadilla del
Camino

IGLESIA SANTA MARÍA ▲
ROLLO DE BOADILLA ★
ALBERGUE EN EL CAMINO ■

N611

Río Valdarna

Río Pisuerga

Río Pisuerga

Itero de la Vega

HOSTAL PUENTE FITERO

ERMITA DE SAN NICOLÁS
AT PUENTE DE ITERO

E80

Quintana
del Puente

Río Odrilla

Alto de Mostelares
900m (2,953ft)

A231

N622

SEE "CASTROJERIZ" MAP

Castrojeriz
Km 448.8

Río Odra

SAN ANTÓN MONASTERY RUINS ★

IGLESIA DE LA IMMACULADA CONCEPCIÓN ▲
MESÓN EL PUNTIDO ●
HOSTAL FUENTESTRELLA ■
ALBERGUE SANTA BRÍGIDA ■

Hontanas

Olmillos de
Sasamón

Río Brullés

Río Arlanza

ALBERGUE ARROYO DE SANBOL ●

Arroyo de
Sanbol

SAN ROMÁN ▲
PLAZA DE LA IGLESIA ★
FUENTE DEL GALLO ★
BAR CASA MANOLO ▼
EL ALFAR DE HORNILLOS ●
DE SOL A SOL ■

N622

Río Arlanzón

Hornillos del Camino

E80

Río Hormazuela

A231

Cuesta de Matamulos
950m (3,117ft)

IGLESIA DE SANTA MARINA ▲
ALBERGUE LIBERANOS DOMINE ■

Rabé de las Calzadas

Tardajos

CAFÉ BAR RUIZ ▼
ALBERGUE HOTEL CASA DE BELI ●

Río Cogollos

ALBERGUE LA FÁBRICA ●

Río Úrbel

E80

N627

MONASTERIO DE SANTA MARÍA
LA REAL DE LAS HUELGAS ★
SEE "BURGOS" MAP

MEDIEVAL TOWN CENTER
CATEDRAL DE SANTA MARÍA
HUMAN EVOLUTION MUSEUM

Burgos
Km 489.7

Río Cubillo

Valdorros

E5

Río Ubierna

N623

CARTUJA DE SANTA MARÍA
DE MIRAFLORES ★

BU30

N235

0   5 mi

0   5 km

To Atapuerca
Archaeological Site

N120

AP1

© MOON.COM

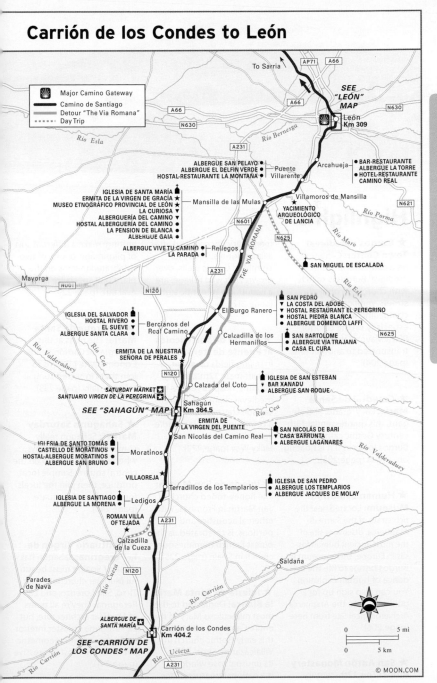

Carrión de los Condes to León

To Sarria

SEE "LEÓN" MAP

León
Km 309

Arcahueja
- BAR-RESTAURANTE
- ALBERGUE LA TORRE
- HOTEL-RESTAURANTE CAMINO REAL

ALBERGUE SAN PELAYO ●
ALBERGUE EL DELFIN VERDE ●
HOSTAL-RESTAURANTE LA MONTAÑA ●
Puente Villarente

IGLESIA DE SANTA MARÍA ★
ERMITA DE LA VIRGEN DE GRACIA ★
MUSEO ETNOGRÁFICO PROVINCIAL DE LEÓN ★
LA CURIOSA ▼
ALBERGUERÍA DEL CAMINO ●
HOSTAL ALBERGUERÍA DEL CAMINO ●
LA PENSION DE BLANCA ●
ALBERGUE GAIA ●
Mansilla de las Mulas

Villamoros de Mansilla

YACIMIENTO ARQUEOLÓGICO DE LANCIA

ALBERGUE VIVE TU CAMINO ●
LA PARADA ●
Reliegos

SAN MIGUEL DE ESCALADA

Mayorga

El Burgo Ranero
- SAN PEDRO
- LA COSTA DEL ADOBE
- HOSTAL RESTAURANT EL PEREGRINO
- HOSTAL PIEDRA BLANCA
- ALBERGUE DOMENICO LAFFI

IGLESIA DEL SALVADOR ▇
HOSTAL RIVERO ▼
EL SUEVE ▼
ALBERGUE SANTA CLARA ●
Bercianos del Real Camino

Calzadilla de los Hermanillos
- SAN BARTOLOME
- ALBERGUE VIA TRAJANA
- CASA EL CURA

ERMITA DE LA NUESTRA SEÑORA DE PERALES ★

Calzada del Coto
- IGLESIA DE SAN ESTEBAN
- BAR XANADU
- ALBERGUE SAN ROQUE

SATURDAY MARKET ▇
SANTUARIO VIRGEN DE LA PEREGRINA ▇

SEE "SAHAGÚN" MAP
Sahagún
Km 364.5

ERMITA DE LA VIRGEN DEL PUENTE ★
San Nicolás del Camino Real
- SAN NICOLÁS DE BARI
- CASA BARRUNTA
- ALBERGUE LAGANARES

IGLESIA DE SANTO TOMÁS ▇
CASTELLO DE MORATINOS ▼
HOSTAL-ALBERGUE MORATINOS ●
ALBERGUE SAN BRUNO ●
Moratinos

VILLAOREJA ★

IGLESIA DE SANTIAGO ▇
ALBERGUE LA MORENA ●
Ledigos

Terradillos de los Templarios
- IGLESIA DE SAN PEDRO
- ALBERGUE LOS TEMPLARIOS
- ALBERGUE JACQUES DE MOLAY

ROMAN VILLA OF TEJADA ★

Calzadilla de la Cueza

Saldaña

Parades de Nava

ALBERGUE DE SANTA MARÍA ▇
Carrión de los Condes
Km 404.2

SEE "CARRIÓN DE LOS CONDES" MAP

Major Camino Gateway
Camino de Santiago
Detour "The Via Romana"
Day Trip

THE VIA ROMANA

Río Esla
Río Bernesga
Río Porma
Río Moro
Río Esla
Río Cea
Río Valderaduey
Río Cea
Río Valderaduey
Río Carrión
Río Cueza
Río Ucieza
Río Carrión

0   5 mi
0   5 km

© MOON.COM

Highlights

★ **Burgos's Medieval Town Center:** Centering on a cathedral and castle, medieval Burgos is so rich with churches, cobbled streets, public squares, and compelling terraced cafés—especially on the colorful Plaza Mayor—that you feel transported to another time (page 204).

★ **Catedral de Santa María:** Lacy, grand, and elegant, this quintessential 13th-century Gothic cathedral in Burgos looks as if it is floating on clouds (page 205).

★ **Human Evolution Museum:** Located near the rich strata of the Sierra de Atapuerca, discovery site of the most ancient human fossils in Europe, this museum in Burgos brings to life the evidence of human evolution. You can also sign up for a guided visit to the Atapuerca Archaeological Site from here (page 206).

★ **San Antón Monastery Ruins:** This 12th-century monastery once looked after ailing pilgrims. Today its crumbled Gothic walls, overgrown with wild foliage, are a hauntingly romantic sight (page 217).

★ **Ermita de San Nicolás at Puente de Itero:** Set in rolling fields of wheat, this intimate 12th-century pilgrims' hospice retains its medieval character. Pilgrims can still stay here and share a communal meal by candlelight, then gaze up at the Milky Way (page 222).

★ **Iglesia de San Martín:** The honey-toned church of San Martín in Frómista, with ethereal acoustics and proportions, is celebrated as the purest French Romanesque church in Spain (page 225).

★ **Iglesia de Santa María la Blanca:** Dedicated to the most miraculous Mary of the entire Camino, La Blanca, this early Gothic church in Villalcázar de Sirga, with its unusual rose window, is a national treasure. After

visiting, make a different sort of pilgrimage: to one of two celebrated taverns on the plaza that specialize in medieval fare (page 229).

★ **Albergue de Santa María:** The nuns at this *albergue* in Carrión de los Condes invite pilgrims to join them in sacred song at 6:30pm daily (page 233).

★ **Sahagún's Saturday Market:** Sahagún really comes to life on Saturdays, when a market sets up on the central square. Sample local produce, then join the locals for a drink on the square (page 240).

★ **Santuario Virgen de la Peregrina:** Sahagún has three of Spain's most beautiful Mudéjar churches—San Tirso, San Lorenzo, and La Peregrina. They're all gems of Mudéjar architecture, but La Peregrina's plaster interior walls, carved with geometric patterns, are most impressive (page 241).

Recommended Overnight Stops

Burgos (Km 489.7, page 201)

Hornillos del Camino (Km 468.6, page 214) or **Arroyo de Sanbol** (Km 462.9, page 215)

San Nicolas (Km 441.3, page 222) or **Itero de la Vega** (Km 438, page 222)

Frómista (Km 424, page 223)

Villalcázar de Sirga (Km 409.8, page 228) or **Carrión de los Condes** (Km 404.2, page 231)

Terradillos de los Templarios (Km 377.8, page 235) or **Moratinos** (Km 374.6, page 236)

Sahagún (Km 364.5, page 238)

El Burgo Ranero (Km 346.6, page 246)

Mansilla de las Mulas (Km 327.4, page 248)

This is the classic *meseta*, the high plateau of Castile and León, framed perfectly between the two regal cities of Burgos and León. In stark contrast to the ascent and descent and forest cover of the first sections of the Camino, here it is all open sky and endless horizon—but with its share of wave-like rolling terrain, in some places 950 meters (3,117 feet) in altitude. The region has a beauty all its own. The wildlife here is stunning and, like pilgrims, is more active at dawn and dusk to cope with the intense sun, wind, heat, and cold. Look for clusters of white butterflies clinging, fast asleep, to vertical stalks of purple thistle, or frogs burbling in canals and creeks. If you get an early start, be sure to turn around and watch the sun rise from the eastern horizon in a rainbow swirl of orange, fuchsia, violet, and lavender.

The landscape of Castile and Léon brings to life the medieval knights and royal battles for power over Iberia, not only between the Christian north and the Muslim south, but also between the rival Christian kingdoms of Castile, León, Navarra, and Aragon. This is the territory of El Cid, a Castilian mercenary with an Arab nickname (*al-sidi*, meaning "lord" or "sir") who fought on many sides, north and south. And here is another irony: As much as the region's history depicts battles between Muslims and Christians, it also offers proof that those centuries were ones of creative flourishing, cohabitation, and diversity—*convivencia*. In Castile, more than anywhere else on the Camino, you will see the influence of Spain's two other major faith communities, Muslims and Jews; It's evident in the aesthetics of the churches and monasteries, especially in Burgos and Sahagún.

You are also now in core *bodega* country. (Bodegas are family wine cellars with underground passages dug into natural or manmade hills.) This is where each family makes and stores their annual wine, and also where they store other harvested and produced foods, from cheeses, sausages, and cured hams to grains, roots, and legumes. The entrance, the room nearest the surface, is often where friends visit the family and enjoy a drink, tapas, and meal. Each bodega has Hobbit-hole-like doors and icons around the entrance that seem both to decorate and protect the contents. Walking the Camino, you'll pass many bodegas as you approach the villages and towns.

Planning Your Time

Walking the full **181-kilometer** (112-mile) stretch of the Camino from Burgos to León will take **7-9 days** if you average **20-25 kilometers (12.5-15.5 miles) per**

Local Markets

- **Burgos:** Weekly produce market on Wednesdays and Saturday; flea market on Sundays; textile and apparel markets on Wednesdays, Fridays, and Sundays (page 209).

- **Carrión de los Condes:** Every Thursday morning, a mixed market selling produce and other local foods, household goods, and textiles (clothes, shoes, linens) sets up on and around the Plaza de Santa María (page 231).

- **Sahagún:** Every Saturday the market sets up in the Plaza Mayor and surrounding streets. This is one of the best markets on the Camino (page 241).

- **Mansilla de las Mulas:** Every Tuesday, the market selling food and general goods sets up around the Plaza del Grano (page 248).

day. This pace allows time to explore a little each day.

Consider 1-2 days to explore **Burgos,** and a day to visit **Atapuerca,** Europe's oldest site for human fossils. Add another day to make a detour from Mansilla de las Mulas to visit the rare 10th-century pre-Romanesque and Visigothic chapel of **San Miguel de Escalada.**

Route Options

Two **detours** reduce the long tracts where the Camino runs parallel to the road after **Frómista** (Km 424). The first is an easy side-step, a few meters farther to the right of the road and the historic Camino, to follow the bank of the Ucieza river from **Población de Campos** (Km 420.6) to **Villalcazar de Sirga** (Km 409.8).

The second detour, 4 kilometers (2.5 miles) after **Sahagún** (Km 364.5), takes the path where once the Roman road, the **Via Calzada** (also called Via Romana and Via Trajana/Traiana), passed. This detour adds little by way of extra distance (less than 1 km/0.6 mi) but takes you away from the road along a 31-kilometer (19.2-mile) stretch, 17.7 kilometers (11 miles) of which lacks support structures. The two paths join as one again at both Reliegos (Km 333.7) and Mansilla de las Mulas (Km 327.4).

If you find yourself short on time, or if you want to **bypass the unappealing industrial outskirts of León,** you can get a bus from El Burgo Ranero, Mansilla de las Mulas, or Puente Villarente to León. You'll gain about one or two days of walking, but unless you wait until Puente Villarente to get on the bus, you'll miss the Roman archaeological site of Lancía, which is just after Mansilla de las Mulas. Another popular option to speed your journey is to **bike from Burgos to León.**

Geography and Terrain

The route from Burgos to León traverses the bulk of north-central Spain's *meseta,* a high plateau. This is big plains and big sky country, though there are still hills, especially on the stretch from **Burgos** (Km 489.7) to **Boadilla del Camino** (Km 429.7). After Boadilla del Camino, the terrain levels significantly and invites a new challenge—seemingly endless and unvaried terrain that can take pilgrims more deeply into their own thoughts.

The trail is well marked. Yellow arrows painted or engraved on stone and wood surfaces continue to guide the way, as do the knee-high stone pillars with engraved and stylized scallop shells. There is not a lot of walking parallel to a road in the first portion of this section, but from **Frómista** to **León,** about 50 percent of the historic Camino passes parallel to the road. Two detours significantly reduce this.

There are three other stretches where there are few or no support structures for more than 8 kilometers (5 miles): the 16.9-kilometer (10.5-mile) section from **Carrión de los Condes** (Km 404.2) to **Calzadilla de la Cueza** (Km 387.3); the 10.6-kilometer (6.6-mile) stretch from **Sahagún** (Km 364.5) to **Bercianos del Real Camino** (Km 353.9); and the 12.9 kilometers (8 miles) between **El Burgo Ranero** (Km 346.6) to **Reliegos** (Km 333.7).

Weather

The *meseta* is open, exposed, and often high-altitude plains that average around 850 meters (2,789 feet). This makes for a place of sweltering heat with little shelter or shade in **summer** that is equally exposed to wind, rain, snow, and frigid temperatures in **winter.** In **spring and autumn,** the climate can fluctuate, but generally these are the most pleasant and moderate seasons. If walking in summer, it is imperative to have sun protection and to carry plenty of water. It is also best to start walking early in the day and finish walking by early afternoon. In winter, bring layers. Days are shorter, and many places may be closed after October, so you will want to walk at the first sunlight; be ready to stop before the sun goes down, and be prepared to stay in hotels if albergues are closed.

Getting There

Starting Points

The most popular starting point is **Burgos,** the second-largest city on the Camino, after Pamplona. The city is most easily accessed by train or bus. Another popular and well-connected starting point is midway, in **Sahagún,** which is most easily reached by train. El Burgo Ranero is a rare village with a transit hub on the *meseta,* connecting to León via bus and train.

Car

The east-west autoroute **A-12/A-231** and **N-120,** named for the Camino, Autovía del Camino de Santiago, is never far from the walking trail between Burgos and León.

Camino bikers in front of the Catedral de Burgos

Highlights of Castilian Food and Wine

Castilian cuisine is born of hearty farmers' and herders' fare that can sustain body and soul in this traditional farming and long-distance sheepherding territory. You'll find full-bodied red wines, rich, sustaining pork and bean stews, succulent pork, lamb, and beef roasts, colorful grilled garden vegetables, strong cheeses, and a special passion for robustly seasoned sausages.

Bread and Pastries

This region has been the breadbasket of Spain since Roman times, so bread is a matter of pride here. Many towns still have traditional bakers that locals frequent to buy their daily bead. Three of the most common breads are **barra** (baguette-style), **colín** (bread sticks that are eaten with tapas), and **pan candela** (a round loaf).

Many times on the Camino you may pick up the scent of anise drifting through the air as you approach a village. In Castile, many pastry makers have special anis-flavored cookies, such as at **Confitería La Perla Alcazareña** in Villalcazar de Sirga (especially their almond cookies, *almendrados*).

Meat

Meat is central to Castilian cuisine. Some specialties are lamb, including **lechazo** (roast suckling lamb), **cochinillo asado** (roast suckling pig), and **cecina** (dry-cured beef). A special poultry dish, **pollo al chilindron,** is braised chicken with paprika, red peppers, tomatoes, onions, and brandy. Cured meats and sausages are big, and in addition to *cecina*, you'll find varieties of cured hams, including **jamón Iberico,** and sausages, such as chorizo, and especially blood sausage, **morcilla.**

Cheese

Pilgrims can delight in the varieties of cheeses—especially amazing semi-cured sheep's milk cheeses, known as **quesos de oveja,** often aged from six to twelve months. These are tangy and robust and take on the special taste of the herbs and grasses on which the sheep graze. Each herding locale will have its own special *queso de oveja,* such as the *queso de oveja Boffard,* made in Frómista. You can buy and taste this particular semi-cured cheese there at the shop, **La Venta de Boffard.**

Vegetable Dishes

Vegetables are robustly handled, roasted,

Air

No convenient flights connect to Burgos's municipal airport (RGS). The nearest airport is **Bilbao** (BIO; www.aena.es/es/aeropuerto-bilbao), coming from several destinations in the United Kingdom, France, and Germany, and from Brussels in Belgium and Lisbon in Portugal. Frequent bus and train departures connect Bilbao to Burgos.

Train

RENFE (www.renfe.es) has several stops along this stretch of the Camino. The train has many connections from all points in the country and also has a line running along the Camino, stopping in Sahagún and El Burgo Ranero between its stops in León and Burgos. Frómista is also accessible via train from Madrid.

Bus

Monbus (www.monbus.es) and **ALSA** (www.alsa.es)—often working in concert—serve destinations between Burgos and León (including Castrojeriz, Frómista, Carrión de los Condes, Terradillos de los Templarios, and Mansilla de las Mulas). The bus is often the most efficient way to get around, as many locals in rural areas rely on this service to get to urban centers for work and shopping.

Wine

Wine has been produced in Castilla and León for more than 2,000 years. The land dedicated to growing vines has declined in the past century, and today, the focus is on quality rather than quantity. The most celebrated wine regions for Castile are the Ribera del Duero, Toro, and Rueda, south of the Camino. You may see the Tierras de Castilla label on many a bottle of wine on the Camino; this full-bodied earthy red is often the house wine and very good. The reigning red grape here is Tempranillo.

White wines here favor the Verdejo grape and sometimes use Viura, two Iberian varietals that have more meat than a sauvignon blanc but are lighter than a chardonnay.

Castilian *Cocido*

stewed, or grilled. Try **parillada de verduras,** a seasonal variety of grilled vegetables (red and green peppers, zucchini, eggplant, mushrooms, artichokes, and the like).

Stews

Hearty stews take the sting off the cold whipping wind of the high plains, including various types of **cocidos,** stews rich in meats, sausages, beans, and vegetables. Some *cocidos* are prepared and served in the same manner as the French *pot au feu:* The broth is served as a soup (often with *fideos,* little stick noodles), and the meats and vegetables are served on separate platters.

Vermouth

After a brief lull, vermouth is resurging in popularity, and Spaniards today love their *vermut.* Some bars even have the elixir on tap, in addition to bottles of various vintages and makers lining the wall. Many enjoy it on ice with an olive and orange slice and sometimes with bubbly water. For a great bar to enjoy this pre-dinner cocktail, head to **Vermutería Victoria** in Burgos.

There's also a direct bus from Madrid to Burgos.

Burgos   Km 489.7

Burgos (pop. 178,966) is a beautiful and prosperous city on both sides of the Arlanzón river. The medieval walls of the enclosed town are a dramatic backdrop to the river and a splendid atmosphere for the nightlife that it draws, especially on weekends. Inside the walled city and around the walls are several interesting churches, the most dominant being Burgos's imposing cathedral, Spain's third largest after Seville and Toledo.

The other churches—San Lesmes, San Nicolas, San Gil, San Esteban, and San Águeda—offer more intimacy by contrast and are worth visiting for a better sense of what medieval Burgos felt like.

Burgos is also home to one of the world's most important human evolution museums, thanks in large part to the nearby archaeological site of Atapuerca. It is also a university town and has a vibrant student population, with tapas bars, restaurants, outdoor cafés, and tree-lined walks and parks. Much of the action takes place along the river that flows through the city. All this makes the city an ideal place to explore for an extra day or two before returning to the Camino. The Camino itself passes

Burgos

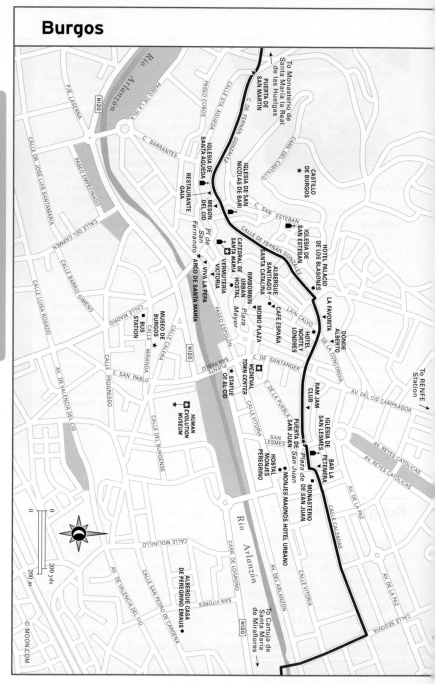

To Monasterio de
Santa María la Real
de las Huelgas

Río Arlanzón

PASEO DE LA ISLA

N120

P.E LASERNA

PASEO CUBOS

PASEO EMPECINADO

C. BARRANTES

CALLE STA. ÁGUEDA

C. DE FERNÁN GONZÁLEZ

CALLE DE FERNÁN GONZÁLEZ

CARR. DEL CASTILLO

PUERTA DE
SAN MARTÍN

IGLESIA DE
SANTA ÁGUEDA

IGLESIA DE SAN
NICOLAS DE BARI

★ CASTILLO
DE BURGOS

RESTAURANTE
GAIA

MESÓN
DEL CID

Pl. de
San
Fernando

C. DE SAN ESTEBAN

IGLESIA DE
SAN ESTEBAN

HOTEL PALACIO
DE LOS BLASONES

CALLE DEL CARMEN

CALLE DR. JOSE LUIS SANTAMARIA

CALLE BARRIO GIMENO

CALLE LUISA ROSADO

CALLE MADRID

ARCO DE SANTA MARÍA

CATEDRAL DE
SANTA MARÍA

SANTA MARÍA
VICTORIA

VERMUTERÍA
VICTORIA

VIVA LA PEPA

RIMBOMBIN

URBAN
HOSTAL

ALBERGUE
SANTIAGO Y
SANTA CATALINA

CAFÉ ESPAÑA

MOMO PLAZA

Plaza
Mayor

PASEO ESPOLÓN

LAIN CALVO

LA FAVORITA

HOTEL
NORTEY
LONDRES

DONDE
ALBERTO

DE LA CONCORDIA

AV. DEL CID CAMPEADOR

To RENFE
Station

CALLE PROGRESSO

AV. DE VALENCIA DEL CID

MUSEO DE
BURGOS

BUS
STATION

CALLE GALERA

CALLE
MIRANDA

C. SAN PABLO

N120

PUENTE
DE SAN PABLO

STATUE
DE EL CID

MEDIEVAL
TOWN CENTER

C. DE SANTANDER

C. DE LA PUEBLA

RAM JAM
CLUB

CALLE DEL BURGENSE

★ ✚ HUMAN
EVOLUTION
MUSEUM

CALLE VITORIA

PUERTA DE
SAN JUAN

SAN
LESMES

IGLESIA DE
SAN LESMES

BAR LA
PETENERA

MONASTERIO
DE SAN JUAN

Plaza
de San Juan

HOSTAL
MONJES
PEREGRINO

MONJES MAGNOS HOTEL URBANO

AV. DEL ARLANZÓN

CALLE CALZADAS

AV. DE LA PAZ

AV. REYES CATÓLICAS

AV. REYES CATÓLICAS

AV. DE LA PAZ

CALLE VITORIA

Río Arlanzón

CARR. DE LOGROÑO

SAN VITORES

CALLE MOLINILLO

AV. DE VALENCIA DEL CID

CALLE SAN PEDRO DE CARDEÑA

ALBERGUE CASA
DE PEREGRINO EMAUS

N120

CALLE SEGOVIA

To Cartuja de
Santa María
de Miraflores

0   0

200 yds

200 m

© MOON.COM

To Monasterio de
Santa María la Real
de las Huelgas

Cycling from Burgos to León

This open stretch of the Camino from Burgos to León is easier to cycle than others, and some pilgrims, particularly those who are walking the whole Camino or a large portion of it, choose to rent a bike in Burgos and cycle the 180.7 kilometers (112.3 miles) to León, where they drop the rental off and continue walking from there.

Bicigrino (Plaza de las Platerías, 1; 627-928-213; www.bicigrino.com; €40/day), based in Santiago de Compostela, offers bike rentals from Burgos to León.

They have pick-up and drop-off addresses in Burgos, Calzadilla de la Cueza, Sahagún, and León. The rental price includes transport to your chosen starting point on this stretch of the Camino, carrying crate, lock, repair kit, speedometer, and pump.

The potentially pricier **Velobur Bikes** (Avenida de la Paz, 7; 947-211-303; www.velobur.es; €30-150/day) will set you up for pick-up and drop-off points from Burgos to León, points in between, and even a little farther past León.

through the heart of the medieval walled town, entering at Puerta de San Juan and exiting at the Puerta de San Martín.

Sights

Most of these sights are within the walls of medieval Burgos, easily navigated if you use the cathedral in its heart as your beacon. The exceptions can be accessed by using the river as your guide, from east to west, in this order: Cartuja de Miraflores; a small jaunt over the river to the Iglesia de San Lesmes; back again to the south bank for the Museo de la Evolución Humana; and then to the Monasterio de las Huelgas on the western end.

Cartuja de Santa María de Miraflores

The 15th-century Cartusian monastery **Cartuja de Santa María de Miraflores** (Carretera Fuentes Blancas; 947-252-586; www.cartuja.org; Mon.-Sat., 10:15am-3pm and 4-6pm; Sun., 11am-3pm and 4-6pm; donation) is set on the edge of a lovely pine forest on the east end of town. Still inhabited by monks of the order who live in seclusion and solitude, the monastery church is nevertheless open to the public. Inside, you can view the tombs of Queen Isabel la Católica's parents, King Juan II and Isabel of Portugal, in the center, and that of her brother, Alfonso, set in the wall. Her parents' tombs, completed in 1498, are perhaps the most dramatic and elaborate of any royal tombs, with a series of symbols and figures surrounding the lifelike carved-marble images of the reclining couple, who rest on a raised star-shaped platform. The monks living here are known for their craftsmanship of rosaries made from rose petals. On Sundays the public can attend **mass** at 10:15am.

Iglesia de San Lesmes

Adelelmo (who would be named Burgos's patron saint, San Lesmes) was a French Benedictine monk who arrived in Burgos in the 11th century to dedicate his life to serving pilgrims in the monastery of San Juan, which was founded here. He died in 1097, and the present church, the Gothic and 15th-century **Iglesia de San Lesmes** (Plaza de San Juan, s/n; 947-204-380; www.aytoburgos.es; free), holds his tomb in the center of its nave. It is open daily, with several religious services throughout the day. Visitors are asked to limit sightseeing visits to before or after services.

After visiting the church, step outside onto the **Plaza de San Juan.** If you stand with the church to your left, you will face the Benedictine **Monasterio de San Juan** (947-205-687; www.aytoburgos.es; Tues.-Sat., 11am-2pm and 5-9pm, Sun., 11am-2pm, closed Sun. afternoon, Mondays

El Cid

Burgos is the city of Rodrigo Díaz de Vivar (1043-1099), better known by his Arabic name, El Cid (derived from the Moroccan Arabic title for "lord" or "sir," *sidi*). His Arabic name, adopted into Castilian, speaks of his mercenary activities in service of both Christian and Muslim kings in 11th-century Spain, depending on whose mission and purse he felt best deserved his efforts at the time. Rather than seeing the true El Cid as fickle, his shifting loyalties speak honestly about the nature of life in 11th-century Spain, where kingdoms vied for control and the dividing lines were not always drawn by religion but by other, more human quirks, such as morality, friendship, and loyalty, not to mention the need to make a living.

A **statue of El Cid** stands on the north bank side of the bridge, Puente de San Pablo. He is astride his horse, Babieca, and thrusting his sword, Tizona, straight ahead, eternally riding into battle. It is a work by Juan Cristóbal and dates to the 1950s. The bridge also holds statuary, a

statue of El Cid, Burgos

promenade of personalities that pertain to El Cid's life, the most important being the nearest to him, both here and in life, Doña Jimena, his wife. These, too, were made in the 1950s.

El Cid and Doña Jimena are buried in Burgos's cathedral, right under the transept. If you wish to experience the church that they knew and attended in life, head to the nearby Iglesia de Santa Águeda.

and holidays), where San Lesmes and his order housed and cared for pilgrims. It is now an interesting art exhibit space, with a lovely enclosed garden that's open to the public during opening hours. In spring, if you look up at the old **bell tower** from the plaza, you will likely see nesting storks raising their young. Just to the right of the old monastery is Burgos's public library, the **Biblioteca Pública**, an ultra-modern building that retains the Gothic door from the old hospital of San Juan.

★ Medieval Town Center

Burgos's charismatic town center is surrounded by thick medieval walls that jut up along the north bank of the Río Arlanzón, containing the cathedral in its heart and the castle above it. With churches and plazas anchoring the interior, vibrant eateries, and locals coming here for a *paseo*, you're sure to be pulled in.

If you are walking the Camino, you'll find the medieval town center simply by following the yellow arrows and scallop shells inlaid into the pavement. Enter the medieval walled city through the gate on the eastern side of town, **Puerta de San Juan,** just off the **Plaza de San Juan,** outside the walls. Once inside the walls, allow yourself to meander. All roads within the walls ultimately will take you toward the cathedral, and to its south, the **Plaza Mayor**, an appealing and unpretentious square, each building painted a different color, with many cafés, restaurants, and bars offering diverse options for eating or for relaxing in the sun at an outdoor table.

From the Puerta de San Juan, the Camino moves past the north side of the cathedral and the **Iglesia de San Nicolas de Bari** (947-260-539; Monday-Saturday, 11am-2pm and 5-7pm; Sundays, before and after mass; €1.50, free on Mondays), a well-endowed 15th-century church once favored by Burgos's merchant guilds. Off this street and up the hill lie the castle ruins, some towers still standing.

Castillo de Burgos

In the 9th century, the king of León, Alfonso III, built a small castle over the remains of an early Roman fortress. Early medieval Burgos formed around this castle and the fortification and protection it offered several surrounding villages, which were known as *burgos*, burgs. It was modified and expanded over the Middle Ages to defend the region from incursions, and survived reasonably intact until it was blown up by Napoleon's troops in 1813.

Today, it's worth the climb up the hilltop to see the archaeological site of the **Castillo de Burgos** (Cerro de San Miguel; 947-203-857; www.aytoburgos.es/direcciones/castillo-de-burgos; €3.70; Jul.-Sept., Sat.-Sun. 11am-8:30pm, 11am-2:30pm). The city has restored aspects of the castle, and you can see the outline of the medieval foundations and some of the walls and towers. There are also good displays that recreate the medieval world from this hilltop, plus a great view down onto the cathedral just below and the city all around.

Iglesia de San Esteban

Just below the castle is the Iglesia de San Esteban. It is rarely open, so enjoy the exterior of this survivor from the 13th and 14th centuries, with its lyrical side porch with thick timbered roof and playful animal engravings around the doorway arch—including a smiling rabbit running towards two scallop shells. Could he be a pilgrim?

★ Catedral de Santa María

For lovers of religious art, Burgos's **Catedral de Santa María** (Plaza de Santa María; 947-204-712; www.catedraldeburgos.es; Mar. 19-Oct. 31, 9:30am-7:30pm, Nov. 1-Mar. 18 10am-6pm, closed Dec.

25 and Jan. 1; €7, €4.50 for pilgrims) is as much a museum as a place of worship, not to mention of pomp and politics.

Begun by King Fernando III in AD 1221, it was completed a mere 22 years later, a feat that gives the church its unified aesthetic. That Gothic structure was then added to and elaborated on, becoming the multilayered walk through Castilian history that you see today.

You can spend several hours here, exploring the many chapels, elaborately carved choir, cloister, and layers of medieval to early modern art. But whatever your timeframe, be sure to see these four highlights:

- **Transept:** The place in the church's cross-shaped ground plan where the arms intersect is beautiful and symbolic. Destroyed by a fire three centuries after it was built, the current vault was reconstructed in 1568 by Juan de Vallejo, who was inspired by the Mudéjar—Iberian Muslim—art of Spain. In the center of the transept's dome is an elegant filigree eight-pointed star, which lets in soft natural light. You've seen this same pattern in the reconstruction of the church of El Puy in Estella (if you have been walking from there), and you'll see it again in the Constable's Chapel beyond the apse here, too. The crossing also stands directly over a rose-toned marble stone, marking the **tombs of El Cid** (1043-1099) **and his wife** Jimena Díaz (1046-1116) underfoot. Their bodies have been here only since 1921, when they were moved here from the monastery of San Pedro de Cardeña just southeast of Burgos.

- **Rose window:** The west entrance's rose window with its six-pointed star—a common decorative motif in Christian, Islamic, and Jewish art—is ethereal and beautiful when viewed from the nave. It can represent many things, but top among them is the Seal of Solomon, symbol of a just and wise ruler. His seal also represents the force of heaven intersecting with that of earth, as with justice and wisdom, creating a perfect harmony. From the nave, you will also find the ornately carved wooden **choir,** built in the 16th century. At that time, it was the style in Spain to set these in the center of earlier churches, obstructing the full line of the nave. While that is unfortunate, take time to look closely at the interesting characters in the engravings. Some are humorous, expressive, and highly animated.

- **Capilla de Condestable:** The octagonal Constable's Chapel is just behind the apse. This is an incredibly ornate Gothic to Renaissance space, largely from the 15th and 16th centuries. Look for the detailed tombs of Burgos's first constable and his wife, Don Pedro Fernandez de Velasco and Doña Mencía de Mendoza, then take a look up at the chapel ceiling to see the Gothic-Mudéjar-fusion eight-pointed star. Similar to the Mudéjar-inspired star in the transept, this one precedes it and is by the late 15th-century architect Simón de Colonia.

- **Cloister:** Saunter through the late-13th- and early-14th-century Gothic cloister. Largely original, it offers a more serene and organic experience of the cathedral.

Iglesia de Santa Águeda

Iglesia de Santa Águeda (Calle Santa Águeda; 947-206-755; Mon.-Wed., 12-1pm and Thurs.-Sat., 5:30-7pm; free), west of the cathedral, is where in AD 1072 El Cid made his patron, King Alfonso VI of León (and imminently also King of Castile), swear that he played no role in the murder of his brother, King Sancho II of Castile. You'll see this history forged in ironwork on the outside entrance door's lock, an image of an altar with El Cid on one side holding his sword, and Alfonso VI on the other wearing the king's crown. The current church, also known as Santa Gadea, is Gothic and from the 15th century, built over the 11th-century site.

Arco de Santa Maria

The iconic passage of the Arco de Santa María was the main entry gate into medieval Burgos during the 14th century. Its present ornate and flamboyant appearance come from the 16th century, when the Hapsburg king of Spain, Carlos V, commissioned the building of a larger gate, its decoration directed toward the imperative that citizens be loyal to the crown.

Puerta de San Martin

If you return back to the Camino's passage through the medieval town and follow it west, it eventually exits at the **Puerta de San Martín**, which marks the general vicinity where Burgos's medieval Jewish and Muslim neighborhoods once stood. Though San Martín's gate is a reconstruction, it retains the signature Mudéjar brickwork of Iberia's Muslims (you'll see more of this in Sahagún). Recent archaeological excavations around the gate of San Martín have revealed many layers of the city's history, including tiles that date to the medieval Muslim neighborhood and structures related to the medieval Jewish one, one of Iberia's most important Jewish communities. From here, the Camino meanders through city-park-lined neighborhoods and onward to the plains.

★ Human Evolution Museum (Museo de la Evolución Humana)

One of the world's most important museums on human evolution, the **Museo de Evolución Humana** (Paseo Sierra de Atapuerca, s/n; 902-024-246; www.museoevolucionhumana.com; €6) showcases finds from the nearby Atapuerca archaeological site, a layer cake of human existence in Europe. The museum contains artifacts from over a million years

Top: the Catedral de Burgos and the Plaza de Santa María in the heart of the medieval town center.
Bottom: the colorful Plaza Mayor in Burgos.

Top Experience

Day Trip: Atapuerca Archaeological Site

As you walk over the low Sierra de Atapuerca mountains to reach Burgos, underfoot is a complex subterranean world that developed over millions of years, as underground water flowed through limestone to create a Swiss-cheese pattern. Occasionally, an opening to one of the underground caverns surfaced and ancient humans and other mammals sought shelter there. Over time, those same openings collapsed and were sealed, preserving some of what was inside as fossils.

Around 1900, a mining company cut a deep trench into the Sierra de Atapuerca, hoping to build a rail line to transport minerals to Burgos. Finding little mineral wealth, they abandoned the project, but exposed several caverns full of preserved animal and human remains. Excavations began in the 1970s and continue to this day. When archaeologists in 2007-2008 unearthed the fossilized lower jaw and teeth of a human who lived around 1.2 million years ago, Atapuerca quickly became known as the place of Europe's oldest human remains. Other discoveries included the remains of 28 individuals who lived around 430,000 years ago.

Visiting Atapuerca

A visit to Atapuerca's archeological site, **Yacimientos de Atapuerca** (947-430-435; www.atapuerca.es, €6), lets you walk into the trench, 15-25 feet wide, where the mining company blew open a passage into the Sierra de Atapuerca. The site contains some 11 excavation sites, but the tour takes you to those most immediately accessible from the trench, including the **Sima del Elefante** (Elephant Pit), where excavators unearthed the 1.2 million-year-old human fossils. It is mind-blowing to stand in the base of the long railway trench, with limestone towering several meters overhead on both sides, and explore a place that's chock-full of fossils.

Allow at least half a day to visit Atapuerca. All visits to the site are guided, and usually occur at 11am and 3:45pm. (While one group is visiting the site, another is visiting the nearby park and didactic center.) It's best to reserve your ticket ahead, via phone call or email (947-421-100;

ago, especially highlighting the earliest humans, *Homo antecessor*, who lived here 1.2 million to 800,000 years ago, and Europe's earliest Neandertals, around 400,000 years old.

This museum is also an important center for research about human evolution. Exhibit spaces are engaging, creative, and interactive: Experience a simulated brain as it fires off neurons for functions such as speaking, then learn about early human art and why we create these symbolic forms of communication. Descriptive panels are also in English.

The museums opening times are: Oct.-June, Tues.-Fri., 10am-2:30pm and 4:30-8pm; Sat., weekends and holidays, 10am-8pm; July-Sept., 10am-8pm. Admission is free on Wednesdays from 4:30-8pm and Tuesdays and Thursdays from 7-8pm; closed Mondays. General admission includes entrance to the nearby **Museo de Burgos** (Calle Miranda, 13; 947-265-875; www.museodeburgos; Oct.-June, Tues.-Sat., 10am-2pm and 4-7pm, July-Sept., Tues.-Sat. 10am-2pm and 5-8pm, Sundays, all year, 10am-2pm; €1), which also displays archaeological remains from the area, from the Paleolithic era through the Roman period and into the medieval era. It also houses a good collection of 19th- and 20th-century art.

Monasterio de Santa María la Real de las Huelgas

Founded in AD 1175 on the land of one of Castilian king Alfonso VIII's country palaces, the **Monasterio de las** reservas@museoevolucionhumana.com). You can also arrange visits in person at the Human Evolution Museum in Burgos (try to do this at least a day in advance).

Getting There

You can arrange visits to the site from near the village of Atapuerca or from the Human Evolution Museum in Burgos.

Arrange for a visit (guided visits only; €12) from the **Human Evolution Museum** in Burgos, which includes the bus ride (€1) and admission for both the archaeological site (€6) and the **CAREX Experimental Archaeology Center** (€5), the didactic center on human prehistory with a good museum on prehistoric art, technology, and sex, and an attached outdoor park where you will learn to throw a spear, paint in caves, and make fire. Buses from the museum in Burgos leave mid-morning and return in late afternoon, stopping at either the village of Atapuerca or Ibeas de Juarros, on the outskirts of the archaeological site, to the north and south respectively, where you pay for your own lunch at one of the villages' rural restaurants.

at the entrance of the Yacimientos de Atapuerca archaeological sites

From Atapuerca Vilage: If you're starting from the village of Atapuerca, go to the **Atapuerca Visitor Reception Center,** 1 kilometer (0.6 miles) from the village and the **CAREX Experimental Archaeology Center**. From the village, turn right off the Camino (Calle del Camino de Santiago) onto Calle Medio, which passes the Albergue El Peregrino on the right. Continue on Calle Medio for 1 kilometer (0.6 miles) all the way to CAREX, on the left, where the guided visits take visitors to the archaeological site, on the other side of Atapuerca village.

Huelgas (Calle de Compases, s/n, 947-201-630; www.patrimonionacional.es/real-sitio; open Tues.-Sat., 10am-2pm and 4-6:30pm, Sundays and holidays, 10:30am-3pm; €6) was Cistercian from the start and a convent for women from the nobility. Its abbess was powerful and oversaw several towns and other Cistercian monasteries. Las Huelgas was also the site of Castile's royal pantheon, tombs that you can visit today, where kings were crowned and knights knighted. Not only was it the center of Castilian royal and religious power, it remains a treasure of Mudéjar architecture blended with the complex's Romanesque and Gothic, reflecting *convivencia*—mixing and living together in harmony—over conflict.

The Mudéjar influence is clear in the tomb engravings, as well as in the roof and ceiling woodwork of the cloisters, the lacey plasterwork on the walls of the **Capilla de la Asunción** and the **Capilla de Santiago**, the multi-lobed archways of the former and the inlaid wooden ceiling of the latter, among many other spaces.

Today Las Huelgas remains an active Cistercian convent, with 32 nuns carrying on monastic life and service (www.monasteriodelashuelgas.org).

Festivals and Events

Every Wednesday and Saturday (9am-2pm) the weekly **produce market** sets up on the east end of town along the Calle El Plantío, running parallel along the north bank of the Río Arlanzón—midway

between the Cartuja de Miraflores and the Human Evolution Museum, though these landmarks are on the south bank. Every Sunday (10am-2pm) is Burgos's flea market, **El Rastro,** on the Plaza de España, to the northeast of the castle and cathedral, where you can browse antiques, books, stamps and old coins, among other things—something like an open-air ethnography museum of daily life from a bygone era. Open-air textile, clothing and shoe **markets** also set up Wednesdays (Parque de los Poetas; 9am-2pm), Fridays (Paseo de Empecinado; 9am-2pm), and Sundays (Calle El Plantío; 9am-2pm).

Food

★ **Meson del Cid** (Plaza Santa María, 8; 947-208-715; €35) has large windows overlooking the cathedral from the Plaza de Santa María and an interior of medieval-style stained-glass windows, ceramic tiles, and crisp white linens. This is the place to try Burgos's famous *morcilla* (blood sausage), either on its own or in *alubias rojas de Ibeas* (a red bean stew with morcilla and chorizo, €9.90). Other signature dishes are the roast lamb (€23), the high-quality *jamón Iberico de bellota* (acorn-fed, free-range cured ham), and clams and artichokes simmered in white wine and herbs.

With its casual country décor, white wood walls, and contemporary cuisine emphasizing fresh, local, and healthy, **Viva La Pepa** (Paseo del Espolón, 4; 947-102-771; www.vivalapepaburgos.com) feels a bit like California. (Check out their smoothies or their tofu and spring greens salad.) They have an elaborate breakfast menu (€3-10) that is unusual in Spain, plus tapas (€7-10), lunch (€13.50), or dinner (€18-26). Though the address is on Paseo Espolón, the gardened promenade on the riverside, it has an entrance

---

From top to bottom: Museo de Evolución Humana in Burgos; the Arco de Santa Maria entrance gate into the walled center of medieval Burgos; bakery shop window in Burgos.

on the other side from the Plaza del Rey San Fernando, which faces the cathedral.

★ **Momo Plaza** (Plaza Mayor, 16; 947-250-423; €5-12) offers excellent regional wines to go with their creative and tasty array of *pinchos*, such as beef-and-onion-stuffed mushrooms, red peppers filled with cod and hot sauce, and mussels stuffed with minced tomatoes, onions, and bread crumbs, then deep fried. They also make superb cocktails.

La Favorita (Calle Avellanos, 8; 947-205-949; www.lafavoritaburgos.com; €12-20) has beautiful stone and brick walls, elegant white tablecloths, and an immense *bodega*—wine cellar—with a wide selection of wines. They serve plates of regional cheeses and several kinds of Ibérico cured hams, grilled blood sausage (*morcilla*), salads, omelets, fois gras cooked in port, and a variety of grilled meats and vegetables.

Restaurante Gaia (Calle de Fernán González, 37; 947-279-728; €11) caters to vegetarians, offering something for nearly every taste thanks to a world-cuisine approach with inspired ideas, diverse ingredients, and bold spices and seasonings.

★ **Bar La Petenera** (Plaza de San Juan; €5-10) is tucked in behind the Iglesia de San Lesmes (apse side) on the Plaza de San Juan. The setting alone makes the bar a place to visit, but the delicious *pinchos*, upbeat servers, and friendly customers will all keep you here. Bar La Petenera feels more like secret neighborhood spot than a tourist attraction. On warm days and evenings, the bar expands with outdoor seating into the plaza.

Donde Alberto (Plaza Alonso-Martínez, 5; 637-016-461; €4-10) is run by the ever-cheerful and upbeat Alberto, who also makes the fresh and innovative *pinchos* that line his counters from one end to the other. Everything is amazingly inexpensive. There is a wide selection of wines. It can get pretty crowded at night, but midday can make for a good lunch venue with fewer people.

Nightlife

This university town is alive with evening and weekend energy. The **medieval town center** is a major hub for multi-generational nightlife, and in many venues, even the Ram Jam Club, you'll see people of all ages. Nearly everyone is out for the evening *paseo* to enjoy the squares and cafés, and to meet up with friends for a drink, an activity that flows seamlessly into a long night of hopping from one tapas bar to the next. If you meander through the **Plaza Mayor** and **cathedral** areas, as well as around the **Puerta de San Juan** and the riverside cafes around the **Arco de Santa María**, many of which also open on to the **Plaza de San Fernando**, you will come upon many enticing places to stop and enjoy the flow.

To join the vermouth resurgence in Spain, and especially Castile, head to **Vermutería Victoria** (Plaza Rey San Fernando, 947-204-281). Founded in 1931, the bar and dining room is an energetic mix of turn-of-the-century Belle Époque floral plaster carved walls and ceiling, classical paintings, and big-band music surging through the vermouth-laced air. As vermouth is considered a pre-dinner aperitif and you are in Spain, anytime before 10pm you'll find the place festive and packed.

Ram Jam Club (Calle San Juan, 29; 629-709-447) is casual with a mellow, café-society feel, where a good selection of inexpensive drinks combines with rich conversation as well as occasional live music. It can get more pulsating during weekends, and is popular with students as well as music lovers of all generations. You can't miss it for its clock sculpture at the entrance, the hour numbers all reading 6, and the wavy lines of the hour and minute hands implying that time can be left at the door. It is also a venue for the cider festival, Fiesta de Sidra, which takes place around the summer solstice in June.

Café España (Calle de Lain Calvo, 12; 947-205-337; www.cafeespana.es) is a classy place holding down the same spot since 1921. Known for its wide variety of coffee drinks, some straight-laced and others spiked, several evenings a week the café can turn out live blues, jazz, and flamenco. Sundays are Poesía y Música nights, where literature and music combine into a soiree of readings, performances, and discussions.

Accommodations
Albergues

Albergue Casa de Peregrino Emaus (Calle San Pedro de Cardeña, 31a; 947-205-363; Easter-Nov. 1; 20 beds; €5) is a recently opened ecclesiastical *albergue*. Clean, well-run, and welcoming, it is popular among pilgrims and is an inexpensive place to stay in the city. It also has a good communal meal, based on donation, and a small chapel with evening service.

Albergue Santiago y Santa Catalina (Calle Lain Calvo, 10; 947-207-952; Mar.-Nov.; 16 beds; €6) is also known as the Albergue Divina Pastora because of its ideal location just above the chapel, Capilla de la Divina Pastora, a stone's throw from the cathedral. They have eight bunk beds, for walking pilgrims only, in their simple but clean and uncrowded single-room dormitory.

Hotels

Hotel Palacio de los Blasones (Calle Fernán González, 10; 947-271-000; www. hotelricepalaciodelosblasones.com; €90-100) is in an old palace in the heart of the pedestrian medieval town. With beautiful thick stone walls and simple decor, it's a lyrical merging of past and present.

Hotel Mesón del Cid (Plaza de Santa María, 8; 947-208-715; www.mesondelcid.es; 49 rooms; €65-75), located in a stunning setting right in front of the cathedral, offers consistent high quality. Rooms are colorful, spacious, and simply but tastefully decorated, with spacious modern bathrooms.

★ **Monjes Magnos Hotel Urbano** (Calle Cardenal Beniloch s/n; 947-205-134; www.monjesmagnoshotel.com; €50-70, call to inquire about special pilgrim prices not advertised online) offers several options at different price ranges. Ismael Díaz Peña takes great pride in running a welcoming and efficient place, which is geared toward pilgrims as much as other visitors. Clean and modern, the hotel is right on the square near the pilgrim church of San Lesmes, and the surroundings are fetchingly historic. On weekends in the warm season, many weddings take place on the facing Plaza de San Juan. Proprietors speak English.

Just around the corner is the **Hostal Monjes Peregrino** (Calle Bernabé Pérez Ortiz, 1; 947-205-134; www.monjesmagnoshotel.com), run by the same English-speaking management as Monjes Magnos. The *hostal* is expressly outfitted for the pilgrim while still offering the comfort of private rooms with baths. Rooms are spare but elegant and airy, with large beds. Common areas have spaces to gather for food and drink. There is a gym, in case you haven't walked enough.

Hotel Norte y Londres (Plaza Alonso Martínez, 10; 947-264-125; www.hotelnorteylondres.com; 50 rooms; €50-65), founded in 1904, is a classy boutique hotel overlooking a sweet little square in the medieval center of town. Some rooms have glass-enclosed balconies looking out on the Plaza Alonso Martínez. Warm, professional, English-speaking staff are ready to assist.

For something a little different, the **Rimbombin Urban Hostal** (Calle Sombrerería 6; 947-261-200; www.rimbombin.com; €55) is deep in pedestrian Burgos between the cathedral and the river. Modern, airy, and light-filled rooms have private baths. A communal kitchen and salon are convenient if you want to gather provisions from Burgos's produce markets and have a meal in.

Getting There

Burgos is a transit hub, and is well connected to the rest of Spain by all modes of ground transportation. The most convenient and easy ways to arrive are by train and by bus.

Car

If you are driving the Autovía del Camino de Santiago, the romantically named east-west **A-12/N-120** highway from Pamplona to Burgos (and onward to Santiago), your entry into Burgos will be on the east side on the **N-120**. The whole drive on the N-120 from Pamplona to Burgos is 200 kilometers (124 miles, 2.5 hours). From San Juan de la Ortega to Burgos it is 30 kilometers (19 miles, 30 minutes).

Burgos is 246 kilometers (153 miles) due north of Madrid on the **A-1**, 158 kilometers (98 miles) southwest of Bilbao and 214 kilometers (133 miles) southwest of San Sebastián on the **AP-68 and A-1**, and 606 kilometers (377 miles) west of Barcelona via Zaragoza on the **E-90 and E-804**.

Burgos has a vast array of car rental companies, including **Thrifty** (www.thrifty.com), **Dollar** (www.dollar.com), **Hertz** (www.hertz.com), and **Avis** (www.avis.com). The RENFE station also has car rentals with **Enterprise** (www.enterprise.es) and **Gavis** (www.gavis.es). The next municipality along this section of the Camino with rental agencies is León.

Train

RENFE trains (www.renfe.com) connect to Burgos from Madrid (3-5 daily, 2.5-4.5 hours, €35), Bilbao (3-4 daily, 2.5-3 hours, €14-19), Barcelona (3-7 daily, 6-8.5 hours, €45-114), and Pamplona (2-4 daily, 2-4 hours, €14-21), among many other destinations. Burgos's large and ultra modern **Rosa de Lima Station** is five kilometers (3.1 miles) north of the city. When you arrive, taxis into town (€12-15) can be shared with 2-3 other passengers, and bus shuttles (€2) transport passengers hourly to the city.

If traveling by train from Burgos, you can purchase train tickets in the city center at the **RENFE office** (Calle Moneda, 23, 947-209-131; Mon.-Fri., 9:30 am-1:30pm and 5-8pm, Sat., 9:30am-1:30pm, closed Sun. and holidays).

Bus

Unlike the new train station, Burgos's **Estación de Autobuses** (Calle de Miranda, 4; 947-265-565) is super-central, set in from the south bank side of the Río Arlanzón across the bridge from the Arco de Santa María. Buses run by **Monbus** (www.monbus.es) and **ALSA** (www.alsa.es) cover regional and national destinations. There are 12-20 buses daily from Madrid (2.5-3 hours, €15-19) as well as from other major hubs, including Bilbao (8-9 daily, 2-3.5 hours, €9-14), León (3-4 daily, 2-3 hours, €16), Barcelona (4-8 daily, 8-9 hours, €32-55), and in France, Biarritz (one daily, 4.5 hours, €25). **Autobuses Jiménez** (902-202-787; www.autobusesjimenez) runs buses connecting Logroño to Burgos (10 daily). There are no direct buses from Pamplona, but the train is direct and efficient.

ALSA has a direct bus to Burgos from Terminal T4 in Madrid Barajas airport (11-14 daily, 2.5-3 hours, €15-27).

Taxi

Call **Radiotaxi Burgos** (947-481-010; www.radiotaxiburgos.es); **Taxi Burgos** (634-430-234; www.taxiburgos.com), with whom you can get discounts if reserving via the internet; or **Abutaxi** (947-277-777; www.abutaxi.com).

Tardajos   Km 478.6

The passage out of Burgos soon turns into rolling countryside and, in a little over 10 kilometers (6.2 miles) arrives at the village of Tardajos (pop. 794). Though little of historical significance is left here, in the 10th century this village had three churches. Long before then, there was a Roman villa here, and possibly before that, a small Celtiberian *castro* (settlement).

Food and Accommodations

This is a great place for a rest at the energetic and upbeat **Café Bar Ruiz** (Calle Pozas, 10; 947-451-433; €4-5), which churns out creative breakfast sandwiches intended to fuel a trekker, such as egg-in-a-hole with cheese and ham.

Two popular *albergues* offer accommodation if you wish to stop here. The **Albergue La Fábrica** (Camino de la Fábrica; 646-000-908; open all year; 14 beds; €12) opened in 2014 in a restored old stone building that was once a flour mill. They have dorm-style bunk beds as well as private rooms, meals, and good hospitality.

The **Hotel-Albergue La Casa de Beli** (Avenida General Yagüe, 16; 629-351-675; www.lacasadebeli.com; open all year; 30 beds; €10) is a new pilgrims' hostel, opened in 2016, with beautiful thick stone walls and elegant private rooms (€35-45) along with dorm-style sleeping (30 beds at €10). The *albergue* also offers a warm welcome, tasty meals, and a relaxing garden in back.

Tardajos also has a **municipal *albergue*** (Calle Asunción, s/n; 947-451-189; 18 beds in three dorm rooms; donation; mid-Mar.-Oct.31) operated by volunteers from the pilgrim association, Asociación de Amigos del Camino de Santiago de Madrid.

Rabé de las Calzadas Km 476.4

Rabé de las Calzadas (pop. 214) has a pretty chapel, **Iglesia de Santa Marina** (Calle Santa Marina, 4), typically open daily, where you can get a stamp in your pilgrim's credential as well as enjoy the heavily fortified stone walls of the 13th-century transitional Gothic church. Storks love the building and in spring you may see them active in their nests on the bell tower.

Accommodations

The ★ **Albergue Liberanos Domine** (Plaza Francisco Riberas, 10; 695-116-901; www.liberanosdomine.com; open year-round; 24 beds; €8) opened in 2009 and is simple but flawlessly clean and efficiently run by joyous *hospitaleras* attuned to the old tradition of pilgrim hospitality on the Camino. They also serve a fresh, simple, and satisfying communal dinner, usually offering soup, salad, pasta, and dessert (€8), and breakfast (€3.5).

Leaving Rabé de las Calzadas

About 4 kilometers (2.5 miles) after leaving Rabé de las Calzadas, you'll pass a section of the Camino, several meters long, known as **Pedras Sagradas** (approximately Km 473.8). Here, passing pilgrims have built mounds and cairns from the stark-white local fieldstones, giving the wild terrain the feel of a Shinto shrine.

You are now ascending to the **Cuesta de Matamulos**, a hill that rises 950 meters (3,117 feet) above sea level. Here, the horizon opens up to a glorious vista below, followed by a dramatic descent into Hornillos del Camino. This stretch is stunning in all seasons, but especially in spring, when red poppies speckle the pale green fields with splashes of color.

Hornillos del Camino Km 468.6

The name Hornillos ("little oven" or "little kiln") hints at some past industry, perhaps smelting, but this town (pop. 58) was and remains an important stop for pilgrims for food and shelter in this off-the-beaten-path country.

The 13th-century Gothic church of **San Román** on the **Plaza de la Iglesia** holds the highest point in the village. In the 12th century, monks from Saint Denis in Paris founded a monastery here that later was transferred to Benedictines in south-central France. Inside the church is a sculpture of the famous Black Madonna of Rocamadour, a reminder of this French connection. Sloping down from the church toward the main street is an inviting village square with **Fuente del Gallo**, the Rooster's Fountain, in the center.

Food and Accommodations

On the main street, facing the church and square, is the lively **Bar y Restaurante** (Calle Real, 14; 947-564-798), serving refreshments, tapas, and sandwiches in the bar and sit-down meals in the dining room, with fresh and good home-cooked options on the daily *menú de peregrino* (€10).

A favorite *albergue*, **El Alfar de Hornillos** (Calle Cantarranas, 3; 654-263-857; www.elalfardehornillos.es; 20 beds; €9) is open from Apr.-Oct. It is family run, in a comfortable space with an outdoor patio and a family-style dining room. They also offer a communal dinner (€9; they are especially known for their paella) and breakfast (€3). Sleeping options are in three rooms, one with four beds, one with six beds, and the third with 10 beds.

De Sol a Sol (Calle Cantarranas, 7 bajo; 649-876-091) is situated in a family home-turned-*hostal* with shared kitchen, dining area, lounge, garden, and clean and homey sleeping spaces with seven rooms, one being a room with bunkbeds (€10/bed) and the others double rooms with private baths (€40-50). For many, it is the owner, Samuel, that makes this place special; he welcomes everyone

warmly and wants to help in any way that he can. When Martin Sheen walked the Camino with his son, Emilio Estévez, and grandson, Taylor Levi Estévez (before the father and son came back to film *The Way*), the three arrived at Samuel's place, but it was full. Out of concern that they have a place to stay, Samuel sent them to his mother's home, where Taylor met Samuel's sister and became smitten; eventually, the two married.

Arroyo de Sanbol
Km 462.9

This little oasis, the Arroyo de Sanbol, also called Sambol, has no inhabitants other than the *hospitaleros* and the pilgrims who stay in the *albergue*. There is pilgrim lore surrounding its natural spring, located a few meters south of the Camino. That spring may be why people built the monastery of **San Baudillo** here in the 11th century. Though little remains of San Baudillo, the spring still flows and some pilgrims say it has curative powers. (Many claim that washing their feet in the locale's freshwater pool relieves them of foot problems for the rest of the Camino.)

Accommodations

Here in this sparse outpost is the municipal, beehive-shaped **Albergue Arroyo de Sanbol** (606-893-407; €5 for a bed; €7 for dinner), which offers rustic—no plumbing or electricity—but impeccably clean and charming accommodation for up to 12 pilgrims. If you desire simplicity and to sleep in deep silence under a big starry sky, this is your adventure. It comes with a great pilgrim meal shared around a large wooden round table. Bedtime is at 9pm.

Hontanas Km 458.1

The village of Hontanas (pop. 73) is named for the many sources of water

that flow through the area. (The name is born from *fuentes* in Spanish, *fontaines* in French, and *fons* and *fontibus* in Latin.) The central church in Hontanas is the **Iglesia de la Immaculada Concepción** (Calle Iglesia, 3), a sturdy 14th-century structure that defines the horizon as you approach. It has a lovely modern twist, a niche portraying a strong ecumenical feel with images of leaders and holy people from many faiths across the world, honoring all of humanity's sacred traditions. For some pilgrims, this open and peaceful atmosphere is reason enough to stay in Hontanas.

Food and Accommodations

The excellent bar and restaurant **Mesón El Puntido** (Calle Iglesia, 6; €4-10) turns out fresh and creative meals morning to night. It's set in a historic stone and wood building along the main street, across from the church.

Next door, **Hotel Fuentestrella** (Calle Iglesia, 4; 947-377-261; www.fuentestrella. com) is modest but serene and clean, with five double rooms (€35-45) and one triple room (€55), all with private bath. An adjoining restaurant offers good meal options—home-cooked dishes, both on a traditional *menú del peregrino* as well as different a la carte offerings. A dining terrace out on the small square adds to the ambiance.

Albergue Santa Brigada (Calle Real, 19; 609-164-697; open Mar.-Oct.; 16 beds in three rooms; €8) is a pretty and clean place to stay. An adjoining bar and shop sell food. They also serve dinner (€8) and breakfast (€3).

From top to bottom: Pedras Sagradas (sacred stones) on the trail just past Rabé de las Calzadas; partially standing walls in the ruins of San Anton's medieval monastery; Bar Casa Manolo in Hornillos del Camino.

====== **Top Experience** ======

★ San Antón Monastery Ruins
Km 452.5

Founded in 1146 by the French order of Antonines, the present ruins of the monastery of San Antón Abad stand alone in the nook of a small ravine, mostly to the left of the Camino. Largely Gothic and from the 14th century, the monastery existed in service to pilgrims as a hospital. The Camino romantically passes under one of the monastery's half-crumbled arches. In the Middle Ages, this site contained a sheltered porch area where pilgrims who arrived after the monastery gates had been locked for the night could find a protected place to sleep. There, the monks also left food and drink in two stone niches set within the wall. The niches survive today, and pilgrims fill them with notes, poems, and other offerings.

Before fully passing under this arch to continue on the Camino, follow the wall to your left to see what else survives of the ruins. Standing in the middle of the monastery, with its collapsed ceiling, decaying Gothic walls, and grass growing across the monastic floor, is a hauntingly beautiful experience. Look at the windows to find the one showing the symbol of the Antonines, the

form of a Tau cross: a cross with three arms, somewhere between a T and a Y. Medieval brothers baked the Tau cross into loaves of bread in order to heal pilgrims of illnesses—especially Saint Anthony's Fire. The Tau was (and by some, still is) considered an esoteric symbol through which Saint Anthony comes to one's aid and administers cures. In recent Camino lore, the Tao cross is also associated with the Templars, who like the Antonines were on the Camino to protect and serve the pilgrims.

You can still sleep in the ruins, in a simple small shelter built against the side of one of the standing moanstery walls, and benefit from the legacy of kindness and a simple but good meal at the donation-based **Albergue San Antón** (Open Oct.-Apr.; 14 beds). The sleeping area and toilets are very clean. There is water but no hot water and no electricity. Dinner is by candlelight.

Castrojeriz   Km 448.8

The approach to the hilltop town of Castrojeriz (pop. 552) is beautiful: the Iglesia del Manzano appears on the horizon, tucked into the protective foot of the castle hill, and grows slowly larger as you approach. The town is small and seemingly sleepy but full service, lively,

Saint Anthony's Fire

During the 11th to 14th centuries, an epidemic of ergot poisoning known as Saint Anthony's Fire plagued northern Europe. It most commonly came from rye grains infected by fungus. It could cause skin lesions, convulsions, hallucinations, and ultimately death.

Interestingly, people were cured of this illness after visiting **San Antón Abad** and other Antonine monasteries that rose to serve the ailing. One explanation was the good bread the monks distributed:

Because the monks' bread was untainted with ergot, the ill were able to clear the ergot from their system. Exercise apparently also helps in the curing process, so it makes sense that, as pilgrims exerted themselves physically on the Camino while eating uninfected bread and other sustenance, they were on their way to a natural cure. It also helped that, on the *meseta*, the main grain grown was, and remains, wheat, which is not as susceptible to ergot as rye.

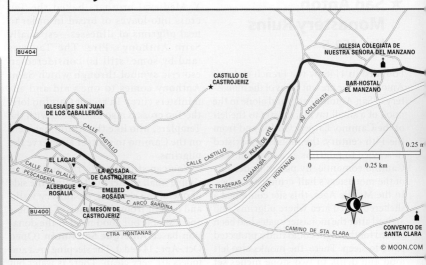

Castrojeriz

IGLESIA COLEGIATA DE
NUESTRA SEÑORA DEL MANZANO

BAR-HOSTAL
EL MANZANO

CASTILLO DE
CASTROJERIZ

IGLESIA DE SAN JUAN
DE LOS CABALLEROS

CALLE CASTILLO

BU404

EL LAGAR

CALLE STA OLALLA

C PESCADERÍA

ALBERGUE
ROSALIA

LA POSADA
DE CASTROJERIZ

EMEBED
POSADA

CALLE CASTILLO

C ARCO SARDINA

EL MESÓN DE
CASTROJERIZ

BU400

CTRA HONTANAS

C REAL DE OTE

AV COLEGIATA

C TRASERAS CAMARASA

CTRA HONTANAS

CAMINO DE STA CLARA

CONVENTO DE
SANTA CLARA

0   0.25 mi

0   0.25 km

© MOON.COM

warm, and with a vibrant community that comes to life after the siesta hour. Underneath the entire town are interconnecting tunnels that hide wine cellars. They are privately owned, but you can get a glimpse of these if you stay in the Posada Emebed, or just ask anywhere you alight if you can get a glimpse of the subterranean world.

Castrojeriz was an Iron Age Celtiberian site that was later dominated by Romans. In the early Middle Ages, Visigoths took this hill, and soon after them, Iberian Muslims and Christians alternated control over the town many times, until it fell permanently into the hands of the latter. Castrojeriz was incorporated into the Kingdom of Castile and León in 974 and was an important commercial and pilgrim town. At one point it had seven pilgrim hospitals and five churches. The Jewish population here was highly valued and protected, and some vestiges of their lives here remain, especially if you stop for a drink or a meal in El Lagar, a bar and restaurant set over what most likely was once the synagogue.

Sights

The Camino passes into the center of Castrojeriz, built on the lower half of the hill's slope, after passing the Iglesia del Manzano on the path's right, and all the while the castle on the hilltop far above, towering protectively over the town, also stands on your right.

Iglesia Colegiata de Nuestra Señora del Manzano

The Iglesia de Nuestra Señora del Manzano, Our Lady of the apple tree, stands on the site where Mary miraculously appeared to Saint James, who was passing through on horseback. When Saint James neared an apple tree in the orchard that grew here, he saw Mary, and his horse left hoof prints in stone marking the spot where he saw the image. Local lore says that rock is still there, on the south-side entrance to the church.

This is the Virgin whose numerous miracles King Alfonso X (1221-1284) of Castile and León celebrated in his sacred songs, the *Cantigas de Santa María*. Out of a total of some 427 songs, five of them were dedicated to the miracles of

Castilian Folklore on the Camino

Like other regions on the Camino, Castile is not without magical creatures, some of which seem to have been folded into more modern Christianity.

Moras

There are tales across Castile of enchantresses and fairies called *moras*. Some think the name *mora* comes from the Spanish for Moorish women from the south, who were were considered exotic by their northern neighbors. But more recent etymologies show an interesting syncretism from an earlier word for ancient inhabitants, *moradores,* that over time took on mythic associations. Either way, these moras share certain divine qualities: They protect the natural world; test mortals; guard hidden treasures; live near rocks, trees, caves, stones and springs; and at times act as agents of justice in human society. They are sisters to Galicia's *mouras,* Asturias' *xanas,* and Basque Country's Mari.

Curiously, the Marys of the Camino exhibit some of the *moras'* qualities. The Marys of Castrojeriz (who was first found in an apple tree) and Villalcazar de Sirga saved many people from death or disaster. There is a Mary in the hermitage of the village of Bercianos del Camino Real who is named after a pear tree. In Sahagún, another Mary, called La Peregrina, is celebrated for her appearance as a guide at night for pilgrims, leading them to shelter with light that emanated from her staff. Another Mary on this stretch, just before Villalcazar de Sirga, arrived on the banks of the nearby river when it flooded and villagers built a shrine in her honor, La Virgen del Río. You can visit her shrine right after you cross the bridge over the very same river.

Reñubero

Reñubero is a storm god (also known as the Nubero across other parts of northern Spain). In Castile and León, where agriculture is the biggest activity, the Reñubero may suddenly appear out of nowhere and wreak large-scale destruction on crops.

Las Ánimas

Disembodied spirits wander here, too. Top among them are Las Ánimas, who can appear as a procession of souls or as a solitary visitor seeking to make contact or pass on a message. The ghosts are respected and honored, but encouraged to keep moving.

Duendes

If you happen to stay in an *albergue* and hear bumps in the night, it is probably a *duende* (house elf, also called a *trasgo* or *trasgu*) making mischief in the kitchen. One particular *duende,* the Martinico, likes to create disarray in homes and also invades people's bodegas. As much as they can cause chaos and trouble, sometimes they feel inclined to help people in need, a thing to keep in mind as a pilgrim out on the road.

this Mary, who especially looked out for stonemasons. Among her miracles, she's credited with saving several masons from falls that would have been fatal without her intervention.

The church foundations reach back to the 11th and 12th centuries, though the reconstructed vaults date to the 16th to 18th centuries. The image of Alfonso X's miraculous Madonna, the 13th-century polychrome-painted stone statue, stands in the heart of the altar, an interesting depiction of Mary holding Jesus in a complete profile view; Mary herself appears as you might see classical images of the Greek earth goddess, Demeter.

Castillo de Castrojeriz

This castle's medieval foundations carry aspects of the town's earlier occupants: the Visigoths built a castle, here, too, and incorporated aspects of the earlier Roman fortress into it (and Romans doubtlessly used aspects of the Celtiberian *castro*).

The builders of the medieval fortification used aspects of both Roman and Visigothic foundations.

The medieval castle actually survived intact until 1755, when it crumbled into ruins during an earthquake that more famously destroyed Lisbon. Today, about one-third of the heavily walled, fortified castle survives, most of it having crumbled into poetic heaps except for one central wall that stands out straight into the sky.

If you want to understand the surrounding landscape's topography, and enjoy exploring castle ruins, make the climb to the top of the hill and enjoy its view over the *meseta*. Both Iberian Christians and Muslims controlled the territory from this hill, on and off in the early Middle Ages.

Iglesia de San Juan de los Caballeros

The heavily fortified, largely Gothic, 13th-century **Iglesia de San Juan** (Calle Cordón, 22; 947-377-011) has, among its sacred symbols, a beautiful and unusual window in the shape of a five-pointed star. The star represents the five wounds of Christ; in medieval sacred geometry, especially for stonemasons and builders, it was the ancient Pythagorean sign of wholeness and divine perfection. In the ancient world, the five-pointed star represented Venus.

This church was originally a Romanesque building, and these foundations define the structure. It was later reformed with Gothic, Mudéjar, and Baroque elements. Ornate Mudéjar woodwork and painting forms the ceiling of the beautifully preserved cloister. In the cloister garden, notice the solar disk tombstones, which are common across Basque Country and Navarra and signify the blending of earlier pagan ideas with later Christian ones. The tombstones are round and engraved with images of intersecting arms that suggest both a radiating sun and an equal-armed cross. In pagan religion, the sun was considered the supreme life-giving and life-regenerating power, an association that translated smoothly to the image and concept of the cross and its representation of Jesus as the bringer of light and rebirth.

Castrojeriz's Igelsia del Manzano, village, and protective castle hill

Convento de Santa Clara

On the southeast outskirts of town are the restored convent ruins of **Convento de Santa Clara** (Camino de Santa Clara; 947-377-011; www.castrojeriz.com; 9am-7pm), with a lovely Gothic monastery church and walled-in compound surrounding it, containing resident and garden spaces. Alfonso X founded this convent in the 13th century, though builders constructed the current church in the 14th century and it was massively restored in the 18th century.

Once a Franciscan monastery, today the convent is run by Clarist nuns and thus is called Santa Clara. They make their living providing large-scale laundry service for businesses, and selling special pastries. (Try their *puños de San Francisco*, Saint Francis's Cuffs, a sponge, puff-shaped vanilla cake roll filled with rich cream, which you can buy directly from them at a the convent.) Daily **mass** is at 8:30pm in the convent church; the hours may be earlier in winter. Additionally, **Lauds** is at 8am (7:50 on Sundays and holidays); the **Eucharist** at 8:30am; **Rosary Benediction** at 5pm; and **Vespers** at 8:20pm (7:30 on Sundays and holidays).

Festivals and Events

Castrojeriz has some vibrant festivals that all involve festive processions, traditional attire, song, dance, and music. **Fiesta de San Juan**—Saint John's Festival—occurs every June 24, celebrating both the summer solstice and Saint John the Baptist's feast day; the **Fiesta de Ajo**—Garlic Festival—happens in mid-July, and the **Fiesta de Sejo**, the town's sacred celebration of their patroness, Nuestra Señora del Manzano, is on the second Sunday in September, with processions and celebrations of the town's folk traditions in music, dance, and food.

Food and Nightlife

Like so many towns across Spain, at siesta hour Castrojeriz can feel like a ghost town, then suddenly explodes into life and activity as people leave their homes, meet friends in cafés, do afternoon and evening shopping, go to church, stroll about, and stop to gossip with neighbors. During this time, late afternoon into evening, the small squares and narrow streets hum with activity, and locals will make you feel a welcome part of it.

On entering town, break for a drink, a snack, or a meal (really good pizza is the main option, as well as the ubiquitous *tortilla*, Spanish omelet) at the inviting **Bar-Hostal Manzano** (Avenida Virgen del Manzano, 1; 620-782-768) right beside the Iglesia del Manzano. You can also check in for the night (double rooms with bath, €35) for a basic, clean, and peaceful rest. The owners sustain a remarkable sense of hospitality as thousands of tired pilgrims walk past on their way to Castrojeriz's center, another few hundred meters ahead.

El Lagar (Calle Cordón, 16; 947-377-441) is a great tapas bar and restaurant for home-cooked meals, but it also was once the likely location of Castrojeriz's synagogue. El Lagar, which means "the wine press," is named after the wine press that once operated here and is still located on the premises.

El Mesón de Castrojeriz (Calle Cordón, 1; 947-378-610), the bar and restaurant connected to La Posada hotel, offers a good dinner menu (including a €10 *menú del peregrino*) featuring traditional Castilian cuisine from this region, such as *cecina* (dry cured beef), *cocido* (*a pot au feu*-style stew with meats, garbanzos, cabbage and other vegetables), various lamb dishes, and rice pudding.

Accommodations

Among the town's seven *albergues,* the super-clean and charming **Albergue Rosalia** (Calle Cordon, 2; 947-373-714; open Mar.-Oct.; four rooms on two floors; 32 beds; €10) is a top pick and wins points for offering single, generous-sized beds—not bunks—arrayed in several small dormitories with rustic low timbered roofs, stucco whitewashed walls and sleek wooden floors. An honor system in the wonderful country kitchen allows pilgrims to cook at their leisure and pay for stocked items that they use, such as eggs, coffee, and pasta.

Of the five hotels in Castrojeriz, the centrally located **Posada Emebed** (Plaza Mayor, 5; 947-377-268; www.emebed-posada.com; 10 rooms, each very different; €50-70) most feels like an elegant medieval manor (though it dates to the 19th century) in the quality of the furnishings and the stately stone walls, while possessing all the modern comforts: large rooms, comfortable beds with plush linens, private terraces with café tables, and a great view across the *meseta*. Additional services include massage therapy (arranged in advance) and bikes for exploring the surrounding area. If you stay here, ask the English-speaking owners to show you the underground wine cellars.

La Posada de Castrojeriz (Landelino Tardajos, 5; 947-378-610; info@laposadadecastrojeriz.es; €45) is a bit more basic, but rooms are still spacious and elegant. A nice interior courtyard patio has a good library and is an enjoyable space in which to relax.

Leaving Castrojeriz

One of the most beautiful vistas of the *meseta* is 3.5 kilometers (2.2 miles) after leaving Castrojeriz. A steep climb leads up the slope of the high ridge, **Alto de Mostelares,** (900-meters/2,953 feet). You are well rewarded for the hard effort to get here with limitless views of the yellow and green wheat fields of the *meseta* looking like a billowing patchwork quilt. Pilgrims have built stone mounds on this hilltop that add to the beauty. Be careful on the descent: The path is at a steep angle and is paved, making it easier to slip. High winds also gust on this hilltop and across the vast wheat fields you are hiking toward. At the end of the slope

where the trail levels out again you will spy another reward, the refreshing Rio Pisuerga with the Ermita de San Nicolás settled along its eastern bank.

★ Ermita de San Nicolás at Puente de Itero   Km 441.3

There is a special feng shui to the surviving vestige of this 12th-century hospice and hermitage, Ermita de San Nicolás, now a refuge. The single rectangular stone building stands at the base of a dale, with a sweeping horizon through wheat fields beyond. The Rio Pisuerga flows nearby, crossed by the lovely **Puente de Itero,** a bridge with 11 arches dating to Alfonso VI's rule in the 11th century.

Accommodations

Before crossing the bridge, stop to visit the inside of the hermitage and consider staying at ★ **Ermita de San Nicolás** (947-377-359; open mid-May through September; 12 beds; €5). It is well run and serene, if rustic. Originally run by Benedictine monks, today it is run by Italian *hospitaleros*, who offer excellent hospitality and serve a communal meal by candlelight (only the bathroom has electricity). The river burbling nearby completes the calm atmosphere. At night, this a great place to view the Milky Way.

Leaving Ermita de San Nicolás

A little over 1 kilometer (0.6 miles) after crossing the bridge next to the hermitage, you'll pass a 16th-century church as you enter into the village of **Itero de la Vega** (Km 438), an oasis in the middle of vast swaths of wheat fields. The village's **Hostal Puente Fitero** (979-151-822; eight rooms; €30-40) is also an *albergue* (22 beds; €6) bar, restaurant (with *menú del peregrino* for €10), and little food shop. The whole establishment is well run and impeccable.

Before you leave, stock up on water and food if you need it; the next stretch is 8.5 kilometers (5.3 miles) without support services until you reach Boadilla del Camino. Three kilometers (1.9 miles) after Itero de la Vega, you'll cross the **Canal de Pisuerga**, a manmade canal built to irrigate farmland in this wheat-growing territory, which defines the 5 kilometers (3.1 miles) to Boadilla.

Boadilla del Camino
Km 429.7

In the center of Boadilla, you pass the farming village's most distinctive feature: the **Rollo de Boadilla,** a towering and intricately carved Gothic cross covered in scallop shells. The 15th-century cross has a macabre history attached to its artistry: This was a post of justice, and people found guilty of serious crimes were hanged here. Its tradition comes from the era of Enrique IV (1425-1474), who granted Boadilla self-governance from outside powers. Near the cross is the 15th- and 16th-century church of **Santa María**, a solid structure that was restored and reformed many times into the 18th century.

Accommodations

Off the same square as the church, **Albergue En El Camino** (Plaza el Rollo; 979-810-284; www.boadilladelcamino. com; Mar.-Oct.) is a favorite pause, in part for its large garden and pool, but mostly for the easy-going warmth of its *hospitaleros,* who also offer great food and drink. They offer 70 beds in four large dorm rooms (€8/bed), and an evening meal for €10; breakfast is €3.

Leaving Bodilla del Camino

Approximately 1 kilometer (0.6 miles) after Boadilla del Camino, the Camino meets up with and runs parallel to the left of the **Canal de Castilla,** which was built for irrigation in the 17th and 18th

centuries. It is rife with frog, toad, and bird life, as well as wild yellow irises, four types of lizards, and water snakes. From here, another 4.8 kilometers (3 miles) remain to Frómista.

Frómista Km 424

To enter Frómista (pop. 790), the Camino crosses a bridge over the Canal de Castilla at the point of an elaborate damming gate that controls the flow of water. You then enter on the main road into town, passing the train station on your left.

Sunflowers, wheat, and barley cover the fields surrounding Frómista, making the horizon a gorgeous melding of bright blue sky and golden undulating earth. In spring, that horizon transforms into a pale green speckled with red poppies. This territory has long been the heart of Spain's breadbasket. Celts and Celtiberians cultivated the land here, and Romans called this town *frumentum* ("cereal" in Latin). By the 11th century, Frómista was an important religious and market center on the Camino. It also was home to an ancient Jewish community that continued to thrive into the 14th century. In 1492, when the Spanish monarchs Isabel and Ferdinand forced conversion or expulsion upon its Jewish and Muslim communities, the economy and agriculture diminished with their decline, here as well as across significant parts of the country.

Frómista today is still about wheat and bread—this is its main industry—but also about cheese, which is celebrated at an annual festival in July. If you can't be here for the festival, be sure to visit the local art exhibit space, café, and sale venue for local cheeses, **La Venta de Boffard**.

For a town of nearly 800, Frómista feels more like 200, but you'll nevertheless find several nice places to eat and sleep. The outdoor cafés surrounding the church of San Martín probably offer the best atmosphere, but don't overlook the

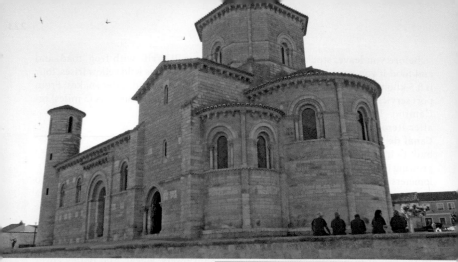

Clockwise from top: Frómista's Iglesia de San Martín; Boadilla del Camino's medieval post of justice, the Rollo de Boadilla; lock of the Canal de Castilla just before Frómista; sculptures on Frómista's Iglesia de San Martín.

more intimate square behind the Iglesia de San Pedro, also with several good cafés and inns.

Sights

Frómista has three churches: the **Iglesia de San Pedro,** fortified, sturdy, largely unadorned but with elegant vaults, from the 13th century; the largely 16th-century **Iglesia de Santa María del Castillo;** and the reason why people visit Frómista, the **Iglesia de San Martín,** one of the jewels of medieval Iberia, built in the 11th century. San Martín is worth all the time you can offer it, both to take in all the stone images engraved in the corbels and capitals inside and out, and also to enjoy the visceral feeling of being in a sacred space built to perfect proportions for the human form.

★ Iglesia de San Martín

The **Iglesia de San Martín de Tours** (Plaza San Martín, 3; 979-810-144; Apr.-Sept., daily, 9:30am-2pm and 4:30-8pm; €1, free on Wed.), was built in AD 1066 and once belonged to an adjoining Benedictine monastery that no longer stands. It is considered the purest French Romanesque church in Spain, and in many ways, it is a prototype for understanding the proportions, harmony, and richly expressive sculpture of the Romanesque style in France as well. Step inside to take in the pleasing pale yellow domed ceiling sweeping overhead, or the many carved capitals recounting Biblical, historical, moral, and humorous tales. A personal favorite, on the second pillar from the back end of the church, on the left in the central nave, depicts the vain raven with a loaf of bread in his beak, and the clever fox who wanted to steal it. The fox praised the raven's magnificence, and when the raven opened his mouth to respond, the loaf fell and the fox took off with it. The imagery culminates in the statue of Jesus at the altar, and, to his right, the compelling dark-toned wooden

sculpture of **La Virgen de la Acogida,** the Virgin of the host. Another aspect of the intimate artistry is how the proportions and shape create perfect acoustics. If you sing here, the resonating sound will wash over you and transport you to another level of sacred experience.

Once, risqué corbels—a veritable Kama Sutra of the Middle Ages—adorned the church's exterior, but many of these were replaced with sedate floral and geometric patterns when the church was restored between 1896 and 1904. (Ironically, those sexually explicit sculptures reflected not inhibition, but an earth-bound and honest view of humanity in 11th-century Europe. In fact, at the time, it was the norm in Europe to show that chaotic world on the outside of churches, and then invite the nonliterate populace to step inside the church, where the chaos and wildness of life is controlled and tamed.)

A few of the saucy corbels do remain, along with many expressive and idiosyncratic characters that depict local folklore and stories. Look especially for the contemplative sage wearing a turban, the woman who has just given birth, the giant baring his sharp teeth, and the playful animals with charming expressions. There are also three sculptures of waterfowl (ducks, geese, and swans), considered symbols of fidelity and also guides and gatekeepers of the heavens. They also may have an association with the medieval-to-early modern-game, the Game of the Goose, where they also act as guides and guardians of pilgrims on the Camino.

Festivals and Events

In the third week of July is the **Feria del Queso** (979-810-001; administracion@Frómista.es), the cheese fair where you can taste the artisanal cheeses (largely sheep's milk) and meats (including *chorizos* and *morcillas*) produced in the region.

Food

To purchase gourmet goods for a picnic before heading back on the trail, especially the sheep's milk cheese from Frómista, *queso de oveja Boffard,* stop at **La Venta de Boffard,** a shop as well as a café, bar, restaurant, art gallery, and garden.

La Venta de Boffard (Plaza San Martín, 8; 979-810-012; www.laventafromista.com; €10-12) is an art exhibit space, music venue, and a food-lover's paradise, combining a love for Palencia's foods (cheese, charcuterie, homegrown greens) with art and ethnography. Run by two English-speaking sisters from Palencian and Basque backgrounds, they welcome everyone warmly and hold pilgrims as special guests. In this spirit, they prepare a gourmet *menú de peregrino* as well as an array of other offerings, such as savory toasts with *bellota* (acorn-fed cured ham), Boffard cheese, and smoked salmon, as well as desserts such as white chocolate flan. The Iglesia de San Martin, just outside on the square, adds to the artsy atmosphere.

El Apostal (Avenida Ejército Español, 5; 979-033-209; www.hostalelapostal. com; €10) is frequented as much by locals as by pilgrims. They offer a straightforward and fresh *menú del dia* that offers three courses with many choices, including vibrant fresh salads, grilled fish, and stuffed red peppers, with just-plucked Persian melon for dessert.

★ **Restaurante Doña Mayor** (Calle Francesa, 31; 979-810-588; www.hoteldonamayor.com; €18) is more than a hotel; it's also a great restaurant and bar. Departing from the typical menu, the Doña Mayor offers an a la carte splurge with dishes such as lemon- and rosemary-grilled salmon, a vegetarian sauté of local vegetables with chickpeas and artichoke mayonnaise, and two varieties of lasagna (spinach or meat). Desserts include blackberry cheesecake, brownies, and lemon-blueberry sponge cake, served on slate planks. In good weather, you can choose to dine in the private garden.

Accommodations

Frómista has a wide array of accommodation among its four *albergues* and almost a dozen pensions, *hostales,* and hotels. Nothing distinguishes the *albergues,* but the range of other accommodation might entice you to splurge for private digs; if you share a room with one or two other pilgrims, the price can be quite sweet.

Named after the 11th-century patroness of the Iglesia de San Martín, the **Hotel Doña Mayor** (Calle Francesa 31; 979-810-588; www.hoteldonamayor.com; 12 rooms; €70-100, which typically includes breakfast) is a modern building in the old center of town with an excellent bar and restaurant. All spaces—guest rooms and dining—are contemporary designs with earthy and appealing woodwork along the walls and floors. Large floor-to-ceiling windows let in copious light. They offer a large buffet breakfast with gluten-free options (€9). Proprietors speak English.

Hostal El Apostal (Avenida Ejército Español, 5; 979-033-209; www.hostalelapostal.com; €30/45/60 with breakfast) is not only a great restaurant but also a lovely inn on a quiet square next to Iglesia de San Pedro. Rooms are a mix of modern and cozy. Proprietors speak English.

Across the street from Iglesia San Pedro, ★ **Hostal San Pedro** (Avenida Ejército Español, 8; 979-810-016; www.hostalsanpedrofromista.com; €30-55) feels like home. The welcoming and engaging proprietor, July (pronounced *who-lee*), has designed her boutique-like *hostal* with great artistic flair. Rooms are painted with saturated, earthy colors, and the floors are sleek gray tiles. Bathrooms are spotless. The whole place is decorated with restored antiques from 19th- and 20th-century Castile. July offers a good buffet breakfast (€4.50) in the communal dining room.

Getting There

Three trains daily depart Madrid, with a change in Valladolid, for **Frómista** (2.5-4.5 hours; €27-40).

Leaving Frómista

You will walk on a dirt path that runs parallel to the right side of the **P-980** from Frómista to Población de Campos (3.4 km/2.1 mi).

Población de Campos
Km 420.6

Just a few hundred meters before arriving in Poblacion de Campos (pop. 137), a village founded in the 11th century, you pass the lyrical hermitage, **Ermita de San Miguel**, a small chapel with transitional Romanesque corbels and Gothic doorway from the 13th century. The villagers of Poblacion de Campos have arrayed picnic tables here for pilgrims to enjoy a rest in the shade of the poplar trees, an oasis in the *meseta*.

The village has two other churches. The 16th-century **Iglesia de Santa María la Magdalena** is on the village's highest hill. Just below it is a hermitage set almost below ground—or, more accurately, the ground level has risen from later building over older settlements—making for a slight climb below street level to enter into the earthy and acoustically rich 13th-century **Ermita de la Virgen del Socorro**.

Food and Accommodations

The rural hotel, **Amanecer en Campos** (Calle Fuente Nueva, 5; 979-811-099; www.hotelamanecerencampos.com) offers lunches and dinners based on home-cooked dishes passed down for generations, including paella, Castilian soups, dishes from locally harvested vegetables, and homemade desserts. They also have 14 country-inn-style rooms (floral bedspreads, colorful walls with floral paintings) for €30-45, all with private baths; breakfast is €3.

The **Albergue La Finca** (on the P-980 across the road from the Ermita de San Miguel; 979-067-028 and 620-785-999; www.alberguelafinca.es; 20 beds; €10) is a stone, brick, and terracotta farmhouse with wonderful modern interiors— wide-planked wooden floors, modern bathrooms, a large country-style dining room, and an open lounge and kitchen with copious natural sunlight. A garden with pool and Japanese bridge are a calm space to rest. Beds (singles, not bunk beds) are in inset wall nooks with curtains, offering privacy. The restaurant and bar serves a *menú del peregrino* (€10) or an a la carte menu, specializing in regional dishes and Castilian wines.

Población's more basic **municipal** *albergue* (Calle Escuelas, 17; 979-811-099; €5) has 18 beds in one dorm room. Both *albergues* are open all year. The town also has three bars for meals, snacks, and drinks, and a shop for provisions.

Leaving Población de Campos

Soon after Población de Campos, the Camino splits. Both paths lead to Villarmentero de Campos. The path heading to the right eventually becomes a **riverside path** and adds 0.9 kilometers (0.6 miles) to the walk. The other continues straight on the **P-980** road that you have been on since Frómista.

The river path is more appealing and passes along the life-giving waters of the Río Ucieza, where you'll see stands of poplar trees and rich bird life, including European robins, canary-like serins, green woodpeckers, owls, hawks, and falcons.

Villarmentero de Campos   Km 417.5

The P-980 leads directly to Villarmentero de Campos (pop. 23). If you took the riverside path, the town is connected by a few-hundred-meter-long country road from the river—look for the distinctive white teepees in a field that identify the village. The 16th-century village church, **Iglesia de San Martín**, is interesting for its Mudéjar—Islamic-style—ceiling. (To go inside, ask a local if someone can unlock it.)

Accommodations

La Casona de Doña Petra (Calle Ramón y Cajal, 14; 979-065-978; www.lacasonadepetra.com; €35-55) with 12 private rooms, offering meals (€15) and breakfast (€5), was once a pilgrim hospice that operated until the late 17th century. Interestingly, when the present (English-speaking) owners restored the place, they discovered a hidden box containing an ancient deed in Hebrew that identified a Jewish resident as the owner.

The **Albergue Almanecer** (Calle Jose Antonio, 2; 629-178-543) offers 18 beds, three teepees (the very ones you saw when you approached the village), and three outdoor hammocks. For outdoor sleeping and sharing the grounds with wandering farm animals (donkeys, chicken, geese), the hammocks (€3) and teepees (€3; the ground is hard) give a novel twist to pilgrim lodging. Inside are comfortable bunkbeds (€6). The couple who runs Almanecer is celebrated for their homemade communal meals, prepared with care and passion. The dining area feels like a country farmhouse, with a wonderful long wooden table.

Leaving Villarmentero de Campos

Both paths—the P-980, or the dirt road back to the river path—lead next to Villalcazar de Sirga. I recommend that you continue on the riverside path, where just before Villalcazar you'll arrive at **Ermita de la Virgen del Río** after crossing a bridge over the Ucieza river. Once a 12th-century Romanesque church, now largely from the 18th century, this

hermitage remains an active sacred center for the people of Villalcazar de Sirga. This Lady of the River has a story similar to that of Logroño's Virgen del Ebro, who was found floating in the Ebro river: Locals found the Virgen del Río's icon floating up the Río Ucieza after a flood, and this shrine marks the spot where she came ashore. The brotherhood of the Virgen del Río, formed in 1650, carries on annual celebrations in her honor on the Monday after Pentecost Sunday (seven Sundays after Easter). The hermitage is open only on feast days, but has a generous covered porch where you can rest as well as some picnic tables on its grounds.

Just before entering Villalcazar de Sirga (approximately 30 meters/100 feet), if you have been walking the river side path, is **Palomar del Camino** (Kilometer 10 on the P-981; 653-916-600; www.palomardelcamino.com; *menú del peregrino* €10, a la carte €15), a good place for food and drink on the left side of the Camino and located in the round, white-stucco 19th-century dovecote (*palomar*) with shady terrace seating. A nice alternative to the lusty meats, stews, and casseroles of Castilian cuisine (which you will find in the restaurants in Villalcazar's central Plaza Mayor), it serves up nourishing and tasty lunches such as fresh salads and empanadas. Proprietors speak English.

Villalcázar de Sirga
Km 409.8

As you enter the small village of Villalcázar (pop. 172), notice the mounds and Hobbit-like holes with doors in the hillsides. These *bodegas* are where local families make and store their wine, as well as their harvest, cheeses, and cured meats. They are also social gathering places; in summer they can be a surprisingly cool.

Villacázar revolves around its celebrated church, Iglesia de Santa María la Blanca, and the Madonna, La Blanca, that it houses. In the 13th century, King

Alfonso X of Castile and León wrote, or commissioned, twelve of his sacred songs, *Cantigas,* about La Blanca's miracles. In fact, La Virgen Blanca performed so many stunning miracles—from restoring a blind man's sight to lifting a 24-pound weight a sinner was sentenced to carry—that Villalcázar became an important pilgrimage destination, and the Camino was actually redicted in the 13th century to pass through it.

It is possible that the Templar Knights used Villalcázar as a base from which to protect and serve pilgrims on the Camino. However, it seems more likely that this service was fulfilled by another knightly order, the Order of Santiago, though tradition and lore still refer to this as a Templar town. The Templar residence, the cloister, the towers, walls, gates, and pilgrim hospices were all largely destroyed by the 1755 earthquake or soon crumbled thereafter. That the church is still here is something. What remains feels epic: you feel the church's towering height as you walk into town.

Sights
★ Iglesia de Santa María la Blanca
Built in the late 12th and early 13th centuries, the transitioning Romanesque-to-Gothic **Church of Santa María la Blanca** (Plaza Mayor, s/n; 979-880-854) is like a fortress, and probably was used as one in times of duress. The high-porched entrance has Christ in Majesty and the Tetramorphs on the upper sculptured line; below them is Santa María la Blanca.

Inside, the church is unusual in that it has three naves and two crossings. You'll find the sculpture of the miraculous Mary of Alfonso X's *Cantigas* in the center of the altar's retable. This sculpture is also distinct in that it is carved of

From top to bottom: teepees for *peregrinos* at the Albergue Amanecer in Villarmentero de Campos; Iglesia de Santa María la Blanca in Villalcázar de Sirga; Iglesia de Santiago in Carrión de los Condes.

stone—like that of Castrojeriz's Virgen del Manzano—and not wood, the more common medium of revered Marian icons along the Camino.

You'll easily locate the chapel dedicated to Santiago; it is in the end of the transept that includes the church's beautiful and unusual rose window. With 14 petals, rather than the more typical 6, 8 or 12, this window is also aligned to let in the midday sun.

The posted visiting hours are May-Oct.15 10:30am-2pm and 4:30-7pm; Oct.16-Apr. Mon.-Fri. by arrangement, Sat.-Sun. and holidays 12-2pm and 5-6:30pm; visits are free unless you arrange a guided tour (€1). Despite these posted hours, the church, especially in the early autumn, is typically open in the mornings, but the afternoons are less certain.

Food

★ **Mesón de los Templarios** (Plaza Mayor; 979-888-022; www.mesonlostemplarios.com), next to the church, and ★ **Meson de Villasirga** (Plaza Mayor; 979-888-022; www.mesonvillasirga.com) are run by the same proprietor, Pablo Payo. He opened the former in 1984 and the latter in 1965. Both are on the Plaza Mayor, kitty-corner from each other. Both serve classic Castilian food, medieval-banquet style, including roasted meats on bread plates meant to be eaten, large casseroles, and special pastries, including the anisseed-laced ones you may have smelled on entering the village. These are among the Camino's most traditional (and sought out) restaurants. Payo opened the original, Mesón de Villasirga, to better serve pilgrims' culinary needs, which it delivers in a large communal hall. The Mesón de los Templarios is also intended for pilgrims and other visitors, but is a bit more formal and transports you more to the

Middle Ages. People habitually drive from Burgos and Madrid just to eat at both places, where a meal typically can run €15-25. If one place is fully booked or closed, be sure to try the other.

★ **Confitería La Perla Alcazareña** (Calle El Ángel, 4; 979-888-020; www.pastelvillasirga.com), family operated for four generations (since 1870), lures locals and visitors alike with the butter-and-anise aroma that wafts from its ovens down all the streets of this little village. The bakery's creations include traditional Castilian almond cookies, *almendrados*, and little almond cakes, *amarguillos*. They also supply the dessert served at Meson de los Templarios and Meson de Villasirga. You'll find the bakery on the Camino as it is about to depart the village, on the right side.

Accommodations

Bar Hostal Las Cantigas (Calle Doctor Durango Solomon, 2; 979-888-027; www.hostallascantigas.es; €30 for a single, €40 for a double; wifi available) gets its name from its location, across the square from the celebrated church of Santa María La Blanca, for whom Alfonso X composed several *cantigas*. It merits a cantiga for its calm, clean, and welcoming atmosphere and excellent bar frequented by locals as well as pilgrims. They serve breakfast (€3.50) and a good, basic, and fresh *menú del peregrino* (€9.50) for dinner.

Casas Rurales Don Camino (Calle Real, 1; 979-888-163 and 620-399-040; www.casa-aurea.es) offers three rural hotels—Casa Áurea, Casa Federico, and Casa La Era—for nightly rent that come complete as apartments (€120-180/night), and, at the other end of the spectrum but also impeccable, the **Albergue Don Camino** (€7/bed). All options offer a private courtyard garden and a wonderful bar and restaurant serving specialties "taught to us by our grandmother, Abeula Áurea."

Carrión de los Condes
Km 404.2

Set on a bluff, sprinkled with compelling medieval churches, and populated with warm, sincere people, Carrión de los Condes (pop. 2,087) is a delightful place to visit. But the true highlight of this town is the singing nuns of the parish and *albergue* of Santa María. Many pilgrims report this as one of the apex experiences of their pilgrimage.

The town was first a Roman settlement, picked for the bluff with the river below and a terrific view of the world beyond. Visigoths next settled here, and in AD 713 North Africans conquered the town. By the 11th century, the town had a population of nearly 10,000 and was massively wealthy and hugely influential. Its wealth derived from large and diverse agricultural harvests and from the movement of people that the Camino opened. As with Burgos, Castrojeriz, and Fromísta, Carrión had a large Jewish community.

Carrión has a rocking **weekly market** around the Plaza de Santa María every Thursday morning, with food and produce vendors setting up alongside merchants selling clothing, shoes, household goods, and textiles. If you need to replace a piece of gear or buy a fruit knife or a corkscrew, this is the place to do it.

Sights
In its medieval height, during the 11th and 12th centuries, Carrión had thirteen parishes and a vast network of pilgrim support structures that could house up to 10,000 people. Today a few survive, the most interesting being the churches of Santa María and of Santiago, San Zoilo's monastery, and if you are interested in Saint Francis of Assisi, the monastery of Santa Clara.

Monasterio de Santa Clara
Saint Francis of Assisi slept in the Monasterio de Santa Clara (Calle Santa Clara 1) in 1214 when he made his pilgrimage to Santiago de Compostela. The cool part is that you can too. The present convent is mostly from the 17th century. Access to the monastery is restricted, but its *albergue* has a wonderful enclosed and porticoed courtyard reached as soon as you pass through the entry gate. The spaces designated for housing pilgrims are well kept. The convent has a small museum of sacred art, **Museo de Santa Clara** (Calle Santa Clara, 12; 979-880-134; www.carriondeloscondes.org; daily 11am-1:30pm and 4:30-9:30; €2), which also showcases the site's Franciscan history. Little of the 13th-century founding monastery survives.

Iglesia de Santa María del Camino
From the 12th century, a compelling aspect of the **Iglesia de Santa María** (Plaza Santa María, 1; 979-880-072; www.carriondeloscondes.org; open daily, Oct.-Mar., 11am-1:30pm and 5-7pm, Apr.-Sept., 9am-2pm and 4-9pm) is its porched entrance, adding more three-dimensionality to the overall south-facing door. The interior has a single nave, with similar transitional Romanesque-to-Gothic arches and engravings. Some of the polychrome decorative painting on the walls is still visible. The most appealing sculpture (of Mary, a lovely 12th-century depiction) is on the west entrance, facing the square where the Thursday market also sets up. You can enjoy a **mass** here daily at 8pm.

Iglesia de Santiago
The surviving part of this 12th-century church, destroyed by fire in the early 19th century, is its west entrance, a great example of Castilian Romanesque. There, Christ in Majesty is surrounded by the 24 Elders of the Apocalypse. Look closely to see characters from daily life in medieval Carrión: a cobbler, a tailor, a monk with book, dancers and acrobats, a scribe, a female zither player, and a blacksmith,

Carrion de los Condes

MONASTERIO DE SAN ZOILO
HOTEL MONASTERIO SAN ZOILO/
RESTAURANTE LAS VIGAS
CALLE SAN ZOILO
CALLE LAS HUERTAS
Rio Carrión
CL615
CL615
BAR CHANFFIX
MERINO
C. PIÑA BLASCO
C. ADOLFO SUÁREZ
EST. COLLANTES
RAMÍREZ
P241
P964
HOSTAL PLAZA MAYOR
C. QUINTANA
IGLESIA DE SANTIAGO
ALBERGUE DE SANTA MARIA
IGLESIA DE SANTA MARÍA DEL CAMINO
P980
CAFETERÍA LOS CONDES
C. STA. MARÍA
AV. DE LOS PEREGRINOS
RESTAURANTE LA CORTE
PADRE GIL
CAFE BAR ESPAÑA
STA. CLARA
MONASTERIO DE SANTA CLARA
Rio Carrión
0   200 yds
0   200 m
© MOON.COM

among others. A later Mudéjar-style bell tower is harmonious with the 12th-century façade. The Iglesia de Santiago contains the **Museo del Arte Sacro** (Calle de la Rúa; 979-880-072; www.carriondeloscondes.org; May-Sept. Tues.-Sun. 11am-2pm and 5-8pm, Mar.-Apr Tues.-Sun. 11am-2pm and 5-7pm; €1 guided visit), a museum of sacred art.

Monasterio de San Zoilo

The **Monasterio de San Zoilo** (Calle San Zoilo, 23; www.carriondeloscondes.org; summers only, 10:30am-2pm and 4:30-8pm; €2) was founded in the 900s in the name of Saint John the Baptist. When the trade of relics—and their ability to draw pilgrims and funds—peaked in the 11th century, the name changed to San Zoilo after a gift of this Cordoban saint's relics in 1047 from the Cordoban emir.

San Zoilo was under the Cluny Order then and was the second most powerful monastery in the Castile of the 11th and 12th centuries, surpassed only by Sahagún down the road. Jews, Christians, and Muslims in Carrión paid their royal taxes to the monastery instead of the king in the 13th century, amping up the financial prosperity of San Zoilo. After the 14th and 15th centuries, the monastery's influence declined. Today, it is an important site of national patrimony and also a luxury hotel that has turned the monks' quarters into guestrooms.

The cloisters have late Gothic arches and date to the Renaissance, built between 1537 and 1604, and are impressive for their unity of style and preservation. Seek out the older Romanesque doorway, which survives from the 11th century and was found hidden behind a wall in 1993.

━━━ **Top Experience** ━━━

★ Albergue de Santa María

Whether or not you stay here (though it is worth it to stay), the nuns who run the **Albergue de Santa María** (Calle del Clérigo Pastor, 6; 979-880-768) welcome pilgrims to gather in the large common room at 6:30pm, when they pull out a guitar and drums and perform sacred and folk songs with their beautiful voices, encouraging everyone to sing. They also lead the prayer service in the church next door, Iglesia de Santa María, with **Vespers** at 6pm, and **mass** and the **pilgrims' blessing** at 8pm. If you stay here, they serve a cheerful communal meal at 9pm.

Food

The **Cafe Bar España** (Plaza Piña Merino, 1; 979-880-047; €4-10) doubles as the town bus and taxi stand. But this also is a great informal place for a bite—whether you intend to keep walking or to wait for the bus—offering freshly made tortillas (Spanish omelets), sandwiches, good breakfasts, and all types of drinks.

Restaurante Las Vigas (Calle Obispo Souto, s/n; 979-880-050; www.sanzoilo.com/restaurante; €25-35) is an upscale choice located in the old monastery kitchen of the Monasterio de San Zoilo, today a warm wood-toned, brick and stone tavern setting. Modern interpretations of traditional dishes include grilled vegetables—*verduras a la plancha*—diversified with grilled leek, green asparagus, cauliflower, zucchini, brussel spouts, and carrots with piquant romesco sauce; cream of pumpkin soup with ham; the quintessential *lechazo* (roast baby lamb) for two (€45); and desserts such as coffee cream-filled pastry rolls with pistachio ice cream.

Restaurante La Corte (Calle Santa María, 36; 979-880-138; www.hostalrestaurantelacorte.com; €12-20), attached to the *hostal* of the same name, is a wonderful place to enjoy a *menú del peregrino, menú del dia,* or a la carte. Some

signature offerings are *cocido* (bean and meat stew), shellfish-stuffed red peppers, and even game, such as venison.

Bar Chanffix (Calle Esteban Collantes, 17; 979-880-435; €8-12) gives a modern twist to traditional Castilian cuisine (such as blood sausage, *morcilla*, and scrambled eggs) while also doing all the things a good bar does: offer every kind of drink and snack along with good robust *menús del peregrino*, salads, tapas (shared plates with 2-3 others, which can make for a great lunch or dinner), and homemade desserts, with terrace and inside seating. Excellent wine selection and vermouth.

An upbeat and inexpensive place, the **Cafetería Los Condes** (Plaza Mayor s/n; 979-880-136; www.cafeterialoscondes.com) serves up large tapas (€6-14), salads and soups (€3-7), combined platters (€8-9), paella (€11), and pizza (€9) on the cheerful corner of the Plaza Mayor right where the Camino passes as it leaves town.

Accommodations

★ **Hotel Monasterio San Zoilo** (Obispo Souto, s/n; 979 880-049; www.sanzoilo.com; €60-105), attached to the monastery, is the town's upscale accommodation, in a lovely riverside setting on the western edge of town right on the Camino. It's often a gathering place for cyclists on the Camino, with good space for bikes. It's a splurge, and the atmosphere can be a little more touristic and formal, with less of the usual Camino camaraderie. But the rooms and location are idyllic, with views of the monastery church and cloister. There is an atmospheric brick-and-tile hotel bar, and the hotel restaurant, **Las Vigas,** serves traditional cuisine.

Hostal Plaza Mayor (Calle Adolfo Suarez, 1; 669-340-131; www.hostal-plaza-mayor-negocio.site; €55, but inquire: they give special prices to pilgrims) opened in 2017, a wonderfully modern place with a fun, plucky sense of color and design while holding down a

Day Trip: Roman Villa of La Tejada

La Tejada (Kilometer 214 on the N-120; 650-410-913), is the best Roman remains within close access anywhere along the Camino. The ruins, discovered in 1970, are of a large Roman villa and a farm. The ruins retain many of its walls and its floor plan is remarkably well-demarcated. But the highlight is the colorful floor mosaics in full pristine condition. Look for complex geometric patterns, cavorting sea creatures, and the dynamic god Neptune looking as if he is blowing waves asunder.

You can walk here (carefully, because you have to walk on the road) from Cal-

zadilla de la Cueza (Km 387.3), a total of 8 kilometers (5 miles) round-trip, following the N-120 south. However, a much better plan is to arrange a taxi from Carrión de los Condes (€20-30, including 20-30 minute wait); have the cab driver wait while you explore the ruins, and then ask them to deliver you to Ledigos or Terradillos de los Templarios—or, walk, carefully, along the N-120 going northwest to pick up the Camino 4.5 kilometers (2.8 miles) just outside of Calzadilla de la Cueza, and continue the 4.1 kilometers (2.5 miles) to Ledigos.

---

classical edge. It is on a cheerful corner of the main square, right on the Camino. It has clean and quiet rooms with private baths, some with terraces.

Turning right past the church of Santa María is the ★ **Albergue de Santa María** (Calle del Clérigo Pastor, 6; 979-880-768; open Mar.-Oct.; 54 beds; €5), run by Augustinian singing nuns. It is a wonderful chance to hear and join in with sacred and folk song—the nuns play instruments as well as sing—an experience many pilgrims have claimed as one of the highlights of their entire Camino. It has a well-equipped kitchen and they offer a communal meal. The sleeping area is very clean and the bunkbeds comfortable. They serve watermelon as refreshment and send you off with blessed six-pointed stars to grace your Camino.

Monasterio de Santa Clara (Calle Santa Clara, 1; 979-880-837; Mar.-Nov.) offers 30 beds in four dormitory rooms of varying size (one only has two beds) at €5-7, with a shared bath in the *albergue* section of the monastery. Their *Hospedería*, hostel, offers nine private rooms with private baths for €25/50 for single/double. Come here not only to sleep where Saint Francis slept (in 1214), but also to enjoy a very inviting atmosphere, from the entrance at the

porticoed courtyard off the street, to the common spaces, kitchen, and ultra-clean (even if in some cases small) sleeping quarters. They do their share of singing here too; if you join the 8:30am Eucharist, you'll be treated to sacred song. Consider purchasing some of their special cupcake-like *magdalenas* for the road from the turnstile gate of the monastery.

Getting Around

The best way to find a taxi in Carrión is at the cafe **Bar España** (Plaza San Merino, 1; 979-880-047), which also happens to be where you can buy **ALSA/Monbus** bus tickets and wait for the bus, which stops out front. Two taxi services here are **Taxi Mariano Hervás Morante** (608-486-059) and **Taxi Jesús García Melgar** (979-880-918 and 639-886-824).

Leaving Carrión de los Condes

The next leg of the Camino is a long 16.9 kilometers (10.5 miles) to **Calzadilla de la Cueza** (Km 387.3, pop. 53) without support structures in between. (Most times there *should* be a caravan-like mobile café along this long stretch, but it can't be guaranteed.) Get an early start, if walking in the warm seasons, to cover most of this terrain before the midday sun. Calzadilla de la Cueza does offer food and lodging, but I do not recommend staying here. Instead, refuel at the village bar if you need a rest and provisions, and then continue on to **Ledigos** or **Terradillos de los Templarios**.

Alternatively, consider a sightseeing variation: Arrange a detour via taxi from Carrión de los Condes to visit the Roman Villa of La Tejada and then ask to be dropped off in Ledigos.

Ledigos   Km 381.1

The legacy of Ledigos (pop. 67), in times past as today, is to offer the weary traveler a place to stay; this village has one of the best *albergues* in Castile.

Inside the **Iglesia de Santiago,** which dates to the 13th century, you'll find several statues of Saint James.

Accommodations

A woman nicknamed La Morena founded ★ **Albergue La Morena** (Calle Carretera, 3; 626-972-118; www.alberguelamorena.com; open all year); today, her granddaughter and her family carry on her work ethic in this *albergue,* exceptional for its hospitality. They serve a great home-cooked *menú del peregrino* (€10) in the restaurant and bar, or you can cook for yourself in the well-equipped kitchen. The lodging is pristine and spacious. Options here cover the spectrum, from dorm beds (€8) to private rooms with shared bath (€35) and private rooms with private bath (€50).

Terradillos de los Templarios   Km 377.8

After a very long stretch on the flat *meseta,* it's a welcoming sight to come over the rise and see the huddle of terra cotta roofs that make up the village of Terradillos (pop. 68). The manufacture of red clay tiles and bricks is associated with this area; Terradillos's name might

actually come from the word *terrados* (roof) and its diminutive, *terradillos* (little roofs).

Terradillos dates to the late Roman period, when there probably was a villa here. Templar Knights controlled Terradillos in the 13th century, though there is no evidence that it supported hospices for pilgrims. The Mudéjar-style church, **Iglesia de San Pedro,** is of the signature Tierra de Campos red-brick style and houses a 14th-century icon of Christ on the cross. Villagers celebrate their patron, Saint Peter, on June 29.

The village also harbors a mystery: this is the place the last Templar Knights hid the fabled hen (or goose, depending on the telling) that lay golden eggs and was a source of their wealth.

Accommodations and Food

For a tiny village, Terradillos has two good *albergues* with good sleeping and eating options.

Just before you enter the village, along the N-120, you'll find what looks like a vast hacienda or modern villa house with a huge yard, open terrace, and angled timber roof entry with a big Templar cross hanging from the meeting joint. This is **Albergue Los Templarios** (979-065-968; www.alberguelostemplarios; Mar.-Oct.), with 52 dormitory beds (€8-10) and nine private rooms (€28-38). The airy dining hall, good food, pristine sleeping quarters, and wide green space make this a great place to stop for the day. Proprietors speak English.

The **Albergue Jaques de Molay** (Calle de la Iglesia, 18; 979-883-679; open Feb.-Nov.; 46 beds, €8-10/bed), named after the last grand master of the Templars (who was tortured and burned at the stake in 1314), offers clean and comfortable dormitory-style beds, with good home-cooked meals, in an enclosed garden space at the other end of the village, just as the Camino is about to exit. The Templar name is a reference to the legend of the Templars' hidden golden hen or goose, possibly still buried here in Terradillos. The true gold is the hospitality, along with the daily meditations written on the chalkboard in the garden. A recent one: "Sometimes you have to lose yourself to find yourself."

The village also has a general store and a bar.

Leaving Terradillos

About midway between Terradillos and Moratinos you will pass the spot where the medieval monastery of **Villaoreja** once stood (Km 376.2). The monastery operated for around 700 years, caring for pilgrims and offering lodging. It is possible that earlier it also was a Roman wayside inn. The Asociación Cultural de Moratinos, the cultural association of the village coming up next, is raising funds to excavate the monastery. Meanwhile, the site is marked with a large stone engraved with its name to the left of the Camino, near a sitting area in a grove. Look closer and you'll also see a modern spiral labyrinth in the center of the grove, a meditative walk that invites a pause.

Moratinos   Km 374.6

A seemingly sleepy little village, Moratinos (pop. 58) has panache. You'll see it right away on the main square, with the brickwork parish church, **Iglesia de Santo Tomás**, decked out in colorful knit-yarn creations that are strung across the church plaza and wrapped around the trees. These "yarn trees" are the project also of the Asociación Cultural de Moratinos, who wanted to add color to their village. It's growing into an international project as other groups join the fun: A group of women from Vandergrift, Pennsylvania, sent in crocheted creations to add to the display, and at least one Canadian *hospitalera* is also knitting away.

Camino Clean-Up

Rebekah Scott, a North American pilgrim, *hospitalera,* and transplant in Moratinos, is committed to improving life on the Camino, including bettering many of the area's *albergues*—for pilgrims and locals alike. In this spirit, she is the CEO and founder of **Peaceable Projects, Inc.** (www.peaceableprojects.org). Visit the website to learn more, and roll up your sleeves and get involved, even right now, as you walk. (They coordinate an annual trash pickup on the Camino every November called **Ditch Pigs**.)

Scott and her husband, Patrick O'Gara, also offer some beds to a few pilgrims in Moratinos (ideally no more than two at a time); they typically open their accommodation to pilgrims in need (including those under vows or with no resources) and in winter, when the other places in the village may be closed. They also have a small apartment for two with a kitchen that they may rent to you, if given advance notice (rebrites@ yahoo.com).

Food and Accommodations

Dine in a *bodega,* one of those cool underground wine cellars you've been walking past, at ★ **Castello de Moratinos** (Calle Bodegas, s/n; 979-061-467; three-course daily menu, €13). The boxy hillside entrance opens to a great bar for drinks, sandwiches (€3-5), and excellent tapas (€6-14). But you can continue deeper into the hill for a full meal in the bodega's subterranean dining areas. (Specialties include lamb chops and grilled langoustine.) It's a good place to sample the local Tierra de Campos cheeses and cured meats, and true to its setting, it features a great list of regional wines, most around €1.50 per glass.

Hostal-Albergue Moratinos (Calle Real, 12; 979-061-466; www.hostalmoratinos.es; open all year) is on the edge of the village as you enter, with an extensive garden, bar, and restaurant. It's a modern, all-facilities *hostal* and *albergue* with cheerful, light-filled, and spotless rooms and bathrooms, both private *(hostal)* and shared *(albergue)*. Some rooms have a private terrace. Rooms in the *hostal,* with private bath, are €40/45 single/double, and with shared bath are €35/40 single/double. Beds in the *albergue* are €10 in the room with six beds, and €15 in the room with only two.

Albergue San Bruno (Calle Ontanón, 9; 979-061-465; 16 beds in two rooms; €9), near the church, feels like a small Italian-style villa, with a spacious garden with fountain and shaded terrace. Rooms are clean, with terracotta floors and cubicle bunk beds. They offer a *menú del peregrino* (pasta and Italian cuisine feature heavily). Alternative natural healing modalities are available.

San Nicolás del Camino Real   Km 372

This hamlet (pop. 41) is filled with a lot of love. Locals are passionate about their village and about the pilgrims who pass through. The church of **San Nicolás de Bari**, the village patron saint, is a classic example of the brickwork Mudéjar style of architecture of this region, and has an added covered porch. In the 12th century, San Nicolás del Camino Real was owned and protected by the Templar Knights, the same century its church was founded. Villagers restored the church in the 18th century. Inquire at the *albergue* if a local can open the church so you can see see the 13th-century icon of Mother and Child inside.

Food and Accommodations

If you happen here on a festival day or a weekend, or someone's birthday or anniversary in the village, you will likely find a festive party unfolding over good food and drink at ★ **Casa Barrunta**

(Calle Ortero, 11; 689-336-189), a ranch-and-tavern-like restaurant on the edge of the village. Step inside; the staff will cheerfully find you a place and ply you with excellent food and drink. This is some of the best food on the *meseta,* served with the biggest heart and professional flair. They offer a great daily menu (€12) and are known for their *cocido,* the *pot au feu*-style spicy meat and chickpea stew, served along with a lusty garden salad (also €12, including dessert, bread, and wine).

On the village square, across from the church, is a good choice for sleeping and eating, the **Albergue Laganares** (979-188-142; www.alberguelaganares.com; 22 beds; €9 bed, one private room €20-30; all share one well-maintained bathroom). A lovely plaza-side café run by the *albergue* serves drinks, snacks, and meals (*menú,* €10, breakfast, €3). Proprietors speak English.

Ermita de la Virgen del Puente   Km 366.9

The Camino will take you across a medieval double-arch bridge over the small Valderaduey river and lead sraight ahead to the solitary Ermita de la Virgen del Puente. Both the bridge and hermitage are set in a refreshing grove of trees with a rest area on the left side (the hermitage on the right), after crossing the bridge. There you'll find curvy modern metal benches, perfect to recline and rest on in the shade.

An Augustinian pilgrims' hospice in the Middle Ages, the Ermita de la Virgen del Puente has an interesting hybridized arch, part Mudéjar with a slight horseshoe shape, and part Gothic pointed arch. The hermitage is only open in summers and on feast days. Until the 1990s, its caretaker and guardian, known by everyone as Paca (her actual name was Julia Tovar), was a force of energy, kindness, and willpower who cared for the chapel as if it were her own home. Paca has since passed, but her granddaughter carries on the family dedication to the hermitage, though the municipality in Sahagún now holds the keys and sees to the upkeep of the place. The image of the Virgen del Puente that once stood on the altar is now kept in the Iglesia de San Juan in the center of Sahagún. From June-August, the hermitage is open daily with an enthusiastic local on hand who enjoys sharing the hermitage's history.

Sahagún Km 364.5

Sahagún (pop. 2,597) is a large town that seems to combine all the joys of close-to-the-land village life with the ease and amenities of city life. If you join the locals for a drink on the Plaza Mayor, you'll begin to feel a harmony here. Sahagún has not lost itself to the glories of its past, nor to existing only for the pilgrim trade. Commerce, agriculture, tourism, and jobs in nearby León keep the town vibrant.

And though it seems like a quiet outpost in Castile today, in the 11th and 12th centuries Sahagún's Benedictine monastery, San Facundo y San Primitivo, was one of the most powerful in Spain. Hints of that past are still here, with a remarkable collection of Romanesque-Mudéjar churches, from the ruins of the monastery to the Santuario de la Peregrina on the small hill just 600 meters (1,969 feet) due south of the Plaza Mayor near where the Camino passes through town. (It is here where you can get your **midway certificate of walking,** if you began the Camino in Saint-Jean-Pied-de-Port.)

Stop by the city hall, the **Ayuntamiento,** on the Plaza Mayor, for practical information, such as bus and train schedules.

Sights

As the Camino makes its way into the center of Sahagún, to its north are the Iglesia de la Trinidad, now the popularly called "four-star" municipal *albergue,* and next to it, the 17th-century Neoclassical Iglesia de San Juan, which holds the tombs of San Facundo and Primitivo. A little farther west from

medieval bridge and hermitage, Ermita de la Virgen del Puente

Sahagún

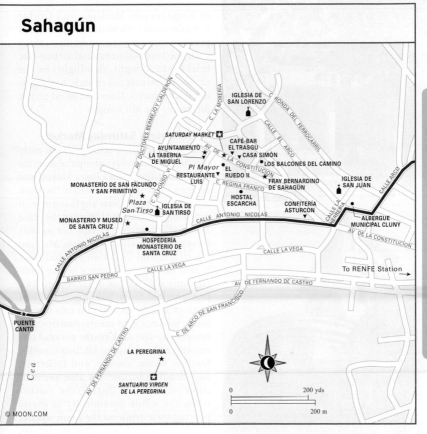

SAHAGÚN KM 364.5

here is the Iglesia de San Lorenzo and the Plaza Mayor. The Santuario de la Peregrina is a slight detour south off the Camino's trajectory through town, and then the Camino passes directly by the Iglesia de San Tirso, the Monasterio de San Facundo y San Primitivo, and the Monasterio de Santa Cruz. The Camino then wends farther to the west to the Río Cea, the site of Facundo and Primitivo's 4th-century martyrdom, today traversed by the sturdy and lovely **Puente Canto,** a bridge built in 1085 under Alfonso VI's patronage.

Iglesia de San Juan
Sahagún's name comes from San Facundo, one of two brothers—Facundus and Primitivus—who were martyred here in AD 303 by Romans, who killed them by throwing them the nearby Cea river. The 17th-century Neoclassical **Iglesia de San Juan** (Calle del Arco; 987-780-001) is where the tombs of the two brothers are kept, as well as the image of the Virgen del Puente. The interior is fairly modern, with a strong Neoclassical style. The church opens for **daily mass** at 10am and 8:30pm and is otherwise closed except on festival days.

Iglesia de San Lorenzo
Founded in the early 12th century, if not earlier, the present form of **Iglesia de San Lorenzo** (Plaza de San Lorenzo, s/n; 987-780-001; www.villadesahagun.es) is a mix

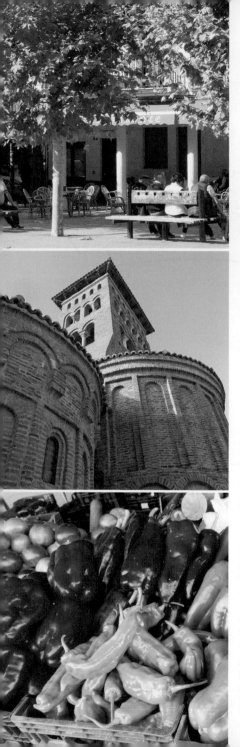

of Romanesque, Mudéjar, and Gothic from the early 13th century. The arcaded porch is one of its prettiest features, along with the three-dimensional lattice-like brickwork. At night, floodlights on the square illuminate the church, highlighting the geometric lines and blind arches formed by the brickwork.

★ Sahagún's Saturday Market

The weekly market sets up in the early morning on Saturdays along the Avenida de la Constitución and Plaza Mayor, and brings a color and dynamism to the town that comes closer than anything else to capturing the medieval glory of the place as a market center. Perhaps not as bustling as then—with its Jewish, Muslim, Christian, and Frankish residents—it is still rich in the produce of the land. Not only will you see amazing produce just plucked from Sahagún's kitchen gardens and fields, but you can sample local cheeses, cured meats, pastries, and breads, and also soak up the array of terracotta cooking dishes, kitchen utensils, textiles, shoes, jewelry, and toiletries. Surrounding businesses also seem to come more to life during the market when the whole community is there, pausing for a drink on the main square. This is one of the best weekly markets on the Camino and can be combined with a day of sightseeing in Sahagún, the red brick churches being but a few paces away (and open).

A statue of **Fray Bernardino de Sahagún** (AD 1499-1590), a missionary and historian from Sahagún who was sent to the New World and who is considered Spain's first anthropologist (given his careful ethnographic study of the Aztecs), overlooks the market from his pedestal on the Avenida de la Constitución.

From top to bottom: Plaza Mayor in Sahagún; Mudéjar brickwork on the apse of Iglesia de San Tirso in Sahagún; garden harvest for sale at Sahagún's Saturday market.

Iglesia de San Tirso

The **Iglesia de San Tirso** (Plaza de San Tirso, s/n; 987-780-001; www.villade-sahagun.es; Oct.-Mar. Wed.-Sat. 10am-2pm and 4-5:50pm, Sun. 10am-2pm; Apr.-Sept. Wed.-Sat. 10am-2pm and 4-8pm, Sun. 10am-2pm) was built either in the later 11th or early 12th century. Similar to San Lorenzo, it has the classic Romanesque-Mudéjar triple apse and geometric brickwork. Along the triple naves are a wonderful collection of tabletop three-dimensional architectural models of Sahagún's medieval churches. Among them is an ambitious reconstruction of the Monasterio de San Facundo y San Primitivo. You may want to take this in before you investigate the ruins of the monastery next door.

The central altar's hybrid horseshoe and Romanesque arch is of a height and width that makes it feel as if you are being embraced warmly and invited to sit and meditate. Inlaid in the floor before it is a six-pointed star of brick with black and white stone. This is a common decorative element in Christian, Islamic, and Jewish art and architecture and represents the Seal of Solomon, a symbol of balance, wisdom, and justice. (The Star of David is an association that became more common in the 19th century.) It's a great reminder both of Sahagún's tri-religious past and of the common source tradition of all the Abrahamic faiths.

Monasterío de San Facundo y San Primitivo

A portion of the church and a few standing walls are all that survive of this once powerful **monastery** (Plaza de San Benito, 1; 987-780-001; www.villade-sahagun.es), built mostly in the 11th to 13th centuries over its earlier Visigothic foundations. But the town has built itself onto these walls, and there is a romantic continuity of past to present. Once, a resplendent Romanesque-Mudéjar complex stretched across a good portion of what is now a park, parking lot, and streets around the current monastery ruins, but much of that structure was destroyed in 1812 by Napoleon's troops. Today, the ruins still offer a romantic pose, especially if you visit at night, when they (and the Iglesia de San Tirso next door) are illuminated with floodlights.

The former monastery church bell tower, now the town's clock tower, is a modern construction from 1835. The town has gradually been restoring the Gothic monastery church, and though it still looks like a ruin, the progress has been immense. The large arch over the street next to the ruins, the **Arco de San Benito,** marks where the original front of the monastery was, but it too is a more modern overlay, from 1662. Hidden on its backside are a few elements from the earlier Romanesque building—a portion of a column and its capital and two round windows.

Monasterio y Museo de Santa Cruz

The most moving part of the **Monasterio de Santa Cruz** (Avenida Doctores Bermejo y Calderón, 10) is its daily **mass** at 8:30am (9am on Sundays) and **Vespers** at 7pm, where sacred song is a part of the prayer service. The monastery is largely rebuilt and more modern than its late 12th-century founding. It has an important sacred art museum, **Museo de Santa Cruz** (987-780-078; www.monas-teriosantacruz.es; Sun.-Thur., 10:30am-1pm and 4-6:30pm; €2). You can sleep here as a pilgrim in wonderful lodging newly taken over by the Padres Maristas, Marist Fathers, an order of men devoted to being the charismatic presence of Mary on earth.

★ Santuario Virgen de la Peregrina

Santuario de la Peregrina (987-780-001; www.villadesahagun.es; Mon.-Sun., 10:30am-2pm and 4:30-8pm; €3) was founded in 1257 as a Franciscan monastery, but restoration work in the latter half of the last century uncovered lacey

The Halfway Certificate

If you began the Camino in Saint-Jean-Pied-de-Port, you passed the midpoint some time after Carrión de los Condes. This warrants a celebration—you've gone almost 400 kilometers (250 miles)! You can mark the moment with a short walk (500 m/1,640 ft) south of the Camino, as it passes through the heart of Sahagún near the Plaza Mayor, to the **Santuario de la Peregrina** to receive your halfway certificate on your way out of town. And while there, waiting for the sanctuary attendant to ink your name in pretty cursive script on the illuminated certifi-cate, consider paying the €3 entrance to visit La Peregrina's church and monastic grounds, especially to see the Islamic-Christian interior of carved and painted plaster, similar to the ornate geometric work seen in the Alhambra in Granada. This was how the Monasterio de San Facundo y San Primitivo was decorated as well, by the same craftsmen, and gives an idea of what it once looked like before it deteriorated to ruins. You can also visit the excavations outside the southern wall that uncovered wall foundations of other sections of the monastery.

and pigmented Mudéjar lattice work under a coat of plain plaster, revealing the greater beauty of the monastery in the Middle Ages. Careful restoration has brought to light the larger extent of this mixed Gothic and Mudéjar (with pinches of Romanesque) monastery.

Not only is this a gem of Mudéjar artistry, this sanctuary houses **La Peregrina,** a 17th-century statue of Mary on the altar who is dressed as a traveling pilgrim with cape, sun hat, staff, and water gourd. She is the whole point: medieval legend, as captured in Alfonso X's 13th-century *Cantigas de Santa María* (song #49), recorded that pilgrims arriving in Sahagún after nightfall encountered a woman on the road, her staff aglow with light, who would meet them and lead them to shelter. (If her statue is not here when you visit, you'll find it in the museum of the Monasterio de Santa Cruz.)

This is also where pilgrims receive their **halfway Camino certificate.**

Festivals and Events

In addition to its Saturday market, Sahagún has a rich cycle of festivals throughout the year (www.aytosaha-gun.es/turismo-y-ocio/ferias-fiestas-y-tradiciones). Some of the most colorful include: The **Fiesta de la Virgen de la Peregrina,** every July 2, with processions, traditional folkloric groups, bonfires, and festive foods; the local pilgrimage, **Romería de la Virgen del Puente** in April, which is unofficially called the *Romería del pan y queso*, bread and cheese pilgrimage, a celebration of the produce of the land and of spring; and every June 12-13, the **Fiesta de San Juan de Sahagún,** a celebration of the town's patron saint.

Food and Nightlife

Several cafés line the **Plaza Mayor,** which is a lively spot for a drink, especially on pleasant evenings when you can take a seat at one of the outdoor tables, such as at the Restaurante Luis or the Taberna de Miguel.

★ **Casa Simón** (Avenida de la Constitución, 47; 987-780-917; www.casasimonsahagun.com; €8-15) can get crowded any night of the week, but there is also a dining area in back, with large windows letting in light from the other side of the building. It is a popular *raciones* (tapas) and *picoteo* (*pinchos* bar) joint, as well as a place to get a good *menú del día* or graze a la carte. Among their signature dishes are croquetas, braised leeks with *cecina* (dry-cured beef), and chorizo grilled with *pimientos de Padrón* (tiny green peppers from Galicia). They have an excellent wine list.

Café-Bar El Trasgu (Avenida de la Constitución, 45; 987-782-011; under €10) is named after the house elf, *el trasgu*, common to Asturian, Castilian, and Leónine folklore, who is known to help as much as to cause charming bits of mischief. The owner is Asturian and offers inexpensive, tasty, and creative mischief in the form of generous tapas (*raciones*), good pizzas, and paella.

For excellent coffee and some of the best pastries on the Camino, stop at ★ **Confitería Asturcon** (Avenida de la Constitución, 62; 987-780-343; €2.50), a great place for a snack or breakfast. All their baked goods are made on the premises, including croissants, rolls, and fruit- or chocolate-filled pastries. (A personal favorite: the flakey, custardy, open-faced apple tart.) The owner is cheerful and welcoming, no matter how many people are clamoring at the counter for treats. There's some café seating inside and a wonderful triangular raised terrace on the Camino outside.

Restaurante Luis (Plaza Mayor, 4; 987-781-085; €12-20) is an institution, serving the same high-quality cuisine over recent decades, both of the local Tierra de Campos as well as with a strong Basque culinary influence. Among the specialties are roasted suckling pig, foie gras, bean stews, and grilled cod and tuna, as well as homemade tarts.

A very good restaurant—also with a good quality lodging on the upper floors—**Restaurante El Ruedo** (Plaza Mayor, 1; 987-781-834; www.restauranteelruedo.com; €11) prides itself on its modern interpretations of classic regional dishes, all made from seasonal, locally grown ingredients. A house specialty: roasted lamb and braised leeks. With a great location on the main square where the whole community aggregates, you can linger here deep into the night and be a part of local life.

La Taberna de Miguel (Plaza Mayor, 12; 987-781-162; €10) is located in a peaceful corner on the other side of the Plaza Mayor, next to the city hall, the Ayuntamiento. Come here to enjoy a glass of regional wine and pincho (€2.5-3) at an outdoor table under dappled shade from the square's plain trees. The interior dining room is entirely wood—bar, floors, tables, some with communal benches—giving a fun rustic tavern feel. Meal specialties include pastas and grilled steaks.

Accommodations

A modern building done in the red brick Mudéjar style, ★ **Los Balcones del Camino** (Calle Juan Guaza, 2; 987-780-145 or 676-838-242; www.losbalconesdelcamino.es; five rooms, three with private bath; €35-60) is a home converted into a small rural hotel that feels as if you are time-traveling to the Belle Époque. Gorgeous wood and inlaid painted-tile floors and stairways accentuate rooms and passageways. A large group can rent the whole house (€260 for the weekend). Hostess Carmen offers warm and helpful reception. The one drawback can be the noise from the street, so weekends might be less peaceful than weekdays.

Hostal El Ruedo II (Plaza Mayor, 1; 987-781-834; www.restauranteelruedo.com; €32-52) is centrally located, with spacious, spotless, and comfortable rooms. A very good restaurant on the ground floor, **Restaurante El Ruedo**, serves seasonal and local fare.

The central **Hostal Escarcha** (Calle Regina Franco, 12; 987-781-856; www.hostalescarcha.com; €20 single, €40 double) is among Sahagún's best deals, on a quiet side street, a delightful family-run *hostal* with clean, basic rooms with en-suite bath. A few paces from the Plaza Mayor for food and drink, the ground floor also has a bar that leads out to a courtyard terrace.

★ **Albergue Municipal Cluny** (64 beds; €5; open year-round), located in the beautifully restored 16th-century Iglesia de la Trinidad, has been called a "four star" *albergue*. Built from the familiar warm brick of Sahagún, they've crafted a light-filled and airy interior, with open stairways, high ceilings, and comfortable bunk beds set in private partitions. It feels like as if you are stepping into a medieval M. C. Escher print, especially when you look up at the stairways and beams. The *albergue* actually shares part of its building with a music hall, and when there are concerts, resident pilgrims get to attend for free, many just enjoying the music from their beds!

In 2018, the Marist Fathers took over running the already good ★ **Hospedería Monasterio de Santa Cruz** (Calle Antonio Nicolás, 40; www. alberguesensahagun.es; 50 beds) and made it excellent, with pristine rooms most with two or four beds per room and some with six or eight; each room has its own ensuite bath. (They request a minimum donation of €5, but if you can afford more, that would be nice.) They offer a communal dinner (also donation), a mass, and above all, the hope that people will feel welcome here and enjoy "a chance to return to the roots of the Camino," with an emphasis on spirituality and service.

Getting There

Sahagún is connected by train from Barcelona, Madrid, Burgos, and León, the last being the most efficient and direct travel hub. The most direct bus conection to Sahagún is from Madrid.

Train

RENFE (www.renfe.es) runs trains from Barcelona (three daily, 7-9 hours, €62-88), Madrid (four daily, 4-5 hours, €35), Burgos (three daily, 1.5 hours, €17), and León (eight daily, 40 min., €6-12).

Sahagún's train station, **Estación de Renfe** (Calle de la Estación, s/n) is 800 meters (0.5 mile) east of the Plaza Mayor in the center of town and a direct 10-minute walk along Calle de la Estación and Avenida de la Constitución.

Bus

ALSA (www.alsa.es) has one bus daily from Madrid (Madrid Estación Sur; 4.5 hours; €23) to Sahagún. There is no official bus station in Sahagún; the main stop is on the outskirts of town near the Hotel Puerta (Carretera de Burgos, 11), which the Camino passes behind (to the right of the hotel), 1 kilometer (0.6 mile) east of the center and a 15-minute walk west to Sahagún's central Plaza Mayor.

Taxi

If you need a cab, call **Taxi Mary** (630-437-921), **Taxi Fede** (639-943-349), or **Taxi Almudena** (669-797-769).

Leaving Sahagún

Four kilometers (2.5 miles) after leaving Sahagún, you have a choice: Stay on the medieval route, known as the **Camino Real**, or detour to the **Via Romana**—also called the Calzada Romana and the Via Trajana/Via Traiana—which follows the old Roman road that parallels the Camino Real a few hundred meters to the north, adding a little over 1 kilometer (0.6 miles) to the whole trek. You won't see much of the Roman road; it is largely under dirt and gravel. The advantage of this detour is to get a little farther away from the highway (A-231) that the Camino Real parallels in places. Be prepared with both choices: Both paths have long stretches where there are no support services of food, water, or lodging, 12.9 kilometers (8 miles) on the Camino Real and 17.7 kilometers (11 miles) on the Via Romana.

The Camino Real continues on to Bercianos del Real Camino. One reason to stay on it is to see the 17th-century hermitage, **Ermita de Nuestra Señora de Perales** (Km 354.9; Lugar Diseminado, 4, Bercianos del Camino; 987-784-179; June-Sept. 11am-1pm and 6-8pm; free) just before this village. Both a rest area and sacred site for the people of Bercianos, it houses the village protectress, **Nuestra Señora de Perales,** Our Lady of Pear Trees. It dates back at least as far as the 12th century, when it was attached to a pilgrims' hospital run by monks from Cebreiro. Now, you may find an elderly couple, current guardians in a long line of caretakers, who visit the shrine frequently with their grandchildren to greet and offer information to pilgrims passing through. Consider stopping to take in the red brick and stucco hermitage, to see Our Lady of Pear Trees on the altar, and enjoy the cool interior. Its angled terracotta roof and arched bell tower rising above the wheat field in the *meseta* has a magnetic pull. This is the site of village festivities and *romerías*—village processions—that take place in the spring and every September 8 to honor the Virgen de Perales.

⚑ Detour: The Via Romana

Calzada del Coto   Km 360.3

This village (pop. 241) centers on the 17th-century brickwork **Iglesia de San Esteban** and on a shrine dedicated to **San Roque,** patron of pilgrims as well as protector against disease and disaster, a win-win for *peregrinos* and locals alike.

Food and Accommodations

Stock up on provisions in the **Bar Xanadu** (Calle Real, 84; 696-881-411) if you are continuing to Calzadilla de los Hermanillos, 8.5 kilometers (5.3 miles) away. Xanadu offers a good *menú del peregrino* with the usual suspects: grilled meats, fried eggs, and good local wines. The one lodging choice here is the clean and modern municipal **Albergue San Roque** (Calle Real; 987-781-233 or 674-587-001; www.aytocalzadadelcoto.es; open year-round, 36 beds; donation), which has a shared kitchen.

Calzadilla de los Hermanillos   Km 351.9

The parish church of this village (pop. 141) is **San Bartolome,** a sturdy 16th- and 17th-century structure that replaces what might have been an earlier Visigothic or Mozarabic (Christians coming from Muslim Iberia) church on the spot.

Food and Accommodations

The stylish, family-run brick and stucco **Albergue Via Trajana** (Calle Mayor, 55; 987-337-610; www.alberguaviatrajana. com; Apr.-Oct.; five double rooms with private bath, €35-40, three dorm-style rooms, €15) also has a restaurant that serves a *menú del peregrino* as well as combined plates of grilled meat, fries, and salad.

Another nice option is the family-run rural guesthouse, **Casa El Cura** (Calle Carretera, 13; 987-337-647; €55), set off on the edge of the village and surrounded by countryside, where you can get meals and lodging (seven different rooms with private bath) while relaxing in the garden, terrace or lounge.

The municipal *albergue* (987-330-023; 22 beds; donation) is in the old school and features modern basic facilities and comfort (hot showers, a shared kitchen).

Leaving Calzadilla de los Hermanillos

After 17.7 kilometers (11 miles) with no support services in between, you arrive at **Reliegos** (Km 333.7). You can either rejoin the Camino Real here, or stay on the Via Romana another 6 kilometers (3.7 miles) to rejoin the Camino in **Mansilla de las Mulas** (Km 327.4).

Bercianos del Real Camino   Km 353.9

Berciano refers to the people from the El Bierzo region of León who settled this village (pop. 193) in the Middle Ages. The church, **Iglesia del Salvador**, lost its tower—it collapsed—in 1998, but the church is still there, as well as a beloved village chapel dedicated to pilgrim and protector, **San Roque**.

Food and Accommodations

The **Hostal Rivero** (Calle Mayor, 12; 987-784-287; www.hostalrivero99.wixsite.com/hostal-rivero; €30-45) has eight private rooms with bath and also serves a three-course *menú* (€10).

The bar and *hostal* **El Sueve** (Calle la Iglesia, 21; 987-784-139) takes pride in serving delicious food, including a *menú del peregrino* (€9), and offers four comfortable and peaceful rooms (€30-45).

The **Albergue Santa Clara** (Calle Iglesia, 3; 605-839-993; alberguesantaclara@hotmail.com; year-round) offers two dorm rooms (10 beds total, €8/bed) and four private rooms (€25-30); try to get one of the private rooms as the dorm is a bit cramped. The reception here is very welcoming and the spaces clean and modern.

El Burgo Ranero
Km 346.6

Some say El Burgo Ranero (pop. 220) gets its name from *el burg granero*, a grain or granary town, and others from *el burgo ranero*, a place abundant with frogs (*ranas*), a part of the town legacy thanks to the nearby pond. Take your pick; they've got plenty of both. The frogs add a nice touch, ribbiting along the small lagoon on the northwest side of town, especially at dusk as the sun begins to set on a hot, dusty day.

El Burgo Ranero's industries, outside of pilgrimage, are wheat and sheep. The village probably came into being in the early 12th century, but is set on a much more ancient pathway where sheep have been moved from pasture to pasture over millennia. (Shepherding and *transhumance*—a word we get from Spanish, the practice of moving sheep from summer to winter pastures and back again—have been practiced here ever since the first farmers and herders inhabited Iberia.)

Food and Accommodations

El Burgo Ranero's accommodations and shops are on the north side of the village, off the Camino trail, but as you walk in—just before the sweet brick, stone, and clay village church of **San Pedro**—you'll pass a few eating options. One in particular, ★ **La Costa del Adobe** (Calle Real, 79; 649-287-580; €9-12), is run by an idealistic and energetic English-speaking couple who work to procure and prepare local, organic, and sustainable foods and to accommodate all dietary needs. Dishes are innovative and traditional at once, such as a grilled vegetable platter, homemade thin crust pizza, and the house specialty, *tortilla guisada*, Spanish omelet stewed in a terracotta dish in a rich tomato and pepper sauce. They also make their own ice cream.

On the north side of town, near the road that leads to the train station, two excellent lodging choices stand side-by-side: The **Hostal Restaurant El Peregrino** (Calle Fray Pedro del Burgo, 36; 987-330-069) and the **Hostal Piedra Blanca** (Calle Fray Pedro del Burgo, 32; 987-330-094; www.hotelruralpiedrasblancas.com) offer the same good value, cozy and spotless rooms. Each has 10 rooms with bath to let for €30-45. Both are family run, and each has an animated bar (where locals play cards, dominoes, and board games) and dining area, offering good pilgrim menus (€10), refreshments, and snacks. Locals laud both *hostales'* restaurants, especially El Peregrino's, as the places to go for traditional, family-style meals.

Across the street from the *hostales* is the **Albergue Domenico Laffi** (987-330-023 and 987-330-047; elburgoranero@gmail.com; 30 beds in four rooms; donation), named after the 17th-century Italian pilgrim who stayed here and who also wrote a colorful account of the Camino, *A Journey to the West*. The volunteer

Top: Ermita de Nuestra Señora de Perales near Bercianos del Real Camino. **Bottom:** El Burgo Ranero's main street, also the Camino, and village church.

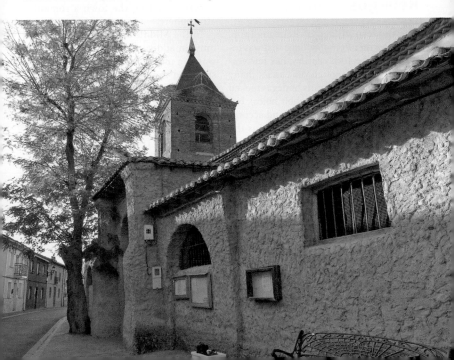

hospitaleros offer helpful and warm reception in a cheerful two-story building with small, spacious, well-kept dorm rooms. It is open year-round; if no one is there to greet you from Nov-Mar., ask for the key at the general store across the street.

Leaving El Burgo Ranero

El Burgo Ranero is a rare transport hub along this stretch of the *meseta*. Every Mon., Wed., and Fri. morning, one **ALSA** (www.alsa.es) bus connects El Burgo Ranero to León (45 min., €4) with stops in Puente Villarente, Arcahueja, and Mansilla de las Mulas. **RENFE** (www.renfe.es) also runs trains to León (two daily, a morning and an afternoon train, 30 min., €4). Schedules for both bus and train are posted on the bulletin board inside the Albergue Domenico Laffi. If walking, stock up on water and food; the 12.9 kilometers (8 miles) to Reliegos have no support services.

Reliegos Km 333.7

The modern village of Reliegos (pop. 176), a former Roman village that was re-settled in the 10th century, has few vestiges of its past (though you can see many wonderful private family bodegas tucked into the hillsides like Hobbit holes), but offers a good place for food and accommodation. The **Via Romana** rejoins the Camino Real here.

Food and Accommodations

For its size, Reliegos has a large array of lodging, some six *albergues* and three *hostales* and inns.

Albergue Vive Tu Camino (Calle Real, 56; 610-293-986 or 670-885-959; www.alberguevivetucamino.com) offers clean and simple living spaces, with a shared dining area and kitchen, a peaceful garden, and dorm-style sleeping (€9 for each sturdy and new wooden bunk bed) and private rooms (€35-50).

La Parada (Calle Escuela, 7; 987-317-880; alberguelaparada@gmail.com) has a great terrace centered around a traditional well and has all facilities and options, including a shared kitchen, small store, restaurant and bar (dinner menu, €10). Lodging options are two private rooms (€30) or 36 beds in six dorm rooms (€7).

Mansilla de las Mulas
Km 327.4

Mansilla de las Mulas (pop. 1618) makes a strong impact on the horizon, its dense town walls—3 meters (nearly 10 feet) thick in some places—enclosing the medieval center. Those walls were first laid down in Roman times, when this was a stopping place on the Via Trajana (Via Traiana) destined for León. King Fernando II of León reinforced the walls and town in the 11th century; they were fortified again in the 13th and 14th centuries. Some 75 percent of the walls survive, lending the town a romantic atmosphere.

In the Middle Ages, Mansilla's economy, in addition to pilgrim commerce, was as a mule market (*las mulas*), which supplied the region with these all-important animals for labor and transport. Today, the old town is full of picturesque plazas (many of them concentrating along the west wall), pedestrian promenades, and riverside paths along the Esla river.

Every Tuesday, a food and general goods **market** sets up on the Plaza del Grano.

Sights
Ermita de la Virgen de Gracía

About 50 meters (164 feet) to the left of the Camino as it nears the medieval section of Mansilla de las Mulas, the Belle Époque 1898 stucco **Ermita de la Virgen de Gracia** (Plaza de Nuestra Señora de Gracia, 1; www.aytomansilladelasmulas.es) stands out for its bold striped cream- and red-painted walls. It may be a modern building, without too much to see inside or out, except that it houses the town's most precious icon, the statue of Our Lady of Grace. The age of the sculpture is unclear, but it was restored in 1950 by the sculptor Victor de los Ríos after it was damaged in an earlier fire. But Mary of Grace, in earlier form, has been venerated here since 1220 (if not earlier), when it is documented that an older church dedicated to her stood here. The hermitage is rarely open, only for festival days. Since 1991, on the first Sunday in September, in honor of her feast day, locals (over 500 in recent years) make a pilgrimage from León's Iglesia de Nuestra Señora del Mercado to this hermitage, an 18-kilometer (11.2-mile) journey, to lay at her feet offerings of flowers and fruits that they have grown on their own land. It is as much a harvest festival as a pilgrimage of gratitude for the abundance of the land and the season under the Virgen de Gracia's protection throughout the year.

Iglesia de Santa María

Iglesia de Santa María (Calle de la Concepción, 7; 987-310-019) is Mansilla's oldest church. It has survived since 1220, while the other five churches from the 13th century have all but disappeared (except for the 13th-century bell tower that survives on the modern Iglesia de San Martín nearby). But even here, the church's earlier medieval form was reformed in the 18th century. Santa María remains a house of worship. There is daily **mass** here at 8:30am, and **Vespers** at 8:30pm.

Museo Etnográfico Provincial de León

Learn about León province's cultural traditions, festivals, folklore, and agrarian life at the **Museo Etnográfico Provincial de León** (Calle San Agustín, 1; 987-311-923; www.etnoleon.com; Tues.-Sat., Apr.-Oct., 10am-2pm and 5-8pm, Nov.-Mar., 10am-2pm and 4pm-7pm; €5). Exhibits include *Guirrios,* traditional Carnival regalia, complete with wonderful radiating psychedelic-patterned head gear.

Food

★ **La Curiosa** (Calle Jose Alvarez, 15; 608-880-588; www.lacuriosademansilla.com; €15-20) shows its innovative spirit in its name ("the curious"), taking traditional cuisine and adding modern, flavorful twists, such as scallops in blue cheese sauce, grilled hake and shrimp kebabs, and escarole with wild mushrooms. It's set in a turn-of-the-century pharmacy building, and the original shelving in the bar displays a wonderful array of elixirs. This is one of the finest places to dine on the Camino.

Alberguería del Camino has an excellent restaurant connected to its *hostal.*

Accommodation

★ **Hostal Alberguería del Camino** (Calle Concepción, 12; 987-311-193; www.albergueriadelcamino.com; €38-56) feels like a Leónese country inn set inside the old walls near the church of Santa María, with tasteful and impeccable rooms in solid wood and cast-iron furnishing. The rustic tavern-style bar and restaurant has several signature dishes (€9-13) dedicated to Mansilla's local cuisine, including a leek tart and *bacalao al Estilo de Mansilla* (Mansilla-style cod that's pan fried then stewed with garlic and spicy smoked paprika).

La Pension de Blanca (Avenida Picos de Europa, 4; 626-003-177; www.la-pension-de-blanca.negocio.site; €25-40) has seven eclectically decorated, neat, and colorful rooms.

Clean, well maintained, and upbeat, **Albergue Gaia** (Avenida Constitución, 28; 987-310-308; www.alberguegaia.com; €8; open Mar.-Jan.) was created by pilgrims-turned-*hospitaleros* Carlos and Marisa Fernández. They have 18 beds (all bunks) in two rooms with kiwi-green walls. There is a well-equipped kitchen

Day Trip to San Miguel de Escalada

Mansilla de las Mulas is just 16 kilometers (10 miles) from one of Spain's gems, the church of **San Miguel de Escalada** (987-310-719; www.turismocastillayleon.com, Mar.-Apr. Fri.-Sun. 10am-2pm, May-Oct. Tues.-Sat. 10pm-2:30pm and 4:30-7:30pm, Dec.-Feb. Sat.-Sun. 10am-3pm; closed Nov.; €2). It was built by Christian refugees from late 9th- and early 10th-century Córdoba in southern Spain, who brought with them an Islamic aesthetic and building style, Mozárabic, that predates the Romanesque. The result is an elegant little church with horseshoe arches and Visigothic and Mozarabic floral, geometric, and plant designs.

The church is dedicated to the archangel and saint of high places, Saint Michael (which is why it was built on a hill), and is a truly intimate and sacred space in the middle of the countryside. The 12-arched porch is one of its distinctive features. Inside, the nave, surrounded on three sides by horseshoe arches, replicates on a small scale a forest of arrayed pillars and arches like those in the Mosque of Córdoba. The builders came from that part of Spain, and as with the mosque, here they reused eclectic pillars and capitals from the earlier Roman building that stood where this chapel now stands. The nave is also rich in engraved floral designs and bird figures, adding to the forest feel. The church was built over an older Visigothic one, and excavators in 1968 discovered vestiges of the Visigothic church's apse underneath the present chapel.

This was likely a part of the medieval Camino, but today, the best way to visit is via taxi from Mansilla de las Mulas. You can arrange for a round-trip excursion to San Miguel de la Escalada, including a 30-40 minute wait as you visit the church, with **Taxi Mansilla** (609-012-383; www.taximansilla.com) for approximately €20-30. The price will vary depending on season and time of day, and you should plan to leave a small tip. You can also inquire into organized excursions or alternative transport with Mansilla de las Mulas's **tourist office** (Plaza de San Antonio Martínez Sacristán, s/n; 987-310-012; www.cultura.jcyl.es).

for communal cooking and a shared dining area with an enclosed patio in back.

Getting Around

If you need a cab, try **Taxi Mansilla** (609-012-383; www.taximansilla.com).

Leaving Mansilla de las Mulas

If you want to bypass the heavily urban and industrial outskirts of León, **ALSA** (902-422-242; www.alsa.es) runs 11 buses daily from Mansilla de las Mulas (€1.65), Puente Villarente, and Villamoros de Mansilla (€1.40) to León.

Archaeological Site of Lancía   Km 324.4

Along the side of the N-601, 3.2 kilometers (2 miles) afer leaving Mansilla de las Mulas, a 1-kilometer (0.6-mile) detour to the right (just before the gas station Galp) leads to **Yacimiento Arqueológico de Lancía** (Villasabariego; 987-310-971; www.institutoleonesdecultura.es/EtnografiaPatrimonio/YacimientoArqueologicoLancia), the partially excavated ruins of the Roman settlement of Lancía. Visits inside the site are usually possible Mon.-Fri. mornings, but you can still see the site when it is closed, from the other side of the fence. The remains unearthed so far in this ongoing excavation are the thermal baths and the public market of the Roman town, which was established in the 1st century AD.

After visiting the site, you can backtrack to where you left the Camino, along the N-601, heading toward **Villamoros de Mansilla** (Km 323) and **Puente Villarente**

(Km 321.5), leaving another 12 kilometers (7.5 miles) to León.

Approaching León

After Puente Villarente (Km 321.5, pop. 234), the stretch into León becomes increasingly industrial, and you may want to catch the bus from here into León to skip it. The settlements are more bedroom communities and feel rather desolate; the Camino passes near the busy road into León. If you decide to walk to León, Puente Villarente and Arcahueja offer some food and accommodation options. After leaving Arcahueja, 7.4 kilometers (4.6 miles) remain until León.

Food and Accommodations
Puente Villarente   Km 321.5
Albergue San Pelayo (Calle Romero, 9; 987-312-677; www.alberguesanpelayo.com; open year round) has a large garden and roomy interiors that can sleep up to 64 people (€8-10/bed) in four dormitory rooms and six private rooms (€30-40). Proprietors speak English.

Albergue El Delfin Verde (Calle Carretera General, 15; 987-312-065; www.complejo-el-delfin-verde.negocio.site; open Mar.-Nov.) has it all: a large swimming pool (in the summer), 15 private rooms (€25-40; breakfast is included), and 20 beds (€5) in three shared dorm rooms, plus a three-course evening meal (€10). Known for impeccable service and hospitality.

Hostal-Restaurante La Montaña (Calle Camino de Santiago, 17; 987-312-161; www.hostalrestaurantelamontana.es; 16 rooms; €30-45), on the west end of town, is a roadside inn with comfortable rooms and a decent restaurant and bar.

Arcahueja   Km 317.2
Bar-Restaurante Albergue La Torre (987-205-896; www.alberguelatorre.es; open year round) has a range of options, from two dorm rooms with 22 beds for €8/bed and four private rooms for €25-40. The bar restaurant serves a *menú del peregrino* (€9). Just beyond town, the roadside **Hotel-Restaurante Camino Real** (987-218-134; open year round; 44 rooms; €65) offers a decent menú and a la carte menu in the hotel restaurant (€13-18).

León and Galicia

León to Sarria

Km: 309–115.5
Total Distance: 193.5 km (120 miles)
Days: 8–10

León to Ponferrada

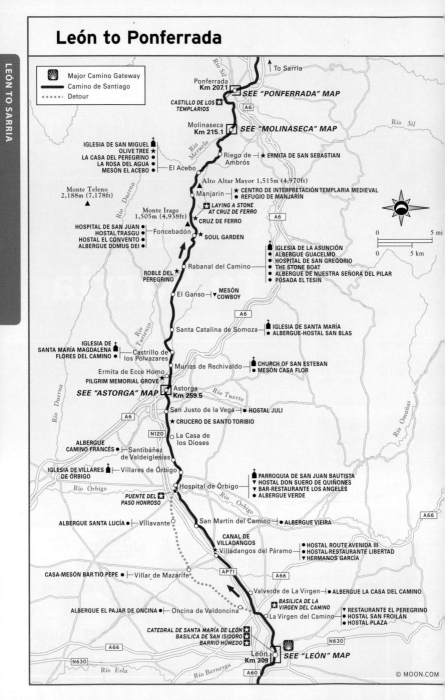

Major Camino Gateway
Camino de Santiago
Detour

To Sarria

Ponferrada
Km 207.1

SEE "PONFERRADA" MAP

CASTILLO DE LOS TEMPLARIOS

Molinaseca
Km 215.1

SEE "MOLINASECA" MAP

Río Sil

IGLESIA DE SAN MIGUEL
OLIVE TREE
LA CASA DEL PEREGRINO
LA ROSA DEL AGUA
MESÓN EL ACEBO
El Acebo

Riego de Ambrós

ERMITA DE SAN SEBASTIAN

Alto Altar Mayor 1,515m (4,970ft)

Monte Teleno
2,188m (7,178ft)

Manjarín

CENTRO DE INTERPRETACIÓN TEMPLARIA MEDIEVAL
REFUGIO DE MANJARÍN

LAYING A STONE
AT CRUZ DE FERRO

Monte Irago
1,505m (4,938ft)

CRUZ DE FERRO

HOSPITAL DE SAN JUAN
HOSTAL TRASGU
HOSTAL EL CONVENTO
ALBERGUE DOMUS DEI

Foncebadón

SOUL GARDEN

ROBLE DEL PEREGRINO

Rabanal del Camino

IGLESIA DE LA ASUNCIÓN
ALBERGUE GUACELMO
HOSPITAL DE SAN GREGORIO
THE STONE BOAT
ALBERGUE DE NUESTRA SEÑORA DEL PILAR
POSADA EL TESÍN

El Ganso

MESÓN COWBOY

Santa Catalina de Somoza

IGLESIA DE SANTA MARÍA
ALBERGUE-HOSTAL SAN BLAS

IGLESIA DE SANTA MARÍA MAGDALENA
FLORES DEL CAMINO
Castrillo de los Polvazares

Murias de Rechivaldo

CHURCH OF SAN ESTEBAN
MESÓN CASA FLOR

Ermita de Ecce Homo
PILGRIM MEMORIAL GROVE
SEE "ASTORGA" MAP

Astorga
Km 259.5

Río Tuerto

San Justo de la Vega

HOSTAL JULI

CRUCERO DE SANTO TORIBIO

La Casa de los Dioses

ALBERGUE CAMINO FRANCÉS
Santibáñez de Valdeiglesias

IGLESIA DE VILLARES DE ÓRBIGO
Villares de Órbigo

Hospital de Órbigo

PARROQUIA DE SAN JUAN BAUTISTA
HOSTAL DON SUERO DE QUIÑONES
BAR-RESTAURANTE LOS ANGELES
ALBERGUE VERDE

Río Órbigo

PUENTE DEL PASO HONROSO

ALBERGUE SANTA LUCÍA
Villavante

San Martín del Camino

ALBERGUE VIEIRA

CANAL DE VILLADANGOS

Villadangos del Páramo

HOSTAL ROUTE AVENIDA III
HOSTAL-RESTAURANTE LIBERTAD
HERMANOS GARCÍA

CASA-MESÓN BAR TIO PEPE
Villar de Mazarife

Valverde de La Virgen

ALBERGUE LA CASA DEL CAMINO

BASILICA DE LA VIRGEN DEL CAMINO

ALBERGUE EL PAJAR DE ONCINA
Oncina de Valdoncina

La Virgen del Camino

RESTAURANTE EL PEREGRINO
HOSTAL SAN FROILÁN
HOSTAL PLAZA

CATEDRAL DE SANTA MARÍA DE LEÓN
BASILICA DE SAN ISIDORO
BARRIO HÚMEDO

León
Km 309

SEE "LEÓN" MAP

© MOON.COM

Ponferrada to Sarria

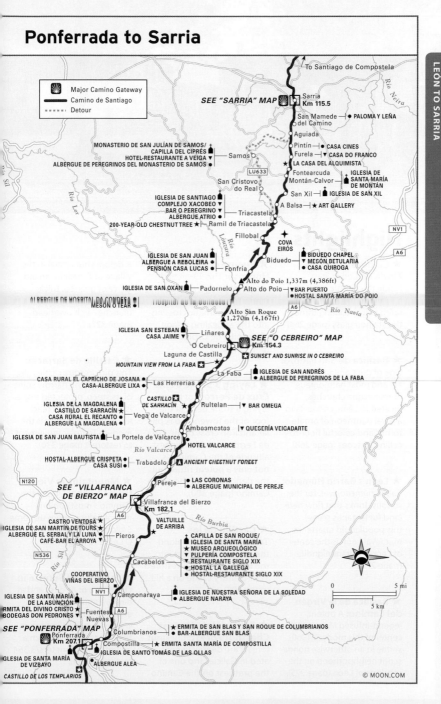

Legend:
- 🐚 Major Camino Gateway
- —— Camino de Santiago
- ······ Detour

To Santiago de Compostela

🐚 Sarria
Km 115.5

SEE "SARRIA" MAP

San Mamede del Camino → ● PALOMA Y LEÑA

Aguiada

MONASTERIO DE SAN JULIÁN DE SAMOS/
CAPILLA DEL CIPRÉS †
HOTEL-RESTAURANTE A VEIGA ▼
ALBERGUE DE PEREGRINOS DEL MONASTERIO DE SAMOS ▼

Samos ○

Pintín → ● CASA CINES
Furela → ▼ CASA DO FRANCO
LA CASA DEL ALQUIMISTA ●

San Cristovo do Real

Fontearcuda
Montán-Calvor ●

IGLESIA DE SANTA MARÍA DE MONTÁN †

LU633

IGLESIA DE SANTIAGO †
COMPLEJO XACOBEO ▼
BAR O PEREGRINO ▼
ALBERGUE ATRIO ●

Triacastela

San Xil → ● IGLESIA DE SAN XIL

A Balsa → ★ ART GALLERY

200-YEAR-OLD CHESTNUT TREE ★ ← Ramil de Triacastela

Fillobal

COVA EIRÓS ✦

BIDUEDO CHAPEL †
MESÓN BETULARIA ▼
CASA QUIROGA ●

Biduedo ●

IGLESIA DE SAN JUAN †
ALBERGUE A REBOLEIRA ●
PENSIÓN CASA LUCAS ●

Fonfría ●

IGLESIA DE SAN OXAN † ← Padornelo

Alto do Poio 1,337m (4,386ft)
Alto do Poio → ▼ BAR PUERTO
HOSTAL SANTA MARÍA DO POIO ▼

ALBERGUE DE HOSPITAL DO CEBREIRO 🏛
MESÓN O TEAR ● ▮

Hospital de la Condesa ●

Alto San Roque 1,270m (4,167ft)

Río Navia
A6

IGLESIA SAN ESTEBAN †
CASA JAIME ●

Liñares ●

O Cebreiro 🐚 SEE "O CEBREIRO" MAP
Km 154.3

Laguna de Castilla

★ SUNSET AND SUNRISE IN O CEBREIRO

MOUNTAIN VIEW FROM LA FABA ★

La Faba ●

IGLESIA DE SAN ANDRÉS †
ALBERGUE DE PEREGRINOS DE LA FABA ●

CASA RURAL EL CAPRICHO DE JOSANA ●
CASA-ALBERGUE LIXA ●

Las Herrerías ●

IGLESIA DE LA MAGDALENA †
CASTILLO DE SARRACÍN ●
CASA RURAL EL RECANTO ●
ALBERGUE LA MAGDALENA ●

CASTILLO DE SARRACÍN ★

Rultelan → ▼ BAR OMEGA

Vega de Valcarce ●

IGLESIA DE SAN JUAN BAUTISTA † ← La Portela de Valcarce

Ambasmestas ● → ▼ QUESERÍA VEIGADARTE

HOTEL VALCARCE ●

Río Valcarce

HOSTAL-ALBERGUE CRISPETA ●
CASA SUSI ●

Trabadelo ●

🏛 ANCIENT CHESTNUT FOREST

N120

Pereje ● ● LAS CORONAS
● ALBERGUE MUNICIPAL DE PEREJE

SEE "VILLAFRANCA DE BIERZO" MAP

Villafranca del Bierzo 🐚
Km 182.1

Río Burbia

VALTUILLE DE ARRIBA ★

CASTRO VENTOSA ★
IGLESIA DE SAN MARTÍN DE TOURS ★
ALBERGUE EL SERBAL Y LA LUNA ▼
CAFÉ-BAR EL ARROYA ▼

Pieros ●

A6

CAPILLA DE SAN ROQUE/
IGLESIA DE SANTA MARÍA †
MUSEO ARQUEOLÓGICO ★
PULPERÍA COMPOSTELA ●
RESTAURANTE SIGLO XIX ●
HOSTAL LA GALLEGA ●
HOSTAL-RESTAURANTE SIGLO XIX ●

N536

Cacabelos ●

COOPERATIVO VIÑAS DEL BIERZO ●

Río Sil

NV1

Camponaraya ● ● IGLESIA DE NUESTRA SEÑORA DE LA SOLEDAD
● ALBERGUE NARAYA

IGLESIA DE SANTA MARÍA DE LA ASUNCIÓN †
ERMITA DEL DIVINO CRISTO ★
BODEGAS DON PEDRONES ▼

Fuentes Nuevas ●

A6

Columbrianos ● → ★ ERMITA DE SAN BLAS Y SAN ROQUE DE COLUMBRIANOS
● BAR-ALBERGUE SAN BLAS

SEE "PONFERRADA" MAP

Ponferrada 🐚
Km 207.1

Compostilla → ★ ERMITA SANTA MARÍA DE COMPOSTILLA

IGLESIA DE SANTO TOMÁS DE LAS OLLAS †

Compostilla ●

IGLESIA DE SANTA MARÍA DE VIZBAYO †
● ALBERGUE ALEA

CASTILLO DE LOS TEMPLARIOS ★

0 ——————— 5 mi
0 ——————— 5 km

© MOON.COM

Highlights

★ **Catedral de Santa María de León:** Step inside this Gothic gem into a Cézanne-like swirl of saturated colors coming through the stained glass (page 264).

★ **Basilica de San Isidoro:** One of the Camino's largest and most harmonious Romanesque churches, located in Léon, connects to a royal pantheon of ornate tombs and colorful floor-to-ceiling frescoes (page 268).

★ **León's Barrio Húmedo:** Called *húmedo,* wet, for the serious drinks that flow here (and for its tapas scene), this popular old quarter in medieval León is the center of León's vibrant nightlife (page 271).

★ **Basilica de la Virgen del Camino:** A potent, legend-infused Mary is at the center of this modern 1960s shrine in an otherwise nondescript neighborhood on the outskirts of León (page 275).

★ **Puente del Paso Honroso:** This 19-arched medieval bridge, made famous by a lovesick knight, remains a dramatic crossing into the appealing village of Hospital de Órbigo (page 280).

★ **Laying a Stone at the Cruz de Ferro:** For many, laying a stone here, at the foot of the towering oak pillar and iron cross of the Cruz de Ferro, set on the highest altitude of the Camino, is not only a potent ritual, but the dénoument of the entire Camino (page 300).

★ **Castillo de los Templarios:** Climb along the ramparts and pass into the keep of this well-restored 12th-century castle on a hill (page 308).

★ **Trabadelo's Ancient Chestnut Forest:** Chestnut forests are deeply venerated in Galicia, and one of the prettiest on the Camino

is before your arrival in the village of Tabadelo: an old grove of gnarled, thick-trunked trees whose ancient branches arch overhead (page 327).

★ **Castilló de Sarracín:** This picturesque castle ruin, situated on the narrow spine of its steep, protected slope, is worth the hike to reach it. Equally interesting is the modern Templar movement to restore it (page 330).

★ **Mountaintop View from La Faba:** One of the Camino's most sublime mountaintops opens up some 5 kilometers (3 miles) before O Cebreiro (page 333).

★ **Sunset and Sunrise in O Cebreiro:** At dusk and at dawn, a rainbow of colors expands across the sky and washes over rippling mountain vistas. See it all from a height of 1,330 meters/3,364 feet (page 334).

Recommended Overnight Stops

León (Km 309, page 260)	**Molinaseca** (Km 215.1, page 305)
San Martín del Camino (Km 283.6, page 279)	**Cacabelos** (Km 190.6, page 318)
	Trabadelo (Km 172.8, page 327)
Astorga (Km 259.5, page 284)	**O Cebreiro** (Km 154.3, page 333)
Rabanal del Camino (Km 239.7, page 297)	**Triacastela** (Km 133.3, page 343)

León to O Cebreiro is diverse terrain; you leave the *meseta* and enter the mountains with two of the Camino's three highest ascents, taking in a fertile valley in between and arriving on the first mountaintop in Galicia, fully leaving León. It is a place of transition, both physically as well as emotionally and, some report, spiritually. You pass from the brick and adobe *meseta* villages into idyllic but rugged mountain hamlets and fertile valley towns built of iron-saturated stone. This mountainous trek can challenge as much as reward, with a beauty that is distinct from both the Pyrenees and the mountains of Galicia because of its remoteness, the height of its peaks, and its landscape, stained orange, red, and deep dark black by natural iron deposits. At Monte Irago the Camino hits its apex, where you can enact one of the Camino's most powerful rituals: leaving a stone you have carried from home, at the foot of the oak trunk and iron cross of the Cruz de Ferro.

This region also is a part of the northwest's core areas of Iberian Celts who built hundreds, perhaps thousands, of *castros* (fortified hilltop settlements) all along the mountains and valleys. You enter also into a wilder region, where Iberia's largest wolf populations still survive—and are making a comeback thanks to conservation efforts. This too is the land of unique and velvety wines, fresh mountain trout, dense and spicy *botillo* sausage, and lush produce from the valley orchard gardens of Molinaseca and Ponferrada.

Planning Your Time

From León to Sarria is **193.5 kilometers** (120 miles). Allow **8-10 days** for walking when covering an average of 20-25 kilometers (12.5-15.5 miles) per day.

Consider 1 rest day in **León** to explore the Gothic cathedral and nightlife scene, 1 day for a spa day in **Astorga** or a rest day in **Ponferrada** for its Templar Castle, and 1 day for an art retreat in **Castrillo de los Polvazares,** for a total of 8-13 days.

Route Options

You have a few options for **detours** on this route. First, just after León, a few hundred meters past La Virgen del Camino, you can detour to **Villar de Mazarife** on a path that leads away from the rural highway and rejoins the main path in Hospital del Órbigo. (This detour has fewer support services.) Later, you can detour to **Castrillo de los Polvazares** (highly recommended; adds just 1 kilometer/0.6 mile to the route). Another detour to the medieval monastery of **Samos** from Triacastela adds 6.5 kilometers (4 miles) to the total trek to Sarria.

The path out of León to La Virgen del Camino is an **unpleasant concrete path** that parallels the busy highway. Consider skipping it by taking a local **bus** that will drop you off right on the Camino in

Local Markets

- **León:** Mercado de Abastos del Conde Luna (Mon.-Sat.) is a covered market on the Plaza del Conde Luna; weekly food markets set up in Plaza Mayor every Wednesday and Saturday; El Rastro de León flea market occurs every Saturday on Plaza Don Gutierre; and a weekly general goods market happens every Sunday, along the Paseo Papalaguinda (page 264).

- **Astorga:** Weekly market with food, household goods, and apparel every Tuesday morning (page 285).

- **Ponferrada:** Food market every Wednesday and Saturday morning (page 308).

- **Cacabelos:** Traditional market every 9th and 26th day of the month (page 319).

- **Villafranca del Bierzo:** Weekly market selling food and general goods every Tuesday morning (page 322).

La Virgen del Camino, 7.7 kilometers (4.9 miles) away. This plan also gives more time to visit the shrine at La Virgen del Camino.

Geography and Terrain

The Camino from León to Sarria covers the most variegated terrain of any stretch, beginning with the western edge of the high plateau plains of the *meseta* and leading into two **rugged mountain ascents,** at **Monte Irago** (the Camino's highest point) and **O Cebreiro** (the second highest point), with the fertile El Bierzo garden valley in between.

The Camino is well marked on this stretch. Approximately 65 percent of the trail runs **parallel to a road,** but at least half of it is on a dirt path near the road, not on the pavement on the bank of the road, so (other than the stretch from León to La Virgen del Camino), it's not unpleasant. The remaining part of the trail (approximately 35 percent) is on dedicated dirt hiking paths. After Hospital del Órbigo (Km 276.2) the trail begins to get wilder and, at many places, departs the rural highway it has been paralleling, instead taking up footpaths through exquisite mountains, valleys, fields, vineyards, and forests. One of the **wildest, most remote, and most stunning sections of the Camino** is its pass through

León's mountains between Rabanal del Camino and Molinaseca.

In this section of the trail, **longer unsupported sections** occur. On the main Camino, **Triacastela to Furela** (9.6 km/6 mi) can be hit or miss for refueling and hydrating stops, especially outside of the period between late spring and early autumn. The **detour to Samos** (10.3 km/6.4 mi) offers unreliable food and lodging. The **Villar de Mazarife** detour also offers fewer support structures.

Weather

Starting at the last edges of the *meseta* high plains in León, exposure to **strong sun** and open terrain is a concern in all seasons; it's hot in summer, with cold winds in winter. This route also contains the highest mountain peaks in the Camino, which can mean **snow** from late autumn into early spring. After passing O Cebreiro, you enter into Galicia's lower green mountains, where it can **rain** any time of year, especially from autumn through early summer.

Getting There

Starting Points

León is a central transportation hub in northern Spain, connected by vast highways and frequent buses and trains from all major urban centers. **O Cebreiro** and **Ponferrada** are also popular starting points, and **Astorga** and **Villafranca del Bierzo** can serve as gateways as well. The latter three are best accessed via bus or train from León, while O Cebreiro is a bit more removed.

Car

The trail and stopping points along the Camino are never far from an easy access road if you are driving this section.

From **León**, take the **N-120** toward La Virgen del Camino and onward to Hospital de Órbigo and Astorga. After Astorga, exit onto the **LE-142** to just past Castrillo de los Polvazares. Exit toward Santa Catalina de Somoza on the **LE-6304** until it merges with the **LE-142** upon entering Rabanal del Camino. Stay on the LE-142, which will meander parallel along the Camino foot trail to Ponferrada. From León to Ponferrada is 109 kilometers (68 miles; 2 hours).

From **Ponferrada,** take the **LE-713** northwest of the town and follow it past Camponaraya and all the way to Villafranca del Bierzo, where it will merge with the **N-VI**. Stay on the N-VI. From Ponferrada to Villafranca del Bierzo is 24 kilometers (15 miles; 30 minutes).

After you pass through **La Portela de Valcarce,** if you wish to hold closest to the Camino trail, you'll begin to take even smaller country roads from here, including taking a left fork off the **N-VI** to an older road called the old **N-VI**. Take the **Carretera Antigua N-VI** until it becomes the **N-006A**, through Vega de Valcarce and on to Ruitelan, where the N-006A remerges with the new **N-VI** to Las Herrerías. From Villafranca del Bierzo to Las Herrerías is 23 kilometers (14 miles; 25 minutes).

Just before **Las Herrerías,** if you wish to stay on the truest reach of the Camino trail, the road will get narrower and steeper. Take the **CV-125/1** just before Las

Herrerías (a left fork off the N-VI) and follow it up past **La Faba** where it intersects with the **CV-125/15**.

To go to **La Faba,** turn left onto the **CV-125/1**. To continue to **Laguna del Castillo** and then **O Cebreiro,** go right onto the **CV-125/15** and follow the switchback turn (right-left) that will take you up hill all the way to O Cebreiro. Las Herrerías to O Cebreiro is 9.1 kilometers (5.7 miles; 40 minutes given the steep and narrow road).

From **O Cebreiro** to **Sarria,** take the **LU-633** west, which passes through Camino stops, including Hospital, Fonfría, Triacastela, and Samos, all the way to Sarria (45 km/28 mi, 55 minutes) or, once in Samos, make a right from the LU-633 onto the **LU-P-5602** heading north, and then west, to Furela, and continue on the LU-P-5602 west to Sarria (50 km/31 mi; 1 hour).

Air

The nearest airports are **Santiago de Compostela (SCQ)**, from which you can get the train to Ponferrada, Astroga, and León, and **Oviedo (OVD),** from which you can catch a train or bus to León and, from there, a train or bus to Astorga, Ponferrada, or Villafranca del Bierzo.

From **Madrid**'s Barajas airport (MAD), both bus and train lines connect directly to León, where you can catch a train or bus to Astorga and Ponferrada, and a bus to Villafranca del Bierzo.

Train

RENFE (www.renfe.es) has a line that runs nearly along the entire Camino (two trains daily), operating from Irún, at the Pyrenees, and stopping in Burgos, Sahagún, León, Astorga, Ponferrada (where you can connect to O Cebreiro by taxi), and Santiago de Compostela.

Bus

ALSA (www.alsa.com) connects towns and villages from León to Villafranca del Bierzo and then after, to Pedrafita do

Cebreiro, 4 kilometers (2.5 miles) north of O Cebreiro village, which is accessible via taxi.

León   Km 309

León (pop. 125,317) is the fourth largest city on the Camino, after Pamplona, Burgos, and Logroño. The approach into the city may be the most industrial (and the ugliest) of the Camino cities, startling some pilgrims after the vast and unpopulated *meseta*. Press on: León has a heart of gold and is one of the most lyrical medieval urban centers, after Santiago de Compostela, on the Camino.

León greets you with broad avenues, golden stone buildings, and sinuous medieval streets that disappear behind the protection of massive Roman walls. Its people are warm, and there is a cheer and creativity in the city's public life, which is especially centered on good food and wine. One of the striking aspects of the city is just how much of the Roman walls are still standing. Many people have built their homes against or between them. In some places, such as behind the cathedral on the east side, townhouses are interspersed with Roman walls, a striped architectural blanket woven from Roman to modern times.

True to many locales in medieval Iberia, León also had a significant Jewish and Muslim population. One of Spain's most famous Jewish citizens was from León: **Moses ben Sem Tov de León** (1250-1305) is said to have either created or compiled the Zohar, the Kabbalah, the most important text in Jewish mysticism.

Sights
Beginning from your entry into León on the Camino, you will pass all historic sights in León in an easy, linear, one-after-the-other fashion, beginning with Iglesia de Santa Ana and ending with Basilica de San Isidoro, within the Roman and medieval walls. You will encounter the monastery, Convento de San Marcos (now a luxury hotel, Parador San Marcos), farther west as you leave León on the Camino. The only exception to the linear progression of sights is the contemporary art museum, **MUSAC,** which is a 5-10 minute walk (750 meters/0.5 miles) north of the Camino from the Parador and monastery of San Marcos. The remaining museums highlighted here are within closer striking distance of the Camino, along with many squares and medieval streets on which to pause for food, drink, and atmosphere.

Iglesia de Santa Ana
As the Camino enters the heart of León, you'll pass the lovely **Iglesia de Santa Ana** (Calle Santa Ana, 44; 987-209-761; www. aytoleon.es; free, open daily) on your right. Folks of the quarter often gather in the small tree-lined square just outside the church to enjoy each other's good company.

This church was built in the 15th century in a Gothic-Mudéjar style that blended medieval Christian and Islamic styles. The current form is largely Neoclassical, but the grounds are historic. Before the church, a temple stood here, including the neighborhood's ancient synagogue. The church is an anchor in the neighborhood and for the Camino, and is a marker of the general vicinity of the medieval Muslim and Jewish neighborhoods of León.

This church is a cherished neighborhood hub for daily prayer and socializing, far more than a tourist site; come here for the peace and for a chance to fold into local life in its most sacred daily expression.

Puerta Moneda
Just past the Iglesia de Santa Ana, the Camino passes into the walled part of León via the gate known as Puerta Moneda, a medieval extension of the

León

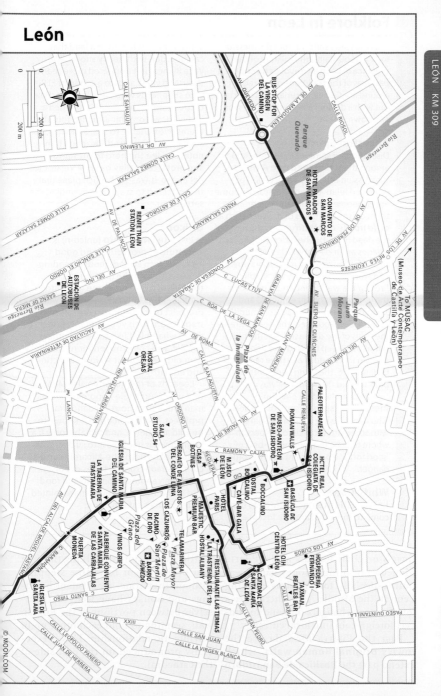

0
200 yds
0
200 m

CALLE SAHAGUN

AV. DR. FLEMING

CALLE GOMEZ SALAZAR

CALLE DE ASTORGA

RENFE TRAIN STATION LEON

AV. DE PALENCIA

CALLE GOMEZ SALAZAR

AV. DEL ING SANCHO SCHO DEL GORRO

ESTACION DE AUTOBUSES DE LEON

Rio Bernesga

SAENZ DE MIERA

AV. FACULTAD DE VETERINARIA

AV. REPUBLICA ARGENTINA

AV. LANCIA

AV. DEL ALCALDE MIGUEL CASTAÑO

C. BARAHONA

PUERTA MONEDA

IGLESIA DE SANTA ANA

C. SANTO TIRSO

CALLE LEOPOLDO PANERO

CALLE JUAN DE HERRERA

CALLE JUAN XXIII

CALLE SAN JUAN

CALLE LA VIRGEN BLANCA

LA TABERNA DE TRASTAMARA

IGLESIA DE SANTA MARIA DEL CAMINO

ALBERGUE CONVENTO DE LAS CARBAJALAS

SANTA MARIA DE LAS CARBAJALAS

VINOS GRIFO

RACIMO DE ORO

Plaza del Grano

LOS CAZURROS

BARRIO HUMEDO

San Martín

Plaza de San Martín

MERCADO DE ABASTOS DEL CONDE LUNA

TELAMARINERA

MAJESTIC

PREMIUM BAR

HOSTAL ALBANY

Plaza Mayor

SALA STUDIO 54

ORDOÑO II

CASA BOTINES

REGERAL

C. RAMÓN Y CAJAL

M.SEO DE LEÓN

EL CID

HOSTAL OREJAS

AV. DE ROMA

CALLE SAN AGUSTIN

AV. DEL PADRE ISLA

Plaza de la Inmaculade

C. ROA DE LA VEGA

C. LUCAS Y TUY

GRAN VIA DE SAN MARCOS

C. JUAN MADRAZO

AV. CONDESA DE SAGASTA

PASEO SALAMANCA

AV. DE LOS PEREGRINOS

HOTEL PARADOR DE SAN MARCOS

CONVENTO DE SAN MARCOS

AV. QUEVEDO

AV. DE LA MAGDALENA

BUS STOP FOR LA VIRGEN DEL CAMINO

Parque Quevedo

CALLE RIOSOL

Río Bernesga

AV. DE LOS REYES LEONESES

To MUSAC (Museo de Arte Contemporáneo de Castilla y León)

Parque Juan Morano

AV. DEL PADRE ISLA

AV. SUERO DE QUINONES

CALLE RENUEVA

PALEOTERRANEAN

ROMAN WALLS

MUSEO-PANTEÓN DE SAN ISIDORO

HOTEL REAL COLEGIATA DE SAN ISIDORO

BASÍLICA DE SAN ISIDORO

HOSTAL BOCALINO

BOCALINO

HOTEL PARIS

CAFÉ-BAR GALA

LA TRASTIENDA DEL 13

RESTAURANTE LAS TERMAS

CATEDRAL DE SANTA MARIA DE LEÓN

HOTEL QIH CENTRO LEÓN

AV. LOS CUBOS

HOSPEDERIA FERNANDO I

TAXMAN BEATLES BAR

CALLE BABIA

CALLE SAN PEDRO

PASEO QUINTANILLA

© MOON.COM

Folklore in León

In a landscape shifting from the *meseta* to high mountains, the folklore of the province of León also evokes transition. It partakes of the traditions of the regions around it—Castile, Asturias, and Galicia—but with a distinct shape-shifting flavor all its own.

Ancestral Spirits

Disembodied spirits wander here, top among them **Huéspeda de Ánimas,** "procession of souls": a procession of deceased relatives and ancestors. In some areas, people welcome and celebrate them on specific times of the year, such as on *la noche de los difuntos,* the night of the dead (Nov. 1), when locals in remote villages around Ponferrada and Villafranca del Bierzo leave their doors open and stoke their hearths with warming fires for the wandering souls. Between the festive days of December 25 and January 6, some mountain communities in León leave food near the hearth fire for the souls of the deceased, but the hope is that they keep moving and don't get stuck in this world. If any have remained by January 6, the living bang pots and pans to send them on their way.

León also shelters a belief in **messenger spirits,** souls of the dead, who may take the form of an animal with some significance to the person for whom they have a message—be it of good fortune or warning against some danger.

White Cows

La Vaca Blanca (the white cow) may come to the aid of anyone lost in a snowstorm—relevant in a land that can be laden with heavy snows. The Vaca Blanca first appeared more than a thousand years ago, to a group of El Bierzo shepherds who were leading their cattle through the mountains when a heavy snowstorm hit and they found themselves unable to see. Suddenly, a white cow appeared, clear and luminous, and led the herd to the narrow and protected valley basin of Villafranca del Bierzo. It was such a rich place that they decided to stay there, founding the settlement.

Unicorns

In León, the **Alicornio** (unicorn) is a creature of protection and good luck, but with added gender-bending powers: It's said the unicorn can turn women into men, and men into women—but only for one day. It was a prospect met with both curiosity and trepidation, for if you suddenly understood what it felt like to be the other gender, you could no longer resume your old life without serious reflection and empathy for all.

Legends of the Alicornio also recount that it can cure male impotence if the man touches its horn—a dangerous prospect, for the Alicornio is known to be wild and fierce, and tamable only if a virgin gives it her breast to suckle. With a touch of its horn, the Alicornio can also cure a person from all types of poisoning, from venomous bites to bad food and bad water. It can even make tainted water sources safe to drink.

town's original Roman walls. Puerta Moneda (meaning "money gate") was built especially for pilgrims entering León in the Middle Ages; there were a lot of money changers on hand to convert foreign coin into local currency.

Past the Puerta Moneda are the town's **original Roman walls,** which extend past the **Basilica de San Isidoro** a little farther north. Walking through and beside them feels like stepping into another time. Apartment buildings and houses have wedged themselves between portions of the Roman wall, seeming to hold each other up in a symbiotic relationship. This is especially pronounced on the east side of the cathedral.

Top: León's Catedral de Santa María. **Bottom:** Barrio Húmedo in León.

Plaza del Grano

This ancient square has many names—Plaza del Grano (grain square), Plaza del Mercado (market square), and Plaza de Santa María del Camino. Its massive Middle-Age cobblestones bring the past to life. (They also challenge tired ankles, so tread carefully.)

Once the site of a local grain and bread market, Plaza del Grano is perhaps León's most atmospheric and serene square, and a terrific place to stay or to have a drink. An 18th-century fountain sits between two venerable old trees; its two marble and stone angels represent the two rivers, Bernesga and Torío, that flow through and nourish León.

The **Iglesia de Santa María del Camino** (often referred to as Iglesia de Santa María del Mercado) is located on the square. The church, a rustic and early Romanesque structure with a local dedication, is worth visiting. Walk around the outside to take in the detailed and quirky sculptures in the corbels, including a wine carrier, a man pulling on his beard, and some folks in saucy poses. In the 6th century, just outside the church, a shepherd found the image of Mary hiding in a blackberry bush. Locals built the church in her honor in 1092, and her presence holds strong not only in the city but in outlying areas.

The church opens for daily **mass,** which is held at 8:30am, 1:30pm, and 6:30pm.

Mercado de Abastos del Conde Luna

Built in 1929, León's central covered market, **Mercado de Abastos del Conde Luna** (Plaza Conde Luna, s/n; 987-259-967; Mon.-Sat. 9am-2pm) is a living museum, with 42 kiosks selling meats, sausages, cheeses, breads, fruits, and vegetables, among other foods grown in the region. This is also a great place to see locals, shop, mingle, and fold into local life while stocking up for the trail.

★ Catedral de Santa María de León

Construction of the **Catedral de Santa María de León** (987-875-770; www.catedraldeleon.org; open daily, 9:30am-1:30pm and 4-7pm) began in 1205. It was envisioned as a pure French Gothic cathedral, similar to Chartres cathedral and to Paris's Sainte-Chapelle, where stained-glass windows dominate, and challenge, the building's structural form. León's cathedral was an intentional replica of the cathedral in Rheims in northeastern France, though a third smaller. Two other churches stood on this site before the current cathedral was constructed. This location once also held a Roman bath, and a thick glass square laid into the stones of the cathedral square's south side gives a view of the thermal world of clean Romans.

The expressive sculptures on the west entrance include the famous Virgen Blanca, the most miraculous Mary of the medieval Camino, who is celebrated in poetry and song. She stands at the mullion, the pillar of the central arch. Above her are scenes of the Last Judgment with Jesus in Majesty.

But inside is where it gets intense and potentially transcendent. As soon as you pass the ticket kiosk and enter the west side of the nave, be prepared for the sensation of stepping into saturated liquid light in hues of cobalt, indigo, golden yellow, ruby red, and emerald green. The delicate vertical lines of the towering Gothic walls and columns soar upward, drawing all your attention to the stained-glass windows they hold. So numerous are the windows that the building's integrity is in fine balance: is there enough stone to hold it all up? (So far, it's survived 800 years, with a lot of restorations.) I find this to be one of the most peaceful interiors of the grand Gothic cathedrals of Europe. The windows, which were made from the 13th to the 15th centuries, have been continuously restored, with ongoing work in the present.

Most of the windows depict scenes from Christ's life or the Bible, but one, on the north side, shows a curious and detailed series of hunting scenes (including one panel with a monkey riding a horse). Some art historians speculate that they came from another building, perhaps a noble's or king's castle, which was destroyed and partially repurposed here in the 15th century.

The cloister off to the north side of the cathedral is 13th century and Gothic, but has a familiar Renaissance overlay for pilgrims who have visited the Monasterio de San Zoilo's cloister in Carrión de los Condes: Juan de Badajoz, the architect who modified San Zoilo's cloister, did similar work here, layering more ornate Renaissance embellishments over the more delicate Gothic arches.

The cathedral's **Museo Diocesano** (987-875-770; www.catedraldeleon. org; daily, 9:30am-1:30pm and 4-7pm) is worth a visit to see the Romanesque sculpture from the third church, and for other sacred art, including Mudéjar (Islamic Iberian) textiles that were popular with medieval northern nobility, and Jewish funerary stones from the long-vanished medieval neighborhood.

General admission to the cathedral is €6, or €9 if combined with visits to the cloister and the church museum, Museo Diocesano. The fee includes audio guides in many languages, including English. It is perhaps the steepest admission for a sacred site on the Camino, but worth every centime. However, daily **mass** (9am, 2pm, and 6pm) is free, giving you a chance to experience the church as it was originally intended: as a place of worship (definitely no gawking, and *expressly* no photos).

From top to bottom: Vinos Grifo on the Plaza del Grano, León; León's Catedral de Santa María; Antonio Gaudí's Casa Botines.

Highlights of León's Food and Wine

León's food and wine is the hearty and rustic cuisine of muleteers, herders, and farmers who inhabit the chestnut- and oak-forested mountains on both sides of Ponferrada, especially the celebrated Maragato and El Bierzo traditions. In this irrigated valley, everything grows well—including fruit trees not seen in neighboring regions, such as cherries, pears, figs, and olives, and especially the *manzana Reineta,* El Bierzo's Designation-of-Origin apple that was coveted in the Middle Ages by pilgrims, as much as it is today, for its perfect balance of sweet and sour. Kitchen gardens thrive, and most you see will be growing *pimientos del Bierzo* (sweet peppers), collard greens, and strawberries.

A combined platter of cured ham, local egg, garden salad, and croquettas

Cocidos and Other Mountain-Style Dishes

León's *pot au feu-style cocido* of stewed meats and vegetables is served as a three-course meal: soup, vegetable, and meat courses, in that order. These cocidos come in many variations, such as **cocido Leonese, cocido Berciano, cocido del Bierzo,** or **cocido montañes** (mountain stew), but all are essentially the same. These León-region cocidos use local sausages, including *botillo* (a smoked meat that is similar to chorizo, and almost exclusively used for stick-to-your-ribs cocidos), as well as local legumes, such as garbanzos and lentils, and vegetables, especially onions, cabbage, potatoes, carrots, and sometimes tomatoes.

Cocido Maragato is another local cocido, found between Astorga and Ponferrada. It uses similar ingredients, but can contain up to seven different types of meat. It is also served in the opposite

order of other cocidos: meats (chorizo, pork belly, chicken, ham, cecina, and other beef), then vegetables (cabbage, potatoes, garbanzos, tomatoes), and finally the rich soup broth with noodles.

Some other original, hearty, mountain-style dishes from this province, almost all stove-top stewed or baked in terracotta *cazuelos,* casserole dishes, are **ancas de rana de Astorga** (frog legs cooked in white wine and garlic with chili peppers and smoky paprika), **al ajoarreiro** (garlic-infused meat or fish), and **alubias con callos** (a stew of paprika, garlic, white wine, and tomato with tripe and locally grown white beans).

Cheeses

Most cheeses are made from sheep's milk (near León in the *meseta*) and cow's milk (near Galicia in the mountains), but there is a narrow stretch on the Camino, in the village of Ambasmestas, that is known for goat's milk cheeses, **quesos de cabra.** At **Quesería Veigadarte,** a goat farm and home kitchen/cheese shop you can visit the farm and purchase fresh cheese from the maker; the farm is well marked, found midway through Ambasmestas. With a

Casa Botines

Catalán architect Antonio Gaudí designed the **Casa Botines** (Plaza San Marcelo, 5; 987-353-247; www.casabotines.es), which was built between 1891 and 1894. It was commissioned by (and first used as) a department store for Leónine textile merchants. In 1931 the building sold and became a local office for Caja España bank, which respected the original building and preserved the original structure.

In 2017, Casa Botines opened as an exhibit space celebrating Gaudí's architecture and other modern artists, overseen by the Fundación España Duero, fresh-baked baguette (look for the bakery van passing through these mountain villages, selling bread from the trunk) and apples, you have a perfect picnic lunch.

León's special Stilton-like blue cheese, **queso de Valdeón**, is made from the local cow's milk or, at times, from a blend of cow, sheep, and goat's milks.

Botillo and Cecina

Botillo is a wide, fat sausage, shaped almost like an American football, made from scraps of meat mixed with garlic and *pimentón* (Spanish paprika), then cured with the smoke of the Holm oak, the *encina*, a native tree. Botillo is a favorite ingredient in El Bierzo cocido; in fact, it's about the only way you'll see botillo used. Don't be surprised if on weekends you see Spaniards from across the country flocking to El Bierzo just to eat botillo and drink local wines, especially Mencía.

Another cured meat celebrated here is the dry-cured beef, **cecina,** which is delicate and nutty, similar to the cured *jamón Iberico*.

Lamb and Game

Lamb dishes are traditional here, especially the *lechazo de cordero* (roasted suckling lamb), *chanfaina* (a garlic, onion, and chili pepper and lamb shepherd's stew that cooks the meat in blood), and perhaps more palatable to visitors not used to the shepherding way of life, the savory *caldereta de cordero*, a lamb stew traditionally cooked in a big hanging black iron cauldron over the open fire and filled with choice cuts of lamb, onion, garlic, parsley, white wine, and smoked paprika.

Such wild territory also has *carnes de caza*, wild game meats, especially from *jabalí* (wild boar), *ciervo* (deer), *liebre* (hare), *perdiz* (partridge), and *codorniz* (quail). During hunting periods, which can fall in every season, look for these meats, usually listed by their name and how they are prepared, as a *cocido* (stew) or *asado* or *al horno* (fire-grilled or oven-roasted).

El Bierzo Wines

Especially between Ponferrada and Villafranca del Bierzo, vineyards dominate the landscape. El Bierzo wine, especially from the Mencía grape, is a rare treat since it is rarely exported. It is velvety, medium-bodied, and more mineral than fruit. It is fabled that a 12th-century French settler brought the cabernet franc vine to this part of Iberia. Over the decades and centuries it evolved into the unique Mencía, suited to the soil and climate of El Bierzo.

The white wines are dominantly made from Godello or Albarín grape varietals and also show the unique taste of the land: somewhere between an unoaked chardonnay and a sauvignon blanc.

Orujo

As in Galicia, many festive meals end with the digestive *orujo*, an eau de vie that is infused with local herbs and considered both medicinal and enjoyable.

Chocolate and Pastries

Astorga has long been a center of chocolate production. Other Astorgan sweets include pastries such as *hojaldres* (puff pastry dripping in honey syrup), *mantecadas* (dense muffin-sized pound cake), and *merles* (custard-filled pastries).

the heir foundation to the social-works branch of Caja España Duero. The **museum** (daily, 11am-2pm and 5-9pm; general admission €5; guided tour and more extensive access, €12) includes not only the interior design and history of Gaudí's whimsical structure and permanent exhibits on Gaudí's visions, dreams, and artistry, but also temporary art exhibits exploring Dalí and Dante's Divine Comedy.

Outside, in front of the main entrance, a memorial bronze sculpture of Gaudí is seated on a bench facing his creation, and there's plenty of room for visitors to join him and admire his work (and have a photo op). True to Gaudí's signature style, the building incorporates modernist, natural, and medieval religious forms (especially Gothic) as a part of its harmonious fusion style.

Museo de León

Near Casa Botines, the city's and region's archaeological museum, **Museo de León** (Plaza Santo Domingo, 8; 987-236-405; www.museodeleon.com; open Tues.-Sat., Oct.-June, 10am-2pm and 4-7pm, Jul.-Sept., 10am-2pm and 5-8pm; Sun. and holidays, 10am-2pm; €1), is the place to see the local Roman remains, especially coins, pottery, sculptures, mosaics, and engraved and inscribed funerary stones.

The museum covers earlier and later periods as well, such as the Iron Age. Its Celtic *torques*, collars, are especially interesting, as are the reconstructions of pre-Roman Iron Age villages with *pallozas*, round stone huts with low thatched roofs. Among its celebrated medieval collections is the *Cristo de Carrizo*, a 35-centimeter-long ivory cross, with a finely carved image of Christ.

A section of the museum is also dedicated to early modern and modern art. Panels are in Spanish. The museum's upper floors offer great views of Gaudí's Casa Botines.

★ Basilica de San Isidoro

The **Basilica de San Isidoro** (Plaza de San Isidoro, 4; www.museosanisidorodeleon. com; open daily, typically 8:30am-9pm; free admission) was constructed over a Roman temple dedicated to Mercury and marks the center of Roman León. It was built to house the relics of San Isidoro, brought here from Seville in 1063. Like Villafranca del Bierzo (Km 182.1), San Isidoro has a **Puerta del Perdón** (Gate of Pardon): It's the right-most outer portal on the south side, where pilgrims who could not make the rest of the trip to Santiago de Compostela could earn pardon. The images on the tympanum depict the days surrounding Jesus's crucifixion, from being taken off the cross, the empty tomb discovered by the three Marys, and his ascent to heaven (inspiration for downtrodden pilgrims).

You enter the basilica through the other south portal, which enters the building in the middle at the nave, left of the Puerta del Perdón. Its themes are from the Old Testament. Inside the three-nave basilica, Saint Isidoro's relics are on the altar.

This is an active house of worship, with a daily cycle of mass and confession. It is worth taking the time to amble all around the church, looking up at the detailed sculptures on the column's capitals. The expressive sculpture reflects earlier Romanesque imagery, while the scalloped arches at the transept reflect an Islamic influence. Notice also the many stones in the walls and pillars all throughout the church that are etched with stonemason marks, some of which are fairly elaborate, with symbols of spirals, arrows, crosses, and triangles. (A favorite displays two triangles touching at their points, forming an hourglass, with a circle and a cross dawn in the middle of the intersection. No one knows what it might have symbolized, its meaning private to the builder himself; it is his distinct signature.)

Notice also at the back end of the nave, next to a scalloped doorway, you will find the **Chi-Rho** (also known as a *chrismon*), a monogram of Christ using the overlapping first two Greek letters of his name, *chi* and *rho*, to form a stylistic circle with six crossing arms. Like the symbol of the fish, it was used by early Christians to depict Christ before the cross was used for this purpose. This one has an alpha and omega (the first and last letters of the Greek alphabet, representing beginning and end) hanging on each of the horizontal arms, a common way to say that Jesus was the beginning and the end. In Chi-Rho, the alpha and omega are normally written in the order a Latin speaker would read them, left to right. Here, like the Chi-Rhos in Puente la Reina, Cirauqui, and Estella (in Navarra, farther east), the alpha and omega are reversed, reading right to left— hinting again, as in Navarra, that some of the builders had Islamic or Jewish backgrounds, since both Hebrew and Arabic are read right to left.

The priest here is very welcoming and will gladly stamp your credential. You can ask him if you see him milling about the nave and transept, or you may find him at a table to the left side of the nave, inkpad and stamp at the ready.

Adjoining the Basilica de San Isidoro is the pantheon and museum, **Museo-Panteón de San Isidoro** (Plaza de San Isidoro; www.museosanisidorodeleon. com; €5; guided tours, some in English), accessed through the outside door to the left of the basilica. The pantheon is among the earliest parts of the overall Romanesque complex, and was built in the 11th century to house León's royal tombs. It contains the most beautiful and well-preserved 12th-century multicolored Romanesque frescos in Spain. The images have an earthy and personal style and are a mix of sacred and mundane themes. There are Biblical scenes as well as animated representations of annual events shown month by month, such as the planting of crops in April, the wheat harvest in July, and the pig slaughter in November. You'll also visit the tombs of León's kings and queens here.

The Museo-Panteón has varying hours throughout the year: Oct.-Apr. Mon.-Sat. 10am-2pm and 4-7pm, Sun. 10am-2pm; May-Jun. Mon.-Thu. 10am-2pm and 4-7pm, Fri.-Sat. 10am-2pm and 4-8pm, Sun. 10-3pm; Jul.-Oct. Mon.-Sat. 9:30am-3pm and 3:30-9pm, Sun. 9:30am-3pm. Visits are by guided tour only, which is included in the ticket price.

Convento de San Marcos
The Knights of Santiago founded the monastery of **San Marcos** (Plaza de San Marcos; 987-245-061; www.visitaleon.

com/san-marcos) in the 12th century. It was rebuilt in the form you see today in the 16th century, with a blocky, massive, and ornate edifice, and functioned as a monastery until 1837. In 1961, the Spanish government turned it into a luxury hotel, as it functions today. It also includes the original cloister and a good museum.

If you saw the movie *The Way,* this is the ritzy place where the four pilgrims stayed when they passed through León. You can enter through the hotel entrance and take in the interior. If you can't afford to stay here, you may want to contemplate a drink in the bar to soak up the atmosphere. Additionally, the monastery-hotel retains the 16th-century church, **Iglesia de San Marcos,** and an extensive **museum** (Oct.-Jun. Tues.-Sat. 10am-2pm and 4-7pm, Sun. and holidays 10am-2pm; Jul.-Sept. Tues.-Sat. 10am-2pm and 5-8pm, Sun. and holidays 10am-2pm; €0.60, free Sat.-Sun.), set in the church's cloister, containing religious works and some local archaeological remains that complement those found in the Museo de León.

MUSAC (Museo de Arte Contemporaneo de Castilla y León)
This Roman and medieval city also has a modern flair that's best seen on its streets and in the **Museum of Contemporary Art of Castile and León** (Avenida de los Reyes Leoneses, 24; 987-090-000; www.musac. es; Mon.-Fri. 11am-2pm and 5-8pm, Sat.-Sun. and holidays 11am-3pm and 5-9pm; €3). This museum showcases artists from the autonomous region of Castilla y León, as well as others from across Europe and the world. The 3,600-square-meter space includes six exhibit halls and an art laboratory.

MUSAC opened in 2005 with the intent to be a center of dialog about modern European and Spanish experiences. One recent photographic exhibit, featuring more than thirty artists, explored the pilgrimage experience on the Camino, focusing on its aesthetic beauty as well as its spiritual, cultural, historical, natural, and anthropological elements. Other exhibits have explored the affect of Franco's dictatorship on the Spanish psyche and the art of modern Castilian writing.

You can't miss the building, which is north of the medieval center and to the northeast of the Camino, near where it passes the Convento de San Marcos. Its hypermodern exterior is features colorful metal and glass panels.

The museum hosts daily activities, and exhibits change regularly, so it is worth just showing up to see what's happening. You can also check the website, which is in both Spanish and English, to see the daily offerings. Programs and panels are in Spanish, but if modern art is effective, most of the exhibits should translate to the viewer visually and viscerally.

Festivals and Markets

León is one of the best places on the Camino in which to experience **Semana Santa** (Holy Week), the week leading up to and including **Easter Sunday**. The whole historic center, with the cathedral at its heart, becomes a part of the Passion of Christ; there is a strong dedication to Mary, with processions and floats making their way to the cathedral. Some 16 religious brotherhoods—*cofradias*—organize the processions, and each of the elaborate, heavy floats are hoisted onto the backs and shoulders of dozens of men. Some of the *cofradias* are over 400 years old. Feasting with family and friends, staying up all night, and dressing to the nines are all par for the course.

In addition to its Mercado de Abastos del Conde Luna, León also has **food markets** every Wednesday and Saturday (9am-2pm) on the Plaza Mayor. León's colorful **flea market**, El Rastro de León, sets up every Saturday on the Plaza Don Gutierre, just south of the Mercado de Abastos. Every Sunday, along the Paseo Papalaguinda, running parallel with the train station but on the other side of the Bernesga river, a **weekly market** that sells general merchandise unfolds; it can be a good place to find a cotton scarf or replacement T-shirt for the trail.

Food

Racimo de Oro (Plaza de San Martín, 8; 987-214-767; www.racimodeoro.com; €18) in the Barrio Húmedo has the tapas scene, as well as fine cuisine, in several different dining rooms in a restored house from the 17th century. They serve many regional dishes; among the most celebrated are the charcuterie platter (*embutidos*), the lentil soup (*sopa de lentejas*), and the grilled lamb.

Q!H Centro Leon (Avenida de los Cubos, 6; €8) is a fabulous, upscale burger joint (on the corner and ground floor of the Hotel Q!H) with a changing weekly chalkboard of wines selected from Rioja, Castile, and León's growers. Burgers can come with fries (or, better, flash-fried Padrón peppers). Try also the calamari with wasabi mayonnaise.

Telamarinera (Calle Platerias, 1; 987-071-862; telamarinera@enoilogicos.com; €13) specializes in fish and seafood—which explains its blue and white ship-like marine décor—that also does classic dishes from Leon with an experimental and inventive angle. There are several small dining areas inside, as well as outdoor terrace seating.

★ **Vinos Grifo** (Plaza de Santa María del Camino, 9; 629-491-405; www.vinosgrifo.es) is a wine bar (€2-3) and restaurant (€10-15) with a terrific location on the Plaza de Santa María del Camino. Any time of the week you can come here to sample newly uncovered gems of regional and provincial wines. Fresh ingredients go into the creative tapas; entrees include vegetarian options.

La Taberna de Trastamara (Calle de Trastamara, 1; 987-255-173; €10-15) serves creative complementary tapas with wine orders in the bar and seasonally inspired dishes. If you decide to stay for a more substantial meal in the connecting dining room, try the stewed morcilla blood sausage with wild mushrooms or the *toro* steak with red peppers.

Restaurante Las Termas (Calle Paloma, 13; 987-264-600; www.hostalalbanylas-termas.com) has a chef dedicated to daily market and seasonal finds and inspired by traditional Leonese recipes (but with experimental license): Try the spider-crab-stuffed roasted red peppers, scrambled eggs with wild mushrooms, shrimp, and ham, and fresh anchovies fried with garlic and little green peppers, *pimientos de Padrón* (menú, €15).

Café-Bar Gala (Calle del Cid, 20; 987-236-024; www.gala.es; €5-10) serves good tavern food, including fresh salads and sandwiches. It's a fun place to stop for informal meals and snacks, along a quiet side street across from the Parque del Cid, where you can watch from the café terrace as locals walk their dogs and relax after a day of work.

★ **PaleoTerranean** (Calle Renueva, 20; 987-172323; €10-17) emphasizes the Paleo diet with Mediterranean underpinnings and goes wonderfully overboard in its creative mixes of vegetables and various meats, fish, and fowl. Try a salad of dry cured duck breast (*cecina de pato*), avocado, sun dried tomatoes, almonds, and cranberry vinaigrette; or an octopus carpaccio with gazpacho tartar; or a vegetarian burger made with red beans and served with lettuce "buns," caramelized onions, lactose-free cheese, and sweet potato chips. (They also serve gluten-free bread.) The dining room décor is of Upper Paleolithic cave paintings.

Nightlife

León has a special tradition around tapas and drinks, known as *el arte del tapeo* (the art of tapas). Unlike elsewhere in Spain, where a drink order may come with a complimentary small but simple bite, here your drink order comes with a fairly elaborate tapa, also called a *tapita*, which is a larger small bite than usual, and one that is creatively concocted by the restaurant or bar chef each day. It is

included in the cost of a drink (typically €1.5-2). Drink sizes tend to be more modest than elsewhere and may be called *un corto,* a short glass, so you can enjoy the feast without getting drunk.

▬▬▬ Top Experience ▬▬▬

★ Barrio Húmedo

Old Roman and medieval León is nicknamed the "wet quarter"—not for any issues for flooding or humidity, but because the neighborhood contains well over a hundred bars. This is where locals come to wet their whistles, slowly making their way from one establishment to the next, enjoying a glass and tapa created by each place. The labyrinth-like streets filled with bars, cafes, and restaurants are located south of the cathedral and west of the **Plaza Mayor**, radiating out from the **Plaza de San Martin**. Happy grazers usually throng to this neighborhood around sunset. But for more nightlife of the club, dance, and music variety, expect a late night as these don't tend to rev up until after 11pm or later.

Top venues in the Barrio Húmedo include **Los Cazurros** (Plaza San Martín, 5; 987-252-233; www.loscazurros.es), which takes its name from particularly rambunctious medieval jugglers and performers. Known for a dynamic local wine offering, it's equally worth visiting for the vibrant and innovative *tapas* and *tapitas* inspired by local products, from charcuterie to vegetables—and especially spicy eggs. The décor reflects the region, with sepia photos and a whole wall mounted with *madreñas,* wooden shoes that farmers and herders traditionally wear. They offer gluten free options.

A wine bar and restaurant with Belle Époque flair, **La Trastienda del 13** (Calle Ancha, 1; 987-007-333; www.latrastiendadel13.es), provides delicious tapas and a wide selection of wines and cocktails on the popular Calle Ancha near the cathedral. Stop in for a *tapita* at the bar or terrace, or enjoy market fresh, creative dishes in the colorful, eclectic dining room off the bar.

Other Nightlife in Leon

Taxman Beatles Bar (Calle Babia, 6; 987-002-211) is run by a passionate Anglophile (he'll be thrilled if you're from Liverpool) and serves a good selection of beers and wine, with black-and-white Beatles photos on the walls, an upright piano, and a display cabinet packed with Beatles memorabilia.

The Majestic Premium Bar (Plaza Conde Luna, 11; 696-946-426; majesticpremiumbar@gmail.com) has an upscale, futuristic ambiance with bottles on backlit neon purple glass shelves; it's like a cocktail party under the sea, with good music. The mixologists here are celebrated for really knowing how to mix an authentic cocktail. Especially popular are the gin and tonics and the mojitos.

Sala Studio 54 León (Calle Burgo Nuevo, 18; 987-255-212) has been hosting local live music, discos, drinks, and dancing since the 1980s. Check out their Facebook page (www.facebook.com/studio54leon) for upcoming music events.

Accommodations

León has an array of consistently excellent accommodations for a wide range of budgets, more than I have found elsewhere on the Camino. Hotels in León get pretty overbooked during Semana Santa, but *albergues* remain for pilgrims only, always assuring *peregrinos* have a bed even during holiday periods.

Albergue

★ **Albergue Convento Santa María de las Carbajalas** (Calle de Ascrial and the Plaza de Santa María del Camino; 680-649-289; €5) is simple and clean, with an expansive entry and many communal spaces, not to mention 140 beds in four dormitories segregated by gender. The highlight here is the chance to attend Vespers (7pm) with the nuns. They also have 25 private rooms (€49-100) in their

Hospedería Antigua next door. There are varied dinner options (€9-25) and breakfast (€8). An active monastery, these Benedictine nuns run one of the best *albergues* in León province. They also hold a pilgrims' blessing (9pm) and Compline (9:45pm).

Hotels

★ **Hotel Parador de San Marcos** (Plaza San Marcos, 7; 987-237-300; www.parador.es/en/paradores/parador-de-leon; 184 rooms; €100 and up) lets you sleep in the 16th-century Order of Santiago's monastery-turned-*parador* (state-run hotel in an historic building), a splendid mix of monastic and royal accommodations. There is a library in addition to the church and monastery museum. There are special room discounts for certain ages: Persons 18-30 get 15 percent off, and travelers over 55 get 10 percent off—plus, everybody gets 15 percent off if they stay two nights. You can also dine here: Chef Agapito Cristóbal Nuñez prepares dishes inspired by traditional Leones cuisine, with specially selected Bierzo and Tierra de León wines (€36).

★ **Hostal Restaurante Boccalino** (Plaza de San Isidoro, 9; 987-223-060; www.hotelboccalino.es; €35-55) has perhaps the best situation right on the square, facing the Basilica de San Isidoro. The rooms are on several floors and are open, clean, with quilted French-style bedspreads and wrought-iron balconies with a view. The attached **restaurant**, with terrace dining on the square, serves dishes with an Italian influence, including seasonal fish dishes, homemade pasta and ravioli, and risottos. Proprietors speak English.

Hotel Real Colegiata de San Isidoro (Plaza Santo Martino, 5; 987-875-088; www.hotelrealcolegiata.es; 46 rooms; €90-115) is a romantic luxury hotel, boasting a lyrical architectural continuity with its illustrious neighbors—San Isidoro's basilica, the pantheon, and Roman León's first foundations. The reception, rooms, and (English-speaking) service are impeccable. There is a restaurant serving traditional and modern Spanish cuisine (€17-20) in a private courtyard and cloister in the center. The rooms are thick-cut stone, with stately traditional woodwork and modern and comfortable furnishings.

Hotel Q!H Centro Leon (Avenida de los Cubos, 6; 987-875-580; www.hotelqhcentroleon.com; €130) is in possession of a great bar (with excellent burgers) on the ground floor and extends its innovative and modern flair to boutique hotel rooms on the upper floors. The rooms feature textured wood walls, bold earthy tones, tile-lined tubs, and French-window views of the cathedral next door (in all 22 guest rooms and bathrooms). You can take a rest day at Q!H's full-service spa, including hammam, sauna, massages, and peels. Promotions on their website offer packages (often for two nights and two people) that are a good value for this luxury hotel. Proprietors speak English.

Hotel Paris (Calle Ancha, 18; 987-238-600; www.hotelparisleon.com; 59 rooms; €61-88) feels like a boutique hotel in Paris. It is equipped with a spa, La Pausa en Paris, with massage therapy and therapeutic water treatments, including a pool with water jets that can iron out back and neck kinks. The attached restaurant-café is a local favorite, and if you love *churros con chocolate*, those Spanish donut-like creations with thick, dark hot chocolate, this is the place. Modern, comfortable, and spotless rooms.

The rooms in the **Hospedería Fernando I** (Avenida los Cubos, 32; 987-220-731; www.hospederiafernandoi.com; 27 rooms; €50) feature ironwork, bed boards painted with medieval city scenes, and frescos on room walls of Romanesque scenes; the overall mood here is quintessentially medieval León, with modern comforts. It's a quirky, delightful blend. Each of the 27 rooms is uniquely decorated with these elements.

The same extends to the medieval tavern atmosphere of its **restaurant** (987-220-601), which features good daily menus (€12.50).

★ **Hostal Orejas** (Calle Villafranca, 8; 987-252-909; www.hostal-orejas.es; 49 rooms; €35-45), a central, family-run hotel, has clean modern rooms, agreeable beds, and spacious baths. The mood and décor is a delightful mix of old and new, medieval and modern, with stained-glass doors and striped wallpaper. A good breakfast is served in the sun-filled breakfast room, and the owner is a font of information about the traditions and highlights of León.

Popular with pilgrims for its central location (50 meters/164 feet to the cathedral) and featuring decent prices for its slightly more upscale quality, **Hostal Albany** (Calle Paloma, 13; 987-264-600; www.hostalalbanylastermas.com; €30-45) has pleasing thick stone and brick walls and large beds with plush duvets, assuring sweet dreams even as the nightlife in the historic center amps up its decibels.

Getting There and Around

Unless you are driving the Camino, getting to León is easiest by train and bus. Buses from several stops earlier on the Camino (El Burgo Ranero, Mansilla de las Mulas, and Puente Villarente) connect to León. Many Camino walkers use these buses in order to bypass the unappealing industrial outskirts leading into the city.

Car

From **Burgos** (183 km/114 mi; 2 hours): Follow **N-120** or **A-231** (both follow the Camino and run nearly parallel to each other) all the way to León.

From **Bilbao** (486 km/302 mi; 5 hours): Exit south on **AP-68;** take **A-1** at Miranda de Ebro, heading southwest to Burgos; take **A-1/BU-30** to **A-231** to León.

From **Santander** (420 km/261 mi; 4.5 hours): Head south on **A-67** to Osorno; exit to **A-231** to León.

From **Madrid** (343 km/213 mi; 3.5 hours): Head north on **A-6** to **A-66** to León.

From **Barcelona** (785 km/488 mi; 8 hours): Go west on **AP-7** and **AP-2** to Zaragoza; take **AP-68** then **A-232** and **AP-1** to Burgos, then **A-231** to León.

From **Santiago de Compostela** (325 km/202 mi; 4 hours): Essentially driving the Camino in reverse, head east on **N-547** to **LU-633** toward Portomarín all the way to O Cebreiro then Pedrafita do Cebreiro; take **N-VI** all the way to Ponferrada, then **LE-142** to Astorga, and **N-120 or A-231** to León.

From **A Coruña**: Exit south on **AC-11** which becomes **AP-9** and then **E-70/A-6** to Lugo; stay on the **A-6** to Pedrafita do Cebreiro and exit south on **LU-633** to O Cebreiro.

With offices for **Europcar** (www.europcar.com) and **Avis** (www.avis.com) right next to León's train station (Plaza de San Marcos, 2), and **Enterprise** (www.enterprise.com) within walking distance of the station, you can pick up or drop off a rental from here.

Train

RENFE (www.renfe.com) runs daily lines from other major cities to León: Madrid (14 trains daily; 2.5-4.5 hours; €30-50), Barcelona (eight daily; 6-9 hours; €54-83), Oviedo (six daily; 2-3 hours; €10-20), Santiago de Compostela (three daily; 4.5-6.5 hours; €26-35). One train runs daily from Irún at the Pyrenees all the way to Santiago de Compostela (11 hours; €48), with stops at Burgos, Sahagun, León, Astorga, and Ponferrada. More frequent trains run between, such as from Burgos to Leon (four daily; 2 hours; €15-24).

From León's train station, **Estación de Renfe** (Calle Astorga, s/n; 902-432-343), reaching the Camino is a 1.5 kilometer (0.9-mile), 20-minute walk east to the Catedral de Santa María. Leave the station and cross the bridge over the river Bernesga. Continue straight on Avenida Ordoño II to the Plaza de Santo Domingo;

from there, continue straight ahead onto Calle Arco de Ánimas, which becomes Calle Ancha. Keep going straight to the Plaza de Regla with the cathedral at its center. Brass scallop shells and yellow arrows in the pavement and on the walls will direct you left and onto the Camino.

Bus

ALSA (www.alsa.es) offers many options to get to León from several hubs: Madrid's airport (two buses daily; 6 hours; €34); Madrid's Estación Sur (two daily; 6 hours; €34); Ponferrada (four daily; 40 minutes; €4); Lugo (five daily; 50 minutes; €6); and Santiago de Compostela (four daily; 3.5 hours; €19).

From León's bus station, **Estación de Autobuses** (Avenida Ingeniero Sáenz de Miera, s/n), which is next to and just south of the train station, reaching the Camino is a 1.5-kilometer (0.9-mile), 20-minute walk: Exit and go left on Avenida Ingeniero Sáenz de Miera to the bridge, Puente de Leones, and take a right to cross the river Bernesga. Cross and continue straight on Avenida Ordoño II to the Plaza de Santo Domingo; from there, continue straight ahead onto Calle Arco de Ánimas, which becomes Calle Ancha. Keep going straight to the Plaza de Regla with the cathedral at its center. Brass scallop shells and yellow arrows in the pavement and on the walls will direct you left and onto the Camino.

Taxi

A taxi from León to La Virgen del Camino will run around €15 (10 minutes). Try **Radio Taxi León** (987-261-415; www.radiotaxileon.com) or **Radio Taxi Amarillo Ciudad de León** (987-106-006; www.radiotaxiamarillociudaddeleon.com).

Leaving León

After passing the Convento/Parador de San Marcos on your right, you will cross the bridge over the Bernesga river, and pass a small tree-covered park (also on your right), where hens and roosters roam.

The Camino then continues west. This is perhaps one of the road's ugliest, most industrial stretches, though the people along it are very nice. If you wish to skip 7.7 kilometers (4.8 miles) of walking on pavement, the **bus** (www.lavirgendel-camino.info/wordpress/horarios-auto-buses; €1.40), with "Virgen del Camino" noted on its digital sign, stops at the corner where the Avenida de la Magdalena opens up after the first traffic round-about, just after passing the park (a hardware store, Ferretería El Crucero, is across the street). You'll see a small sign on the sidewalk and a large white "BUS" painted on the asphalt. Buses run every half-hour, 6:15am-10pm. The bus drops you off on the Camino in La Virgen del Camino, in 7.7 kilometers (4.8 miles).

La Virgen del Camino
Km 301.3

La Virgen del Camino (pop. 2,600) has grown from an outlying chapel dedicated to Our Lady of the Camino, who is said to have appeared here to a shepherd in the 16th century, to a suburb of León. The chapel stands immediately to the right of the Camino, which here runs parallel to the right side of the N-120. Even today, Mary is a living and active presence in the lives of locals as well as the city.

Sights
★ Basilica de la Virgen del Camino
In 1505, Alvar Simón, a shepherd, saw a star and followed it until Mary appeared to him. Simón told the local bishop about the vision, and that Mary asked him to build a church in her honor. But the bishop was unconvinced. To prove the veracity of his vision, Mary told Simón to throw a stone, and that she wanted him to build a church on the site where it stopped. He did so. Miraculously the stone grew as it rolled until it reached the size of a boulder and came to a stop. The bishop authorized the holy site and locals constructed it in 1513.

The current **Basilica de la Virgen del Camino** (Avenida de Astorga, 43; 987-300-001; www.virgendelcamino.

Basilica de la Virgen del Camino

dominicos.es; open daily through-out the day; free) is from 1961. Though modern, the basilica is appealing. Over the entrance door are metal modern-ist sculptures by José Subirachs, show-ing a towering and serene Mary flanked on both sides by the Apostles. The exte-rior walls and door surfaces are covered in engravings of Christian symbols, in-cluding the faith's earliest symbol, the fish, set centrally on the door. Inside, the rectangular space is open and simple, but the upper walls are inset with col-orful stained-glass windows that filter the natural light into myriad rainbow tones. On the altar is the original 16th-century icon of Mary, engraved to honor the shepherd's vision and this sanctuary's construction. It is set within a brilliant il-luminated niche that radiates white light all around her and makes you feel as if a vortex is pulling you in. You can stamp your pilgrim's passport here. If no one is present, you'll find the stamp on a table near the entrance.

Food

Restaurante El Peregrino (Avenida de Don Pablo Díaz, 7; €5-8), right across from the Basilica de la Virgen del Camino, serves breakfasts and basic bar food throughout the day, such as om-elets, sandwiches, and salads, including a spring greens, goat cheese, and walnuts salad. This is a fun place to visit after you take in the modern sanctuary across the street—still visible from the bar—and want to digest the experience and grab some sustenance.

Accommodations

Hostal San Froilán (Calle Peregrinos, 1; 987-302-019; www.hostalesplaza-sanfroilan.com; 22 rooms; €31-45) and **Hostal Plaza** (Avenida de Astorga, 96; 9 rooms; €31-45) are run by the same (English-speaking) management, and both places are decent roadside hotels offering basic clean rooms with bath.

But up ahead are even better options; the nearest is in 4.3 kilometers (2.7 miles), in **Valverde de la Virgen.**

Leaving La Virgen del Camino

Leaving La Virgen del Camino, you enter a dusty stretch punctuated with mounds and hills of Hobbit-hole-like *bodegas* (underground wine cellars). The earth is pleasingly saturated with ochre and gold tones, mirroring those of the stones of the city of León.

A few hundred meters past La Virgen del Camino, you will pass over to the left side of the N-120. Soon after, you will have the choice to continue on the more historic medieval Camino, which con-tinues to run parallel to the N-120, or to detour slightly farther south toward Villar de Mazarife and rejoin the main Camino path in Hospital de Órbigo (Km 276.2). The only advantage of the detour to Villar de Mazarife is to take you a little farther away from the N-120, but the landscape is much the same and adds another 4.2 kilometers (2.6 miles) to the trek.

If you stay on the more historic Camino, you will walk on a dirt path with the N-120 to your right and have more services and options.

The best next option for food and ac-commodations on the historic Camino is in **Valverde de la Virgen** (Km 297.5).

Detour: Villar de Mazarife

If you take the detour to Villar de Mazarife farther south, the gain is being away from the N-120 and deeper into a more remote landscape (though it's not drastically different from that of the his-toric Camino). This route, especially the 9.8-kilometer (6-mile) stretch from Villar de Mazarife to Villavante, offers fewer stops for food and lodging. It also adds 4 kilometers (2.5 miles) to the trek to get to **Hospital de Órbigo** (Km 276.2), where the two paths join as one.

Accommodations and Food
Oncina de Valdoncina   Km 297.5

A classic *meseta* village 3.8 kilometers (2.4 miles) after you leave La Virgen del Camino, Oncina de Valdoncina offers the one place to stay between here and Villar de Mazarife in over 8 kilometers (5 miles): Olga's **Albergue El Pajar de Oncina's** (Calle Arriba, 4; 677-567-309; elpajardeoncina@gmail.com; nine beds in one bunkhouse, €10; communal meal, €9; open all year), a neat and basic *albergue* with a good communal meal that can be vegetarian upon request. Beds are all bunks. Wood balconies facing the geranium-potted inner courtyard give an insight into a traditional high-plateau home, and how these households stay cool in summer. Pilgrims with dogs can let the dogs sleep in the courtyard. Ask Olga for a packed lunch (*comida para llevar*) to prepare for the 10 kilometers (6.2 miles) between Oncina and Villar de Mazarife. Be sure you also fill up your water bottles for the trek.

Villar de Mazarife   Km 287.5

Villar de Mazarife (pop. 360) is the best stopping place on the detour for lodging and food, especially at the **Casa-Mesón Bar Tio Pepe** (Calle Teso de la Iglesia, 2; 987-390-517; www.alberguetiopepe.es; five private rooms, €50; 22 dorm beds in 5 bunkhouses, €9), which overlooks the village church. It offers a sun-dappled patio, a garden, a fresh, generous, and home-made *menú del dia* (€10), and breakfast (€3.50), and is open all year. The building is a 70-year-old traditional *meseta* house, restored in 2007 for the purpose of welcoming pilgrims.

The next opportunity for food and accommodations is in 9.8 kilometers (6 miles), at Villavante. Be sure to stock up on water and food before departing.

Villavante   Km 277.7

As you enter Villavante (pop. 265), terracotta walls, bright blue lettering, and a series of café tables lining the street announce the *albergue* and bar of **Santa Lucía** (Calle Doctor Vélez, 17; 987-389-105 or 692-107-693; www.alberguesantalucia.es; Apr.-Oct.; communal meal €9, breakfast €4) where the warm *hospitalera*, Carmen Tabuyo, offers both spotless dorm beds and private rooms (23 beds in one bunkhouse, €9, and three private rooms, €25-40). The *albergue*, which opened in 2012, also has a quiet interior brick and tile patio and a communal kitchen. Inquire with Carmen if you want to schedule a session with a massage therapist.

From Villavante, this Camino detour continues another 5 kilometers (3.1 miles) before rejoining the more historic Camino at the 19-arched medieval bridge entering **Hospital de Órbigo**.

Valverde de la Virgen   Km 297.5

Food and Accommodations

The **Albergue La Casa del Camino** (Camino El Jano, 2A; 987-303-455; www.alberguelacasadelcamino.com; open all year; 32 beds €8; breakfast, €3) opened in 2016. This peaceful and spacious pilgrims' dorm offers individual beds, not bunks, in a hacienda-like home with a large stone fireplace, surrounded by an expansive garden with a circle of hammocks under a thatch-roofed canopy. There are therapeutic areas for foot showers and sole-massaging sand paths. A neighboring kitchen garden grows vegetables for the daily *menú* (€10). This haven is directly to the right of the Camino, on the other side of the N-120.

Leaving Valverde de la Virgen

The Camino continues along a dirt path that runs parallel to the left side of the N-120, weaving at times through native brush and low, rolling, mustard-toned terrain. A few times you will walk past private bodegas, the locked doors set into the mound or hillside and bearing various protective talismans—such as mounted statues of saints, painted geometric designs, crosses, and bundles of herbs—to guard the cool subterranean cellars, where homemade wine and seasonal harvests are stored.

Villadangos del Páramo Km 288.2

Villadangos del Páramo (pop. 1,106), bisected by the N-120, is known as the site where Queen Urraca of León and Castile fought a battle against her husband, Alfonso I of Aragón, in 1111.

When Urraca married Alfonso I in 1109, at the behest of her father, Galicia revolted and was harshly put down by Alfonso I. Repulsed, Urraca and her allies resisted the heavy hand of the new king. Alfonso and his soldiers then ambushed Queen Urraca's men as they camped. A medieval account noted that Alfonso I had some 600 horsemen and 2,000 foot soldiers, while Urraca had just 265 horsemen, who were mostly slaughtered.

Urraca and Alfonso I of Aragon reached a truce in 1112, the same year they dissolved their dysfunctional marriage. Urraca retained control over Galicia, Asturias, and León. When she died in 1126, her kingdom was at peace.

Here in Villadangos, nothing of the battle remains. Even the church is modern, a 20th-century construction. Every August the town people stage a recreation of the famous battle, called La Mantanza ("the killing"), in the central Plaza Mayor.

Food and Accommodations

As you near Villadangos del Páramo, 1.6 kilometers (1 mile) before the village center, the roadside **Hostal Route Avenida III** (987-390-151; www.hotelavenidaiii.com/en; year-round 65 rooms; €35-55) looms boldly with a big block letter sign to the left. It's a large, modern, four-story, terracotta-colored roadside hotel, for drivers as much as for pilgrims, and has all the amenities of roadside diners and inns. Rooms are spotless and the restaurant offers a standard and good *menú del día* (€11), plus the rich three-part *pot-au-feu* stew, *cocido Leonés* (€15). Proprietors speak English.

The central, basic, and neat **Hostal-Restaurante Libertad** (Calle Padre Angle Martínez Fuertes, 25; 987-390-123; 23 rooms; €35-45) has a café on the street level where locals pause with pilgrims to refuel for their work day or weekend. They serve the usual bar food of sandwiches, Spanish omelets, salads, and tapas such as charcuterie and cheese plates, olives, and a worker's *menú del día* (€10).

Leaving Villadangos del Páramo

The Camino passes through the main street (N-120) and then veers to a parallel side street, Calle Real, to the right, and departs the village on a footpath away from the road. Just before exiting town, there's a good bakery and general store, **Hermanos García** (Calle Real, 44; 987-390-129) to your right that sells provisions, including fresh baked goods, fresh fruits and vegetables, olives, cheese and cold-cuts, and bags of dried fruits and nuts.

You'll next cross over the irrigation canal, **Canal de Villadangos**, followed by a wild wooded park. Here you may glimpse a lot of bird life, including hawks, for nearly 2 kilometers (1.2 miles) before returning to run parallel with the N-120, crossing to the left side of the road. From there, fields of corn and wheat will flow along your left, the road to your right, all the way to San Martín del Camino.

San Martín del Camino
Km 283.6

San Martín del Camino is a quiet farming village with 354 inhabitants. Nothing remains of the original 13th-century pilgrim town or the 17th-century hospice that stood right on the main street, Calle Real. The church is from 1963, though the bell tower survives from the 1600s.

Accommodations

The reason to stop in this town is the ★ **Albergue Vieira** (987-378-565; www.alberguevieira.es; year-round; 36 beds in six rooms €7/bed, two private rooms €30; communal dinner €10), which opened in 2013 and is named for the Camino's scallop symbol, *la vieira*. Amelia, who speaks some English, runs an efficient and spotless place, with pastel-toned rooms and comfortable metal-frame bunk beds. She greets each pilgrim as a member of the family.

Gathering everyone around wooden tables in the common room, Amelia serves delicious home-cooked vegetable and meat casseroles, stews, and roasts, drawing heavily on produce from her daughter's farm and from other local producers. A plate of 2-3 types of local sheep's milk cheeses is always on hand to sample, as are local white and red wines—plus, Amelia makes a mean gin and tonic. Breakfast is plentiful, with eggs, bread, fruit, yogurt, and cheese (€4).

Leaving San Martín del Camino

The Camino runs parallel to the N-120 for another 5 kilometers (3.1 miles), then angles right onto country dirt paths and groves of trees on the way to **Hospital de Órbigo**. If it rains, even only slightly, watch the path under your feet, for all along this stretch snails and caterpillars may come out to revel in the precipitation. Notice that the terrain is changing, slowly shifting from mustard-yellow towards a darker, iron-rich earth. The fields around you grow many large-scale crops, including corn, potatoes, and sugar beets.

Hospital de Órbigo's medieval bridge, Puente del Paso Honroso

Don Suero's Jousting Tournament

The year was 1434. The knight Don Suero, rejected by the woman he loved, locked an iron collar around his neck and declared he would hold a tournament along the long bridge of Hospital de Órbigo for the two weeks leading up to Saint James's feast day. In 1434, that fell on a Sunday and made it a holy year, meaning more pilgrims were on the road to Compostela: hence, a larger crowd.

Nobles got behind this dare and helped promote the tournament, and champions arrived to joust with Don Suero. The town set up a 146-paces-long tournament area near the bridge, complete with viewing boxes for the crowd. At the end of the two weeks, Don Suero prevailed, having broken the lances of 300 opponents. With that, he took off the iron collar and declared himself free from the bonds of love that had so injured him. He also made the pilgrimage to Santiago de Compostela as a final gesture of release, completion, and gratitude.

Don Suero may well be one of the last knights to hold a medieval jousting tournament, and the bridge is called **Puente del Paso Honroso** ("bridge of the honorable passage") because of this event.

============ **Top Experience** ============

★ Puente del Paso Honroso   Km 276.7

You'll know you've reached Hospital de Órbigo when you spot its most distinctive feature, the 19-arched bridge, Puente del Paso Honroso. This is also where the two routes, the historic Camino and the detour, rejoin as one.

The knight Don Suero made this bridge famous, but the bridge was first constructed in the 13th century and precedes Don Suero by at least 200 years. It is physically delightful to cross the long, sinuous bridge, passing over the river and marshy groves, facing the mountains up ahead, and at last entering a town that retains its medieval atmosphere. Part of the bridge's appeal is that it begins at a higher elevation and descends into town, making for a dynamic approach.

The 19 arches of the bridge have had a rough time, as the bridge has gone through several periods of destruction and rebuilding. Here is the history of the arches, going east to west, from the approaching point and ending at the town of Hospital de Órbigo: Surviving from the 13th-century construction are arches 3, 4, 5, and 6. Arches 7 to 16 were rebuilt in the 17th century. And after the English blew up the bridge to prevent the approach of Napoleon's forces, locals rebuilt arches 1, 2, 17, 18, and 19 in the 19th century. Despite this rough history, the bridge retains its sturdy, cobblestoned medieval personality. Pleasingly, it pulls the colors from the surrounding landscape and town into a unified focal point.

When you step off the bridge and enter Hospital de Órbigo, prepare to time-travel to the 12th and 13th centuries, with cobbled stones, storefronts engraved with Templar and Maltese crosses, knightly shields, and coats of armor. All of these features easily bring to life the time of one Don Suero, who so loved the lady who rejected him.

Hospital de Órbigo
Km 276.2

The whole town of Hospital de Órbigo (pop. 976) retains its medieval atmosphere. It is a full-service town, and the Camino cuts right through the center of it, passing every amenity—including a small grocery store, a bakery, several cafés, and at least four *hostales* and three *albergues*. All are caught up in the medieval legacy of the town's knightly legend, not only of Don Suero, but also of the Knights Templar and the knights of the Order of Malta. You'll notice their crosses all around town: white equal-armed crosses with red flags, and inlaid white stone crosses, in the walls and doors of several buildings.

Midway through town, you'll see Órbigo's 12th-century **church**, dedicated to **San Juan Bautista** and built of the native stone, with a single nave and rectangular bell tower. An equal-armed cross in black and white stone is inlaid at the top of the entrance archway. Most of the current structure is fairly modern and the most interesting aspects are on the outside, such as the pleasant covered porch entrance and the statue of Saint John the Baptist over the door.

Every **June** the town re-enacts Don Suero's tournament with a **medieval festival** that includes jousting as well as food, drink, and fanfare.

Food and Accommodations

Hostal Don Suero de Quiñones (Calle Álvares Vega; 987-388-238; €45-65), found to the left as you cross the bridge into town, has a raised semi-formal dining area and a terrace with great views of the bridge. Named after the 15th-century knight, the hostal has agreeable mid-range rooms with private bath. The restaurant offers meals from breakfast to dinner, with a variety of popular dishes, including *ensalada mixta* (garden salad topped with tuna, corn, carrots, olives, and white asparagus), *salpicón de marisco* (mixed shellfish sauté), and diverse *tortillas* (omelets with varieties of vegetables, ham, and chorizo). Proprietors speak English.

A few paces down, the ★ **Bar-Restaurante Los Angeles** (Calle Doctor Santos Oliera, 6; 987-388-250; €10-15) is run by cheerful staff offering up a well-wrought pilgrims' menu, including locally caught trout, prepared in a rich *sopa de trucha* (trout soup) or grilled

with *jamón Serrano* and served with garden salad and fries. The homemade *tarta de queso* (cheese cake) baked in a flan mold is especially rich but not too sweet, and if you've been looking for a perfectly blended sangria, theirs should satisfy your thirst.

Slightly off the Camino path to the left, **Albergue Verde** (Avenida de los Fueros de León, 76; 698-927-926; www. albergueverde.es; open all year; 26 dorm beds, €11; one private room, €30) is a timber and stucco barn turned into an elegant hacienda-style pilgrims' lodging with high ceilings, power-massage showers, and solid wood bunks. Surrounded by green lawns and palm trees, Albergue Verde is best known for their organic garden, yoga-massage-meditation room, and sustainable vegetarian meals (including hummus with roasted peppers, cream of mushroom soup, chocolate cake, and zucchini bread). Proprietors speak English.

Leaving Hospital de Órbigo

Follow the yellow arrows out of town, where the main road through Hospital de Órbigo turns from black asphalt to a wide earth path. Here the road splits, one following the *"Astorga/Camino Way"* to the right, and the other the *"Astorga by Highway"* to the left. The "Highway" path runs parallel to the N-120 for 10 kilometers (6.2 miles) to rejoin the Camino Way at the Crucero de Santo Toribio (sometimes spelled *Cruceiro* de Santo Toribio). It has no food or accommodations, and little appeal, though it is 1.2 kilometers (0.7 miles) shorter and doesn't include the mild climb and descent of the "Camino Way." Staying on the Camino Way is more beautiful, wilder, and rewarding, passing through low red hills, wheat fields, and groves; this path also seems to be the original path of the Camino and has more food and accommodation support.

From here to Astorga, the Camino enters some beautiful and remote territory and slowly climbs in altitude. Right now you are at about 800 meters (2,625 feet) and will climb another 100 meters (328 feet) to Astorga. Notice how the mountains of León loom ahead but are getting larger and nearer, at times taking on the rainbow colors of the horizon.

Villares de Órbigo
Km 273.8

The Astorga/Camino Way leads through corn fields and a stand of polars, and soon you enter the village, Villares de Órbigo (pop. 272), tucked into the foot of the somewhat distant hills. Follow the painted yellow arrows through the village center, past the **church** to the right of the Camino (on the village's north end) with its stocky square red stone bell tower. The church is fairly recent, from the 18th century, with a Baroque retable and is dedicated to four patron saints: Santiago, Our Lady of the Rosary, Saint Anthony, and Saint Francis of Assisi.

Leaving Villares de Órbigo

The Camino leaves the village along another wide dirt path, marked with yellow arrows, through wilder territory where groves of trees and wildflowers transplant the earlier cornfields. Keep your eyes open for wildlife, including hawks and falcons that hunt small game from the treetops and ride air pockets in the sky. You will pass a triangular raised **fountain** that flows with drinkable water (as noted in its sign, *agua potable*). The earth is so dark here that the well-groomed Camino looks like a great orange highway cutting through pale yellow fields.

Santibanez de Valdeiglesias   Km 271.2

Santibanez de Valdeiglesias has a total population of 323, including outlying homesteads, but the village itself could be missed in the blink of an eye. Its most distinctive feature is its 18th-century **church** dedicated to the Ascension and the Trinity. This place is in the heart of corn country, so much so that locals call it *el laberinto de maíz* (the corn labyrinth).

Food and Accommodations

Santibanez offers solid food and lodging at the centrally located **Albergue Camino Francés** (Calle Real, 68; 987-361-014; www.alberguecaminofrances. com; open Mar.-Oct.), which opened in 2014. The *albergue* features an attached bar and restaurant serving breakfast (€2-4) and a lunch and dinner *menú del día* (€9.50). Everyone is welcome to partake, whether staying here or not. Bright and light-filled rooms are arrayed on two floors around an interior courtyard, with a bunkhouse for up to 12 people (€8.50) and one private room (€35). Proprietors speak English.

Leaving Santibanez de Valdeiglesias

After Santibanez de Valdeiglesias, the path persistently ascends at a mild grade. Just when you feel it may never end, you will come upon La Casa de los Dioses, a "free pilgrim paradise." Other than La Casa de Dioses, there are no support services until San Justa de la Vega, 8 kilometers (5 miles) away.

La Casa de los Dioses
Km 267.5

La Casa de los Dioses feels like a small encampment on the Mongolian steppe: Yurt-like shelters made of blankets give warmth, as does a hot kettle of tea. Bowls of fruit are arrayed on tree stumps, and a food stand is arrayed with cheeses, hard-boiled eggs, yogurt, juices, and vegetables. Hot soup is another possibility. Drop what you can afford in the money jar and take what you need.

David Vidal, originally from Barcelona, is here on this lonely stretch to offer food, drink, and shelter to pilgrims. He calls his shelter and rest spot La Casa de los Dioses because he wants everyone to feel welcome, whether they believe in one god or many. His shelter is based on the honor system, and there is no electricity, gas, or water. He hauls the fuel and water here and keeps the roadside rest-stop running with humility and grace. Take a rest and refreshment here and then continue to Santo Justo de la Vega or Astorga for lodging. Here you can also unwind by walking a spiral labyrinth made from smooth river rock. Nearby, David has planted several varieties of roses, including a rare lavender one that has a strong, pure fragrance.

Leaving La Casa de los Dioses

Follow the Camino to a towering cross, **Crucero de Santo Toribio** (Km 264.9), that marks the highest lookout view of the valley in which Astorga sits, giving a tremendous first glimpse of the city of San Justo de la Vega. The cathedral's dark twin bell towers, made from rock of the surrounding hills, jut above the landscape.

San Justo de la Vega
Km 263.5

San Justo de la Vega (pop. 1,912) is not a beautiful town, but it has beautiful aspects, such as its surrounding fields and kitchen gardens, speckled with fluffy white sheep, and its 17th-century church of San Justo, a simple but pretty adornment on the town's highest hill.

Accommodations

San Justo also has the agreeable **Hostal Juli** (Calle Real, 56; 987-617-632; 12 rooms; €30-50), the best lodging between here and Astorga (3.6 km/2.2 mi away), with bright and boldly painted contemporary rooms with windows opening to the countryside and a large stained-glass window of Saint James in the lobby. An attached bar-café serves meals and snacks all day and into the evening (€5-15).

Leaving San Justo

The Río Tuerto is right ahead as you leave San Justo de la Vega; you'll cross it and cotinue toward Astorga. From this distance, the town's imposing Roman-era walls and the twin towers of its cathedral come into view.

About midway, 1.5 kilometers (1 mile) before reaching Astorga, you will pass a pastry factory on your left that churns out thousands of *hojaldres de Astorga,* little flakey square cakes dripping in honey. You can't enter or purchase the treats here, but a back door to the factory is often open, and pastries are set near the door to cool—a preview to entice you to try some *hojaldres* once you arrive in town. These pastries will be wrapped and boxed for sale in shops far and wide, but I've noted some Astorgan pastry shops below where you can buy *hojaldres* direct. Save some room: Astorga is also a chocolate capital.

Just on the outskirts of Astorga, you cross a nutty zigzagging bridge (some pilgrims call it "the jolly green giant," and others "the *peregrino* torture tower") over the railroad tracks. It seems to add a kilometer (roughly half a mile) to the walking, but was designed to keep pedestrians safe and away from the tracks. After passing some residential areas and then climbing up toward the old Roman section of Astorga, you will pass a traffic roundabout in whose center is a large sign noting the city's Roman name, Asturica Augusta. Soon after this, you will climb along a street that takes you up through the Roman wall on the southwest side of town and into the center of the walled city. You may notice some pilgrims arriving on another Camino route, the **Via de la Plata**, coming from the south. The Via de la Plata traditionally begins in Sevilla, in Andalucía, and merges with the Camino

Francés here in Astorga, continuing to Santiago de Compostela as one path.

Astorga   Km 259.5

Astorga (pop. 11,153) was the capital of the Celtic Astures until it was taken over by Romans, who turned the fortress into a major town at the intersection of many roads, many of them bent toward mining and the transport of goods and materials. Pliny called it an *urbs magnifica*, magnificent city.

With the Christianization of the Roman Empire, Astorga also became one of Iberia and Europe's first seats of a bishop, a *bishopric*, as early as the 3rd century. With the rise of the medieval pilgrimage, Astorga became another intersection of roads—this time two major pilgrim routes, the Camino Francés and the Via de la Plata, which originates in the south. Both essentially follow earlier Roman roads. In the 12th century, Astorga boasted 21 pilgrim hospices, the second largest number on the Camino after Burgos.

The entire modern city is built over the Asture and Roman one. Because it retains (with a lot of restorations over the centuries) its thick Roman walls, the act of stepping into Astorga, climbing up its hill, and passing through the gateway called the Puerta del Sol, the gateway into the walled city, feels like walking into a city that is both medieval and Roman, with stone walls and street plans harkening to both eras.

Astorga also marks the beginning of the territory of León known as the **Maragatería,** home of a people called Maragatos. The Maragatería is defined

From top to bottom: Rest stop at La Casa de los Dioses; mosaic floor in Astorga's Domus Roman Villa ruins; Astorga's Maragato clock tower on the townhall on the Plaza de España.

Astorga

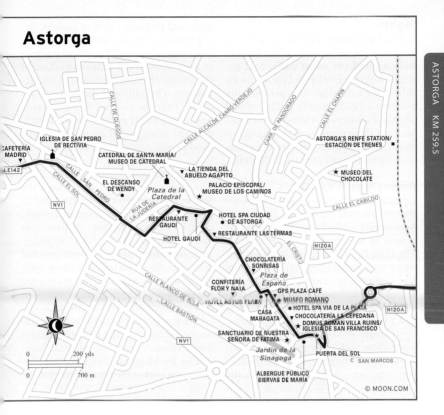

by the unique culture of strong mountain people, including *arrieros* (traditional muleteers) who transported goods over the mountains before there were railways and trucks, and who were key to Astorga's rebirth as a center for chocolate making.

Astorga's **weekly market** is Tuesday morning on the Plaza de España, selling local foods as well as general household goods and clothing.

Tours

Consider taking an hour to sign up for a guided tour, the "Ruta Romana," at the **Museo Romano** (Plaza San Bartolomé, 2; 987-616-937; www.turismocastillayleon. com; €5 tour and museum; some tours are in English). The tour covers Astorga's surviving Roman sights, including the forum, villa, two thermal baths (not open to the public except on a tour), and even the sewer.

Both the tour and the museum bring to life the colorful personalities who once lived here, as discovered through their engraved memorial stones from the 1st to 3rd centuries, including nobles, slaves, poets, craftspeople, and a professional beggar—as well as one fortuneteller named Lucius Valerius Auctus, from Astorga in the 2nd century, who lived until age 56, had a stutter, and read the future through interpreting the flight of birds and from reading the entrails of sacrificed animals.

Sights

Beyond exploring within the walls of Roman Astorga, be sure to take time to walk around the **outer walls,** best accessed from the gate behind the northeast side of the cathedral, to experience the more than 2 kilometers (1.2 miles) of wall and the 27 towers that survive (the most intact of these round towers bulging out from the fortified walls are visible as soon as you pass the gate near the cathedral).

Domus Roman Villa Ruins

Open at all hours, with a covered open-air shelter built over the remains, the **Domus Roman villa** (Calle Padres Redentoristas) is next to the Iglesia de San Francisco. The floor layout and parts of the indoor water works (plumbing) survive, but the highlights are its beautiful, decently preserved mosaics from the 2nd and 3rd centuries, featuring floral patterns with birds and a bear. The central figure, Orpheus, is no longer visible, though he once appeared here with a lyre given to him from Apollo. According to specialists, the animals represent the body and the lyre the soul (and Orpheus's skill to enchant living things with his music). That someone chose to place such spiritual imagery in their home seems to say something of the focus, or intended focus, of the occupants. This villa was also centrally located, near the forum (public square), and had a small private thermal bath; perhaps someone of economic means lived here.

Museo Romano

The high-vaulted space that houses the **Museo Romano** (Plaza San Bartolomé, 2; 987-616-937; www.turismocastillayleon.com; Oct.-Jun. Tues.-Sat. 10:30am-2pm and 4-6pm, Sun. and holidays 10:30am-2pm; Jul.-Sept. Tues.-Sat. 10am-2pm and 4:30-7pm, Sun. and holidays 10am-2pm; €3; €5 with the Ruta Romana tour; some panels in English) may once have been either a Roman prison or the main entrance to Astorga's forum. It is now a museum dedicated to the city and region's Roman history and archaeological finds.

The building, as much as the displays, is a part of the overall installation.

Catedral de Santa María, Astorga

The Maragatos

León is home to a distinctive historic region and community, the Maragatería of the Maragatos of El Bierzo, a place and people concentrated between Astorga and Foncebadón. The Maragatos traditionally were mountain communities of persons with semi-nomadic skills, transporting goods over the mountains to the coast and plains of Iberia with their trusty and sturdy breed of mules. No one knows where the muleteers (*arrieros*) came from: Perhaps they were a native group that were always here, or perhaps they were descended from Berbers who resettled here in the 8th century, or from Goths from one of the invading Germanic tribes. That they have retained their colorful costumes, dance, and music traditions and festivals, speaks of a thriving culture of survival. One of the best places to see Maragato life and festivities is

the Camino through the center of Castrillo de los Polvazares

during the feast day of Mary Magdalene, on July 22, in the Maragato village of **Castrillo de los Polvazares** (Km 253.2). Maragatos were also key to why Astorga became, and remains, a center for delicious chocolate making.

A 49-meter long, 5-meter wide (161 feet long, 16 feet wide) tunnel, with tall overhead arches about the height of two people, it's an elegant space despite the fact that it may once have imprisoned slaves. Exhibits use archaeological artifacts—funerary stones, pottery, coins, gold jewelry, alabaster vessels, glass, mosaics, even a pair of dice—that come from excavations in the city. Didactic films also recreate the town and bring its Roman citizens to life.

Sanctuario de Nuestra Señora de Fatima

While the outside of this chapel sanctuary dedicated to Our Lady of Fatima preserves the 12th-century Romanesque engravings of the **Santuario de Nuestra Señora de Fatima**, the interior has a different appeal, with its mix of early modern, Baroque, Renaissance, and Neoclassical. Note the placement of the statue of Our Lady of Fatima in the center of the altar, against a black background; she appears to be levitating in a black

cosmic sky, maybe even with the splash of the Milky Way behind her.

The garden facing the church's entrance is the **Jardín de la Sinagoga** (Garden of the Synagogue), marking one of the two medieval Jewish neighborhoods of Astorga; some of the best views are from this hilltop.

Plaza de España

This plaza is the heart of social life in Astorga, where grandparents come to play soccer with their grandkids, including some pretty talented young girls. It is also the site of the town hall, the **Ayuntamiento**, a Baroque building from the 17th century that has a special **clock tower:** two metal figures, a man and a woman dressed in black and red Maragato attire, stand on the façade before the bell and ring in the hour with metal hammers that turn in their hands. They've been at it since 1748 and are fun to watch: grab a glass on the square just before the hour and enjoy the show from there.

Chocolate in Astorga

You may not know it before you arrive, but Astorga is a chocolate mecca on the Camino and has been intimately tied to the cacao bean from the moment it was brought to Spain from the Maya and Aztec of Central America by Hernán Cortés in 1520. Soon after, the marquis of Astorga, Álvaro Pérez Osario, married Cortés's daughter, María Cortés de Zuñiga; a substantial part of her dowry was cacao, already coveted for its nutritional value—not to mention its economic value (and, apparently, its aphrodisiacal value as well).

Astorga itself was a key to the transport of cacao into Spain. Ships loaded with cocoa beans from the New World arrived in Galician ports, and the most reliable way to transport the cargo over the mountains of León was to employ the trusted Maragato muleteers. Some townfolk got the bright idea to process the cacao here, too, instead of simply exporting cacao from the city, and the dry and cool mountain climate turned out to be ideal for shaping, cooling, and packaging chocolate.

Chocolate was so popular nationwide, and such an industry in Astorga, that in 1636 a church document noted a debate about the danger of chocolate in causing

chocolate in Astorga

the devout (especially priests) to break their fasts. Nevertheless, the chocolate industry in Astorga peaked during the 18th and 19th centuries. A census in 1752 listed eight chocolate-making families in the city. Since 1991, there have been six families still producing traditional, local chocolates.

Notice that the streets through which the Camino meanders are lined with shops selling locally produced chocolate. The Museo de Chocolate is a good place to purchase it as well. There are chocolate vartieties from white to dark, and local producers pride themselves in the high quality of their product; it's nearly all good, and it's fun to try a few places and compare.

Museo de Chocolate

The **Museo de Chocolate** (Avenida de la Estación, 16; 987-616-220; www.aytoastorga.es; Tues.-Sat., 10:30am-2pm and 4-7:30pm, Sun. and holidays, 10:30am-2pm; €2.50, €4 if combined with the Museo Romano), covers the history of chocolate making, from its Central American origins to the industry in Astorga, including the families whose names are synonymous with chocolate. Displays include ancient Mesoamerican cacao grindstones. You'll also learn chocolate-making techniques, and even the science behind the health benefits of chocolate. The museum is housed in a tiny modernist palace that's the ancient home of one of the city's chocolate makers. It's located an easy 5-minute walk outside the walls. Admission includes a chocolate tasting, and the shop is a good place (with good prices) to purchase chocolate.

Gaudí's Palacio Episcopal and the Museo de los Caminos

The **Palacio Episcopal** is fairly new (a century old) and was inspired by the spiritual insights of Antoni Gaudí. Some pilgrims claim that the palace has a more spiritual feel than the cathedral, and I have to agree.

Gaudí was commissioned in 1889 to build this residence for the bishop of Astorga. Gaudí leaned toward naturalistic forms with an idyllic neo-Gothic twist to create an uplifting sacred space. On the interior, this includes lacy, towering lines, and forms using the pale white granite from the local hills (an interesting contrast to the orange and red stone of the cathedral), with detailed, floral stained-glass windows and painted tiles.

Although the palace is understated compared to Gaudí's other designs, the bishop felt it was too flamboyant for him to live in. In 1963, the building was re-purposed as a pilgrimage museum, the **Museo de los Caminos** (Plaza Eduardo de Castro, 5; 987-616-822; www.diocesi-sastorga.es/organismos/museos/museo-de-los-caminos-1; May-Oct., Mon.-Sun., 10am-2pm and 4-8pm; Nov.-Apr., Mon-Sun, 10:30am-2pm and 4-6:30pm; €6). Exhibit panels (in Spanish) cover the full rise and expansion of the pilgrimage to Santiago de Compostela. The museum also showcases prehistoric and Roman archaeology, along with artifacts from the early Christian and medieval periods of Astorga. Some of the more intimate pieces are keepsakes and talismans left by pilgrims over the ages, including shells, prayer beads, and pilgrim passports. Inside, be sure to take in the Gothic lines soaring skyward and the floral windows and tile work, Gaudí's signatures in his passion for exalting natural forms into sacred acts.

Catedral de Santa María and Museo de Catedral

The **Catedral de Santa María** (Plaza de la Catedral, s/n; 987-615-820; www.tur-ismoastorga.es; Apr.-Oct., Mon.-Sun., 10am-8:30pm; Nov.-Mar., Mon.-Sun., 10:30am-6pm; €5; €3.50 for *peregrinos*), a 15th- to 18th-century cathedral, features a Baroque exterior, while the interior retains a classic Gothic form that is calmer and less adorned than the ornate entrance. The main highlight here is access to the cathedral museum, the **Museo de Catedral** (same hours as cathedral; free with entry to the cathedral and cloister).

This is one of the more interesting cathedral museums. The collection includes an early Christian marble sarcophagus from AD 310, from late Roman and early Christian Astorga, with elaborate carvings depicting Old and New Testament scenes. It was originally discovered in the area of San Justo de la Vega.

The museum also exhibits capitals from the Romanesque cathedral that previously stood on this site, a collection of expressive 12th- and 13th-century wood-carved icons of Mother and Child, several illuminated medieval manuscripts, including the delightful beasts and angels of the Beato de Silos (1091-1109), and a 15th-century painting of the 1st-century Queen Lupa—a rare imaginative representation of the mythic Celtic queen of Galicia.

The brief text panels are in Spanish, but the museum is worthwhile even if you don't speak Spanish, as much of the collection is self-explanatory.

Iglesia de San Pedro de Rectivia

As you are about to depart Astorga on the Camino heading west, you will pass the A-frame-shaped, mosaic-covered church of **San Pedro de Rectivia** (Calle San Pedro, 0; 987-615-556; www.astorga. co/es/turismo). Built in 1970, the modern mosaics utilize ancient techniques from Roman times and inlay images of the two Caminos, the Via de la Plata and the Camino Francés (Camino de Santiago), and their intersection at Astorga. At the center of the lower levels of this triangular church are words in Arabic, Hebrew, and Latin, reflecting an ecumenical awareness that all three Abrahamic faiths revere the same god. Look also for exquisite images of places along the Camino, from Extremadura to Astorga and from Navarra to Galicia.

This modern church has foundations in the Middle Ages; people founded it then to serve pilgrims on the Camino, especially those coming from Extremadura on the Via de la Plata.

In recent decades, Astorgans decided to build a new, congruous temple on the site of the old church. The church is rarely open outside of Sunday mass and holy festival days, but its exterior is remarkable and shows some of its finest elements. And if you chance upon the church when it is open, during services or festivals, the interior has colorful modernist/cubist-style panels by stained-glass artist Enrique Morán.

Food

Astorga possesses celebrated foods, including locally cultivated garbanzos and lentils, *cecina* (dry cured beef), *hojaldres* (little square puff pastries dripping with honey syrup), and *mantecadas,* dense pound-cake-like muffins. Notice that the streets through which the Camino meanders are lined with chocolate, charcuterie, wine, cheese, and pastry shops (usually selling all these items in one place, plus dried lentils and garbanzos), as well as cafés and restaurants serving *cocido Maragato.* The chance to taste the city's delicacies are all around you.

Cocido Maragato is similar to other *cocidos*: a rich, *pot au feu*-style stew that boils several meats (especially pork and beef) and vegetables (especially potatoes, cabbage, carrots, and garbanzo beans) together and then serves the cooked stew in three parts—soup, vegetables, and meats. It almost always consists of seven meats, usually a combination of different cuts of pork and beef and types of sausages; the three-part meal is served in a specific order, starting with the meat plate, then the vegetables, and then the soup. It is almost always seasoned with a sauté of paprika, pepper, garlic, and caramelized onions.

Restaurants

The place for authentic, stick-to-your bones *cocido Maragato* is ★ **Restaurante Las Termas** (Calle Santiago, 1; 987-602-212; www.restaurantelastermas.com; €22), near the old Roman thermal baths and 50 meters (164 feet) from the cathedral. The setting is as traditional as the fare: a timber and stone town home in the heart of Astorga, with tables covered in crisp white linen. Come with an appetite, and remember that Maragato tradition dictates that the *cocido* is served in a specific order (as compared to Castilian or other regional *cocidos*): the meats and vegetables arrive before the soup. Included is a homemade custard with a square of *mantacada* sponge cake for dessert.

Another celebrated and comparable place for *cocido Maragato* is **Casa Maragata** (Calle Husar Tiburcio, 2; 987-618-880; www.casamaragata.com; €23), which opened in 1992 a few paces to the southwest of the cathedral. It features a slightly more informal dining room than Las Termas, but with a similar ebullient enthusiasm over the regional dish and its dining guests.

Restaurante Gaudí (Plaza Eduardo de Castro, 6; 987-615-654; www.gaudi-hotel.es), affiliated with the **Hotel Gaudí** (below), has large picture-window views from the dining room of Gaudí's Palacio Episcopal across the square. They serve a creative, if pricey (but so is much of Astorga), *menú del día* (€18-20) that includes the traditional *cocido Maragato* but also has roasted suckling lamb, varieties of grilled fish (including hake and eel), *pulpo á feira* (paprika seasoned octopus), and rabbit stew. The less formal bar and cafeteria, opening to the square, is a nice spot for *pinchos* and tapas.

The **Hotel Astur Plaza** (Plaza de España, 2-3; 987-617-665; www.hotelasturplaza.es) has a more down-to-earth restaurant than Hotel Gaudí, offering traditional cuisine and the usual *menús del peregrino* at a more reasonable price for pilgrims (€10.50) and offering popular dishes, such as grilled fish, roasted chicken, and seafood (grilled langoustine and, at times, baked scallops), but also a traditional *cocido Maragato* menu (€20).

GPS Plaza Café (Plaza de España, 16; 987-796-853; www.gpsgrupo.com), with outdoor café tables on the Plaza de España and an indoor bar, offers a good choice of snacks and meals throughout the day—but stands out for its array of breakfasts (€3.50-5.50), including an "English" breakfast (eggs, bacon, sausages, toast, with coffee/tea and fresh orange juice), a "Mediterranean" breakfast (toast rubbed with tomato and topped with cured ham, served with coffee/tea and fresh-squeezed OJ), the usual Continental breakfast, and the chocolate city's own *churros con chocolate* (aka "Spanish" breakfast).

Cafetería Madrid (Carretera Madrid-Coruña, 237; 987-615-808; €4-8) is a total neighborhood joint run by a woman with the energy of the wind. Located just behind the modern, mosaic-covered church of San Pedro de Rectivia, it's a nice last stop for coffee, breakfast, sandwiches, or snacks before hitting the trail (which passes to its left on the way out of town). Cafetería Madrid is especially hailed for its wedges of thick, fresh, perfectly prepared Spanish *tortillas* (omelets) with caramelized onion and softened, crisped potato.

Chocolate and Pastries

The *hojaldres de Astorga* you may have noticed at the factory on the way into town will be boxed for sale in shops far and wide, but there are some Astorgan pastry shops where you can buy *hojaldres* direct. The chocolate and pastry shops listed below—many of which sell packaged local pastries (*hojaldres* and *mantecadas*), lentils, cheeses, pork and beef sausages, and wine—are strategically and conveniently positioned right on the Camino or a mere few feet off of it.

Chocolatería La Cepedana (Calle Padres Redentoristas, 16; 987-615-593; www.chocolaterialacepedana.com) is for buying and carrying (or for sitting and drinking) all the forms of chocolates

on hand, made on the premises by La Cepedana since 1903.

Confitería Flor y Nata (Calle San José de Mayo, 2; 987-615-849; www.merles.es) is the place for freshly churned-out pastries of many varieties, especially a custard tart called *merles* that takes the puff-pastry foundation of *hojaldres* but bakes it with an egg-custard filling.

Chocolatería Sonrisas (Calle Pío Gullón, 5; 987-616-112): maybe you just want to settle in to a café table and try the local hot chocolate, perhaps with *churros*, the traditional way? This is your place, "chocolate smiles," making a dense, dark, more-pudding-than-drink hot chocolate produced by the city's cacao kings.

Since 1946, **La Tienda del Abuelo Agapito** (Avenida Doctor Mérida Pérez, 26; 987-615-728; www.tiendadeastorga.com) has been selling it all: chocolates by Astorgan Alvarez Benedi (for making real hot chocolate, as well as for eating, pure or mixed with almonds), Leonese chorizo, wines from Ribera del Duero (Castile), local sheep's milk cheese, and of course, *mantecadas* and *hojaldres*.

Accommodations

The first lodging you'll see is the high-end **Hotel Via de la Plata** (Calle Padres Redentoristas, 5; 987-619-000; www.hotelviadelaplata.es; €95-120 for a room; €12 for the spa), a four-star hotel with a full-service spa. Proprietors speak English.

★ **Hotel Gaudí** (Plaza Eduardo de Castro, 6; 987-615-654; www.gaudi-hotel.es; 35 rooms; €80) is in the most central and interesting part of Astorga, the Plaza de Gaudí, with Gaudí's bishop's palace and the cathedral across the square. Most rooms have a view across the square (to be sure, ask for one that does). Like the palace, the hotel draws on modern and medieval aesthetics and blends them harmoniously in the rooms. The restaurant is also excellent, even if the *menú del día* is €18, higher than almost anywhere else on the Camino (or

Do as the Romans: Spa Day in Astorga

Astorgans honor their Roman past with two elegant modern places that offer thermal spa treatments on the Camino. If you book ahead, look for the special spa packages, or inquire about them when you check in. There may be special prices offered to *peregrinos*.

Look for **Hotel Spa Via de la Plata** (Calle Padres Redentoristas, 5; 987-619-000; www.hotelviadelaplata.es; €95-120 for a room; €12 for the spa), on the Camino as you enter Astorga. This four-star hotel opened in 2011, offering a full-service spa with massages, peels, facials, thermal pools, and body wraps, including *vinoterapia*, a wrap with extracts from vines and pressed grapes. The large thermal pool is sleek and modern, but feels as if you could be in the Roman thermal bath, only a stone's throw behind the hotel in the old town center. Enjoy waters of different temperatures and jet currents. If you book online, or inquire ahead, you may be able to book a stay that combines lodging and spa treatments (60-minute sessions per person) for as little as €80 per night for two. Proprietors speak English.

Closer to the center of the old city, **Hotel Spa Ciudad de Astorga** (Calle los Sitios, 7; 987-603-001; www.hotelciudaddeastorga.com; €80, rooms) is a new, fully modern spa hotel with Art Nouveau décor, offering thermal pools, a Turkish bath with color therapy (*cromoterapía*), a Finnish sauna, and jet shower massages. Hotel guests can use the spa for €14 a session, and walk-in guests for €15. Sessions are 1 hour 15 minutes. Spa hours are Mon.-Sun., 9am-10pm. Proprietors speak English.

in Spain, for that matter). Proprietors speak English.

Hotel Astur Plaza (Plaza de España, 2; 987-617-665; www.hotelasturplaza.es; 37 rooms; €60-85) is another modern, spacious, and centrally situated hotel, this one on the historic town's Plaza Mayor (also called Plaza de España). It has a good restaurant on the square, with more modest prices than Hotel Gaudí's for the *menú del día*. Some rooms overlook the square. Proprietors speak English.

★ **El Descanso de Wendy** (Calle Matadero Viejo, 11; 987-617-854; www.eldescansodewendy.com; six rooms; €45-90) is a boutique hotel run by Maria Méndez Contreras, a businesswoman and designer with endless enthusiasm and taste. (She also runs the bath and hardware store around the corner.) Named after Maria's cat, Wendy, who sadly is not on the premises, each room is decorated with plush furnishings, modern art, and intense colors. Guests have use of a fancy common kitchen and terrace with views of the cathedral. Breakfast (included) is cooked to order: baked goods, omelets, fresh juice, coffee, tea, and seasonal fruits.

Albergue Público Siervas de María (Plaza de San Francisco, 3; 987-616-034; www.caminodesantiagoastorga.com; open all year; 156 beds in several dorm rooms; €5) was a convent until 2004, and opened as a pilgrims' *albergue* in 2006. It is in a cool building with neo-Romanesque and neo-Gothic windows, three stories tall and painted taupe with cream trim; it stands where the 1,000-year-old pilgrims' hospital, San Feliz, once stood. Centrally located, next to the Jardín de la Sinagoga and Domus Villa and Roman Museum, and three churches (Fatima, San Francisco, and San Bartolome), the inside is spotless, comfortable, and at ease.

Getting There

Astorga is well connected by train and bus, which are the best ways to access the city.

Car

Astorga is connected by highways coming from Madrid, León, Oviedo, and A Coruña. Destinations farther east and north, such as Barcelona, Pamplona, Burgos, San Sebastian, Bilbao, and Santander, will all approach Astorga via León.

From **León** (51 km/32 mi; 40-50 min.): Take either the **AP-71** (for efficiency) or the **N-120** (for scenic driving and frequent stopping on the Camino) west to Astorga.

From **Madrid** (333 km/207 mi; 3.5 hours): Exit northwest on the **AP-6** to Astorga.

From **Oviedo** (152 km/94 mi; 2 hours): Exit south on the **AP-66** to **León** then take the **AP-71** or **N-120** to Astorga.

From **A Coruña** (265 km/165 mi; 2.5 hours): Pick up the **AP-9** south, then the **A-6** southwest past Lugo, Ponferrada, and to Astorga.

Train

Astorga's train station is on the east side of town, outside the Roman walls, and the rails cross near where the Camino enters the settlement. **RENFE** (www. renfe.com) has several trains stopping in Astorga: from Santiago de Compostela (three trains daily; 4-6 hours; €24-48), Ponferrada (eight daily; 1 hour; €7-16), León (eight daily; 30-45min.; €6-14), Madrid (four daily; 3-6 hours; €28-39, and Barcelona (three daily; 7.5-9.5 hours; €41-72). Trains from Oviedo and other northern points, such as Santander and Bilbao, connect to Astorga via León.

Bus

ALSA (www.alsa.es) buses run frequently from León to Ponferrada, with a stop in Astorga (16 buses daily; 40-50min.; €3.65); and from Santiago de Compostela (six daily; 5-6 hours; €24); Santander (six daily; 6-8 hours; €26-42); and Barcelona (one night bus daily; 12-13 hours; €57); from Madrid's Barajas Airport (five daily; 4-5 hours; €26-38) and from Madrid's Estación Sur (six daily; 4 hours; €26).

Taxi

Parada de Taxis (987-616-000) is the central taxi dispatch.

Leaving Astorga

Leaving Astorga, the Camino is well marked. As you make your way west, you will pass the splendid, modern church of **Iglesia de San Pedro de Rectivia.** On the 27.6 kilometers (17 miles) from Astorga (900 meters/2,953 feet) to Cruz de Ferro (1,505 meters/4,938 feet), it is a steady but paced climb, with some stretches where you climb down then up again, interspersed with level stretches. The 3 kilometers (1.9 miles) from Astorga to Ermita de Ecce Homo slopes gently downhill, opening an expansive view of the layers of mountains ahead of you.

Ermita de Ecce Homo
Km 256.5

When you reach Ecce Homo, be sure to look back for great views of Astorga with the distinctive twin bell towers of the cathedral.

The little 17th-century hermitage of Ecce Homo is built on a human scale. The rounded doorway arches just overheard, and leads into a single-nave chapel with a sculpture of Saint James. The hermitage's porch is a protected alcove with stone benches on three sides, offering a sheltered space to rest or enjoy a picnic. The whole chapel exudes a strong spiritual energy, with the pilgrims' prayer in several languages, including English, set on a pillar of the chapel's porch entrance.

On the garden side of the chapel is the **Pilgrim Memorial Grove**, founded by pilgrim and Camino resident Rebekah Scott to honor American pilgrim Denise Thiem, who was tragically killed near here on the Camino in 2015. It serves as a dedicated place to honor all foreign pilgrims who died along the Camino.

Leaving Ermita de Ecce Homo

As you continue west, look at León's mountains. The tallest peak to your left/south is **Monte Teleno** (2,188 meters/7,178 feet), a place of legend for the Maragatos, in part because of the numerous and enriching waterways that flow from its snow-covered peaks.

Murias de Rechivaldo
Km 255.2

A quintessential Maragato village, with its thick orange-red stone homes, terracotta roofs, and chalkboard signs advertising hearty mountain laborers' fare, Murias de Rechivaldo (pop. 113) straddles the two sides of the LE-142 rural road.

Murias's church, on the northwest edge of the village and on the right side of the LE-142, is from the 18th century and is dedicated to **San Esteban**. Its most striking feature is the massive stork's nest perched on the bell tower.

Food and Accommodations

Mesón Casa Flor (Carretera Santa Colomba, 52; 987-603-148; year-round; eight rooms, €49; 10 beds in two dorm rooms, €10) is a family-run inn right on the LE-142, on the right side of the road, with cozy private rooms as well as *albergue*-style dorm rooms. There's also a nice bar and dining area, with varied *menú del peregrino* (€10), including another chance to taste the regional specialty, *cocido Maragato*. Breakfast is €3.

Leaving Murias de Rechivaldo

You have the option here to take the Camino left, off the left side of the LE-142 and directly to **Santa Catalina de Somoza** (in 3 km/1.8 mi), or—my strong recommendation—the much more scenic route, ironically following the LE-142 on its right side, for another 2 kilometers (1.3 miles) to the jewel village of **Castrillo de los Polvazares**. This is the prettiest of all

the Maragato villages that the Camino passes, and very likely was on the original main route of the Camino. Castrillo also has a sublime artists' retreat and pilgrim B&B, **Flores del Camino,** a unique offering on the entire Camino where you can rest and even make some sacred art. The detour adds about 1 kilometer (0.6 miles) to the walk.

To take the Castrillo de los Polvazares detour, from central Murias de Rechivaldo, turn right onto Calle Nueva and take it to the **Albergue Municipal** (669-067-433), which will be on the left. From the municipal *albergue*, cross the road (LE-142) and turn left, passing **Mesón Casa Flor** on your right (across the road from the *albergue*); in 200 meters (656 feet), take the footpath that parallels the right side of LE-142. The path is very pleasant, about ten meters away from the road, and separated from it by thick shrub growth and trees that block the view, though the LE-142 does not get a lot of traffic and is a calm country road. Enjoy the native black, white, and orange/red stones underfoot, polished and inlaid by the passage of time, feet, wind, and water. This trail goes straight to Castrillo de los Polvazares, reinforced by a large sign announcing the village.

⬧ Detour: Castrillo de los Polvazares
Km 253.2

Once the Camino arrives on the edge of Castrillo de los Polvazares (pop. 107), make a right over the bridge and the road will take you straight into the village. The village gets its name from the *polvaredes* (dust storms) kicked up by high winds or passing horse-drawn carts.

The village's beauty comes from the unified style of its bridge, buildings, and streets, all of which are built from the local red- and rainbow-colored stone.

Nearly all the homes are traditional farmhouses and have wide arched doorways with heavy wooden double doors, which once allowed mules and mule carts through and into the interior courtyards. Today, villagers paint their doors different colors, from plum to teal, adding to the village's appeal.

Walk around the village to fully experience its dense stone architecture, which can feel as if you're walking through a town carved out of a mountain. On the corners of some buildings are massive corner stones that seem to serve both as sturdy foundations and magical talismans. At least one of the stone benches built into the front entrance of the homes is said to contain a repurposed petroglyph from the surrounding hills, its surface showing the pockmarked dot patterns ancient herders or early farmers chiseled into the stone.

The village church, **Iglesia de Santa María Magdalena,** is dedicated to Mary Magdalene, and her feast day of **July 22** the town celebrates the **Fiesta de la Magdalena** in traditional Maragato attire (women in flowing long dresses and colorful scarves and men in black fitted jackets and trousers with bright belts and trim), featuring processions with the church icon of Mary Magdalene, music, song, dance, and festive foods.

Accommodations

You'll encounter ★ **Flores del Camino** (Calle Real 36; 691-221-058; www.flores-delcamino.com; five rooms; non-pilgrim: lodging €50 one person, €60 two people, breakfast €5, meals €10; pilgrim with credential: lodging €40 one person, €50 two people, meals by donation) midway down the main street, right in the heart of the village. (Look for a large wooden green door on the right.) This soulful art retreat is run by past pilgrims and accomplished artists Basia Goodwin and Bertrand Gamrowski (who speak English). They will accommodate many possibilities, from simple lodging to a transformative creative retreat.

Retreats are diverse, but popular themes are studying and learning to draw sacred geometry, painting sacred Eastern Orthodox icons, learning Persian miniature illustration, and

Flores del Camino artist's retreat and bed-and-breakfast

creating stained-glass windows. Some retreats delve into the meaning and experience of pilgrimage, and there is the possibility to visit the recently discovered 4,000-5,000-year-old petroglyphs of Peña Fadiel (Petroglifos de Teleno), 22.5 kilometers (14 miles) to the southwest. (If you're interested, inquire at Flores del Camino.) One-day retreat packages for non-pilgrims, which include accommodation, three meals a day, and a whole day course, are €150 for one person and €210 for two people sharing a room. Pilgrims should also inquire about retreat packages.

A stay at Flores del Camino offers a window into the sacred art of the Camino. It also offers a chance to sink into a beautiful village, watch the sun set over Monte Teleno, and then catch your breath at the shocking beauty of the Milky Way, which is stunningly bright in the deep, dark night that descends on this old village.

Basia and Bertrand also manage the village **municipal** *albergue* (€5), and those who stay there can still arrange their meals at Flores del Camino (by donation for pilgrims) and can even do a retreat there (€20 1.5-hour retreat course, €40 half-day, €70 full day). All passing through are welcome to stop in and peruse the art gallery of stained-glass rose windows and sacred geometry drawings and paintings, among other sacred art.

Leaving Castrillo de los Polvazares

Take the village's central street, the Calle Mayor, heading west. A yellow arrow pointing to the left appears at the base of a roadside *crucero* at the end of the street. Turn left here and follow the waymarkers for 1 kilometer (0.6 miles) to return to the path that runs parallel with the LE-142, which will be on your left. When LE-142 intersects with LE-6304, the Camino follows to the right side of LE-6304 and continues straight ahead into Santa Catalina de Somoza.

Santa Catalina de Somoza   Km 250.7

The entry into Santa Catalina (pop. 47) is lined on both sides with stone walls overgrown with morning glories. The first structure you'll notice as you approach the village on the Camino is the **Iglesia de Santa María** and its bell tower on the left. Be sure to go around to the other side of the church to see its west entrance, adorned with modern but primitive-style paintings of a circle enclosing an equal-armed cross and square, possibly representing heaven and earth, the cardinal directions, and the eternally flowing beginning and end relevant to many spiritual traditions. The church was built in 1708 and restored in 1982.

At the other end of town, as you are about to leave, an innovative woodcarver sells handmade walking staffs on the street on the right side. His staff stand is the first of many that will appear fairly regularly up ahead, inspired by the locals' entrepreneurial spirit as well as the approaching mountains.

Food and Accommodations

When you first enter Santa Catalina you'll see the **Albergue-Hostal San Blas** (Calle Real, 11; 987-691-411; contacto@ hospederiasanblas.com; year-round; 20 dorm beds in two rooms, €7; eight private rooms, €30-40) a multi-option accommodation near the church, offering both dorm beds and private rooms plus a small grocery store in the same building complex.

Leaving Santa Catalina de Somoza

The Camino runs through the center of Santa Catalina and exits running parallel to the LE-6304 all the way to El Ganso. This is a great vantage point from which to see the sacred **Monte Teleno** (2,188 meters/7,178 feet), slightly to your left when you face west and look at the mountains straight ahead. The low rolling hills between here and those mountains are carpeted in the native Holm oak. One of the common wildflowers here is the *clavel Maragato* (Maragato carnation), a five-petaled lavender or pink flower of the genus *Dianthus*.

El Ganso   Km 246.5

Nothing is left of the original 12th-century settlement of El Ganso (pop. 23). But the name El Ganso refers to a goose, so it's no surprise that some esoteric seekers, drawn to the Game of the Goose, speculate as to whether this tiny, dilapidated village has any clues. (The only one I can speculate on is the ladder carved into the modern church door on the entry porch—possibly a reference to Sophia, the goddess of wisdom, whose ladder of knowledge and growth connects earth to heaven.)

Food

El Ganso is known for its recent, and run-down, Camino landmark, **Mesón Cowboy**, a cowboy-style cantina serving pilgrims since 1998. As much as it evokes the Wild West, it's also a reminder that this, too, is cowboy country, Maragato-style, with horses, mules, and herding a way of life.

Leaving El Ganso

The Camino from El Ganso to Rabanal del Camino continues to run parallel to the right side of the LE-6304 country road. Midway, you climb slightly, with a pine forest to the left of the path. This is a special place to pause and watch the acrobatics of a large population of titmice. If you hear gentle taps echoing through the wood, look for woodpeckers.

At a point 2.2 kilometers (1.4 miles) before Rabanal del Camino, the dirt path veers right, slightly more away from the LE-6304, passing over a bridge and down a small slope into oak forest, the right side of which is lined with a fence and thousands of crosses that passing pilgrims have made by inserting tree twigs and branches into spaces of the wire fencing. The terrain is fairly uneven and rocky, with a slight climb before evening out and veering back to running parallel with the LE-6304.

When you come out of the trees, you'll cross the LE-6304 at the wooden footbridge over a ditch and make your way to the left side of the road. There you'll see the massive **Roble del Peregrino**, the "pilgrims' oak," a grand old oak trunk, now a massive stump, left as a memorial to this grand tree's existence, on a field that blooms with crocuses in the autumn. The tree's legacy is in having given thousands, maybe millions, of pilgrims a place to rest. It was believed that the leaves of this tree protected pilgrims who carried them, as a sort of natural talisman.

Carefully cross back to the right side of the LE-6304, where the Camino continues and runs alongside the right side of the road. Just before entering Rabanal del Camino, the LE-142 intersects with the LE-6304. The Camino continues to follow the LE-6304 into town, where the road becomes the Calle Real, the central street that passes through the village.

Rabanal del Camino
Km 239.7

Rabanal del Camino (pop. 74) is an intimate village where the houses have potted geraniums and calendula growing out of the stone cracks along the walls, and as many cats basking in the sun as pilgrims passing through.

Rabanal is mostly a 12th-century garrisoned Templar town, with the now-familiar mountain Maragato architecture of sturdy, multicolored stone homes. It was mentioned in the 12th century *Codex Calixtinus* as an important pilgrim stop. One story attributes the town's name, Rabanal, to the Muslim wife of one of the

Templar knights, a plausible likelihood given that the 11th and 12th centuries of Iberia were more in *convivencia,* living together in harmony, than in *conquista,* conquest.

Sights
Iglesia de la Asunción
The centrally located 12th-century Iglesia de la Asunción has been somewhat rustically restored, and is presently overseen by the active Benedictine Monasterio de San Salvador del Monte Irago (the church is therefore also called Iglesia de San Salvador). They offer daily **Vespers** (7pm) and **Compline** (9pm) prayer, in the form of Gregorian chant with the evening pilgrim service and blessing. Included is a **blessing of the stones** that *peregrinos* have carried and will place at the base of the Cruz de Ferro (Km 231.9). You can also attend **Lauds** (7:30am) and **mass** (12pm) here.

Food and Accommodations
Across the plaza from the church is the British Cofraternity of Saint James's *albergue,* the **Albergue Guacelmo** (987-631-647; 40 beds in three dorms; Nov.-Mar.; donation), a popular *albergue* for its backyard garden, relaxed if run-down atmosphere, and afternoon cup of tea. But the *albergue* is special because it is in the restored 12th-century **Hospital de San Gregorio**. The CSJ named the modern *albergue* after Guacelmo, an 11th-century hermit who came to these mountains in monastic retreat and founded the **Hospital de San Juan**, now in ruins, on the outskirts of Foncebadón up ahead. It is Guacelmo who set the iron cross, the Cruz de Ferro, on the oak trunk on Monte Irago, putting a Christian symbol on top of the older pagan one.

A traditional Maragato home, ★ **The Stone Boat** (Calle Real, 7; 652-660-504; www.thestoneboat.com; three rooms with bath, €40-70, breakfast included), is a new (2018) B&B and art gallery focused on "the pilgrims' quest." The effort of fellow *peregrina,* Kim Narenkevicius, after 15 years of traveling "as pilgrim and seeker," offers hospitality and support to other journeyers. Also possible are communal dinners; inquire if interested. All meals are procured from sustainable, local, and organic sources. Kim is also an artist and writer and envisions writing and creative retreats, so also ask about these if interested.

Albergue de Nuestra Señora del Pilar (Plaza Jerónimo Morán, s/n; 987-631-621; www.alberguelpilar.com; 76 beds, €5; four rooms, €35) is a warm family-run *albergue* that offers dinners and breakfasts (€8 and €3) and also has a bar with a terrace. Note: the *albergue* remains open all year, but the bar closes in late autumn and winter. Dorm beds are a mix of bunk beds and individual free-standing beds.

Posada El Tesin (Calle Real, s/n; 635-527-522; www.posadatesin.com) is a spacious stone building at the beginning of the village, just to the left as you enter, with four private rooms (€40-60), and an attached bar and restaurant (**Cantina Tesin**, with a basic but well prepared *menú* for €10, and breakfast, €3-7) with a large street-facing terrace.

Leaving Rabanal del Camino
Take the Camino straight through the center of Rabanal on Calle Real and exit past a fountain (not marked as drinkable) and covered traditional washing pool (to your right); stone walls and a dirt path demarcate the Camino. It will soon enter a passage that is pure wild territory for the next 5.6 kilometers (3.5 miles); you will be on a narrow dirt and stone hiking trail that climbs up out of Rabanal's valley and over undulating mountainous terrain toward the mountaintop of Foncebadón. It is a blissful stretch. You are now officially in the thick of León's mountains.

Be sure to fill your bottle with water in Rabanal del Camino (especially on hot, sun-exposed days) and take any provisions to fuel your climb. It is a more challenging hike from the recent prior kilometers, but steady as well, with few areas of steep ascent or descent.

Foncebadón   Km 234.2

As you enter Foncebadón, turn around to see the mountains you just climbed. This village was the traditional home of muleteers and monks, and an important pilgrims' stop in the 11th and 12th centuries. The settlement remained vibrant through the Middle Ages and into the early modern era, but by 1815, Foncebadón's population was in decline. In the 1990s, no one lived here. But thanks to the popularity of the Camino in recent years, the local population now stands at a thriving 18.

Foncebadón is in the midst of a renaissance. Famous in both Paulo Coehlo's and Shirley MacLaine's accounts of the Camino as the abandoned village with vicious dogs, it now boasts several nice dogs, at least two hostels and four *albergues,* and two little grocery stores. You see construction as you enter and leave, and I think each year for several years to come, pilgrims will find this place even more transformed.

Some old-time pilgrims lament the loss of the rustic hilltop village and its legends of ordeals and hardship. (Read Coehlo's *The Pilgrimage* to get a feel for how the wild dogs of Foncebadón were really a part of the pilgrim's spiritual initiation.) But fear not: This is indeed a place of spiritual initiation, for the Cruz de Ferro, in 2.3 kilometers (1.4 miles), has served this purging purpose for centuries. Foncebadón is also an ideal, protected rest stop before making the final climb to the Camino's highest peak (a relatively gradual and pleasant final ascent).

Food and Accommodations

The ★ **Hostal Trasgu** (Calle Real, s/n; 987-053-877; four rooms; €36-55) is a great place to stay, each room outfitted with what feels like classy garage-sale and attic finds. The restaurant serves a solid, at times innovative, *menú del peregrino* (€10) with fresh, seasonal ingredients, including grilled hake and roasted red peppers, and spicy eggs and jamón Iberico with fries. The *trasgu* is a house elf in Leon, Asturias, and Galicia, a character who is inclined to help around the house. It must be working, for there's a lot going on here; the owner also runs an excellent grocery store on the premises.

Hostal El Convento (Calle Real, s/n; 987-053-934; 14 rooms; €36-50) is run by an enterprising couple. When they bought the place as a ruin, the husband looked for a plausible history—one being that this may, or may not, have been a medieval convent. If not that, it easily could have been a pilgrims' hospital or village homestead. Either way, you will sleep well in this now-well-restored and modern *hostal*. Many of the rooms have a view of the mountains to the west. The restaurant and bar serve meals and snacks throughout the day.

Albergue Domus Dei (Calle Real, s/n; peregrinosfluc@terra.com; Apr.-Oct.; 18 beds in one bunkhouse; donation), which opened in 2007, is basic but atmospheric, set in the restored village church and run by *hospitalero* volunteers of the American Pilgrims of the Camino. It is at the upper end of town, to the right, near where you exit on the Camino for the Cruz de Ferro.

Leaving Foncebadón

Leave through the center of Foncebadón. Soon after leaving the village, 300 meters (984 feet) to your left, look for the ruins of **Hospital de San Juan,** built by a hermit named Guacelmo in the 11th century. And to your right, you will pass a recent pilgrim creation called the **Soul Garden,** where stones inscribed with uplifting messages intermingle with wild flowers and heather.

Continue to climb toward Monte Irago, the Camino's highest point, and on it, the Cruz de Ferro, an ancient pagan

ritual site topped with a sacred oak tree trunk and cross. About 1 kilometer (0.6 miles) before reaching Monte Irago, the Camino will intersect with and cross the LE-142 and then run parallel to it on the road's right side. On your right, a pine forest lines the path all the way up to the Cruz de Ferro; it is rife with cheerful bird life. You'll see the cross a few hundred meters before you reach it.

Top Experience

★ Cruz de Ferro
Km 231.9

Here at **Monte Irago** (1,505 meters/4,938 feet)—the highest altitude on the Camino—you're standing on an ancient ritual site that dates back as far as 2,500 years. A sacred oak tree trunk sits on the site as well. In the 11th century, the hermit Guacelmo set an iron cross, the Cruz de Ferro, on the oak trunk, putting a Christian symbol on top of the older pagan one. At this altitude, the nearest point to heaven that the Camino reaches, it's a potent link between heaven and earth.

With ancient roots that precede Christianity, the Cruz de Ferro is considered the most ancient monument of the Camino. The site may have been a crossroads veneration site for Iron Age Celts and then for Romans, each leaving a rock on this high point for their own gods. Since the time of Romans, the muleteers and other travelers (incluing pilgrims) have continued this practice. To this day, leaving a stone here is a significant rite of passage. The mound of stones below the cross is seven meters (23 feet) high and 30 meters (nearly 100 feet) in diameter, a testimony to how many people have come here and left a rock. Leaving

From top to bottom: Mesón Cowboy rest stop in El Ganso; pilgrims at the Cruz de Ferro; Posada El Tesin in Rabanal del Camino.

your stone can be a powerful ritual, and you may want to take a few moments to think about what ritual you want to enact: gratitude, letting go, forgiveness, or some combination?

The oak trunk is also significant, one of several manifestations on the Camino of the World Tree, also called the Axis Mundi, a concept shared by many ancient sacred traditions around the world. The Axis Mundi is a tree that connects the earth with heaven and is a means of communication and travel between realms. It is also a spiritual guide, a road map for the soul's journey upward, but without disconnection from rootedness on Earth. Oak is often identified for this role. You'll see this theme again, beautifully depicted with an ornate cross (*cruceiro*) and an ancient oak tree, in Galicia at Lameiros (Km 77.4).

Set on the ledge of the pine forest, to the right of the cross, is a small **hermitage** and another small **shelter**, built in 1980 for pilgrims. The chapel has a see-through grate, which pilgrims have embellished with wild heather, through which you can glimpse inside to the altar with a rustic and appealing statue of Saint James. Notice the slate paving stones on the hermitage's porch: many are engraved by pilgrims with messages and names.

Leaving the Cruz de Ferro

The Camino continues to run parallel to the right side of the LE-142 and through native oak forest. At the indentation of the first steep dale you will find the tiny hamlet of Manjarín tucked into the hillside where the path descends slightly as it heads toward the hamlet.

Manjarín Km 230

Manjarín (pop. 1) is largely a vacant hamlet but for the dedicated efforts of its one resident, modern-day Templar knight Tomás Martinez de Paz, who identified

this place as his calling in 1986 and returned full-time in 1993 when he settled in the ruin of this village. He has restored parts of it purely in service to pilgrims and the Camino. He picked this location to assist pilgrims on a remote stretch with little support.

Among the cluster of village buildings that Tomás has been restoring is an open-air shelter, **Centro de Interpretación Templaria Medieval,** Center of Interpretation of Medieval Templars, where you can learn about Templar history via information sheets and maps plastering its walls. It's also a place to enjoy Camino lore, along with Tomás's perspective and fellow-pilgrim camaraderie. You can also buy food, drink, and Camino-oriented souvenirs here, spend the night, and get your credential stamped in the first building to your right. Some pilgrims feel drawn to the place for its romantic and seeker's vibe, and others pass it without a thought, or find it a bit too basic.

Food and Accommodations

Tomás has rebuilt part of the village ruins to house pilgrims in a rustic but fully enclosed, warm, and atmospheric *albergue.* Some hard-core pilgrims say that this is the real Camino, where one lives simply and relies on the hospitality of such dedicated souls as Tomás. **Refugio de Manjarín** (no phone or internet; open all year; donation) operates on a first-come basis; lodging is rudimentary, with around 10 spots on the floor with mattresses in the fully enclosed refugio building, and another possible 20 spots on the floor in a stone building that is open and exposed to the elements. There is no heat, electricity, or plumbing, just an old-style outdoor latrine (a shack with a hole in the ground) and no showers. The communal meal, served by Tomás and/or other *hospitaleros* who are also fellow knights, is filling but basic. With no creature comforts, the draw of this place is its rustic atmosphere and the imagined old-time pilgrimage experience; it's the stuff of medieval tales and knightly lore. The lack of modern conveniences makes this an ideal place to see the Milky Way at night, with no light pollution competing with the trail of stars.

Leaving Manjarín

Past Manjarín, the Camino climbs again to another summit that offers great vistas and perspective. At the true highest point of Monte Irago's pass, midway between Manjarín and El Acebo, you'll stand on the right (south) edge of **Alto Altar Mayor** (1,515 meters/4,970 feet) for a full view of the approaching village of El Acebo at your feet below and of the large town of Ponferrada in the distance, nestled in the bowl of a mountain valley.

Past Alto Altar Mayor, the path begins to gradually (2 km/1.2 mi) and then more dramatically (1 km/0.6 mi) descend to El Acebo.

El Acebo Km 223

El Acebo (pop. 52), meaning "holly," is a delightful village set midway on the slope down into the valley, surrounded by mountains but with a sweeping view of the bowl-like valley where Ponferrada sits, 16.5 kilometers (10.3 miles) away. Along the village edge, raspberry bushes grow over the stone walls. The village itself is built of stone, and filled with kind people and friendly dogs. Here, and in Riego de Ambros (Km 219.6), you'll notice the bundles of herbs tied to doors, balconies, and windows. This an ancient pre-Christian practice toward warding off bad luck, and attracting and keeping well-being, that is also practiced in Basque Country and Navarra.

Perhaps it is El Acebo's perch midway between mountain and valley and the angle of the slope, or perhaps it is the native herbs growing in the hills, but the air here is invigorating and sweet. I love spending the night in El Acebo, and doing so sets you up for a quiet morning of walking before the folks staying in Rabanal del Camino or Foncebadón converge on the path.

Sights
Iglesia de San Miguel

As you near the end of the village, on the left side of the Camino is El Acebo's church, the 15th-century Iglesia de San Miguel, whose interior holds a statue of John the Baptist, the wild man of the Bible and a perfect personality for the deep wilderness of the Camino along this stretch. It's located on the highest spot of the hamlet, a sure sign it is dedicated to the archangel Michael, protector of high places. An ancient **olive tree**—the first you'll see on this stretch of the Camino—is planted near the church wall in the church square, **Plaza El Sagrado,** which means "sacred square." Look at the roots that have grown into the stone wall below it (and are partially holding the wall up): Locals and *peregrinos* have carved words and images (faces, grape leaves hinting at Bierzo wines coming up) in their dense, gnarled wood. Confirm with any of the villagers, but **mass** typically is held Sunday at 5pm, which is likely the only time you'll catch the church open.

Food and Accommodations

Most places in El Acebo offer both room and board, whether a hostel or an *albergue* or a combination of both, and all are easily found on the central road through the village, which is also the Camino.

★ **La Casa del Peregrino** (987-057-875; three rooms, €35-50) is the first place to the right as you enter the village. It's a wonderful place to stay, with a warming central fire in the dining room, a cozy bar to the side, and four elegant rooms of the same thick earth-toned stone, wide-plank wooden floors, and limestone-tiled baths. A varied and solid *menú del peregrino* (€10) includes seasonal delights such as local strawberries with fresh cream and entrées of perfectly grilled steak and fresh garden salads. Enjoy your meal while seated around the central fireplace in the dining room. Rooms have tall French windows, and some lead out onto traditional wood-beam balconies with excellent views of village life below and the mountains beyond.

La Rosa del Agua (Calle Real, 52; www.larosadelagua.com; 616-849-738; €40-50) offers three B&B-style rooms and takes as its emblem the seed of life, the six-petaled flower that represents harmony and the merging of heaven and earth. The enthusiastic young couple who own La Rosa are passionate about service, pilgrims, and the Camino as a sacred path. The thick-walled stone rooms with bath are fitted with hydromassage showers. To the side of the house is a mountainside garden, lounge, shared kitchen, terrace, and general store selling homemade meat and tuna-filled *empanadas*, fresh salads, cheeses, fruits, and sandwiches.

Mesón El Acebo (Calle Real, 16; 987-695-074; www.mesonelacebo.es; two rooms, €24-36; 32 beds in two dorms, €7) feels like a medieval pilgrims' inn— low timber roof, dense stone walls, small tables, and a central bar, waiting for you to take a seat and join the fray. It is in the heart center of the village, right to the left of the Camino. Rooms are basic and comfortable, and the bunk beds are roomy and have partitions to offer some privacy. The Mesón makes a delicious bowl of *caldo Leonés* (€4.50), similar to caldo Gallego, a thick, leafy, dark-green bean and pork soup. They also pride themselves in their *botillo* (you are firmly in *botillo* country)—the fat smoked pork sausage that is a specialty of the El Bierzo region.

Leaving El Acebo

From El Acebo to Molinaseca is some of the most wild, unspoiled, and sublime territory on the Camino. There is a strong energy to this territory; the path gets narrow and rocky, and climbs deep into the valley that takes you to Molinaseca. When the trail goes through narrow crags between high, dense rock and trees, it can feel as if you've left the modern world far behind. Butterflies and dragonflies are everywhere here.

Riego de Ambros
Km 219.6

The Camino enters Riego de Ambros (pop. 40) via a descent along a lane lined with stone walls and towering chestnut trees that drop their nuts onto the path. The village is inviting in the way El Acebo is, but where El Acebo felt firmly of the mountains, Riego feels more like the transition into the valley.

In the center of this originally 12th-century village is the small Baroque **Ermita de San Sebastian**, patron saint of athletes and adventurers as well as a protector against plague and calamity. You'll find him and his single-nave chapel on the left of the Camino. Climb up to its chapel grounds and light a candle for those you love, or to protect your path.

Leaving Riego de Ambros

The Camino leaves Riego on a rocky path that descends through chestnut trees that are even older than those on the approach to town. These are worth slowing down for, to see the wide, tall trunks, twisting as if in a dance. Just be careful that you don't slip on the path, which is often plastered with fallen nuts. In 2 kilometers (1.3 miles), look for the grove of oak trees with a stone circle and cairn in the center; the rich bird life seems drawn to this place, more than surrounding areas.

The Camino is marked with painted yellow arrows all the way to Molinaseca, but some are painted on the corners of rocks, at different heights, and can be easy to miss. You can double-check your progress by looking for the many stone

Clockwise from top: entering El Acebo; the Cruz de Ferro and the hermitage dedicated to Santiago on Monte Irago; Molinaseca's Puente de los Peregrinos; ancient olive tree and Iglesia de San Miguel in El Acebo.

cairns that passing pilgrims have stacked on the trail boulders and rock faces, a sure sign that you are on the Camino.

Nearer Molinaseca, groves of poplars, interspersed with oak and chestnut, paint the valley yellow in autumn. You'll experience a bit of hide-and-seek with Molinaseca in the valley ahead, as it appears and disappears from view as you plunge down into the narrow trail and ravine.

Molinaseca Km 215.1

As you approach Molinaseca (pop. 895), you've fully descended from one side of León's mountains and face a vast fertile valley ahead, with as much Mediterranean as Atlantic flora, which you will cross before climbing to the other side of León's mountains.

Molinaseca, meaning "dry mill," is a beautiful, well-irrigated mountain town built along the Río Meruelo. The town and its valley are known for their apples, pears, and chestnuts, the fat chorizo-like smoked sausage called *botillo*, red peppers, and wine. Moreover, the Meruelo river is full of trout. (All of these, plus fresh-baked bread, you will find in a general store immediately to the left of the Camino right after you cross the bridge into town).

The town feels as if halted by time: enduring stone homes with thick wood beams and traditional wood balconies line the streets. But Molinaseca's most distinguishing feature is its medieval bridge. In warm weather, there is a swimming area set off along the river, north of the bridge (to your right as you cross the bridge). There, and along the whole west side of the river and bridge, are many areas to laze along the bank and enjoy the dappled shade and outdoor cafés of the old town.

Sights

As soon as the Camino hits the edge of Molinaseca, before you even cross the river, you will pass the **Iglesia de la Quinta Angustía,** set apart from the rest of the settlement. Though the church was built in the 11th century, a fire destroyed it; the locals rebuilt it in 1512, and so it has a much more modern form. You can attend **Vespers** here daily, at 7pm.

Soon after the church, the Camino turns left and crosses Molinaseca's seven-arched 12th-century Romanesque pilgrims' bridge, **Puente de los Peregrinos,** which crosses the Río Meruelo with large cobbled stones. You'll feel as if you are back in the Middle Ages, so much that you can almost hear the swish of the pilgrim's long woolen cape. The bridge leads directly into the old town, **Casco Antiguo,** along the Calle Real, which is the Camino, a central sweep through this small town.

When you come off the bridge, look left (and detour if inclined) onto Calle el Rañadero, to the church on the highest point on this side of town, **Iglesia de San Nicolás de Barí.** This 17th-century church celebrates Saint Nicolás of Barí, the protector against disaster, including shipwrecks, fires, and poverty. It is surrounded by sacred olive trees, like so many of the churches along the trail in El Bierzo. San Nicolás church is often open during the day and early evening, and has some interesting sacred art inside, especially the two statues flanking the nave, both of San Roque (along with Saint James, the other patron saint of pilgrims, and also a protector against disaster and disease), and the florally engraved stone baptismal font to your left. Near the font is also where you should find the stamp for your pilgrim's credential.

Return to the Calle Real/Camino, which passes several small squares opening to either side. The most picturesque are the **Plaza de Garcia Rey,** to the right of the Camino, and a few paces farther ahead and on the left, the **Plaza del Rollo.**

Many of the homes here have coats of arms and engraved symbols over their

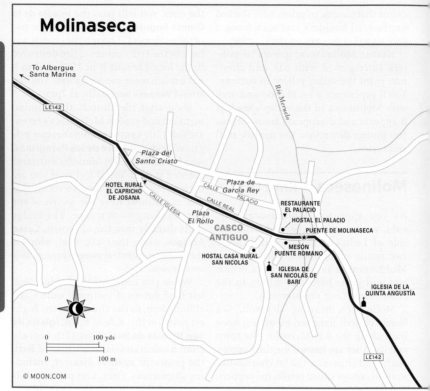

Molinaseca

To Albergue Santa Marina

LE142

Río Meruelo

Plaza del Santo Cristo

HOTEL RURAL EL CAPRICHO DE JOSANA

CALLE IGLESIA

Plaza de García Rey

CALLE PALACIO

CALLE REAL

Plaza El Rollo

CASCO ANTIGUO

RESTAURANTE EL PALACIO

HOSTAL EL PALACIO

PUENTE DE MOLINASECA

MESÓN PUENTE ROMANO

HOSTAL CASA RURAL SAN NICOLAS

IGLESIA DE SAN NICOLAS DE BARI

IGLESIA DE LA QUINTA ANGUSTÍA

0   100 yds

0   100 m

© MOON.COM

LE142

stone doorframes, some with Latin inscriptions. One, a third of the way down the street from the bridge and to the right, is of a triangle with a cross atop it. According to the homeowner, some local historians believe the symbol may have indicated the home of a *meiga* ("white witch," as León and Galicia's traditional herbalists and healers are known).

Another home, the **Casa de Cangas y Pambley,** midway through the heart of the tiny town, and also to the right, is more elaborate and marked with raised and carved coats of arms, with a tree, knight, river, and tower. The tree represents the house of an ancient noble family (deep roots); the knight represents nobility; the river signals that the knight was well educated; and the tower is a symbol of generosity and the service given by the knight/noble to his land and king.

Straight ahead, as you leave the Casco Antiguo, the **Plaza del Santo Cristo** is easy to identify for its ornate cross, the **Crucero del Santo Cristo**. Near the cross is a modern sculpture, **Monumento Peregrino**, in honor of the pilgrims; this one is depicted as none other than Saint James, the original pilgrim to Compostela.

Food and Accommodations

Molinaseca is full of all ranges of enjoyable accommodations that line both sides of the Calle Real/Camino, or found just off it on a side street.

The stone, stucco, and slate-roofed traditional **Hostal-Restaurante El Palacio** (Calle el Palacio, 19; 987-453-094; www. casaelpalacio.com; 15 rooms, €35-50), immediately to the right after crossing the bridge, has a magnetic riverside café, full-service restaurant, and comfortable private rooms with bath; the rooms have good riverside views, which include the pretty sweep of the bridge into town.

Across the path from El Palacio, to the left, is another riverside café with good food, **Mesón Puente Romano** (Calle la Presa, 1; 987-453-154; www.mesonpuenteromano.com; €10-15), serving traditional Molinasecan cuisine for over 30 years, including roasted meats, fish (trout!), seafood, and salads.

Hostal Casa Rural San Nicolas (Calle la Iglesia, 43; 645-562-008; www.hostalcasasannicolas.com; six rooms, €30-40), at the foot of the San Nicolas church to the left, has rooms with old-fashioned cast-iron beds, dense grey granite stone walls, and traditional wood-beamed balconies looking out onto the church and kitchen gardens around the river.

At the other end of Calle Real, to the left, the ★ **Hotel Rural El Capricho de Josana** (Plaza del Santo Cristo, 1; 987-453-167; www.elcaprichodejosana.com; eight rooms; €43-61) is both a rural hotel (Victorian décor meets modern simplicity) and a restaurant, with a creative chef who draws upon the kitchen-garden wealth of the valley. Even the *menú del peregrino* (€9) shows his innovations, a mix of usual suspects popular with peregrinos (spaghetti Bolognese, fried eggs with sausages and fries, roasted chicken with salad) with original dishes (such as spinach-pesto lasagna). El Capricho de Josana also has great tapas (toast with truffled cecina, varieties of shellfish including scallops, and razor clams). The chef and serving staff, who speak English, are jocular and joyous; it feels like a party, with you as a valued guest. They all take pride in the food and in Molinaseca's kitchen-garden, valley-fresh foods, including local vegetables and fruits from the many orchards (apples and pears) and also local produce, such as the celebrated *botillo*.

Albergue Santa Marina (Calle Fraga Iribane, s/n; 653-375-727; alfredomolinaseca@hotmail.com; open Mar.-Oct.; 59 beds in five dorm rooms, €7; dinner, €9) is 1 kilometer (0.6 miles) on the way out of Molinaseca, on the right side of the Camino, and has an open view of kitchen gardens and expansive, wild green spaces all around. The *albergue* opened in 2007 and is a modern stone and ochre-toned stucco building, with spotless and comfortable sleeping and living spaces; it is run by the welcoming *hospitaleros* Alfredo and Cristina Blanco. A sunny terrace set back from the street lets you enjoy the sloping hill views and wave to passing pilgrims continuing on to Ponferrada.

Leaving Molinaseca

The 8 kilometers (5 miles) to Ponferrada are well marked and straightforward, and parallel the road leading into the large town. Much of the walk passes through residential suburbs of Ponferrada, the most ancient being **Campo** (Km 210.5). Campo's 17th-century church, **Iglesia de San Blas**, is identifiable by its most beautiful aspect, a grove of olive trees and an ancient oak tree next to its wall. All around you are patchwork fields covered in vines, promising good Mencía and Godello reds and whites. Some of the fruit trees in the valley around Ponferrada are apple and cherry, which bear fruit from summer to autumn.

Ponferrada   Km 207.1

Once occupied by native Iberians, Ponferrada (pop. 65,788) is protected on all sides by hills and mountains and the two rivers, the Sil and the Boeza, that water the settlement. Romans took over Ponferrada, as they did much of this area, for their mining operations. Like Astorga, Ponferrada became a large and prosperous Roman settlement, and it was also overrun by Visigoths (in the 5th century) and North Africans (in the 9th century).

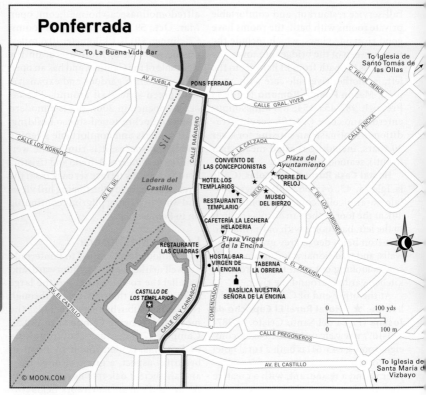

Ponferrada

To La Buena Vida Bar →

AV. PUEBLA

PONS FERRADA

To Iglesia de
Santo Tomás de
las Ollas

C. FELIPE HERCE

CALLE GRAL. VIVES

CALLE RAÑADERO

Sil

CALLE LOS HORNOS

AV. EL SIL

Ladera del
Castillo

C. LA CALZADA

CONVENTO DE
LAS CONCEPCIONISTAS

Plaza del
Ayuntamiento

HOTEL LOS
TEMPLARIOS

TORRE DEL
RELOJ

RESTAURANTE
TEMPLARIO

MUSEO
DEL BIERZO

CAFETERÍA LA LECHERA
HELADERÍA

RESTAURANTE
LAS CUADRAS

Plaza Virgen
de la Encina

HOSTAL-BAR
VIRGEN DE
LA ENCINA

TABERNA
LA OBRERA

C. EL PARAÍSIN

AV. EL CASTILLO

CALLE GILY CARRASCO

CASTILLO DE
LOS TEMPLARIOS

COMENDADOR

BASÍLICA NUESTRA
SEÑORA DE LA ENCINA

CALLE ANCHA

C. DE LOS JARDINES

0   100 yds

0   100 m

CALLE PREGONEROS

AV. EL CASTILLO

To Iglesia de
Santa María de
Vizbayo

© MOON.COM

In 1178, Templars made Ponferrada a main stop on the Camino to protect and serve pilgrims and the road. In the 13th century they built the massive castle that defines the iconic image of Templar Ponferrada. Hidden inside the castle is the ability to draw water from the Sil river without leaving the keep.

The modern town of Ponferrada is still concentrated on the confluence of its two rivers, though it now has large outlying areas, with small neighborhoods and enclaves, that explain its large population. Entry into the town takes you through some of the outlying neighborhoods, some new suburbs and others old villages, and the feel is very modern, somewhat industrial, interspersed with a lot of small gardens and orchards. But then you turn the bend on the Camino, right into the historic center of Ponferrada, and

the castle looms ahead, a spitting image of quintessential crusader castles in the Holy Land, transplanted to seemingly remote northwestern Iberia. Go toward the castle; it leads to the rest of the medieval town at its feet to the right.

Ponferrada's weekly **food market** sets up every **Wednesday** and **Saturday** morning on the Plaza del Mercado de Abastos, on the other side of the Sil river from the Templar castle. You can buy clothing here as well as food, among other items.

Sights

Top Experience

★ Castillo de los Templarios

The **Castillo de los Templarios** (Avenida del Castillo; 987-402-244; www.ponferrada.org/turismo/es/monumentos/

castillo-templarios; €6) is better than any castle Hollywood could conjure. It is immense, with thick, high walls and toothy rampart and towers. Walk across the bridge to the massive twin-towered gate and feel immediately transported to the 12th and 13th centuries, the time of knights, pilgrims, and passionate causes. Look up at a Tau cross engraved overhead at the gate's arch, a reminder that the Templars ruled from here as one of their headquarters, where they protected pilgrims as well as other sacred interests. Look also at the capitals embedded in the entry gate: two humble Romanesque-era human heads eternally hold watch.

Step over the drawbridge to the interior and see firsthand why this was the site chosen by native Iberians for their hilltop castro, and by Romans (and later, Visigoths, and even later, King Fernando II) for their fort. This place, at the intersection of two rivers, with fertile forests and valley, and on a high precipice with excellent views on all sides, assured protection as well as good food and water. Once inside, you can stand in the center of the large inner courtyard, walk along battlements and to the towers, look through the arrow slits at the town below, visit the keep, and imagine yourself a Templar knight in defense of pilgrims on the Camino.

The posted hours are Jun.-Oct. 15, Mon.-Sun., 9am-9pm; Oct.16-May, Mon-Sun., 10am-2pm and 4pm-7pm, but double-check these before planning your visit. The city is inconsistent with them and they vary often, compared to those posted on the municipal site.

After exploring the castle, take a walk through the park, **Ladera del Castillo,** that passes along the back side of the castle and has a steep slope down to the Sil river below. It has a dirt trail that will lead you into the old town through the back way, entering on small streets that lead to the Plaza Virgen de la Encina. The park is rich with specimen trees, including holly, wild cherry, and (a favorite among bears) the Madroño tree, really a bush, that has round red fruits that ferment naturally on the branch—the reason why the bears in Iberia are fabled to like them.

Basilica de Nuestra Señora de la Encina

The Plaza Virgen de la Encina is the social and town center of medieval Ponferrada and the home of its most celebrated church, **Basilica de Nuestra Señora de la Encina** (www.basilicadelaencina.es; daily, 9am-2pm and 4:30-8:30pm, free), based on a founding legend that weaves pagan spirituality with Christian.

The legend goes that, during the building of Ponferrada's fortified castle by Templars in the 12th century, a knight went into the forest seeking more wood for the construction, and spotted Mary's image on an ancient oak. (Oak trees were considered sacred by pre-Christian peoples in Iberia.) *Encina* means Holm oak; hence, Our Lady of the Oak. The legend is recreated in the modern sculpture by Venancio Blanco installed in 2003 in the center of the square.

The Basilica de la Encina was originally built in the 12th century, but was largely rebuilt in a heavy, fortified Baroque style from 1573 to 1660. The image of the patroness of Ponferrada is on the altar, set in a 16th-century retable. Even more appealing is her image engraved in stone on the outside west door's tympanum, where she feels to me like the ancient tree-bound Madonna. Below this Marian tympanum, the engraved border for the door's lintel is covered with nine-petaled flowers, an unusual number, since six and eight are more common and easier to draw geometrically. From sacred geometry, this may represent the Trinity tripled, magnifying not only the sacred Father, Son, and Holy Ghost, but also the more ancient sacred trinity of Maiden, Mother, and Wise Elder, a part of the ancient Eurasian worldview that harmonized heaven and earth through complementary earthly opposites (male-female, light-dark, sun-moon).

The **Plaza Virgen de la Encina** has a lot of appeal as well: Arcaded passages lined with café tables run along some sides of the plaza, making for a good place to take a seat and watch the town locals begin their evening ritual *paseo*. Check out the manhole covers in the square, with their scallop shells and Tau cross of the Templars.

Convento de las Concepcionistas, Museo del Bierzo, and Clock Tower

This trinity is clustered on the narrow, cobbled path, **Calle Reloj**, leading off the Plaza de Virgen de la Encina, with the arched passage of the clock tower marking the other end. Just before reaching it, the convent is to your left and the Museo del Bierzo is across the narrow path to your right.

A Franciscan order, the **Convento de las Concepcionistas** (Calle Reloj; 987-410-823) was founded in 1524 and expanded in the 17th century. It is easily identifiable from its solitary and almost Art Deco-style Madonna set in the arch over the thick rounded entry doors. The church marks the spot of an earlier church, dedicated to San Sebastian, from the 15th century, and parts of the older church, the choir, are preserved from that earlier edifice. The convent remains an active monastery; you can attend **mass** daily at 8:30am (9:30 am on holidays).

Directly across from the convent, in a building from the same century (built 1565-1572), is the **Museo del Bierzo** (Calle Reloj, 5; 987-414-141; www.ponferrada. org/turismo/es/museos/museo-bierzo; Oct.-Feb., Tues.-Sat.,10am-2pm and 4-6pm, Sun. 10am-2pm; late Mar.-Sept., Tues-Sun. and holidays, 10am-2pm and 4:30-8:30pm; in March, hours may vary so check these; panels in Spanish; €2.70). This is Ponferrada's old city hall and jail, now a beautifully arrayed archaeology and ethnology museum. The entrance gives way to a vestibule, with two staircases leading up to exhibit floors and straight ahead to a hidden interior courtyard. The collection is of all things Ponferrada and El Bierzo, from prehistory to the recent present. Some highlights on view: Paleolithic and Neolithic stone tools; Iron Age axes and daggers; Roman coins; and medieval religious art. More recent highlights include a room-sized weaver's handloom and a collection of festive mountain attire. Stand outside in the central courtyard, with its thick stone support pillars and protective arcades, and look up to see the Torre del Reloj peeking over the rooftop.

The **Torre del Reloj,** clock tower, is largely from the 16th century but was built over the ground plan of the medieval town. It frames the true delight of this section of town, the 30-meter (98-foot) passage from the Plaza Mayor on the Calle Reloj, dripping with the medieval atmosphere of towering stone buildings, hanging wooden balconies, and cobbled stones. Go through the gate at the base of the clock tower, which is the passageway into another elegant square, **Plaza del Ayuntamiento,** featuring the town hall and several restaurants.

Iglesia de Santo Tomás de las Ollas

Officially dating to the 10th through the 13th centuries (but as early as the 9th if you talk to the church caretaker), **Santo Tomás de las Ollas** (Plaza Campín, 8, 1 km/0.6 mi northeast from the town center), is an old pre-Romanesque church with an enigmatic 11-sided round apse that resolves into just nine arches. Ollas means "pots" and may refer to the local industry of this place.

The original church of Santo Tomás de las Ollas was just a single nave with no side chapels. In 1700, the parish added a large side chapel with a Baroque retable. Following the Mozarabic tradition, a screen between the apse and nave kept the monks from being seen by the laity. The current church entrance is from the 12th century and is a classic rounded

Romanesque arch. That door is to the side and faces south; the original Mozarabic door was probably under the bell tower, on the west side (facing Ponferrada).

As for Santo Tómas de las Ollas's most distinctive feature, its 11-sided polygon apse curiously capped with nine horseshoe arches: One possible explanation lies in the theme of "100-doors" (the 99 names of God, and then the final step into the kingdom, via a metaphoric 100th door: 9×11+1). This theme appears earlier on the Camino, at the Iglesia de Santa Maria de Eunate, replicating an idea prevalent in the mystical traditions of both Christianity and Islam: meditating on the 99 names of God as if they are each a gate, inducing a trance state that opens the final and ultimate 100th door to union with the divine.

You will need the caretaker to let you in, and will find her next door, in house #7 on the church's square. A knowledgeable and cheerful woman, she is happy to open the church and give you an informal historical tour (in Spanish) and will also allow you the time and space to enjoy the chapel in silence if you wish. She accepts donations for her effort, all of which go to the upkeep and constant restoration of the church. Whether she gives you a tour or simply opens the door for you, give her what you can; €1-2 is a good offering.

Floodlights outside the church (paid for by people's donations) beautifully illuminate the stones from which it's built. Opposite the caretaker's home, on the same square, is a stable of goat-sized miniature ponies who graze on the other side of the tall stone wall.

It's a 2-kilometer (1.3-mile) trek round-trip to get here. Take Calle Ancha east, off the northeast corner of the Plaza del Ayuntamiento, and follow it

From top to bottom: Castillo de los Templarios in Ponferrada; Ponferrada's Plaza de Virgen de la Encina and Clock Tower; Ermita Santa María de Compostilla.

around the south side of Parque de Gil y Carrasco. There, Calle Ancha flows into Avenida Astorga. About 200 meters (656 feet) after following Avenida Astorga, you will pass a part of the university, Campus Universitario de Ponferrada, on your left. Turn left after you pass it, onto Calle el Medio. You'll see signs directing you up the hill of Calle el Medio and leading straight to the church, on the left side. From the church's hill, look west to see one of the best views of Ponferrada, showing how the town is built in the crevices of the valley formed by the two rivers, the Sil and Boeza.

Iglesia de Santa María de Vizbayo

Santa María de Vizbayo (Camino la Ermita, s/n, Otero; 987-424-236; open summers, July-Sept., 10am-1pm and 4-7pm, closed the rest of the year; free) is the El Bierzo region's oldest Romanesque church. Built in the 11th century, with earlier Mozarabic elements, it is not open for visits; however, the exterior is worth a look for art history and architecture buffs: It is in a transitional style from Mozarabic to Romanesque, with horseshoe arches, and it has an intimate covered porch entrance, the door showing signs of having once been painted with a colorful fresco. A few carved corbels survive under the roofline, one of a man's face and another that looks like an acrobatic monkey flaunting a full frontal—a sure sign of its early Romanesque origins, before the earthier images on churches were cleaned up. Notice the sacred olive trees planted on the church grounds.

To reach Vizbayo from the Templar castle, head east on Avenida el Castillo, which runs to the castle's south, then make a right on Calle Cruz de Miranda. An ornate road cross, a *crucero*, marks that intersection. Take Cruz de Miranda over the Boeza river and continue straight, following the signs for Santa Maria de Vizbayo, which will take you to the right and uphill, past a small neighborhood vineyard (on the left), to the top where the church is. From there, look back to Ponferrada for a view of the Templar Castle, the Basilica de la Encina, and the mountains to the north and west of you. It's a 2-kilometer (1.3-mile) round-trip trek.

Food

Cafetería La Lechera Heldadería (Plaza Virgen de la Encina, 4; €4-9) is a café, tapas bar, and a pastry and ice cream shop all rolled into one, with café tables along the arched passageway on the Plaza Virgen de la Encina. Inside, Tiffany-style stained-glass lamps designed with dragonflies (so similar to the real ones flitting about the Camino here) are strung overhead. This is a great place for a snack or simple lunch (sandwiches, salads). Many Ponferradans enjoy their *merienda* here, a late afternoon ritual similar to English tea, taking pastries and coffee with friends.

★ **Bar La Virgen de la Encina** (Calle Comendador, 4; 987-409-632; www.hostallaencina.net; €3-8), the warm earth-toned brick, stone, and wood bar attached to the hotel of the same name, is a fun place to gather with locals to try the year's production of El Bierzo's hard cider, *sidra,* and the local white and red wines made from the Godello and Mencía grapes. A beer list and vermouth selection round out the offering, noted daily on a chalkboard hanging on a central pillar. Alcoholic drinks come with innovative and complementary bite-sized tapas, including varieties of local *cocidos* (stews) served in little bowls.

Run by the Hotel-Bar La Virgen de la Encina next door, the more formal **Restaurante La Cuadras** (Calle Tras la Cava, 2; 987-419-373; www.hostal-laencina.net) offers equally fresh and inspired meals, with white linen and red and white checkered tables arrayed around a wood balcony/mezzanine dining area. In good weather, you can dine at tables outside, under awnings hung over the lawn of the Templar castle wall. For full-on El Bierzo cuisine, try their *botillo* with pork sausage, cabbage, potatoes, and garbanzos, or the *morcilla con manzana* (blood sausage with a puree of local apples), or, in the fall, the chestnut flan made from locally gathered nuts.

In the medieval center of town, just off the Plaza Virgen de la Encina, ★ **Taberna La Obrera** (Calle Paraisín, 8; 679-845-673; www.laobreraponferrada. es; €10-15), "the Worker," uses the famous 1943 American feminist image of Rosie the Riveter ("We can do it!") as its icon to celebrate all hard workers in this cheerful, large, open-space bar for tapas and drinks. Touches of Americana pervade the place, including the front of an old Dodge van turned into a bar. They specialize in original, tasty, and creative tapas, including local cheese plates, a five-spice hummus dip with veggies, salmon tartar with avocado, and even fish and chips.

Nightlife

Restaurant and nightspot **Taverna La Obrera** (Calle Paraisín, 8; 679-845-673; www.laobreraponferrada.es) becomes quite the center for friends going out on weekends and holidays. Enjoy the edible and drinkable alliteration "*tapas y tragos*," (tapas and drinks) that includes not just wine and beer but also a wide selection of cocktails with innovative tapas.

Located on the other side of the bridge, the Pons Ferrada, a one-kilometer (0.6 mile), 15-minute walk from the Plaza Virgen de la Encina, is **La Buena Vida Bar** (Avenida Compostilla, 10 bajo; 987-403-573; www.labuenavidabar.com, 10:30pm-4am), which means "the good life bar." Enjoyed by locals for its sleek, open, red-and-black interior and good, inexpensive selection of beer, wine, and cocktails, La Buena Vida amps up its late-night vibe with eclectic music—from rock to reggae—that is conducive to dancing.

Accommodations

Hotel Los Templarios (Calle Flórez, 3; 987-411-484; www.hotellostemplarios. es; 18 rooms; €45-60), down a narrow side street near the castle and off the Plaza Virgen de la Encina, plays up the medieval tone with large modern rooms and baths mixed with Templar-inspired décor—thick wood furnishing, armor and shields, blood-red Templar crosses and flags, plush red velvet upholstery, and best of all, a dedication to serving the pilgrim cause. The associated **Restaurante Templario** carries the decorative theme into the dining room, with white linens and a *menú del dia* (€12) with several Leónese dishes, such as *albondigas en salsa* (meatballs in tomato sauce), *carrilleras en salsa* (pig cheeks), *pastel de espinacas* (spinach tart), and *arroz con botillo* (rice with the celebrated *botillo* sausage). Proprietors speak English.

★ **La Virgen de la Encina** (Calle Comendador, 4; 987-409-632; www.hostallaencina.net; 13 rooms; €30-50) is a *hostal* in the old city, built of the same ancient rock as the church and Templar castle, located a stone's throw from its front door. It exudes the medieval atmosphere of knights and pilgrims, right down to the wood cabinet in the elevator vestibule with two Saint Jameses engraved on its dense doors. The **bar** on the first floor draws locals as much as pilgrims with its selection of local wines and ciders and tapas. The upper floors have rose- and rust-toned rooms that compliment the heavy, dark wood furnishings. Sleeping here is as close as it gets to feeling like a medieval pilgrim with some means for a remarkably modest price.

Albergue Alea (Calle Teleno, 33; 987-404-133; www.alberguealea.com; Mar.-Nov.; 18 beds in four dorm rooms; €10; open Mar.-Nov.), opened in 2014, is a delightful new addition to the Camino. Run by the cheerful *hospitaleras*, Amelia and Esperanza, the *albergue* is dedicated to pilgrims and is a pristine home away from home, including generous and delicious communal dinners and fortifying breakfasts (€8 and €3, with vegetarian options). Cheerful white-trimmed, block-framed windows let in soft natural light.

Getting There and Around

Car

Ponferrada is well connected by highways coming from Madrid, León, Oviedo, and A Coruña. Destinations farther east and north, such as Barcelona, Pamplona, Burgos, San Sebastian, Bilbao, and Santander, will all approach Ponferrada via León and Astorga.

From **León** (113 km/70 mi; 1.5 hours): Take either the **AP-71** (for efficiency) or the **N-120** (for scenic driving and frequent stopping on the Camino) west to Astorga, and continue on the **A-6** (efficiency) or the **LE-142** (scenic) to Ponferrada.

From **Astorga** (59 km/37 mi; 1.5 hours): Depart west on **LE-142**; soon after Castrillo de los Polvazares, go right onto **LE-6304** and follow it to Rabanal del Camino, where you will get back on the **LE-142** all the way to Ponferrada.

From **Madrid** (395 km/235 mi; 4 hours): Exit northwest on the **AP-6** to Ponferrada, via Astorga.

From **Oviedo** (215 km/134 mi; 2.5 hours): Exit south on the **AP-66** to León and follow directions from there to Ponferrada.

From **A Coruña** (202 km/126 mi; 2 hours): Pick up the **AP-9** south, then the **A-6** southwest past Lugo to Ponferrada.

Enterprise (www.enterprise.com) car rentals are at the train station.

Train

RENFE (www.renfe.com) has daily trains to Ponferrada: from Santiago de Compostela (three trains daily; 3-5 hours; €20-26), Astorga (eight daily; 1 hour; €7-16), León (nine daily; 2 hours; €12-19), Madrid (four daily; 4-7 hours; €32-42), and Barcelona (three daily; 9-10.5 hours; €42-72,).

Trains from Oviedo and other northern points, such as Santander and Bilbao, will connect to Ponferrada via the train from León.

Ponferrada's **train station** (Avenida del Ferrocarril, 15) is on the northwest bank of the Río Sil, across from the Castillo de los Templarios that is on the Sil's southeast side. It is 1.2 kilometers (0.75 miles) walking (15-20 minutes) to the Castillo de los Templarios, a nice place to pick up the Camino. Take Avenida del Ferrocarril southeast toward the first roundabout (about 400 meters/0.25 mile), make a left onto Calle Ortega y Gasset and in about 200 meters (660 feet) make right onto Calle Hermanos Pinzon; follow it through a small riverside park to the intersection with Avenida del Castillo and make a right. Avenida del Castillo will lead you across the river and to the castle where you can pick up the arrows and scallop shell markers for the Camino as it passes the right side of the castle and enters the Plaza Virgen de la Encina.

Bus

ALSA (www.alsa.com) connects to Ponferrada: from Madrid's Barajas Airport (two buses daily; 5 hours; €31) and Madrid's Estación Sur bus station (two daily; 4-5 hours; €31-43); from Santiago de Compostela (four daily; 4 hours; €19); from León (12 daily; 2 hours; €10), Barcelona (one night bus daily; 12-13 hours; €61), and Santander (three daily; 7 hours; €40), among other cities and towns. More locally, ALSA connects Ponferrada to Villafranca del Bierzo (9 daily, both directions; 30min.; €1.65).

Ponferrada's **bus station** (Avenida de la Libertad, s/n) is on the west bank of the Río Sil and close to where the Camino begins to exit Ponferrada after crossing the iron bridge, Pons Ferrada, over the river from the east to the west side. This is the best place to pick up the trail, a 1.2-kilometer (0.75-mile), 15-20 minute-walk from the station. Cross over Avenida de la Libertad heading south on Calle Gral. Gómez Núñez. Go straight to the first roundabout, and make a left onto Avenida Puebla, which will take you straight to the Pons Ferrada and bridge crossing over the Sil. Don't cross, but look for Camino markers that will direct you left and north to leave Ponferrada. But do cross if you want to visit the medieval town on the west side of the river.

Taxi
Call **Radio Taxi Ponferrada** (www.radio-taxiponferrada.es; 987-009-900).

Leaving Ponferrada
Arrows and scallop shells direct you over the **Pons Ferrada** bridge and west out of town. Astorga's bishop, Osmundo, commissioned this bridge over the Río Sil for pilgrims in 1082. By 1178, it needed to be reinforced with iron supports, hence its name: *pons ferrada* (iron bridge), which is how Ponferrada gets its name. When you cross it, you will see stone, not iron, but iron is a part of its strength.

The Camino then leads through residential areas punctuated with parks and tree-lined streets, as well as some dirt paths, a pleasant change from the large towns and cities. To aid pilgrims, some residents in these suburban outskirts have attached symbols of the Camino, such as brass scallop shells and arrows made of real scallop shells, to their garden walls and gates.

Compostilla   Km 204.6

As you leave the town of Ponferrada fully, you will pass through a school ground in the suburban community of Compostilla, and soon after passing through the school grounds, you will come upon the levitating Mary of Compostilla.

Sights
Ermita Santa María de Compostilla
In the west-central section of Compostilla and on the right of the Camino is **Ermita Santa María de Compostilla**, a post-1960 construction

mimicking the medieval Romanesque chapel that used to be here, with rounded arches and, most delightfully, full-color frescos on the side porch, painted in 1993 and signed by the artist with the single name, Ajerbe. These frescoes open to view as you walk past the chapel, and depict the 12-month cycle of agricultural labor (planting, harvest, wine-making, pig slaughter, rest, and the like), as well as the Annunciation with Gabriel and Mary, and Christ Pantocrator, with wonderfully expressive images of the four evangels of the Tetramorph. (I especially love the way Mark's lion seems to growl with pleasure at the presence of Christ in the center.) Those eight-armed wheels rotating around Jesus's head are no accident. Eight in Christianity is the symbol of rebirth and resurrection, a meaning it holds in common with Islam, where eight represents the gateway to heaven. You can extend this to the eight-fold path of Buddhism, the path to enlightenment, which is another way to talk about resurrection and heavenly access.

As you reach the apse end of the little church, look to the right for the statue dedicated to Santa María de Compostilla. Her image stands atop a stone cairn, a miniature version of the Cruz de Ferro, and many locals have left flowers and other offerings at her feet.

Continuing a few paces past the hermitage, also to your right, is a **mural** painted on what looks like a small utilitarian stucco building, but the image is hardly utilitarian: It is of Santa María de Compostilla, levitating. Ajerbe also painted it, possibly in 1993, the same date as the hermitage murals, but no date is noted. The dedication written below her image says, "To the memory of the village of Compostilla and the hermitage of Our Lady of Compostilla that in these places they met her." This very likely refers to all the places Mary has appeared, far and near, all of which are connected to Saint James and his life, and his later death and burial in Spain. The Marian-Jamesian theme is reinforced by the *crucero*, an ornate cross at the crossroads next to this mural. It is unusual because instead of Jesus on the cross, it depicts Saint James as a pilgrim with staff and shell. On the other side of the cross are Mary and Child.

Leaving Compostilla

A pleasant country road, the width of one car, leads you to Columbrianos. Be sure to look at the mountain views to your left, vineyards and apple trees in the foreground, settlements in the middle ground, and dark blue and purple mountains in the distance. You are walking through the garden valley of Ponferrada, and will see many plants that typically do not thrive in mountain settings. Fruit trees thrive in this more temperate climate, and vines get the strong sun and cold nights required for good wine.

Columbrianos   Km 202.4

What I love most about Columbrianos is its **church**, located on the left side of the Camino and surrounded on all sides by olive trees and vineyards. In autumn, you may see locals harvesting these holy olives to cure, press, and eat. Also look for the 1998 mural of Saint James, dressed in an embroidered pilgrim's cape, on the outside wall of the small modern **Ermita de San Blas y San Roque** in the center of the village, on the Camino's right.

Food

Soon after the hermitage, to the left, is another delight: ★ **Bar-Albergue San Blas** (Calle San Blas, 5; 675-651-241) where I had the best coffee of El Bierzo, not to mention a delicious tomato and garlic rubbed toast with *jamón Serrano* and fresh OJ for breakfast (€5.50). The slate and stone building houses three private rooms (€25-30) and 20 dorm beds in

three shared rooms (€10). Owners Jesús and Rosa Mari also serve lunches and dinners (€10-12).

Leaving Columbrianos

The Camino continues to be well marked, passing through orchards, vineyards, and kitchen gardens overgrown with rosemary bushes and collard greens to be used in *cocido* or sautéed with bacon. Each village is centered on its church, a sure sign that you are on the original medieval Camino, built around the road and local holy sites as much as the one at the end, in Santiago de Compostela.

Fuentes Nuevas
Km 199.9

Fuentes Nuevas (pop. 2,750 both the village and surrounding rural residences) is simply fun to walk through. It's an older village surrounded by what are more rural suburbs of Ponferrada. Its old village center is passed by the Camino along its central street, Calle Real. All along this street, village doors and garden fences are adorned with statues of Saint James, scallop shells, and hanging black kettle pots (the original pots used for cooking over open fires in much of northern Spain, but especially the northwest). As you enter the village, at the crossroads, you'll find an ornate *crucero* with Saint James on one side and Jesus on the other (a bit unusual, since most cruceros depict Mary on one side and Jesus on the other).

Sights
Ermita del Divino Cristo

Soon after the crucero, you enter the village proper. To your left you will see the small 15th-century **Ermita del Divino Cristo** (Calle Real, 2, on the left side of the Camino), which was fully rebuilt by the people of Fuentes Nuevas in 2003. The hermitage door is usually open all day, although an iron grill in the shape of two pilgrims walking prevents you from entering. You can still see the whole single-room space through the grill, with an image of Jesus on the cross dominating the center. The small retable is fun: it has a smiley-face sun and moon, representing many things, including Jesus as the alpha and omega, beginning and end, and the turning of time and the cycles of life. The outside wall of the hermitage has a neo-Romanesque fountain in a baptismal font shape, with engraved faces on the rim and pedestal. It's marked *agua potable,* so the water is drinkable.

Iglesia de Santa María de la Asunción

A few paces farther along, in the village center, is the **Iglesia de Santa María de la Asunción** (Calle Real, s/n, in the middle of the village and on the right side of the Camino), with its olive tree in front, and a covered porch entry with a rustic stone engraving of Mary and Child over the door. Often, a helpful local is seated at a table in the garden or at the door, ready to offer you a stamp, a *buen Camino,* and advice should you desire it. Take a few moments to visit the church: It has unusually wide arches and several rich, multicolored frescoes, and the whole scale of the chapel gives a pleasant feel. Of medieval origin, and retaining some aspects of its early proportions, the chapel was rebuilt in the 18th century.

Wine-Tasting

Fuente Nuevas also has a local wine-maker, **Bodegas Don Pedrones** (Calle Flora, 5; 647-698-485; donpedrones@ yahoo.es; €1-3) that invites *peregrinos* in particular to stop for a wine tasting with *pinchos;* it's typically open during the day. You will find it three-quarters of the way through Fuentes Nuevas, a few paces off the Camino, to the left down Calle Flores.

Camponaraya   Km 197.3

Continue along the country road through Fuentes Nuevas to arrive in Camponaraya (pop. 2,800). The name comes from a confluence of the words *campo* (countryside) and *Naraya* (the river that flows through here), and it has been this small town's name since the 16th century, though the settlement itself dates back to the peak of the medieval Camino in the 11th and 12th centuries. Camponaraya once had a pilgrims' hospital. The town's principal church is **Iglesia de Nuestra Señora de la Soledad,** to the left toward the exit end of town, a modern structure dedicated to the town's patron, Our Lady of Solitude.

This is not really a pretty town, and it's also long. The entry into it, from its outskirts on the Camino, feels pleasant and rural; but then a right turn onto the road LE-713, which the Camino follows along sidewalks through town, gives it an industrial feel. It is a ten-minute walk through the town, and you'll depart by still following parallel to the LE-713, on the left side of the road.

Events

Camponaraya is proud of its two religious festivals. On January 23 they hold the mid-winter festival of the village patron saint, San Ildefonso. A larger and more colorful festival takes place in the warmer season of late summer (often the time of the wine harvest), celebrating the village patroness, La Soledad, on the third weekend in September.

Accommodations and Food

Just before you turn the bend into the more industrial part of town is a small *albergue,* the **Albergue-Bar Naraya** (Avenida de Galicia, 506; 987-459-159; www.alberguenaraya.es; 26 beds in five dorm rooms, €9), opened in 2014, with a friendly restaurant and bar serving meals and snacks 6am-10pm. Lunch and dinner options emphasize an Italian theme, with various fresh-made pasta dishes from pasta Bolognese to lasagna, plus *pimientos de Padrón* (little fried green peppers from Galicia). This is a good, quiet place to stay; it still feels like part of a small village, with spotless rooms, new and agreeable bunk beds, and a covered terrace. In 200 meters (656 feet) you will enter Camponaraya on the main street.

Leaving Camponaraya

One kilometer (0.6 miles) after leaving Camponaraya, paralleling the LE-713, you'll pass the **Cooperativo Viñas del Bierzo** (Km 196.3, Prolongación Camino de Santiago, s/n, Camponaraya; 987-463-009; www.granbierzo.com) on your left. Pilgrims are welcome to stop in at this wine cooperative to sample a glass and a small *pincho* (€1).

After the wine cooperative, the Camino crosses over the A-6 highway on a high footbridge, then continues on a dirt path into wilder grass and herb-covered hills, interspersed more and more densely with vineyards all the way to Cacabelos. Midway, you might find a temporary refreshment stop, **La Siesta** (€2-10), a camper van with a picnic table and benches and a canvas canopy in a dense grove of poplar trees. La Siesta serves breakfast, lunch, drinks, and freshly made fruit smoothies. Enjoy it if it is there, but don't count on it for provisions: be sure you have enough water and provisions in Camponaraya for the 6.7 kilometers (4.2 miles) to Cacabelos. The way is well posted.

Cacabelos   Km 190.6

When the Camino first enters Cacabelos (pop. 5,152), it feels like a small, single-road village of stucco and stone homes, with traditional hanging wood-beam and rail balconies. Soon, the town expands into an extended settlement. The Camino leads right into the center of medieval Cacabelos, with the modern town arrayed beyond it. Notice the garden-valley climate here, not only the vast vineyards but also the olive and fig trees growing side by side.

Medieval Cacabelos dates to the 10th century but was inhabited, most likely due to its key location on the Cúa river, since prehistory. It became an important pilgrim town in the 11th and 12th centuries, centering around its Iglesia de Santa María. As with many towns on the Camino de Santiago, including nearby Villafranca del Bierzo, Cacabelos had a significant French population that resettled here to build up the Camino. Like so many towns in this region, Cacabelos also has Roman roots. Romans brought vines with them, a legacy that has enhanced the whole El Bierzo region. Cacabelos is in the center of this wine country, and any place in town where you stop for a drink will serve up the local vintage.

I love staying overnight here, an alternative to the equally appealing Villafranca del Bierzo up ahead. Consider an hour to take in the local archaeology museum and the Santa María church. The remainder of Cacabelos unfolds as a more modern but still intimate and pedestrian-friendly town, with all the amenities.

Sights

The first historic site in the old town center is the 15th-century Capilla de San Roque. Just past San Roque's chapel, the old town opens up into intimate, cobble-stoned pedestrian streets. The Camino becomes the **Calle Santa Maria,** which leads from San Roque chapel to the Iglesia de Santa María. These two churches act as parentheses containing the old town. In between them are tiny squares, narrow streets, and hanging balconies with colorful flowers overhead, especially potted geraniums.

Capilla de San Roque

The 15th-century **Capilla de San Roque** (Calle Santa María, 59), in the old town center on your right, is a small chapel dedicated to the other pilgrim saint, this one from France. If the chapel is open, typically in the morning (9am-1pm) and afternoon (4-6pm), you'll see a local seated at a table in the simple, small, one-room chapel to offer you a stamp in your pilgrim's passport.

Iglesia de Santa María

Like the Iglesia de Santa María in Fuentes Nuevas, the **Iglesia de Santa María** (Calle Santa María, 1 ; 987-781-233 or 987-549-416; Mon.-Sat. 10am-1:30pm and 5-8pm, Sun. and holidays 10am-1:30pm; free) of Cacabelos also has wonderful wide Romanesque arches defining the interior apse, nave, and side chapels. Their width and height—wider than usual and lower than usual—have a tunnel effect that seems to propel the viewer forward into the sacred space of Our Lady on the altar. Only these architectural elements of the 1108 church survive; most of the church was reconstructed in the 16th and 17th centuries, and the sculpture on the altar of Mary is 17th century Baroque.

The south-facing entrance outside the fortress-like church has a rustic 13th-century Romanesque image of Our Lady set in the tympanum. If you wander around the outside wall of the apse, counterclockwise from the south door, just beyond it is an equally rustic and charming stone image of Saint James tucked into an upper niche.

Museo Arqueológico

The **Museo Arqueológico** (Calle las Anguastias, 24; 987-546-993; www.cacabelos.org; Tues.-Sat., 10am-2pm and 4:30-7:30, Sun. and holidays, 11:30am-2pm; €2.50; some panels are in English), set in a stone and timber 19th-century town home, is worth a 30-60-minute stop. The exhibits highlight Cacabelos's archaeological and ethnographic past, especially the nearby *castro* hilltop settlements—the most famous being Castro Bergidum in Pieros, also known as Castro Ventosa, which the Camino passes 2 kilometers (1.3 miles) after Cacabelos. The exhibit recreates the Iron Age peoples' attire (woven tunics, pants and dresses), their pottery, and their iron-forged tools.

Interesting displays also cover local Roman conquest history, an important period that also brought wine-making to the territory. You can also have your photo taken in a recreated chariot; just suspend disbelief when you see the modern rubber wheels (I think it gets used in festival processions). The museum is also a didactic center, and the town hosts special lectures and events that bring the regional history to life. Sometimes they do more creative exhibits, such as Harry Potter-style wizardcraft.

Events

Cacabelos has a small but well-attended covered market, **Mercado de Abastos** (Calle Doctor Santos Rubio, 1), open in the mornings and centrally located. Here you can purchase local foods such as fresh almonds, cheeses, wines, fruits, vegetables, and sausages.

The **9th** and **26th** day of every month, Cacabelos hosts its **traditional market**, selling general goods as well as local produce, foods, and wine on the Plaza del Ayuntamiento.

Food

Pulpería Compostela (Calle Santa María, 42; 987-546-351), right on the Camino, serves more than delicious paprika-seasoned boiled octopus; there are also wine-steamed *mejillones* (mussels), calamares with lemon, a sampling plate of charcuterie, and more. Their €10 *menú del peregrino* includes these dishes and more (such as salads, soups, steaks, grilled chicken, and fish). The staff manages to remain upbeat and deliver great food even during the most demanding times, when tables are full with hungry and tired pilgrims.

The formal and romantic dining room of the **Restaurante Siglo XIX** (Calle Santa María, 2; 987-546-555; www.hostalsigloxix.com; €10-12) matches the 19th-century Belle Époque style of its attached *hostal* with its pinstriped walls, gold-embossed mirrors, and white linen tablecloths. The menu is dedicated to contemporary Mediterranean cooking, including regional Bierzo dishes with seasonal and local ingredients. Siglio XIX offers both a la carte and a *menú del día*; dishes include escarole salad with thick bacon and a poached egg, cod with leek salsa, and homemade rice pudding. They have a good selection of El Bierzo wines. There is also a more informal café with outdoor seating on the church square.

Accommodations

Hostal La Gallega (Calle Santa María, 23; 987-549-476; www.hostalgallega.com; open all year) is centrally located, between the Capilla de San Roque and Iglesia de Santa María. It offers neat, basic, and restful rooms, both *albergue*-style (29 dorm beds in seven spotless bunkhouses, €10) and hotel-style (19 private rooms, €25-40), with all facilities, including a washing machine in the lobby. La Gallega is run by a helpful, industrious couple who also manage the connected street-front café, which is great for breakfast, dinner (€10), or a drink.

Hostal-Restaurante Siglo XIX (Calle Santa María, 2; 987-546-555; www.hostalsigloxix.com; eight rooms; €50-80) has a great location, on the corner looking out onto the Iglesia de Santa María. You'll know the place for its 19th-century Belle Époque ironwork grapevines, wrapped around the stone pillar on the corner of its arcaded entrance and on its walls. Inside is just as romantic for a bygone era, with reclining Belle Époque divans and East Asian ceramics. Some rooms have glass-enclosed balconies.

Leaving Cacabelos

Following the Camino past the Iglesía de Santa María and then the Museo Arqueológico, you will cross over the Río Cúa and soon pass on your right, an outdoor display of an 18th-century **wine press.** Here, grapes were pressed down to pulp and vats collected the juice for fermentation. This one is made of chestnut wood and is the size of a small boat.

The Camino parallels the road in this section. A few paces after the wine press, also on the right, is the municipal ★ **Albergue de de Nuestra Señora de las Angustias** (Plaza del Santuario, s/n; 987-547-167; €5) inside the church of the same name ("Our Lady of Sorrows"). Some locals push flowers and herbs through the church window grates; these may be offerings to Our Lady, or perhaps they represent an ancient pagan use of herbs and flowers as talismans for well-being and protection against harm. Access to the exemplary municipal *albergue,* which opened in 2001, is through the door to the garden, to the right of the church entrance. Aromatic sage and rosemary grow on the grounds. Ask if you can pluck some; it is a good antidote to smelly boots if you stuff a spring or two in each shoe overnight. Solar panels on the roof fuel the *albergue,* which is composed of 70 beds, arrayed in several shared cubicles, two beds to a room, with door and privacy.

Wine country thickens from here to Villafranca del Bierzo, and vines radiate out in rounded rows along infinite rolling hills, punctuated by groves of pine and poplar. The red wine grape varietal that is king here is Mencía, and two white varietals are Godello and Doña Blanca.

Pieros   Km 188.9

This hamlet of 36 people has two gems: the remains of an ancient *castro*, and a church with an unusual triangular façade.

Sights

Castro Ventosa

Just as you enter the village, to your left is a road that wraps up and around to the sign-posted Castro Ventosa, which is the present name of the Castro Bergida or Bergidum, the original prehistoric settlement of both Cacabelos and Pieros. Today Castro Ventosa is a vineyard, and all of the castro is largely unexcavated and under vines—but on the edges of the kidney-bean-shaped hill, the one visible element of this old castro are the old walls of dense stone that the Romans refortified. It's a 1.8-kilometer (1.1-mile) climb to the west-facing walls, where you can see these wall remains of the Castro Ventosa. There, another small road continues west down the other side of the hilltop slope and reconnects with the exit end of Pieros in 1.6 kilometers (1 mile).

Iglesia de San Martín de Tours

Iglesia de San Martín de Tours is accessed from the center of the village, on the one small road perpendicular to the Camino on the right. Take that road down the hill into the small valley of the village below. San Martín has an almost triangular stone façade and was built in 1086. Along with a hospital and lepers' colony, Templars protected and oversaw medieval Pieros as a part of their watch in El Bierzo. Apple trees and vines surround the church. It is rarely open, but just taking in the unusual exterior façade and being in this mini-valley is worth the 300-meter (984-foot) trek down. Because it is set off from the village, you may see wild boar (or at least their tracks) rooting around the church grounds for grubs and other goodies. If you do see one, keep your distance; their tusks are quite dangerous.

Food and Accommodations

At the entrance to the village, 50 meters (164 feet) off the Camino to the right, is the **Albergue El Serbal y la Luna** (Calle Pozo, 13; 639-888-924; albergenedepieros@gmail.com; 20 beds in three rooms; €5). In addition to breakfast, lunch, and take-out food for the road, this *albergue* is popular for daily communal vegetarian dinners (€9). They also offer meditation and alternative therapies.

A modest-looking rustic snack shack on the left side of the LE-713, and the Camino, as you are just about to leave Pieros, ★ **Café-Bar El Arroya** (LE-713; 607-299-112; www.castrobergidum.com), makes superb to-order meals, including a generous bacon and eggs breakfast with local rustic bread (for an incredible €3). Several tarped areas on the café's garden grounds offer outdoor seating, with a view of the vineyards behind the café that lead up the hill to Castro Ventosa/Bergida. El Arroyo also sells local olive oil and wine.

Leaving Pieros

Less than half a kilometer (a quarter of a mile) after Pieros, the Camino turns right and forges a footpath through the vineyards and rolling hills; this is the terrain for the 6.3 kilometers (4 miles) to Villafranca, first passing through the vineyard-enshrouded village of **Valtuille de Arriba** (Km 186.5). Rolling hills, dark red and brown earth, vineyards, almond and pear trees, and oak groves define the way. If it weren't for the large metal posts and electric wires running overhead, this would be one of the most beautiful landscapes of the entire Camino. Stop and look behind you for dramatic views of the mountains, vines, and Cacabelos. You'll also get a better vantage point to see Castro Ventosa, the biggest mound in the foreground, if you look directly south from here toward Pieros.

After Valtuille de Arriba, you enter the Burbía valley's wine-growing area. This stretch to Villafranca is also called *el camino de la Virgen* and is a deeply spiritual landscape for locals, intimately tied both to wine and to Mary, who is seen as the protector of the land, fruit, and wine. Legend has it that a medieval pilgrim from France brought the first Cabernet Franc grapevine to the area, which over time adapted to El Bierzo's climate and soil and evolved into the unique Mencía grape varietal that grows only here. (To my palate, Mencía is indeed unique, but comes closest to what Oregon-grown Pinot Noir tastes like.) Several other winemakers grow their vines here, many also specializing in the white wine Godello, another varietal unique to this part of Spain; it's a bit meatier than a sauvignon blanc but lighter than a chardonnay. You will climb up and over the last vineyard's hill and dale into the next valley, nestled at the foot of the mountains, and then enter Villafranca del Bierzo, first passing the most important sight in the small town, the **Iglesia de Santiago** and its **Puerta del Perdón**, door of pardon. The area around you here is called **Los Ancares** and is a Reserva de la Biosfera (biosphere reserve) with maples, hazel and oak among the many tree varieties; wild goats, bears, wolves, otters, and eagles are among the wild animals.

Villafranca del Bierzo
Km 182.1

Set in its steep, lush valley, Villafranca del Bierzo (pop. 3.055) is a pretty little town with glass-enclosed balconies and stone and stucco homes. It was founded by French monks from Cluny around the year 1070, and the town holds its historic form into the present both because of good development choices and because the town is wedged in a narrow river valley with little room to expand. The monks also very likely played a part in cultivating the unique wine traditions and grapes rooted here over the centuries.

In Villafranca, you've arrived at the 10th of the 13 stages of the Camino, as defined by the *Codex Calixtinus*. But if this is it for you, take comfort that at Villafranca's Puerta del Perdón you can receive full blessings and redemption if you cannot make it all the way to Compostela. Villafranca also was, and for many remains, the staging area to rest up and stock up for the climb to O Cebreiro. (However, stocking up is less critical than it once was, as many small villages now host food and accommodation between here and the mountaintop 28 km/17.4 mi away.) People here are gregarious and proud of being residents of a pilgrim town, offering help and services to best prepare you for the next stretch of the Camino.

The whole center of town is appealing. On a sunny day, look for the ad hoc tarp and picnic tables set up just in front of the Colegiata de Santa María, where an industrious man boils octopuses in a large vat of water on the sidewalk, serving up *pulpo á feira* (boiled octopus seasoned with Spanish paprika, olive oil, and sea salt) with wine to patrons enjoying the dappled shade of the public place. To the right of the Colegiata de Santa María is **Parque de la Alameda,** where the **Tuesday weekly market** sets up, selling food and general goods.

Sights
The Camino leads through the center of the town, meandering down one hillside, flowing across the Burbía river, and beginning its ascent up the hill on the other side as it exits town toward Pereje. On the way, it traverses several streets and passes by the main sights, and is well marked with scallop shells embedded on the pavement and on walls.

Iglesia de Santiago
On the entry edge of arriving in Villafranca, the Camino leads the pilgrim to the north door of the 12th- and 13th-century **Iglesia de Santiago** (Calle de Santiago; 987-540-028; Jul.-Sept., Tues.-Sun., 10:30am-1:30pm and 5-8pm; free). This church and its north door, known as **La Puerta del Perdón** (gate of pardon), comprise Villafranca's most famous and important site, for this is

Villafranca del Bierzo

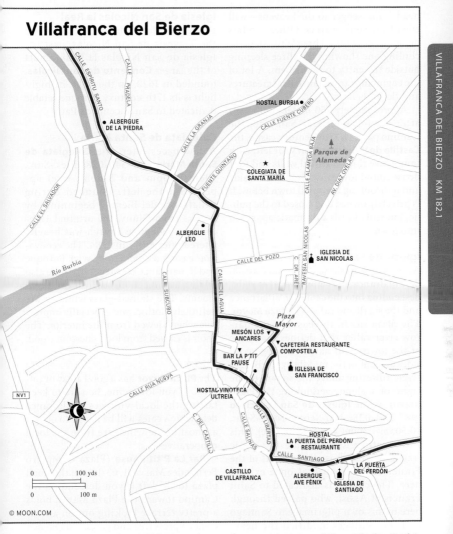

© MOON.COM

where *peregrinos* who could not make it all the way to Santiago could fulfill their pilgrimage and receive pardon for their transgressions. Along with the Puerta del Perdón in León's Basilica de San Isidoro, this is the only other place outside of Santiago de Compostela to earn redemption of one's sins on the Camino. Today the gate does not serve this purpose, but in the Middle Ages, those too sick to continue would climb (or be carried) up the five stone steps and through the Gothic arch to receive pardon from a witnessing priest waiting within.

The building is now used as an exhibit space, and the door and church are rarely open outside of summer. But you can still stand on the church steps, touch the door, and take in the transition Romanesque-to-Gothic engravings on the 13th-century north door's capitals. Perhaps the one on the left—the bird with a human head, a messenger to the heavens—will even hear your prayers. Other capitals depict scenes of the Three Wise Men, including one showing the three sleeping outside the entry to Bethlehem. A lot of the engravings are of fantastical creatures and floral themes.

Approximately 150 meters (500 feet) after leaving Iglesia de Santiago, the Camino passes a 17th-century castle, the **Castillo de Villafranca**, on your left, with impressive thick fortified walls and four dense round towers, set into the hillside and overlooking the small town below. It is privately owned and closed to the public, but still affords a dramatic approach into town.

Iglesia de San Francisco

After the Iglesia de Santiago and Castillo de Villafranca, the Camino snakes right, descending into the center of Villafranca and the small and café-rich **Plaza Mayor.** The plaza sits in the basin of the narrow river valley that defines the shape of the town, with narrow slopes on all sides and cut in the middle by the Burbía river. Towering above the square to the right, on a slope overlooking the Plaza Mayor, is the **Iglesia de San Francisco** (987-540-028; Jul.-Sept., Tues.-Sun., 10:30am-1:30pm and 5-8pm; free). This 13th-century Romanesque-to-Gothic transition church is all that's left of the Franciscan convent that once existed here. The church is dedicated to Saint Francis of Assisi, who passed through here on his own pilgrimage to Santiago in 1214. Builders modified the heavily fortified church in the 17th century. Among its most beautiful aspects is its 15th-century Mudéjar-style wooden ceiling, which is considered one of the largest in northern Spain.

One of the best reasons to climb up to this church is to turn around and look at its view of the Castillo de Villafranca; from here you can fully see its enclosing walls and four watchtowers, as well as the rounded hilltop landscape around it.

Iglesia de San Nicolas la Real

From the Plaza Mayor, follow along the Travesía de San Nicolás, past the Iglesia de San Nicolas la Real, a part of the larger **Convento de San Nicolás**, founded in 1620, on the right. Its highlight is its 17th-century Baroque retable dedicated to San Vicente de Paúl.

Colegiata de Santa María

A few paces later, the **Colegiata de Santa María** (987-540-028; Tues.-Sun., 10am-1:30pm and 5-8pm; free) appears on the left. Founded during Villafranca del Bierzo's beginnings by monks from Cluny, the original 11th-century collegiate church was heavily altered after a fire in 1784. The renovation gave it a stockier, heavier Baroque and Renaissance construction while also folding in some more ethereal Gothic elements. The stained-glass windows are definitely Gothic, and especially impressive when viewed from the interior. The choir is carved from local chestnut wood.

Food

The **Plaza Mayor** has a good array of eateries. If you love wine, be sure to keep tasting the local vintages. Villafranca del Bierzo's cafés will be happy to oblige, as most house wines are from the local cooperatives.

Bar La P'tit Pause (Plaza Campairo Fernández Marva, 1; €3-10), on the small plaza to the left if you descend on the Camino toward the Plaza Mayor, holds a pretty terrace looking out on an ancient Cypress tree and garden. Its French name and Iberian location belies some of its German cuisine, plus vegetarian and vegan foods, *and* some French quiches. Try their many varieties of vegan burgers (including tofu and mushroom, lentils and chia seed, BBQ seitan, and kale and quinoa), or the five-vegetable lasagna. For meat lovers: the meat lasagna, beef burgers, and German sausages are good. German beer is on hand, if El Bierzo wine isn't your cup of tea.

La Puerta del Perdon (Calle Prim, 4; 987-540-614), a part of the boutique hotel of the same name, has picture-window views from the cozy dining room looking out on the Castillo de Villafranca, and prides itself on local and seasonal ingredients. Some specialties are roasted oxtail, a wide selection of salads (including the best take on the ubiquitous *ensalada mixta*, embellishing this Spanish go-to salad with mache greens instead of romaine lettuce), croquetas made from El Bierzo *botillo*, and squid-ink black rice with grilled shrimp.

Mesón Los Ancares (987-542-317; €15) faces the Plaza Mayor with a view of Iglesia de San Francisco, and serves classic favorites, from Galician style octopus to El Bierzo *cocido, caldo Gallego* (leafy green pork and bean soup), saffron-stewed chicken, and roasted lamb.

★ **Cafeteria Restaurante Compostela** (Plaza Mayor, 12; 987-540-315; €11) features inside dining or al fresco on the Plaza Mayor, right under the towering Iglesia de San Francisco, at sunny tables with umbrellas. The warm and enthusiastic staff serves creative combined platters (try the *jamón Iberico* with fried eggs, salad, fries, and croquetas), daily menus, and a selection of tapas and drinks. The local grilled trout is perfectly fried and puckering fresh. The staff are always happy to see you, as if you're the first pilgrim they've ever served.

On sunny days, look also for the octopus man setting up with tents and picnic tables on the pavement in front of the Colegiata de Santa Maria, boiling and serving fresh *pulpo á feira* and wine.

Accommodations

On entering Villafranca, to your left and right after and next door to the Iglesia de Santiago, is the legendary **Albergue Ave Fénix** (Calle Santiago, 10; 987-542-655; www.albergueavefenix.com; open all year; 80 beds in five rooms; €6). Opened in 1992 and rebuilt by hand by the owner, Jesús Jato, after a fire in 2001 destroyed the earlier *albergue,* the new structure was recently refurbished in 2016. Communal meals are €6-7 and breakfast is €3. Near the entrance, look for the wooden Loving Box: If you are sad, open it to take one of the messages inside it that were left by other pilgrims; if you are happy, write a message on a piece of paper and deposit it in the box for others. Jesús also hosts the *queimada,* the ceremonial sharing of the beverage called *orujo* that's more common in Galicia, when he feels it is appropriate to do so. (This is hit or miss; it's not something that can be scheduled.) The ritual is performed in Spanish, but orujo's ethereal spirit translates easily enough. Lately, some find this *albergue* too rustic and unkempt, but it remains a beloved Camino icon nonetheless.

Hostal La Puerta del Perdón (Plaza de Prim, 4; 987-540-614; www.lapuertadelperdon.com; €55-100), a boutique *hostal* in a townhouse with traditional glass-enclosed balconies, offers seven guest rooms—a number important to the owners for its mystical qualities (such as the seven chakras, days of the week, and the colors of the rainbow). This whimsy pervades the place, each room having its own name and theme: El Mar, El Camino, El Bierzo. Guests are offered dinner from locally harvested and produced foods (see above). Proprietors speak English.

Hostal-Vinoteca Ultreia (Calle Puentecillo, 8; 987-540-391; www.hostalultreia.com; four rooms; €45-65), on the Camino right before the Plaza Mayor, is a traditional inn that is also a wine lovers abode. If you wish to taste El Bierzo wines without leaving your hotel, this is the place to book. The vinoteca is a special wine bar on the grounds, stocked with some of the best of the regional vintages. Ask the owner to sample a few in a tasting, or pick one to savor slowly.

The family-run **Hostal Burbía** (Calle Fuente Cubero, 12; 987-542-667; www.hostalburbia.com; €35-45) treats guests like family from the moment they arrive, and go out of their way to assure a great stay in the hotel and the town. Set 300 meters (328 yards) off the Camino to the right, on a quiet side street running parallel with the Río Burbia, the *hostal*'s backyard faces the river and green hillside, which is enjoyed from restful, peaceful, and exemplary rooms.

Albergue Leo (Calle Ribadeo, 10; 987-542-658; www.albergueleo.com; 32 beds, €10; €2.5 breakfast; open Mar.-Nov.) is a traditional country house in the heart of town, restored in 2014 and run by *hospitaleras* María and Ángela, who will make you feel like a treasured family member. The seven high-ceilinged dorm rooms, kitchen, and bath facilities are exemplary. A fireplace and sweet-voiced guitar in the salon is a natural magnet for guests. The central location, on a quiet side street, is amazing for a traditional farmstead.

The enthusiastic *hospitaleros* and former piglrims from Madrid Livia and Unai opened **Albergue de la Piedra** (Calle Espiritu, 14; 987-540-260; www.alberguedelapiedra.com; Mar.-Nov.; €2; breakfast) in 2008. It stands at the other end of town, west toward Pereje, after you cross the Río Burbia and on the banks of the Río Valcarce; it's hard to miss for its bright yolk-yellow-orange stucco walls. Three floors house fresh, flawless, and spacious rooms: one dorm room with 10 very comfortable beds (€10), and four private rooms (€30). Rooms have large windows with full views of the surrounding mountains.

Getting There

The best way to reach Villafranca del Bierzo is by bus.

Car

Villafranca is in a narrow valley, with main access roads from Lugo and Ponferrada that connect to roads coming from Madrid, León, and A Coruña. Destinations farther east and north, such as Barcelona, Pamplona, Burgos, San Sebastian, Bilbao, Santander, and Oviedo, all approach Villafranca del Bierzo via León and Ponferrada.

From **León** (135 km/78 mi; 1.5 hours): Take either the **AP-71** (for efficiency) or the **N-120** (for scenic driving and frequent stopping on the Camino) west to Astorga, and continue on the **A-6** (efficiency) or the **LE-142** (scenic) to Ponferrada and continue to Villafranca del Bierzo.

From **Madrid** (416 km/258 mi; 4 hours): Exit northwest on the **AP-6** to Villafranca del Bierzo via Ponferrada.

From **A Coruña** (185 km/115 mi; 2 hours): Take the **AP-9** south, then the **A-6** southwest past Lugo to Villafranca del Bierzo.

Bus

ALSA (www.alsa.com) connects Villafranca del Bierzo from Madrid's Barajas Airport (two buses daily; 5 hours; €32) and Madrid's Estación Sur bus station (two daily; 6 hours; €32); from Santiago de Compostela (four daily; 4 hours; €21); from León (three daily; 2.5 hours; €11), Barcelona (one night bus daily; 13-14 hours; €62), and Santander (one daily; 9 hours; €37), among other cities and towns.

More locally, ALSA connects Ponferrada to Villafranca del Bierzo (nine daily in both directions; 30min.; €1.65).

There is no bus station in Villafranca del Bierzo, but the bus will drop you off in the center of town at the **Parque de la Alameda.** From there, walk toward the river Burbía and pick up the trail markers—arrows and scallop shells on walls, on the ground, and on posts—that will guide you onto the Camino at Calle Ribadeo and continue west out of town.

Bike

Though most prefer to walk, some pilgrims enjoy the option of renting a bike from **One Day Bike** (638-041-823; €20) in Villafranca del Bierzo to ride to the drop-off point in Las Herrerías (Km 162.4) and resume walking from there.

Leaving Villafranca

Scallop shells and arrows guide you to the bridge over the Burbía river westward on the 4.9 kilometers (3 miles) to the hamlet of Pereje. Much of the Camino from here to La Faba (Km 159.2) will run parallel to the N-VI. It is a less busy rural highway than the nearby A-6, and for most of it you will see little traffic, but still be careful at places where you need to cross the highway or walk very near its bank.

From Villafranca del Bierzo to Las Herrerías, you may see a roving **baker** in his van, selling bread from the back hatch, or a **Bibliobus,** a library on wheels, serving the village residents directly. This is one way the surrounding communities have resolved to keep their villages alive and its largely elderly population sustained in body and mind. Everyone is welcome to purchase bread from the bakery van, and it is a great way to meet the locals as well as to enjoy fresh-baked bread warm from the ovens.

Pereje   Km 177.2

The little town of Pereje (pop. 33) has existed since the early 12th century. There's little going on here today, but it is an option for food and lodging if you want to rest before covering the next 4.4 kilometers (2.7 miles) to Trabadelo.

Accommodations

There is a rural inn, **Las Coronas** (Calle Camino de Santiago, 44A; 987-540-138; four rooms; €36-56), on the right when you enter the town; it has seemed more run-down in recent years than it was when I first visited it in 2007, but the welcome is still warm and a decent bar offers refreshments and snacks (€3-10).

A few paces farther along, the municipal *albergue,* **Albergue de Peregrinos** (Calle Camino de Santiago, 61A; 987-542-670 or inquire at Las Coronas; €5), on the right, is in a refurbished traditional village home with wood-beamed

front porch. It features single beds, not bunk beds, in two reasonably roomy and handsome stone and wood dorm rooms housing a total of 30 people. You'll need to get food down at the village inn's bar, or bring your own to cook in the communal kitchen.

★ Trabadelo's Ancient Chestnut Forest   Km 173.8

One kilometer (0.6 miles) before reaching Trabadelo, the Camino passes between old chestnut trees lining both sides of the path, their branches criss-crossing overhead. Many trunks are so wide that if you hugged them, your arms would barely make it halfway around.

In autumn, locals gather chestnuts here, a practice that hunters and gathers have enacted for millennia and that local farmers and herders continue. Chestnuts in Iberia, France, and Italy have been called the "bread of the poor," because they have singlehandedly saved whole communities from starvation in bad winters. In addition to bread made from nut flour, locals make chestnut soups and varieties of sweets.

But this place is more than about sustenance: this forest also sustains the spirit with its tranquil beauty. I like to slow down here, listening to the wind through the leaves, taking in the dappled shade, pondering the twisting and massive trunks, smelling the nutty air, and gathering my own nuts to take into Trabadelo to roast.

Trabadelo   Km 172.8

Trabadelo (pop. 103) is a village whose livelihood is based on the Camino business and the lumber industry. A lumber mill takes up the middle of the village, but the operation carries on rather

Clockwise from top: El Bierzo region vineyards; chestnut forest just before Trabadelo; castle ruins at Vega de Valcarce; Albergue Ave Fénix, Villafranca del Bierzo.

quietly, so Trabadelo retains its sleepy, chilled-out feel. It is the home of several kind and engaging older women who act as the village guardians; they will offer local information to anyone who asks.

Trabadelo was here in the 9th century, since the first century of the Camino's existence. Signs of that past don't survive. Even the village church is firmly closed and has a more modern edifice. The attraction of Trabadelo is the slow-paced village life. Over the years, many pilgrims have passed through, a steady stream since at least AD 895.

Accommodations

Trabadelo has a few *albergues,* along with a roadside hotel for truckers and drivers, but my favorite by far is ★ **Hostal-Albergue Crispeta** (987-566-529; osarroxos@gmail.com, open all year, 32 beds in five dorm rooms, €8; five private rooms, €20-32) a complex of rooms, bar, and restaruant located on both sides of the Camino as you enter the village. One autumn when I arrived in Trabadelo, the owner of this *hostal* was making a big vat of quince jam over a single burner in her garden. For dessert that evening, as a part of an excellent *menú del peregrino,* I had her homemade *cuajada* (yogurt custard) with the just-made quince jam, still hot, on top. The *hostal* has clean, private rooms and equally spotless shared dorm rooms. The Pereje River runs past the back yard, and the only noise you'll hear at night is the river's musical burbling. The bar has a small dining room and serves a pilgrims' menu (€10) with such options as garlic soup with pimentón (smoked paprika), steak and salad, and that homemade cuajada with membrillo. Traditionally it is served with honey, a great alternative if it is not membrillo season. Some villagers keep beehives, so chances are that the honey is also local.

★ **Casa Susi** (located midway through Trabadelo, on the left; 683-278-778; www.facebook.com/alberguecasasusi; alberguecasasusi@gmail.com; April-Oct.; €5) is a small *albergue* run by the Australian-born Susi (Susan Swain, who is bilingual in Spanish and English) offering 12 single beds (not bunk beds) in one room and two full bathrooms. A home cooked communal meal is offered each evening (donation).

Leaving Trabadelo

Leaving Trabadelo, the Camino is well marked, never far from the N-VI road or the Valcarce river. In just under 4 kilometers (2.5 miles), you'll pass a roadside hotel on the right, **Hotel Valcarce** (Carretera N-VI, Salidas (Exits) 419-420; 987-543-180; www.valcarcehoteles.com; 50 rooms, €30-50 and up), that also has a full-service cafeteria serving good breakfasts and other meals (€5-12) and snacks and a small grocery section for local foods. Be very careful here; it is a rare time that you will have to cross the road with a lot of oncoming or exiting traffic (from the roadside hotel and the nearby A-6). Once across, the Camino veers slightly left, away from the A-6, and into and through the center of the village of La Portela de Valcarce.

La Portela de Valcarce Km 168.7

As you enter the tiny but quirky hamlet of La Portela de Valcarce (pop. 50), notice the prehistoric-looking stalks of collard greens growing in a raised garden plot on the right; they add a nice backdrop to a life-size stone sculpture of Santiago el Peregrino. About a dozen meters (40 feet) later, almost as you leave town, look for a resident's garden gate, decorated with plaster sculptures of an elderly farm couple with humorous facial gestures: a local artist's rendering of traditional Galician country folk. A friendly village dog is often in there to poke his head out through the fence posts, calmly inspecting every pilgrim who walks by. Calle Carretera National VI, a small road parallel to the N-VI, is the village's main street.

At the far end of town, on the left, the 17th-century village church, **Iglesia de San Juan Bautista** (Calle Carretera National VI, 10) is worth a visit (it's often open). A single room built of the native gray-white granite, the church is beautiful in its simplicity. The altar holds a statue of Saint James, while a side niche holds another of Mary and Child. The stone baptismal font has a seed of life, a six-petaled flower, painted on the intersection of the crucifix behind it; it's a symbol of harmony between heaven and earth, and a more ancient representation of Solomon's Seal, more popularly recognized today as the Star of David.

Ambasmestas   Km 167.5

Ambasmestas (pop. 43) in Castilian would translate to *mezcla de aguas*, "mix of waters," referring to the two rivers that converge here, the Valcarce and the Balboa. These two waterways provide an abundant water supply, explaining why the kitchen gardens are so robust. Carretera Antigua N-VI is the older, smaller frontage road off (and parallel to) the newer N-VI that passes through the village.

Ambasmestas is also a rare place where goats' cheese is produced, along with the ubiquitous cow's milk cheeses. About three-quarters of the way through Ambasmestas, look to your left for **Quesería Veigadarte** (Carretera Antigua N-VI, 6; 987-543-223; www.veigadarte. blogspot.com; 8:30am-7pm), the artisanal cheese maker and goat farm where you can buy the locally made goat's milk cheese from creamy and fresh to aged and cured to blends, such as with herbs, *membrillo* (quince jam), garlic and parseley, *pimentón* (Spanish paprika), and chestnuts (around €5 and up). If the gate is open, step in and knock on the door.

Vega de Valcarce
Km 166

The name describes what this village is: a fertile valley plain of the Valcarce river. Vega de Valcarce (pop. 205) has a dynamic village center with cafés, an array of lodging, and food shops. It is also the center of a recent Templar revival movement, centered on the castle ruin that you can see on the high hill on the left side of the village as you depart.

Sights
Iglesia de la Magdalena

In the village center, on the right, the 16th-century **Iglesia de la Magdalena** (Carretera Antigua N-VI, 17; 987-411-254; open daily during the day; free) is an oasis of cool and calm to step into if you wish to pause and meditate. You can also stamp your pilgrim's passport here; you'll find a stamp and pad set on a side table. While here, look for the simple decorative mark, over the keystone of the door to the left of the apse, of the three lines that form the goose footprint. It could just be decoration, but it looks intentional, and given that this village is a part of a Templar renaissance, it may signal a connection to the Game of the Goose and the Camino.

★ Castillo de Sarracín

The castle ruin on the high ridge over the village, known as Castillo de Sarracín, was possibly founded in the 9th century, though nobody knows by whom. (Perhaps it was the Lords of Sarracín, powerful landowners in the region.) In the 14th century, another castle was built over the older one, and the ruins you see when you look up at the ridge date to this era. That ridge is so sheer and narrow that the castle's position is strategic: Only one of its four sides can be reached without risking a steep drop off the slope of the rocky hill.

To visit the castle, start at the Iglesia

de la Magdalena, and with your back to the church, cross the road (N-VI Antigua, which is also the Camino) and take the LE-5101 (called here Calle Puente Nueva), perpendicular to the Camino and directly in front of you. Take it straight ahead to the Ayuntamiento (town hall, on the Plaza de Ayuntamiento) on your right. Follow the LE-5101 as it wraps to the right around the Ayuntamiento (still on your right) and heads southwest toward the hill on which the castle stands. From the LE-5101, and after approximately 700 meters (0.4 miles) from your starting point at the Iglesia de la Magdalena, you'll see a small footpath on the right side of the road that leads straight up to the castle ruins.

Given the steep climb, allow an hour for the round-trip hike, and another half-hour to enjoy the ruins of its intact outer walls, its half-standing (and half crumbled) inner walls, arched passageways, keep, and watchtower, and the surrounding views. You can visit the castle for free any time of day during the daylight hours—the path leads to an arched entrance with an iron gate that is unlocked during the day—but avoid climbing here when the light is low (before dawn and after dusk). Be sure to take in the view on all sides of the castle. To the north is the almond-sliver shape of Vega de Valcarce, tucked at the foot of the hill far below; to the south and west, appreciate the green mountains you are hiking into. If you bypass the climb, you can still see the castle from the valley floor by looking up to your left. But I strongly suggest making the climb to take in the full extent of this massive fortress in half-ruin.

One man is determined to restore the castle and bring its history to light. Hungarian Attila Otott Kovacs walked the Camino almost a decade ago and climbed to Castillo de Sarracín, where he had a profound mystical experience. This led him to relocate to Vega de Valcarce, where he has been raising funds to restore the medieval castle on the hill. He believes that Templars used the castle as a part of their protection and service to pilgrims on the Camino. Kovacs's plan is to fully restore the original castle while making it self-sufficient and eco-friendly. He hopes that creating an authentic experience where the past meets the present will inspire such work on other places of patrimony. He also hopes that, with its restoration, he can create special lodging for pilgrims, opening others to have their own experience with the castle.

To learn more about the efforts to restore the castle and turn it into an ecological pilgrim *albergue*, contact **The Camino Castle Project** (635-978-634; www.caminotemplarcastle.com).

Food and Accommodations

To your left on entering Vega de Valcarce, the house with the pumpkin cart in the entryway is **Casa Rural El Recanto** (987-543-202; open all year; €35-40), a rural inn as well as an on-the-premises bakery, set in a quiet and verdant edge of the village. The bakery, Panadería El Recanto, is reason enough to stop; it makes breads and pastries, but also good foods for lunch—empanadas, sandwiches, tortillas, crepes, salads, and hamburgers. Or you can decide to slip off your pack for the day and stay, the waft of fresh baking bread your only ordeal to overcome. The four immaculate rooms are each named after a different season and decorated with the colors of its namesake.

In the center of Vega de Valcarce, on the right, is the **Albergue La Magdalena** (Calle Carqueixeide, 2; 684-045-491; alberguelamagdalena@hotmail.com; Mar.-Nov.; eight beds and bunks in one dorm room, €9; four private rooms, €18-26), named after the village church and patroness, with full meal service in a modern stone and stucco village town home.

Leaving Vega de Valcarce

In 2.2 kilometers after Vega del Valcarce, on the narrow passage nearing the final climb to O Cebreiro, in the village of Ruitelan (Km 163.8; pop. 20), is one of the best cafés on the entire Camino. ★ **Bar Omega** (N-VI, Ruitelan; 987-543-040) is on the right as you enter the east end of the hamlet. Everything is made to order from fresh ingredients and done with energy and flair; the servings are generous. Even a simple order of tortilla Española—one serving being a half-circle rather than a mere wedge— is made with just-laid eggs and garden-plucked lettuce and tomatoes, all for €5.50. The outdoor seating faces a little garden; there's indoor seating as well. The setting, in the green valley near the Valcarce river, is as energizing as the food.

Las Herrerías   Km 162.4

Las Herrerías (pop. 39) is built along the banks of the Valcarce river. Operating a large iron forge near the river, people in Las Herrerías used to smelt iron ore (*hierro*) that was mined nearby. Today the village is a quiet getaway spot for vacationers, and the locals largely make their living from the pilgrim trade, as they did in the Middle Ages.

To reach the heart of town, cross the old bridge that is built in the Roman style but dates to the 15th century. On the other side, notice the pieces of cloth, string, and paper tied to the trees along the bank of the river. It's a ritual to tie an offering to the trees here, or to acknowledge and release something from your life as you continue to walk. While this is a millennia-old practice across Europe and Asia, here it is entirely a modern pilgrim ritual.

Food and Accommodations
Casa Rural El Capricho de Josana (Calle Camino de Santiago, s/n, Las Herrerías de Valcarce; 987-119-300; www.elcaprichodejosana.com; 13 rooms; €36-50), at the upper side of the slope at the entrance to Las Herrerías, before the

Camino descends toward the river, Río das Lamas, has a cozy roadside bar serving snacks and meals (€10-12) and also luxurious private rooms (bathrooms have soaking tubs) in a traditional stone and slate country home. The quality and warmth of the welcome have held since my first time here in 2007.

Set at the foot of the hill with horses and cows (and the occasional chicken) grazing nearby, **Casa-Albergue Lixa** (Calle Camino de Santiago, 35; 987-134-915; www.casalixa.com; open Mar.-Oct.; 30 beds in four dorm rooms, €11; five private rooms, €40-50) is an ancient village home, restored in 2016 as an *albergue* and rural inn run in a tranquil manner with pristine accommodations and food options for all preferences. If you've been craving a big, juicy, 100% beef hamburger, this is the place.

Leaving Las Herrerías
Las Herrerías is the last settlement before you begin the ascent to O Cebreiro, but there is food and lodging on the ascent. More than midway up is La Faba, in 3.2 kilometers (2 miles).

When you enter Las Herrerías, the Camino leads you to turn left off the N-006 and take the village road through and past the village, climbing up. Soon the Camino will fork off the road onto a narrow footpath directing you to La Faba; this is for foot traffic only (cyclists have to take the road, which continues to the right). The foot trail is a sublime but challenging hiking trail that ascends from here to O Cebreiro, passing through more dense and old chestnut forests.

La Faba   Km 159.2

The Camino enters up a steep slope and turns left to enter the village of La Faba (pop. 35) and passes through the center of the village, which after the climb can feel like a true oasis with its cool, narrow stone streets and sturdy granite and slate roof houses, all huddled together along the southwest face of the mountain. A welcoming village **café** is on the left in the center of the hamlet.

Sights
Iglesia de San Andrés

To see La Faba's church, **Iglesia de San Andrés** (Calle de la Iglesia, 1), rather than going left and continuing on the Camino when you enter town, go right toward the lower end of the village. San Andrés is a fairly modern church, reconstructed in the 18th century, but its bell tower gives it a pretty backdrop with the mountains all around and below it. There is a pilgrims' service here in the evenings. The popular **Albergue de Peregrinos** is right next to the church where you can inquire about visiting the church if it is closed.

To continue on the Camino toward O Cebreiro, return to the ascending and central village path through La Faba. The steep slope persists on the 4.9 kilometers (3 miles) remaining to O Cebreiro.

★ Mountaintop View

As you leave the village of La Faba, pause to take in the view. You are now leaving the tree line and passing through heather, brush, and pasture lands on the mountaintops. La Faba's Iglesia de San Andrés is nestled below the village, in a stand of trees, multicolored mountains rolling out beyond the bell tower beyond into the distant horizon. This is one of the best mountaintop views of the whole Camino, competing with those of the Pyrenees passing from Saint-Jean-Pied-de-Port to Roncesvalles, and just past Monte Irago approaching El Acebo.

Food and Accommodations

Consider staying at the German Friends of the Camino Association, **Albergue de Peregrinos de la Faba** (Calle de la Iglesia, s/n; 630-836-865; www.lafaba. weebly.com; open mid-Mar.-Oct.; 66 beds in three dorm rooms, €5; evening meal by donation), a favorite pilgrim's jaunt next to San Andrés church. It is an impeccably clean and well-organized place with a beautiful view to the valley below. They offer very basic cooking (vegetarian meals possible), and at times massage therapy is available.

Leaving La Faba

In a little over 2 kilometers (1.3 miles), you'll reach **Laguna de Castilla** (Km 156.8), the last hamlet before the final 3-kilometer (1.9-mile) climb to O Cebreiro. This is also the border between León and Galicia. Above the trees, the climb is all open, but the terrain is steep. At times the trail is narrow and cut deep into the mountainside, so that all you may see are the brush, grasses, and flowers growing along the trailside.

Right when you think the trail will never end, the granite rock face on your right gives way to a manmade wall of the same stone. You are at the outer reaches of the **Iglesia de Santa María** in O Cebreiro. Be sure to look over your shoulder, to the left, for yet another spectacular view of the mountains. It's worth returning to this spot at sunrise, to see the dawn's jewel-toned colors washing over the same vista.

O Cebreiro   Km 154.3

Arriving in O Cebreiro (pop. 30) after a steep and seemingly endless climb, you'll feel like you're on top of the world. O Cebreiro marks a final major threshold over the Cantabrian mountains. You've now also entered Galicia, the final autonomous community of the Camino.

Here, you'll see why Iron Age Iberians loved to build on high places, picking strategic lookout points for their fortresses called *castros*. O Cebreiro—the third highest peak on the Camino, at 1,330 meters (3,364 feet)—was very likely one such site, one that has

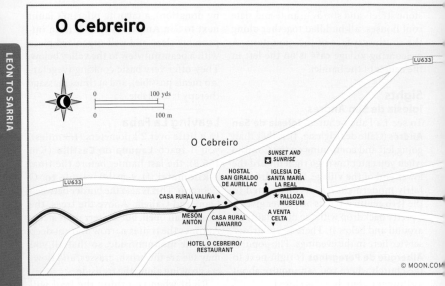

O Cebreiro

LU633

0   100 yds
0   100 m

O Cebreiro

SUNSET AND
SUNRISE

HOSTAL   IGLESIA DE
SAN GIRALDO   SANTA MARÍA
DE AURILLAC   LA REAL

LU633

CASA RURAL VALIÑA ●   ★ PALLOZA
                               MUSEUM

MESÓN   CASA RURAL   A VENTA
ANTÓN   NAVARRO   CELTA
                      ▼

HOTEL O CEBREIRO/
RESTAURANT

© MOON.COM

maintained the continuity of the *castro* architecture in its round stone houses with thatched roofs, known as *pallozas*. From the 9th century and onward, O Cebreiro was exclusively a settlement to support pilgrims on the Camino. Today, the only survivors from the Middle Ages are the continued style of palloza building and the excavated and reconstructed 9th-century church of Santa María, the first structure you see as you take your last steps on the climb up.

O Cebreiro thrives today thanks to the Camino; locals are welcoming and passionate about their village's legacy. Expect curiosity and engaging conversation, and perhaps a bit of flirtation. (Watch for the fellow who is always in one of the cafés with his wonderful wolf-like dog, who will try to convince you that the Camino's purpose is for finding a spouse; in the same breath, he might also tell you he's single.)

O Cebreiro is also known for a miracle that took place in the Iglesia de Santa María la Real, when a priest is said to have turned bread and wine into actual blood and flesh. This miracle made O Cebreiro famous across medieval Europe

and brought pilgrims flocking to behold the sacred chalice, known by some as the Holy Grail, that held the holy blood. This miracle inspired Richard Wagner to set his opera, *Parsifal*, here; it also inspires the very real **Asociación Santo Grial,** composed of locals, many in business in O Cebreiro, who are proud of being a part of the Camino and serving pilgrims on this mystical mountain. You'll see their name all around town.

Sights

Top Experience

★ Sunset and Sunrise

For such a small place, O Cebreiro has a lot to enjoy, the most important being its natural setting, perched on the precipice of some of the Camino's most spectacular views: be sure to take in the sunrise to the east and the sunset to the west. Both are easily done as the village is compact, round, and huddled with views all around, but here are some prime spots:

The ideal spot for the sunrise is the **stone wall** that lines the road and parking lot facing east and to your left when you

Top: Mountain view from above La Faba hamlet. Bottom: Iglesia de Santa María la Real, O Cebreiro.

first arrive and are about to enter into the village on the Camino (before the Palloza Museum and the church). The wall is a splendid place to sit, dangling your legs over the steep eastern slope, and watch the sun rise over the mountains.

There are two ideal spots for the sunset. For a more solitary experience, head to the lower west side of the village, just below where the lowest and westernmost palloza stands (to your right, in the center of town, when you arrive on the Camino). There is a small public **garden** space on the west-facing slope that's a good sunset spot. The more social option is to grab a seat and drink at the one stone picnic table in front of **Mesón Antón**, in the center of the village. Face west and let nature take over. Antón gives out little snacks to go with the drinks, and his picnic bench is often the main hub of pilgrim life just before dinnertime, making the sunset a gregarious affair.

Iglesia de Santa María la Real

The first structure you see as you take your last steps on the climb up is the **Iglesia de Santa María la Real,** possibly the oldest surviving church on the Camino, with foundations that date to around the 830s and which were excavated in the 1960s and 1970s. The walls, nave, apse, and tower of the old church were faithfully reconstructed to the early medieval plan. The baptismal font is from the 9th or 10th century, and the chalice and paten are from the 12th, as is the Romanesque sculpture of Mary. This medieval sculpture is a highlight for its intimately carved facial gestures and details in the clothing.

This is the site of a famous miracle, and some consider it a powerful place. The story begins in the late 13th or early 14th century. A dangerous snowstorm kept most worshippers from coming to mass, but one devout man climbed up the steep mountain from the village of Barxamajor. (If you've just climbed up the mountain yourself, you can appreciate this villager's dedication.) The priest

was surprised, as he was only half-heartedly celebrating the Eucharist and doubting its miracle of transforming wine to blood and bread to flesh. But the peasant's dedication made him carry on. To his utter surprise, as he raised the chalice and held up the bread, the wine turned into thick red blood and the bread into actual flesh.

That cup, a beautiful work of 12th-century Romanesque metalwork that some refer to as the Holy Grail, is on display in the church, along with vials of the blood and the paten used in the Eucharist miracle. The wooden sculpture of Mary, also still in the church, turned her head to get a better look at the miracle, and hence is called *La Virgen del Milagro,* the Virgin of the Miracle.

The tomb of the 20th-century parish priest and Camino maverick, Elías Valiña Sampedro, is on the left side of the nave. It is he who mapped out the historic route, endeavoring to trace the original medieval pathway of the Camino Francés. He wrote the first modern guide to the Camino, *The Pilgrim's Guide to the Camino de Santiago,* and laid the foundation for all subsequent guides and trail restoration efforts.

Look also for the postcards sold at the church entrance by artist Miguel Castellanos Sotos, showing the image of Mary with psychedelic auras and chakras associated with the icon and place.

The parish priest holds daily evening **mass**, typically at 7pm. The feast days, celebrating the Lady of the Snows, are September 8 and 9. You can get your pilgrim passport stamped here with the 12th-century image of O Cebreiro's Santa María.

Palloza Museum

Across from Iglesia de Santa María la Real is a *palloza* (traditional round thatched home), the first you'll see in O Cebreiro. These oval structures with conical thatched roofs slope low to the ground to endure high winds and heavy snow fall, and to create an easy-to-warm interior. The inside was typically divided into two halves, one side where the animals were sheltered at night, and the other where the people cooked and ate and then climbed to a second-story loft to sleep. This was a symbiotic system, where animals and people kept each other safe and warm.

O Cebreiro's *pallozas* are not inhabited today, but you can see inside this one, which is one of four that comprises O Cebreiro's **Xan López Palloza-Museo** museum complex (982-367-053; www.museos.xunta.gal/en/cebreiro, mid-June to mid Sept., Tues.-Sat., 11am-6pm; mid.-Sept-mid-June, Tues.-Sat., 8:30am-2:30pm; free). It contains the main displays, including traditional tools of life in dairy country, such as a stone trough, an iron cauldron on the hearth, wood furnishings, agricultural implements, and spinning and weaving tools.

The complex's three other *pallozas* are located to your right as you pass into the center of the village on the one main street. These have varied access, one being used as a storage space and the other two opened upon request to show examples of traditional domestic life.

Food

O Cebreiro endures harsh winters, given its altitude and exposure, and makes an especially hearty version of that warming, tasty Galician comfort food, *caldo gallego.* Each inn here prides itself on its own house recipe for this stew of collard greens, beans, potatoes, and pork. Almost all the places to eat in O Cebreiro are also classic country inns, serving their own variations on the *menú del peregrino.*

The restaurant and bar of the **Hotel O Cebreiro** (982-367-182; www.hotelcebreiro.com; lunch/dinner €10-14, breakfast €4), just down the lane in front of the church, is a favorite gathering place, and has a cozy wrap-around dining area where pilgrims can join tables or find a table for two with some privacy. The family that runs this inn and restaurant is industrious and energetic, and many of the dishes are homemade. Don't be surprised if you see two women of the family seated amiably during a slow spell, peeling chestnuts gathered from the forest. Try the local cheese if it is offered on the dessert list.

A Venta Celta (O Cebreiro, 21; 982-367-137; ventacelta@hotmail.com) is popular for its pilgrim menu (€10), which typically offers vegetable and meat stew, pork chops, *caldo gallego,* and two types of salad. If the owner is not serving dinner, she still has on hand her homemade *caldo gallego.* A Venta Celta is also well known for its *pulpo a feira*—paprika- and sea salt-seasoned octopus. Daily specials are prepared from scratch and served in a large dining area with thick timber beams overhead, strung with bundles of dried herbs and garlic. Many come here for a fortifying breakfast (€3-4) before pressing onward onto the trail.

In the heart of the village, **Mesón Antón** (982-151-336) is the supreme place to enjoy a drink before dinner. Grab a seat at the thick wooden table outside to enjoy both the camaraderie of other pilgrims and to watch the sun set over the curved thatched roofs of the neighboring *palloza.*

Accommodations

All the listings are open year-round. Other than the municipal *albergue* at the end of town, all the listings here are found clustered along the single road through the village, **Rúa Cebreiro,** have no address numbers, and are centrally located; look for the names posted on the entrances as you walk through the village, which will take you no more than two minutes at a leisurely saunter.

Casa Rural Valiña (982-367-125 and 982-367-182; €40-50) is named after the village's parish priest who is the celebrated modern-day reviver of the Camino. It has five snug rooms with bath, and is appropriately right across from the church where Valiña held mass and

Os Ancares Cheese Festival

Coinciding with Semana Santa (holy week, the week leading up to and including Easter Sunday) each year, the region surrounding O Cebreiro holds a cheese festival (Fiera do Quexo do Cebreiro in Galego, and Feria de Queso del Cebreiro in Castilian) that celebrates the protected denomination-of-origin cheese (*queso con Denominación de Origen Protegida*) known as **D.O.P. Os Ancares**. It is made from the unique cow's milk from regional *vacas rubias* (a Galician cattle breed) and benefits from the hillside grazing ecology of this mountain territory.

Each year the festival is held in one of three locations: Pedrafita do Cebreiro (4 km/2.5 mi northeast of O Cebreiro via LU-633), Triacastela, and As Nogais (18.5 km/11.5 mi north of O Cebreiro, via the LU-633 and A-6). If you are in this area around Semana Santa, ask in O Cebreiro or Triacastela for the year's festival location.

This is not only a chance to sample the cheese from many local makers, but also to taste local breads, sausages, and varieties of pastries, and to enjoy local song, folkloric dance, and a midday (meaning around 2pm in Spain) festive meal. For more information call 982-367-103 or visit the Facebook page for *Feira Do Queixo Do Cebreiro*, which is in Gallego, but the dates and times are easy to pick out.

If you can't make the cheese festival but want to try the cheeses, ask at any of the inns in O Cebreiro, such as the **Hotel O Cebreiro,** either to have the cheese for dessert after dinner, or a tapa at the bar. This will light up the owner's face and probably initiate a passionate gourmet discussion, including what wine to pair with the excellent cheese.

prayer services (when not on the Camino painting yellow arrows on the trail from Navarra to Galicia).

Next door, and also next to the church, is **Casa Rural Navarro** (www.casaturismoruralnavarro.com; four rooms; €30-40), with walls painted with warm, saturated earth tones. The rooms and bathrooms are pristine (though some of the bathrooms are a bit small).

The **Hostal San Giraldo de Aurillac** (982-367-182; www.hotelcebreiro.com; six rooms; €45 single/€60 double), just in front of the church as you take the main street through town, derives its name from the Benedictine monks of San Giraldo d'Aurillac from south-central France, who were given O Cebreiro to build up and support pilgrims in the late 11th century. This building was restored in 1965. Warm stone walls, crafted woodwork, and immaculate rooms make for a restful and homey stay.

By the same management as San Giraldo, and in the same compound, is the **Hotel O Cebreiro** (five rooms; €45 single/€60 double). It is located in the old town jail and town hall, which was restored in 2002 to accommodate the growing popularity of the Camino. Both *hostal* and hotel have comfortable, inn-style private rooms with thick stone walls and traditional wooden furniture, including some rooms with wood headboards featuring carved scallop shells.

The comfortable and well-priced **A Venta Celta** (O Cebreiro, 21; 982-367-137; ventacelta@hotmail.com; five rooms; €30 single/€40 double) has basic rooms with private bath, thick granite walls, and beds strewn with warm blankets and bedspreads. The rooms are accessed around the back of the café and restaurant run by the same owner. A traditional well with a cast-iron Celtic-style disk marks the base of the exterior stone stairs that lead up to the rooms.

The centrally located and privately run **Albergue Casa Campelo** (679-678-458 and 982-179-317; casacampelo@outlook.com) is the only other *albergue* in O Cebreiro after the municipal one (below), but offers private rooms as well. There is one dorm room with 10 beds for €12, and there are four private rooms for €45.

Casa Rural Carolo (982-367-168; €40-48), right across from Casa Campelo, has 10 small, clean, and straightforward rooms.

The clean and basic municipal **Albergue de Peregrinos** (660-396-809; two rooms with bunk beds, 106 beds; €6), is at the end of the village, to your left, as the Camino exits through the center to the wooded trail beyond.

Getting There and Around
Car
From **Lugo** (70 km/43 mi; 1 hour): Take **N-VI** southeast to Pedrafita do Cebreiro and then exit onto **LU-633** south for the remaining 4 kilometers (2.5 miles) to O Cebreiro.

From **Ponferrada** (53 km/33 mi; 1 hour): Head west on **A-6** (or on **N-VI**, a smaller, more tranquil rural highway that runs parallel with the larger A-6). Exit onto **LU-633** at Pedrafita do Cebreiro, heading south 4 kilometers (2.5 miles) to O Cebreiro.

From **Bilbao** (486 km/302 mi; 5 hours): Exit south on **AP-68**; take **A-1** at Miranda de Ebro, heading southwest to Burgos; take **A-1/BU-30** to **A-231** just west of Burgos, all the way to the south of León; exit onto **AP-71** at Virgen del Camino (7 km/4.3 mi past León); near Astorga stay on the AP-71, which becomes A-6. Head west on **A-6** to Pedrafita do Cebreiro; exit onto the **LU-633,** heading south 4 kilometers (2.5 miles) to O Cebreiro.

From **Santander** (420 km/261 mi; 4.5 hours): Head south on **A-67** to Osorno; exit onto **A-231** heading west to Virgen del Camino, and then exit onto **AP-71** continuing west and merging with **A-6** near Astorga. Take it to Pedrafita do Cebreiro and exit onto the **LU-633** to O Cebreiro.

From **A Coruña** (162 km/101 mi; 2 hours): Exit south on **AC-11** which becomes **AP-9** and then **E-70/A-6** to Lugo; stay on the **A-6** to Pedrafita do Cebreiro and exit south on **LU-633** to O Cebreiro.

Bus
ALSA (www.alsa.es) offers many options to get to **Pedrafita do Cebreiro,** 4 kilometers (2.5 miles) north of the village of O Cebreiro and the closest bus stop. From Madrid's airport (two buses daily; 6 hours, €34); Madrid's Estación Sur (two daily; 6 hours, €34); Leon (two daily; 2.5-3 hours, €12); Ponferrada (four daily; 40 minutes, €4); Lugo (five daily; 50 minutes, €6); and Santiago de Compostela (four daily; 3.5 hours, €19).

There is no bus station in Pedrafita do Cebreiro, just a stop, on Avenida de Castilla and the Plaza de España, right in front of the town hall. From Pedrafita do Cebreiro, you will need to get a cab (€7-10, 10 minutes) to O Cebreiro.

Train
RENFE (www.renfe.es) does not go to O Cebreiro. The nearest train stop is in Ponferrada.

Taxi
Taxi Ana Belén (670-681-832) offers services throughout Lugo province. You can also call **Taxi Fermín Gómez Diaz** (609-674-303), **Taxi Pepines** (982-367-165), or **Taxi Rubio** (626-587-796).

Liñares   Km 151

This hamlet (pop. 48)—named after the local flax fields grown here in the Middle Ages to make linen—restored and maintains the **church of San Esteban** (a few steps off to the left of the Camino in the village center), founded in AD 1120. A resident unlocks it in the morning and keeps it open throughout the day. Many other villages ahead of you—Hospital da Condesa (Km 148.5), Padornelo, Fonfría, and Biduedo (Km 139.7)—have historic village chapels that also mark out the medieval Camino, but these are rarely open to show their treasures. Many of these churches also incurred the wrath of time but have been restored, some holding small aspects of their medieval form but mostly taking on more recent aesthetics. At San Esteban you can enjoy this intimate sacred space restored to its medieval style, with its single nave, handful of simple pews, altar with Saint Stephen and Mother and Child, and an altar with a sculpture of Saint James off to the side, near where you can stamp your pilgrim's credential. Two ancient baptismal fonts stand to your left and right as you enter.

Accommodations and Food

Just before the church of San Esteban, you will pass **Casa Jaime** (982-367-166; meals, €3-10; four rooms, €40) as you enter the village, on your left. At this all-in-one stop, you can get meals, snacks, drinks, groceries, toiletries, other trekking supplies, and if desired, a clean private room for the night.

Leaving Liñares

Soon after Liñares, you arrive at the **Alto San Roque** (Km 149.9), one of the higher altitude points, reached with a gradual and comfortable ascent to 1,270 meters (4,167 feet) and with a tremendous view. Named after a hermitage to San Roque that no longer exists, today it is marked with a modern bronze sculpture of Saint James the Pilgrim walking with determination into the wind, a constant companion at this height.

Notice also the growing prevalence of outcroppings of stark white quartz. It is so common in the region that many of the stone walls use the white quartz as capstones or vertical fences to add beauty.

Hospital de la Condesa   Km 148.5

With 42 people living here today, nothing indicates that this was once a destination, starting in the 9th century (with the building of a substantial pilgrims' hospital) and throughout the Middle Ages. But pilgrims still get a special welcome from amicable villagers. Chickens and

roosters, who wander freely about town, pick up the slack when humans aren't around to greet you, making the place feel like a peaceable kingdom. The village church was built in 1963, replacing an earlier one from 1130, but manages to feel older with its thick local gray-white stone walls and traditional bell tower.

Accommodations and Food

To the right as you enter the village, **Albergue de Hospital da Condesa** (Hospital da Condesa, 11, 982-161-336 or 660-396-810) is the municipal *albergue,* plain but neat and in good repair, open all year, and with 18 beds (€6) in two dorm rooms.

A few paces farther, in the center of Hospital and also on the right side, **Mesón O Tear** (Hospital da Condesa, 14 982-367-183) is a traditional village house, with two private rooms rented out for €30. The dining room has an antique hand loom that recalls this area's flax production for linen textiles. A copious *menú de peregrino* (€10) may at times include a traditional *cocido,* pot au feu-style stew. They may open only on weekends in the late autumn to early spring, but are open every day in the summer.

Leaving Hospital de la Condesa

Soon after Hospital, the trail begins one final ascent, which can get fairly steep as you approach and pass up and through **Padornelo** (Km 146, pop. 10). It is also beautiful, on a narrow country lane, at times flanked by deep hedgerows.

Iglesia de San Oxan, in the center of Padornelo, dates to the 15th century and is dedicated to Saint John after the order that protected this section of the Camino, the Hospitallers of San Juan de Jerusalén. Its name, Oxan, curiously mirrors the Armenian name for John, Ohan. (The "x" in Gallego is pronounced like the "j" in Castilian and the "h" in English.)

The **cemetery** you pass upon leaving this small hamlet marks the spot where once upon a time a medieval hospice and a church dedicated to Santa María la Magdalena once stood. The next 500 meters (1,640 feet) is steep but short, and soon after leaving Padornelo you arrive at the final peak of the Camino, the Alto do Poio. The trail emerges and levels out right at the terrace of Bar Puerto: Welcome to Alto do Poio.

Alto do Poio   Km 145.6

Alto do Poio (pop. 12) stands today as a lookout point more than a settlement. At 1,337 meters (4,386 feet) this is really the third highest point on the Camino, beating O Cebreiro out by 7 meters (30 feet), but O Cebreiro still gets this honor for its dramatic location. (It's almost all downhill from here!) Alto do Poio was once also under the protection of the Hospitallers of San Juan de Jerusalén Today, no sign of the medieval hermitage that once stood here survives, except the small church dedicated to Santa María la Magdalena del Poyo. In modern times, new angels of the Camino oversee this remote spot and cater to pilgrims' needs: Not only will you find a well-earned view, but also the Bar Puerto, an excellent place to stop and rest and enjoy refreshments or a meal.

accommodation and Food

Bar Puerto (Alto do Poio, 2; 982-367-172; €2.50-6) offers a bar with a roaring fire and an outdoor terrace with a view of mountains all around. A cold drink and sandwich in the sunshine can refresh a summer hike, and in autumn to spring, an ample bowl of the thick homemade stew, *caldo gallego*, can warm and refuel by the fireplace. Open all year. Bar Puerto also runs an *albergue,* one bunkhouse with 18 beds (€6).

More comfortable accommodation is across the small road from Bar Puerto, at the homey **Hostal Santa María do Poio** (Alto do Poio, 15; 982-367-167; www.pensionsantamariadopoio.com), with 16 beds in two shared dorm rooms (€9) or 14 restful double rooms with bath (€30-40). The **restaurant** on the ground floor specializes in roasted leg of lamb, sautéed collard greens and bacon, and local cheese and honey. You can buy local products from the little store they run here as well. The proprietors speak some English.

Fonfría   Km 142.2

From the Latin *fons frigida*, cold fountain, Fonfría (pop. 45) is the site of an excellent cold water fountain but also of a human legacy: a lady who for at least two decades has been selling homemade crepes from her front stoop. Seeing her is hit or miss—whenever she feels like making and selling crepes—but if she is in the mood, you'll find her on the Camino as it passes through Fonfría, offering her goods. She does expect a donation, and other pilgrims have learned that anything less than €1-2 is not enough.

In the Middle Ages, Fonfría was known to guarantee pilgrims who stayed here a warm fire, salt, water, and beds with two blankets—coveted staples then as now. Sick pilgrims were also allotted an egg, bacon, and bread. The monastery and hospice that once stood here are no more, but the restored 16th-century church, **Iglesia de San Juan** (San Xoán in Gallego), is to your left as you leave the village. Though rarely open, you can still glimpse inside through openings in the church door and see the simple but sweet chapel with Saint John the Baptist holding the altar center.

Food and Accommodations

This small village has three *casas rurales* (rural hotels), and a celebrated pilgrims' **Albergue A Reboleira** (Calle Camino de Santiago, 15; 982-181-271; www.albergueareboleira.blogspot.com; open only Mar.-Oct.) appreciated for its location, warm welcome, capable management,

and good pilgrims' evening meal (€9). It can house up to 70 pilgrims in four dormitory rooms (€8) and also has eight private rooms (€32 single/€40 double). The bunk beds are great, built from thick log posts and rustic wood frames. It also serves breakfast (€3) and has a good bar where you can buy provisions and taste locally made cheeses.

Pensión Casa Lucas (Fonfría, 25; 690-346-740; www.casadelucas.es; three rooms; €37-55) also has a café and bar with a dining room (with meal service) and wood-burning fireplace. All the rooms are immaculate and pleasant, but try to get the room with the exposed stone walls for the added beauty and the feeling of sleeping in a traditional country home in Galicia. The owners love to encourage all pilgrims, whether staying the night or passing through, to warm themselves around the fire and rest.

Leaving Fonfría

From here to Triacastela you will make a dramatic descent from high altitudes into lush and forested valleys. All along, notice the hillside fields marked off with stone boundaries, defining the grazing pastures for the region's celebrated dairy cows. You can request and sample locally made cheeses (called *queixo de Cebreiro*) in local establishments.

Biduedo   Km 139.7

This hamlet (pop. 29) possesses what is considered the **tiniest chapel on the whole Camino,** which is barely wide enough to fit two people standing with arms extended side by side. It is a soulful work of rural sacred architecture, with multicolored stone and a thick, beautifully arched doorway formed by laying

From top to bottom: the tiny village chapel, Capilla de Biduedo; Mesón Betularia, Biduedo; Statue of Santiago on the bell tower of Triacastela's Iglesia de Santiago.

flat stones in a fanning pattern that looks like sun rays forming an arc. It is greatly loved by the village, as evidenced in the surrounding earthy garden and the character-rich collection of statuary and vases of flowers on the altar inside.

Food and Accommodations

Biduedo also has a great place to rest, have a meal, or even lodge if you've had it for the day and wish to stop. Uphill on the left of the Camino as you enter the village and across the street from the tiny chapel is **Mesón Betularia** (982-187-299), which cooks a variety of omelets to order, as well as salads, full meals (€10), or sandwiches (€3.50-7). They also manage a rural inn next door, **Casa Quiroga** with nine rooms (€35) that you can inquire about in the bar of Mesón Betularía. Enjoy the mountain view sloping down from the inn from the dining tables on the slate porch.

Leaving Biduedo

As you approach the village of **Fillobal** (Km 136.8; pop. 11), look to your right and locate the quarry in the valley below, where stone has been cut since the Middle Ages. That quarry stands near the ancient cave site of **Cova Eirós**, where recent excavations have unearthed Neandertal stone tools, processed animal bone remains, and early cave paintings. This makes it clear that ancient humans, first Neandertals and later Homo sapiens, long ago discovered this as a great place to live. Locals in Triacastela are very proud of this deep ancestry. Cova Eirós is closed to the public, but visualizing its early inhabitants—some of the first human residents of this corner of Europe—is inspiring.

Less than 1 kilometer (0.6 miles) before Triacastela, passing through the chestnut and oak forest nestled in the valley, the little hamlet of **Ramil de Triacastela** (Km 134) harbors an **over 200-year-old chestnut tree** in its center. It is one of many sacred trees on the route (the cypress at Samos being another), most of which grow near churches, except this one. It is so large that it would take 3-4 people standing fingertip to fingertip to embrace the whole tree. As you pass by, you might stop and greet the tree. Doing so will add to your good luck and blessings, or so the lore of the Camino goes.

Triacastela   Km 133.3

As you pass through the tree-lined path into Triacastela (pop. 658), the first thing you'll see is the church bell tower surrounded by the town cemetery and vast countryside. It is a long, green town, formed by the serpent shape of the passing Camino, with all its support services on the main road or not too far off. The rest is untroubled countryside with grazing horses, caramel-colored dairy cows, and the occasional cat keeping the field mice in check. You can see why the people who live here and serve the pilgrims are content: the stresses of the modern age seem as though they haven't arrived.

The town dates back to the 9th century, and its name comes from three castles that once stood here, very briefly, in the 10th century. No sign of them remains, except for the town name, its shield, and the engravings of three castles carved into the church's bell tower.

According to the *Codex Calixtinus,* pilgrims passing through Triacastela each received a piece of limestone—less common in other regions of Galicia but plentiful here—which they carried for 88 kilometers (55 miles) to Castañeda, just east of Arzúa. There, kilns turned the limestone to lime for mortar in the building of Santiago de Compostela's cathedral. It was a clever way of riding on free labor—perhaps with promises of salvation and penance—and also gave pilgrims a chance to feel more invested in the holy destination at which they had spent weeks of hardship to arrive.

Sights
Iglesia de Santiago

Triacastela's church, set in the middle of the town's cemetery, is a mix of its 12th-century Romanesque foundations—the apse is all that survives—and largely 18th-century Baroque reconstructions. The interior is a simple single nave and the altar holds a retable with a sculpture of Saint James as a pilgrim in the center. It is a sweet place to sit and meditate or contemplate the day. The welcoming parish priest holds **mass** here at 6pm daily.

Food

Expect basic but good standard fare in the form of *menú del peregrino* and snacks and sandwiches in Tricastela's eateries, which are entirely geared to the pilgrimage.

At **Complejo Xacobeo** (Rúa Santiago, 12; 982-548-037; www.complejoxacobeo), you can order tapas a la carte (€2-7), or go with a combined plate (salad, fries, and grilled meats or an egg dish; €5-6), or go with the tried and true *menú del peregrino,* which is also their *menú del dia* (choices include three types of salads, grilled salmon or trout, green beans with potatoes, fish soup or *caldo gallego,* €10). Dishes are traditional rustic Galician cuisine, including homemade desserts.

Bar O Peregrino (Rúa do Peregrino, 8; 626-434-600; wwwcomerentriacastela.com), across from the Albergue de Triacastela, is a great place to hang out and relax and enjoy the evening (or midday) menu (€10) in a colorful contemporary dining area, or out on the terrace with a full view of the valley and hills surrounding Triacastela. The selection isn't too innovative, but the dishes are fresh, tasty, and well-prepared, especially the house-made *caldo gallego.*

Bar Restaurante Esther (Avenida Castilla, 15; 982-548-455; €6.50-10), in the center of town, has informal and roomy seating both inside and out on the terrace. In addition to a decent *menú de peregrino* with more choices than the norm, they also prepare combined platters. Try the wonderful spicy baked egg dish, *huevos a la cazuela,* or the Creole chorizo.

There are two small **grocery stores** in town.

Accommodations

Unless otherwise noted, all the accommodations are open year-round.

Triacastela has some seven *albergues* and six hostels, most of which line the main street through town. My favorite is the ★ **Albergue Atrio** (Calle Peregrino, 1-3; 982-548-488; www.albergue-atrio.negocio.site; 20 dorm beds, €9 each; three private rooms, €40-45), run by a dedicated couple who restored two village farmhouses and joined them into one, preserving and accentuating the high, timbered ceilings and thick stone walls. Large windows let in sunlight, the dormitories are spacious, and the lockers come with keys. Immaculate men and women's bathrooms, a communal kitchen, and a garden with pond and clothes-washing area further enhance the place. Atrio offers breakfast (€4) but no other meals.

Pensión-Albergue Lemos (Avenida Castilla, 24; 677-117-238; www.pension-alberguelemos.com) is new (opened in 2016) and squeaky clean. The buildings, rooms, and facilities are in top condition and aimed toward utilitarian function as well as comfort. The pension has 10 private rooms (€35-40) and one bunkhouse with 12 beds (€9).

Casa David (Avenida Camilo José Cela, 8; 982-548-144; www.casadavidtriacastela.com; seven rooms; €35-50) has a hidden enclosed garden in back that you can't see from the street; it is really appealing, sweeping into the sloping countryside beyond. But the interior is also an oasis of comfort, a traditional stone home with plush and restful beds. The bar on the first floor serves a good continental breakfast (€5) and is open all day and evening for drinks, snacks, and meals. Open all year except on Christmas.

Casa Olga (Rúa do Castro, 2; 982-548-134; www.casaolga.net; four rooms; €38-55) is a family house a few dozen meters from the center of town, not much but enough to give it its own peaceful, rural setting. The four rooms are unadorned, restful, and quiet.

Leaving Triacastela

There are two paths to Sarria from Triacastela, and both are lovely. If you stay on the route that passes through San Xil, considered the original medieval Camino, you will be treated to tiny, lyrical, fairyland-like hamlets with little chapels, one after the other, strung along the lush valleys of ancient chestnut forests covered in moss and ferns. If you detour to Samos, you will enjoy similar valley villages (though far fewer), but you will also have the chance to visit one of the oldest still active monasteries in Spain, with the option to stay in the monastery's *albergue*.

As you exit Triacastela, if you desire to go toward **San Xil,** follow the yellow arrows to the right. Though there will be seasonal places open along the way, the next guaranteed place for food and water is in **Furela** in 9.6 kilometers (6 miles) so it is a good idea to stock up on food and water in Triacastela, just in case.

If you wish to visit **Samos,** follow the yellow arrows to the left. The road parallels the Río Oribio to **San Cristovo do Real** (also spelled San Cristobo) in 4.3 kilometers (2.7 miles). The trail turns off the LU-633 to the right in San Cristovo. After San Cristovo, continue on the trail, which ambles through a lush tree-covered river valley to **Lastires** (in 2.5 km/1.6 mi) and then **Samos** (another 3.5 km/2.2 mi). The Samos detour will add 6.4 kilometers (4 miles) to the trek to Sarria. If you take this detour, there are even fewer reliable places for food and drink until Samos, 10.3 kilometers (6.4 miles) away, so it is also a good idea to plan to hike to Samos with food and water fully stocked.

◈ Detour: Samos
Km 122.8

Samos (pop. 190) is a warm, full-service village with all amenities. Its highlights are the monastery, the venerable 1,000-year-old cypress tree on the monastery grounds, and the surviving 10th-century Mozarabic chapel of San Salvador, 200 meters (656 feet) from the monastery. Every October, Samos holds a chestnut festival, **Fiesta de la Castaña,** a chance to try all the soups, breads, pastries, candies, and preserves made with the native nut.

Sights
Monasterio de San Julián de Samos
Founded in the 6th century, the **Monasterio de Samos** (982-546-046; www.abadiadesamos.com; visits Monday-Saturday, five per day; Sunday and holidays, three visits per day; €4) came under Benedictine control by the 10th century, as it has remained to the present with some dozen brothers still in residence. Most of what you see is from the rebuilding of the monastery, after fires and raids, in the 16th-18th centuries. Another fire destroyed significant parts of the monastery in 1951. But despite the more modern structures, the ancient feel of one of Spain's oldest active monasteries comes through the walls and the hidden valley surroundings.

The brothers perform the daily cycles of sacred prayer at 7am (**Matins**), 8:30am (**Lauds** and **mass**), 1:45pm (**Sext**), 4pm (**None**), 7:30pm (**Vespers**), and 10pm (**Compline**). In between they work, take meals, have times of rest and recreation, and share spiritual discourse. If you stay in Samos overnight, one option being right here in the monastery, you can join the brothers for Vespers.

Allow 30-45 minutes to tour the monastery, led by one of the Benedictine brothers. Part of the guided tour will take you through the chapel and the cloister, including up to the second floor where a series of frescoes, painted in 1963 by Enrique Navarro, depict the life of Saint Benedict, founder of the Benedictine order.

Another interesting aspect of the monastery grounds, and its oldest surviving remains, is its Pre-Romanesque Mozarabic chapel, called both the **Capilla del Ciprés** and also the **Capilla del Salvador**, from the late 9th century. It's just a little older than the 25-meter (82-foot) tall, 1,000-year-old **cypress** leaning into its wall. The chapel and tree are 200 meters (656 feet) from the monastery and make for a serene amble across the monastery grounds. The cypress has been designated one of 50 notable trees in Spain given its age and sacred setting.

Food

Travelers appreciate **Hotel-Restaurante A Veiga** (Avenida Compostela, 6; www.hotelaveiga; 982-546-252; €23-30) for its traditional but innovative Galician cuisine and extensive menu, modified daily depending on available fresh ingredients. Deviating from the usual *menú del peregrino* that often is the only option on the Camino in places this small, they offer a large a la carte menu, which includes such dishes as *crema de calabacín* (pumpkin soup), *sopa de pescado* (fish soup), *alubias con almejas* (clams with white beans), and *lubina con pimientos* (sea bass with peppers). A Veiga also offers a decadent array of 31 desserts (typically €3), many homemade, including fresh strawberries with cream, *freixos* (crepes), and coffee *orujo* cake.

Right across from the monastery, **Restaurante Albaroque** (Calle San Salvador, 1; 982-546-087; €10-15) is the place to sample fresh-harvested Galicia-style scallops (grilled with olive oil and good sea salt), symbol of the Camino. But

also try the *revuelto de alga's y erizo* (sea urchin and algae egg scramble), *pulpo á feira,* and steamed mussels. This is also the location of the village bar, drawing colorful characters.

Accommodations

You can stay in the **Albergue de Peregrinos del Monasterio de Samos** (982-546-046; www.abadiadesamos. com; 70 beds; donation) for a good taste of monastic life; the thrill is staying in the monastery as if a lay brother. The impeccably clean accommodations are simple bunk beds in a large dorm room. There is no heat, so winter can be trying, but the showers are hot and the kitchen has ample cooking facilities and dining tables. Open year round.

A favorite among pilgrims seeking more privacy is **Casa Licerio** (Avenida Compostela, 44; 653-593-814; casalicerio@gmail.com; €30-45 including breakfast), a spotless B&B capably run by former pilgrim Ashley Weaver. She offers ten beds in four cozy rooms, each with a private bath, along with a warm welcome and a daily pilgrims' reception at 6pm.

Leaving Samos

Before you leave Samos, stock up on food and water. The trail from Samos will rejoin the main Camino route in **Aguiada** (Km 120), 10.3 kilometers (6.4 miles) away, and there are no food or lodging options in between.

Follow the way-markers leaving Samos from the west, which follow along the left side of the LU-633 for 2.2 kilometers (1.4 miles) to the hamlet of Teiguin. There, the trail turns right, away from the LU-633. Way-markers will guide you on the remaining 8.1 kilometers (5 miles) through a narrow valley and the tree-covered hamlets of Pascais, Gorolfe, Veiga, and Sivil. After Sivil, it is another 2.3 kilometers (1.4 miles) to rejoin the main Camino route in Aguiada.

A Balsa   Km 131.5

If ever there was a Shire village on the Camino, this is it. A Balsa is replete with grazing cows in lush fields fed by burbling streams, stone cottages tucked into the hillside, hens, roosters, and baby chicks running along the stone bridge and kitchen gardens, and midway through the village, a small artist's gallery and prayer niche set along the path.

The **artist's gallery** is the creation of English painter Arthur Lowe, who walked the Camino in 2006 and was so taken by this place that he returned here to live and restored this tiny settlement (once a cattle barn). The art gallery is the upper level, set on a small slope which descends behind it to a kitchen garden below. A small painted sign, simply noting "Art Gallery," marks the site, to your left as you pass through the center of A Balsa; an impish ceramic garden gnome will mark the place if you miss the sign. Sometimes the place is open and you may see Arthur. His small gallery shows his pen-and-ink and water-color works, and also contains a small altar where you are welcome to sit and pray or meditate. Sometimes meditative music is playing, and at times there is a thermos of hot water and tea bags for passing pilgrims.

Food and Accommodations

A Balsa's pleasant atmosphere makes it a good place to stop for the night, especially at the **Albergue Ecológico El Beso** (633-550-558; www.elbeso.org; 16 beds in one room; €10), which typically opens from Apr.-Nov., but it is best to check their website to be sure. El Beso ("the Kiss" in Spanish) is a restored stone house tucked on the right side of the village. The owners, Marijn Voogt and Jessica Moro prepare conscientious, ecologically minded, and delicious vegetarian dinners €11) and breakfast (€4).

Leaving A Balsa

Soon after the art gallery, the Camino continues through A Balsa and snakes across a bridge and passes a small chapel on the village edge that is dedicated to **Our Lady of the Snows** (*las Nieves*). There is a grill on the door and you can look in at the rustic wood-carved altar with Mary. The path then leaves the hamlet on a steady upward climb through dense, and even more enchanted, chestnut and oak forests where the trees gather around and feel like ancient earth spirits. Don't be surprised to find freely grazing cattle moving about the forest here.

Soon the path will pass by a very modern and somewhat incongruous fountain, with a green-and-white-striped scallop shell framing the water spigots that rush water into a large reflective pool. The pool, however, beautifully reflects the surrounding trees and magnifies the beauty of the forest. In another 1.5 kilometer (1 mile) through this forest, you'll reach San Xil.

San Xil   Km 130

The hamlet of **San Xil** (pop. 25) huddles on the slope above its church, with small kitchen gardens growing pumpkins and collard greens and bordered with standing slabs of the local gray-white granite. If you take the 300-meter (984-foot) detour to your left off the Camino to visit the church, **Iglesia de San Xil,** a local German Shepherd may very well act as guide to the chapel, happy for company in this sleepy hamlet. The church itself is modern but with a pretty stone, stucco, and wood vestibule.

Leaving San Xil

The path after San Xil rises above the forest and skirts along hillsides, with open vistas of fields and small dairy farming villages, through intermittent forests of oak, chestnut, birch, and pine. Each village ahead possesses a tiny single-nave church, many modern and rebuilt with less lyrical or historic aesthetics.

Montán to Calvor
Km 126.1 – Km 120.5

Sights
Iglesia de Santa María de Montán

After San Xil, the Camino passes Iglesia de Santa María de Montán (Km 126.1), which is set in an isolated little nook in the valley. A largely restored and modern building, its façade and entrance survive from the 12th century and are appealing. Its most distinctive feature is its hybrid entrance arch, set in a protective vestibule, with a curve that is part horseshoe-shaped, an influence from Christians (Mozarabes) arriving here from the Iberian Muslim south, and part rounded, like the more classic Romanesque arch. It stands to the right of the Camino, at the lowest point of the valley and on the edge of Montán (pop. 45), with no support structures. As you continue past, be sure to turn around and look at the church tucked into the valley floor.

Casa del Alquimista

Around 200 meters after passing the signs for Casa do Campo (a rural house that has been turned into a cafeteria and bar), a sign will appear directing you left on a detour for another 800 meters, to a private home called **Casa del Alquimista** (Lousada de Samos; 619-729-636). Here, you are invited to enjoy the extensive art exhibit and hospitality of owner Antonio Armiche Bello. Bello is inspired by sacred geometry as well as the ancient inhabitants of this land—especially the *castro* builders—and most of the paintings are done using ground minerals, flint, and local and semi-precious stones. Bello generously offers a place

of retreat for those wishing to pause on their Camino. My favorite aspect is the meditation room, surrounded by sacred art with a large Middle Eastern carpet in the center arrayed with meditation cushions; it really is a peaceful place to meditate if you are inclined.

Food

Just 500 meters (1,640 feet) after the village of Montán is the teeny-tiny farming hamlet of **Fontearcuda** (Km 125.6, pop. 2), which sporadically hosts a donation-based makeshift **lounge and food bar,** set into a dilapidated old barn in the middle of the village and to your left, part under roof cover and part open barnyard, all largely open to the elements. Young people like to gather here, and many enjoy the hippie vibe; philosophy swirls in the air along with the tea sipping. You can get water, juices, tea, coffee, fruits, cheeses, hard-boiled eggs, and the like, in exchange for an offering in the jar.

Approximately 300 meters after leaving Fontearcuda, you'll see signs leading to a rural house **Casa do Campo** (off the trail about 50 meters/164 feet to the left), that has been turned into a cafeteria and bar. It's a good option if the previous option is closed.

The first building before entering the hamlet of **Furela** (Km 123.7, pop. 25) is **Casa do Franco,** a café on the left of the Camino. It is typically open by 8:30am and into the evening. The owner makes great to-order omelets with various fillings (chorizo is one favorite; the mushroom omelet is another). Also, there are fresh sandwiches, hot and cold, and fresh-squeezed fruit juices (€5-8).

Good food and lodging are next forthcoming in the village of **Pintín** (Km 121.9, pop. 26) at the pension, restaurant, and bar of **Casa Cines** (982-167-939; seven rooms; €35-60). They are full-service, with dinner menu (€10) and breakfast (€3).

Casa Cines also offers transportation, in the case of overflow, to the more rudimentary municipal *albergue* in **Calvor** (Km 120.5, pop. 25). **Albergue de Peregrinos de Calvor** (Antiguas Escuelas, Calvor; 660-396-812 and 982-531-226; 22 beds, €6) is a solitary, clean, and simple bunkhouse and there are no other support services or residences in the vicinity. With no food options, be sure to bring your own for a picnic dinner (ask for takeout from Casa Cines). Though nothing remains, Calvor sits atop the older Iron Age site of Castro Astorica.

Aguiada to San Mamede del Camino
Km 120 – Km 119.3

In **Aguiada** (Km 120, pop. 40), the route that detoured from Samos rejoins the main Camino. This hamlet has no café or lodging but possesses a compelling and relatively modern rural chapel dedicated to Mary, with a retable at its altar that depicts an almost Botticelli-like Mother Mary as she ascends to heaven. The chapel flanks a farmer's field, so don't be surprised if cows peer at you from the other side of the fence.

Accommodations

If a well-outfitted *albergue* is what you really want, hold out to **San Mamede del Camino** (Km 119.3, pop. 9) where you'll encounter one of Galicia's best *albergues*, ★ **Paloma y Leña** (San Mamede do Camino, 4; 982-533-248; www.palomaylena.com), literally translated as "dove and firewood" (but more likely the name aspires to elicit the feeling of peace and warmth). A part of its fame is the abundant and creative vegetarian communal dinners (€9) and the immaculate and intimate sleeping options, including six private rooms (€30-45) and 20 beds distributed between three shared dorm rooms (€10, breakfast included). The *albergue* is set on the verdant edge of surrounding forest all on its own, and also has stables for horses.

Approaching Sarría

Though you are never far from the country road LU-P-5602, cattle crossing signs (and cattle at any turn) remind you that you are still in deep rural country, even as Sarria looms 3.8 kilometers (2.4 miles) away.

Leaving San Mamede, the path runs parallel to the right side of a reasonably calm road through pine forest, although more and more houses and settlements appear as you near the outskirts of Sarria. Just before Sarria, the quantity of places to stay and eat increases exponentially, compared to the past 21 kilometers (13 miles). **La Pension de Ana** (Cima da Agra, 11; 982-531-458; www.pensionana.com; €25-35) is a pleasant place on the left just before Vigo de Sarria, with energetic and engaging English-speaking hosts, a terrace and side yard garden, and immaculate and restful rooms.

The path then continues through **Vigo de Sarria** (Km 116.5) and approaches and crosses the Río Sarria with an appealing tree-lined riverside promenade. Continue over the river and continue straight ahead to the medieval passage through Sarria, a steep climb of steps up the town's hill on Rúa Maior, where most of the lodging—but not all of the best—competes for your business, much as they have since the Middle Ages.

Galicia

Sarria to Santiago de Compostela

Km:	115.5-0
Total Distance:	115.5 km (72 miles)
Days:	5-6

Sarria to Santiago de Compostela

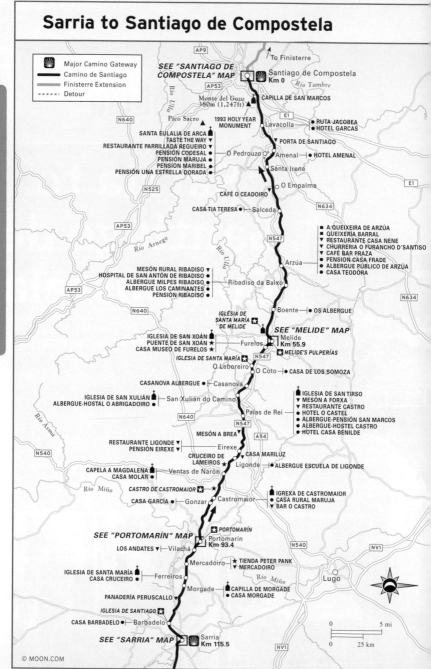

Major Camino Gateway
Camino de Santiago
Finisterre Extension
Detour

To Finisterre

SEE "SANTIAGO DE COMPOSTELA" MAP

Santiago de Compostela
Km 0
Río Tambre

CAPILLA DE SAN MARCOS

Monte del Gozo
380m (1,247ft)

1993 HOLY YEAR MONUMENT

Pico Sacro

Lavacolla

RUTA JACOBEA
HOTEL GARCAS

SANTA EULALIA DE ARCA
TASTE THE WAY
RESTAURANTE PARRILLADA REGUEIRO
PENSIÓN CODESAL
PENSIÓN MARUJA
PENSIÓN MARIBEL
PENSIÓN UNA ESTRELLA DORADA

PORTA DE SANTIAGO

Amenal — HOTEL AMENAL

O Pedrouzo

Santa Irene

O Empalme

CAFÉ O CEADOIRO

CASA TIA TERESA — Salceda

A QUEIXEIRA DE ARZÚA
QUEIXERÍA BARRAL
RESTAURANTE CASA NENE
CHURRERÍA O FURANCHO D'SANTISO
CAFÉ BAR PRAZA
PENSION CASA FRADE
ALBERGUE PÚBLICO DE ARZÚA
CASA TEODORA

Arzúa

MESÓN RURAL RIBADISO
HOSPITAL DE SAN ANTÓN DE RIBADISO
ALBERGUE MILPES RIBADISO
ALBERGUE LOS CAMINANTES
PENSIÓN RIBADISO

Ribadiso da Baixo

Boente — OS ALBERGUE

IGLESIA DE SANTA MARÍA DE MELIDE

SEE "MELIDE" MAP

IGLESIA DE SAN XOÁN
PUENTE DE SAN XOÁN
CASA MUSEO DE FURELOS

Furelos

Melide
Km 55.9

MELIDE'S PULPERÍAS

IGLESIA DE SANTA MARÍA

O Leboreiro

O Coto — CASA DE LOS SOMOZA

CASANOVA ALBERGUE — Casanova

IGLESIA DE SAN XULIÁN
ALBERGUE-HOSTAL O ABRIGADOIRO

San Xulián do Camino

IGLESIA DE SAN TIRSO
MESÓN A FORXA
RESTAURANTE CASTRO
HOTEL O CASTEL
ALBERGUE-PENSIÓN SAN MARCOS
ALBERGUE-HOSTEL CASTRO
HOTEL CASA BENILDE

Palas de Rei

MESÓN A BREA

RESTAURANTE LIGONDE
PENSIÓN EIREXE

Eirexe

CRUCEIRO DE LAMEIROS

CASA MARILUZ

Ligonde — ALBERGUE ESCUELA DE LIGONDE

CAPELA A MAGDALENA
CASA MOLAR

Ventas de Narón

CASTRO DE CASTROMAIOR

CASA GARCÍA — Gonzar

Castromaior

IGREXA DE CASTROMAIOR
CASA RURAL MARUJA
BAR O CASTRO

PORTOMARÍN

SEE "PORTOMARÍN" MAP

Portomarín
Km 93.4

LOS ANDATES — Vilachá

Mercadoiro

TIENDA PETER PANK
MERCADOIRO

IGLESIA DE SANTA MARÍA
CASA CRUCEIRO

Ferreiros

Morgade

CAPILLA DE MORGADE
CASA MORGADE

PANADERÍA PERUSCALLO

Lugo

IGLESIA DE SANTIAGO

CASA BARBADELO — Barbadelo

SEE "SARRIA" MAP

Sarria
Km 115.5

0   5 mi
0   25 km

© MOON.COM

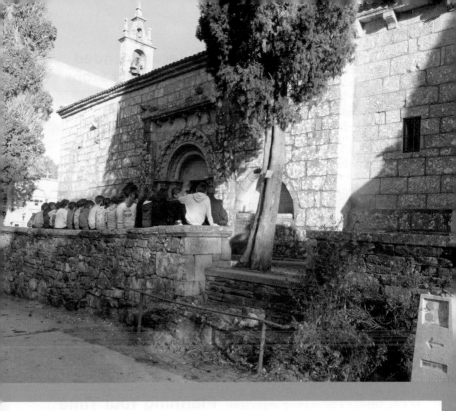

Highlights

★ **Iglesia de Santiago:**
Barbadelo church's enigmatic
engravings include a primitive Christ image with sun-
like forms, which may harken
to pre-Christian ideas about
an all-important sun deity
(page 365).

★ **Portomarín:** Few
approaches are as dramatic
as Portomarín's bridge, high
over the Miño River, but it's
the town's arcaded passageways dotted with enticing
outdoor cafés that will cause
you to linger (page 369).

★ **Castro de Castromaior:**
This 2,400-year-old Celtic
hilltop settlement is one of
the highlights of the whole
Camino, with 360-degree
views of the surrounding
mountains (page 374).

★ **Leboreiro's Iglesia de
Santa María:** After discovering an image of Mary in
a fountain, locals moved it
inside this church—only to
have it mysteriously return
to the fountain. Interestingly,
the story mimics that of
pagan mouras/lamiñaks,
which are central to Galician
folklore (page 381).

★ **Melide's *pulperías*:**
Sample Galicia's most lauded
culinary delight—paprika-
seasoned octopus—in a
festive atmosphere, where
locals share communal
tables, swap stories, and may
break out into song on any
night of the week (page 385).

★ **Iglesia de Santa María
de Melide:** This 12th-
century Romanesque church
preserves multicolored frescos and a Visigothic altar. If
you can catch cheerful José
Antonio, who is something
of a modern-day Templar
Knight, he'll be happy to give
you the full tour (page 386).

Along with the Pyrenees and Navarra, the Camino through Galicia might be the prettiest stretch of the trail. The mountains in Galicia have a very different personality than those at the French and Spanish border. Spiraling inward, they feel like a lost emerald kingdom, revealed and then concealed by daily mists at dawn and dusk. The seemingly endless layers of mountains that continue right to the Atlantic may explain why some of Iberia's highest concentration of Iron Age *castros* (round hilltop fortresses)—some associated with early Celtic speakers and the earliest around 2,500 years old—stand in the area where the Camino passes. The estimates for castros in Galicia are in the thousands, and the numbers seem to increase the closer you draw to Santiago de Compostela (itself an ancient hilltop), especially from the areas around Triacastela and Sarria to Arzúa. This may be a good hint as to why this location, already sacred to earlier peoples, became the site of one of Christianity's three most important holy cities and pilgrimages, along with Jerusalem and Rome.

The Camino here passes through ancient native chestnut, oak, and pine forests huddled along myriad creeks, and through remote gray stone and slate-roofed hamlets where residents still live a subsistence economy of farming and herding. You can buy fresh cheese, fruits, and vegetables as you pass through.

Now fully immersed in the green mountains, hills, river valleys, and rich forests that define the rest of the trek to Santiago de Compostela, you also enter more deeply into a unique folklore, language, and culinary experience. In this green land of magic, spells, and *meigas* (healing witches), you may be offered a potent brew called *queimada* (literally meaning "burned"), a coffee and orange zest-laced brandy-like drink, its surface lit afire. The host ladles out the hot drink into earthenware cups and hands

Recommended Overnight Stops

Sarria (Km 115.5, page 357)

Portomarín (Km 93.4, page 369)

Eirexe (Km 75.6, page 376)

Melide (Km 53, page 382)

Arzúa (Km 39.1, page 388)

O Pedrouzo (Km 20, page 391) or **Amenal** (Km 16.6, page 392)

it to all present, often uttering a blessing or prayer. This is a Galician ritual for communal bonding, and one that locals say will *quemar* (burn) all bad karma and energy from a person and prepare him or her to approach to Santiago with a clean slate.

Planning Your Time

The Camino from Sarria to Santiago de Compostela covers **115.5 kilometers (72 miles)** and is **5-6 days** of walking if you average **20-25 kilometers (12.5-15.5 miles) a day**. I recommend you make an early start each day to allow a leisurely walk without feeling rushed.

Before and after Sarria, you may encounter an organized form of **panhandling** on the Camino, usually two people approaching you with a clipboard and asking you to give money to a cause. (They may start the conversation with "Do you speak English?") These are likely scams, and it's best to continue calmly without stopping. If you really want to contribute to a local cause, find a local charity and donate there.

Route Options

Twenty kilometers before Santiago de Compostela there is a very small **detour**

Local Markets

- **Sarria:** Tri-monthly cattle and produce market, the 6th, 20th, and 27th of every month (page 360).

- **Melide:** Produce and goods market every Sunday (page 382).

- **Arzúa:** Produce and goods market the 8th and 22nd of every month, in the central Recinto Feiral Terra do Queixo market space (page 389).

to O Pedrouzo, which offers the widest range of accommodations on this stretch. Another very small detour leads to the excavation site of Castro de Castromaior, one of the highlights of the whole Camino.

Geography and Terrain

The entire way from Sarria to Santiago de Compostela is through low green mountains and rolling hills, pastures, valleys, and forests that deliver plenty of wild beauty and are dotted with historic

hamlets. Santiago de Compostela itself is nestled in a fertile river valley. This is one of the prettiest (and also easiest) portions of the Camino to hike, with constantly changing scenery, many places under tree cover.

The way is well marked and well supported throughout. The longest stretches without food and accommodations are from **San Xulián do Camino** to **Melide** (11.5 km/7.1 mi), and from **Arzúa** to **Salceda** (10.8 km/6.7 mi). Even on less-supported stretches, trailside cafés seem to pop up out of nowhere, some with canopies and small kitchens, selling drinks, meals, and packable provisions such as sandwiches and bottled water.

If you plan to stay in the **municipal albergues** in Galicia, note that many have a fully functioning kitchen but with no cooking utensils, which makes it impossible to really cook anything.

Weather

In Galicia, **rain** is pretty much guaranteed. Be prepared for it in any season, but especially autumn, winter, and spring. You can always pick up a rain poncho

trail marker in Galicia

Crowd Control

Because 26 percent of all pilgrims who walk the Camino de Santiago begin walking from Sarria, the greatest challenge to this stretch is the crowds. (If you've been walking from starting points farther east, the sudden increase in pilgrims can come as a shock.) But there are strategies to pace and spread out the impact.

- **Avoid the most popular overnight spots.** These are Sarria (Barbadelo is a good alternative), Portomarín, Palas de Rei, Arzúa (Ribadiso de Baixo, 3 km/1.9 mi down the road, is an enticing option), and O Pedrouzo.

- **Get an early start each day.** This gives you some moments of solitude

on the trail before the crowds arrive. Many of those crowds are also people on package tours, who are dropped off and picked up from the trail and walk it from mid-morning to mid-afternoon. (They usually have their hotel pre-arranged—some in accommodations off the Camino—and are not staying in the *albergues*.) In late spring, summer, and early autumn try to be on the trail before 8am. In late autumn, winter, and early spring, the more mellow seasons, aim to start walking with the rising sun or a little after since days are shorter and you want to maximize the daylight but not walk in the dark.

or inexpensive umbrella in Sarria, where several shops carry all manner of pilgrim supplies, including rain and trekking gear.

Getting There

Starting Points

Sarria is the most common starting point in Galicia. In fact, it is the most popular starting point on the entire Camino, where an annual average of 25 percent of people walking the Camino begin their journey. This is because it is the most convenient place to start the final 100 kilometers (62 miles) of the Camino, the only mileage that counts in the eyes of the church in order to earn a pilgrim's certificate, the Compostela. Sarria is well served by train and bus.

Buses also serve **Portomarín** from Sarria and from Lugo.

Car

To drive the Camino, coming from O Cebreiro, follow the **LU-633**; at Ventas the LU-633 gives way to the **C-535**

to Palas de Rei. From Palas de Rei to Santiago de Compostela, follow the **N-547**. Access is the same by car as by foot to all stopping points on the Camino when you follow these roads. Where these roads don't pass directly through destinations on the trail, there are marked, smaller access roads to reach the same settlements. The driving route is way-marked, with blue signs with a yellow scallop shell, to guide drivers along a road parallel to the trail.

There are no car rental companies in Sarria; dropping off a rental car driven in from other hubs is not possible, either. The nearest car rentals are in Lugo: **Budget**, www.budget.com; **Avis**, the most centrally located; and **Keddy** (www.keddy.com). Other options for car rentals are in Palas de Rei and Santiago de Compostela.

Air

The nearest airports are in **Santiago de Compostela (SCQ),** from which you can catch a train (1-2 daily) to Sarria, and in **A Coruña (LCG),** from which there are seven trains daily to Sarria.

Train

RENFE (www.renfe.es) has a line that runs nearly along the entire Camino (two trains daily), operating from Irún at the Pyrenees, and stopping in Burgos, Sahagún, León, Astorga, Ponferrada, and **Santiago de Compostela**. Daily, from Barcelona to Sarria there are three trains (one is direct and two change in Madrid); from Madrid to Sarria there are four trains daily, all of which change in Ourense; from Santiago de Compostela to Sarria there is one train to Sarria and from A Coruña there are seven trains daily.

Bus

ALSA (www.alsa.com) connects towns and villages from Pedrafita do Cebreiro (4 km/2.5 mi north of O Cebreiro) to Santiago de Compostela, as well as from from León, Lugo, A Coruña, and Madrid. From Santiago de Compostela to Sarria, **Monbus** (www.monbus.es) has one bus daily, and from **Lugo to Sarria,** eight daily buses.

Bike

The trail is way marked where bike access and foot access diverge; bikers at times share the footpath and at times are directed to the road, which never deviates too far from the trail. Way-marking, with icons of walkers (footpath) and cyclists (bike path), is with blue and yellow signs.

Sarria   Km 115.5

Sarria's hilltop location and rich waterways made it a destination long before the Middle Ages. And although the 12th-century pilgrim's guide, the *Codex Calixtinus*, made no mention of Sarria, it was still a popular pilgrim stop. (As with Triacastela, Alfonso IX, the 13th-century king of León and Galicia, championed this town and poured proceeds into building it up with support structures dedicated to the pilgrimage, including a monastery and several hospitals.)

Compostela Tip

Take note: If you wish to earn a certificate, a Compostela, from the cathedral in Santiago de Compostela, walking from Sarria forward, you need to acquire a **minimum of two stamps per day** in your pilgrim credential. Fortunately, practically every place on the Camino will have a stamp to offer. The locals really get into this tradition and love designing stamps for their businesses. Many will have them out front on the counter, but if you don't see one, be sure to ask.

Today, Sarria (pop. 13,330) is the most common starting point for people wishing to walk the Camino and earn a certificate (Compostela) from the church, which recognizes only the final 100 kilometers (62 miles). This fact also alters the mood of the Camino for those who have started their walk from farther away: Suddenly there are many more people and all are unfamiliar faces, fresh and new to the Camino. From here forward, places fill up faster, especially in the summer, though more accommodations are cropping up to meet the demands.

Modern Sarria has a pragmatic, industrial feel, and is set up with a wide range of good lodging options. The riverside is more mellifluous, and is a nice place to gather for a snack or before-dinner drinks with friends.

Sights

While much of the medieval town does not survive, Sarria does retain important reminders of this past. One is the main street—**Ruá Maior/Calle Mayor**—that grew out of the passage of the medieval Camino, and then (as now) was lined with inns, shops, and cafés vying for the pilgrim trade. Some of the older buildings here retain the coats of arms of the powerful noble families of Sarria. The town also retains one of Galicia's most lyrical Romanesque churches, San

Highlights of Galician Food and Wine

Galicia's fertile landscape and proximity to the ocean translates into diverse and delicious foods from both land and sea.

Cheese

People take pride in their regional cheeses, each defined by the valley and cows' milk from which they are crafted. The **tetilla** cheese, unmistakable from its breast shape (hence the name), is common across the Camino in Galicia. It is a creamy, medium-yellow, and semi-cured cheese with a mild flavor. Semi-soft but dense and creamy cheeses from the **Melide** and **Arzúa** area are famous. If you are lucky to be walking in autumn when locals make quince jam and paste, be sure to ask for the dessert of *queso con membrillo,* cheese with quince paste.

Caldo Gallego

Caldo Gallego, a pork and bean stew rich in dark leafy greens (collards, kale, or mustard tops), as well as potatoes, onions, and garlic, is ubiquitous in pretty much every bar, café, restaurant, and household, each chef putting her spin on this iconic dish.

Empanadas

Galician **empanadas** (large pie-sized dough pockets) and **empanadillas** (smaller empanada) are cousins to the Cornish pasty with flaky crust and savory fillings, the most common being mussels with onions and red peppers, tuna and onions, beef, rabbit, and in some places *pulpo* (octopus).

Seafood

Pulpo á feira—boiled octopus seasoned with Spanish paprika, sea salt, and olive oil and served on a wooden platter, accompanied with local white wine—is synonymous with Galicia.

Try all things from the sea here, such as *percebes* (gooseneck barnacles that look like dinosaur claws but harbor meat tasting like oysters crossed with lobster), clams, mussels, oysters, squid, octopus, cod, tuna, hake, sardines, eel (especially the braised eel, *lampera estofado*), and most especially, the scallops that give the Camino its symbol, known as *vieira*. Try also the trout (*trucha*), fresh from the rivers.

Sopa de Castañas

During chestnut season (autumn and winter), you may find this creamy chestnut soup on the menu, made from nuts gathered from the forests through which you walk. The chestnuts are boiled and shelled, sautéed in pork fat with onions and garlic, then puréed and finished with a bit of wine or sherry vinegar and a drizzle of olive oil before serving.

Salvador, and the still-active monastery of La Magdalena. A heavily fortified **castle** from the 14th and 15th centuries once stood on Sarria's hill, but it is now reduced to a fragment with a surviving and rebuilt tower. Access to the hill is closed, but you can see the tower from the street just below the small hill. A lot of the old castle is still in Sarria, too: Its stones were reused to build the town's walkways.

Aspects of more historic and soulful Sarría reveal themselves as you make the final climb up Rúa Maior near the church of San Salvador, the castle ruins, and the raised orchard just under the castle ruins, where apple trees drape their branches over the thick granite walls.

Iglesia de Santa Marina

Though it is a modern church built over the now-nonexistent 12th-century church, the **Iglesia de Santa Marina** (Rúa Maior, 65; pilgrims' mass 6pm) holds the place where thousands of pilgrims first arrived in Sarria and went to worship.

Pimientos de Padrón

Pimientos de Padrón
In an order of these little green peppers, about one in ten is hot and the rest are sweet. They are almost always sautéed in olive oil and served crispy and hot with a dash of sea salt.

Dessert
Galicians make traditional crepes (*freixos*) that are similar to those found in Brittany, but usually served as a sweet with a dusting of sugar. Among the most frequent desserts you'll be offered is the *tarta de Santiago*, a dense almond cake with a powdered-sugar sword of Santiago dusted on the surface.

Wine
Albariño, the effervescent dry white best known from the Rias Baixas along the coast, is one of more than a dozen grape varietals grown in Galicia. Three other celebrated growing regions, Valdeorras,

Ribeiro, and Ribeira Sacra—which the Camino passes through just after Sarria—produce wonderful local wines as well. Other grape varietals worth looking for are **Godello, Dona Branca,** and **Palomino Fino** for white wines and **Mencia, Garnacha, Tempranillo,** and **Loureira,** among others, for reds. Many house wines offered in cafés and restaurants along the Camino are locally made, from a wine cooperative or local grower; they come unlabeled, can be mixed varietal blends or single varietals, and typically are very good (and the least expensive).

Orujo
The local after-dinner drink, *orujo,* is made from the residue of pressed grapes, stems, and seeds left over after wine-making. Once distilled, *orujo* is offered three ways: straight as it is (a clear liquor), infused with locally harvest herbs (a yel low liquor), or infused with coffee (a dark brown liquor). It is mostly a homemade enterprise. Makers pride themselves on the quality, especially of their *orujo con hierbas,* orujo with herbs, selecting secret herbs that grow in the surrounding valley or mountain to alchemically transform the elixir. *Orujo* is believed to have healing medicinal properties and often when it is offered, it is offered as a gift and a gesture of shared well-being. *Orujo* is also the key ingredient in the ritual brew called *queimada.*

They are honored with a modern mural depicting medieval pilgrims with capes, staffs, and water gourds walking on the Camino. Interesting sacred sculptures, from an 18th-century *cruceiro* (ornate cross) to a more modern vision of Jesus coming up from the earth, populate the churchyard.

Iglesia de San Salvador
As you climb the hill toward the castle, following the Camino as it leaves Sarria, the 13th-century **Iglesia de San Salvador**

(Rúa do Castelo, 7) is almost at the top and across from the castle ruins. It features a tympanum with Christ in Majesty surrounded by two trees, or vines, each with six leaves, and Jesus's hands held above his shoulders, the right giving a blessing and the left palm open. It has a delightful folk style seen in some earlier Romanesque churches in Galicia; it is a curiosity here since this is a later-Romanesque church transitioning to the more angular and exalting Gothic style that is usually less organic.

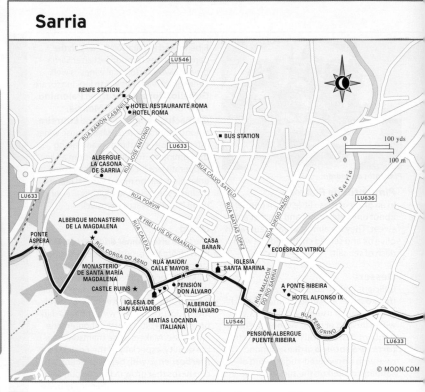

Sarria

© MOON.COM

Monasterio de Santa María Magdalena

Housing a community of the Mercedarian Order—Order of the Blessed Virgin Mary of Mercy—the destroyed and restored **Monasterio de Santa María Magdalena** (Avenida La Merced, 60; 982-533-568; www.alberguedelcamino.com) was founded by Italian pilgrims in the 12th century; Augustinians took it over in the following century. If you approach the church entrance, chances are one of the fathers will hear you and open the door (locked, except for when the *albergue* is open to admit pilgrims wishing to spend the night). It is worth a visit to see the cloister and church inside, and also to receive a warm welcome and a stamp for your credential.

Festivals and Events

The town celebrates a five-day **festival in honor of Saint John** (San Xoán) June 21-25, and becomes one big and colorful party with music, dance, folkloric and religious processions, and bullfights.

Sarria hosts a Celtic pork festival, **Fiesta del Cocido del Porco Celta,** the last weekend in January, that celebrates cured meats and grilled and stewed dishes made from the large black and pink native Galician pig, with its big, floppy ears. It is called Celtic pork because it comes from an animal Galicians say they have been raising since at least the Iron Age, some 2,500 years ago.

Sarria has a tri-monthly **cattle and produce market,** the 6th, 20th and 27th of the month at the Campo da Feria (fairgrounds) on the edge of town, reminding everyone that this industrial town

Clockwise from top: Iglesia de Santa Marina, Sarria; signs leading to the Italian albergue and restaurant Matias Locanda Italiana; Iglesia de San Salvador; Pension Don Álvaro, Sarria.

is about farming as much as it is about pilgrimage.

Food

For its size, Sarria doesn't have a huge array of exciting restaurant options. Many places have more of a get 'em in and get 'em out atmosphere and average but decent food. Still, there are a couple of gems:

★ **Matias Locanda Italiana** (Rúa Maior, 4; 982-886-112; matiaslocanda. es; €8-15) is consistently popular with pilgrims looking for a good dinner. This Italian restaurant takes pride in the quality of its food—a long list of homemade pizzas and several types of salad, a rarity on most Spanish menus, including the *ensalada locanda* (mixed greens, cherry tomatoes, walnuts, apple, blue cheese, and corn). It is attached to the *albergue* of the same name.

The ★ **Hotel Restaurante Roma** (Calle Calvo Sotelo, 2; 982-532-211; www.hotelroma1930.com) is a great place to stay and eat. Go with the more extensive *menú del dia* (€16) or a la carte menu (€11-18) offering a wide variety of traditional Spanish cuisine, including several types of grilled fish, *coquilles Saint-Jacques* (baked scallops), and *almejas a la marinera* (clams cooked in white wine, garlic, and parsley).

A Ponte Ribeira (Rúa do Peregrino, 29; 982-530-005; www.alfonsoix.com; €15 *menú del día*; €25 a la carte) is located inside the restaurant in Hotel Alfonso IX, and is a destination on its own. Inside, warm red brick walls surround tables topped with crisp white cloths. Specialties include a grilled whitefish and langoustine skewer, and a garden salad with grilled goat cheese and fresh Cebreiro cheese. Service is excellent.

The contemporary vegetarian restaurant **EcoEspazo Vitriol** (Rúa Diego Pazos, 18; 604-004-112; €8.50-13.50) focuses on cuisine inspired by organic, fresh, and sustainable foods, in a funky coffeehouse setting. The English-speaking staff is passionate about good food and service. Try the *crema de violetas* (purple potato cream soup), the Buddha Bowls (fresh veggie bowls with dipping sauce), and the vegan hamburger with salad and nacho chips. They also have a small organic grocery selling packable foods for the trail.

Accommodations
Albergues

The **Albergue Don Álvaro** (Calle Mayor, 10; 686-468-803; www.alberguedonalvaro.com; 40 beds divided into four dorm rooms; €9), is located in a traditional house with courtyard garden, a terrace for relaxing, and higher rooftop terrace for hanging laundry to dry in the sun. Pilgrims are drawn magnetically to the communal fireplace off the garden, where the owners offer an after dinner drink of their homemade *orujo* around a roaring fire.

Albergue Monasterio de la Magdalena (Avenida La Merced, 60; 982-533-568; www.alberguesdelcamino.com; 60 beds, €10; open from 9:30am) is a basic *albergue* but with some well-considered details: barriers set between bunk beds to offer more privacy, lockers with keys, a large kitchen and cooking area, and numerous clean toilets, shower stalls, and sinks. The entrance is past the church entrance, marked by signs to help you find the front door, and is in the same complex as the church and cloister.

Pensión-Albergue Puente Ribeira (Rúa do Peregrino, 23; €9 bunk, €20-30 room with shared bath, €25-40 with private bath) feels like staying in a monastery in all the good ways. Expect a kind (and English-speaking) staff and pristine if simple rooms that are modern, open, light-filled, and restful.

French windows, traditional wood ceilings, exposed stone walls, and central fireplace make **Albergue La Casona de Sarria** (Rúa San Lázaro, 24; 982-535-556; www.lacasonadesarria.es; dorm bed, €10; room with bath, €35-45) a treat. This cozy boutique hotel also doubles as an *albergue*. The English-speaking owners, Marcela Caballera Gaete and her husband Antonio, restored this 1940 farmhouse from near-ruins. It's positioned near the Río Pequeño, a bit north of where the Camino will cross the river to continue west.

Hotels

Located behind Albergue Don Álvaro (and run by the same couple who runs the *albergue*) is the ★ **Pensión Don Álvaro** (982-531-592 and 686-468-803; www.alberguedonalvaro.com; €37-45), a gem of a boutique hotel. Rooms have rooftop views of Sarria, floral décor, and spacious private baths with good showers; note the beautiful floor-to-ceiling Cubist painting in the lobby (by the husband). Hotel guests share the garden, terrace, fireplace, evening drink, and kitchen with those in the *albergue*.

The **Hotel Roma** (Calle Calvo Sotelo, 2; 982-532-211; www.hotelroma1930.com; 24 rooms; €50 single/€60 double), a more traditional hotel, maintains comfortable rooms with colorful bedspreads, plush linens, and simple but classy wooden furnishings. The overall quality has remained high since I first stayed here in 2007.

Casa Barán (Calle Mayor, 53; 982-876-487; www.casabaran.com; €75) is a boutique hotel with four luxury rooms in a home with beautifully restored stone walls. The elegant rooms feature pristine linens, quilted bedspreads, very comfortable beds, and elegant Galician-style glass-enclosed balconies. Proprietors speak English.

You won't miss the **Hotel Alfonso IX** (Rúa do Peregrino, 29; 982-530-005; www.alfonsoix.com; €60), towering to your right as you approach Sarria's center and just before you cross the Río Sarria. This luxury hotel, with crisp-pressed white sheets, French wallpaper, and toned-down Louis XIV-style furnishings, also has a good restaurant, **A Ponte Ribeira,** and (a boon for hot days)

a swimming pool in the enclosed garden. The hotel takes its name from King Alfonso IX of León and Galicia, whose most enduring legacy may be the university he founded in Salamanca in 1212. Proprietors speak English.

Getting There and Around
Car

From **O Cebreiro** (48 km/ 30 mi; 1 hour): Take the **LU-633** to Sarria.

From **A Coruña via Lugo** (130 km/80 mi; 2 hours): Take the **AG-11** south to the **AP-9** heading southeast, which turns into the **A-6** destined for Lugo. Continuing past Lugo, take **LU-546** heading south directly to Sarria.

From **Ponferrada** (115 km/71 mi total): Take **A-6** heading west (for 95.6 km/59 mi); exit onto **CP 16-11** heading south (for 9 km/5.6 mi), and take **LU-546** the remaining 10 kilometers (6.2 miles) south to Sarria.

From **Bilbao and Santander:** Follow the **A-8 west** across the north of Spain as it enters Galicia and turns south toward Mondoñedo (423 km/263 mi; 4 hours), but don't exit. Stay on A-8 another 16 kilometers (10 miles), to just past Abadín, and be prepared to exit soon after onto **LU-113** (for 32 km/20 mi), then take **N-640** to **A-6** to **LU-546** for the remaining 41 kilometers (25 miles) to Sarria.

From **Madrid:** Exit Madrid via **M-30** and take the **A-6** heading northwest into Galicia for 483 kilometers (300 miles), via Ponferrada; exit onto **CP-16-11** heading south (9 km/6 mi), then **LU-546** south to Sarria (another 10 km/6.2 mi).

Bus

Monbus (www.monbus.es) serves Sarria with one bus daily from Santiago de Compostela (three hours; €12.50) and eight daily buses from Lugo (30 minutes; €2.60). The bus station (Rúa Matías López, s/n) is 800 meters (0.5 miles) north of the Camino where it enters Rúa Maior near Iglesia de Santa Mariña (Rúa Mayor, 65), a 12 minute walk. Go south

Top: Ponte Aspera. **Bottom:** The trail through oak forest after Sarria.

on Rúa Matías López to Rúa Escalinata Maior, turn right and continue straight.

Train

RENFE (www.renfe.es) runs trains to Sarria from Santiago de Compostela (1-2 trains daily; 2 hours; €20), from A Coruña (seven trains daily; 2-3 hours; €14-35), from Barcelona-Sants (three trains daily: one direct with sleeping compartments, 13 hours, €50; two with train change in either Madrid, 10 hours, €42-89; or in Monforte de Lemos, 12 hours, €28), and from Madrid-Chamartin, with a train change in Ourense (four daily; 6-8.5 hours; €50-80).

The **train station** (Rúa Calvo Sotelo, s/n) is 1.1 kilometers (0.7 mile) north of the Camino: Exit and take Rúa Calvo Sotelo straight ahead, walk southeast until you reach Rúa Matías López; take it (a slight right), heading south to Rúa Escalinata Maior, turn right and continue straight.

Taxi

Both **Peregrino Taxi** (679-444-996; www.peregrinotaxi.es) and **Taxi Camino de Santiago** (626-120-842) serve Sarria.

Leaving Sarria

You will see the **castle site** at the top of the hill, highlighted with the aid of a historical plaque, to the left side of the Camino as it passes on its way out of town. You'll also pass the **Monasterio de Santa Maria Magdalena** (on the right side), and then the path will turn left to cross the medieval **Ponte Áspera** bridge over the Celeiro River, leading you briefly along railroad tracks and then toward an enchanted oak forest with massive ancient trees. These give way to another hilltop pastureland with groves of pine trees between the fields for the next 3.6 kilometers (2.2 miles) to Barbadelo.

Barbadelo, a small settlement today, was mentioned in the *Codex Calixtinus*, where the author rants against the scammers and profiteers of the Camino. Today

it is no different: From here on out, you may begin seeing more panhandlers and scam artists. The best thing to do is to not engage them and keep walking calmly on; given all the pilgrims walking now, you will rarely find yourself alone.

Barbadelo   Km 111.5

If you are walking from Sarria in the early morning, it is very likely the world will be covered in a thick mist. This gives a magical quality to the walk, especially through the oak forest just after Sarria. However, it also risks enclosing you so that you will miss one of the more enigmatic churches on the Camino, the Iglesia de Santiago de Barbadelo. As you near the village, be sure not to miss the sign for Barbadelo's medieval church, next to the signpost for Casa del Carmen, to your left.

The church is set off from the center of Barbadelo (pop. 13), a tiny rural settlement. It is a very hospitable community, geared since the Middle Ages toward feeding and housing pilgrims, and today has good food and lodging options, especially if you want to avoid the crowds in Sarria.

Sights
★ **Iglesia de Santiago**
Set 200 meters (656 feet) off to the left of the Camino just as you approach Barbadelo, **Iglesia de Santiago** (open for mass on Sunday and holidays July-Sept.7:30pm, Oct.-June 6pm) once belonged to a monastery founded in the 10th to 11th century. The current building dates to the 12th century. Its bell tower is its most distinguishing feature as you approach, appearing like a fortress at the head of the long and narrow church.

However, it is its tympanum, both outside and inside, that sets it apart from other churches on the Camino. Look for its curious images, including a very primitive-looking Christ standing in the

Horreos

In Galicia you will begin to see stone granaries, called *horreos*, that appear as small rectangular houses on stilts, all of it made of the local grey granite. These *horreos* are used to store grain, feed for livestock, and any form of harvest the farmer and kitchen gardener desires. The stilts and large round disks between their upper ends, where they meet the granary's body, are there to protect the contents from rodents as well as from the pervasive damp of this green land. Many *horreos* show the mix of beliefs that persists here: you'll see symbols carved on the granary doors or set upon the roof from both pagan (such as a sun disk, a trisquele, or a hand folded in a fist over the thumb) and Christian (a cross) outlooks to protect against bad luck.

Galician *horreo*

center with sun-like forms on both sides, and below him, a demon-like creature flanked by serpents.

No one is completely certain what the serpents and flanking demons mean. They, like the church's primitive Christ image with sun-like disks, may harken to pre-Christian ideas. In the case of Christ and the disks, these may be blending Jesus's role as the god of light with the earlier sun deity who was once worshiped in this area of Galicia all the way to Finisterre (which marks, according to local lore, a pre-Christian Camino to the land's end).

The serpents, too, may tie in to older ideas about serpents as symbols of the energy of the earth, sometimes called the *woivre* or *voivre*. In this outlook—based in part on archaeology and folklore, and in part on a modern revival movement of these ideas—the whole Camino is a great subterranean serpent that energizes and revives us. As if walking on an underground channel of feel-good energy, it can initiate us into a deeper awareness of life and clear our baggage. In this philosophy, the earth energy may also come

above ground at certain points, usually where churches are built, many over older sacred sites.

Perhaps the demons are there to remind those walking this path that the Camino delivers light as much as it does challenges and ordeals (metaphoric demons)—forcing us to face ourselves, warts and beauty, toward becoming more whole.

The church is likely to be closed outside the summer season. Ask at the nearby *albergues* for a local with the key so that you can go inside and see the interior of the tympanum.

Food and Accommodations

★ **Casa Barbadelo** (982-531-934; www. barbadelo.com; 48 beds in six dorm rooms, €10; 11 private rooms, €45), directly on and to the right of the Camino as you enter the village, is a large stone complex of several buildings and landscaped gardens with everything you could need. There's a terrace, a dining area with a full-service restaurant seating up to 80 people, a café making food to order all day and into the evening, a pool, meandering garden spaces, a small shop for provisions and souvenirs, and best of all, pristine lodging—dorm rooms sleeping up to eight people with shared baths, as well as private ensuite rooms. The **restaurant** doubles as a common room with fireplace and has a good library. Specialties include grilled fresh scallops with olive oil and chives, and a tasting board of cured meats and local cheeses.

Leaving Barbadelo

More oak forest and sinuous roads through small farmsteads lie ahead, along with possible visits from a vocal donkey and a beautiful black stallion. After 6 kilometers (3.7 miles) you'll find the family-run ★ **Panadería Peruscallo** (609-836-437) in the hamlet of Peruscallo (Km 105.5), a farmstead abutting a café and bakery on the Camino (to the left) that serves omelets, sautéed *pimientos de Padrón*, sandwiches, and salads, as well as fresh-baked breads. You can stamp your pilgrim's passport with the bakery stamp, which is usually on the front counter or on a table outside during busy periods.

From here to Morgade, the Camino weaves in and out of pastures and oak forest, taking you over some passages that retain the large medieval pavement stones of the millennia-old pilgrims' path. You will pass dozens of *horreos* along the way, most filled with dried corn for the farm animals. Most farmsteads mark their borders and pastures with slabs of the ever-present local granite, stood vertically and edge to edge to create gap-free stone fencing.

From top to bottom: Camino through Barbadelo and fog shrouded path to Iglesia de Santiago; Casa Morgade; Iglesia de Santa María with its outdoor font in Ferreiros.

Morgade   Km 103.7

Morgade (pop. 4) came into being in 1200 as a hospital for pilgrims. Today it remains dedicated to supporting pilgrims and is also an agricultural and herding village.

Accommodations and Food

Morgade centers today on **Casa Morgade** (982-531-250; www.casamorgade.gal; Mar.-Nov.), a rural *albergue* and hotel in the village center, to your left as you enter town. You'll feel the magnetic vibe as soon as you near it, with its friendly café out front spilling out onto the tiny village street. Inside are accommodating rooms, an enclosed courtyard terrace, and a salon with a wood-burning fireplace. Of the six rooms, one is a shared bunkhouse with six beds (€10) and five are private rooms (€30-42). Breakfast is included and a communal meal in the evening costs €9.

Leaving Morgade

As you leave town, there's a small chapel, **Capilla de Morgade**, to the right of the Camino, with a Templar cross engraved in the entrance's keystone. Inside, the walls are covered with graffiti, many declarations of love from passing pilgrims. The church is closed most of the time (to prevent more graffiti).

The path continues through forests with pastures, but now you'll also pass through vineyards that are part of Lugos province's Ribeira Sacra wine region. Farmsteads setting up *donativo*-style (donation) tables of local foods (cheeses, fruits, cakes, and donuts)—a random and at-whim occurrence across the whole Camino—increase from here to Portomarín. These are based on the honor system: If someone isn't there to greet you, there is usually a contribution jar, so drop some money in for whatever you take. Many of the products are home baked, locally harvested (apples, honey, berries), and homemade (cheese).

The path makes a slight descent down into the village of Ferreiros, where food, lodging, and a pretty medieval church await.

Ferreiros   Km 102.4

Ferreiros (pop. 27) was a thriving pilgrim stop in the 12th century. Today, the tiny village still gathers around its most important feature, the 12th-century **Iglesia de Santa María**, with its handsome baptismal font set outside—not inside—the church's western door in the center of the village cemetery.

The entire church preserves its 12th-century form, and the west entrance is especially ornate, with lions and other animal figures with animated faces and expressions. Look for the lions gazing down at you with playful smirks, or the one on the right capital baring its teeth. The church is rarely open except in summer. Thankfully, the west entrance is one of its finest features.

Accommodations and Food

Just before you fully descend toward the church, you will pass **Casa Cruceiro** (Ferreiros, 2; 982-541-240 or 639-020-064; www.cascruceriodeferreiros.com; Mar.-Nov.), an *albergue* (right side) and restaurant across the street (left side). The restaurant has a wide selection of refreshments, tapas (from €3), meals (€8-12), and breakfast (€3.50). Try their homemade lentil soup, grilled fish, or various egg dishes. The *albergue* has 12 dorm beds (€10) and two private rooms (€35-40).

Mercadoiro   Km 98.7

Aside from an *albergue* and trail-side restaurant complex, the only other structure in the tiny oasis of Mercadoiro (pop. 1) is the general store, **Tienda Peter Pank** (689-435-041 or 634-707-368; www.peterpank.wixsite.com), named after an edgy, rebellious punk-like Spanish comic book character, and run by the congenial Guillermo Lamas and Olga Rodríguez, who greet pilgrims as if they are the first to ever walk through their door (they speak some English, too). They sell original art as well as provisions, drinks, sandwiches, and Camino-themed souvenirs (this is the place to get a hand-cast cowbell, that ever-present sound on this trail, shared so often with local cows and their sing-song chimes). Guillermo and Olga also sell trekking clothing and some gear.

Accommodations and Food

★ **Mercadoiro** (982-545-359; www.mercadoiro.com; Apr.-Sept.) is really more a hotel, *albergue,* and popular trail-side restaurant complex than an actual village. They specialize here in many homemade dishes (€4-12); this is a great place to sample *caldo Gallego*, the tuna or beef *empanadas*, and a plate of local cheeses. They also serve a pilgrims' menu. Three dorm rooms with beautifully restored and exposed stone walls and low thick beam wood ceilings have 3-4 bunks that can sleep 6-8 people (a total of 22 beds, €12). There are four double rooms with private bath that are of the similarly appealing stone and wood farmhouse architecture (€50-60).

Three kilometers (1.9 miles) from Mercadoiro, the hamlet of **Vilachá** (Km 95.7, pop.19) has a good vegetarian restaurant and bar, **Los Andates** (Vilacha, 18; 681-611-761; www.losandantes.simdif.com; €3-8). It's worth all the trail markers dotting your approach: heart-shaped wooden cutouts with a countdown of distances noted as you draw nearer, starting from 2.5 kilometers (1.6 miles) away and ending 50 meters (164 feet) from the bar. The options include vegetarian salads, sandwiches, combined plates (grilled vegetables, salad, potatoes, croquettes), and pizza, plus homemade desserts.

★ Portomarín   Km 93.4

Cross a high modern bridge to enter Portomarín (pop. 1,528). The town was founded as a crossing over the Miño River in Roman times. Until the 1950, Portomarín was located lower down on the banks of the Miño river. In the 1950s and 1960s, Franco backed the building of the Belesar reservoir to bring water-powered electricity to the area, and water from the the dam submerged the medieval-to-mid-20th-century town in a matter of years.

Before all was lost, the town people carefully disassembled and reassembled their two Romanesque churches—the whole of San Nicolas, and the western façade of San Pedro—and transported them, along with a few historic mansions, higher up the slope. In doing so, they managed to preserve the churches, the two icons that preserve the town's medieval character.

As you cross the modern bridge into town, study the water closely. You can make out walls and outlines of the houses that now are all under the water. Below and running parallel with the new bridge is what remains of the original 10th-century bridge. It is still accessible by foot when water levels are low, if you climb down to the water's edge from town. The high modern bridge gives an amazing view of the mountains and river that define so much of Galicia. (It can also elicit a feeling of vertigo.) The bridge leads to steep stone stairs—a part of the medieval bridge, transplanted higher up—that present one final ordeal before you cross into town.

The small, current town's **arcaded passageways,** lined with many cheerful options for a glass or meal, add to Portomarín's appeal, even though they are modern constructions, built in the 1950s and 1960s. They and their cafés

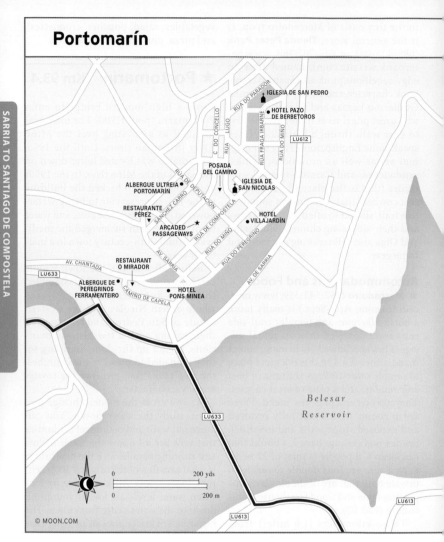

Portomarín

Labels on map:
IGLESIA DE SAN PEDRO
RÚA DO PARADOR
HOTEL PAZO DE BERBETOROS
RÚA FRAGA IRBARNE
C DO CONCELLO
RÚA LUGO
RÚA DO MIÑO
LU612
POSADA DEL CAMINO
RÚA DE DEPUTACIÓN
ALBERGUE ULTREIA PORTOMARÍN
IGLESIA DE SAN NICOLAS
RESTAURANTE PÉREZ
SÁNCHEZ CARRO
RÚA DE COMPOSTELA
HOTEL VILLAJARDÍN
ARCADED PASSAGEWAYS
RÚA DO MIÑO
RÚA DO PEREGRINO
RESTAURANT O MIRADOR
AV. SARRIA
AV. CHANTADA
LU633
ALBERGUE DE PEREGRINOS FERRAMENTEIRO
CAMIÑO DE CAPELA
HOTEL PONS MINEA
AV. DE SARRIA
Belesar Reservoir
LU633
0   200 yds
0   200 m
LU613
LU613
© MOON.COM

are a delightful place to spend your evening, even in a light rain under the protection of the arches. Like the two churches, these arcaded passageways give the modern town of Portomarín a feeling of timelessness, as if the town has been here all along, not only for a mere six decades. They also create a congruity between the rescued and rebuilt 12th-century Iglesia de San Nicolas and the arcades lining the street and leading the eye to the plaza at the center, where the church stands. This may be the single most enjoyable aspect of Portomarín, the creation of such a congenial public space.

Sights
Iglesia de San Nicolás

The **Iglesia de San Nicolás** (Plaza Conde de Fenosa, s/n; www.concellodeportomarin.es; daily 10am-1pm and 4-8pm; free), also known as the Iglesia de San Juan, to reflect its association with the order of the knights of Saint John, was built in the 12th and 13th centuries, both as a place of worship and as a place of defense and protection. The heavy towers and walls were designed as a fortress for when the town came under attack. The Romanesque carvings all around the outside are delightful, such as the half-waterfowl/half-human figures on the capitals, the west entrance's tympanum with Christ Pantocrator (Christ All-Powerful) surrounded by the 24 Elders of the Apocalypse and their musical instruments, and the north side's depiction of the Annunciation, with Mary looking very dubious about the whole affair as an angel alights to tell her what is coming. Be sure to visit the inside to get a full feel for this church's massive stature as both fortress and temple. **Mass** is held at 7pm each day and is followed by the **pilgrims' blessing**. The play of late afternoon light through the rose window is worth a visit in its own right.

Iglesia de San Pedro
Dedicated to Saint Peter, the medieval part of **Iglesia de San Pedro** (Traversía Circunvalación, 30; www.concellode-portomarin.es; usually closed)—the west entrance—dates to the late 12th century. (The remainder of the church was built in the 1950s and 1960s, after the townspeople transported the original west entrance to higher ground.) It is a beautiful façade, with two sturdy bull's heads carved in the upper corners of the stone doorframe. The sculptor perfected their gaze to look at you as you pass through. The church grounds are planted with oak, the most common and most sacred tree, found planted around churches all across Spain and especially

From top to bottom: arcaded passageway with cafes in Portomarín; Iglesia de San Nicolás in Portomarín; offerings on the trail after Portomarín.

on the Camino. Oak trees were (and are) venerated by pagans and Christians alike, as symbols of strength and wisdom and the joining of heaven and earth through roots, trunk, and branches.

Festivals and events

Portomarín happily is the location of an annual *orujo* festival—**Festival del Aguardiente**—coinciding with Easter weekend. It includes traditional dances and music, and plenty of opportunities to taste the firewater, as well as to experience *queimada*. A copper *orujo* distillery stands in the center of the square in front of San Pedro church to commemorate the town's passion for this traditional liquor.

Food

Restaurant O Mirador (Rúa do Pelegrin, 27; 982-545-323; omiradorportomarin. com; *menú del día*, €10; a la carte, €7-20), near the bridge, has tall windows facing the river and the mountain vista. Both bar and restaurant attract patrons for drinks, tapas, or a three-course meal. They specialize in wild caught fish, grilled meats, seafood, and traditional stews. Top picks include the *parrillada de verduras* (grilled vegetable plate, €9.50) and *navajas a la plancha* (grilled razor clams, €14).

★ **Posada del Camino** (Rúa Lugo, 1; 982-545-081; www.restauranteposad-adelcamino.com; €10) has held to solid standards ever since I first discovered it in 2007. It has a good *menú del día* or a la carte options, and is an atmospheric place to sit and enjoy a drink or meal, looking right out over Iglesia de San Nicolás. Watch the sun move across the outer carved walls of the medieval church while the engaging staff make sure you have a flow of good food and wine.

Restaurante Pérez (Praza de Aviación, 2; 982-545-040) offers good home cooking with satisfying *caldo Gallego*, lentil soup, and good fish dishes. Pérez gives you four fixed-price menus to pick from, ranging €9-14. The *menú especial* is the most expensive option. What makes it "special" is a wide range of first-course options, plus two special dishes for a second course: veal chops or a rich lamb stew.

Accommodations

The new, gray brick and slate-roofed **Hotel Pons Minea** (Avenida de Sarria, 11; 610-737-995; www.ponsminea.es), on the upper banks of the Miño river, offers both dorm-style *albergue* accommodation (24 beds with four shared baths, €10, includes sheets and towels) and six private rooms with bath (€40 single/€50 double), all spotless and comfortable despite the spartan decor. The modern, sleek hotel also has a happening café that is known for its *pulpo á feira*. They also turn out a popular breakfast with coffee, fresh orange juice, and (if you ask for it) eggs, ham, cheese, and tomato to go with good crusty bread (€5-6).

Facing the Iglesia de San Pedro on its peaceful square is the **Hotel Pazo de Berbetoros** (Calle San Pedro, s/n; 982-545-292; www.pazodeberbetoros.com; €70-100), the surviving portion of a 1712 luxury estate that builders rescued and relocated during the 1960s Belesar dam project. Today, it's a five-room boutique hotel with plush contemporary and turn-of-the-20th-century country-manor styles, plus an enclosed private garden. Proprietors speak English.

The **Albergue de Peregrinos Ferramenteiro** (Avenida Chantada, 3; 982-545-362; www.albergueferra-menteiro.com; €10) is spotless, spartan, and efficiently run, with comfortable basic bunks that are spaced far enough apart to make the 130-bed dorm room easier to inhabit. The large picture windows add to this sense of space and ease. Set on the less congested west end of town where the Camino leaves Portomarín, the setting is peaceful, with views of the river below, and offers easy access to the center of town and its numerous restaurants.

Hotel Villajardin (Rúa do Miño, 14; 982-545-054; www.hotelvillajardin. com; €40-60) may have the town's best views of the river (especially if you get an east-facing room on the upper floors). It's unfussy, relaxed, and well maintained, with spotless rooms. A bar and restaurant serve drinks and meals. Proprietors speak English.

Albergue Ultreia Portomarín (Calle Diputación, 9; www.ultreiaportomarin. com; €40) is an immaculate *albergue* with bright, upbeat contemporary décor and both dorm-style and private rooms. It's family-run, with Carmen Rey (who speaks English) at the helm, making everyone feel special. The communal spaces are well thought-out and offer all that you need if you stay in to cook or want to do laundry.

Getting There and Around

From the nearest car-rental hub in **Lugo,** leave Lugo by taking the **N-VI** south toward Madrid/A-6/Monforte/LU-546 (pay close attention because the N-VI has two exits from Lugo); follow signs for **LU-612** toward Portomarín/Estrada Vella de Santiago, and take it all the way to Portomarín (27 km/16 mi; 30 min.).

Empresa Portomarín (www.empresaportomarin.com) connects to Portomarín from Sarria (Mon.-Fri two buses daily, Sat.-Sun. one daily; 30 min.; €3) and Lugo (Mon.-Fri. two daily, Sat.-Sun. one daily; 30min.; €3).

Call **Peregrino Taxi** (679-444-996; www.peregrinotaxi.es), **Taxi Camino de Santiago** (626-120-842), or **Portomarín**: **Taxis Monterroso** (982-545-088).

Leaving Portomarín

On your departure from the center of Portomarín, you will make your way west out of the center of town, turning left and climbing down, making a switchback

heading east for a few meters on the **LU-633** at the lower end of town before turning right onto a car and foot bridge over a small tributary of the Belesar dam. From there, the Camino heads straight west through another ancient oak and chestnut forest. You will climb in altitude slightly (and easily), so that as you near Gonzar, you're back on higher pastureland interspersed with pine forest.

In **Gonzar** (Km 85.6, pop. 41), **Casa García** (Gonzar, 8; 982-157-842; Mar.-Oct.; €4-10), immediately to the left at the village entrance, is a café with outdoor terrace churning out fresh omelets, sandwiches, salads, baked goods, and refreshments. A family of friendly calico and striped cats also share the space but go about their own business. Casa Garcia also has a medium-sized *albergue* with 48 beds (€10) in two bunkhouses and four additional private rooms (€35) in a stone homestead, including a common room with an inviting fireplace and a large back garden.

Castromaior   Km 83.9

In 2004, the village of Castromaior (pop. 30) completed the restoration of their **Igrexa de Castromaior**, a 12th-century Romanesque church with a classic arch and harmonious proportions. In the center of the village and to your left as you pass through, the church wall that faces the small cemetery retains some enigmatic marks that look like folk engravings of various styles of crosses; perhaps they commemorate those who are buried here, or they may simply reinforce the sacred power and protection imbued within this place.

Food and Accommodation

Casa Rural Maruja (Calle Castromaior, 8; 982-189-054; €35), next door to the church, is Castromaior's only accommodation and covers the basics: no-frills and somewhat worn-out, but spotless and quiet rooms with bath and decent beds. The perk is the chance to sleep in this tiny village and save ample time the next day to visit the nearby castro.

Look for the ★ **Bar O Castro** (Castromaior, 11; €4-9) just before you leave the village. It has no name posted, but you won't miss it—there are no other bars—and it is the place to stop for a homemade dish of yogurt from the local cow's milk (the best I've ever eaten), or the patroness's fresh raspberry smoothie, which is also deliriously good. Her chalkboard offers such delights daily, changing with the seasons and local ingredients, including a daily menu (€9). She is also knowledgeable about the ancient castro, which is less than 1 kilometer (0.6 mile) up ahead. There is an aerial photo of the ancient hilltop site framed on the bar's wall, to better orient you to what you are about to see.

Leaving Castromaior

As you leave the village of Castromaior, signs will direct you both to the Camino and to the **Castro de Castromaior.** The latter is just a slight, 200-meter (656-foot) detour (to the left) that I strongly recommend; I consider this to be one of the highlights of the entire Camino. The detour isn't entirely well-marked, but two signs in particular indicate you are nearing the castro. After the second sign, continue another 150 meters (492 feet), and when you see a stone postmarker for the Camino, look to your left for a large horizontal information panel 10 meters (39 feet) off the Camino. Head to the board, which describes the basic history of the castro, and then take the track to the right of the board, which leads straight to the main opening of the hill fort.

═══ **Top Experience** ═══

★ Detour: Castro de Castromaior
Km 83.4

Some 2,400 years ago, on this hilltop, Iron Age peoples built a substantial *castro* (hilltop fortress) and enclosed it with a series of round fortifying walls. Archaeologists began excavating this *castro* in 2004, and while most of it is still under mounds of sediment and grass, the excavation has already revealed a large hill fort town, along with the walls that surround it.

The settlement's protective outer walls have yet to be excavated, and are presently ring-shaped earthen mounds. You'll pass through each ring wall on a dirt path as you approach the protected settlement. Just before the innermost wall, a sign appears to tell you the *castro* settlement is up ahead. Once you step through the inner wall's entrance and climb up to the center of the windy hilltop and castro, you will see why Iron Age peoples built here: a **360-degree view** offers perfect visibility and yet the hilltop is practically unseen from below, offering its residents enhanced protection. From here, look for the **excavated houses** of the *castro* that lie within the innermost protective wall; you'll also be able to make out the outlines and homes still under the earth and also of the other two walls encircling the Iron Age town.

Archaeologists have uncovered three separate occupations here. They've found evidence of wood-and-thatch abodes from the Iron Age settlement 2,400 years ago, as well as stone structures dating to the Roman invasion around 2,000 years ago.

The excavation has no barriers and is open 24/7 and free to visit. The village of Castromaior (www.castromaior.es) is seeking support to continue the excavations and also plans to build a museum.

After you have visited the site, continue across the platform of the inner circle, away from where you entered. The exit is to the right of the only stand of trees in the circle (a yellow arrow on one of the trees points the way). After a slight climb up and over the castro wall, you'll see the Camino—indicated by a visible iconic stone pillar with scallop shell—and soon you can rejoin the pilgrimage trail.

Ventas de Narón
Km 79.9

The Camino passes through the heart of this hamlet (pop. 23), passing in the center a delightful raised pasture surrounded by a stone wall with grazing sheep who will gladly come and greet you. Continue on toward the end of the village to a tiny chapel dedicated to Mary Magdalene, **Capela a Magdalena.** It is built from the stones of an older hospital, overseen here by the Templar Knights in the 13th century, that collapsed after it was abandoned in the 19th century. Villagers wanted to commemorate the past and took the stones to create this chapel. Some of the stones retain engraved images of the Templar cross. The thick-trunked oak tree facing the chapel door speaks of the continued sacredness of trees, a pagan legacy with a poetic Christian expression.

Food and Accommodation

Immediately to your right as you enter Ventas, the sturdy stone **Albergue-Hostal Casa Molar** (Calle Ventas, 4; 696-794-507; casamolar_ventas@yahoo.es) offers lodging in two dorm rooms (18 beds total; €10) and two private rooms (€30). The friendly, down-to-earth owners greet you as if you are family and offer good pilgrim menus (€9.50). There is a covered terrace out front with a full-service bar and restaurant.

Iron Age hilltop fortress of Castro de Castromaior

Cruceiro de Lameiros
Km 77.4

From Ventas, the Camino continues through hilltop pasturelands and oak and pine forests and in 2.5 kilometers (1.6 miles), you'll reach the elaborate and expressive cross, the Cruceiro de Lameiros, on the left side of the road, standing near an ancient and venerated oak. The base of the cross shows engravings of a mason's building tools on one side and a skull and bones on another. Looking up to the top, the cross depicts a crucified Jesus on one side. On the other side, his mother's arms hold him in a maternal embrace.

The oak tree and the cross are echoes of the same idea. The oak is an ancient pagan representation of an *axis mundi,* a portal that connects earth with heaven and serves as a spiritual highway from one realm to the other. This idea of an axis mundi, also known as the "world tree," is found in many traditions and cultures around the world. Similarly, the *cruceiro*'s base is planted in the mortal earthly realm, represented both by the mason's tools and the bones. The pillar is the portal, and the cross at the top represents the heavens.

This is also one reason why you keep seeing oak trees—and at times cypress and olive—planted around churches and chapels all along the Camino. But the veneration of the oak trees is also a persisting Iron Age tradition, one also cherished by the Celtic speakers of Atlantic Europe, including here in Iberia. To them, and to the Christian expressions that took over after them, the oak represents strength, wisdom, and transcendence.

In less than 1 kilometer (0.6 mile) from the Cruceiro de Lameiros, you'll reach the village of **Ligonde** (Km 76.4, pop. 77) with food and lodging options.

Food and Accommodations

As you near the western end of Ligonde and to the right on the Camino, the clean and small municipal **Albergue Escuela de Ligonde** (Ligonde, 2; 982-153-483 or 679-816-061; year-round; €8) is a well-managed place with 20 beds in one basic but agreeable stone room; when you arrive, ask for Isabel. As is typical of municipal *albergues* in Galicia, there is a kitchen but no cooking utensils. You can get meals in another 300 meters (984 feet) west on the Camino, at **Casa Mariluz** (982-169-141; €10) where you'll find a good *menú del peregrino* and combined platters, such as a fresh garden salad with calamari, and fried eggs or baked cod casserole with peppers and tomatoes. Watch for the cheerful chickens underfoot that like to run about the place.

Eirexe   Km 75.6

Just after Ligonde, the neighboring hamlet of Eirexe (pop. 73, including the surrounding farmsteads)—also spelled Airexe—is a small cluster of buildings in a grove of trees, reflecting the serene and self-sufficient life of farm, fields, and kitchen gardens. At night, the Restaurante Ligonde becomes the center of village life—this one, and several other villages in the vicinity. Fortunately, it sits across the street, and outside of earshot, of the two accommodations in Eirexe. One of the best-run inns is right here, as well as an impeccably clean but basic municipal *albergue.* Nearby is a tiny chapel dedicated to Santiago.

Food and Accommodations

Don't be surprised if the chef at ★ **Restaurante Ligonde** (660-971-787; www.restauranteligonde.com; €10) comes out with a large plate of tiny morsels to share with you and other patrons at the bar. The pilgrims' menu is traditional—salad, soup, grilled fish, chicken,

A Gourmet Pilgrimage

Foodies ready for a splurge—and dreaming of something other than the *menú del peregrino*—should detour 8.5 kilometers (5.3 miles) south from Palas de Rei to owner and chef Maria Varela's **A Parada Das Bestas** (Lugar Pidre, 27, in the hamlet of Pidre; 982-183-614; www. aparadadasbestas.com; €45), which literally means "The Beasts' Stop." A native of Palas de Rei, Maria and her husband, Suso, are passionate about the land's produce. Their menu, inspired by the traditional food Maria's grandmother Balbina prepared, is a fusion of modern cuisine with traditional Galician cooking.

Varela also resurrects medieval dishes that may have been served on the Camino in the Middle Ages. Among her signature dishes is *capón de pidre estilo peregrino,* capon roasted in succulent wine and brandy (among other ingredients) with chestnuts and blackberries.

You can also stay here, in the 300-year-old homestead restored as a country inn, with seven private rooms (€75-85) and a few apartments for 4-6 people (starting at €161). Rooms retain the original home's farming legacy, with 19th- and early 20th-century décor and thick stone walls. Enjoy the wood-burning fireplace, the outdoor pool, and the large meandering garden that blends into the countryside.

A taxi from Palas de Rei will cost on average €15 each way and take 10-15 minutes; try **Taxi Palas de Rei** (675-625-112; www.taxi-palasderei.com).

pork, or beef, and an array of desserts—and is good, fresh home cooking. You can linger in the communal cheer and then saunter the 20 meters (66 feet) across the small road to the village pension or *albergue.* Breakfast typically is offered starting around 8am; inquire about the hour—it can vary with the seasons—before you turn in.

The *xunta* **(municipal)** *albergue* here is clean and basic, but next door to it is one of my favorite places on the whole Camino, the ★ **Pensión Eirexe** (Airexe, 18; 982-153-475; pensionereixe@yahoo.es; €25 single/€30 double). With the help of her mother, Cruz Diaz runs her place with spotless efficiency and warmth, and visitors feel welcome in their combined cheer. The rooms are clean, with homey little touches, such as a vase of flowers or a hand crocheted table cover. Windows in back open to the field, garden, and roaming chickens. The nighttime air is so fresh, you sleep more deeply and awake incredibly restored.

After Eirexe, in 4.8 kilometers (3 miles), and in the middle of nowhere (but directly on the left side of the Camino), 20 meters (66 feet) south of the rural road

N-547, is ★ **Mesón Brea** (Lugar A Brea, s/n; 982-374-129), a roadside café with a tree-covered terrace and warm stone interior. Brea makes hot breakfasts upon request, plus the thick and extra-savory *tortilla Española* (Spanish omelet). Their *menú del dia* (€10) changes daily.

Palas de Rei   Km 68

Palas de Rei (pop. 799) is a working farm town with several tiny neighborhood like hamlets around it. The Camino meanders sinuously through the town, giving you a good feel for its rural and deeply agrarian character, such as tractors rolling through and the occasional cow, donkey, chickens, and passing sheep herd.

Sights
Iglesia de San Tirso
As you enter Palas de Rei, you pass its most historic icon, the **Iglesia of San Tirso** (Calle de la Iglesia, s/n; 9:30am-1pm and 3:40-7pm Tues.-Sun.; mass at 7pm). A church has stood on this spot, in one form or another, since the 9th century. The structure has been declared by

some to be too modern to merit interest, but they have overlooked the original Romanesque façade that preserves the look of the original late-12th-century church.

Despite the present modern structure, the interior is inviting and offers respite for anyone seeking a quiet retreat. Also, take a close look at the sculpture of Mary, both inside as you enter, and also outside on the church grounds: She is standing on a big three-dimensional spiral, not a serpent. This slight-of-hand takes the symbolic association of the serpent back to its more primal, and pagan, roots across Europe and Asia, representing the life force as it unfurls and expresses itself in the material realm on Earth. Mary, too, takes on a more ancient association as the cosmic mother earth, whose creation and expression on Earth is that very life force.

Festivals and Events

San Tirso's festival in Palas de Rei is every January 28 and celebrates the town's patron saint with processions and festive food and drink. In late April is Palas de Rei's **Feira do Queixo** (cheese festival), celebrating the region's *queso de Ulloa*.

Food

Mesón A Forxa (Traversía da Igrexa, 2; 982-380-340; €10-12) combines market-fresh ingredients, contemporary cooking, and traditional Galician dishes, noted daily on their street-front chalkboard, including a garden salad with walnuts, cheese and raisins; shrimp and spinach egg scrambles; and grilled octopus with garlic and paprika and potatoes.

Restaurante Castro (Avenida de Ourense, 24; 982-380-321; €10-16) is another treasure of farm-fresh ingredients, serving traditional Galician recipes prepared with contemporary flair in a bright wood and stone dining room. Both the *menú del peregrino* and the *menú especial* are good values and offer great selections

of dishes, such as saffron clams, varieties of paella, sirloin steak with blue cheese and grilled vegetables, and homemade chocolate cream cake. (There is also a more informal café with bar at the same place, where you can check in for the **hostel.**) Proprietors speak English.

Accommodations

Just as you enter Palas de Rei, you'll see the **Hotel O Castelo** (Calle Cruceiro, 14; 618-401-130; www.hotelocastelo.com; eight rooms; €38-60) to your right in a quiet part of town. The otherwise plain rooms are decorated with original paintings by a local artist of bold and large floral works, some with a Japanese aesthetic.

Next door to the Iglesia de San Tirso, the **Albergue-Pensión San Marcos** (Travesía da Igrexa, s/n; 982-380-711; Mar.-Dec.; 24 dorm room beds, €10; seven private rooms, €50) features brand-new, meticulously clean rooms. The *albergue* has three dorm rooms, while the pensión offers comfortable beds against a backdrop of floor-to-ceiling images of local nature, such as fallen chestnuts, sunflowers, and a golden wheat field across the *meseta*. The whole complex opened in 2013. Breakfast is €4.

Albergue-Hostel Castro (Avenida de Ourense, 24; 982-380-321; www.alberguecastro.com; €10) is a gregarious and enjoyable *albergue*. There are five rooms with six beds and four rooms with four beds, all with minimalist white and neon décor; the light metal Scandinavian-style bunk beds have curtains and copious room to move around in. Proprietors speak English.

Rooms at **Hotel Casa Benilde** (Calle Mercado; 982-380-717; €45-71), a few paces right off the Camino, are pleasant, relaxing, and pristine. The English-speaking staff are wonderfully engaging and eager to make sure you enjoy your stay, including learning and remembering your name from the moment you contact them.

Leaving Palas de Rei

Over the next 26 kilometers (16 miles), from here to Ribadiso de Baixo, you will cross over no less than eight small rivers and creeks, part of the wider, rolling-hill-and-river-valley landscape that defines both provinces of Galicia traversed by the Camino. The first portion of the walk, from here to Leboreiro, goes through native oak forests with dense tree canopies that protect from sun as well as rain.

San Xulián do Camino
Km 64.5

San Xulián do Camino is a vibrant village built around a 12th-century Romanesque church, **Iglesia de San Xulián.** There are a lot of mixed styles in the church architecture that speak of different influences. Its simplicity and proportions, including unadorned corbels and strong plant motifs, are probably from the Cistercians. Its pre-Romanesque-styled arches, almost forming a horseshoe shape, could be Mozarabic or Asturian in influence. Collectively, they work, making for a

harmonious place of worship. On All Saints Day, November 1, and the days leading up to it, you will find a flurry of activity in the cemetery around the church as women clean their ancestors' graves and array them with fresh flowers.

Accommodations

Albergue-Hostal O Abrigadoiro (Lugar San Xulián, 15; 676-596-975; www.albergue-o-abrigadoiro.negocio.site; May-Sept.; 12 beds, €10-12; and three private rooms, €28-40; communal meal, €10) is a snug vine-covered home-turned-*albergue* in the village center, to your left before you reach the church. The hosts are spunky and outgoing, and love greeting and taking care of pilgrims. They also run an immaculate and cozy place, prepare a delicious evening meal (with excellent wine), and enjoy singing with guests after dinner, gathered around the piano.

Leaving San Xulián do Camino

From San Xulián to Melide, there are few options for lodging directly on the Camino, and some of them close down for the winter months.

Leboreiro's unique *horreo* (granary) and Iglesia de Santa María

Galician Folklore on the Camino

One character stands supreme in Galician folklore, with a connection to the wider regions of the Camino: the **moura.** Considered the Mother Earth by many, the moura is often found in folktales as a female being who dwells in and around the ancient dolmens, standing stones, and castros of prehistoric Galicia. She resides in subterranean places as a guardian of the land and nature. She is strong, beautiful, and formidable, and when human eyes see her, she is usually seated near a cave, dolmen, or watery place, combing her long and luxuriant hair. She often tests mortals who cross her path. Similar characters to the moura are found across northern Spain, such as **lamiñaks** (Galicia to Basque Country), **xanas** (Asturias and León), and **Mari** (Basque Country and Navarra).

The Camino has its own moura/lamiñak story: **Leboreiro's Mary,** whose statue returned to the edge of a nearby fountain no matter how many times she was moved to the village church. This Mary is none other than the pre-Christian moura, woven Into the Christian tradition as it made its way into Galicia.

Traditional Galician folklore and traditional Galician society afford a lot of self-governance to women, so it isn't surprising to find so many female leads. There also are practicing **meigas** (also called "white witches," healers in service of the community's well-being) and **curanderas** (traditional herbalists and healers). Galicia also has strong male characters, including **curanderos** and druids—some still present today and practicing in Santiago de Compostela as well as in the countryside, like their female counterparts.

The mist-filled valleys inspire many stories, some of trickster characters a lot like house elves, called **Trasgos,** and others of wandering souls called **Santa Campaña:** If you see them, you had better let them pass without seeing you, for they can pull you into their eternal wandering. People carve crosses, solar disks, and other talismans on buildings and *horreos* to protect home and harvest and attract only good luck.

At the budget end of the spectrum, is the basic and clean **municipal *albergue*** (982-173-483; year-round; 20 beds; €6) in **Casanova** (Km 62.2), to which you need to bring your own food. If you find it locked, seek out Mari Carmen Morandeira Vázquez at the only other buildings that are across the small street, and she will let you in. She can also stamp your pilgrim's passport.

At the more opulent end, in **O Coto** (Km 59.4), **Casa de los Somoza** (s/n; 981-507-372; www.casadelossomoza.es; Mar.-Nov.; 10 private rooms, €47-55) has a full-service bar and restaurant (€18). Contact them ahead of time, by phone or email, to be sure they have a room. Proprietors speak English.

Just before Leboreiro, you leave the province of Lugo and enter the province of A Coruña. You are now 3-4 days of walking—depending on your pace— away from Santiago de Compostela.

Leboreiro   Km 58.7

Noted in the *Codex Calixtinus* as a good pilgrim stop, Leboreiro (pop. 71) was a popular place in the 11th to 13th centuries. Thereafter it seems to have tapered off and received little mention in later pilgrim accounts. But its folk legend of the magical Mary, seen combing her hair in a fountain nearby, persists to the present.

Leboreiro is a peaceful and pleasing village to walk through. As you near the church of Santa María, you will see a thatched, cone-shaped container about the height of a person set on a low masonry wall. This is yet another style of granary for storing harvested foods such as corn. From there, the Camino turns slightly right and arrives at the church. After the church, the path continues over the Río Seco on a single-arched medieval bridge 120 meters (394 feet) beyond the church and passes through kitchen gardens, fields, and forests toward Furelos and Melide.

Sights
★ Iglesia de Santa María

The current church of Santa María is an 18th-century rebuilding of the 13th-century original, but it elegantly retains the Romanesque elements in the entrance, windows, corbels, and overall proportions. The church is associated with a legend: It's said that villagers discovered a sculpture of the Mother Mary seated in the local fountain, combing her hair. Numerous times they took it from the water and set it in the church, only to discover that of its own accord, it returned to the fountain. But, when the villagers eventually carved an image of Mary on the tympanum over the church's entrance, the original sculpture of her remained inside the church. But not all the time: As recently as the 1960s, local villagers reported that this image of Mary would return nightly to the fountain where she could still be seen combing her hair. This is the spitting image of the pre-Christian female divinities—mouras, xanas, lamiñaks, and Mari—that populate the folk stories of northern Spain. The fountain of legend doesn't survive, but it is possible that it was a natural spring coming from the Río Seco river behind the church.

If you are walking through Leboreiro in summer, the church is open daily, and you will have a chance to see the **original icon of Mary** on the altar inside. Other times of year, the church remains firmly closed, and the key resides with the priest in Melide. But the **tympanum** outside features an impressive image of Mary, as well. It dates to the 14th century and

depicts two angels swinging censers—incense burners—on either side of Santa María, whose facial expression and posture reflect her commanding nature.

Walking around the church and through the cemetery that surrounds it, note the corbels, the carved stones at the joints where the roof edge meets the church walls. There is one in particular that might arrest you, a very explicit penis. Romanesque art, unlike Gothic, liked to depict earthy and human qualities, and there are some in northern Spain, including San Martín in Frómista, that had even more explicit depictions of human sexuality. This one is sedate by comparison and may even come from an earlier influence, the Roman world, where fertility sculptures such as this one were obsessively common.

Furelos Km 54.9

A four-arched medieval bridge, **Puente de San Xoán**, crosses the Río Furelos into the village of the same name (pop. 159). As you cross the bridge, notice the impressive old stones—they also belong to the original medieval road. They are so massive, worn, and deep-set that you can almost imagine being a medieval pilgrim here, crossing over on foot, maybe following a cart or mule.

On entering the town, to the left side at the foot of the bridge, stands a small and informative ethnographic museum and tourist information center, **Casa Museo de Furelos** (Tues.-Sun. 10am-2pm and 5-8pm,), which opened in 2010. Step inside for a moment to gather local recommendations from the helpful attendants and also to take in the exhibits on farming and culinary traditions and festivals of the region.

A little farther along to the right is Furelos's 13th-century **Iglesia de San Xoán** (church of Saint John). During the peak of the pilgrimage in the 11th and 12th centuries, Furelos, and many of the

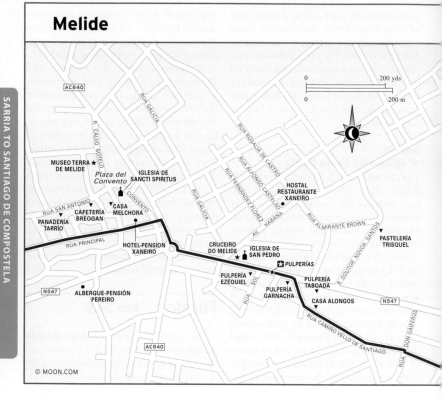

Melide

(Map showing: AC840, RÚA GALICIA, R. CALVO SOTELO, MUSEO TERRA DE MELIDE, Plaza del Convento, IGLESIA DE SANCTI SPIRITUS, RÚA ROSALÍA DE CASTRO, RÚA ALFONSO CASTELAO, RÚA FERNÁNDEZ FLÓREZ, HOSTAL RESTAURANTE XANEIRO, RÚA SAN ANTONIO, CAFETERÍA BREOGAN, CASA MELCHORA, PANADERÍA TARRÍO, CONVENTO, RÚA GALICIA, AV. HABANA, RÚA ALMIRANTE BROWN, PASTELERÍA TRISQUEL, RÚA PRINCIPAL, HOTEL-PENSION XANEIRO, CRUCEIRO DO MELIDE, IGLESIA DE SAN PEDRO, PULPERÍAS, R. DOUTOR NOVOA SANTOS, N547, ALBERGUE-PENSIÓN PEREIRO, PULPERÍA EZEQUIEL, RÚA SOL, PULPERÍA GARNACHA, PULPERÍA TABOADA, CASA ALONGOS, N547, AC840, RÚA CAMINO VELLO DE SANTIAGO, RÚA DON GAIFEROS, © MOON.COM, 0-200 yds, 0-200 m)

surrounding villages you've passed on the Camino, were active with people, lodging, churches, monasteries, and hospitals. The Order of Hospitallers of San Juan, who protected and oversaw this village and many of the others, ran the hospital here, and resided here.

South of Furelos from the Camino, archaeologists have unearthed much older guardians of the land and people, such as 2,000-year-old burial mounds called *mamoas*. The deeper you walk into this region on the Camino, the more castros, dolmens, and mamoas there are. Most are unexcavated or do not offer a lot to see, but indicate the deep ancestry of prehistoric peoples here. The best place to get to know them is up ahead, in the Museo Terra de Melide.

Melide Km 53

The area around Melide (pop. 4,798) teems with prehistoric remains, from 2,000-year-old burial mounds to Iron Age Celtic castros, to Roman roads, to medieval remains from the rise of the Camino in the 9th-13th centuries, all that testify to how old this locale is.

Melide also has more modern delights and is one of the famous pilgrim stops for the Galician specialty *pulpo á feira*, boiled octopus seasoned with sea salt, smoked paprika, and olive oil. Many more *pulperías*—eateries specializing in octopus—will begin to appear as you walk toward the ocean. There are four in Melide that are as popular with locals as with visitors.

Melide is proud of its other culinary creations, too, especially its creamy and delicious locally made cheeses, several types of bread, and a celebrated cookie called *melindres de melide,* which you will likely smell before you see: The perfume of their key ingredient, anise, laces the air as you walk into town.

Sights
Iglesia de San Pedro
If the **Iglesia de San Pedro** (Rúa Cantón San Roque; 981-505-003; www.turismo-melide.com; open for mass Sun. 11am) looks familiar, that may be because the church doorway is the model for the architectural design printed on the €10 bill. (To confuse matters, the doorway was actually salvaged from another church, that of San Roque, which is why this church is also called the Capilla de San Roque.) While it may not be the most ornate of Romanesque doorways, it is elegant in its proportions. San Pedro overall is a 19th-century restoration of a 12th-century Romanesque church. Inside are the 14th-century tombs of three local nobles, Diego Garcia, Roi Lopes, and Lopes's wife, Inés Eanes.

The plaza next to the church also holds a historic marker, the ornate and dynamic cross, **Cruceiro do Melide.** Considered Galicia's oldest stone-carved *cruceiro,* from the 14th century, it depicts Mary and Saint John standing with Jesus on the cross on one side, and Christ in Majesty on the other.

Plaza del Convento
This historic square retains its medieval form and holds several historic sites, the most prominent being the **Iglesia de Sancti Spiritus** (Plaza del Convento, 2;

From top to bottom: tympanum of Leboreiro's Iglesia de Santa María; Melide's Iglesia de San Pedro on the €10 bill; Arzúa at night around the Iglesia de Santiago.

981-505-003; www.turismomelide.com; open daily during the day and early evening), a largely Baroque structure with pinches of earlier Gothic calm taming the flamboyant style. Founded in 1375, it once belonged to a Franciscan monastery and was rebuilt several times during the 15th and 18th centuries. It remains an active place of worship among the locals.

Museo Terra de Melide

Founded in 1978 as a center of study for Melide's local archaeology, the **Museo Terra de Melide** (Praza do Convento; 981-507-998; www.mtmelide.es; Monday-Saturday, 11:30am-1:30pm; Sunday 11am-2pm; closed on holidays; free) covers all the strata, from prehistory to the present. This museum is a great chance to glimpse the region's past. One exhibit room is dedicated to the Camino's history, and has pieces of medieval sculpture and mural painting. Other gallery spaces cover Neolithic finds from Melide's earliest farmers, Iron Age metalworks and pottery remains from the surrounding castros,

and displays on daily life of the region in recent centuries, including traditional crafts of blacksmithing, shoemaking, stone and wood work, and traditional music. The building itself is interesting, set in the old pilgrims' hospital founded in 1502. Though panels are in Gallego and Spanish, most of the exhibits are self-explanatory and easy to follow during a leisurely visit of an hour or less.

Festivals and Events

Melide hosts the **Fiesta de Melindres** (www.turismomelide.com) on two days in mid-May, with bakers by the dozen offering the celebrated sweet along with other baked goods and local foods.

The town erupts into animated festivities of music, dance, processions, and foods for the week-long **Fiesta de San Roque** (Aug. 15-21) and the **Fiesta de Nuestra Señora del Carmen** (July 21).

A large cattle market, **Fería Grande,** at the town's fair grounds is held the last Sunday of every month.

At Melide's large **weekly market** (Sun.), you can see the fresh octopus

Pulpería Garnacha in Melide

that is shipped overnight from fishing boats from nearby Galician ports, and also shop for general goods, regional produce, and food products (especially honey, cheese, and bread). The market sets up along centrally located streets and squares in town, especially the Rúa do Convento, Praza das Coles, and Praza da Alfóndiga (the latter two locations are also good for daily food purchases from vendors selling garden-harvested produce, local cheeses, breads, and sausages that make great provisions for the trail).

Food and Nightlife

As in the rest of Spain, the *paseo* (evening stroll with family and friends) and eating out with friends defines nightlife in Melide. If you want to be like the locals, start at one end of town and slowly make stops at a few tapas and *pincho* bars along the way, sampling, chatting, and enjoying as you go.

★ *Pulperías*

Melide is regionally celebrated for *pulpo á feira* (octopus Gallego-style, seasoned with paprika, sea salt, and olive oil). Step into one of the town's three *pulperías* to try it. (These communal and festive eateries also offer much more to savor if octopus is not your thing.)

In ★ **Pulpería Garnacha** (Rúa Camiño Vello de Santiago, 2; 605-883-268; www.pulperiagarnacha.com; €11-25) a woman prepares the pulpo to order right in front of you at the entrance, while stirring a large cauldron of boiling octopus, surrounded by stacks of wooden plates that will hold the disks of sliced meat (€9.50). Two dining areas with long communal wooden tables line the large space that can get packed on weekends. The long bar is stocked with every elixir. All dishes are offered as *raciones*, servings meant to be shared; ask for a *media ración*, half-serving, if you want less. They also offer platters of charcuterie, large salads, and *pimientos de Padrón*, among many other choices.

Just up the street is **Pulpería Ezequiel** (Avenida Lugo, 48; 686-583-378; www.pulperiaezequiel.com; €9-15), offering similar options in a smaller space, which also gets jam-packed on weekends and festival days. Other house specialties are *pimientos de Padrón*, varieties of clams and langoustines, chorizo stewed in wine, homemade cheesecake, and *tarta de orujo*.

Pulpería Taboada (Avenida Lugo, 22; 619-246-602; €14) is a pulpería and also a tableside grill joint with bar seating or a more formal separate dining room. You can get good *pulpo á feira* here for sure, but try the slightly crispy grilled octopus for a tasty variation.

Other Food Options

When it isn't busy, **Cafetería Breogan** (Rúa San Antonio, 3; 981-509-018; €3-10) is easy to overlook on passing, but the stone-fronted bar becomes full of color and animated local life at night, serving great bar food with cheer. It's named after the mythic founder of Galicia. Do like the locals and shimmy up to the bar and put in an order for drinks and a selection of *raciones*.

For something entirely different, head to **Casa Alongos** (619-229-334; www.casaalongos.com; €6-13), with its candy-striped walls, checkered green tablecloths, and market-fresh foods and attitude. The seasonal produce and catch dictate the dishes here, and the chef then takes it up a notch, with creative items such as a homemade vegan burger or the radical *hamburguesa de pulpo* (octopus burger), made with ground octopus seasoned with *pimentón* (Spanish paprika) and served on artisanal bread with caramelized onions, lettuce, tomato, and local cheese. The homemade desserts include a puckering-fresh *helado de frutas* (red fruit ice cream) and a rich *crema de chocolate*.

Bakeries

You can buy *melindres*—popularly also

known as *rosquillas de feria* (fairground shortbreads)—all across town. They actually look more like partially glazed donuts, and are made with good flour, rich butter, egg yolks, and a hit of anise seed liquor. Here are three favorite bakeries:

Pastelería Trisquel (Rúa Doutor Novoa Santos, 32; 10am-2pm and 5-8pm) is a new café and pastry shop with lime-green walls. Passionate pastry chefs bake fresh batches of many pastries daily, including the celebrated *melindre*.

Panadería Tarrío (Calle de San Antonio, 21; 981-505-382; 8am-2:30pm and 5-8pm) is known not only for *melindres* but also good bread and great empanadas. Stock up here for picnic staples for the trail.

Casa Melchora (Rúa Camiño de Ovedo, 6; 981-507-829; 10am-2pm and 4:30-8:30pm) is famous for their *melindres* as well as other traditional pastries, especially *almendrados* (dense, chewy almond cookies).

Accommodations

Though it could use a fresh coat of paint, the central, spotless, and comfortable **Hotel-Pension Xaneiro** (Rúa San Pedro; 981-505-015; www.hotelxaneiro.com; 37 rooms; €25 single/€40 double) is a decent value for basic rooms and central location in the heart of historic Melide, on a quiet pedestrian street right on the Camino.

A few blocks east of Hotel-Pension Xaneiro is the **Hostal Restaurante Xaneiro** (Avenida Habana, 43; 981-506-140; www.hotelxaneiro.com; €35-55), run by the same family. It's equally spotless but slightly more upscale, with an Old Europe feel. The helpful hosts are good sources of local information. A good restaurant on the ground floor serves a daily menu (€9) and a la carte options (€10-15), including *pulpo*. This is a good place for *empanadas* and *caldo Gallego* as well.

Albergue-Pensión Pereiro (Rúa Progreso, 43; 981-506-314; www.alberguepereiro.com) opened in 2013 and offers new, clean, and relaxing informal rooms and common spaces—including a good kitchen. The bunk beds are solid wood, and the dorm rooms (several with two, four, or eight beds in them; €10) leave a lot of room to move around. The private rooms with bath are plain, light-filled and equally spotless (€40). Proprietors speak English.

★ Iglesia de Santa María de Melide
Km 52

One kilometer (0.6 mile) from the center of Melide as the Camino proceeds west lies this beautiful Romanesque church from the late 11th century. **Santa María de Melide** (Rúa Santa María, s/n; 981-505-003; www.santiagoturismo.com; open for Sunday mass at 11am) preserves two ornate doorways on the south and west sides, and also has multicolored frescos from two periods inside. The more recent frescos were painted in the 15th century, but seem to honor and replicate the earlier 12th-century styles. Depicted are the Trinity and the four Evangels represented by the Tetramorph of winged man, winged lion, winged ox, and eagle. The older paintings, geometric motifs and bands, are the parts that date to the 12th century.

Santa María has many other elements from different times, some even more ancient, such as the altar, an 8th-century Visigothic piece reused from an earlier chapel. Also look for unusual engravings, such as the geometric forms and numbers that decorate the western door and the whimsical animals over the southern entrance and on the interior capitals.

The church has a champion as well, an engaging volunteer, José Antonio, who opens the church for visits and guided tours when he is not working his full-time job (usually on holidays and weekends). Passionate about the Middle Ages

■■■ **Top Experience** ■■■
The *Queimada* Ritual

Queimada, meaning "burnt," is a drink made either in a cast-iron cauldron or in a terracotta cooking pot. The process begins with *orujo,* a strong spirit made from the remains of the winemaking process (similar to how brandy is made). The *orujo* is poured into the cauldron with a few tablespoons of sugar, a few whole coffee beans, lemon peels, and sometimes orange zest. The maker stirs and recites a traditional poem or spell for blessings. She or he then lights the surface of the liquid, and lets the burning finish the flavor of the drink. Everyone gathered is offered a cup of the flaming elixir.

This ritual is often performed at times of transition, such as on All Saints' Day or the coming of winter, or as a rite of passage in a community of friends. It is also offered in some places, such as at **Os Albergue** in Boente, to pilgrims, who are themselves beings in constant transition and prepares them for arriving in Santiago de Compostela, to chase away evil spirits, to burn off bad karma, and to infuse them with positive energy for the final stretch.

Other opportunities to partake in *queimada* on the Camino are at **Albergue Ave Fénix,** back in Villafranca del Bierzo (Km 182.1) and ahead in Santiago de Compostela's **Casa Casino.**

---

and knowledgeable about Templar history, he will gladly show you the Templar connections to this church, as well as discuss its earlier foundations, not only from the Visigoths, but further back to the Iron Age Celtic speakers who possibly also worshipped here.

What is clear is that this spot has been held sacred for a long time by many different peoples. Sure enough, there are underground sources of water, which Jose Antonio says pass exactly under the baptismal font in the adjoining room off of the church nave. When I was last there, three pilgrims from Madrid wearing Tau crosses—the wooden T-shaped cross of San Antonio (some also connect it to the Templars)—arrived with pendulums and dousing rods to map the waterways under our feet.

José Antonio speaks English, and takes pride in learning the basics in as many languages as he can, usually from passing pilgrims. (Ask to see the notebook where he keeps track of his linguistic experiences!) Also ask him about the Game of the Goose: He has two illustrations of the esoteric game associated with the Camino and is happy to discuss its mystical, Camino, and Templar connections.

Boente   Km 47.5

The roadside hamlet of Boente (pop. 115) was once called Santiago de Boente, and was noted in the *Codex Calixtinus*; it was a more common pilgrim stop in the 12th century than it is today. But if you hope for the chance to experience the ritual of *queimada,* with its deeper ritual of clearing and transformation, stop at **Os Albergue** (981-501-853; 30 beds, €11). Os Albergue is run by *hospitaleros* who cook healthy meals (€10) and at times perform the *queimada* ritual as a gift to guests. They hold the *queimada* after dinner, in Spanish (but ask a fellow pilgrim to translate), and offers a chance for you to reflect, share with others, and to release anything you no longer need so you can walk more lightly toward Santiago. This is definitely the draw of this place but also be prepared for the accommodations to be very rudimentary, and, some say, uncomfortable.

Another elixir in town carries local lore: Near the village *cruceiro* is the **Fonte de Saleta** (fountain of Saleta), whose waters some believe possess healing properties. The water is not clearly marked as drinkable; I advise that you do not drink from it.

Ribadiso da Baixo
Km 42.2

Among the many rivers and valleys traversed since Palas de Rei, the passage from Boente to Ribadiso defines one of the prettiest, culminating at the Iso river just before Ribadiso de Baixo (pop. 9) with its **medieval bridge.** This graceful single-arch bridge stretches across the grassy slopes along the banks of the Río Iso. A patch of green just below the bridge beckons for a lazy riverside picnic.

This small riverside village is incredibly enticing, given its fresh country air and lack of congestion, a mere 3 kilometers (1.9 miles) from Arzúa. If you want a quiet, full-service place, consider stopping here for the night.

Food
If you're hankering for a hot meal or a cold beer, cross the bridge into Ribadiso to find **Mesón Rural Ribadiso** (€9-12) a few feet to the right. This terrific café has an indoor fireplace and backyard terrace that flows into the neighboring pasture, where cows graze near laundry drying on a line. The food, even the simplest of meals, is excellent. For dessert, try the local semi-soft Arzúa cheese with a dense slice of *membrillo* (quince paste), delivered with joy by the two women who run the place.

Accommodations
Just before Mesón Rural Ribadiso, you will pass the **Hospital de San Antón de Ribadiso** (Ribadiso s/n; 981-501-185 or 660-396-823; €6), founded in 1523 and restored in 1993. This was a pilgrims'

hospital, and today resumes its original function as the basic *xunta* (municipal) **albergue**, with 70 beds in three dorm rooms.

In addition to the municipal *albergue*, across the path, to the Camino's left, are two other *albergues,* the **Albergue Milpes Ribadiso** (Ribadiso, 7; 981-500-425; alberguemilpes@gmail.com; year-round; 28 beds, €10), and the **Albergue Los Caminantes** (Ribadiso; 981-500-295; Apr.-Oct.; info@albergueloscaminantes.com; 56 beds, €10). For private lodging, the contemporary **Pensión Ribadiso** (Ribadiso, 22; 981-500-703; www.pensionribadiso.com; €60) offers graceful, pristine, modern rooms with floor-to-ceiling windows and traditional stone walls.

Leaving Ribadiso
Departing Ribadiso is a brief but slightly steep climb out of the Iso river valley. When you get to the top, in less than 2 kilometers (1.2 miles), look to your left for a layered view of the mountains you've been gradually climbing through. The approach from here into Arzúa is a straight and easy passage along the main road (N-547) that passes into the town and serves also as the Camino into Arzúa.

Arzúa   Km 39.1

Still thick in ancient *castro* territory, Arzúa (pop. 6,261) is remarkable for its gregarious community life and the dynamic energy running through the heart of town. Locals share a passion for good food, and take pride in producing a lot of it locally. Many food shops—green grocers, cheese and charcuterie, wine, and general goods—line the main thoroughfare, which is also the Camino.

While all of the terrain the Camino traverses in Galicia is celebrated dairy and cheese country, Arzúa, known by Spaniards as *la tierra de queso* ("the land of cheese"), is its capital. The local cheese, *queso de Arzúa* is, like tetilla, made from the blended milk of three special breeds of cow that graze the hills and mountains of Galicia—specifically Freisian, Alpine Brown, and Rubia Gallega—but Arzúa's graze the special meadows, grasses, and hills of this particular locale, giving it its special flavor. Chances to taste *queso de Arzúa* are ample. All along the main street in town are shops and cafés where you can ask for a sample or purchase a few hundred grams or a disk of the semi-soft, creamy, flavorful cheese. Many cheesemakers—often cottage industries—will also be by the roadside near their farm or homestead, advertising any available cheese for purchase. You will also notice that cheese appears more frequently on the dessert menu, most often felicitously paired with the locally made dense quince paste, *membrillo*.

Arzúa is a rather modern town with few medieval remains. You'll find the typical pilgrim town layout here, with almost all the businesses arrayed along the long serpent-shaped body of the Camino. The parish church, **Iglesia de Santiago** (Rúa do Carme, 6; 981-511-003; open daily for mass 7pm), is a modern 20th-century church that stands on the ancient site of prior churches also dedicated to Saint James.

Cheese Shops

Food shops are open during the usual business hours of 9am-1:30pm and 5-9pm. Two cheese shops, the first right on the Camino as it passes into Arzúa and the other a few meters north in the center of town, are good places to sample cheeses and make some picnic purchases for the next day of trekking.

A Queixeira de Arzúa (Rúa de Lugo, 70; 981-500-510) may have up to a dozen local makers of the famous Arzúan cheeses on any day, as well as other regional products such as sausages, liquors, and jams.

Queixería Barral (Rúa Doutor Fernández de la Riva, 6; 687-515-515; www.queixosbarral.com) is one of the established cheesemakers from the area, specializing in D.O.P. (*denominación de origen protegida*, protected denomination of origin) Arzúa and Tetilla cheeses. The former is slightly firmer and tangier than the latter, which is creamier and milder. Both are made with milk from cattle that graze in surrounding hillside pastures.

Festivals and Events

Arzúa hosts an **annual cheese fair** in early March and also has a twice-monthly **market,** the 8th and 22nd of every month, showcasing a substantial selection of cheeses; it's located in the Recinto Feiral Terra do Queixo covered market (Travesia da Feira A; 8am-2pm), just north (right) off of the Camino in central Arzúa and not far from Quiexería Barral.

Arzúa also has an **ecological fair** held in October, also in the Recinto Feiral "Terra do Queixo" market space, that focuses on natural, local, and organic products and services.

Food

★ **Restaurante Casa Nene** (Rúa Cima do Lugar, 1; 981-08-107; €25) might be one of the best places to eat on the entire Camino. It reflects a modern twist on Galician cuisine with some French and Italian elements folded in. A well-considered wine list accompanies what is not a typical Spanish menu: more choices of salads and grilled vegetables are offered, as is a seaweed (harvested in Galician waters) risotto with wild mushrooms, the priciest item on the menu (€27). There is also a cheese board—a must in Arzúa—as well as seven gourmet desserts.

The tapas bar and restaurant **Churreria O Furancho d'Santiso** (Calle de Lugo, 9; 981-50-12-22) is a gregarious place for pilgrim diners as well as a popular place to bring a date. There is an excellent *menú del peregrino* (€10) and a la carte menu (€15-20) where even simple dishes are executed with the freshest ingredients and brightest flavors, such as perfectly grilled chicken breasts, vibrant green salads, and a creamy saffron-toned *caldo gallego*.

Café Bar Praza (Rúa Lugo, 2; 981-500-949; www.cafebarpraza; €5-8) is a central hub—bar, café, and eatery—on the prominent corner of the main road and the town square, and is run by a woman who does everything with thought and care. A popular place all day for drinks, snacks, and a bite, her breakfast offerings—including local ham and eggs with crusty bread and fresh-squeezed juice—are divine and can practically fuel the whole day.

Accommodations

The 10 double rooms (some with the potential to be triples) in ★ **Pension Casa Frade** (Calle Ramón Franco, 10; 981-50-00-19; www.casafrade.arzua-comercial.com; €30/single, €40/double) feel like your favorite aunt's home, with crocheted bedspreads, yellow walls, and dark wooden floors. This is in fact an old family home converted into an appealing guesthouse. The café on the ground floor is open for coffee or afternoon drinks, and is frequented by many locals as well as guests.

Albergue Público de Arzúa (Rúa Cima do Lugar, 6; 660-396-824; 56 beds, €6) is made of the same warm rainbow-toned gray granite as the tiny, neighboring 14th-century chapel dedicated to Mary Magdalene. Located along one of Arzúa's more picturesque streets off the main drag, this is an intimate yet spacious and clean establishment with delightful traditional wood and stone.

The semi-luxury **Casa Teodora** (Calle de Lugo, 38; 981-500-083; www.casateodora.com; €36-45) is in the very center of all the action on the main street, at a point where the main street forks into a lower and an upper road. Teodora is a delightful place to stay, even with the sometimes impersonal attitude of the reception. They also have a good **restaurant** in a warm stone dining room on the first level with a decent *menú del dia*. Traditional Galician cuisine is presented colorfully and creatively, with dishes such as Galician hake grilled and stewed with red peppers, green peas, and potatoes and grilled steak or pork tenderloin with Arzúa cheese.

Leaving Arzúa

The next accommodations on the Camino after Arzúa are 11.2 kilometers (7 miles) ahead, in **Salceda** (Km 28.3; pop. 120), including the warm-hearted **Casa Tia Teresa** (Salceda, 14; 628-558-716; casatiateresa@gmail.com), a modern country home on the edge of corn field and forest, to the left on the Camino and the N-547. The hotel, run by an upbeat and humorous (and English-speaking) husband-and-wife team, offers five private rooms with both shared (€35) and ensuite baths (€40-45). Rooms are exemplary, with natural light, cast-iron beds, quilted bedspreads, parquet floors, and tile bathrooms. There's also a restaurant and bar. The restaurant serves delicious home-cooked meals, such as grilled langoustine and savory empanadas, among other choices (€4.50-12.50). The bar at Casa Tia Teresa also has bottles of the Camino-inspired craft beer from Santiago de Compostela, *Cerveza del Peregrino*.

O Empalme Km 23.8

This is a small place on the N-547 where the Camino passes, making it a roadside destination for drivers and walkers alike. The whole point to stop here is its café, O Ceadoiro (on the left of the Camino).

Food

The food at ★ **Café O Ceadoiro** (Santa Irene, 18; 981-511-348) is local and delicious. The owners, big-hearted and jovial, run a bar and a dining room, both lively with local and pilgrim business. They pride themselves in excellent local wines and high-quality, locally grown and produced ingredients. When I asked for a plate of *pimientos de Padron*, they went into their garden and plucked the peppers just for my order, and then discussed the merits of which white wine to pair with the dish. Other dishes to try are the *empanada de carne* (beef empanada), lentil stew, and grilled squid.

Santa Irene   Km 22.6

Leaving O Empalme, the Camino never departs too far from the N-547, but walking through the village of Santa Irene (pop. 18), to the left of the Camino, makes the rural highway feel more removed.

The village has a 17th-century stone **fountain** dedicated to Santa Irene. Its central niche once held a sculpture from 1682, but it was stolen by an unknown thief in 1989. Pilgrims continue to place stones in the empty niche, as they do all across the Camino, stacked like small cairns, known as *milladoiros*. Village legend attributes miraculous and healing properties to the waters of this fountain. Because the water is not potable, locals use it to water their vegetable gardens, a form of alchemy allowing one to ingest the magical waters safely and nutritiously.

If you were to follow the stone pathway to the left of the fountain a few dozen meters off the Camino, also to the left, you'll see the **village church** of Santa Irene, an all-stone 18th-century rectangular church. It is rarely open. Inside it is entirely plain, except for a Baroque retable on the altar. Retrace your steps back to the Camino as it passes through this village; soon after Santa Irene the trail crosses and returns to walking parallel to the N-547, on the right side of the road.

Leaving Santa Irene

After Santa Irene, in 3.8 kilometers (2.4 miles), the Camino has a 0.5-kilometer (0.3-mile) detour to the left (Km 20), to the town **O Pedrouzo**, also known as **Arca**, which offers you the widest range of lodging and meals. If you skip this left-forking detour, you'll stay on the Camino, passing through a eucalyptus forest toward the hamlet of Amenal.

Both O Pedrouzo and Amenal offer a good last night on the Camino, and I like them both. I am slightly more fond of Amenal simply because it is a tiny hamlet with one hotel (and nothing else), guaranteeing a quiet night of rest. If a time of quiet reflection set in eucalyptus and pine forest is your desire, consider Amenal (though it is slightly pricier than most accommodation, starting at €45). If a more social atmosphere, or wider range of lodging, feels right for your last night on the Camino, then O Pedrouzo/Arca is the place.

⬦ Detour: O Pedrouzo   Km 20

Locals call their town (pop. 850) by both names, O Pedrouzo and Arca, a place that serves as the last large stop on the Camino with a wide range of lodging before Santiago de Compostela, with at least six hotels and seven *albergues*.

Arca has no surviving historic monuments; the modern church of **Santa Eulalia de Arca** (Calle Pedrouzo, 7; 981-511-003) stands on the site of an earlier church and offers a daily pilgrims' **mass** at 7:30pm.

Food
★ **Taste the Way** (Avenida de Lugo, 9; 615-104-141; www.tastetheway.com; €8-20) a self-slated "gourmet tavern on the Camino," lives up to its claim. Galician-style omnivore and vegetarian dishes are a departure from the usual meat, salad,

and potatoes menu common on the Camino. Consider the arugula and asparagus salad, *pulpo á feira* with grilled collard greens, cream of pumpkin soup, crab, gooseneck barnacle, or sea urchin paté, or the vegetarian lasagna.

At the other end of the spectrum, go whole-hog at the **Restaurante Parrillada Regueiro** (Avenida Santiago, 25; €10-15), a grill house offering heaping servings of steamed clams, roasts, ribs, steaks, fries, and salads.

Accommodations
Wood-paneled walls and terracotta floors warm the rustic, immaculate, and straightforward rooms of **Pensión Codesal** (Calle Codesal, 17; €45-50), but more endearing is the cheer of owner Ramiro, who welcomes each visitor as if they were the first to walk through his door. He speaks some English, and any language barriers are obliterated by his joy and desire to help. Rooms have ensuite baths.

At **Pensión Maruja** (Rúa Nova, 9; 981-511-406; €15-25), the quiet and informally elegant rooms are detailed with original artwork or antique prints, fine quilted bedspreads, and large windows that let in natural light and views of the beautiful countryside. María, the owner, makes you feel as if you're coming home.

Pensión Maribel (Rua Os Mollaos, 23; 981-511-404; www.pensionmaribel.com; €35-45) is pristine, and Maribel isn't afraid of colors and rich textures. She's just as enthusiastic about her guests and goes out of her way to help make your stay comfortable, including packing a picnic lunch for the next day upon request. All rooms have ensuite baths.

Pensión Una Estrella Dorada (Avenida de Lugo, 10; 630-018-363; €30-40) gets a golden star, as in its name, for kindness, dedication, opulent and impeccable rooms (even though all must share a bath); it is more like an old-time, high-class residential house. A well-equipped kitchen is open for guests' use.

Leaving O Pedrouzo
Simply follow the way-markers for the Camino departing on the north side of town on **Rúa Concello**. These will lead you to rejoin the Camino in less than 1 kilometer (0.6 miles), where you will veer left (west) toward Amenal.

Amenal   Km 16.6

If you bypass the detour to O Pedrouzo, or return to the fork to resume the Camino, you will arrive in Amenal, a tiny hamlet with no services for pilgrims other than a single hotel.

Food and Accommodation
The ★ **Hotel Amenal** (Amenal, 12; 981-510-31; www.hotelamenal.com; €45/single, €80/double) stands on the edge of a peaceful eucalyptus and pine forest and offers a peaceful slumber for your last night on the Camino before reaching Santiago de Compostela. Though it's a modern hotel, the atmosphere in the bar and dining room is akin to that in the *albergues,* offering a chance to meet other pilgrims and share a meal. The rooms are immaculate and spacious, with massive firm beds and thick cotton sheets and towels. If this hotel is full, the staff also oversee a similar hotel 3 kilometers (1.9 miles) away, meant for pilgrim overflow. They transport pilgrims there and back to the Camino the next morning, for free.

Leaving Amenal
The path meanders through dense eucalyptus and oak forest from Amenal to Lavacolla.

In 4.2 kilometers (2.6 miles) after Amenal, to your right and directly on the Camino, is a good café in the hamlet of San Paio. **Porta de Santiago** (Lugar San Paio, 28) serves snacks and refreshments throughout the day, beginning with breakfast (typically open by 8am). For a twist on the morning meal, ask for the *pan de tomate con jamón* (tomato-rubbed toast with olive oil and Serrano ham), served with coffee and fresh OJ (€6.80).

Lavacolla Km 10

In medieval times, pilgrims washed their private parts in the freshwater stream that to this day sweeps through the modest settlement of Lavacolla (pop 305). (In fact, the town name derives from this ritual: *lava mentula* in Latin, *lava culo* in more vulgar Spanish.) There's an important metaphor to the ritual: to cleanse one's body in preparation to cleanse one's soul. Consider making ritual ablutions here; that is, cleanse your mind and leave behind any extra metaphorical baggage that the Camino has not yet lifted—or at least take inventory of what the walk has taught you about yourself and the world.

Food and Accommodations

If rain or desire to slow the walk down inspire you to lodge here, Lavacolla has four rural inns, all of which serve dinner and breakfast.

Ruta Jacobea (Lugar Lavacolla, 41; 981-888-211; www.rjacobea.es; 20 rooms; €60-75; breakfast, €9), a big modern complex of stone and metal, is a quality hotel, formal restaurant, and casual café-bar. The chef creates contemporary Galician cuisine, with dishes such as lobster and scallop paella that use fresh local ingredients from land and ocean. A la carte options can make for a pricier meal, but the hotel also offers a good *menú del día* (€10-15). Note that this is also an airport and business hotel, so be prepared for more impersonal service than what *peregrinos* get on most of the Camino; it is still of high quality. Proprietors speak English.

For a more personal touch, and better budget choice, the **Hotel Garcas** (Calle

From top to bottom: pilgrims and locals on the Camino after Arzúa; the 1993 Holy Year Monument on Monte del Gozo; the first view of Santiago de Compostela's cathedral spires.

Noval, 2; 30 rooms; €45-50; breakfast, €5) is another modern hotel with an enclosed terrace café. To reach it, head 150 meters (492 feet) off the Camino to the left (before reaching Hotel Ruta Jacobea), on the left (south) side of the N-634a. Rooms are homey, with multicolored fabrics and restful beds. The restaurant has a daily menu (€10). Proprietors speak English.

Leaving Lavacolla

With the copious promise of rain in Galicia, you may find that you do not need to wash the dust of the road off here, that the weather—charmingly called *chubascos* (tempests)—will do it for you as you walk.

For such a momentous passage, the stream where medieval pilgrims once washed themselves is now small and overgrown with forest undergrowth along its banks, as you cross over the narrow footbridge just before leaving Lavacolla. After crossing the bridge, begin a slight climb toward Monte del Gozo. The vista opens up gradually to reveal stunning views of the mountains and river valleys that surround Santiago de Compostela toward the south.

Monte del Gozo Km 4.9

The 380-meter-high (1,247-foot) Monte del Gozo (in Spanish; Monte do Gozo in Gallego) is the historic hill from which medieval pilgrims first caught sight of Santiago de Compostela's cathedral spires and cried out with emotion, *Mont joie!* ("Mount Joy!") You can still catch a glimpse of Santiago de Compostela from here, even though the tree cover at mid-distance blocks the cathedral spires.

From Monte del Gozo's hilltop you can see the fabled **Pico Sacro** to the southwest, the hill of legend where Queen Lupa, the indigenous ruler of that territory 2,000 years ago, tested Saint James's disciples.

They overcame the wild bulls and the dangerous dragon and continued 12 more kilometers (7.5 miles) northwest, taking Saint James in his stone sarcophagus to the ancient burial hill that today is Santiago de Compostela. From the Monte del Gozo, 4 more kilometers (2.5 miles) remain for you to do the same.

Sights
1993 Holy Year Monument

In 1993, as part of the holy year festivities, officials built this modern (and terribly incongruent) monument at the top of Monte del Gozo, to honor both Pope John Paul II's visit to Santiago in 1989 and that of Saint Francis of Assisi in 1214. Beyond the industrial sport-trophy look of the monument, the hill and its view of the surrounding rolling hills and green valleys near Santiago de Compostela is still stunning. The government also built new pilgrim housing (resembling army barracks) below the monument, to house up to 400 pilgrims. These are still in use, but with Santiago de Compostela so near at hand, much more felicitous housing awaits you in 4.9 kilometers (3 miles).

Capilla de San Marcos

Standing at the hilltop next to the 1993 monument, and facing the mountain vista, looking toward Santiago de Compostela, the small and plain Capilla de San Marcos is to your right.

This is a rather nondescript chapel, and often not open outside of summer, but it is most famous for being the last place before entering Santiago de Compostela where you can get your pilgrim passport stamped. The structure is modern, but it marks the historic site of the much-altered (and gone) medieval chapel, most likely from the 12th century. It actually marks the original site of the lookout point at which pilgrims stood to see for the first time the cathedral spires of Santiago de Compostela. In medieval times, pilgrims raced to the lookout point, and the first to reach it would be declared "king."

The chapel also has an unusual entrance, one that faces east rather than west. Legend has it that a fatigued San Marcos arrived here and built a chapel for rest, setting the door facing the direction from which he had arrived.

The chapel has a low stone wall surrounding its tree and grass grounds, offering a nice place to sit and contemplate your journey.

Leaving Monte de Gozo

It's all downhill from here. Follow the arrows and signs past the Capilla de San Marcos. Over the next 2 kilometers (1.2 miles), you'll continue through green rolling countryside while descending into the river valley of Compostela. During these kilometers, take pleasure in the hide-and-seek game the spires of the cathedral play with you, becoming visible for the first time only to disappear again as you pass near tall stands of trees.

Approaching Santiago de Compostela

The path enters Santiago de Compostela on the west side at the neighborhood of San Lázaro. The urban passage is well marked, moving along Rúa Dos Concheiros, which flows into Rúa San Pedro and crosses into the medieval walls of Santiago at the Puerta del Camino, leaving a final few hundred meters to reach Kilometer Zero at the cathedral. Urban way-markers are everywhere: on the pavement, on street signs and posts, and on the sides of buildings.

You have at last arrived, but don't be surprised if locals largely ignore you: They see thousands of pilgrims arriving here monthly, not only from the Camino Francés, but also from Portugal (Camino Portugués), as well as other pilgrim routes south, north, east, and west (including the Camino del Norte, Camino Primitivo, Camino Inglés, and Via de la Plata). In fact, some pilgrims suggest that the scallop shell is the symbol of the Camino because its shell pattern traces the many paths that lead to the center, here at Compostela.

As you make your way to this center, you may feel a bit betwixt and between, perhaps a mix of elation and deflation. But every so often, as you make your way to the cathedral, someone you pass may make eye contact, smile, and offer a quiet nod, acknowledging that you have just accomplished something huge: a holy trek, a great adventure, a simplification of life, a lesson in self-reliance, a broadening of horizons, a lightening of your heart and spirit, a deepening of your trust in life, and a wild walk into nature, culture, and history, all the while enriched with the kindness and generosity of everyone you met along the way.

Santiago
de
Compostela

Km: 0

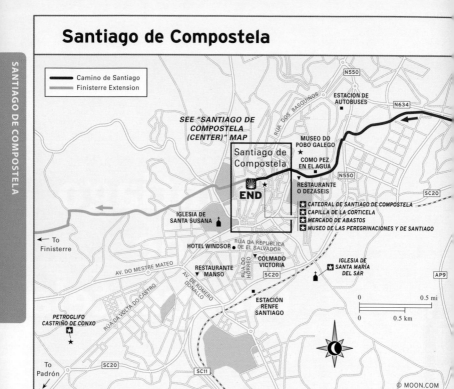

Santiago de Compostela

The pilgrim's final trek into the center of Santiago de Compostela is a long, green, and sinuous walk filled with anticipation. Upon entering the city, pilgrims beeline straight for Km 0, the Plaza de Obradoiro and the cathedral, under which Santiago's nearly 2,000-year-old bones are believed to be entombed.

Santiago de Compostela (Km 0; pop. 95,092) is a mythic medieval city whose arched stone passageways, cobblestones, and grey granite squares give off rainbow colors when it rains. (And it rains a lot.) Along with the green moss and ferns growing on old stone walls and the many symbols of pagan Galician folklore, from Celtic designs to *meigas*

and *curanderas* (white witches and traditional healers), the city reminds you at every turn that it is older than Saint James, a fertile green place between two rivers, the mountains, and the ocean that has drawn people since prehistory. But Santiago's real magic is that it is very much a city of the present, with gregarious restaurants and cafés, shop windows full of *tetilla* cheeses and cooked *pulpo* (octopus), and artisans hawking traditional handcrafts as they have for a millennia. There is the piquant scent of peppers frying, the soulful echo of a lone bagpiper playing Galician folk tunes, and wandering bands of university *tunas* who, like troubadours before them, sing medieval songs, hoping for a coin.

Highlights

★ **Catedral de Santiago de Compostela:** A holy site since Roman—if not pre-Roman—times, this cathedral is famous as the site where legend claims Saint James is buried. Hugging the statue of Saint James on the high altar is an emotional rite of a passage for pilgrims (page 404).

★ **Capilla de la Corticela:** A 9th-century chapel within Catedral de Santiago de Compostela, La Corticela may be the oldest church on the Camino and has a quiet, intimate atmosphere (page 408).

★ **Mercado de Abastos:** One of northern Spain's most colorful and dynamic daily markets vends produce, cheeses, meats, fish, wine, and liquors from local farmers, herders, and fisherman. Take your seafood to a designated kiosk, and they'll cook it for you on site and set a table for your lunch (page 411).

★ **Museo de las Peregrinaciones y de Santiago:** An interactive and engaging museum on all things pilgrimage-related, including the origins of labyrinths and the esoteric Game of the Goose (page 412).

★ **Iglesia de Santa María del Sar:** Built by the cathedral's master builder, Master Mateo, this Romanesque jewel of a church is sinking slowly into the spongy earth on the banks of the river Sar, adding to its treacherous but romantic setting (page 415).

★ **Petroglifo de Castriño de Conxo:** This surviving 3,000-year-old petroglyph in the city attests that this holy and hilly place was considered sacred long before the time of Saint James (page 416).

Santiago de Composela (Center)

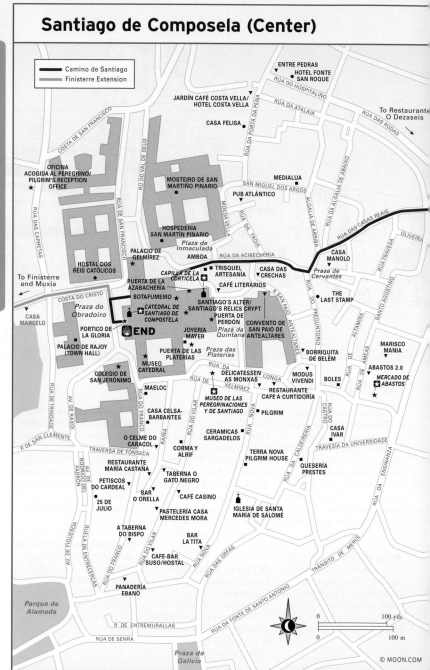

Legend:
- Camino de Santiago
- Finisterre Extension

RUA DO HOSPITALIÑO

ENTRE PEDRAS
HOTEL FONTE
SAN ROQUE

To Restaurante
O Dezaseis

RÚA DAS RODAS

RÚA DA ATALAIA

JARDÍN CAFÉ COSTA VELLA/
HOTEL COSTA VELLA

RÚA DA PORTA DA PENA

CASA FELISA

RÚA DE VAL DE DEUS

COSTA DE SAN FRANCISCO

RÚA DE SAN FRANCISCO

MEDIALUA

SAN MIGUEL DOS ARGOS

ALGALIA DE ABAIXO

RÚA DA ALGALIA DE ABAIXO

RÚA DAS CASAS REAIS

OFICINA
ACOGIDA AL PEREGRINO/
PILGRIM'S RECEPTION
OFFICE

MOSTEIRO DE SAN
MARTIÑO PINARIO

PUB ATLÁNTICO

MOEDA VELLA

RÚA DA TROIA

ALGALIA DE ARRIBA

OLIVEIRA

RÚA DAS CARRETAS

HOSPEDERÍA
SAN MARTÍN PINARIO

PALACIO DE
GELMÍREZ

Plaza de
Inmaculada

AMBOA

RÚA DE ACIBECHERÍA

CASA
MANOLO

RÚA TRAVESA

SANTO AGOSTIÑO

To Finisterre
and Muxia

HOSTAL DOS
REIS CATÓLICOS

CAPILLA DE LA
CORTICELA

TRISQUEL
ARTESANÍA

CASA DAS
CRECHAS

Praza de
Cervantes

COSTA DO CRISTO

PUERTA DE LA
AZABACHERÍA

CAFÉ LITERARIOS

THE
LAST STAMP

CASA
MARCELO

Praza do
Obradoiro

BOTAFUMEIRO

CATEDRAL DE
SANTIAGO DE
COMPOSTELA

SANTIAGO'S ALTER/
SANTIAGO'S RELICS CRYPT

PUERTA DE
PERDÓN

Plaza da
Quintana

CONVENTO DE
SAN PAIO DE
ANTEALTARES

R SAN PAIO ANTEALTARES

RÚA DO PREGUNTOIRO

END

PORTICO DE
LA GLORIA

JOYERIA
MAYER

PALACIO DE RAJOY
(TOWN HALL)

PUERTA DE LAS
PLATERÍAS

Praza das
Platerías

BORRIQUITA
DE BELÉM

RÚA DE AMEAS

ALTAMIRA

MARISCO
MANIA

COLEGIO DE
SAN JERÓNIMO

MUSEO
CATEDRAL

RÚA DA

RÚA DE
XELMÍREZ

DELICATESSEN
AS MONXAS

CONGA

MODUS
VIVENDI

BOLES

ABASTOS 2.0

MERCADO DE
ABASTOS

RÚA DE FIGUEROA

AV. DE RAXOI

MAELOC

RÚA DO FRANCO

RAIÑA

RÚA DO VILAR

RÚA NOVA

RESTAURANTE
CAFE A CURTIDORÍA

RÚA DO CASTRO

RÚA DE TRINDADE

R DE SAN CLEMENTE

CASA CELSA-
BARBANTES

MUSEO DE LAS
PEREGRINACIONES
Y DE SANTIAGO

PILGRIM

CASA
IVAR

TRAVESA DA FONSECA

O CELME DO
CARACOL

CERAMICAS
SARGADELOS

TRAVESIA DA UNIVERSIDADE

RÚA DA CALDEIRERÍA

RÚA DA ENSINANZA

AV. DE FIGUEROA

RÚA RODRIGO DEL PADRON

RESTAURANTE
MARÍA CASTAÑA

CORMA Y
ALRIF

TERRA NOVA
PILGRIM HOUSE

QUESERÍA
PRESTES

RÚA DE ENTRECERCAS

PETISCOS
DO CARDEAL

25 DE
JULIO

BAR
O ORELLA

TABERNA O
GATO NEGRO

CAFÉ CASINO

RÚA DO VILAR

RÚA DO FRANCO

A TABERNA
DO BISPO

PASTELERÍA CASA
MERCEDES MORA

IGLESIA DE SANTA
MARÍA DE SALOMÉ

BAR
LA TITA

RÚA NOVA

RÚA DAS ORFAS

TRÁNSITO DE MERCÉ

Parque de
Alameda

CAFE-BAR
SUSO/HOSTAL

PANADERÍA
EBANO

RÚA DA FONTE DE SANTO ANTONIO

0   100 yds

0   100 m

R. DE ENTREMURALLAS

RÚA DE SENRA

Praza de
Galicia

© MOON.COM

Planning Your Time

Ideally, **4 days** will let you really soak up Santiago de Compostela, but a minimum of **2 days,** intensely packed, can also cover the wealth of this city. If you desire to make a day trip to Padrón, allow half a day to a full day for that.

Most pilgrims arriving in Santiago head straight to the Praza de Obradoiro and the cathedral, which contains the tomb of Saint James. Note that **packs are no longer allowed in the cathedral,** so you'll either have to check into your accommodations first or trust other pilgrims on the square to watch your pack as you take turns entering.

During the **Festival de Santiago** (July 15 through July 31), the city takes on a festive atmosphere as they celebrate Saint James's feast day with music, dance, food, theatre, and sound and light show on the cathedral square.

Getting There

Car

If you're driving the Camino to Santiago from **Sarría** (125.3 km/78 mi; 2.5 hours) or **Portomarín** (96.2 km /60 mi; 2 hours) in the east, take **LU-633** then the **N-547** through A Brea and Palas de Rei; the N-547 then merges with the **A-54** to enter Santiago from the northeast.

From **Porto, Portugal** (250 km/155 mi, 3 hours), **E-1/A-3** connects to **AP-9** after passing the border at Tui and enters Santiago from the south.

A Coruña (74 km/50 mi, 1 hour) links to Santiago from the north on the **N-550** or the **E-1**.

The most direct route from **Madrid** (608 km/378 mi, 6 hours) takes the **AP-6** northwest toward Benavente, the **A-52** west then north to Ourense, and the **AP-53** to Santiago.

Nearly all the main car agencies have offices in Santiago, especially concentrated around the train station: Look for **Hertz** (www.hertz.com), **Budget** (www.budget.com), **Avis** (www.avis.com), **Alamo** (www.alamo.com), **Europcar** (www.europcar.com), and **Enterprise** (www.enterprise.com). You'll also find Europcar, Hertz, Enterprise, and Avis at the airport.

Air

Santiago de Compostela's airport (SCQ) has connecting flights with Ryan Air, Iberia, Veuling, and Qatar Airways from Barcelona (BCN) and Madrid (MAD), and other European cities including Dublin, London, Paris, Amsterdam, and Frankfurt. **A Coruña's airport (LCG),** 75 kilometers (47 miles) north of Santiago and connected by train, has connecting flights from Madrid, Barcelona, Lisbon and London with TAP, Iberia, Veuling, Qatar Airways, Air France, Delta, and British Airways.

Airport **buses** run nearly every half-hour to the airport with pickup points at the central Plaza de Galicia, near the historic city, and also at the train station, before heading to the airport (35-45 min; €4). **Taxis** take about 20-25 minutes and cost around €25. **Pilgrim** (Rúa Nova, 7; 910-607-539; www.pilgrim.es) offers airport transfers to and from Santiago's airport (allow 30-40 minutes, €30 for up to four people) as well as from there to Sarria (€130, but cheaper for more than four people).

Train

RENFE (www.renfe.com) connects Santiago de Compostela with direct trains from Madrid (seven trains daily; 5-7.5 hours; €28-56), Barcelona (three daily; 9-12.5 hours; €42-119), and A Coruña (29 daily; 30-40min.; €6-16).

Santiago de Compostela's **RENFE station** is 1.6 kilometers (1 mile) directly south of the cathedral, a 20-minute walk along the street Rúa do Hórreo heading due north to the Plaza de Galicia, and then another 500 meters (1,640 feet) due north to the cathedral.

Bus

ALSA (www.alsa.com) connects towns and villages to Santiago de Compostela all along the Camino. The **bus station** in Santiago de Compostela, on Praza (Plaza) de Camilo Díaz Baliño, is 1.6 kilometers (1 mile) to the northwest of the cathedral, a 20-25 minute walk. While train is a more pleasant way to travel longer distances, ALSA runs buses from Barcelona to Santiago (two daily, both overnight buses; 15-17 hours; €79), departing the Barcelona Nord bus station, with a stop 15 minutes later at the train station, Barcelona Sants, and then traveling all night to Santiago. ALSA also runs buses from Madrid to Santiago (8-9 hours; €46-60), from Madrid Barajas airport, terminal T4 (four daily), and from Madrid's Estación del Sur (six daily).

Taxi

Radio Taxi (981-569-292) operates 24 hours and can make trips to the airport (around €25; 20-25 minutes). The only time you really will need a taxi in Santiago de Campostela, a delightfully small city suited to walking everywhere, is if you opt not to take the bus (€4) or Pilgrim air transfer service (€30 for up to four people) to get to the airport.

Sights

The vast majority, if not all, of *peregrinos* first head straight to the Plaza de Obradoiro that faces the west entrance of the Catedral de Santiago, Kilometer 0, in the heart of medieval Santiago de Compostela, to fulfill their goal of arriving at the tomb of Saint James inside the cathedral. After gathering their wits and emotions on the square, they enter through the cathedral's western gate, walk down the nave, and climb the high

Local Markets

- **Santiago de Compostela:** Santiago might have the most colorful daily covered and open-air market of the entire Camino right in the medieval center, the Mercado de Abastos. In addition to this, there's a weekly market every Thursday (page 411).

- **Padrón**: Weekly market every **Sunday** (page 426).

altar straight ahead to deliver thanks and hug the statue of Santiago at the altar's center.

Many other historic buildings stand all around the cathedral, including several on the Plaza de Obradoiro. But before taking in these sights, pilgrims usually complete the second most important ritual of arrival, and head to the Oficina Acogida al Peregrino (Pilgrims' Reception Office) to receive their certificate of completion, the Compostela. (Many come here after they check in to their accommodations.)

You can walk Santiago de Compostela like a labyrinth and keep the spirit of the Camino going right here in the city. All roads lead to the cathedral at the center and radiate out from there as well. All sights are an easy walk to reach, including the two peripheral sights, the Romanesque gem Iglesia del Sar, 1.5 kilometers (0.9 miles) from the southeast end of the cathedral, and the remarkable petroglyph, Castriño de Conxo, 2.6 kilometers (1.6 miles) to the southwest.

Praza do Obradoiro (Plaza de Obradoiro)

The large Praza do Obradoiro, meaning "workshop square" in Galician, refers to this as the place where stonemasons set up their workshops to build the cathedral. It is the cathedral's most important square. Here, you are right in front of the

Who Was Saint James?

From the Bible, we know that Saint James was one of Jesus's twelve disciples, son of Zebedee and Salome. James the Greater, as he was known, was one of the three in Jesus's innermost circle, along with John and Peter, and was present at the most significant moments of Jesus's ministry. James was also the first of Jesus's *apostles* to be martyred, by beheading, in the Holy Land in AD 44.

But no historical source connects James to Spain or Iberia, where he became known as Santiago. This connection draws from legends that began to circulate several hundred years after his death. According to these legends, James came to Iberia around AD 40 to evangelize, but only attracted a handful of followers. At his lowest moments, Mary came to him to speak words of encouragement. Once, Mary appeared to James in Muxía, riding a stone boat steered by angels. After she left, she left the stone boat behind, a part of the fabled *piedras sagradas* (sacred stones) that you will find arrayed on Muxía's coast, right in front of the church built in Mary's honor, the Santuario da Virxe da Barca. Another time, Mary appeared to James in Zaragoza, where she arrived riding a jasper pillar through the sky, surrounded by angels. After she returned to the Holy Land, she left the pillar, which stands today in the center of Zaragoza's Basílica del Pilar. In fables, James was in Iberia for four years, then returned home to the Levant, where Herod Agrippa had him beheaded.

It's said that, after his death, two of James's most devout disciples took his body and boarded another magical stone boat guided by angels that carried the them with Saint James's body to the coast of Galicia. Eventually, they made their way inland to the hill at Santiago de Compostela and buried James. His tomb was forgotten until around AD 814, when a hermit named Pelayo followed a trail of stars that led him to Saint James's luminous tomb. He alerted the local bishop, Theodomir, who went back with Pelayo

Saint James

and confirmed that the tomb was that of Saint James the Greater. Soon after the tomb's discovery, Alfonso II of Asturias commissioned a chapel to be built over it. By 899, the next king, Alfonso III, ordered a larger church. The Catedral de Santiago de Compostela you see today is the third one, begun in 1075 and finished in 1188. While archaeological excavations under the Catedral de Santiago can't confirm if one of the Roman-era tombs belonged to Santiago, they did find a 9th-century tomb belonging to the bishop Theodomir, who was with Pelayo at the time of Santiago's tomb's discovery.

Pelayo's journey was the beginning of what would become the great Christian pilgrimage to Santiago de Compostela. It is no coincidence that it happened in the 9th century, a time when the north of Iberia was sandwiched between the imperialistic designs of Charlemagne to the north and the newly founded Islamic kingdom centered on Cordoba to the south. The north forged its own legitimacy and foothold in between these two powerful adversaries, thanks in large part to Santiago and the Camino.

cathedral's west entrance, significant as the entrance medieval pilgrims first approached to enter the cathedral (and the one you'll use to enter as well). This square, along with Saint James's tomb inside the cathedral, are collectively and symbolically considered Kilometer 0.

Before heading into the cathedral, most pilgrims pause on this plaza, perhaps taking off their packs to sit and stretch. Stepping into this square can unleash a mix of emotions: soaring joy usually dominates, but there may be a bit of sorrow as well, along with spontaneous eruptions of celebration as pilgrims hug, laugh, cheer and cry together, whether they've met before or not. The experience was similar for medieval pilgrims, many of whom truly believed that by arriving they had achieved redemption and lifted the weight of sin from their souls. New security measures at the cathedral do not allow pilgrims to enter with their packs, so many take turns watching each other's packs.

Pilgrims arrive here at all times of the day throughout the year, and it can be a constant stream in peak season but still an active place all year round at any time of day. In the very center of the square, look for the inlaid scallop shell, set there in 1987 to recognize the Camino de Santiago as a European Cultural Itinerary by the European Council. Touching it brings a sense of grounding and completion, and some also feel it brings good luck.

The Plaza de Obradoiro didn't look like this until 1526, when Spain's king Carlos V ordered the demolition of the buildings in front of the Hostal de los Reyes Católicos and opened up the square to offer the sweeping view you get today. Before you step into the cathedral, notice that the square is bordered on all sides by monumental architecture, most of it from the 15th century and later. One exception is the 12th- and 13th-century bishop's palace, **Palacio de Gelmírez**, to the left of the cathedral.

Top Experience

★ Catedral de Santiago de Compostela

This cathedral, located on the east side of Praza do Obradoiro, stands on the hill where Santiago's tomb was discovered in the 9th century, buried there since the 1st century on an already-known Iron Age and Roman-era burial hill. News of the discovery soon spread, and by the end of the 9th century, pilgrims were beginning to make their way from across Europe to Compostela. At first, a small church covered the tomb, but each century demanded a larger church. Stonemasons built the present structure from 1075 to 1188; it's a Romanesque church whose most celebrated stonework is the 12th-century western entrance, the Portico de la Gloria, hidden behind the later Baroque façade one sees when standing on the western Obradoiro square. Its long building period explains the many stonemasons' marks—engraved signatures—on the walls and pillars inside the cathedral. Their marks are a part of the magic of the building. Some are quite talismanic, with spirals, crosses, triangles, and other symbolic forms.

The larger 12th-century cathedral absorbed places around it, including the 9th-century chapel of Santa María de la Corticela that is now a chapel inside the cathedral, and one of its sweetest spots. Through the 13th to 15th centuries, chapels were added, and in the 16th and the 18th centuries, the cathedral was expanded and altered even more, adding the overwhelming Baroque exterior. The interior and parts of the façades still retain aspects of the original 12th-century Romanesque. The southwest corner of the cathedral is its attached cloister, a solemn restoration from the 16th century.

Highlights of the cathedral are the Portico de la Gloría, the main altar, Santiago's relics crypt, the *botafumeiro* (massive swinging incense burner), the Capilla de la Corticela, and the four

Clockwise from top: Catedral de Santiago de Compostela; reverse Chi-Rho on the south entrance of the cathedral off Plaza de las Platerías; pilgrim souvenirs for sale; engraved stone in the center of the Plaza de Obradoiro.

exterior facades of the cathedral, not to mention the exquisite stonework, Romanesque capital sculptures, and the curious stonemason's marks throughout.

Visiting the Cathedral

Note that packs are no longer permitted in the cathedral. Visiting the **Catedral de Santiago de Compostela** (7am-8:30pm daily) itself is free (7am-8:30pm daily), but to gain deeper access to closed sections, there are several options:

- **Rooftop tour** (eight tours daily from 10am-1pm and 4-7pm, 1 hour each, €12; or when combined with museum admission, €15).

- **Tour of the archaeological excavation under the cathedral** (one tour daily at 4pm, 1 hour; €10) to see the ancient necropolis.

- **Tour of the tribune** (the balconied interior perimeter of the cathedral's second level, where you can stand near the upper arches and capitals; one tour daily; 1 hour; €10)

- **Cathedral archive tour** (1 hour; every Tues. and Thurs., 11am; €15) allows you to see the *Codex Calixtinus.*

Purchase tickets at the Museo Catedral. All but the rooftop tour also include admission to the museum. Guided tours are almost all in Spanish, but sometimes English-language tours get slated in, so inquire about the possibility that day.

Pórtico de la Gloria

The cathedral's west entrance, the **Puerta de Obradoiro,** protects and hides the original 12th-century Romanesque entrance, the **Pórtico de la Gloria** (Gate of Glory), one of the glories of medieval architecture on the Camino, by master builder, Maestro Mateo. Once exposed to the outside, this gate was the entrance that medieval pilgrims would behold upon arriving.

When you enter, look for Santiago seated in the central pillar of the central arch, a halo of semi-precious gems inlaid around his head with his welcoming gaze directed at you. Above him is Christ in Majesty surrounded by the four evangels, and the arch above them is dominated by the 24 Elders of the Apocalypse in joyous music-making and celestial play. Everyone is celebrating your arrival. It is one of the most joyous portals anywhere.

Below Santiago and facing you when you enter is the **Tree of Jesse,** showing Jesus's lineage from King David. At its base is a handprint worn into the marble by millions of pilgrims. (Touching is no longer permitted.) To the left are Old Testament themes, and to the right, images of heaven and hell.

Here, too, you will find the reason for Galicia's *tetilla*, breast-shaped cheese. First, locate the smiling prophet on the arch to James's right (your left). Follow his gaze to locate the topless Queen Esther on the left side of the arch behind you. The story goes that the stonemason bestowed her with ample breasts, which shocked the bishop (and explains Daniel's smile). The bishop demanded that the mason give Esther a breast reduction, and the mason obliged. But word got out, and citizens rebelled creatively against the bishop's censoring: Cheesemakers began shaping cheeses into voluptuous breasts.

The Pórtico de la Gloria was begun in 1168 and finished in 1188, after the rest of the cathedral was completed. We know the sculptor was Master Mateo because he signed and dated his work (in the lintel stone on the central arch of the Pórtico). He is here in form, too, kneeling at the bottom of the central pillar on the altar-facing side. Artists and writers used to come here to touch their head to his for creative luck. This is no longer possible, as barriers are now in place to protect the ancient stone masterpiece from further degradation.

This stunning gate has been closed to the public from 2007-2020 for restoration

Picking Up Your Compostela

Perhaps the most important stop before or after you visit the cathedral is the pilgrims' reception office, **Oficina Acogida al Peregrino** (Rúa Carretas, 33; 981-568-846; www.oficinadel-peregrino.com; Easter week/Semana Santa-Oct. daily 8am-8pm, Nov.-before Semana Santa 10am-7pm). It's about a five-minute walk downhill and north of the cathedral to pick up your hard-earned Compostela. The process for a Compostela is straightforward, but the lines may be long, especially in the late afternoon and early evening when the wait can exceed an hour. But waiting in line often unleashes more trail magic, as people you met all along the Camino seem to appear at the same time.

When it is your turn, you will present your stamped credential(s), answer the question (whether you walked the Camino for religious, cultural-religious, or secular adventure), and be handed a beautiful illuminated certificate on ivory-

Oficina Acogida al Peregrino, where pilgrims get their Compostelas.

toned paper in Latin inscribed with your name and the date. It is not mandatory, but you can make a small contribution (a few centimes to €1-2), if you wish, in return for your Compostela.

---

work, but panel displays here and in the Museo de las Peregrinaciones offer a chance to see images of the Pórtico.

Santiago's Altar

Immediately past the Pórtico de la Gloria, straight ahead along the central nave, you will see the large Romanesque jewel-encrusted and gold-covered statue of Santiago sitting in the center of the high altar. It is tradition to climb the stairway to the *camarín*, the small space behind the statue, so that you can hug this statue, give thanks, and ask for blessings to be delivered to those who helped you along the Camino. It can be a remarkably poignant experience. The power of this moment hits many, whether they walked a few days or a few weeks.

Santiago's Relics Crypt

After visiting James above ground, many go directly below his statue to stairs leading below ground to the relics crypt,

where his silver reliquary is kept. The shape of this crypt follows the form of the original Roman mausoleum where Saint James was buried in AD 44, and where bishop Theodomir identified Santiago's tomb in the 9th century. Held within the silver chest here are not only Santiago's purported remains but also those of his two devout disciples, Atanasio and Teodoro, who brought his body to Iberia and buried him here.

Botafumeiro

The *botafumeiro* is a 1.5-meter (5-foot) tall swinging incense burner that, since the Middle Ages, has been used both for ritual purposes and to disinfect and perfume the air filled with so many unwashed pilgrim bodies. (Its name in Spanish, *echa humo*—"smoke thrower"—describes it well.) It hangs on the crossing of the transept and directly in the center of the cupola overhead and requires eight people to hoist and swing.

It is quite a dramatic thing to see and to feel the swoosh of air and fragrance whisking past your face. There have been two other *botafumeiros* over the centuries, but this third one, made of brass with silver plate, has been in use since 1851. It replaced the second one, with which Napoleon's troops absconded in the early 19th century.

You will see the *botafumeiro* in use during mass on important holy days throughout the year, including on Easter Sunday, Santiago's feast day (July 25), the Ascension of Mary (Aug. 15), All Saints' Day (Nov. 1), Christmas (Dec. 25), and Epiphany (Jan. 6). It can also be booked, for a reasonably hefty fee (for which you will need to inquire about in the cathedral), by individuals who may want a special mass said. As the Camino has grown in popularity, more and more people are paying the fee simply to be able to see the *botafumeiro* swung. Because of this, your odds of seeing it in action are good, but still the luck of the draw.

★ Capilla de la Corticela

My favorite part of the cathedral is this chapel, La Corticela, in the northeast corner at the end of the transept's northern arm. It was originally a 9th-century church under the rule of the Benedictines at the Monasterio de San Martín Pinario next door, and was separate from the cathedral. It was absorbed during the cathedral's expansion in the 12th century and reconfigured as a chapel within the larger temple. The Romanesque entrance is by Master Mateo, who oversaw the Pórtico de la Gloria. This may well be the oldest surviving church of the Camino, even though it is now considered a chapel within the cathedral. It is the oldest church of the city and marks a time near the discovery of Santiago's tomb.

La Corticela is derived from the Latin *curtis,* meaning an enclosed or cut-off area. It has a quiet, intimate atmosphere, in which you can tune in more easily to the pull of this ancient place. If you sit here

a while, you will also witness locals coming and going, some leaving offerings and others writing wishes on slips of paper to leave in a basket on a platform on the left side. You are welcome to do the same. The place gets busier during final exam week, when students come here for good luck.

La Corticela is also dedicated to foreigners and pilgrims and is their chapel in Santiago de Compostela for important life events; some *peregrinos* arrange to return here to get married or hold a baptism or communion.

Museo Catedral

The **Museo Catedral** (Plaza del Obradoiro; 881-557-945; www.catedraldesantiago.es; 9am-8pm in summer and 10am-8pm in winter, 1 hour; €6), set around the large cloister, is especially interesting for its Romanesque art and for its collection of medieval tapestries, plus several from designs by Rubens and Goya. Most of the text panels are in Spanish, but there are audio guides in English (included with admission). This is also where you purchase tickets for guided visits to the cathedral.

Cathedral Façades

In addition to the famous Obradoiro square and façade on the west, the cathedral's three other façades and corresponding squares—south, east, and north—are also of historic interest.

Puerta de las Platerías (South)

Puerta de las Platerías is named after the *plateros* (silversmiths) who crafted and sold silver souvenirs to pilgrims. They still do, in the shops all around the cathedral, and many are pretty, including scallop-shell pendants and rings. This façade and entrance are the cathedral's most Romanesque, and retain large parts of the 12th-century church's arches and sculpture, although they are assembled in a haphazard order after being reconstructed following the destruction of the local revolt against the bishop Gelmírez in 1117. Notice the **Chi-Rho** (the early, round rosette-style symbol of Christ formed by overlaying the Greek first two letters of his name) at the intersection of the two arches of this gate. As in Cizur Menor, Cirauqui, Estella, and León, the alpha and omega are inverted in this Chi-Rho, reading right to left, which indicates that a Hebrew- or Arabic-speaking stonemason may have contributed to the construction of this cathedral. This gate and side of the cathedral overlooks the **Plaza de las Platerías**, where you'll find the iconic fountain with the horses jumping out of the water toward you.

Puerta de Perdón (East)

Just off the Plaza de Quintana is the cathedral's east-facing apse, and the east entrance to the cathedral, the Puerta do Perdón, which opens only on Santiago's feast day on a holy year, when July 25 falls on a Sunday. On this day, pilgrims can pass into the cathedral from here and earn complete indulgences (in regular years, one only gets a partial indulgence). The Puerta de Perdón has some Romanesque elements: the 24 saints and prophets installed in pairs are by Master Mateo, and were originally a part of the choir stall. You'll also find Santiago el Peregrino here, along with his two disciples, Atanasio and Teodoro.

Puerta de la Azabachería (North)

On the north side is the Plaza de Inmaculada, and off it the north entrance into the cathedral, Puerta de la Azabachería, which retains the arch from the Romanesque cathedral. The gate is named after the craftspeople who sold jet-stone jewelry here to pilgrims (and still do, in shops all around). The Spanish word for jet, *azabache*, comes from Arabic and means "black stone." Jet comes from Asturias, and has been considered protective and talismanic since the Middle Ages.

Also on the Plaza de Inmaculada, facing the north side of the cathedral, is the **Monasterio de San Martín Pinarío** (Plaza de la Inmaculada, 3; 981-560-282; www.hsanmartinpinario.com), built on the site of a 10th-century bishop's chapel. The San Martín Pinarío monastery grew into its massive size by the 17th century, and is so large that it has three cloisters along with its own church (built in the 17th and 18th centuries). Today, a large portion of the monastery is a hotel whose fourth floor is reserved for pilgrim lodging at amazing pilgrim prices. Whether you stay here or not, you can enter the hotel to experience the massive scale of this once powerful monastery and take in the long stone hallways and one of the cloisters open to view on the ground level.

Other Historic Buildings on the Plaza de Obradoiro
Hostal de los Reyes Católicos

The **Hostal de los Reyes Católicos** (Praza do Obradoiro, 1; 981-582-200; www.parador.es) stands on the north side of Plaza del Obradoiro. Once a pilgrims' hospital and now a luxury *parador* (state-run hotel) offering opulent lodging to paying guests, the hospital was built from 1501-1509 and was commissioned by Isabel and Ferdinand—the Catholic Kings—to remedy the declined state of the city's older pilgrim hospitals. You can step inside and into the lobby to see the stonework and tapestries, and also consider dining here or having a drink at the bar.

Today, the *hostal* upholds a tradition of feeding pilgrims, but in a more restrained manner, extending a free meal only to the first ten pilgrims each day to receive their Compostela from the Pilgrims' Reception Office. There, those first ten receive a ticket for the free meal when they are issued their certificate. For this reason, some pilgrims delay getting their Compostela until the next morning, rising early in hopes of scoring a meal ticket. You usually have to get there

Clockwise from top: Catedral de Santiago de Compostela from the Plaza de Inmaculada; Colegio de San Jerónimo; farmers selling their harvest on the edges of the Mercado de Abastos.

before they open at 8am (from Easter week to Oct., or 10am from Nov.-Easter) to have a chance of being among the first ten. Some people are intent on getting a ticket and may stake out a place by the door long before opening time.

Colegio de San Jerónimo

On the south end of the Plaza del Obradoiro is the **Colegio de San Jerónimo,** a part of the university built in the early 16th century in the Renaissance style, but with a late Gothic door brought from a pilgrims' hospital that was once on the north side of the cathedral. This doorway is engraved with the images of Mary and Child, surrounded by several saints including James (on the left), John the Baptist, Peter, Paul, and Saint Francis of Assisi. It has been a part of the university since its founding and today is the vice chancellor's office.

Palacio de Gelmírez

Palacio de Gelmírez (Praza do Obradoiro, adjoining the northwest corner of the cathedral; Mon.-Sat., 10am-2pm and 4-8pm, Sun. and holidays, 10am-2pm; entrance included with cathedral museum visit, €6), to the left of the cathedral on Praza de Obradoiro, was named after the bishop Diego Gelmírez, for whom it was built. The palace was destroyed soon after its construction, during a local revolt in 1117. It then took 150 years to fully rebuild. Its style spans the early 12th and mid-13th centuries and is a mix of Romanesque and Gothic, rare among buildings that are neither church nor monastery. It is well worth visiting for its grand reception and dining halls and its Romanesque vaults, its multi-lobed Mudéjar arches (the style of Muslim craftsmen in Christian Spain), and its rose window, plus the corbels in the Synodal Hall depicting medieval feast scenes. A favorite scene shows a royal couple who are being wed holding their hands over a loaf of bread. Another shows a dancing bear. Along with the cathedral,

this palace is one of the oldest buildings on the square.

★ Mercado de Abastos

In the 19th century, the Count and Countess de Altamira repurposed territory used for gardens to create a single central market in the city, the **Mercado de Abastos** (Rúa Ameás, s/n; 981-583-438; www.mercadodeabastosdesantiago.com; Mon.-Sat., 8am-2pm), bringing together several markets that were distributed across the town. The city built the current form, with 10 long gray granite-covered buildings and open air arches, in 1941. Their intent was to mirror the Romanesque arches of the original 12th-century city.

This is one of the most distinctive and colorful markets in Spain, both the covered and open-air sections, the latter wrapping around the former over a space that covers a large city block. Here you can find everything you need for a picnic or souvenirs, from local cheeses (including *tetilla*), sausages, meats, fish, vegetables, seasonal fruits, and elixirs. Farm women set up outside the covered market areas, all along the outskirts of the gray granite food halls, selling produce, almost always organic and direct from their own farms, gardens, and orchards. The other vendors are superb, too, and also sell local and regional produce, but not all have that direct connection to the cultivation and harvest as do these women. Sellers of household goods, clothes, and crafts also set up on the perimeter.

If you purchase shellfish or meat, you can take it to the market bar, **Marisco Mania** (Building 5; 981-575-720), set inside one of the long covered market stalls, and for €5 they will cook it for you and serve it to you there.

In addition to the daily Mercado de Abastos, every **Thursday,** the weekly market sets up on the Esplanada Salgueiriños, northwest of the Cathedral, with 200 stands.

★ Museo de las Peregrinaciones y de Santiago

Installed in a spacious 18th-century palace, the **Museo de las Peregrinaciones y de Santiago** (Plaza de las Platerías, 2; 981-566-110; www.museoperegrinaciones.xunta.gal; Tues.-Fri. 9:30am-8:30pm, Sat. 11am-7:30pm, Sun. and holidays 10:15am-2:45pm; €2.40/€1.20 for pilgrims) is a museum dedicated entirely to the theme of pilgrimage, from its first occurrences in human society, to its manifestations across the globe, to the Camino itself, with views into its deeper spiritual nuances.

You will also see a magnificent gold-hued plate print of an early Game of the Goose that connects it to labyrinths and pilgrimages, and a collection of medieval instruments. Here too are archaeological artifacts of all Galicia's *peregrinos,* from the Neolithic to Roman to medieval, including 2,400-year-old Iron Age gold torques and other jewelry and Roman-era pottery. Three-dimensional models reconstruct all the churches that once stood over Saint James's tomb, beginning with the Roman mausoleum discovered by Pelayo and Theodomir in the early 9th century. Text panels are in English, Spanish, and Gallego.

The museum is spread across four floors; allow 1-2 hours to take in the exhibits.

Museo do Pobo Galego

The **Museo do Pobo Galego** (San Domingo de Bonaval, s/n; 981-583-620; www.museodopobo.es; Tues.-Sat. 10:30am-2pm and 4-7:30pm, Sun. and holidays, 11am-2pm; €3) is a remarkable ethnographic museum set in the Monasterio de Santo Domingo de

From top to bottom: Museo de las Peregrinaciones; Plaza de Obradoiro; Iglesia de Santa María del Sar.

Pagan Symbols in Santiago de Compostela

Santiago is full of pagan symbols that harken back to pre-Christian influences here, such as spirals, triskeles and tetraskeles (three- and four-spiral-armed spinning sun disks), and Celtic knots, as well as images or sculptures of *meigas*, traditional Galician "white witches," benevolent healers and important folkloric characters. These symbols and icons are all over the medieval town, engraved in wood or stone lintels over storefront doorways, or in the local handcrafts and jewelry on display in shop windows. They reflect contemporary people's passions for the more ancient culture of Galicia and the forms found in the region's archaeological excavations, which you can witness in exhibits in the two museums, **Museo do Pobo Galego** and **Museo de las Peregrinaciones.** You will also see many large and small Santiago el

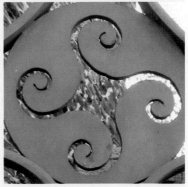

pagan tetraskele

Peregrino sculptures, scallop shells, and Santiago crosses engraved on doorways and walls and for sale in shops overflowing with pagan souvenirs.

Bonaval, a monastery from the 13th century with heavy 16th- and 17th-century additions. The museum has everyday household and craft workshop artifacts from different time periods, along with dioramas that reconstruct homesteads, festival costumes, and craft workshops. A section on traditional healing arts shows how Galician healers use herbs, stones, protective amulets, and blessed water, and even ritually built fire, to pull out negative influences and restore well-being. You'll also find artifacts and models of traditional crafts and work spaces, such as farming implements, fishing boats and nets, a blacksmith's metal workshop, a leatherworker's tools, and collections of masons' tools for cutting and engraving stone. The deeper past is here, too, with some excellent examples of 5,000-year-old Neolithic stone engravings and 2,000-year-old Roman sculptures of human forms with Latin inscriptions identifying the Roman god Jupiter (found near Negreira, which is on the Camino de Finisterre to the west).

In each gallery, a multilingual laminated text accompanies the exhibits, where mounted texts are in Gallego, intentionally done this way to alert you to the language as *the* primary exhibit here of Galicia's heritage.

A visit here is worth a leisurely 1-2 hours, and a great thing to do on rainy day. You can also visit the 12th- to 16th-century church from an interior door, where it shares a wall with the rest of the museum. It's an appealing space that includes the tomb of Galicia's celebrated 19th-century poetess, Rosalía de Castro, whose poetry captured the spirit and heart of the land and its people.

Iglesia de Santa María de Salomé

This small church (Rúa Nova, 31; 981-584-168; www.santiagoturismo.com), located in the center of a stretch of the cobblestone Rúa Nova street, just a few meters from the cathedral and on the same hill, is a holdover from 12th-century Santiago, standing out between the colorful street's stone buildings and arcaded passageways. Parts of the original 12th-century church survive, but most of it is 15th-century. Overlaying the Romanesque façade is the addition of a 14th-century Mary, **Nuestra Señora de la Leche** (Our Lady of the Milk), set in top of the entrance arch, offering the sustenance of her breast to the baby Jesus in her lap as much as to you, for she looks right at you. Inside is a small space beloved by locals for worship and prayer and a calm place on a busy street.

Workers unearthed a tomb under Rúa Nova, not far from the church. The finding reinforced the ancient nature of this hill as a burial hill, not only for Saint James's tomb but for many others of the same era.

The church is open daily for mass, Mon.-Sat., 1 pm and 9pm and Sun and holidays, 12pm and 9pm. It is open for visits (free) during summer months, June-Sept., Mon.-Sat., 10:15am-1pm and 4:14-6pm (no visits on Sunday).

Iglesia de Santa Susana

The **Iglesia de Santa Susana** (Rúa do Campiño da Ferradura; www.santiagoturismo.com) is a 12th-century Romanesque and Gothic church just to the southwest of the cathedral. The pretty 600-meter (0.4-mile), eight-minute walk to the church is worthwhile on its own. From the cathedral, it leads into the oak forest and wild terrain that surround Santa Susana. The church was consecrated by Santiago's bishop Gelmírez, who oversaw the cathedral's 12th-century construction, among other buildings.

The church is very rarely open, and the only surviving original part is the entrance. But the hill on which the church stands is of interest, for it identifies the location of what most likely was an Iron Age castro that defined prehistoric Santiago before Romans arrived. Some speculate that the hill once had dolmens that were removed by later cultivators and builders. Archaeologists refer to this site as **Castro de Santa Susana.**

medieval bridge over the Sar river to Iglesia del Sar

Ancient Santiago de Compostela

Two possible etymologies of the city's name contain traces of its ancient histories. Compostela is the Latin word for either a burial ground, a *compostum*, or a field of stars, *campus stellae*. Both work, but as with most of this route, the more dynamic version won out and we have Saint James of the Field of Stars.

One indication that Santiago de Compostela was likely inhabited since the Neolithic Age (over 4,000 years ago) is the name of one medieval gate, which no longer exists—the Porta da Mámoa, gate of the dolmen (standing stone burial mound). Another indication are the **petroglyphs** once scattered across the city, some surviving and being moved, others unintentionally destroyed, and yet others, surviving in place, including one that you can visit, the Castriño de Conxa. Yet other signs of deep ancestry are the contours of the medieval city itself, taking the shape of the earlier Roman settlement that itself traced the classic lines of an Iron Age *castro*. This is especially pronounced on the neighboring hill just west of the cathedral, today covered by oak trees in the Parque de Alameda, on which stands the **Iglesia de Santa Susana.** It is possible that over 2,000 years ago a *castro* existed under that church.

After Neolithic, Bronze, and Iron Age peoples and then Romans, the Suevi took over Santiago in the early 5th century, and another Germanic tribe, the Visigoths, followed them in the 6th. Soon after, Santiago seems to have been for-

Bronze Age petroglyph of Castriño de Conxo

gotten until the early 9th century, when the hermit named Pelayo followed that trail of raining stars and discovered Saint James's long-forgotten tomb.

The Asturian king Alfonso II made the first royal pilgrimage here in the mid-9th century, and the pilgrimage blossomed (and with it, the city), hitting its peak in the 11th and 12th centuries, especially during the time of Santiago's bishop Diego Gelmírez (bishop from 1100-1140). Gelmírez's vision of a grand sacred city directed building campaigns that largely define what we see today, even though a lot of the 12th-century Romanesque buildings were rebuilt or refashioned in the 17th and 18th centuries, in chunkier Baroque style.

★ Iglesia de Santa María del Sar

Master Mateo, the cathedral's master sculptor, is probably the master craftsman who created the Romanesque **Iglesia de Santa María del Sar** (www.catedralsantiago.es; 881-557-945; open daily, 11am-2pm and 4:30-7:30pm; €2), located 1.5 kilometers (0.9 miles) southeast of the cathedral. Built around the same time as the Pórtico de la Gloria, Santa María del Sar gives you the chance

to taste, on a smaller scale than the cathedral, the 12th-century spirit of Santiago de Compostela. This church was also associated with the Templars. It's named after one of Santiago's two rivers (the Sar and the Sarela), and its nearness to the banks of the Sar has compromised its stability, so that it looks like a ship that is slowly sinking, the arches at slightly askew angles. This also explains the heavy buttressing outside. The arches are Romanesque transitioning to Gothic, and on a grand scale and left bare. The eastern window holds a pretty eight-petaled rose window with a 17th- or 18th-century image of Our Lady of the Sar on the altar below. Diego Gelmírez consecrated this church in 1136.

A small **museum** in the complex houses religious artifacts—from sculptures to ceremonial attire—from medieval Santiago de Compostela and is included with admission.

★ Petroglifo de Castriño de Conxo

The nearly 3,000-year-old petroglyph of Castriño de Conxo dates from the late Bronze Age or early Iron Age. Its impressive images are engraved on a large, gray granite rock face, which is at least twice the height of a person and wider than a person's arm span. The images show a hybrid bird/man with a human-sized bird body, outstretched wings, and a human head. He appears to wear a crown, or has something like an aura or rays emitting from the top of his head, and is surrounded by images of Bronze Age daggers engraved into the stone. Another bird/man with a similar crown/aura seems to have been engraved near the left wing of this one but has faded more over time. Some archaeologists think these images depict a warrior society with status and prestige attached to fighters, but they also may relate more to supernatural expression.

The petroglyph is open access, free, and best visited in full daylight. It's located 2.6 kilometers (1.6 miles) southwest of the cathedral, off of Rúa da Volta do Castro, in the neighborhood of Santa Maria de Conxo, which gives it its name. It is also on the route where the Camino Portugués, from the south and Portugal, enters the city. To get to the petroglyph, take Avenida de Rosalia de Castro, which passes the south side of the Parque de Alameda and heads southwest; the street name will eventually become Rúa da Volta do Castro and soon after, you will pass by the private farm and banquet hall of **Finca da Rocha** (Rúa da Volta do Castro, 34) on the right side. Stay on Rúa da Volta do Castro until the end of that block a few meters ahead, just before passing an industrial garage, also on the right. You should see a small sign announcing the petroglyph. Make a right there at the sign onto the narrow dirt path that wends through ferns and to the right and up the hill behind the Finca da Rocha. When the footpath forks, always opt to veer right and go up the hill. You will enter tree cover and climb a narrow footpath. Near the small hill's summit, look for the chain-linked fence of the backyard of Finca da Rocha below to your right and the large gray oval granite rock of the petroglyph right in front of you on the ground. A small information plaque (in Gallego) is posted to its left.

The petroglyph has no barriers or protective infrastructure. Savor the immediate access to a 3,000-year-old work of art, but please do not climb on it, touch it, or do anything else that can alter it or harm it.

To learn more about the petroglyph, visit Finca da Rocha's website, http://rochaforte.info (in Spanish).

Shopping

Since the Middle Ages, vendors in Santiago de Compostela have been selling specially crafted souvenirs to pilgrims, some of them quite beautiful. All along the cobblestone streets radiating around the cathedral are artisanal and souvenir shops holding down the same medieval spaces as their predecessors, especially along **Rúa do Franco, Rúa do Vilar, Rúa Calderería,** and **Rúa Nova.** Popular souvenirs include silver jewelry (scallop shells, crosses, mini-bota-fumeiros, and Celtic designs), tiny stone (or resin-molded) sculptures of Santiago el Peregrino, and jet-stone jewelry (the most traditional form is a fist pendant,

Pilgrim Services in Santiago

Need to pick up luggage you sent forward along the Camino, or leave luggage to lighten your load while you explore the city? Want help planning your next adventure, or perhaps just the camaraderie of kindred spirits? Fortunately, there are places in Santiago de Compostela that offer these services and more to pilgrims and their particular needs.

After you get your Compostela and before leaving the pilgrim office (oficina de Acogida al Peregrino), go across the courtyard to another office to get practical information for walking to the coast and to get the free pilgrim's passport, *credencial do peregrino*, for **Finisterre** and **Muxía**.

If you need a home away from home and a place to decompress and connect with fellow *peregrinos*, or just to reflect in solitude, **Terra Nova Pilgrim House** (Rúa Nova, 19; www.pilgrimhousesantiago.com; closed Wed. and Sun., open all other days, 11am-6pm) is a welcome center and wonderful post-Camino place for fellowship and support. You can come here to talk about your experience, get advice for what to do next and how, be it returning home, seeking new adventures in and around Santiago, or walking the Camino de Finisterre to the coast. You can also do laundry here, print boarding passes, store luggage, or cook in the communal kitchen.

Pilgrim (Rua Nova, 7; 910-607-539; www.pilgrim.es) is a multi-purpose place for nearly all *peregrino* needs. You can

Pilgrim

shower (€2), store luggage (€3/day), have your laundry washed (€10-14), arrange airport transfers to Santiago's airport or to Sarria (€30-130), or sign up for a tour to Finisterre and Muxía (9 hours; €35; every day, departing at 9am) or a private city tour that includes sampling local craft beer (2 hours; €25).

Casa Ivar (Travesía da Universidade, 1; www.casaivar.com), run by Ivar Rekve, the founder of the great online network Camino de Santiago Forum (www.caminodesantiago.me), is a brick-and-mortar service that will store your luggage if you send it ahead of you. You can store your bags here for up to 60 days for €15-25, depending on size. Ivar will also arrange delivery to your accommodations in Santiago for an additional €5. Hours to pick up your bags: Mon.-Fri., 10am-2pm and 4-5pm, Sat., 10-11am, and Sun., 8-8:30pm. This storage service is available from Easter to Nov. 1.

---

the fingers wrapped around the thumb, used to deflect the evil eye and other bad luck).

Jewelry

Jewelry shops abound on the streets surrounding the cathedral that sell good quality silver and jet, as well as other jewelry of various stones and metals. For more traditional designs, visit **Corma y Alrif** (Rúa do Vilar, 20; 981-575-431; www.joyeriacorma.com), and **Joyería**

Mayer (Plaza de las Platerías, 2; 981-582-536; www.joyeriamayer.com). For more modern designs, try **Amboa** (Rúa da Acibechería, 33; 981-563-932) and **Maeloc** (Rúa do Franco, 1; 981-584-174; www.amboamaeloc.com).

Ceramics

Santiago is home to the gallery and store for **Ceramicas Sargadelos** (Rúa Nova, 16; 981-581-905; www.sargadelos.com), whose works you've likely already seen in bars on the Camino, in the form of those Celtic-inspired blue and white ceramic beer taps in the shape of a woman. Here you can peruse the fuller expression of this modern Galician ceramic producer, known for its fusion of modern aesthetics and traditional Galician folk and Celtic designs for porcelain bowls, cups, plates, sculptures, totemic pendants, and wall ornaments.

Other Souvenirs

For other handcrafted items, such as ceramics, and whimsical souvenirs, try **Como Pez en el Agua** ("like a fish in water") on Rúa San Pedro, 79 (981-575-147; www.comopezenelagua.es), and **Trisquel Artesanía** (Rúa de Acibechería, 31; 981-576-870). For leather, the on-premises workshop with storefront **Medialua** (Algalia de Arriba, 27; 639-833-961; www.medialua.es) creates beautiful belts, bracelets, handbags, folios, book covers, and more. For woodwork, ceramics, and functional household crafts, check out **Boles** (Ruela de Altamira, 3; 629-881-312).

Festivals and Events

The peak event in Santiago de Compostela is Saint James's feast day, July 25, which is such a big deal it really begins on July 15, peaks on July 24 and 25, and then keeps going until July 31. The whole event is known as the **Festival de Santiago.** The medieval town of Santiago is turned into a variegated festival, with diverse music (including classical, Galician folk, blues, and jazz) at indoor concert venues and at outdoor parks and squares, art exhibits in many galleries and historic buildings, and theater productions at several theaters, as well as open-air street theater on the medieval squares. At 11:30pm on July 24, the city hosts a sound and light show on the Plaza de Obradoiro, in front of the cathedral's western side, that includes projected images onto the cathedral and bagpipe

and dance troupes on the square performing traditional Galician folk songs and dances. The next morning, July 25 and Santiago's feast day, the cathedral holds a 10am **mass** that includes the swinging of the *botafumeiro*. The old citywide festivities continue until July 31 with more listings of theater, music, and art. The best way to plan for the two-week feast is to check out the extensive schedule of events on www.santiagoturismo.com.

Food

Restaurants and Cafés
Around the Cathedral

After checking in to their accommodations, showering, and leaving their packs, many pilgrims like to have a celebratory meal, often at ★ **Casa Manolo** (Praza de Cervantes, 981-582-950, www. casamanolo.es, lunch 1pm-5pm daily, dinner 8pm-12am), hailed as a pilgrim meeting place for over three decades. Known as the place to find Camino friends, but popular also with university students and professors, the open dining atmosphere caters to talking across tables. Dining rooms on two levels possess warm wooden floors and large windows with natural light. The ample three-course pilgrims' menu (€10, wine not included) highlights classic Galician home cooking with many choices. It is the only menu offered here and may be the best quality and value in all of Santiago.

Few places have a better location than the book and art lovers' **Cafe Literarios** (Praza da Quintana, 1, 981-882-912; €10), positioned at the top of the stairs overlooking the cathedral's Puerta del Perdón, with Santiago smiling back at you. A sign over the door says "Refugees Welcome," setting the establishment's progressive tone. The menu is simple: *tortillas*, paellas (classic, seafood or vegetarian), *croquetas* (croquettes), and desserts (including carrot cake and *tarta de Santiago*). Servers are artsy, complementing the Neoclassical mural set between warm stone walls. In warm weather you can enjoy a table with a view out on the square.

The Michelin-starred **Casa Marcelo** (Rúa das Hortas, 1; 981-558-580; www.casamarcelo.net; €5-40) features Galician-Peruvian-Japanese fusion cuisine that pops with flavor and mouthwatering inventions. Patrons can sit at tables around the edges or at the sleek, long, red communal table in the center with barstools. The attentive chef is likely to come talk to you, and the upbeat staff serves vanguard dishes such as *dim-sum de bacalao* (cod dim sum), Thai mussels, and *alcachofas del amor* (stuffed and fried artichokes), plus sashimi-inspired plates interweaving Old and New World flavors.

Try a seafood platter and the small pub scene of a few tables and standing room at **Taberna O Gato Negro** (Rúa Raina, s/n; 981-583-105). Enjoy grilled langoustine and crabs and steamed *percebes* (for 2-4 people, €25-40), or an array of tapas including steamed mussels (€6.50), *pulpo á feira* (€11.50), and other Galician comfort foods such as *empanandas* (€3.50), *almejas a la marinera* (wine and herb stewed clams, €12), and *caldo Gallego* (€3.50), with a good selection of wines from the Ribeiro. You'll identify the tavern by its metalwork black cat hanging over the wide stone entrance.

Bar O Orella (Calle Raina, 21; 981-582-459; www.restauranteorella.com; €7-12) is another small inside/outside dining casual pub with some classic favorites, including grilled and lemon-kissed *zamburiñas* (bay scallops), perfectly fried calamares, *pulpo á feira*, mussels, *chipirones* (little squid), *caldo Gallego*, lamb chops, steak, *pimientos de Padrón*, and *orellas/orejas* (pig ears). Menus are bilingual, and there's a large mounted menu behind the

From top to bottom: Casa Manolo; Galician octopus; a small food shop in the medieval town.

bar with the offerings and a great selection of regional wines.

O Celme do Caracol (Rúa Raiña, 18; 981-571-746; €10-20) is a congenial place of pale pinewood floors and furnishings serving casual tapas, seafood (pulpo, razor clams, cockles, and scallops), grilled fish and meats, tasty lentil burgers, and creamy vegetable rice with walnuts. They put their politics on display with a sign that says, *Espazo libre de violencias machistas*—place devoid of patriarchal violence. That goes down as easily as the chocolate cake with vanilla ice cream and balsamic sauce and the *bombas de mozzarella* (deep-fried mozzarella cheese wontons, aka "bombs," with quince dipping sauce).

Restaurante María Castaña (Rúa Raiña, 19; 981-562-137; €10-20) is famous for seafood and Galician-grown seaweed and kelp creations, including a sea lover's *algas con berberechos*, seaweed with cockles.

★ **Café-Bar Suso** (Rúa da Vilar, 65; 981-586-611; €5-12) serves excellent *caldos* (thick soups) and tortillas, enhanced by the steady cheer and warm welcome of this institution for pilgrims and locals. Often university professors and students are here enjoying a cup or glass and discussing the philosophies of the day. Locals stop in for a pick-me-up meal, such as a savory green bowl of *caldo Gallego* or a wonderful made-to-order French omelet with salad. The owner remains as cheerful and passionate about good food and wine today as she was when I first began coming here in 1995. This flawless quality extends to the **Hostal Suso** upstairs.

For creative and delicious vegetarian fare, **Entre Pedras** (Hospitaliño, 18; 981-564-097; facebook.com/entre.pedras; €5-8) is entirely vegetarian, with delicious veggie burgers, salads, sandwiches, falafel, and quesadillas. They also offer wonderful little tapas, *tapitos*, when you order a drink from the bar, such as a small bowl of flash-fried tofu

in sautéed garlic and spinach on a bed of basmati rice.

At Mercado de Abastos

Consider a real market experience with a sit-down grilled lunch with seafood and meat you bought at the market. Take your purchases to ★ **Marisco Mania** (Mercado de Abastos, building 5; 981-575-720; www.mariscomania.com) and for €5, they will cook it for you to dine on right there. Drop off your seafood and make a reservation two hours before you wish to eat. When you return, they will have a place set for you and the feasting can begin. They sell drinks, bread, and desserts. Note that they will not cook fish, cephalopods, or vegetables, only *mariscos* (shellfish: clams, crabs, lobster, shrimp, scallops, etc.) and *carne* (meat). Proprietors speak English.

Abastos 2.0 (Rúa das Ameas in the Mercado/Plaza de Abastos, at Casetas 13-18; 654-015-937; www.abastoscompostela.com) prepares modern Galician cuisine (using daily fresh finds from the market) with a modern twist. Order a tasting menu of six different plates (€21), a more elaborate multi-course tasting menu (€50), or a la carte options such as deliciously charred grilled octopus (€13). Also available are classic market-fresh *pinchos* and tapas, including *percebes* (gooseneck barnacles), Padrón peppers, and empanadas.

On the Outskirts of the Medieval Town

The places listed here are on the outskirts of the medieval town, but within walking distance.

Installed in a former stable, **Restaurante O Dezaseis** (Rúa de San Pedro, 16; 981-577-633; www.dezaseis.com; €15-25) concentrates on the natural taste of fresh ingredients and kicking up traditional Galician cuisine to contemporary tastes. Their most famous dish is perfectly grilled octopus (not the traditional boiled), giving a crisp and pleasantly charred snap to the natural oyster-lobster-like flesh, hit with top-grade olive oil and *pimentón*. It feels like eating in a warm country farmhouse kitchen with a big family (it is quite popular with locals). A good way to sample the best offerings at the best price is with the daily *menú*.

Restaurante Cafe A Curtidoría (Rúa da Conga, 2-3 Bajo; 981-554-342; www.acurtidoria.com) offers creative and classic cuisine with strong Asian, Mediterranean, and Galician influences. People come here on their lunch break as much as visitors, and the three-sided windows make even the grayest day seem cheerful and luminous. A creative and reasonable *menú del dia* (€14) may have innovations such as beer-marinated roasted chicken and/or classics such as sautéed mixed vegetable pasta.

Chef Alberto Larea's style at ★ **Restaurante Manso** (Avenida Villagarcia 21; 881-959-657; www.mansorestaurante.com; €18-29) is to use ingredients curated from Galicia's coast and interior in combinations and flavors that highlight their uniqueness. Consider mackerel tartar with avocado and marsh grasses, crab and algae ravioli, grilled duck breast with polenta and vegetables, or wild boar with creamy wild mushroom rice. Plating is like an edible Gaudí—colorful, organic, flamboyant, and elegant. The astute staff is dedicated to top service and high cuisine, in a dining space with the clean lines and harmony of Japanese design melded with the classic arches, stone, and wood aesthetic of historic Santiago.

Pastry Shops and Bakeries

Santiago is a city of rustic breads, delicate pastries, and the iconic almond cake, *tarta de Santiago*. This is also the land of mini-empanadas, *empanadillas,* little savory pastry pockets packed with anything from tuna, cod, mussels, and octopus to beef, mushrooms, and red peppers

with caramelized onion. Some classic places to find the city's baked goods:

Pastelería Casa Mercedes Mora (Rúa do Villar, 50; 981-565-724; www.mercedesmora.com) opened in 1926 and has continuously produced some of the best bakes in the city, including the famous almond cake, *tarta de Santiago*. Casa Mora is attributed with the invention of the finishing touch, dusting the top with Saint James's cross. Try also the *bombas de crema* (cream bombs: light pastry orbs filled with cream), *milhojas* (cream- or custard-layered mille-feuille), and *bagoas de Compostela* (tear-shaped chocolate and almond biscuits).

For convent-baked almond cake, egg yolk and butter tea cookies, *almendrados* (almond cookies), and puff pastry cakes, head to the turnstile window to put in your order with the Benedictine sisters at the **Convento de San Paio de Antealtares**, near the cathedral (Rúa de San Paio de Antealtares, 23; 981-560-623; www.monasteriosanpelayo.org; daily 9am-1pm and 3:30-7pm).

Panadería Ebano (Rúa do Vilar, 77; 981-576-217) is the place for to go for empanadas and *empanadillas*, plus fresh-baked breads, including the house walnut bread.

The old-fashioned grocery store, **Colmado Victoria** (Rúa do Hórreo, 53; 981-562-628), is a Santiago institution midway on the road between the cathedral and the train station; it's also famous for its artisanal breads, empanadas, and *empanadillas,* not to mention other local foods you may want to carry away for a picnic.

Cheese Shops

Tetilla, given its genesis in Santiago's 12th-century bishop's concern over the size of Queen Esther's breasts in the western gate of the cathedral, is associated forever with Santiago de Compostela and found all across the city, in humble grocery stores and in exclusive cheese shops. You will also find many cheeses from the

surrounding countryside, both of cow's milk and goat's milk, and also the famous cheese of Arzúa.

The violet awning and red walls of **Delicatessen As Monxa** (Rúa de Xelmírez, 17; 981-581-957) foregrounds the famous breast-shaped, creamy, nutty, semi-soft yellow *tetilla* cheeses in cases along the wall. This is a good place to purchase regional wines, liquors, chocolates, and also "the best *tarta de Santiago*," made by various convents in the city.

Quesería Prestes (Rúa da Caldeirería, 27; 881-031-154) is named after the international award-winning Galician cheesemaker based in Vilalba, Lugo, and this shop is a cheese mecca, with dozens of regional varieties including young to aged varieties of San Simón (*tetilla*), and other varieties of cow and goat's milk cheeses, including a blend (*mezcla*). Look also for the smoked cheeses, the blue cheese, fresh creamy soft goat cheeses, and a spicy semi-hard *picante* cow's milk cheese spiked with *pimentón*, smoked Spanish paprika. Cheese-partnering wines and beers are also on sale here.

Bars and Nightlife

The nightlife scene in Santiago de Compostela is mellow but vibrant, and influenced by the university community. The students, as well as professors and staff, enjoy evening ambles through the medieval center of Santiago, going from one tapas and *pincho* bar to another and stopping in for live music in small intimate venues—or, on pleasant evenings, hanging out at a hidden garden café with fairy lights hung in the trees. Sometimes the music wanders over to you along the squares and cobblestone streets in the form of a *tuna*, a university musical

From top to bottom: *Tetilla* cheese; tarta de Santiago almond cake; Jardín Café Costa Vella.

group dressed like troubadours (in tights and tunics with velvet capes and caps), who play lutes and sing medieval songs. If you stop to enjoy their music, be sure to give them a coin (or more) in thanks.

Pinchos and Tapas Bars

Tapas and *pinchos* crawls unfurl at many of the cafés and bars (some with upstairs dining rooms for full meals) all throughout the old quarter surrounding the cathedral, and especially on **Rúa do Franco, Rúa Raiña, Rúa Vilar,** and **Rúa Nova,** the four streets running parallel (more or less) to each other and opening to the south side of the cathedral.

Petiscos do Cardeal (Rúa do Franco, 10; 981-108-292), the cardinal's *pinchos* in Gallego, is a favorite spot for diverse little bites. The pretty painted tile floor and long wood bar with tree trunk bar stools add fun to the downstairs, while there is a more formal dining area upstairs.

★ **A Taberna do Bispo** (Rúa do Franco, 37; 981-586-046), the "bishop's tavern," is an explosion of color. Delight in the displays and countertops of tapas, *pinchos*, and seafood platters to share, such as steamed clams, grilled razor clams, mussels, and grilled stuffed squid, brought daily from the coast.

For the ultimate *tortilla Española* (now that you've eaten so many wedges of this classic Spanish potato-and-onion omelet all along the Camino), head to **Bar La Tita** (Rúa Nova, 46; 981-583-981) for their fluffy, perfectly cooked and caramelized version. This is a popular spot with students, other locals, and *peregrinos* for drinks and a snack throughout the evening.

Bars and Cafés

The difference between bars and cafés is not great (some places even refer to themselves as bar-cafés), and both remain lively places after dark. Some special favorites include:

Jardín Café Costa Vella (Calle Puerta de la Peña, 17; 981-569-530; www.costavella.com) is the adjoining garden café to **Hotel Costa Vella**; it's to the right of the hotel, through a wide doorway leading into a walled paradise of rambling verdant spaces with café tables, benches, and a fountain at its center. Candles and fairy lights add to the enchantment, and most drinks cost around €2-3. Locals come here for deep conversation, atmosphere, and at times, live music.

On the weekends, at 10:30 pm, experience *queimada* at **Cafe Casino** (Rua do Vilar, 35; 981-577-503), if you have not already been offered it along the Camino in Galicia. You can ask for a *chupito*, a cup of the liquid (€5), after the *queimada* ceremony, when it is made and lit afire. Come here any night of the week for drinks, and for the atmosphere of the Belle Époque, with its high ceilings, tapestries, and leather lounge chairs. Some evenings, a pianist plays jazz and classical on the piano near the bar.

Pub Atlántico (Rúa da Fonte do San Miguel, 9; 981-572-152) has a fresh, earthy, modern, minimalist atmosphere and is a popular venue with writers, filmmakers, visual artists, and other creatives for conversation and cocktails, including bright mojitos and their house invention, *flores de otro mundo*, "flowers of another world," made with violet syrup, real flowers, lime juice, and gin.

Live Music

Since 1971, **Borriquita de Belém** (Rúa de San Paio de Antealtares, 22; 653-471-551; www.borriquitadebelem.blogspot.com. es) has been a venue for live music, from folk and jazz to blues, flamenco, and reggae, and for good regional wine served from barrels.

Tap into live folk music, Galician style, at **Casa das Crechas** (Via Sacra, 3; 607-772-29; info@casadascrechas.com), with musicians from northwest Iberia as well as across the world. A wide array of drinks includes Japanese-inspired cocktails, such as Midori liquor with lime, melon syrup, and beer.

Modus Vivendi (Praza Feixo, 1; 607-804-140), in an 18th-century stable, has low *bodega*-style stone arched ceilings and passageways and nooks, including one that holds the small music stage.

Accommodations

Albergues
The Last Stamp (Rúa do Preguntoiro, 10; 981-563-525; www.thelaststamp.es; open all year except Dec.15-Jan. 15) *albergue* couldn't have a better location on the east side, on the hill 300 meters (984 feet) above the cathedral, on a quiet corner in the medieval town. Opened in 2013 in a traditional stone building, there are eight dorm rooms with 62 beds (€15) with an interior courtyard and well-outfitted kitchen and dining area. Evocative pen-and-ink images of the Camino are drawn directly onto the white wall, and Galician glass-enclosed balconies and thick stone define the spaces, all flawlessly maintained. Proprietors speak English.

Hotels and *Hostales*
The refurbished 17th-century ★ **Hospedería San Martín Pinario** (Plaza de la Inmaculada, 3; 981-560-282; www.hsanmartinpinario.com; €50-70) offers traditional monastic lodging next to the cathedral. In addition to the 81 more luxurious rooms, they also set aside 57 modest but very comfortable monk's cell-sized rooms (€23, including generous buffet breakfast) on the fourth floor for pilgrims, each with its own bathroom, towels, writing desk, and rooftop views of the old city and green hills. The grand granite complex makes for a remarkable stay, and it takes longer to exit the monastery than to walk to the cathedral next door. Staff speak English.

The **Hotel Windsor** (Rúa da República de El Salvador, 16; 981-592-939; €60) is in the modern town, an easy 10-minute walk to the cathedral and 100 meters (328 feet) from the airport bus stop. This is a classic business hotel, with comfortable and clean but pragmatic and minimalist modern rooms. Proprietors speak English.

At **25 de Julio** (Rúa Rodrigo de Padrón, 4; 981-582-295; www.25dejulio.com; six rooms, €80-125), named for Saint James's feast day on July 25, romantic melds with Caribbean: bright colors, tropical-print pillows mixed with lace-trimmed bed linens, and almost psychedelic-toned prints of forests and hills, plus a pinch of Impressionism a la Van Gogh's *Starry Night*. Spotless and spacious, some rooms have rooftop views, and others overlook the pleasant street and sidewalk café of the pension's inviting bar and lounge. Proprietors speak English.

At **Hotel Costa Vella** (Calle Porta da Pena, 17; 981-569-530; www.costavella.com/en; €60-100), the English-speaking owner, Roberto, hosts visitors and locals in this popular sunset spot. The garden, an oasis outside the hotel, mirrors the elegance of the stone and wood panel rooms, which feature handsome furnishings from prior centuries, wood-carved headboards, and glass balcony-enclosed views of the old city's rooftops. A small café on the ground floor is cozy in winter, and in good weather, you can enjoy breakfast (€6) in the garden.

A "gastronomic hotel" in a repurposed old convent, ★ **Casa Felisa** (Calle Porta da Pena, 5; 981-582-602; www.casafelisa.es; 12 rooms, €25-40 shared bath/€45-60 private bath) is a friendly and hospitable family-run inn with gourmet tasting menus in the restaurant (€27-48) and a private garden. Flawless rooms feature granite walls and glassed-in balconies. Breakfasts are generous and fortifying. A stone grotto in the dining area holds Mary and candles, cheering up gray days. They create new takes on

Galician classics such as hake in Albariño and octopus and langoustine kebabs. Proprietors speak English.

Hostal dos Reis Católicos (Praza do Obradoiro, 1; 981-582-200; www.parador.es; 137 rooms, €200-430) is a late-15th-century pilgrims' hospital (commissioned by *los reyes catolicos*, the Catholic royals Isabel and Ferdinand) that today is the most historic lodging in town, as well as a part of the *parador* network of historic buildings turned into opulent accommodations across Spain. Rooms surround an inner cloister-style courtyard with Italianate sculpted hedges. Some rooms are more modest, but all are generally done in luxurious linen, velvet, and jacquard tapestry textiles, in a largely muted and neutral palette. Staff speak English.

★ **Hotel Fonte de San Roque** (Rúa Hospitaliño, 8; 981-554-447; www.hotelfontedesanroque; 15 rooms; €40-80) is one of the most uplifting places to stay in Santiago de Compostela, with an exuberant staff who brighten each time you walk through the door. The rooms, with 19th-century décor, are fresh, inviting, and immaculate. Set in a 19th-century stone building with classic glass-enclosed balconies, on a high street near the cathedral in the medieval town, it is central to everything, built next to where once stood the city's 11th-century walls. Ask for a room with one of the glass-framed balconies.

★ **Hostal Suso** (Rúa do Vilar, 65; 981-586-611; www.hostalsuso.com; eight rooms, €50-80) has been a favorite place of mine since I first discovered it in 1995, and today it remains a wonderfully run place, with a popular pilgrims' and locals' bar on the entrance level. The rooms are fresh and modern with very comfortable beds, and the double-paned windows mean you can get a room with a view and also sleep through the din of the popular street below. Proprietors speak English.

Another longtime favorite, **Casa Celsa-Barbantes** (Rúa do Franco, 3; 981-583-271; www.casacelsa.com; 16 rooms; €55-90) was once known as Hostal Barbantes. I knew the warm but no-nonsense Celsa Gonzalez, who ran this hotel from 1983 until she handed it over to her granddaughter in 2016; she now runs it with the same impeccable skill and style as her grandmother, but with her own updated style, including a modern hipster spin on the décor: cheerful, bright spring colors and simple Scandinavian design. Very central, on a busy street for tapas; try to get an upper-floor room where the sound from the street is muted. Proprietors speak English.

Day Trip to Padrón

Twenty-two kilometers (17 miles) southwest of Santiago is **Padrón** (pop. 8,463), where the rudderless boat bearing Saint James's deceased body and his two living disciples arrived around AD 44. The boat, steered by angels from Jaffa, sailed across the Mediterranean and up the coast of Portugal to this spot in northwestern Spain, where they moored at a pillar connected to a temple dedicated to Neptune. (In Gallego, *pedrón* means "mooring post.")

When it landed, Santiago's magical boat startled the wedding guests of the daughter of the territory's Celtic queen, Lupa. The bridegroom was on a horse that startled, too; it ran into the ocean and the two drowned. Santiago's first postmortem miracle in Iberia was to pull them out, both covered in scallop shells, and revive them. That is one reason why, some say, the Camino is represented by scallop shells.

Padrón is worth a visit today for its Santiago legends and sights, as much as for its present warmth. Mingle with fishermen, merchants, home cooks, and craftspeople while exploring the beginnings of James's after death legacy. A perfect day would be to make a day trip from Santiago by **train** (13 trains daily, 15 min., €3-4), coming in the morning for the Sunday market, then visiting the church, climbing to Monte Santiaguiño, and returning to Santiago de Compostela by early afternoon. You can also reach Padrón from Santiago by **bus** (5-8 buses daily, 30 min, €2.20) with Monbus/Arriva (982-292-900; www.monbus.es), but it's slower and less convenient than the train. The bus station in Padrón is 350 meters (1,148 feet) north of the old town center (a 5-minute walk). The train station is 800 meters (0.5 mile) west of Padrón's center of town, a 10-minute walk that takes you to the other side of the Sar river.

Market

Padrón has a huge and colorful weekly market, with some 750 stands, that sets up every Sunday (9am-2pm) next to Iglesia de Santiago, along the Paseo del Espolón on the bank of the Río Sar. You can wander along the open-air stalls of fresh produce, cheeses, and sausages; someone will be roasting chestnuts in autumn, and sometimes steaming vats of *pulpo á feira* and red wine will be available (for breakfast!). A *churrería* cart churns out donut-like coils of deep fried dough to enjoy with thick hot chocolate, and many merchants sell books, household goods (including one selling copper-distilling equipment for homemade *orujo*, eau de vie), and artisanal goods, such as ceramics, handmade lace, woodwork, leather goods, and more. It spans the equivalent of many city blocks along the river, and is a fun way to spend a Sunday morning.

Iglesia de Santiago

This church dedicated to Saint James, which is also the town's parish church, could be considered ground zero for Jamesian lore. It was built over **Neptune's pillar,** the Roman-era stone pillar, once dedicated to Neptune, where Saint James's boat anchored. The original mooring post is under the altar, beneath a protective door that opens to reveal it. (Yes, it is under the altar! Consider that over the past two millennia, the Sar river had silted up the coastline here, covering earlier layers of earth and stones.

Monte Santiaguiño in Padrón

What was once at ground level, including Neptune's pillar, is now below ground.) The pillar is worn into a bowl shape, and the devout bend down to cast coins onto its crown to ask for blessings. The 15th-century pulpit, carved from a single large stone, is engraved with an image of Santiago. The church typically is open daily, morning and late afternoon to early evening.

Monte Santiaguiño

Though the more oft-told legend tells us that Saint James came to Padrón in death, local lore also says he first came here in life, in AD 40, and preached the word of Jesus from this hill, Monte Santiaguiño. Like all the other places (including Santiago) where Santiago appeared in life and death, Monte Santiaguiño was once a pagan site known for its spiritual power.

The hillside is a delightful small park, with a tiny 19th-century chapel, **Ermita de Santiaguiño,** at its base. The pile of large boulders at the top of the hill marks where Santiago is said to have preached. The stones are clearly marked with a stone cross and an image of Santiago. They also offer a great view of the town below.

It is a steep but steady 20-minute hike to Monte Santiaguiño, worth it for the pretty forest and natural stone cairn marking where Santiago once stood. Cross the bridge over the Sar on the south side of the Iglesia de Santiago, and look for signs directing you to the footpath and stone stairs that lead up the hillside to Monte Santiaguiño. Immediately on the other side of the bridge, notice the **Fonte do Carme**, a 16th-century fountain whose arched stone facade shows an engraved image of Saint James in his sepulcher, with his two disciples standing before Queen Lupa when she converted and was baptized.

Camino Finisterre

Finisterre and Muxía

To Finisterre:	89.3 Km (55.5 miles)
Days:	4
To Muxía:	86.9 Km (54 miles)
Days:	4
Finisterre to Muxía:	29.3 Km (18.2 miles)
Days:	2

Camino Finisterre

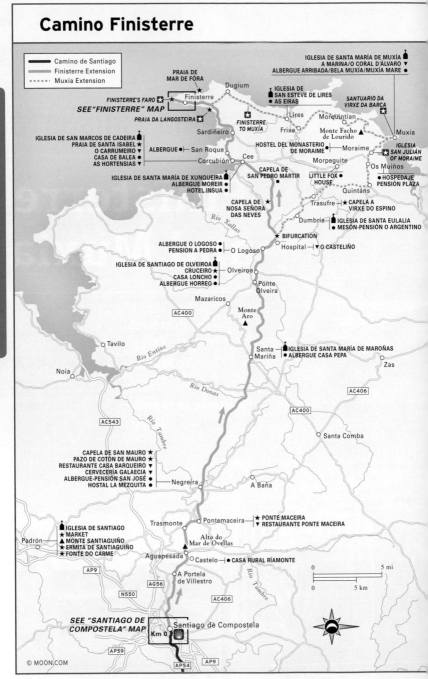

Camino de Santiago
Finisterre Extension
Muxía Extension

PRAIA DE
MAR DE FÓRA

Dugium

FINISTERRE'S FARO ★
SEE "FINISTERRE" MAP
Finisterre

PRAIA DA LANGOSTEIRA ★

PRAIA DE SANTA ISABEL ★
IGLESIA DE SAN MARCOS DE CADEIRA ★
O CARRUMEIRO ●
CASA DE BALEA ▼
AS HORTENSIAS ▼

ALBERGUE ● San Roque

Corcubión

Sardiñeiro

Cee

IGLESIA DE SANTA MARÍA DE XUNQUEIRA ★
ALBERGUE MOREIR ●
HOTEL INSUA ●

CAPELA DE
SAN PEDRO MÁRTIR
■

CAPELA DE
NOSA SEÑORA
DAS NEVES ★

Río Xallas

ALBERGUE O LOGOSO ●
PENSION A PEDRA ●

O Logoso

IGLESIA DE SANTIAGO DE OLVEIROA ★
CRUCEIRO ★
CASA LONCHO ●
ALBERGUE HORREO ●

Olveiroa

Ponte
Olveira

Mazaricos

AC400

Monte
Aro ▲

Tavilo

Río Entins

Noia

Río Donas

AC543

Río Tambre

CAPELA DE SAN MAURO ★
PAZO DE COTÓN DE MAURO ★
RESTAURANTE CASA BARQUEIRO ▼
CERVECERÍA GALAECIA ▼
ALBERGUE-PENSIÓN SAN JOSÉ ●
HOSTAL LA MEZQUITA ●

Negreira

A Baña

Santa
Mariña

IGLESIA DE SANTA MARÍA DE MAROÑAS ★
● ALBERGUE CASA PEPA

Santa Comba

AC406

AC400

Zas

IGLESIA DE SANTIAGO ★
★ MARKET
▲ MONTE SANTIAGUIÑO
★ ERMITA DE SANTIAGUIÑO
★ FONTE DO CARME

Padrón

Trasmonte

Pontemaceira

★ PONTE MACEIRA
▼ RESTAURANTE PONTE MACEIRA

Alto do
Mar de Ovellas

Aguapesada

Castelo ● CASA RURAL RÍAMONTE

AP9

A Portela
de Villestro

AG56

N550

AC406

Río Tambre

SEE "SANTIAGO DE
COMPOSTELA" MAP

Santiago de Compostela

Km 0

AP59

AP54

AP9

© MOON.COM

IGLESIA DE SANTA MARÍA DE MUXÍA ★
A MARINA/O CORAL D'ÁLVARO ▼
ALBERGUE ARRIBADA/BELA MUXÍA/MUXÍA MARE ●

IGLESIA DE
SAN ESTEVE DE LIRES ★
● AS EIRAS

SANTUARIO DA
VIRXE DA BARCA ★

Lires

Morquintian

Frixe

Monte Facho ▲
de Lourido

Muxía

FINISTERRE
TO MUXÍA

HOSTEL DEL MONASTERIO
DE MORAIME

Moraime

IGLESIA ★
SAN JULIÁN
OF MORAIME

Morpeguite

Os Muiños

LITTLE FOX ●
HOUSE

● HOSPEDAJE
PENSIÓN PLAZA

Quintáns

Trasufre

★ CAPELA A
VIRXE DO ESPINO

Dumbria

IGLESIA DE SANTA EULALIA ★
● MESÓN-PENSIÓN O ARGENTINO

★ BIFURCATION

Hospital ▼ O CASTELIÑO

0   5 mi

0   5 km

Highlights

★ **Praia da Langosteira:** This large and sweeping beach right before arriving in Finisterre is where many pilgrims dive into the ocean to ritually wash away the long days of the pilgrimage, and hunt for scallop shells to commemorate the end of their journey (page 443).

★ **Lonxa de Fisterra, Finisterre's Fish Auction:** Take in a daily ballet of fishing boats, fishermen, and heaps of colorful fish and shellfish, at the auction where food professionals come to bid on some of the continent's freshest catch (page 444).

★ **Finisterre's *Faro* (Lighthouse):** This lighthouse is situated at the end of the final 3.2-kilometer (2-mile) climb from Finisterre, a dramatic and steep rise with views of infinite ocean and sky (page 448).

★ **Iglesia San Julián de Moraime:** All that's left of the Monastery of Moraime is this Romanesque church, whose tympanum is carved with an image of the Last Supper that depicts a child-size Saint John the Baptist joining the scene (page 456).

★ **Santuario da Virxe da Barca:** This ancient sacred shrine of Our Lady of the Boat sits on a bottleneck of land between ocean and bay: the perfect perch for both sunrise and sunset (page 458).

★ **Finisterre to Muxía:** One of the most challenging days on the entire Camino takes you into wild forests, steep mountains, hidden valleys, and untamed Atlantic coastline on the trail that connects Finisterre and Muxía (page 462).

Santiago de Compostela is the gateway from Galicia's verdant interior to the wild and beautiful coast known in ancient times as the end of the known world, *finis terrae,* where land and ocean meet. Today, *peregrinos* head there to see the road naturally end and the sun set into the vast watery horizon, a rite of rebirth carried out by ancient people at these same places. They also go to savor seafood pulled directly off the boats and to gather a scallop shell from the beach. Some perform other rituals of closure: swimming in the ocean; casting off trail worn boots and clothes; and gazing out at the endless ocean after following a seemingly finite path across northern Spain. Here, too, many also discover that their lives are no longer ordinary, thanks to the Camino, and that the journey itself never really ends.

Peregrinos have two options when it comes to end points: Finisterre, due west of Santiago de Compostela, is traditionally considered Kilometer 0, while Muxía, to the northwest of Santiago and due north of Finisterre, is more off the beaten path—and locals feel it may well be the true end of the Camino. This is a subjective matter and can be justified in either direction, and is best left for each person to work out through the adventure of walking. One thing is certain: this path is not linear anyhow—has the Camino ever really been linear?—and the whole landscape is rich with ancient and spiritual associations.

As you draw nearer the coast, you will find a special fish stew, *caldeirada,* appearing more and more. Something like the bouillabaisse of Galicia and northern Portugal, *caldeirada* is made with a firm white fish, often hake, but also tuna or mackerel, among others, and cooked in a broth with green peppers, potatoes, onion, garlic, tomatoes, and saffron. This is the basic recipe, but more elaborate *caldeiradas* can also have squid, clams, shrimp, and mussels added in with the fish.

Planning Your Time

If you plan to make the trek on foot to either Muxía (**86.9 km/54 mi** from Santiago de Compostela) or Finisterre (**89.3 km/55.5 mi** from Santiago de Compostela), allow **4 days.** Add **2 more days** if you then want to trek to Muxía from Finisterre (**29.3 km/18.2 mi**) or vice versa. If you plan to bus to Muxía and Finisterre, allow 1-2 days for each, or 2-3 for both. You can also mix up the options, such as busing to Muxía from Santiago de Compostela and then hiking to Finisterre and taking the bus back. Some folks with ample time even walk back. If you opt to do this, note that markers are less clear in reverse, except for the trail between Muxía and Finisterre that often gets trekkers going in both directions. Note that Hospital, where the trail splits to go southwest to Finisterre and northwest to Muxía, is at both Kilometer 29.8 and at Kilometer 27.4. This is because the distance between Hospital and Finisterre (29.8 km) is different from the distance between Hospital and Muxía (27.4 km).

Both Finisterre and Muxía offer their versions of a Compostela. Like the Compostela, to earn these, you must walk to each town; you can't take the bus. For the **Fisterana,** you must walk from Santiago de Compostela and gather stamps (two per day). To get the **Muxiana,** you must walk from either Finisterre to Muxía, getting a stamp in Finisterre and Lires, or you must walk from Santiago de Compostela along the route to Muxía via Dumbria, getting stamps (two per day). While you won't qualify for a certificate if you take the bus (unless you walk the coastal route to Muxía from Finisterre), you can still get stamps in Finisterre and Muxía in your credential to enjoy as mementos of the journey.

Route Options

The two paths to the coast are one road when they depart from Santiago, and

Recommended Overnight Stops

Santiago de Compostela to Finisterre

* **Negreira** (Km 68.3, page 437)

* **Santa Mariña** (Km 46.8, page 438)

* **Cee** (Km 15.4, page 440) or **Corcubión** (Km 13.9, page 441)

* **Finisterre** (Km 3.2, p. 443)

Santiago de Compostela to Muxía

* **Negreira** (Km 68.3, page 437)

* **Santa Mariña** (Km 46.8, page 438)

* **Dumbría** (Km 22.5, page 454)

* **Muxía** (Km 0, page 457)

remain one for 60 kilometers (37 miles), so you don't have to decide which coastal destination to visit until 0.9 kilometers (0.6 miles) after Hospital, at what is called the *bifurcación*, the bifurcation or fork in the path. Head left to Finisterre, and right to Muxía.

If you have the time, make the full trek and let your spirit decide at the fork in the road which fishing town to reach first. You can then walk the coastal route to the other town, then catch the bus back to Santiago. The majority of *peregrinos* who do the full circuit like to head to Finisterre first and then end at Muxía, where the legends of Saint James and Mary are the strongest. This is the direction I too prefer, because Muxía is a smaller, mellower fishing village, a nice conclusion to a long journey, but you should know that more buses connect Santiago to and from Finisterre (4-6 per day) than Muxía (2 per day, one in the morning and one in the afternoon).

Geography and Terrain

The Camino de Finisterre and Muxía is well way-marked, but not always as obviously as the Camino Francés. Remain aware and you will find the arrows, shells, and signs with little trouble. If you decide to walk *back* to Santiago from either town, note that the route is not as well marked in reverse.

This entire coastal route is slightly **less well-supported** than the traditional Camino, so you will be walking in a lot of rural and wild territory without as many cafés and accommodations options. In particular, in the direction of Finisterre, the 14.4 kilometers (9 miles) from **Hospital to Cee** is wholly wild and without support structures, and on the **coastal trail between Finisterre and Muxía,** there is only one guaranteed place to refuel and lodge, and that is Lires, 13.6 kilometers (8.5 miles) after Finisterre and another 15.7 kilometers (9.8 miles) to Muxía.

The first 60 kilometers (37 miles) before the bifurcation are the **hardest,** with several up-and-down climbs and descents. The other hardest part of this terrain—one steep climb and repeated up-and-down walking—is the 29.3-kilometer (18.2-mile) coastal trail between Finisterre and Muxía, but it is among the prettiest sections as well, for its diverse landscape of mountains, forests, and ocean. The Camino Finsterre leads through **deep rural territory,** where hamlets and small villages are the norm. Whether you head to Finisterre or Muxía, you'll traverse rippling hills and low mountains fed by many waterways that flow through the green valleys and dales.

Weather

You are assured of **rain** any time of year in this part of Galicia. Check the weather forecast before leaving Santiago de Compostela to determine how much of the trek might require rain gear, and give yourself extra time to navigate the potentially rain-soaked trails. Temperatures, happily, tend to be **temperate** and reasonably comfortable year round compared to the interior, thanks to the ocean's moderating effect.

Getting There

You can of course walk from Santiago de Compostela to Finisterre and Muxía. It's also possible, and more common among most pilgrims, to arrive in either town by bus. The two towns are connected by bus service via the main hub town of Cee but only on weekdays. Taxi is the best way to get between the two towns on weekends when the bus does not run.

Bus

Monbus (www.monbus.es) has buses that connect Santiago de Compostela with both Finisterre and Muxía. More buses run daily between Finisterre and Santiago de Compostela (4-6/day) than Muxía (2/day). There are no buses that connect Finisterre and Muxía directly. To do that, you need to go through Cee from Finisterre and change for a bus to Muxía. This route runs only on weekdays; on weekends, a taxi is the best way between the two coastal destinations.

Taxi

The most direct way to get between Finisterre and Muxía is in a taxi (30 minutes, €30-35), an option that can be efficient both time- and money-wise if you share the ride with other pilgrims.

Taxi Loncho (981-747-673; www.casaloncho.com) also offers transfer of 1-4 packs to their next accommodation for €5 if you decide you want to walk but

Local Markets

- **Negreira:** Market every **Sunday** (page 438).

- **Cee**: Food and goods market every **Sunday** (page 441).

- **Finisterre**: Weekly markets every **Tuesday** and **Friday** (page 451).

- **Muxía**: Market days every **Tuesday** and **Friday** (page 459).

want to send your pack ahead on any portion of the Camino de Finisterre from Santiago de Compostela to Finisterre and/or Muxía.

Tour

If you have only one day, consider a day tour from Santiago de Compostela: **Pilgrim** (Rua Nova, 7; 910-607-539; www.pilgrim.es) runs a 9-hour tour departing daily at 9am to both Finisterre and Muxía (€35), as does **Tour Galicia** (Rúa do Franco, 53; 608-666-842; www.tourgalicia.com) for the same price. Both companies have some English-speaking staff.

Santiago de Compostela to Hospital
Km 89.3 – Km 29.8

The entire stretch from Santiago de Compostela to Hospital is defined by green hills, many rivers and streams, and huddled pretty gray granite villages and dense forest. It is a beautiful trail, and also one that involves a lot of up and down climbing. Count on the first 46 kilometers (28.6 miles), especially, as a stretch of constant ascent and descent. The steepest and most demanding climb is on the 2.8 kilometers (1.7 miles) to **Alto do Mar de Ovellas**

Finisterre, Muxía, or Both?

Both paths to the coast are beautiful and rewarding, passing through rising and falling hills and forested tracts speckled with the gray-stone hamlets that largely define this corner of Galicia. Generally speaking, the routes are also about the same levels of difficulty, in part because they share the first 60 kilometers (37 miles). The endpoints, Finisterre and Muxía, are equally legitimate, legend-saturated, and gorgeous towns where the way of the stars meets the way of the ocean. So if you must, how will you choose between them?

coastal trail marker to Muxía and Finisterre

Finisterre

Meaning "earth's end," and the place where medieval people thought the world really did end at the edge of the infinite ocean, since the 1980s Finisterre has been treated by pilgrims as the traditional Kilometer 0. The **land's-end view** here can be pretty dramatic, reached by climbing up the spine of Monte Facho and looking out over the ocean from the precipice, the lighthouse marking the spot where polished boulders below have endured pounding by water and wind. Finisterre is also a **larger settlement** and has a **daily fish market** with a large fishing fleet.

The challenge of the way to Finisterre is the long stretch, from Hospital to Cee, that has no support. The last 3 kilometers (1.9 miles) of that section also descend dramatically to near sea level just before reaching Cee.

Muxía

Fewer pilgrims make the trek to Muxía from Santiago de Compostela, so it can have a slightly more "off the beaten path" feel. In the high season, the route is slightly better supported than the one to Finisterre. The way to Muxía also contains one of this terrain's most interesting Romanesque churches, the 12th-century **Iglesia de San Julian de Moraime,** 4.5 kilometers (2.8 miles) south of Muxía. Muxía itself is a more quiet and

intimate fishing village that feels less commercially developed, and makes for a serene finish to the Camino. Like Finisterre, Muxía also has a seaside church, **Santuario da Virxe da Barca,** which is in a far more dramatic location than the one in Finisterre, right on the edge of the rocks and pummeled by the waves.

One challenge of Muxía is that restaurants and accommodations close from early autumn through late spring.

Both

If you have 5-6 days, you can have it all. I advise first walking from Santiago to Finisterre (3-4 days), enjoying a day there, and then walking the coastal route north from Finisterre to Muxía, ending your Camino there. You can even use Muxía as your home base to then walk the 4.5 kilometers (2.8 miles) to the Iglesia de San Julian de Moraime, south of Muxía and on the trail that leads to Muxía from Hospital.

Alternatively, if you have 3-4 days and want to experience the best of the coastal trail options, I would suggest taking the bus from Santiago de Compostela to either Finisterre or Muxía and walking the **coastal path connecting them,** which is way-marked in both directions and is perhaps the prettiest and wildest of all the paths. You can then take the bus back to Santiago de Compostela (there are 4-6 buses/day from Finisterre to Santiago, and 2 buses/day from Muxía to Santiago.

(Km 74.9) at an altitude of 272 meters (892 feet). The path peaks at 375 meters (1,230 feet) at Hospital (Km 29.8) just before where the path forks, with one route leading to Finisterre and the other to Muxía.

Leaving Santiago de Compostela   Km 89.3

Depart Santiago from the cathedral's west side, with the *parador* to your right, and head west down **Rúa das Hortas.** Cross over Rúa do Pombal and continue straight onto **Poza de Bar** through the **Parque de San Lorenzo** and its 13th-century Convento de San Lorenzo on the left, where you will begin to pick up the scallop-shell way-markers mounted on the familiar concrete pillars. You will cross a small bridge over the Sarela river; the path will go slightly left and become a dirt path, continuing through a wooded area toward the tiny village of **Sarela de Abaixo** (Km 87). This is the best place to turn around and look at the city and cathedral towers.

☝ Detour: Castelo   Km 78.3

Soon after passing the hamlet of Ventosa, 10.5 kilometers (6.5 miles) after Santiago de Compostela, you will have the option to take the forking road to the right for 500 meters (0.3 miles) to the small village of **Castelo** (pop. 232), which offers the single lodging option in the 21 kilometers (13 miles) between Santiago and Negreira. **Casa Rural Ríamonte** (Calle Castelo, s/n; 981-890-356), a modern country home of stucco, stone, and terracotta roof, with tile and wood floors and a relaxing terrace overlooking a large lawn and garden, offers a shared dorm room (six beds, €12) and four private rooms (€50-70), some with private bath, as well as dinner (€12) and breakfast (€3). Proprietors speak English.

To return to the Camino from Castelo, retrace your steps to the fork in the road and return to the main path toward **Augapesada** (Km 77.5) where the steep and demanding climb begins to **Alto do Mar de Ovellas** (Km 74.9) and then descends toward Pontemaceira.

Pontemaceira   Km 72.3

The hamlet of Pontemaceira (pop. 68) is defined by the bridge, which you will cross to enter the village and continue on the Camino, that gives it its name, Ponte Maceira ("apple bridge"). This whole hamlet has been beautifully restored to preserve its historic houses. Here, and in Negreira ahead, you'll begin to see some of the old stone mansions and country homes, *pazos,* that define the settlements along this route. Many have ornate stone coats of arms engraved on the outer walls.

Pontemaceira has also preserved three of its riverside water mills, one having been restored and turned into an upscale restaurant. It's well worth taking the time to enjoy this, and then walking the remaining 4 kilometers (2.5 miles) to Negreira.

Sights
Ponte Maceira

This five-arched bridge traverses the wide Río Tambre, with rushes and reeds growing along its banks. The foundations of the bridge most likely date to the Roman era, but the bridge itself was rebuilt in the 13th and 14th centuries and restored in the 18th. According to a Jacobian legend, Santiago's disciples fled across this bridge, Roman soldiers on their heels. A divine force cracked the bridge in the middle, preventing the Romans from making the crossing while allowing Santiago's followers to make it safely to the other side.

Legends aside, it is known that Romans relied on the bridge to connect the maritime road to the interior, and medieval pilgrims used it as well—including those who arrived by boat and were making their way from the coast to Santiago de Compostela for the first time. Before crossing the bridge to make your way west to Negreira, consider a pause at the excellent Restaurante Ponte Maceira, a few paces to your right on the east bank of the Tambré river.

Food

★ **Restaurante Ponte Maceira** (Pontemaceira, 3; 981-881-680; www. restaurantepontemacaera.com; €13-35) is located on the east side of the river Tambre before crossing the bridge. This old mill turned field-and-river-to-table restaurant creates innovative comfort cuisine daily, including the specialty, roasted chicken with tapenade. The mill's millstones are still in place. Dining is inside the mill house or on the terrace, both with a view of the river and bridge. Dishes fill the eyes as much as the mouth, with creations like black rice with squid, herb and olive oil-grilled *zamburiñas* (bay scallops), and grilled octopus on mashed potatoes with red onion and red pepper relish.

Negreira Km 68.3

You'll enter Negreira (pop. 3,896) the same way medieval pilgrims did: via the arched gate and fortified medieval wall of the **Pazo de Cotón de Mauro.** This country mansion dates to the Middle Ages but has been restored many times, including in the 18th century. Built into the right side of the fortified wall is the chapel, **Capela de San Mauro,** dedicated to Saint Amaro, a pilgrim who sailed west across the ocean to discover an island that was an earth-based paradise.

Negreira offers all services and good options for food and lodging. The town has likely Roman roots: From 1876-1958, locals uncovered several granite stones with Roman inscriptions and engravings, all now on display in the Museo do Pobo Galego in Santiago de Compostela. Two of the stones are dedicated to the Roman god Jupiter. A maritime Roman road probably passed here, as in Pontemaceira, that connected Negreira to Padrón and Caldas de Reis to the south. The Germanic Suevi tribe dominated Negreira after the Roman decline. The medieval town began to grow in the late 9th century but was sacked by Viking pirates in 979, and then by Almanzor from southern Iberia in 997. The town was rebuilt by 1113, and by then

to Negreira

was receiving pilgrims on their way to or from the coast.

Negreira's **market** day is **Sunday**, setting up near the Pazo de Cotón.

Food and Accommodations

Restaurante Casa Barqueiro (Avenida de Santiago, 13; 981-818-234; www.casabarquiero.es; €10-15) has inside and outside dining and specializes in surf-and-turf Galician cuisine; it's especially known for grilled meats, vegetables, and seafood dishes, including *chipirones á la plancha* (grilled tiny squid). Try also the lobster saffron rice and the homemade cheesecake.

For comfort food, like fried eggs and bacon, garden salads, and tortillas, head to the central **Cervecería Galaecia** (Rúa da Cachurra, 1; 981-885-649; €5-12).

Before entering Negreira, you'll see the **Albergue-Pensión San José** (Rúa Castelao, 20; 881-976-934; www.alberguesanjose.es), a modern building with modern facilities with warm open spaces of wood, tile, and rust-red, lemon-cream, and ochre-colored walls. The *albergue* offers dorm rooms (50 beds in three rooms, €12) and 15 private rooms (€30-45). There is a large dining room, well-outfitted communal kitchen, and relaxing back garden with covered terrace.

Run by a cheerful family, **Hostal La Mezquita** (Calle del Carmen, 2; 636-129-691; www.alberguehostalmezquita.com) is fun and funky, with its apple-green rooms, white jacquard bedspreads, and dark wood-framed French doors that let in light and open to a small balcony. There are two dorm room (17 beds total, €12) and eight rooms with private bathrooms (€35-50). The congenial bar, restaurant, lounge, and laundry facilities are open to all patrons. *Menú del día* for €10.

Leaving Negreira

It is a good idea stock up on provisions and fill water bottles in Negreira to hedge your bets against cafés that may or may not be open for the 33.4-kilometer

(20.8-mile) stretch between here and Olveiroa. Prepare for a steady and at times steep 9.5-kilometer (5.9-mile) climb from Negreira. The path levels out for the final 8.8 kilometers (5.5 miles) to Santa Mariña.

Santa Mariña Km 46.8

Santa Mariña (pop. 115) is centered on its **Iglesia de Santa María de Maroñas**, founded in the 12th century and rebuilt in the 18th. It offers a good midway stop for accommodations between Negreira and Olveiroa.

Food and Accommodations

★ **Albergue Casa Pepa** (Santa Mariña, 4; 981-852-881; www.casaalberguepepa. es) is a stone country house with inviting terrace and connected restaurant. Run by energetic and upbeat hosts you can stay in the one private room with bath (€40) or in one of the five shared dorm rooms (38 total beds, €12). They cook traditional Galician dishes from scratch and makes sure guests feel as if they are in their own home. The dining room has a large fireplace.

Leaving Santa Mariña

The next 3 kilometers (1.9 miles) after Santa Mariña (alt. 325 meters/1,066 feet) are uphill. This is followed by 7.2 kilometers (4.5 miles) of descent, at times steep, to **Ponte Olveira** (Km 36.7/34.4) and then the final 1.8 kilometers (1.1 miles) on more level ground to **Olveiroa,** with an altitude of 280 meters (919 feet).

Olveiroa Km 34.9

Entering Olveiroa (pop. 109), you are now thick in *hórreo* country. The abundance of these Galician stone granaries, set on stilts to prevent mold and stave off rats and mice, adds charm to the village, as does the *cruceiro,* the ornate cross, at the crossroads, and the small gray granite village church nearby, the **Iglesia de Santiago de Olveiroa**. Although small, Olveiroa still has good options, with two *albergues* and one hostel. One of the *albergues* has private rooms.

Accommodations

★ **Casa Loncho** (981-747-673; www. casaloncho.com; €40) is in a traditional rural townhouse complex, with a restaurant and nine private rooms with exposed stone and plenty of natural light. The *menú del día* is homemade and changes daily, inspired by seasonal and local ingredients. There is a pool and sauna, and if you wish to arrange it, a space for massage therapy. The same family operates the **Albergue Horreo** (52 beds in six dorm rooms, €12), which features well-equipped, spacious, and spotless dorm rooms and an agreeable bar and restaurant. Breakfast is €3-5. There is also a small general store on the premises.

Leaving Olveiroa

Take note that you will find no support services for food and lodging on the 14.4-kilometer (9-mile) stretch between Hospital and Cee, if you plan to walk the route to Finisterre. Be sure to stock up with water and food in Olveiroa, O Logoso, or Hospital.

O Logoso (Km 31.2)

The village of O Logoso has two good accommodation and food options, both run by the same friendly staff, the **Albergue O Logoso** and **Pension A Pedra** (981-727-602; www.alberguelogoso.com). The latter is especially delightful, in a traditional stone townhouse with four cozy private rooms with bath (€30). The *albergue* is simple but agreeable, and features a nice enclosed terrace bar and restaurant (20 beds in three dorm rooms, €12).

Hospital (Km 29.8)

A final stop for food is in **Hospital** (Km 29.8) at the café-bar **O Casteliño** (Hospital, s/n, to the left of the Camino; 981-747-387), run by Javi Rey in a restored traditional stone building with a garden.

You can get snacks and drinks here and a *menú del peregrino* (€10).

Leaving Hospital

With modest up-and-down walking, the path continues to the point where it splits in two, 900 meters (0.6 miles) after passing Hospital. The split is marked by a double pillar trail post set at a roundabout (Km 28.9) on the road, and marked with the familiar scallop shells and yellow painted arrows.

To go to Finisterre, take the arrow pointing left. In 500 meters (0.3 miles) the path will leave the road and take up a foot trail that leads to Cee in 14.4 kilometers (9 miles). Remember to stock up on food and water before leaving Hospital.

To go to Muxía, follow the right arrow and continue weaving on and off the small road to Dumbría (in 3.7 km/2.3 mi).

Hospital to Finisterre
Km 29.8 - Km 3.2

This passage is wild and softly rolling hill country covered in scrub, heather, and ferns, and at times passing into tree cover. It's on fairly level terrain, with a slight descent that becomes suddenly steep and dramatic at the **Cruceiro de Armada** (Km 18.9).

Capela de Nosa Señora das Neves Km 24.9

At 4.4 kilometers (2.7 miles) after the bifurcation, the terracotta-roofed **Capela de Nosa Señora das Neves** (Our Lady of the Snows) appears to the left of the trail, tucked in a grove of trees. Built in the 15th century and rebuilt in 1780, it melds older Romanesque architecture with more recent Neoclassical. The covered porch holds an interesting primitive stone sculpture of Our Lady, where many leave messages, flowers, herbs, and candles. The chapel is locked except on festival days, the most important being in September when locals of the surrounding communities hold a small pilgrimage, a *romería*, to the chapel.

This site was very likely an important place to pre-Christian people as well. Two water sources here explain the place's sacredness. One is a spring located near the *cruceiro* at the bottom of the stairs on the bell-tower side of the chapel, which is attributed with wellness properties, especially for nursing mothers, both human and other mammals. The other is a granite well with a bird carved onto the upper stone rung where the rope and pail are hung. The bird hints at the continuity of ancient sacred places being centered on water. In old northern-Iberian folklore, some feminine divinities—often the mother goddess or mother earth—dwelled in watery places and used birds as messengers. (Sometimes birds were also used to represent the divinities directly.) Today, she is reincarnated as Our Lady of the Snows and, like her predecessors, is the protective patroness of the land and sea.

Leaving Nosa Señora das Neves

Continue along the way-marked path, a blissful dirt road. Approximately 2.5 kilometers (1.6 miles) after Nosa Señora das Neves, you will gain your first view of the Atlantic Ocean. Soon after, the Capela de San Pedro Mártir appears on the right side of the trail.

Capela de San Pedro Mártir
Km 21.1

San Pedro's chapel is rustic and dates to 1741, but stands on the foundation of an earlier building that likely hearkens to the medieval period, and possibly earlier, as signified by the fountain nearby. This fountain also has healing properties, including relieving those suffering from arthritis. Surely it works wonders on tired feet as well.

This locally beloved chapel is closed most of the year, except on festival days, particularly in May when the local communities come here for a local pilgrimage, *romería*, and celebration; the healing fountain is the main draw year round.

Leaving Capela de San Pedro Mártir

A couple of kilometers (a mile or so) after leaving the chapel, you reach the **Cruceiro de Armada** (Km 18.9), a standing stone cross marking the first view of Finisterre's bay and the Cabo Finisterre. Just after this, the route begins a steep descent into the village of Cee, from 275 meters (902 feet) to 10 meters (33 feet) above sea level. At the edge of Cee, the Camino at last arrives at the coast and along the bay. It then enters the inviting town and skirts around the edges of the estuary on which the town concentrates, following town's seaside promenade and crescent-shaped beach.

Cee   Km 15.4

The modern-looking and cheerful town of Cee (pop. 3,700) feels smaller than it is. Much of it huddles along **Playa de Concha,** the town's crescent-shaped beach along the protective bay that opens out into the Atlantic. The Camino follows this sweep, along the seaside promenade known as the **Paseo Maritimo,** which shows off the town's beauty and its more ancient core the nearer you get to the water.

Cee is easy to navigate: you follow the shoreline and the path is well marked. You can also take off your shoes and walk along the curved sweep of Playa de Concha barefoot, all the way to the entrance of Corcubión, the next town over. But before you do, pay a visit to the town church, **Iglesia de Santa María de Xunquiera**.

Cee has Celtic roots: The Celtic-speaking Nerios tribe, documented by Roman chroniclers of the area, inhabited Cee. Cee's name possibly comes from the Latin word for whale, *cetus*, a reminder of the ancient economy along this shore. Local legend attributes the founding of the settlement to the miraculous appearance of the Virgen de

Junquera ("Virgin of the Reeds") in the estuary grasses, many centuries ago. A sanctuary was built where they discovered her, and the settlement of Cee grew out of this. In more recent history, the town of Cee developed in the 12th century, when the nearby villagers shifted from agricultural activities to fishing and whaling and moved closer to the shore.

Every **Sunday** is the open-air food and general goods **market** in Cee, on the Rúa Domingo Antonio de Andrade and the Praza do Mercado, near the town hall in the center of town.

Sights

Iglesia de Santa María de Xunqueira

The **Iglesia de Santa María de Xunqueira** (Plaza do Mercado, s/n) is located in the center of the historic town, 300 meters (984 feet) north of the Playa de Concha of the Camino/Paseo Maritimo. A 15th-century Gothic building that was rebuilt after 1809, when Napoleon's troops destroyed much of Cee, there is not a lot to see here; inside, however, is a sculpture of the Virxe da Xunqueira, whose feast day in Cee is celebrated on August 15. The church is open throughout the day and early evening for **mass** and **Vespers**.

Food and Accommodations

The bright and spotless **Albergue Moreira** (Calle Rosalía de Castro, 75; 981-746-282; www.alberguemoreira.com) is right on the path of the Camino into Cee, in the traditional fishermen's neighborhood a few steps inland from the harbor (a 3-minute walk away). There is one dorm room which houses up to 14 people (€12), plus four double rooms (€30), all with shared baths (a total of four).

The elegant **Hotel Insua** (Avenida de Finisterre, 82; 981-747-575; www.hotelinsua.com; 48 rooms; €55-80) is in the center of town, with rounded balconies, floor-to-ceiling windows, and a street-level restaurant known for specialty seafood dishes.

Leaving Cee

The Camino continues to follow the seaside path, Paseo Maritimo, around the bay of Playa de Concha. If you took your shoes off to walk on the beach, you'll want to put them back on where it ends, before walking to Corcubión.

Corcubión   Km 13.9

The seaside path from Cee leads to Corcubión (pop. 1,375), farther south along a protective seawall promenade (**Rúa Alameda**) that passes above the narrow beach, **Praia (Playa) de Santa Isabel** (visible mostly at low tide). Where this promenade enters the historic center of Corcubión at the harbor, the Camino veers right and inland into the historic town center, and will pass to the right of the historic **Iglesia de San Marcos de Cadeira**.

About half the size of Cee, Corcubión is huddled on the same protected estuary bay that opens to the Atlantic. It also shares the same history as Cee: it was inhabited by Nerios, Celtic speakers, before Romans took over the area; in 1809, it was also destroyed by the Napoleonic invasion and later rebuilt. Also similar to Cee, the people of Corcubión lived farther back from the shore until about the 13th century, when they shifted to this beautiful curve of beach and estuary. The move seems to be related to the decline of piracy (mostly Vikings) along these shores, making it safer to live nearer the water.

In early August, Corcubión holds the **Fiesta de la Almeja**, a clam festival, where all things clam (including various tastings, complimented with crisp regional Albariño and Ribeiro white wines) dominate the town.

Sights

Iglesia de San Marcos de Cadeira

Corcubión's **Iglesia de San Marcos de Cadeira** (Plaza Párroco Francisco Sánchez, 11), on the left of the Camino's passage through town, was originally a 12th-century church that was rebuilt in

the 14th and 15th centuries in an appealing Neogothic style. As in Cee, this church also had to be restored after the 1809 invasion. The interior has an interesting wide-vaulted ceiling, with wider-than-usual Gothic arches (sometimes called "maritime Galician Gothic") that make the small church feel like an upside-down boat. A small and pretty **rose window** behind the altar lets in natural light. The altar itself is simple and unadorned, allowing you to appreciate the late-medieval Gothic stone work. A small niche on the right side of the nave holds the church's namesake, a Baroque-style statue of Saint Mark, whose feast day is celebrated on April 25. The church is typically open during the day.

Food and Accommodations

O Carrumeiro (Porto de Corcubión, s/n; 981-706-110; €10-15) is right on the harbor and serves off-the-boat grilled fish and seafood and other dishes, with a daily *menú* featuring traditional seaside dishes such as *caldeiradas*, a rich fish stew.

Boutique chic meets rural maritime hotel in the fresh and original **Casa de Balea** (Calle Rafael Juan, 44; 981-746-645; www.casadebalea.com; 6 rooms; €50), featuring a whaling-themed décor. Its cast-iron beds, fireplace, terrace with open views of the ocean and countryside, and garden with nooks to read and relax, offer enjoyable immersion into this idyllic little town on the coast.

Dine, dance, and sleep right on the beach at **As Hortensias** (Praia de Quenxe, s/n; 981-747-584; www.ashortensias.es; 16 rooms; €32-50). The dining room and terrace overlook the bay.

Leaving Corcubión

The Camino path turns right and

From top to bottom: Galician *horreos* near Olveiroa; Praia da Langosteira; finding a scallop shell on Praia da Langosteira.

inland (your back will be to the bay) at the church of San Marcos de Cadeira to climb up the hill overlooking Corcubión. In 1.5 kilometers (0.9 miles) after Corcubión, it passes through the village of **Vilar** (Km 12.4), followed by the village of **San Roque** (Km 11.9); this is a brief but steep climb that is the last before Finisterre. Vilar has no support services, but San Roque has the small **Albergue San Roque** (679-460-942; year-round; donation), which has 16 beds and offers a communal meal, often featuring a big salad, pimientos de Padrón, pasta, local bread, and wine.

One of the best views of the land's end is at Km 7.2, 2 kilometers (1.2 miles) after **Sardiñeiro** (Km 9.2), where you take in the full curve of the estuary and the finger of land and rising mound, jutting into endless ocean and sky, that defines the Cabo Finisterre (Capo Finisterre). The large sickle-shaped beach you see in the middle distance is the Praia da Langosteira (Km 4.5). The Camino continues along a dirt path, following the coast until touching down on the beach at Praia da Langosteira.

★ Praia da Langosteira   Km 4.5

Crescent-shaped Praia da Langosteira ("shrimp beach") is a long (2 km/1.2 mi) stretch of soft white sand that leads south to the town of Finisterre. Take your shoes off and walk barefoot if you like. The beach often is covered in kelp and seashells—including scallop shells—at medium and low tides.

This beach is where some pilgrims like to perform a rite of the Camino, taking a ritual plunge to rinse away the last bit of psychic and physical grime from their long pilgrimage. It faces the bay and is protected from the stronger currents of the open ocean, making it an ideal place for a plunge, though you should always pay attention to the tide and the current for this entire coastline, including its inlets and bay: This is not called the "coast of death" (Costa da Morte) for nothing.

But on calm days, despite the fact that the water tends to be on the cold side most of the year, this beach is safer than the ocean-facing beach (Praia de Mar de Fóra) on the other side of Finisterre.

Leaving Praia da Langosteira

If you're tired (or salty and wet from plunging into the ocean), consider booking a place at the **Hotel Langosteira** (Avenida de Coruña, 6; 981-740-543; www.hotellangosteira.com; 11 rooms, €46-52), right near the beach at the beginning of Finisterre town.

After the Praia de Langosteira, the path turns fully south and enters into the center of the narrow finger of land that defines Finisterre and Cabo Finisterre. It is not only *finis terrae,* "land's end," but also a perfect north-south peninsula that can witness both the setting and rising sun, a perfect place for experiencing the cycle of rebirth for which this tip of land has drawn people since time immemorial.

Finisterre   Km 3.2

Finisterre (pop. 2,781), Fisterra in Gallego, is at the southern tip of a north-south-aligned finger of land that juts into the Atlantic. During the Middle Ages, when the ocean was considered to be a great mystery, many considered it the "end of the Earth." Many pilgrims arriving here had never before seen the ocean. Today, it's a seaside resort as well as an important fishing town, but approaching Finisterre still feels as mysterious as it must have in the Middle Ages: You arrive from the interior to the sudden opening of infinite water and sky. The climb to the lighthouse offers one of the prettiest sunsets on the Camino, and the ancient stones there still carry magical properties for many. Finisterre probably was a ritual place dating back to prehistory, and every inch of the landscape feels saturated with symbolic meaning. This is the end of the path, a point of pause between thresholds, and the beginning of something as yet unknown.

When you arrive in Finisterre town and harbor, you still have another 3.2 kilometers (2 miles) to the faro (lighthouse), Kilometer 0, at the end of Cabo Finisterre (Finisterre's cape, the wild peninsula that juts into the Atlantic farther south of Finisterre town). Arrows from the center of town will guide you there. Allow a day to explore the town and the cape where you'll find the lighthouse, under which you can climb to the rocks that hover over the ocean, with places to sit and dangle your feet over the rocks with a panoramic ocean view.

If you walked here, getting stamps along the way in your *credencial do peregrino* (pilgrim passport or credential), you can get a certificate of completion similar to the Compostela, called the **Fisterana.** To gather the certificate, go to the **Ayuntamiento** (town hall) on Rúa Santa Catalina, 1 (981-740-001) with your credential. For visitor information, including about visiting local churches, visit the centrally located **tourist office** (Rúa Real, 2; 981-740-781; turismofisterra@hotmail.com) near the north end of the harbor.

Sights
Finisterre Town
The town's **fishing harbor** occupies the one little nook of protective curve along this coast, which can be battered by strong storms (which explains the name of this coastline, Costa da Morte, coast of death). It's a colorful place to watch boats come and go, or to enjoy a meal or drink at a waterfront café. Several of the town's sights cluster here, including the fish auction and the Museo del Mar.

Monument to Immigrants
Finisterre's large protective harbor is defined by a large pedestrian square, **Paseo da Ribeira**, and lined with several inviting restaurants. Starting at the roundabout at the north end of the harbor is a large public **monument to immigrants** dedicated to Galicians who emigrated. Emigration is a common occurrence in this corner of Spain, where people have largely lived in subsistence economies and experienced hard times over many centuries, especially in the 19th and 20th. You've probably seen such monuments in towns and villages as you've walked the Camino de Finisterre. Galicians make up large communities of expatriates around the world, especially in the Americas.

★ Lonxa de Fisterra
Lonxa de Fisterra (Porto de Fisterra; 981-740-079; www.lonxadefisterra.com; free), Finisterre's fish auction, occupies the large, sleek, metal and glass building standing in the harbor's center. Here, visitors can witness the haul of fish coming off the fishing boats and going to auction. Depending on conditions at sea, this occurs almost daily, starting at 4pm, and lasts until sometime after 5pm. Come at any time in this window, step up the stairs to the mezzanine, and watch fishermen and food professionals bidding on that day's colorful catch. Images and text panels are mounted all around the Lonxa mezzanine's balcony, identifying the different fish that you are likely to see for sale at the auction below. Visitors cannot buy fish from this wholesalers' auction, but you can enjoy the fish right on the harbor at the many seaside restaurants.

A massive **anchor** standing outside the Lonxa is a memorial dedicated to all who have dedicated (and given) their life to the sea.

Museo del Mar
At the far southern end of the harbor is the Castelo de San Carlos, Finisterre's defensive fort from the 18th century, which is now a maritime museum, **Museo del Mar** (981-740-079; Jun.-Aug., 11am-2pm and 5-8:30pm; €1), exhibiting the town's and region's fishing culture. This spacious one-room museum displays small

Clockwise from top: Finisterre's fishing harbor; Finisterre rocks; Finisterre's harbor and *lonxa* (fish auction); Iglesia de Santa María de Arenas.

Finisterre

AC445

0 ——— 200 yds
0 ——— 200 m

CALLE LA CORUÑA

RÚA PATIÑES

RÚA PRADO DA VIÑA

AV. DE A CORUÑA

AC445

RÚA SANTA CATALINA

PASEO CALAFIGUEIRA

HOTEL LANGOSTEIRA

AYUNTAMIENTO DE FISTERRA

RÚA CABELLO

RÚA ATALAIA

RÚA ALCALDE FERNÁNDEZ

RÚA FEDERICO ÁVILA

RÚA REAL

RÚA CAMPO

HOSTAL MARIQUITO

O CÉNTOLO

RESTAURANTE LORCA CALAFIGUEIRA

ALBERGUE DO SOL E DA LÚA

PASEO RIBEIRA

LONXA DE FINISTERRE, FINISTERRE'S FISH AUCTION

PLAZA CONSTITUCIÓN

HOTEL ÁNCORA

A LAREIRA

AC445

RÚA ARRIBA

RÚA DE PRAZA

R. ARA-SOLIS

R. MANUEL LAGO PAIS

CAPELA DE NOSA SEÑORA DO BO SUCESO

RÚA ALFREDO SARALEGUI

MUSEO DEL MAR/ CASTELO DE SAN CARLOS

RÚA ARA-SOLIS

RÚA VIRXE DAS AREAS

RÚA ALCALDE FERNÁNDEZ

IGLESIA DE SANTA MARÍA DE ARENAS

To Cabo Finisterre

© MOON.COM

Cabo Finisterre

ERMITA SAN GUILLERME

PIEDRAS SAGRADAS

Monte San Guillerme

Monte Facho

BAR O REFUXIO O SEMAFORO

HOTEL/ RESTAURANTE O SEMAFORO

FINISTERRE'S FARO

traditional fishing boats and their various fish nets and lobster, crab, and octopus traps, as well as shrimping nets that were developed over the centuries to navigate the treacherous coastline and open sea along the Costa da Morte. It also has displays about the evolution of the local fishing industry, from small-scale to commercial-scale fishing. The displays are in Gallego (Galician), but for the passionate fisher, this will be a half-hour well spent. You can work out a good deal of what is being said from the artifacts, and from a central diorama of a fisherman, fisherman's wife, and traditional nets and boat.

Praia de Mar de Fóra

This 500-meter-long (1,640-foot) scallop-shaped beach, **Praia de Mar de Fóra,** faces the open ocean. It is a protected natural area that remains stunningly wild and beautiful. It is also absolutely dangerous to swim here, given the dramatically high tides, strong currents, and winds that give this whole coastline its name, Costa da Morte, "coast of death." Do not take this lightly; if you want to do any swimming in the ocean, head back to the Praia de Langosteira. People come here to savor the remote and wild beauty of the windswept and ocean-carved beach, to comb for shells, and for moments of quiet contemplation.

This beach faces the open ocean, on the opposite side of the peninsula from where the town is located, 1 kilometer (0.6 miles) due west of the fishing harbor. The beach is accessed via paths from the town that climb over the ridge from the bay side to the ocean side, a 15-20 minute walk: From the harbor's Monument to Immigrants on the Praza de Santa Catalina, turn your back to the water and face the town (west) and walk up Rúa Federico Ávila for about 200 meters (656 feet); follow it to the Rúa Alcalde Fernández and make a left, walk for 40 meters (131 feet), and then make a right onto Rúa Potiña. Stay on this street for about 350 meters (0.2 miles) until it intersects the Camiño Insua. Make a right and follow the Camiño Insua, which will curve left and head due west, marked with signs for Praia de Mar de Fóra.

Cabo Finisterre

As you leave the harbor, heading south toward Cabo Finisterre, on the upper southern end of the town, you'll pass the 18th-century Baroque chapel, **Capela de Nosa Señora do Bo Suceso** (Our Lady of Good Happenings) on the **Plaza de Ara Solis.** Inside, on the altar stands a statue of the **Virgen de Socorro,** Our Lady of Help/Relief. Unfortunately, the church is rarely open except for local events. But it serves as a good landmark for the path, which leaves the upper part of the fishing town and heads toward Cabo Finisterre. The next landmark is the more historic (and legend-rich) Iglesia de Santa María de Arenas.

Iglesia de Santa María de Arenas (Igrexa de Santa María das Areas)

Set at the base of the road outside of town and leading to the lighthouse, the 12th-century Romanesque **Igrexia de Santa Maria das Areas** (Rúa Alcalde Fernández, 14), Our Lady of the Sands, houses a 14th-century Gothic statue of Jesus called **Santo Cristo da Barba Dourada,** Christ of the Golden Beard, showing him on a crucifix. In local lore, this statue arrived on an English vessel that was caught in a treacherous storm at sea along this coast. The sailors threw the sculpture overboard to lighten the vessel, and as soon as they did, the storm ceased. A local fisherman pulled the image out of the water and understood that this Jesus wanted to live here.

The image is now kept in a side chapel inside the church. It has a realistic appearance, from bleeding wounds to reddish beard. Some claim that the sculpture's hair and nails grow like a mortal human's (and have to be trimmed). Medieval pilgrims came to this church to gather extra blessing from this Cristo da Barba Dourada.

The main altar holds the 16th-century sculpture of **Santa Maria das Areas**, Finisterre's patroness, which is paraded through town on her feast day on **September 8**. The church is rarely open, so inquire at the tourist office (Rúa Real, 2; 981-740-781; www.turismofisterra.com) if you wish to go inside. The outside has interesting features, including several Romanesque carved corbels and capitals.

Top Experience

★ *Faro* (Lighthouse)

It's a climb to get to the *faro* (lighthouse) at the end of Cabo Finisterre: The town of Finisterre is at 10 meters (33 feet) above sea level and the lighthouse stands at 130 meters (427 feet). From the town center and/or from the Iglesia de Santa María de Arenas, follow the way-markers that lead you past the church (on the right) and up the hill on a footpath to the left of the road that also leads to the lighthouse. Climbing up to the lighthouse is a steady ascent, with the forests and rises of Monte Facho to your right and the steep drop to the bay and ocean to your left.

Just before the lighthouse you'll find the **Kilometer 0** marker, a familiar white stone post with blue and yellow scallop shell. Stepping past it to the lighthouse, built in 1853, you arrive at the meeting point of land, ocean, and sky. Add in the sun, and you are at the intersection of all four alchemical elements: earth, air, water, and fire. This has been a site of veneration for millennia, and the beauty and power can easily fold you in.

The lighthouse itself is a sentinel for ships, calling fishermen home after days, and sometimes weeks, at sea. It also marks the spot where thousands of pilgrims have faced the end of the road, as well as the infinite horizon of possibilities with the new perspectives earned from walking the Camino. It also stands as a sentinel for pilgrims, who are keen to gather just below its base, on the rocks on which it is built and which angle toward the ocean. You can climb here carefully and dangle your feet over the edge for views of endless blue waters. On those rocks below the lighthouse, as a closing

kilometer 0 and Finisterre lighthouse

Finisterre's Sun Altar

Somewhere near Finisterre's lighthouse there once stood a Roman devotional altar (possibly built earlier by the Phoenicians or, before them, the native Iberians), called the **Ara Solis**, that was dedicated to the dying sun. It suggests that Finisterre was at the heart of a sun-worshipping pilgrimage of death and rebirth, setting and rising. The altar was a large stone slab set on two standing stones. From it, people watched the sun set below its slab line and then the ocean. Like the host being dipped into the wine of the chalice, this sun dipped down into the curve of the Ara Solis and affected the moment of transformation from finite and mortal to infinite and immortal. Galicians believe that their flag and coat of arms, the host and chalice, also symbolizes this ancient Ara Solis.

Because it was destroyed, no one is sure exactly where the Ara Solis stood, but the whole territory here is promising, given its special orientation and height between east-facing bay (ideal for sunrises) and west-facing ocean (ideal for sunsets). Essentially, this north-south jutting finger of land, between bay and ocean, with its high mountain and facing another high mountain on the east on the other side of the bay (Monte Pindo), makes for perfect solar alignments for sunrises and sunsets during certain times of the year. It's thought that the **lighthouse,** Monte Facho around the **Piedras Sagradas,** and **Ermita de San Guillerme** are all strong possibilities for the center of this sun altar, which would have maximized both the rising and the setting sun and represented the cycle of birth-death-rebirth central to many ancient sacred systems, not to mention Christianity.

---

ritual, pilgrims used to burn their trail-worn clothes and boots, symbolically releasing their old selves and embracing the new—another ritual of death and rebirth behind the pagan practice of sun worship. Fires are now strictly forbidden, but other ways of finding closure are still at hand, including watching the sunset from this ultimate lookout point.

A footpath north of the lighthouse leads to two spots. Follow it to a fork. If you go left, along the ocean side, it will lead you up to the ridge of Monte Facho and to the **Piedras Sagradas** (Sacred Stones)—sets of large stones standing in a row next to each other that have been shaped by the elements. If you go right at the fork, the footpath leads to the **Ermita San Guillerme** on the bay side of Monte Facho and its own little hill, called **Monte San Guillerme**. The Ermita San Guillerme's placement on Monte San Guillerme sets it up to look straight out across the bay in a line with **Monte Pindo**, a hill on the other side of the estuary.

Piedras Sagradas

Climbing along the upper spine of the finger of land defining the Cabo de Finisterre to its highest point, **Monte Facho,** you'll see some of the best vistas of both harbor and ocean side. (There are no direct paths from town to get here; the most direct way is from the path from the lighthouse.) At the apex you'll find three clusters of sun-bleached gray-white boulders, two of which are referred to as **Piedras Sagradas** or **Piedras Santas**. These are attributed with certain graces by the people who visit them. Some locals say it was here that Mary came to enjoy a rest. Others think this may be where the pagan sun altar, the Ara Solis, was located. We'll never know for sure, because with the Christianization of the area, as much as pagan practices and lore were absorbed, they were equally destroyed.

These stones also seem to be part of a healthy competition as to which place had more legends connected to James and

Mary. Finisterrans say Saint James came here to preach, that Jesus touched down here, and that Mary came here to encourage Santiago in his evangelizing, as she did in Muxía. One thing is sure: This is a transcendent place for its natural beauty. Regarding the magical properties of the stones, many stones scattered across the Cabo Finisterre were attributed with fortuitous and fertile powers, including stones at the Ermita de San Guillerme. In 2010, folklore scholar Marta Plaza Beltran wrote about these stones and their powers in fertility, not only for begetting children but also for petitioning for rain and a fertile crop. They're also said to be conduits between seekers and the divine.

The Piedras Sagradas are the highest boulders on Monte Facho. Among them, two of the most famous sacred stones are **pedras de abalar,** oscillating stones, that move in order to offer prophecy. (You'll be able to identify them from this very distinct physical property, as the other stones are more firmly seated.) If you want to try the prophecy, ask your question. If the stones move, they affirm it; if they remain still, they negate it. Beltran traces this practice back to the Celtic period here, some 2,700 years ago. Muxía also has an oscillating stone, also at the ocean's edge.

Ermita de San Guillerme

The ruins of an early hermitage, **Ermita de San Guillerme** (Saint William's hermitage), rests atop earlier standing stones situated just below the high point of Monte Facho, on the bay and harbor-facing side of Cabo Finisterre. They appear as crumbling walls of a small structure that was built against several large (one towering overhead) oblong and round boulders; the whole of the ruin is

From top to bottom: Piedras Sagradas on Cabo Finisterre; Restaurante Lorca Calafigueira; *caldeirada.*

not much larger than a small one-room cabin. It appears that San Guillerme intentionally built his hermitage against these stones, incorporating some elements of them into his hermitage both to over take their pagan meanings and displace them with Christian ones, but also to take over what was already a sacred site to add spiritual power to his hermitage. Those standing stones carried magical properties, as documented by the 18th-century Benedictine friar Martín Sarmiento, who traveled through the area. He noted that local couples seeking children would come to these stones to "petition" them. (He was delicate in his use of language: They probably came here and effected unabashed physical magic to seal the deal.)

A horizontal stone within the walls of the ruins is called **Cama del Santo**, the bed of the saint. Legend has it that couples lay together here to invite divine powers to give them children. More likely, this particular stone is an old sepulcher, and the true fertility stone lies in broken pieces around you. The whole place was destroyed in the 18th century, but the hermitage was probably built some time between the 8th and 12th centuries.

No one is sure who this San Guillerme (Saint William) was. He may have simply been a local hermit who, like so many in the Middle Ages, sought to mimic the desert fathers of the Bible and retreated into the wilderness to lead a life of quiet contemplation. Both the native polished stones and the outline of the hermitage are still visible here.

The location is gorgeous, set in the forested hillside of its own little hill, Monte de San Guillermo, with a view of the bay below. Some theorize that this is where the Ara Solis stood. The place's alignment between the rising sun over the bay and the setting sun over Monte Facho and the ocean behind it supports this theory. This arc of the sun seems to align Monte Pindo, a hill across the estuary, with Monte Facho and places the hermitage

in the center of the sun's arc, possibly affecting strong earth and sky magic for those prehistoric peoples who witnessed it from here.

Market Days and Festivals

The weekly market with 40 kiosks sets up every **Tuesday** and **Friday** on the Paseo da Ribeira along the north side of the harbor.

The last weekend in **July**, Finisterrans hold the **Festa da Praia**, beach festival, with food, song, and festivities throughout town. The third weekend in **August** is the **Fiesta del Fin del Camino**, the end of the Camino festival, that is also a festival of **anchovies**—so anticipate feasts of this fresh-caught delicacy as well as more eating, drinking, singing, and color. On **September 8** they honor their patroness, **Santa María das Areas**, Nosa Señora da Areas in Gallego, with processions, song, and more feasting in town.

Food
Finisterre Town

Fresh from the ocean and cooked with talent and pride, ★ **Restaurante Lorca Calafigueira** (Paseo Ribeira, 39; 661-460-719; €12-20) serves up the best of the day's catch, hand-carried a few meters from the harbor, including perfectly grilled razor clams, a grilled medley of various fish, cockles, and mussels, and the delicacy, steamed *percebes* (gooseneck barnacles). This is the best place in the harbor for atmosphere as well as food, with both open-air and covered terrace tables with ocean-blue linens. The staff is exceedingly attentive and capable.

O Centolo (Paseo el Puerto; 981-740-452; www.centolo.com; €12-25), at the north end of the harbor, is as much a locals' hangout as a visitors' harbor-front dining area, serving fresh catch from lobster to tuna, with casual tables on the harbor under a protective porch or inside around the gregarious bar. In addition to crab and lobster, one of their specialty dishes is *cazuela de rape* (pronounced *rah-peh),* a tomato and garlic-baked monkfish.

A Lareira (Rúa Alcalde Fernández, 46; 981-740-214; €20-25) is in a modest building that explodes with life, color, and flavors when you step inside or onto the partially protected outdoor terrace. Popular with locals for a meal out, the staff are very friendly and the chef delivers great food, the forte being all things cooked on the central open-flame grill, from seafood to meats, particularly the langoustine, clams, fish, and scallops. Other choices include colorful salads, an over-the-top seafood paella with razor clams and scallops, and the homemade *caldeirada* (fish stew).

Cabo Finisterre

Right next to the lighthouse and next door to Hotel O Semaforo, ★ **Bar O Refuxio O Semaforo** (Faro de Finisterre; 981-110-210; €5-10) is a small café run by a man passionate about heirloom foods, ciders, and wines from the surrounding region, including local steamed clams, mussels, or octopus, marinated sardines, sandwiches made from *porco celta* (Celtic ham), and *queso de Arzúa*. The ham and cheese are sourced from native pigs and cows, that were regionally domesticated (some think) as far back as, and originating with, the indigenous Celtic-speaking Iberians. Sample these with the six-course tasting menu (€20). If you want to enjoy the same attention to local sourcing of ingredients and freshness but want a more elaborate and formal tasting menu (€40) with a more extensive wine list, try the **Restaurante O Semaforo** next door.

Accommodations
Finisterre Town

A beachfront option, on the beach of the same name, is **Hotel Langosteira** (Avenida da Coruña, 6; 981-740-543; www.hotellangosteira.com; 11 rooms, €46-52), featuring a cheerful staff and setting. The contemporary building and décor exude an aquatic feel inside and out, with blue and white tiles, fish murals, and wave designs—the whole intention is to get you to savor the sea and sleep deeply to the lullaby of lapping waves.

The immaculate **Albergue Do Sol e da Lúa** (Calle Atalaya, 7; 881-108-710; alberguedosol@hotmail.com), "from the sun and the moon," opened in 2010 in a fresh and modern building, with three dormitories holding a total of 18 beds (€11 and up, depending on room size) and three private rooms (€20-27), plus a meditation room and a welcoming host who wants his guests to feel at home on their seaside sojourn. Breakfast for €4.

Located in the heart of Finisterre's harbor, both ★ **Hostal Mariquito** (Rúa Santa Catalina, 44-46; 981-74-00-44; www.hostalmariquito.es; 17 rooms, €30-45) and its attached café are managed by an efficient and engaging owner who runs them with efficiency and character. Rooms are larger than is typical in Spanish *hostales* in this price range, and there are open spaces for the sun and sea air to enchant the simple but contemporary, graphic, and slightly folksy art and décor. Some weekend evenings there is live music in the café.

Hotel Ancora (Calle Alcalde Fernández, 65; 981-740-791; www.hotelancorafinisterre.com; €46-60) is a modern seaside hotel with 27 rooms and three apartments. The rooms emphasize a romantic mood, with canopied beds arrayed with swan-shaped towels and flowers, in a balance that melds tasteful kitsch with classic style in colors of ocean and sky. The owner is enthusiastic and loves welcoming guests.

Cabo Finisterre

★ **Hotel O Semaforo** (Faro de Finisterre; 981-110-210; www.hotelsemaforodefisterra.com; €90-150) is a boutique hotel and restaurant—or, as they call it, a "delicatessen hotel," a place to stimulate all five senses—right next to the lighthouse. It is its own adventure to spend the night

Top: glimpse of the ocean, and an *horreo,* on the trail from Finisterre to Muxía. **Bottom:** lighthouse and ocean view at Cabo Finisterre.

at land's end, in luxe rooms outfitted with king-size beds, fluffy duvets, thick sheets and towels, and a view of everything. Watch the sunset with a glass of wine and enjoy a five-course tasting menu in **Restaurante O Semaforo**—including dishes such as razor clams, scallops, *caldeirada* (fish stew), and a selection of desserts, with wine included (€40).

Getting There and around
Car
From **Santiago de Compostela** (83 km/52 mi; 1.5 hours): Depart Santiago de Compostela south on **SC-20** to **AG-56** heading west. Exit before Brión to **CP-0203** and then to **AG-544**. After Negreira, merge with **AC-546** to Pereira where it becomes **AC-441** (which goes all the way to Muxía); take it for 18.4 kilometers (11.4 miles), then exit left onto **AC-442** and soon, left again onto **AC-552**, then take **VG-1.4** to the **AC-445** to Finisterre. The **AC-445** goes all the way to the tip at Cabo Finisterre.

From **Muxía** (31 km/19.2 mi, 40 minutes): Leave south from Muxía on **DP-5201** and follow it along the coast through Frixe until it intersects with **CP-2301** where you will turn right and head toward Lires. Stay on the CP-2301 through Lires and continue south to Finisterre; turn right onto the **AC-445** at the Praia da Langosteira to go into the center of town.

Bus
Monbus (902-292-900; www.monbus. com) operates buses from Santiago de Compostela via Cee to Finisterre (6 daily Mon.-Fri., 4-5 daily Sat.-Sun.; 1.5-3 hours; €13.10). The Finisterre bus depot, which is really a bus shelter, is in the center of town, in front of the roundabout dedicated to emigrants.

There are no direct buses between Finisterre and Muxía, only taxis (or foot power). But for a more indirect route, on weekdays, Monbus runs buses from Muxía to Cee (four daily Mon.-Fri.; 30

min.; €1.95), and from Cee you can get another bus to Finisterre (seven daily Mon.-Fri.; 20 min.; €1.55). On weekends, a taxi is the only way between Finisterre and Muxía.

Taxi
Outside of the buses from Cee, or walking, the most direct way from Muxía to Finisterre is by taxi (30-35 min.; €30-35). From the town of Finisterre, you can also catch a taxi to the lighthouse at Cabo Finisterre (7 min.; €10-15), but most people like the drama, and ritual, of walking up the rise of Monte Facho to the "end of the earth." It's rare to need to take a taxi from Santiago de Compostela to Finisterre, but it is possible (80 minutes, around €100-120).

Call **Taxis in Cee** (981-745-002 and 981-745-951) or **Taxis in Finisterre** (981-740-255).

Hospital to Muxía
Km 27.4 – Km 0

To walk to Muxía, take the right fork northward 900 meters (0.6 miles) after passing Hospital (Km 27.4) at the bifurcation. (The left goes to Finisterre.) After Hospital, the path makes a steady descent all the way to Muxía, the steepest being the 4.9 kilometers (3 miles) from Hospital to Dumbria. You will be traversing rolling green country, at times along open fields and at times passing under oak and pine tree cover. Remote and sparsely populated, the hamlets and farmsteads are built from the native granite and dot the countryside in periodic clusters of pale gray.

Dumbría   Km 22.5
A village of 476, **Dumbria**'s name may be derived from the Celtic for a fortified place, perhaps referring to the many fortified hilltop castros all across this territory. The village's church is the 17th-century **Iglesia de Santa Eulalia**, near a modern cemetery.

Food and Accommodations

Mesón-Pensión O Argentino (Calle Dumbría, s/n; 981-744-051; www.oargentino.com; seven rooms, €30-40) is both a traditional rural tavern with good home-cooked meals and an inn, in a modern country house that includes a communal kitchen and salon. The restaurant also has tasting plates of local products, such as cheeses, cured meats, and prepared dishes with seasonal and locally harvested vegetables. A three-course *menú* is €12.

Leaving Dumbría

After Dumbria, the trail continues to descend but becomes more moderate, with a few smaller rises and falls until entering Muxía. More than two-thirds of the trail from Dumbría to Muxía is dirt trail, and the remaining portion is usually calm country roads. As always, use caution when walking on or crossing the roads.

Capela a Virxe do Espino
Km 19.1

Before Quintáns and Os Muiños, 3.5 kilometers (2.2 miles) after leaving Dumbría, you will pass through the hamlet of **Trasufre** (Km 19; pop. 51). Look for the **Capela a Virxe do Espino** just before the village, and its nearby healing fountain, *fonte sagrada*, down the hill on the small stone wall-edged road below. Many visitors here come to cure skin problems: They run a handkerchief or cloth under the water of the stone fountain, wash their skin with it, and then drape or tie the cloth on the railing on the path opposite the fountain, leaving their ailment there where the natural elements will dissolve it. An annual *romeria*, local pilgrimage, takes place in September, with many people coming out for the procession, the mass,

From top to bottom: Iglesia San Julián de Moraime; sacred cedar tree on the grounds of the Iglesia de San Julián de Moraime; the sacred stone, pedra dos cadrís.

the healing ritual at the stone fountain, and a food and music festival around tents that set up around the chapel.

Quintáns Km 11.2
Accommodations and Food

In Quintáns (pop. 174), the **Hospedaje Pensión Plaza** (Calle Quintáns, 194, on the central plaza; 981-750-452; www. plazapension.com) has homey rooms, some with sea-blue and others with sandstone-red walls, comfy beds with colorful quilted or plaid bedspreads, and smallish but spotless baths (€30-40). The attached ★ **restaurant** is a destination among locals and visitors for the fresh seafood hauled here daily. They are especially famous for their crab dishes, lobster rice, and shellfish paella. They grill almost everything—meats, scallops, langoustines, crabs—right on the open brick fireplace. A good *menú* is offered for €9.

Moraime Km 4.5

Moraime, along with Muxía itself, is the crown jewel of this entire route from Hospital. This is the ancient site of an early monastery and church, built here for its prior sacred association among the native Celtic speakers. Today, only the 12th-century Romanesque **Iglesia San Julián de Moraime** survives. The only other structure here is a restored and modern *albergue*-style hostel next door, built over part of the remains of the medieval monastery (probably where the monks slept).

Moraime was founded by Benedictine monks, but nearby excavations of a preChristian necropolis prove that pagan natives, Romans, and Visigoths lived in this area before the monks built here. Local lore reinforces this, describing the earth here as inherently sacred, which may be why the monks chose this spot for their settlement. In the 12th century, when Moraime and the surrounding communities were only marginally Christian, the Benedictines began converting the pagan population, who in turn melded their important local pagan beliefs into the new Christian practices; this is a strong theme everywhere in Galicia, especially along remote coastal areas such as this area.

Sights
★ Iglesia San Julián de Moraime

The 12th-century **Iglesia San Julián de Moraime,** tucked into the hillside of a protective fold of land, is all that survives of Moraime. Stepping inside feels like stepping into a cave: The stairway leads down into the porch of the western entrance, then down again into the nave. The church is usually closed, but you still can step into the porch and look through the windows to see the altar and the 16th-century frescos painted on the sides of the nave. Those frescos were restored in 2017 and represent the seven deadly sins.

The most distinctive aspects of the church are on the outer south entrance, where you'll see a tympanum, in a primitive medieval style unique to Galicia, carved with an image of the Last Supper. Just six of the 12 apostles are present. Jesus stands in the center of them, and an eighth figure, the size of a child, impishly presses through the group to reach the table right under Jesus's upheld right hand. Some art historians think the smaller figure is Saint John the Baptist.

The possible presence of Saint John the Baptist references a delightful local pagan and Christian expression about the cycle of the sun and its symbolism of the cycle of death and rebirth: John the Baptist has long been the other half in the dance of light with Jesus. We've seen this before, most famously at San Juan de Ortega in Castile. Saint John's feast day is the summer solstice, as Jesus's feast day is six months later, on the winter solstice. John's day arrives with the fullness of light, to announce that light will remain in the world even as it diminishes, and Jesus's day arrives to promise light's growth, once again at its darkest moment.

Several grand trees stand on the church grounds, the most distinctive being a large, **ancient cedar** whose branches stretch into a large bowl canopy. In earlier European lore, cedars were seen as protective trees that symbolized the strong and evergreen (eternal) nature of Christ and, sometimes, Mary. This tree is massive, unlike any other trees in the area, and carefully cared for on the church grounds; it is very likely one of these sacred cedars that represented Christ and possibly Mary.

The church is typically closed, but you can arrange guided visits with the Hostel del Monasterio de Moraime next door; these should be available Mon-Sat (10am-6pm) for €4, and free on Sundays (1-5pm). Visits take a little less than an hour and are in Spanish. It is best to call or email (881-076-055; www.hostelmonasteriodemoraime.com) ahead of your arrival if you want to schedule a visit outside of the summer season, since the hostel is run in a part-absentee manner.

Accommodations

Hostel del Monasterio de Moraime (881-076-055; www.hostelmonasteriodemoraime.com) offers 58 bunk beds, built in Japanese-style sleeping cubicles, in four dorm rooms (€17), and two luxury private rooms with bath (€120-140). Outside the summer season, the hostel is not always staffed: You pay in advance and enter the building by unlocking the door using a special code, and then check yourself in and self-cater.

Leaving Moraime

From Moraime, you begin to smell the first waft of sea salt and kelp perfuming the air from the ocean. As you make your way through the forest north of here, you'll soon glimpse the ocean; it will appear through the parting of the trees on the path, eventually opening to the protected beaches on Muxía's estuary (the finger of land jutting north that holds

the village) and the immense blue ocean stretching all around and beyond.

Muxía   Km 0

Muxía (pop. 1,527) is built on a narrow neck of land pointing north into the Atlantic. One side holds a protective harbor; the other is whipped daily by the ocean. Before 1985, Muxía was called by its Gallego name, Mugía, which may be related to the verb *mugir*, meaning to roar or bellow. It's a fitting name: the waves do roar and bellow against the rocks daily with the high tide.

Where Finisterre can feel like a commercial seaside resort, Muxía still feels like a traditional fishing village; it is a delightful place to end your Camino. This is also a sublime place to watch the sunset over the stones and ocean, and it's equally stunning to watch the sunrise over the harbor, lighthouse, and green rolling hills, a benefit of the spit's north-south orientation; it allows for perfect east-west alignment and views, similar to Finisterre but with more human-scale contours. The ideal spot for both the sunrise and sunset is the Santuario da Virxe da Barca, a climb north of the village, huddled in its protective cove. This also is one of the two traditionally acknowledged places in Iberia where Mary is said to have visited Saint James when both were still alive (the other place is Zaragoza).

If you walked here, be sure to take your pilgrim's credential with its stamps to the *xunta* (municipal) *albergue,* **Bela Muxía albergue,** or to the tourist information desk in either the municipal town hall, **Ayuntamiento de Muxía** (Calle Real, 35; 981-742-001; www.concellomuxia.com; Mon.-Fri., 8:30am-3pm) or the **Casa de As Beiras** (Rúa Virxe da Barca, 49; 981-742-365; Mon.-Fri. 3:30-8:30pm, weekends) to receive your certificate, the **Muxiana.**

Sights

■■■■ Top Experience ■■■■

★ Santuario da Virxe da Barca

The Santuario da Virxe da Barca (Sanctuary of the Virgin of the Boat) is Muxía's most picturesque monument, standing on the northernmost end of Muxía's small peninsula, 900 meters (0.6 miles) north of the center of the village (a 12-minute walk). Legends say that Mary came to Saint James on this site, arriving in a stone boat guided by angels, to encourage him not to lose hope in spreading the gospel. Locals built the seaside Santuario da Virxe da Barca in honor of this sacred visit. Before its twin towers, a few meters to the west, on the water and the wind-polished stones defining the shore, you can see what locals claim are the stone sail, hull, and rudder of the boat.

The church has been rebuilt at least four times, and it is possible that the original church was first built over an earlier pagan temple, one associated with the sacred stones identified as Mary's boat. The present church was rebuilt in the 17th century, and it was repaired in 2015 after a fire in 2013 damaged it and much of its sacred treasures inside.

The church is usually closed except for on feast days, the most important being the *romería* here on September 8-9, but it is its location—on the edge of the tip of Muxía's peninsula and ocean-facing coastline, with the large sacred boulders to its west—that is picturesque and significant. Those stones, aka Mary's boat, have long-time curative and prophetic capabilities, documented over many decades by Galician folklorists. They claim, as do the locals, that these stones are older than Christianity's presence on this shore. Among these stones are the **pedra de abalar** (the oscillating stone that is considered the nave of Mary's stone boat), **pedra dos cadrís** (the boat's sail, called "kidney rock" for its shape), and **pedra do temón** (rudder stone). A fourth is called **pedra dos namorados** (lovers' stone), where couples come to declare their love and commitment. The kidney-shaped sail is by far the most famous, and prominent, of the four shapely and magical stones, and it's a ritual to climb

sacred stones, *piedras* (or *pedras*) *sagradas* before the Santuario da Virxe da Barca.

through the opening it creates to seek healing and well-being. The *pedra de abalar* was also famous for its ability to deliver prophecy. In a severe storm in 1978, the waves crashed down on it, moving it from its original place and breaking it in half. People came to this stone to petition it for many types of questions, such as the state of fishing that season, the fidelity of one's partner, or the guilt or innocence of an accused person. As on Monte Facho at Finisterre, if the stone moved, it meant yes and confirmed the question. If the answer was no, it would not budge.

The annual local pilgrimage here is on Mary's birthday, September 8, with processions to visit the church and carry its sculpture of Mary through town and back. People also come here, sometimes on Christian holy days, to visit the magical stones, especially the healing one. This is also an incredible spot to catch the sunrise or sunset. For the sunset, sit just below the sanctuary church, near the stone that looks like a sail arched in the wind. For sunrise, go another 100 meters (328 feet) north of the sanctuary to the neighboring **lighthouse** and settle yourself on any of the large boulders there, facing east; be sure also to turn west to see the sunrise colors reflected onto the sky and ocean.

To get to the church, follow the central street in the village, Rúa Atalaia (70 meters/230 feet left of the harbor), and head north. Continue straight on Rúa Atalaia, which becomes Rúa da Virxe da Barca and leads straight to the sanctuary and the sacred stones on its west side.

Iglesia de Santa María de Muxía

The 14th-century Iglesia de Santa María de Muxía, just on the other side of the same ridge of rocks as the Santuario da Virxe da Barca, 450 meters (0.3 mile) to the south, gives a double helping of Marian magic in Muxía. This is a gem of the Romanesque-Gothic building style particular to this area. The church is built into the side of the hill. A steep

stone stairway leads up to the bell tower, separate from the church, and beyond it there is a path leading to a short 60-meter (197-foot) climb up to **Monte Corpiño**, the highest point of the village at 67 meters (220 feet). It offers a spectacular view of both sides, ocean and inland, as well as of the full spine of narrow land on which Muxía is built. (This is another nice spot to watch both the sunrise and sunset.)

The church interior gives a wonderful taste of maritime Gothic building: The distinct proportions include wider arches and lower vaulting, and the capitals are carved with medieval characters, some in tunics and tights, and what look like lollipop trees or kelp.

Market Days and Festivals

Muxía has a weekly **market** every **Tuesday** and **Friday,** during which 40 stands set up in the central street of Rúa Areal.

Every year, between **September 9-15**, there is a small pilgrimage and festival period, a **romería**, honoring the **Virxe da Barca**, Our Lady of the Boat, that brings people from all across Galicia, not just locals. Like so many cases of Marian shrines built over early pagan sites, these ancient connections link back to earlier peoples' spiritual connection to the land, the natural elements, and the sense of something numinous and potent happening here.

The last Sunday in **July** is another colorful festival, this one taking to the sea, the **Fiesta del Carmen**, where decorated fishing boats make a maritime procession from Muxía across the estuary to the village of Camariñas. That path is considered another ancient path of the rising and setting sun.

Food

★ **A Marina** (Avenida A Marina, 30; 981-742-490 and 629-17-21-24; €10-20), on the central corner where the village meets the harbor (and near where the bus to Santiago de Compostela stops), is an upbeat social hub. It offers the best views and some of the best eating options for daily catch, artfully prepared in heaping plates to share (*raciones*) or individual dishes to savor. Among the many steamed, grilled, and baked seafood options is a delightful *caldeirada* (fish stew). This is also a place to try the delicacy *percebes,* gooseneck barnacles (€14 for *una ración*).

O Coral d'Álvaro (Rúa Marina, 22; 981-742-501; www.restauranteocoral.com) also has delightful harbor-side views and offers daily ocean- and garden-fresh fare, including a varied daily three-course menu (€15) and seafood paella for two (€30). Some of the innovative dishes include *revuelto de algas* (scrambled eggs and seaweed) and *pulpo flambeado* (octopus flambé).

Accommodations

The challenge of Muxía is that it has good ranges of food and accommodation, but most are only open from late spring to early autumn. Those listed here are open year-round.

★ **Albergue Arribada** (Calle José María del Río, 30; 981-742-516; www.arribadaalbergue.com; 38 beds, €12-15; private rooms, €40-55) is possibly the best *albergue* on the entire Camino, another reason to come to "the end of the earth." Run by an exuberant and capable young woman, the place is pristine, and she has given every space careful thought, resulting in ease, comfort, and efficiency in an airy seaside building of contemporary design (it almost feels like a cruise boat on the inside). The common kitchen is fun to cook in and a grocery store is just around the corner. The *albergue* is located in the heart of the village between the harbor and ocean.

Bela Muxía (Rúa da Encarnación, 30; 687-798-222; www.belamuxia.com; 52 beds, €15; private rooms, €50) is another great option. It is also here where you can ask for your certificate, the **Muxiana,** if you have the stamps to show that you walked here. Along with the crisp modern metallic fixtures and blindingly white-washed walls, the real sparkle of Bela Muxía (along with the enthusiasm of Angel, the *hospitalero*), is a rooftop terrace with surrounding views of big sky, ocean, bay, and rolling forested hills. Ask Angel about the special history and energy of this place, and especially its sacred stones.

Muxía Mare (Rúa Castelao, 14; 981-742-423; www.alberguemuxiamare.es; 16 beds, €13; private rooms, €37) is 50 meters (164 feet) from the ocean; some rooms have a waterfront view. Large windows open wide to let in light and salt air. Private rooms are small and simple but pleasant, especially with the large windows and exemplary maintenance. Dorm rooms are also simple, spotless, and open to air and light. The incredibly hospitable and gregarious (and multilingual, including English) staff are a large part of the delight of staying here.

Getting There and Around
Car

From **Santiago de Compostela,** head west on the **AG-56** toward Brión, then northwest on the **CP-0203** and to the **AC-544,** which then connects to **AC-546** and the **AC-441/AC-440** that will take you to Muxía (74 km/46 mi; 1.5 hours).

From **Finisterre,** leave north on **AC-445** and make a left onto **CP-2301** through Lires; make a left onto **DP-5201** heading north through Frixe and inward to Muxía (31 kilometers, 40 minutes).

Bus

Hermanos Ferrín (981-873-643; www.grupoferrin.com) runs two buses, seven days a week, to and from Santiago de Compostela via Negreira, one in the morning and the other mid-afternoon; the departure hours vary by weekday, weekend, and holiday (1.5 hours; €8). The bus drops you off right at the harbor, near the concentration of cafés and

Little Fox Retreat

On the road from Muxía and 8.9 kilometers (5.5 miles) to the south, via Moraime, is the **Little Fox House** (Morpeguite, 71; 981-190-455; www.thelittlefoxhouse. com), A Casa do Rapasito in Gallego, a retreat in the village of **Morpeguite** (pop. 47). Four-time pilgrim Tracy Saunders—who speaks English, Spanish, and Gallego—opened the Little Fox House as a "post-Camino retreat," seeking to fill a need among some *peregrinos* to have a pause between ending their Camino and returning home. It is a place to rest, reflect, and enjoy communal meals with other *peregrinos*.

Set in a small village in the green Galician countryside and run singlehandedly by Tracy, this is a donation-driven house that suggests a contribution of €25/day per person (for a single bed in a shared double room) or €35/50 for a private double room for one or two people. The amount includes lodging and all daily meals (including wine), wifi, and use of the washer and dryer. For those who cannot afford the suggested donation rates, inquire with Tracy about staying in exchange for labor, such as helping with meals, in the garden, and cleaning. It feels like going home before having to go home, with thick cotton sheets and duvets on the beds, a fireplace, a guitar for playing, walls covered in books, and a garden. Tracy also offers tours that reveal the hidden secrets of this coastal area, including Finisterre and Muxía, and the region's dolmens, castros, castles, lighthouses, and shipwrecks.

You can walk here from Muxía by walking the Camino in reverse from Muxía to Moraime (4.5 km/2.8 mi), and then the remaining 4.4 kilometers (2.7 miles) south of Moraime to Morpeguite: walk carefully on the bank of the AC-440 (for 200 meters/656 feet), then the remaining 4.2 kilometers (2.6 miles) on the DP-2303 country road to the retreat. A taxi from Muxía is also a good option (10 min.; €12-18). You can also contact Tracy in advance to see if she can propose another manner to get you here.

accommodations in the center of the village. Everything in Muxía and the sanctuary is within easy walking distance from here.

No buses connect Muxía directly to Finisterre: The only direct way there is to walk or to hire a taxi. For a more indirect route, **Monbus** (www.monbus.es) runs buses on weekdays from Finisterre to Cee (seven buses daily; 20 min.; €1.55), where you can then take a bus from Cee direct to Muxía (four daily; 30 min.; €1.95). On weekends, walking and taking a taxi are the only transport options—direct or indirect—between Muxía and Finisterre.

Taxi

The only direct way, outside of walking, to Finisterre is by taxi (30-35 min.; €30-35). Call **Taxi José Manuel Fandiño Areas** (659-427-197; www.taxienmuxia. com), **Taxi Muxía** (981-742-070), or **Taxi Loncho** (981-747-673; www.casaloncho. com). On weekends, walking and taking a taxi are the only transport options—direct or indirect—between Muxía and Finisterre. From Santiago de Compostela, a taxi to Muxía would take 1.5 hours and cost around €100-120.

Leaving Muxía

If you're walking to Finisterre, follow the way-markers on the seaside promenade and the sidewalk paralleling the exiting road on the ocean side of the town, directing you south along the coast and soon taking you up into the dense hills. The steepest climb of this trail is up **Monte Facho de Lourido**'s north side, with a more gentle and gradual descent on the south side.

★ Finisterre to Muxía

This 29.3 kilometers (18.2 miles) is possibly the wildest stretch on the entire Camino, rivaling some stretches in the mountains of León. This terrain is dense with hills, some steep, and lush green valleys, and the trail climbs quite a lot, whether you begin in Muxía or Finisterre. I find this to be among the toughest, but also among the most beautiful, of all the stretches on the Camino, and the rewards for your effort are great, from the dramatic views of the ocean at either end to the amazing fresh-from-the-sea meals you can enjoy in Finisterre, Lires, and Muxía. With Saint James's tomb behind you, let these reasons be your holy grail to keep going.

The trail is well way-marked in both directions, but there is only one certain option for food and accommodations, at Lires 13.6 kilometers (8.5 miles) after Finisterre. With another 15.7 kilometers (9.8 miles) to Muxía, you will want to depart with full water bottles and food, and then refill and restock in Lires. You can walk the route in one day, or break for the night in Lires.

The directions here lead from Finisterre to Muxía, but it's also possible to walk this route in reverse. Departing from Muxía sets you up for making the trail's steepest climb up Monte Facho de Lourido, with a gentler descent on the other side; in reverse, if you start in Finisterre, you will have a gentler climb up Monte Facho Lourido but then a steep descent. The remainder of the trail is equal in both directions, a stunning passage through surprising mountains and hilltop vistas and into narrow river valleys and lush forest.

Leaving Finisterre   Km 29.3

Take the central street that passes the town hall heading north until you see the road, **Rúa Aldea San Martín de Abajo,** where you will turn left to see a marker pointing north to **San Martiño de Duio** (Km 27.6). After walking through San Martiño de Duio, continue following the way-markers through the hamlet of **San Salvador** (Km 26.2). The area around these two villages is believed to mark the location of **Dugium** (Duio in Gallego), an ancient castro site first occupied by the Nerios (Celtic speakers), followed by the Romans. According to legend, this was the Roman encampment from which Roman soldiers pursued Saint James's followers across Ponte Maceira, just before Negreira.

Continue following the signs, mostly yellow arrows and occasional posts with scallop shells. If you look toward the ocean (to your left) 2.5 kilometers after San Salvador, you should be able to make out the hill of **Castro de Castromiñan,** an unexcavated Iron Age hilltop fortress 1 kilometer (0.6 miles) away. At the settlement of **Castrexe** (Km 20.7), you'll gain a breathtaking view to your left of the ocean and the **Praia do Rostro** beach, a sweeping crescent-moon-shaped beach with *horreos* on the bordering fields. Continue following way markers to Lires.

Lires   Km 15.7

Nearly perfectly midway, 13.6 kilometers (8.4 miles) north of Finisterre and 15.7 kilometers (9.8 miles) south of Muxía, and straddling the Río Lires, the little oasis of **Lires de San Esteve** (pop. 149) is heavenly for its kind locals and much appreciated food and lodging. It lies in a protected, narrow valley setting of river, patchwork vegetable gardens, and grazing fields spotted with contented sheep, horses, and cows. Its name is lyrical, too, meaning lyres. Its **Iglesia de San Esteve de Lires** is 18th-century Baroque.

Food and Accommodations

★ **As Eiras** (Lires, 82; 981-748-180; www.ruralaseiras.com) is a well-run *albergue* (20 beds, €12), *hostal* (four rooms, €33), and café-restaurant (€5-10). Its

The End Is Just the Beginning

However you have undertaken these last kilometers, be they to Santiago de Compostela or onward to the coast, from here the circle is nearly complete. Now you need to return home, and often this fact gives people an oscillating mix of elation, melancholy, excitement, and hesitation.

Most modern pilgrims make their way back to Santiago by bus and then board a bus, plane, or train to head home. This demands a rapid assimilation from the pilgrim experience to everyday life, especially compared to medieval pilgrims, who had a long walk (or horse ride) home. Today, as in medieval times, one of the most sublime aspects of pilgrimage is how it takes you outside of yourself, yet deeper into your true nature and your hopes for life. One of the hardest aspects of being a pilgrim, then as now, is taking that new knowledge back to old settings.

The gift of the pilgrimage is that life is now lived fully awake and consciously, and this aids all pilgrims in whatever befalls or betides them upon their return. They also have a new network of friends from all across the world to help, and most likely, renewed and strengthened bonds with the many friends and family to whom they return.

The most common feeling at the end of the Camino is embodied in the question that surfaces for many: *What now?* At no time in the walk, before or after, are you more in the pinnacle and power of transformation with this profound question than now, at the end of your journey. The answer dares us to be who we really are, and to create and/or celebrate the life we really want. Some pilgrims say that this is when the Camino really begins, and never ends.

---

accommodation options, both shared rooms and private ones, are clean and comfortable, in a serene setting in the heart of the village where locals and pilgrims mingle in good cheer. It's managed by a warm staff who treat each person's concerns with kindness and full attention. The café is great for a rest, refreshment, and good meals, including homemade chicken noodle soup with a rich broth spiked with paprika, but also arrays of garden salads, sandwiches, tortillas, and seafood dishes, all harvested from its local gardens and its ideal coastal location.

Leaving Lires

Refill your water before leaving Lires.

The villagers in **Frixe** (Km 13) have set up a wonderful little self-service shelter, with a public toilet and vending machine selling snacks and drinks. (But don't count on this, in case they haven't restocked the machine.)

The hamlet of **Morquintián** (Km 9) has an ornate *cruceiro* and fountain (not drinkable) and a picturesque *hórreo*, plus a 12th-century Romanesque church dedicated to **Santa María**. The highest climb is ahead of you, to 269 meters (883 feet) at **Monte Facho de Lourido** (Km 6.6), which offers great views of the mountainous and hilly terrain you've covered and a hint of the ocean as you near Muxía (Km 0).

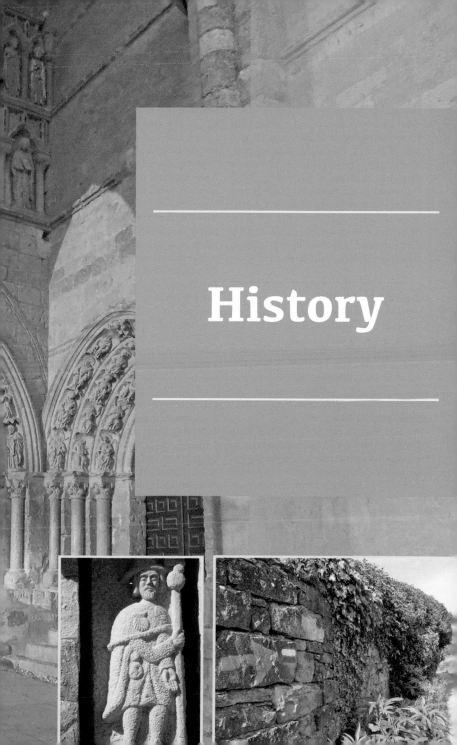

History

The Camino de Santiago as a Christian pilgrimage began in the 9th century, with the purported discovery of Santiago's tomb in northwestern Spain. That discovery alone speaks of older pathways that would make it such an appealing place to bury a saint, and one of Jesus's Twelve Apostles at that. Medieval pilgrims used the older roads forged by millions of feet before them, from prehistoric nomadic hunting and gathering peoples to Neolithic farmers and herders, from Celtic speakers to Romans. In this sense, the idea of the Camino as a 1,200-year old pilgrimage is really the path's newest layer.

Early History

Though the Camino as we know it is defined by the medieval Christian pilgrimage, the territory in southwestern France and across northern Spain has been a significant corridor of nomadic migrations for as long as 1.2 million years.

Paleolithic Era

Archaeologists call the whole territory from southwestern France across northern Spain the Franco-Cantabrian Region, because this terrain is unified by groups of prehistoric peoples who lived here in the Paleolithic era, when humans made stone tools and lived as nomadic hunter-gatherers. These early humans were drawn to this region by its rich sources of food, water, and shelter. It is no accident that one of Europe's oldest native peoples, the **Basques,** live in the intersection of this ancient region.

Evidence of early human inhabitation has cropped up along the Camino, and several sites are open for the curious visitor to explore. In 2007-2008, archaeologists working at **Atapuerca,** 21 kilometers (13 miles) east of Burgos, discovered human remains that may date back as far as 1.2 million years, the oldest found anywhere in Europe.

Neolithic and Bronze Ages

In later prehistory (15,000-10,000 years ago), **Mesolithic hunter-gatherers,** followed by **Neolithic early farmers and herders** (7,000 years ago), forged paths across the rich territories of northern Spain. Some of those routes remain in use today, namely by herders who crisscross the Camino, moving their animals from summer to winter pastures as ancient Iberians have done for millennia. Your chances of encountering these sheepherders are good while walking the Camino across Navarra, La Rioja, Castile, León, and Galicia.

The whole northern territory of the Camino is also rich in **dolmens** (standing stones), which are associated with the early farmers of the Neolithic era. Most are around 5,000-4,000 years old. They are especially concentrated in Navarra, La Rioja, and Galicia. Some still stand near the medieval hilltop wine town of **Laguardia,** which is an easy day trip by bus from the Camino at Logroño.

Neolithic and later Bronze Age peoples (around 4,000 to 2,700 years ago) also created **petroglyphs,** stone surfaces engraved with dots, spirals, labyrinths, crosses, deer, and what seem to be solar or lunar markings. These appear in northern Spain, from Asturias to León and Galicia. In fact, in the city of Santiago de Compostela proper, one is preserved, the **Castriño de Conxo,** and you can visit it.

Celtic-Speakers and Celtiberians

Celtic speakers were a diverse group of Atlantic coast-dwelling tribes from Ireland to Iberia that were interrelated through coastal seafaring, shared language, and trade. They were also an important part of Iberia, and left strong traces of their settlements, crafts, and cultures. It's now thought that Celtic speakers may have first originated along the Atlantic (perhaps around 4,000 years ago), not in central Europe, and that their

Atlantic culture made its way into interior Europe later (around 2,500 years ago), via the river mouths along the shore lines of France and Spain.

The oldest Celtic speakers may have come from either Ireland or Iberia. Remains of Iberia's Celtic speakers are all along the Camino, some mingling so much with the earlier Iberians that their cultures are referred to as Celtiberian. Celtic speakers and Celtiberians built settlements known as castros (fortified hilltop villages and towns). These are especially present in the area near La Rioja, such as in Logroño, which has Celtiberian foundations; they become more concentrated across Castile into León and Galicia. Castro sites are most numerous in Galicia, right up to the Atlantic coast at Finisterre and Muxia. Castro de Castromaior, just a 200-meter (656-foot) detour off the Camino in Galicia, is beautifully intact and well worth a visit. Santiago de Compostela itself may be on an old castro site, which some archaeologists refer to as Castro de Susana, named after the Romanesque and Gothic church that is built on the neighboring hill to the hill of Santiago's cathedral.

Romans

Neolithic and Bronze Age peoples, and especially the Celtic speakers, forged paths that connected their settlements to other significant sites, such as sacred places centered on water sources and mountaintops. (A few examples of these sacred natural places are the **Ebro** river that you cross upon entering Logroño; **Monte Teleno,** the mountain that dominates the horizon just after Astorga; and the Cruz de Ferro on **Monte Irago,** the highest mountain on the Camino, just after Foncebadón).

When the Romans infiltrated and gradually conquered Iberia, between 2,200 and 2,000 years ago, they made use of these prior routes to build their extensive road system for the transport of people and goods, such as silver, gold, tin, grains, and wine, across the empire. Romans also built major cities and extensive villas across the Peninsula, including important centers that you pass on the Camino—from **Pamplona** to **Logroño, León,** and **Astorga.** Even the **Catedral de Santiago de Compostela** stands on an old Roman burial hill. Large tracts of the medieval Camino also utilized Roman roads, most notably the well-preserved **Roman road and bridge** just after Cirauqui, where pilgrims will actually step over grooves left by the wheels of Roman carts.

Medieval Era

Early Medieval Period (AD 400-1000)

With the decline of the Roman world, several Germanic tribes invaded Iberia in the early 400s, including the **Alans,** the **Suevi,** and the **Visigoths.** The latter eventually dominated and ruled Iberia (466-711) with divisive (and bigoted) polices toward the native populations, which made Iberia ripe for yet another invasion, one encouraged by the down trodden locals.

In 711, **Berbers** and **Arabs** from North Africa invaded and over the next decades quickly dominated Iberia. Their Islamic policy of tolerance toward peoples of other faiths and backgrounds—especially Jews and Christians—helped assure their deeply rooted presence in the Peninsula for many centuries to follow. Many Visigoths and those of Roman-Hispanic descent were granted land immediately after the invasion, but some fled to the north, to the other side of the Cantabrian mountains, aspiring to set up their own kingdoms; this initiated the birth of the kingdoms of **Asturias,** then **León** and **Galicia, Navarra,** and **Aragón.** It also initiated the seeds of the idea of the Reconquista (Reconquest), which by the Middle Ages became a strong ideology of unifying the kingdoms toward a common cause to take back Iberia for themselves.

In the 700s, North Africans also pushed into France, making toward Poitiers (in 732) where **Charles Martel, Charlemagne**'s grandfather and head of the newly formed Frankish kingdom of the Carolingians, deflected the advance and sent the invading troops back over the Pyrenees. Here, indeed, is the root of Charlemagne's ambition: he became king of the Franks in 768, and by 800 had unified almost all of western Europe (except Iberia) under his power, the first time a single power had controlled that vast territory since the fall of Rome. With the rise of a similarly imperialistic dynasty in Córdoba, in Islamic Iberia, Charlemagne aspired to take all of the Peninsula into his empire, too.

Pinched between Córdoba to the south and Charlemagne's campaigns in the north, the tiny kingdoms of northern Iberia needed to come together. They never really did manage to do that, but soon, the legends of Saint James in Galicia arose, and with them, the Camino. This gave northern Iberians a unified identity, not to mention a road right along the path of the frontier lands dividing the Peninsula's north and south.

Discovery of Saint James's Tomb and Rise of the Camino

Saint James the Greater (Santiago in Spanish), one of Jesus's twelve disciples, was beheaded in the Holy Land in AD 44. Although no historical documents connect him to Spain, legends began to circulate after his death. It's said that Saint James spent several years in Iberia evangelizing before returning to the Holy Land, where he was martyred. His two closest disciples then delivered his body in a stone boat guided by angels to Galicia, burying him on a hill at Santiago de Compostela.

In more legend, around the year 814, the hermit Pelayo followed a trail of stars to discover the tomb of Saint James. A chapel was soon constructed over the tomb, on the site of the modern **Catedral de Santiago de Compostela.** Pelayo's journey became the root of the pilgrimage as we know it today. King Alfonso II of Asturias made the first royal pilgrimage to Santiago de Compostela sometime between 818 and 842, traveling a path through the Cantabrian mountains that's now known as the Camino Primitivo. In 950, Le Puy en Velay's bishop, Godescalc, made the first official pilgrimage from outside Iberia, beginning in south-central France, using old Roman roads, and crossing the Pyrenees to reach Santiago's tomb.

At this time, the Caliphate of Córdoba, also known as **al-Andalus,** was still strong and unified; the northern Iberian kingdoms of Leon, Castile, Navarra, and Aragón were not. Under the leadership of Almanzor, troops from al-Andalus raided León and Zamora in 989, Carrión de los Condes and Astorga in 995, and Santiago de Compostela in 997. During the raid on Santiago de Compostela, Almanzor's troops famously took the cathedral's bells back to Córdoba, though Almanzor protected Santiago's tomb from being disturbed in the fighting. Upon Almanzor's death in 1002, the southern kingdom of Córdoba began to splinter into several city-states. The north, meanwhile, was becoming more unified and organized. This also was the era of **El Cid,** Rodrigo Díaz de Vivar (1043-1099), the mercenary who served both the kingdoms of the Muslim south as well as the king of Castile, Alfonso VI (1040-1109). This also was the time when the **Camino**'s popularity began to rise.

Camino Heyday: 11th and 12th Centuries

The Camino grew in popularity in the 11th and 12th centuries, becoming one of the most dynamic places in Europe and receiving explorers, adventurers, scholars, artists, artisans, and merchants from across the Continent, Africa, the Mediterranean, the Middle East, and

Asia. This is also when the greatest development efforts of its medieval history took place. Among its apex developments was the building of the **cathedral in Santiago de Compostela,** along with many other commissions of beautiful and expressive Romanesque architecture and sculptures that capture, to this day, the rich religious and sacred traditions not only of European Christians but also of Iberian Jews, Muslims, and pagans. This is also when masons built the many pilgrim hospices, hospitals, roads, and bridges to give pilgrims safer passage (especially by the sainted engineers, **Santo Domingo de la Calzada and San Juan de Ortega**).

Curiously, in many ways the heyday of the Camino and of the northern kings could not have happened without the Muslim kingdoms of the south. As their power waned, they had to pay tribute to the northern kings, especially Fernando I of Castile (r.1037-1065) and his son, Alfonso VI (r. 1065-1109). These kings in turn gave an annual payment (largely gold from al-Andalus) to the powerful **Benedictine order of Cluny** in Burgundy. Cluny had begun as an order in the 10th century, but became a leader of western monasticism by the 11th and 12th centuries. Through Cluny and the commission of many Romanesque churches as well as monasteries, hospitals, and hospices, the Camino developed into a remarkable destination, and Europe's greatest adventure for the devout, the penitent, and the rebellious. Other northern kings also aided in the development of the Camino, including Sancho III of Navarra (1000-1035) and Sancho Ramírez, who ruled Aragón from 1063-1094 and Navarra from 1076-1094. They encouraged French immigrants to settle along the Camino and build up its towns and commerce. (These settlers, and the influence from Cluny, combine to reflect the name of this most famous route of the Camino de Santiago: *el Camino Francés,* the French Way.)

During this era, many Franks and other northern Europeans arrived and settled along the Camino, as did Jews and Muslims, many of whom were farmers and craftspeople. The Muslim style of art and architecture forged in Christian Spain, referred to as **Mudéjar** for its distinctive Islamic geometric patterns and styles, is visible across the Camino, such as in a trio of churches in **Sahagún.** Christian builders from Islamic Spain also arrived to live on the Camino. They, too, had a distinctive style, known as **Mozárabe,** a mix of Islamic and Visigothic styles with a pinch of Roman, such as the church of **San Miguel de Escalada** near Mansilla de las Mulas and **Santo Tomás de las Ollas** in Ponferrada.

The Camino's heyday centuries are also defined by the rise of many military-religious orders of knights who came to develop and protect the pilgrimage route and pilgrims. Among them were the Knights of the Order of Saint John (also known as the Hospitallers and the Knights of Malta), the Order of San Antón (who ran the **Monasterio de San Antón,** now elegant ruins on the way to Castrojeriz), the Order of Santiago, and the Order of Calatrava. But none is more famous or present across the Camino than the **Knights Templar.** Founded in 1118 by nine knights in Jerusalem living near the Temple Mound (hence the name, Templar), they took vows of celibacy, poverty, and service, especially to protect pilgrims to Christian holy sites. On the Camino they hold a special aura, not only as powerful knights but also as keepers of mystical Christian spiritual traditions that some modern pilgrims seek to uncover by walking the Camino. Signs of the Templar presence still survive all along the Camino, but Ponferrada stands out for its massive **Templar castle** that served as one of their key headquarters.

The *Codex Calixtinus*

In the mid-12th century, the French monk and pilgrim Aimery Picaud is believed to have penned the first pilgrims' practical and spiritual guidebook to the Camino, the *Codex Calixtinus*. It was actually a compilation of five separate books; Book Five was the actual pilgrims' guide, offering opinions about the different peoples and regions along the Camino Francés—as well as advice and warnings about ease, accommodations, thieves, bridges good and bad, safe and treacherous water sources, and where one could eat well and plentifully, versus regions with no cuisine or decent food. Read today, the *Codex* is both endearing and snarky, at times sublime and others petty. It remains a wonderful read, and captures the same mood of international adventure and social intrigue on the modern Camino. Written in Latin, the original *Codex Calixtinus* is preserved in the archives at Catedral de Santiago de Compostela (visible on special tour). There are a few good translations in English, especially its more gripping and practical Book Five, among the best being by medieval scholar William Melczer, *The Pilgrim's Guide to Santiago de Compostela*. Melczer's translation is as lively as the original text, and his detailed and colorful footnotes help the modern reader to understand the full context.

There are four other books in the *Codex Calixtinus*. Book One is a collection of hymns and sermons; Book Two, a detailed listing of the 22 miracles performed by Santiago; Book Three, a collection of the legends about Santiago evangelizing in Spain, his martyrdom, and his return for burial in Galicia; and Book Four, sometimes called the Turpin Chronicle, details the stories of Charlemagne and Roland on which all the fables of Charlemagne are based.

Late Medieval Period (AD 1200-1500)

Through the 11th and 12th centuries, the south and north of Spain coexisted competitively but also harmoniously. However, by the 13th century, the kingdoms of the north had gained territory, control, and confidence. The last Muslim kingdom, of Granada, held ground by paying tribute to Castile's kings from 1246-1492. In Christian territories, Iberia's Jews began to experience rising attitudes of intolerance, which peaked in 1391 with horrific attacks across Castile against the Jewish communities. To protect themselves, many Jews either converted to Catholicism or moved to the safer Muslim kingdom of Granada. The north remained dangerous for anyone other than Christians, including pagans, Jews, Muslims, and, by the early 1500s (with Martin Luther's reforms), Protestants.

The Catholic kings Isabel and Ferdinand in 1492 ended the Kingdom of Granada and absorbed it into Castile and Aragón and unified all of Spain into one Catholic nation, their original agenda and intent, no longer happy to just collect tribute. This unified Spain is the geographical shape of country we see today. Granada's Jews were first forced to convert in 1492, as were Granada's Muslims starting in 1499. Those who did not convert were expelled. These policies not only ended the rich cross-cultural flourishing that had built the Camino, they also contributed to the lessening popularity of the Camino itself. Pilgrimage had fallen out of fashion, as a rational world that valued the material over the spiritual took hold. Instead of pilgrimage, Spain (and Europe) was about to dive head-first into conquests abroad. Ironically, they took Santiago with them—not the peaceful pilgrim, but instead the sword-swinging warrior (popularly known as **Santiago Matamoros**) who was used as a symbol in the conquering of the non-Christian worlds of the Americas.

Early Modern to Modern Era

Early Modern Era (1500-1860)

By the 15th and 16th centuries, pilgrimage to Compostela was already in decline. With fewer pilgrims walking, and fewer knightly orders to defend the route, the pilgrimage was a dangerous enterprise. Bandits and rogues traveled the Camino, preying on defenseless travelers. Protestant reforms outside of Spain further diminished interest in Catholic pilgrimage, which was seen as extravagant and superstitious.

By the early 19th century, the trend in Spain was toward more liberal and secular government, and many, including landless farmers, saw the vast uncultivated lands held by monastic orders as a social and economic detriment. In 1835, the ruling minister of Spain banished the Jesuits. The next minister expelled most of the remaining religious orders, emptying nearly all the monasteries and convents. From 1835-1860, a good portion of Spain's monasteries, including those along the Camino, were abandoned or fell into disrepair. Many were gutted and sacked, their art sold to collectors and their stones carted off for use in other construction. This, along with the Napoleonic invasion of Spain in 1809, explains why so many places have required massive restoration efforts in more recent years.

Since the late 19th century, other religious orders have come to Spain, occupied old monasteries, and worked not only to rebuild them but also to turn them into productive living centers of spiritual devotion, service, and communal enrichment. Many of the monasteries

From top to bottom: depiction of Saint James as a pilgrim; Roman mosaics and villa ruins in Astorga; Romanesque sculpture of birds on Frómista's Iglesia de San Martín.

on the Camino today are occupied by these newer orders.

Franco and the Spanish Civil War (1936-1939)

The history of Spain's 19th century, and the first half of the 20th century, reads like a swinging pendulum of succession and control between liberal and conservative groups, until 1936, when the Franco regime plunged the country into a bloody civil war (1936-1939). Spain is still healing from this war and Franco's dictatorship, and the Camino is one place among many where it cannot be pushed under the surface. In efforts to improve the trail, workers have inadvertently uncovered mass graves where people were executed and buried during the Civil War and the early Franco years. One is marked on the border of Navarra and La Rioja, right as you are entering **Logroño,** and another is found in the forest tract on your way from Villafranca Montes de Oca to **San Juan de Ortega.**

The Modern Camino

1980-1990s

The Camino that we experience today can really be traced to the 1980s and 1990s, largely thanks to the efforts of O Cebreiro's parish priest, **Elias Valiño Sampedro,** who from the 1960s to 1980s dedicated himself to retracing, mapping, and marking the path of the medieval Camino. It is he who is responsible for the beloved convention of painting bright yellow arrows as way-markers on the path. Sampedro also wrote the first modern Spanish guidebook to the Camino, *The Pilgrim's Guide to the Camino de Santiago,* published in 1984 and translated into English in 1992. This, along with a 1989 French guidebook by Abbé George Bernès, Georges Veron, and Louis Laborde Balen, *The Pilgrimage Route to Compostela in Search of Saint James,*

became the foundation for all other guidebooks that followed.

Pope John Paul II visited Santiago de Compostela twice, in 1982 and 1989; the Spanish built a memorial to commemorate his visit on **Monte de Gozo** hill, in 1993, to coincide with the Holy Year that year, when Santiago's feast day, July 25, fell on a Sunday. Monte de Gozo is the last hill pilgrims pass before seeing the spires of Santiago's cathedral for the first time. In 1987, the European Community named the Cami**no a European Cultural Itinerary.** In 1993, **UNESCO** declared the road a U**niversal Patrimony of Humanity.**

The Camino Today

Since the mid-1990s, with surging numbers since 2007, the Camino has been achieving popularity similar to its heyday in the 11th and 12th centuries. Each year, 10,000 to 15,000 more people walk the Camino than walked it the year before:

- 1986: **2,491 pilgrims** received a Compostela.

- 2005: **93,924 pilgrims** received a Compostela.

- 2010: **272,135 pilgrims** received a Compostela.

- 2018: More than **300,000 pilgrims** received a Compostela.

The year 2010 was a holy year (when Santiago's feast day, July 25, falls on a Sunday), which partly explains the surge in numbers that year. The release of the movie *The Way,* in November 2010, has since contributed to greater numbers of pilgrims on the Camino. But when you consider that these numbers don't even include the many pilgrims (as many as 50 percent) who do not gather a certificate upon finishing, the numbers are impressive. Travelogues and movies in France, Spain, Japan, Brazil, Canada, the USA,

Camino Timeline

AD 44: Saint James is martyred in the Holy Land. His disciples deliver his body to Galicia, burying him at Santiago de Compostela.

711: North Africans and Arabs invade and gain control of Iberia—except for a narrow territory where Christian kingdoms later developed the Camino.

778: Charlemagne sacks Pamplona. Just outside of Roncesvalles, locals retaliate against his troops, led by Roland.

814: The hermit Pelayo follows a trail of stars to discover Saint James's tomb. Locals build a chapel over the site.

818-842: King Alfonso II of Asturias makes the first official pilgrimage to Saint James's tomb.

950: Bishop Godescalc of Le-Puy-en-Velay in France makes the first known pilgrimage to Santiago's tomb from outside of Spain.

997: Almanzor, under the Caliphate of Córdoba, sacks Santiago de Compostela but protects Santiago's tomb.

1034-1109: Santo Domingo de la Calzada, the hermit, engineer, and most celebrated builder of roads and bridges on the Camino, dedicates himself to building roads, bridges, hospices, and churches on the Camino.

1075: Construction begins on the third and current Catedral de Santiago de Compostela.

Early 1100s: The ambassador for Almoravid king Ali ibn Yusuf of Morocco observes that the road to Santiago was so congested by pilgrims that it was hard to move along it. The popularity of the Camino reaches its height in the 11th and 12th centuries.

1109-1163: San Juan de Ortega survives a shipwreck returning from Jerusalem and in gratitude built the hospice in the wildest stretch of the road, in San Juan de Ortega, making it safer, and devotes the rest of his life to serving pilgrims.

1118: Order of the Templar Knights is founded to protect Christian pilgrims; their presence on the Camino soon grows.

c. 1131: The first pilgrim's guide, the Codex Calixtinus, is written.

1188: Master Mateo finishes the Portico de la Gloría (western gate) of Santiago's cathedral. The cathedral is now complete.

1221: Construction begins on Burgos's Gothic Catedral de Santa María.

1254-1284: The Cantigas de Santa María (420 sung poems in honor of miracles enacted by Mary) are composed. Several honor the Camino's most potent Mary, Nuestra Señora La Blanca in Villalcazar de Sirga.

1258: Construction begins on León's Gothic Catedral de Santa Maria.

1517: Martin Luther's 92 Theses kicks off the Protestant Reformation, reducing interest in religious pilgrimage.

1879: Archaeological excavations confirm that the hill under Santiago's cathedral was an ancient burial mound contemporary with Saint James's life.

1960s-1980s: Elias Valiño Sampedro dedicates himself to retracing, mapping, and marking with yellow arrows the whole length of the Camino.

1987: The European Community names the Camino a European Cultural Itinerary.

1993: UNESCO declares the Camino de Santiago a Universal Patrimony of Humanity.

and Germany, among other nations, continue to draw new pilgrims.

Camino trekkers are a diverse bunch. About 50 percent of pilgrims are from Spain (45 percent) and France (5 percent), the two most historic nations associated with the Camino, and the rest are from around the world. In recent years, over 140 other nationalities walked the Camino. The largest groups were from Italy (8 percent), Germany (8 percent), the USA (5 percent), Portugal (5 percent), Ireland (2 percent), the UK (2 percent), Korea (2 percent), and Australia (2 percent), followed by Brazil and Canada. Alongside the devout Christian pilgrims are Jewish, Muslim, Buddhist, pagan, secular, agnostic, atheistic, and otherly-oriented pilgrims. About half the pilgrims are women and half are men.

Trekkers also come from all walks of life. Students walk it on their "gap year," as do recent retirees as they figure out what lies ahead. Many pilgrims are professionals, self-employed or office nine-to-fivers, who see it as a way to clear one's head while meeting people from all over the world. Wives/husbands and mothers/fathers walk it to reconnect with themselves and work out what to do after children have grown. Divorcees, widows, and widowers do so for healing, wholeness, and clarity. And the list goes on. Also, walking the Camino more than once is also becoming a trend as returning pilgrims use it as a reset button on their everyday lives, discovering it is more fresh and powerfully rejuvenating each time.

Many, but not all, people who decide to walk the Camino arrive calling themselves pilgrims. Even for those who don't start out doing so, something curious happens once they start walking: Locals call them **pèlerins** (in France) and **peregrinos** (in Spain), and soon they embrace the term themselves, whether or not they are religious or spiritual journeyers. Especially because the title *peregrino* is directed toward walkers by locals deeply committed to service to the Camino, the term possesses an initiatory and transformative power that reveals the quest and adventure ahead, leading even secular travelers to start thinking of themselves as pilgrims in some way or another.

Essentials

Before You Go

How Far to Walk

How far to go is not only a matter of how many days you have, but also how far to walk each day. A good rule of thumb for this is to plan shorter days at the beginning, so that your body can adjust to the terrain and to carrying a pack for 6-8 hours a day. This lets you find your own rhythm and avoid early injuries. Once you are acclimated, you can add more kilometers a day or find your sweet spot. Some trekkers love taking their time to take in the natural beauty and the small churches and shrines along the way, and may prefer to average 12-18 kilometers (7.5-11 miles) a day. Others get their high from rushing it, and love to cover 25-35 kilometers (15.5-22 miles) a day. Most fall somewhere in between, and a good average is **21-25 kilometers (13-15.5 miles) per day.**

Equipment

Nothing ruins this trek like too much baggage. A good place to start is to make a list of everything that you think you will need, and then go through it item by item, questioning why you need each thing. If it serves anything other than actual use in the everyday trek, leave it at home. (The Camino's support structure has had over a thousand years of anticipating pilgrims' needs, and you can find anything you need in an unplanned circumstance, or even things that you use each day and need to replace, from band aids to batteries.) A good rule of thumb is to carry no more than **10-15 percent of your body weight.** You should anticipate carrying **2-3 pounds of water and food each day,** so be sure your pack's final weight is 2-3 pounds under the mark.

The three most important items are:

- **Trekking shoes,** such as light hiking shoes or sturdy cross trainers, that you've broken in and that fit you

perfectly. Hefty hiking boots are usually overkill on the Camino, unless you need the extra support. Some *peregrinos* even hike in running shoes. Find the shoe that fits your body, and do not let anyone else, even well-meaning trekking store clerks, tell you what feels right. Do not buy new shoes the week before you leave; this almost always creates problems, from blisters to more serious foot and leg problems.

- **Socks** designed for blister prevention (double-layered, seamless, not 100% wool or cotton). Wright Socks are a good brand. From spring to autumn, I like ankle-length socks. A nice trick for layering warmth is to take a pair of woolen, knee-length socks whose toes and heels are shot, and cut them off at the ankle to create a pair of leggings you can slip on, as needed for added warmth. A perk is that these won't need to be washed as often as socks.

- **Pack:** Choose a light, moderate-sized (30-40 liter/1,830-2,440 cubic inches) pack that fits your torso, hips, and shoulders well.

Also bring a small **first-aid kit.** You can purchase travel-size first-aid kits from trekking stores, and add your own ingredients to augment them. I have used ibuprofen and arnica gel the most, and always outfit my kit to include these. You should not need to carry a lot for blisters if you take measures to prevent them. Plus, almost every place on the Camino stocks up on blister aids such as Moleskin and Compeed, as well as arnica and ibuprofen.

Training

There are no areas on the Camino where the altitude is so high that you'd need to acclimate, but it's still important to prepare for the trek. There are a lot of opinions about how to train, but the truth is that any form of training will set you ahead physically and psychologically once you reach the Camino. Do what you can and commit to it. The most basic program involves a weekly routine of walking, stretching/yoga, and once or twice a week, a full hike (over 8 miles) with your backpack at full weight. (Walking with your pack will also help you decide if you *really* need all the things in there.) Try to begin this regime a minimum of two months (six months is ideal) before you depart. Even if all you can do is 2-3 miles a day and stretching daily, plus a few 8-mile test treks with pack, that will set you well ahead.

Visas

No visa, only a passport, for France or Spain is required for members of the **European Union** and in the **Schengen zone.** Citizens of the United Kingdom, post-Brexit (so far), can still visit Europe without a visa, but should double-check as this law could change.

Visitors to Spain and France for 90 days and less from **Canada, the USA, Australia, New Zealand,** and almost all of **Central and South America** (with some exceptions) also do not need a visa, only a valid passport. Most citizens of Asia and Africa, including **South Africans,** in addition to a valid passport, will need to apply for a Schengen short-stay visa, which will allow for a stay of up to 90 days (or a longstay visa that will allow a visit of more than 90 days); you will also be asked to show proof that you have enough funds to support you while in Europe (usually, a current bank statement will suffice), and that you are covered with travel insurance.

For everyone outside of the EU, it is always wise to double-check with the Spanish Embassy in your country as well as your own country's state department, and also to visit the European Union's official website (www.ec-europa.eu/commission/index_en) to learn the current requirements.

Travel Insurance

Check with your health insurance carrier to see if they cover expenses abroad. If they do not, there are many inexpensive options. One of the most common and respected is through **Allianz** (www.allianztravelinsurance.com); this is sometimes even offered as part of the purchase price of your airline ticket, and may be less than $50. Another reputable company is **World Nomads** (www.worldnomads.com).

Getting There and Around

Starting Points

Of the more than 200,000 people on the Camino Francés each year, about 25% start walking from **Sarria,** by far the most popular starting point. Travelers beginning in Sarria are usually motivated by the confluence of several things, including limited time and a desire to gain a taste of the Camino experience, but the main reason is the desire also to collect a Compostela.

The next most popular starting points are **Saint-Jean-Pied-de-Port** (12%), **León** (4%), **O Cebreiro** (4%), **Ponferrada** (3%), and **Roncesvalles** (3%). But many entry points, such as **Pamplona, Logroño, Burgos,** and **Astorga,** are accessible via the same networks of buses and trains—so start where you want, given your time, inclination, and desired experience.

Air

The most common international entry points to reach the Camino are **Paris** (CDG), **Madrid** (MAD), and **Barcelona** (BCN), which are well connected to Camino destinations via both bus and train. From these airports, you can also get connecting flights to the following regional airports (the first three are nearest the eastern end of the Camino; the latter two are nearest the west end):

Packing Checklist

Essential Gear:

❑ **Light pack** (40L/2,440 cu in or less) that fits your body well.

❑ **Water bottle(s)** that can carry a minimum of 1.5 liters (1 half-gallon). I prefer two lightweight stainless steel bottles to camelback water reserves, because they are easier to clean thoroughly and don't taste of plastic.

❑ **Trekking shoes**, such as light hiking shoes or sturdy cross-trainers.

❑ **One (1) pair of after-trekking shoes** that can double as slippers in *albergues* and about-town shoes for dinner. Flip-flops or Tevas can be good for the shower.

❑ **Three (3) pairs of double-layer socks**, so that you have one clean, dry pair at all times, in case it rains or you step in a puddle.

❑ **Two (2) pairs of quick-dry hiking pants,** one that can be rolled up to serve as shorts or capris.

❑ **Two to three (2-3) tee-shirts** (1-2 short-sleeve and 1-2 long-sleeve, depending on season). I prefer cotton to moisture-wicking fabrics, which stink after a few days, even after being washed.

❑ **One (1) lightweight sweater or fleece:** a cashmere sweater is as light and practical as fleece, layers well for lightness and warmth with t-shirts and a rain jacket, gets smelly less frequently, and looks elegant in the evening.

❑ **One (1) rain poncho** that can double as a picnic blanket or seat.

❑ **Three (3) pairs of quick-drying underwear**

❑ **Two (2) bras** for women, ideally comfortable sports-style bras.

❑ **Sun hat** (for spring to fall).

❑ **Warm cap** and **gloves** (winter).

❑ **Sunglasses**.

❑ **Sunscreen**.

❑ **First aid kit**.

Essential Gear for *Albergues*:

If you'll be sleeping in *albergues* (rather than hostels, rural inns, or hotels), you'll also need:

❑ **A lightweight sleeping bag,** gauged to the season you are walking, and/or a sleeping-bag sheet as an extra layer for winter nights (and as the

- **Bilbao** (BIO), served by Aer Lingus (www.aerlingus.com), EasyJet (www.easyjet.com), Iberia (www.iberia.com), Air France (www.airfrance.com), and Lufthansa (www.lufthansa.com), among others

- **Pamplona** (PNA), served by Air Nostrum (www.airnostrum.com)

- **Biarritz** (BIQ), served by Ryan Air (www.ryanair.com) and EasyJet (www.easyjet.com)—the nearest airport to the eastern end of the Camino

- **A Coruña** (LCG), served by Air Europa (www.aireuropa.com), Air Nostrum (www.airnostrum.com), Gestair (www.gestair.com), Iberia (www.iberia.com), TAP (www.flytap.com), and Vueling (www.vueling.com)

- **Santiago de Compostela** (SCQ), served by Aer Lingus (www.aerlingus.com), sole sleeping gear for summer nights). I have a 20-ounce three-season sleeping bag, and when I use a sleeping sheet, I use one treated with permethrin as an added barrier against bedbugs. (Prolonged use of permethrin is not advised.)

❑ **A traveler's towel** or a cotton bandana that doubles as towel and headgear, preferably one that dries quickly.

❑ **A small dry sack** (ultra-light, such as Sea To Summit's 2-liter sack) for your valuables (passport, wallet, phone, camera) to take with you to the shower in *albergues* that lack lockers.

❑ **A head lamp** in case you need to go downstairs at night to get to the bathroom.

Optional Gear:

❑ **A lightweight cotton scarf** for warmth, sun protection, coverage when you get out of the shower, or to use as a sheet over an albergue bunk bed. This can also serve to cover bare shoulders when entering a church.

❑ **A rain jacket** that also doubles as an extra layer for wind or added warmth.

❑ **A light but warm jacket** if you are walking in **winter.**

❑ **Ultra-light dry sack** the size of your pack (such as Sea to Summit's **35-liter** sack) to line the inside of your pack, which will assure it stays dry in hefty rain. It also serves double-duty as a pillow when stuffed with clothes, as a laundry bag, and as an outer-pack shell (if you have to check your pack on an airline) to protect the straps from tear.

❑ **A compass.** Consider jettisoning all modern tech (it will lighten your load) and learn to use an old-fashioned, lightweight compass. Hook it onto your pack and feel very much the explorer.

❑ **A guidebook with maps** (such as this one).

❑ **A journal and pen.**

❑ **A camera** with **extra memory cards** (available on the trail but sometimes hard to find).

❑ **A smartphone,** or a simple **flip phone** for emergencies. (You can buy a simple phone for very little in Spain and top up minutes as you go.)

Air Europa (www.aireuropa.com), Air Nostrum (www.airnostrum.com), EasyJet (www.easyjet.com), Gestair (www.gestair.com), Iberia (www.iberia.com), Lufthansa (www.lufthansa.com), Ryan Air (www.ryanair.com), and Vueling (www.vueling.com)

Getting from the Airport to the Camino

To reach **Saint-Jean-Pied-de-Port and Roncesvalles:** The nearest airports are

Biarritz, Bilbao, and **Pamplona.** From any of these, you can take an Express Bourricot shuttle to either Saint-Jean (1-2 hours) or Roncesvalles (1-2.5 hours). It's also possible to reach Roncesvalles and Saint-Jean-Pied-de-Port from Pamplona via ALSA bus (1-2 hours).

To reach León: The nearest airports are **Santiago de Compostela** or **Oviedo.** You can catch a train to León from either Santiago de Compostela (4.5-6.5 hours) or Oviedo (3 hours). The **Madrid** airport also has direct bus (6 hours) and train (4.5 hours) connections to León.

To reach Ponferrada: The nearest airport is **Santiago de Compostela,** where you can catch a train (4 hours) or a bus (4 hours) to Ponferrada. From the **Madrid** airport there are buses (5 hours) to Ponferrada.

To reach O Cebreiro: The nearest airport is **Santiago de Compostela,** where you can catch a bus (3.5 hours) to Pedrafita do Cebreiro. From the **Madrid** airport there is a bus (6 hours) to Pedrafita do Cebreiro. From Pedrafita, you can catch a cab for the remaining 4 kilometers (2.5 miles) to O Cebreiro.

To reach Sarría: The nearest airport is **Santiago de Compostela**. From Santiago de Compostela, you can catch a train (2 hours) or a bus (3 hours) to Sarria. From **Madrid** a train, via a train change in Ourense, goes to Sarria (8 hours).

Train
From London and Paris
Eurostar (www.eurostar.com) lets you purchase one ticket for travel from London to Bayonne (five trains daily; 8 hours; £270/€302) with one train change in Paris. You depart London St Pancras Station and arrive in Paris Gare du Nord, where you will need to catch Métro line 4 to Paris Montparnasse station for a train to Bayonne. With a separate ticket from **SNCF** (www.oui.sncf), take the regional train from Bayonne to Saint-Jean-Pied-de-Port (1.5 hours; €11).

France's rail company, **SCNF** (www.oui.sncf), connects trains from Paris to Saint-Jean-Pied-de-Port (8 hours; €124-200) with a change in Bordeaux and Bayonne.

Within Spain
Spain's national rail, **RENFE** (www.renfe.com), has a line that runs the length of the Camino, operating from Irún, at the Pyrenees, and stopping in Burgos (€25-38), Sahagún (€32), León (€35), Astorga (€40), Ponferrada (€40), and Santiago de Compostela (€48). RENFE trains also connect Barcelona and Madrid to a number of Camino destinations, including Pamplona (direct: 4.5 hours from Barcelona, €36-67; 3-4 hours from Madrid, €24-65), Logroño (4 hours from Madrid, €30-62; and 5 hours from Barcelona, €36-70; both change trains in Zaragoza), Burgos (direct: 6.5-8 hours from Barcelona, €42-100; 2.5-4.5 hours from Madrid, €21-36), and Sarria (13 hours from Barcelona, some are direct, €41-95; and 10 hours from Madrid, €30-55, all trains to Sarria change in Ourense).

Purchase tickets online to assure the best price (though do note that the RENFE site in particular can be finicky). You can also buy your ticket (including all connections) at your first train station/entry point in France (at a SNCF station) or Spain (at a RENFE station). If purchasing in the station, I prefer to purchase from the ticket vendor rather than the vending machine. That way, if there is any issue with the credit or debit card, the ticket seller can enter the number manually and confirm the purchase. The ticket-vending machines are hit or miss at times, for reasons that seem to stymie even the SNCF and RENFE employees.

Bus
From London
Though air is by far the most efficient way, economically and time-wise, to arrive in France or Spain from London (followed by train), **Euroline** (www.eurolines.eu) runs buses from London to Bayonne (3-10 buses daily, 24 hours, €45-100), Bilbao (2-8 daily, 26 hours, €90-160), Pamplona (three buses every Fri. only, 30 hours, €77-200), and Burgos (3-6 buses on four days of the week, which can vary each week, 36 hours, €115-170). The dramatic range in prices is based on many factors—the day of the week, which bus you reserve, if there is a festival or holiday—but tend to be highest during the peak summer months (July and Aug.).

Within Spain

The bus company, **ALSA** (www.alsa.com), connects just about all starting points on the Camino with Madrid and Barcelona, and nearly all destinations on the Camino to each other, including Pamplona, Logroño, Burgos, Sahagún, León, Astorga, Ponferrada, and near O Cebreiro at Pedrafita do Cebreiro.

ALSA also runs buses from Biarritz's airport to Pamplona, from Barcelona to Pamplona, and from Pamplona to Roncesvalles and Saint-Jean-Pied-de-Port. They also run direct lines from Madrid's Barajas airport to Pamplona, Burgos, and León. To reach Sarria by bus, **Monbus** (www.monbus.com) is the most direct route from Santiago de Compostela. More regional bus companies reach smaller towns and hamlets on the Camino not served by ALSA; these smaller companies are listed in their respective destination chapters.

Ferry
From Ireland and the U.K.

Brittany Ferries operates four routes to Spain from Ireland (www.brittanyferries.ie) and the UK (www.brittany-ferries.co.uk):

An overnight sail from **Cork, Ireland** leaves for **Santander, Spain** (33.5 hours), which is 3 hours from Pamplona. Other routes depart **Portsmouth, England** for **Santander** (24 hours) and **Bilbao** (28 hours), which is 1.5 hours from Logroño and 2 hours from Pamplona. The fourth route connects **Plymouth, England,** to **Santander** (19.5 hours).

Each route runs one ferry per week. Ferries can range in price, €99-510, depending on season and whether you embark on foot or with a car. Prices go up the nearer the departure date, so it is worth inquiring well in advance.

Taxi

Taxis can be a valid option for getting from a gateway airport to your starting place if the shuttle and bus schedules do not align with your plans. You usually can find other pilgrims to share a taxi with you, bringing the cost down significantly. Taxis in Spain typically charge a little over **€1 per kilometer,** so a 15-kilometer (9.3-mile) ride will be around €20 and a 30-kilometer (18.6-mile) ride around €35.

On the Camino, from stopping point to stopping point, taxis are readily available and you can ask at the local café-bar, albergue, or hotel to call you a taxi. Drivers do not expect a tip, but if you give a euro or two for good service, they'll be elated.

Car

The Camino's towns and cities are accessible by major highways from **Madrid, Santander, Bilbao,** and **Barcelona.**

Car Rentals

All the major international car-rental companies have offices in the major cities and larger towns (Madrid, Barcelona, Bilbao, Pamplona, Logroño, Burgos, León, Ponferrada, and Santiago de Compostela) that connect to the Camino, including **Europcar** (www.europcar.com), **Hertz** (www.hertz.com), **Avis** (www.avis.com), **Enterprise** (www.enterprise.com), **Thrifty** (www.thrifty.com), and **Dollar** (www.dollar.com).

Some agencies may set a minimum age to rent, around 21 or 23 years old, and most will add on an extra surcharge for young drivers (typically under 25). In France, the young driver supplement may be as much as €30-40 per day on top of the rental price, and in Spain around €20 per day in addition to the rental fee. There are no official maximum age limits to drive or rent a car in France and Spain but some agencies may set an upper limit to 70, 75, or 80 years of age, or may want to see that your license was renewed within the last five years. Be sure to inquire ahead of time with the rental company.

Road Rules

You must be **18 years old** to drive in France and Spain. You must have your **passport** and a **valid driver's license** to rent a car and drive legally in France and Spain. The information for those coming from outside Europe about whether you also need an International Driving Permit (IDP) is confusing and often states that you do not need one to drive in France or Spain. In both countries, officially, you are expected to have an IDP to accompany your valid driver's license from home. An IDP is not a license but a translation of your current license into an international form that is recognized around the world. You can apply for one via the officially recognized national auto club that is allowed to issue these, such as the American Automobile Association (www.aaa.com) in the USA, and the Canadian Automobile Association (www. caa.ca) in Canada. You will still need to carry your driver's license with you.

Both France and Spain are stringent about drinking and driving, and there are frequent patrols that may stop drivers for random roadside breathalyzer tests. Both France and Spain hold legal blood-alcohol levels at a maximum of **0.5mg/ml,** which is lower than in the UK and USA. One glass of wine or a beer will typically take your blood level to between 0.2-0.3mg/ml. It's best not to drink until after you reach the destination where you plan to spend the night, and therefore won't be driving any more that day.

About 20 percent of Spain's roads have **tolls,** and on most large highways you will have occasional toll stops (these can range from €5-25, depending on your entry and exit point). The smaller, scenic roads near the Camino are toll-free. The same holds for driving in southwestern France.

The speed limit in both France and Spain is typically **110-130km/hour (68-80 mph)** on large highways, **80km/hour (50 mph)** on open roads in France, and **90km/hour (55 mph)** on open roads in Spain, and **50km/hour (30 mph)** in towns; but in some urban or village areas it can be **20-30km/hour (10-20 mph).**

Driving the Camino

Driving the Camino is slightly longer than walking it, around **810 total kilometers (503 total miles)** from Saint-Jean-Pied-de-Port to Santiago de Compostela and 920 kilometers (572 miles) total to the coast at Finisterre or Muxía. A **minimum of two weeks** is enough to cover the whole stretch, but three weeks is ideal, and will allow you to use the more scenic and smaller roads that parallel the Camino rather than the highway.

Driving does have its advantages. First, it allows you to time your arrival in towns, so you can stop for lunch and eat when the locals do, around 2pm, and then use the siesta hours, around 3-5pm, for rest and to drive to that night's accommodations in time for the early evening when places open up again; you will be installed and ready to sightsee and enjoy the nightlife. As a driver, you will not have access to most *albergues,* but you will still be able to share the pilgrim experience by staying in the same towns and villages in rural hotels, *hostales,* and *pensiones.*

Driving Directions

Saint-Jean-Pied-de-Port is best reached via Bayonne and Biarritz. The best way to reach **Roncesvalles** is via Pamplona. Both towns are connected via the mountain road (**D-933** in France and **N-135** in Spain) over the Pyrenees. After Roncesvalles, driving along the **N-135,** which follows and parallels the Camino de Santiago, will take you all the way to Pamplona.

From Pamplona, the **A-12** highway runs parallel to the Camino to Burgos and is called the **Autovía del Camino de Santiago.** It gives quick access to major hubs such as Pamplona, Estella, Logroño, and Burgos. But for a more leisurely and

20-Day Driving Itinerary

* **Day 1:** Fly in to **Biarritz**, rent a car at the airport, and drive to **Saint-Jean-Pied-de-Port** for the day and overnight.

* **Day 2:** Saint-Jean-Pied-de-Port to **Pamplona**, stopping in Roncesvalles, then lunch and sightseeing in Pamplona and an evening of *pintxos* and wine.

* **Day 3:** Pamplona to **Viana**, with brief stops at Santa María de Eunate, Puente la Reina, Cirauqui, Estella (lunch), Los Arcos, and Torres del Rio.

* **Day 4:** Viana to **Villafranca Montes de Oca**, stopping in Logroño, Nájera, Santo Domingo de la Calzada (lunch), and Tosantos.

* **Day 5:** Villafranca Montes de Oca to **Burgos**, stopping in San Juan de la Ortega, and at the Atapuerca archaeological site (lunch in Atapuerca village).

* **Day 6:** Rest and sightseeing day in Burgos.

* **Day 7:** Burgos to **Carrión de los Condes**, with stops at Ruinas San Antón, Castrojeriz, Frómista, and Villalcazar de Sirga (lunch).

* **Day 8:** Carrión de los Condes to **Sahagún**, with a detour to see the Roman villa of La Tejada, and stop in Moratinos or San Nicolás del Real Camino for lunch, arriving in Sahagún to check in to lodging and visit churches that are opening up for the evening.

* **Day 9:** Sahagún to **León**, stopping in Mansilla de las Mulas, visiting Roman Lancia and Mózarabic San Miguel de Escalada, and arriving in León for lunch, rest, and an early evening of sightseeing.

* **Day 10:** León to **Castrillo de los Polvazares**, stopping in La Virgen del Camino, Hospital de Órbigo, Astorga (lunch), and arriving at Flores del Camino in the village of Castrillo de los Polvazares.

* **Day 11:** Rest day and artist's retreat at **Flores del Camino**.

* **Day 12:** Castrillo de los Polvazares to **Ponferrada**, stopping in Rabanal del Camino, Cruz de Ferro (to lay a stone), El Acebo, Riego de Ambros, Molinaseca (lunch), and Ponferrada.

* **Day 13:** Ponferrada to **Triacastela**, with stops in Cacabelos, Villafranca del Bierzo, O Cebreiro, and Biduedo (lunch).

* **Day 14:** Triacastela to **Eirexe**, with stops in Samos, Sarria, Barbadelo, Mercadoiro (lunch), Castro de Castromaior, and Eirexe.

* **Day 15:** Eirexe to **Santiago de Compostela**, with stops in Leboreiro, Melide, Arzúa (lunch here or in O Empalme), and Monte de Gozo.

* **Days 16 and 17:** Santiago de Compostela.

* **Day 18:** Santiago de Compostela to **Finisterre**, with stops in Pontemaceira, Negreira, Cee, and Corcubión (all are good places for lunch).

* **Day 19:** Finisterre to **Muxía**.

* **Day 20:** Muxía to **Santiago de Compostela**, where you can return the car and fly or train toward home.

pretty drive, the smaller highway— **N-1110/N-111A** then **N-120**—also parallels the Camino. From Burgos, the N-120 continues to León and past to Astorga, where the **LE-142** will next carry you near the trail to Ponferrada.

The Camino By Bike

It takes about two weeks to cycle the Camino. Interestingly, this time frame aligns with the 13 stages outlined in the 12th-century pilgrim's guide (the *Codex Calixtinus*), in which the medieval author suggested it took only 13 days to get to Compostela from the Pyrenees. This has made some think that the author was advising pilgrims to ride horses; others think it was a metaphorical reference. Do it however you wish, but if you want to aim for the stages in the *Codex Calixtinus*, they are:

* **Day 1:** From **Saint Michel** (near Honto on the Pyrenean crossing, soon after leaving Saint-Jean-Pied-de-Port) to **Biskaretta-Viscarreta** (33.4 km/20.8).

* **Day 2:** Biskaretta-Viscarreta to **Pamplona** (30.8 km/19.1 mi).

* **Day 3:** Pamplona to **Estella** (48.6 km/30.2 mi).

* **Day 4:** Estella to **Nájera** (78.8 km/49 mi).

* **Day 5:** Nájera to **Burgos** (94.4 km/58.7).

* **Day 6:** Burgos to **Frómista** (65.7 km/40.8 mi).

* **Day 7:** Frómista to **Sahagún** (59.5 km/37 mi).

* **Day 8:** Sahagún to **León** (55.5 km/34.5 mi).

* **Day 9:** León to **Rabanal del Camino** (69.3 km/43 mi).

* **Day 10:** Rabanal del Camino to **Villafranca del Bierzo** (57.6 km/35.8 mi).

* **Day 11:** Villafranca del Bierzo to **Triacastela** (48.8 km/30.3 mi).

* **Day 12:** Triacastela to **Palas de Rei** (65.3 km/40.6 mi).

* **Day 13:** Palas de Rei to **Santiago de Compostela** (68 km/42.3 mi).

The **LE-713** connects Ponferrada to **Villafranca del Bierzo**, where it merges with the **N-VI** through **La Portela de Valcarce** and **Vega de Calcarce** to **Herrerías**. This reaches the base of the final ascent of the route, over O Cebreiro's mountain, where the foot trail and the road part ways until O Cebreiro. The driving route is way-marked with blue signs with a yellow scallop shell to guide drivers along a parallel path to the trail. From O Cebreiro to Ventas, follow the **LU-633**; at Ventas the LU-633 gives way to the **C-535** to Palas de Rei. From Palas de Rei to Santiago de Compostela, the road to follow is the **N-547**. Access is the same by car as by foot to all stopping points on the Camino when you follow these roads. Where these roads do not pass directly through destinations on the trail, there are marked, smaller access roads to reach the same settlements.

Bike

On average, some 92 percent do the Camino on foot. Some 7 percent cycle it, and the remaining 1 percent do it by horse, donkey, or wheelchair. For those on wheels, about half the Camino is on roads and about half on dirt paths that are also near paved roads, which cyclists are expected to take whenever possible—especially when the trail is narrow and rocky—to keep the foot trail safe for trekkers. Often the deviations for bikers are marked when the trail requires this added clarity.

To cycle the whole Camino takes on average **two weeks,** covering **50-80 kilometers (30-50 miles) per day.** You can also combine walking with cycling, and some pilgrims enjoy renting a bike in Burgos to cross the *meseta*, returning it in León. Many places along the Camino, especially in the cities, offer bike rentals expressly for the Camino. **Bicigrino** (www.bicigrino.com; €40/day) offers pick-up and drop-off addresses in Burgos, Calzadilla de la Cueza, Sahagún, and León, as well as other start and stop points across the entire north. **Velobur Bikes** (www.velobur.es; €30-150/day depending on promotions) does pick-up and drop-off points from Burgos to León and points in between, and even a little farther past León.

With a bike, you can still stay in most *albergues,* but priority is given to walkers; at most, you'll need to wait until 6pm to be given a bed. Such restrictions do not apply to other accommodations. Most lodging, *albergues* and others, have options for overnight bike storage.

On the Camino

Trail Conditions
The Camino is **well marked** for some 95 percent of its 900 kilometers/560 miles (including the stretch to Finisterre and Muxía), but constant vigilance is a good idea for staying on the trail. Most markers are either yellow arrows painted on signs, posts, walls, and rocks, or scallop shells made of ceramic, stone, or concrete, many posted on kilometer pillars along the path. In the Pyrenees, on the border with France and Spain, and into Navarra, horizontal red and white stripes painted on posts and signs also mark the way. You will also notice that pilgrims leave stones on the pillar way-markers, as well as on large boulders on the trailside, creating cairns. This is another way the Camino is unofficially marked, and it's also a good way to check if you are still on the trail.

The **terrain** of the Camino is quite varied. More than half the time, it's on dirt or rocky footpaths. Other times, it parallels a country lane, small road, or rural highway. On a few occasions, it is right on the bank of the road, and only very rarely right on it, but it is these times when you need to be especially cautious with oncoming traffic. A few times you may also need to cross a road, at which point you'll need to muster extra caution. Many of the more treacherous parts of the Camino in recent years have had protective barriers installed, or have been rerouted.

A few sections of the Camino can readily be skipped, more because they are unpleasant urban walking than for any dangers. The worst of these are leaving Logroño, and entering and leaving León; in all cases, you can catch a bus for a few kilometers to skip these parts.

Pilgrim's Credential
A pilgrim's credential– **credencial del peregrino** in Spanish and **carnet de pélerin** in French—is also known as your *passport.* It's an accordion-folded document slightly longer than a regular passport. A stamped credential is first and foremost a passport that lets you stay in *albergues* (and gives discounts in some museums), and also that documents where you began and where you've walked. But it also is necessary if you wish to earn a certificate of walking.

Credentials usually cost **€2**. You can pick up a credential at all the gateway cities and starting points, such as at the pilgrim's welcome office in Saint-Jean-Pied-de-Port. Many *albergues* (especially the municipal ones, including those in Pamplona, Puente la Reina, Estella, Logroño, León, Ponferrada, and O Cebreiro) and churches and monasteries also have credentials (such as in Sarria, at the Iglesia de Santa Mariña and the Monasterio de la Magdalena). You can also get one mailed to you before departing from your national pilgrims' association, such as the American Friends of the Camino (USA), Canadian Company of Pilgrims, Confraternity of Saint James

(UK), Australian Friends of the Camino (Australia and New Zealand), and Confraternity of St. James South Africa.

You'll get your credential stamped every day, usually at the place you stay, but almost every place along the Camino—including shops, cafés, and restaurants—has a stamp they enjoy sharing. Churches also often have a stamp that you will find as you enter. For some pilgrims, their stamped credential is the best souvenir of their walk. If you are walking all the way from Saint-Jean-Pied-de-Port to Santiago de Compostela, you will probably easily fill 2-3 passports before you are done. It's fine to stamp other things, if you wish, such as in your journal, a map, or whatever other parchment you wish to use to create a document of your journey with these unique imprints.

Earning Your Compostela

The **Compostela** (the certificate of completing the pilgrimage) is a beautiful document in Latin, with your name and the date you arrived in Santiago de Compostela, and illuminated with medieval illustrations from the 12th-century *Codex Calixtinus* and the 15th-century *Breviario de Miranda*. The Compostela is issued by the church, which only considers the last 100 kilometers (62 miles) as qualifying for walkers (or the last 200 km/124 mi, if you cycled). You must present your credential in the pilgrim's reception office in Santiago de Compostela, and be sure that it has **two stamps per day, minimum**, from Sarria forward (and two per day from Ponferrada if cycling); all stamps before Sarria (Ponferrada) do not matter for this certificate.

While the **Compostela** is the most valued certificate, it is actually one of four other certificates that you can earn while walking the Camino, each one with its own quirky criteria. If you walk from Saint-Jean-Pied-de-Port to Sahagún (the Camino's midway point) and collect one stamp per day, you can get a halfway certificate, a **Carta Peregrina**. Earn a **Fisterana** by walking from Santiago de Compostela to Finisterre and collecting two stamps per day. You can earn a **Muxiana** in just a day by walking the challenging route from Finisterre to Muxía and collecting two stamps for that day, one in Finisterre and one in Lires. You can also earn a *Muxiana* for walking from Santiago de Compostela to Muxía, stamping your credential a minimum of twice per day.

Accommodations

Essentially, there are three types of accommodations on the Camino: pilgrim dorms called *albergues;* low-cost and budget inns called *pensiones* (many with shared bathrooms); and *hostales* (with private baths), traditional hotels, and *casas rurales* (all with private bathrooms).

Albergues

Pilgrim dorms, called *albergues*, are the traditional pilgrims' accommodations on the Camino. There are four types of *albergues:* **municipal** or *xunta* (municipal, run by the town or village); *parroquia* (parish, run by a religious organization); *privado* (private, run by private individuals and families); and *asociación* (run by nonprofit pilgrim associations, typically from different countries, and usually run by volunteers). Most open in the afternoon and stay open until about 10pm, which is lights out, when everyone is expected to be in bed and quiet. Some even lock the doors, so it is good to observe the curfew. Most have set prices but some albregues run on a *donativo* (donation) basis; try to leave at least €5 minimum if you can. Typically, municipal *albergues* are bare bones and the least expensive (€5-7). Next in price are those run by parishes and associations (€5-12), followed by private *albergues* (€10-15), which offer more creature comforts. Most albergue types offer an evening *menú* or communal meal (€10-12), and many also offer breakfast (€3-5).

If you stay in an albergue, you will be sleeping in a room with other people, at times as few as four, and at others, as many as 50 (but on average, around 8-15 people). Almost all the *albergues* are **mixed-gender dorms,** though a few have separate women's and men's sleeping quarters. Many, especially the private *albergues,* also have private rooms that cost two to three times more than a dorm bed (€20-40). Beds are almost all **twin size,** and most are **bunk beds.** Bathrooms vary: Some are gender mixed and others separate. Some have private shower stalls and others are open. (All have private toilets!) If you plan on staying in *albergues,* you'll want to pack a light, small, quick-dry traveler's towel and either a light sleeping bag or sleeping bag sheet, depending on the season. Consider bringing flip-flops to wear in the shower.

Albergues are only meant for those walking or cycling the Camino and who have a credential (but don't sweat it: if you lose your credential, you can buy a new one and get it stamped at the albergue). Additionally, walkers get priority over cyclists. Many only allow cyclists to check in after 6pm, 3-4 hours after the albergue opened for walkers, and only if there are any beds left over.

Pensiones and *Hostales*

Pensiones and *hostales* are usually small family-run hotels (€22-60), some including breakfast at extra cost (€4-6) and some with attached restaurants and cafés. Many *pensiones* offer homey private rooms with a shared bathroom. *Hostales,* not to be confused with hostels, almost always come with your own private bath. As a rule, almost all these establishments are clean and comfortable, with minimalist but pleasant decor.

From top to bottom: a pilgrim's pack; the Compostela; the many forms of pilgrims' credentials.

Hoteles and *Casas Rurales*

Hoteles and *casas rurales* (rural bed and breakfasts) are at the higher range (€40-100+) and are the most plush options for pilgrims, with elegant rooms, cozy lounges, and many services and creature comforts for the asking (sometimes including laundry service, massage, and spa treatments). Hotels will always offer private rooms with an ensuite bath. Casas rurales are almost always private rooms with attached bath, but at times the private bath is across or down the hall, and very rarely, it might be shared with one other guest.

A special category of luxury hotels are the state-run **paradores,** historic former monasteries, mansions, or palaces that have been beautifully restored and converted into hotels. The Camino has a few, the most astounding being the Parador San Marcos in León. The other famous Camino parador is the Hostal de los Reyes Católicos, a repurposed 16th-century pilgrims' hospital right next to the cathedral in Santiago de Compostela.

If you are staying in an upper-end hotel, it is customary to leave the cleaning staff a tip of around €1 for each day that you stay there.

A special network of hotels on the Camino, called **Posadas del Camino** (www.posadasdelcamino.com), have banded together and offer a 10% discount card after you've stayed in your first Posada hotel in the network. You can find the list on their website, which lists 21 participating hotels fairly evenly spread out across the Camino, starting from Hotel Akerreta in Akerreta (just after Zubiri in Navarra) to Hotel Capitol in Santiago de Compostela. Be sure to ask for the 10% discount card before departing from your first Posada hotel.

Food and Drinking Water

Generally speaking, cafes and bars are reasonably frequent on the Camino, appearing every few kilometers or so. You can eat there, or often you can ask for *un bocadillo para llevar* (a sandwich to go) and indicate if you want it to be a *bocadillo de tortilla* (egg omelet sandwich), *de jamón* (with ham), or *de queso* (cheese). Most bars will have these ingredients on hand and will make you a sandwich on the spot for around €3-5. One advantage of stopping at cafés rather than picnicking is that paying customers can use their bathroom facilities and also ask if they can fill your water bottle with water from the tap.

For long stretches (noted throughout this guide), you may want to pack a lunch and take a trailside break in the middle of the day. It's smart to keep snacks such as nuts and dried fruit in your pack, along with plenty of water. There are many **public fountains** alongside the road, in town squares, and on the trail, but only the ones that are marked *potable* (drinkable) should be used to fill water bottles.

Breakfast

Spanish breakfast is light: typically toast or a croissant with coffee, though tea is also available. Many bars also make *zumo de naranja natural* (fresh-squeezed orange juice) to order. Heartier fare is available for pilgrims, and you almost always can get a *pincho de tortilla* (thick wedge of potato omelet) with fresh bread and whatever beverage you want. A *pincho de tortilla*, *café con leche* (espresso with steamed milk), and glass of fresh-squeezed OJ costs around €5.50 and can really fuel the morning well.

Most *albergues* offer breakfast, at extra cost (€3-5), where you can get toast, coffee, juices (from a carton or bottle), and sometimes yogurt, cheese, ham, fruit, and hardboiled eggs. With the many cafés on the Camino, you can also decide to get an early start from your albergue and break for breakfast along the way.

Menú del Peregrino (Pilgrim's Menu)

The *menú del peregrino,* "pilgrim's menu" (€9-12), a basic three-course meal offered at local restaurants and *albergues,* evolved

The Bed Race

Part of the Camino's magic is letting each day unfold unplanned, and many pilgrims relish the chance to travel without reservations. For some, however, especially those planning to walk during the peak months from May to September, the "bed race" can cause stress. You have some options to mitigate this.

Get an Early Start
The common strategy employed by most pilgrims is to start early (around 5:30 am) and stop early (by 1 or 2pm), so that you aren't the last one rolling into town. In the peak of the summer season, though, on some days, you may arrive in town to find all the beds already taken.

Make Reservations
You can either make reservations in advance, or as you go. Bear in mind that this will restrict your trek and commit you to a stopping place, even if a more appealing one appears after you've booked.

Ask a Local for Help
This is my favorite strategy, and I have always found a place to stay, even in the direst of situations or peak seasons. If you find no beds in town, ask the *hospitalero* (*albergue* staff) or inn keeper to help you find alternative accommodations. They are the best resources for knowing who has an inn or hotel just a kilometer or two off the Camino; they can also call for you. Often, the person running those inns will come and pick you up, and return you to the Camino the next morning.

Walk During Low Season/ Shoulder Season
During the shoulder seasons (mid-March to May and late-Sept.-Nov.) the competition for accommodation is lower. From Dec.-Feb. there is no bed race at all (but also bear in mind that around 60 percent of accommodations on the Camino close in the low season, especially the *albergues*). The vast majority of accommodations listed in this guide remain open all year; those that close in winter are noted.

---

to meet the tastes of international eaters while still offering classic Spanish dishes at affordable prices. It's typically served for dinner, and includes a starter dish (salad, pasta, soup), a main dish (grilled meat/fish/eggs and potatoes and vegetables, a substantial stew), a dessert (custard/flan, pudding, ice cream, fruit), bread, and water, and usually (but not always) wine, beer, or other beverage. Restaurants usually offer several choices for the three courses. The pilgrim's menus at *albergues* are more family style, with just one offering for each course, and the latter tend to be more vegetarian friendly.

Pilgrim's menus are fresh, almost always from local ingredients, but they are often economical and basic dishes that do not showcase the best cooking of a region. For that you may need to step outside the *menú del peregrino* option and pay a little more (€13-15) for either an **a la carte** offering or a slightly more upscale ***menú del día*** (daily menu, €13-18), geared toward working locals on their lunch break.

Meal Times
The Spanish in the north sit down to lunch around 2pm and dinner around 9pm. While they still rise early, they accommodate this schedule with the siesta hour, around 3pm until 5pm. In times past this was a challenge for *peregrinos,* but the Spanish in recent times have devised a way to cater to everyone's needs, offering *menús del peregrino* earlier in the evening, around 6:30-7:30pm. After feeding hungry pilgrims, locals then cook their own dinner for their Spanish customers and their families.

Tipping
Servers in France and Spain earn living wages so the practice of tipping is

The Siesta and *Paseo*

For non-Spanish *peregrinos*, the **siesta** may take some getting used to. In mid-to-late afternoon, things shut down and go seemingly dead. This is when locals are taking a rest from a long day.

Just as dramatically, the whole town erupts to carnival-level life in the early evening as shops and cafés re-open and the whole town floods out for shopping and visiting with friends. This is when locals partake in the ***paseo,*** the early

evening stroll after a siesta that is a traditional part of everyday public life in Spanish towns large and small. In larger places, churches also open at these times and it is a great time to see inside them, both to view their interiors and to observe the daily gossip sessions among neighbors in a back pew.

Another perk of Spanish timing: Shops tend to stay open later, around 8 or 9pm, so it's possible to purchase provisions for the next day.

different. Along the Camino, tipping is not really expected for the *menú del peregrino or menú del día*. At special meals in restaurants, leaving 3-5 percent of the total bill is typical (if you really loved the meal, leave 5-10 percent). In cafés, over drinks and snacks, it is fine to leave nothing, but sometimes patrons leave a few centimes to show appreciation for a hardworking bartender or waiter.

Restrooms

There are no public restrooms on the Camino. Many people relieve themselves on the side of the trail, but this should be avoided, as with the growing number of pilgrims on the trail, it creates garbage, takes its toll on the environment, and compromises the integrity of the many nearby waterways and farmers' fields. Instead, when you need to use the restroom, purchase a drink or snack at a bar or café so you can use their facilities. It's a great way to rehydrate and refuel, too.

If you absolutely must relieve yourself trailside, don't do so near farmer's fields, or closer than a few hundred feet from a stream or waterway. Carry a plastic bag to pack out toilet paper to where you can dispose of it safely. And if you do more than pee, yes, you should pick up your waste, wrap it well, and throw it away in a waste bin.

Camino Etiquette
On the Trail

There is important etiquette on the trail and with other *peregrinos*. First, be sure to dispose of trash (including TP and human waste) in proper receptacles. Both locals and *peregrinos* have been infuriated by the amount of trash, and TP, that has accrued in farmers' fields, the trail, forests, and gardens.

Other trail etiquette is to make way for people who are trying to pass, and if passing, to thank the person. It is a small gesture that goes a long way to keep the Camino congenial. If cycling, it is imperative to slow down before approaching those on foot and make your presence known long before trying to pass, so that you don't startle walkers carrying heavy packs and cause them to lose their balance.

Locals tolerate just about any type of dress in public and churches, but dressing modestly is a nice way to show respect; you may want to drape a light scarf over bare shoulders before entering a church.

In *Albergues*

In the *albergues,* it is key to honor everyone's boundaries. With other *peregrinos,* this means to only take up your bunk or bed space, and to keep the *albergue* clean, and to leave it clean. Be quiet and considerate, and don't turn on lights or headlamps if heading to the restroom at night while others are still sleeping. If you leave early, make as little noise as possible, and absolutely do not rustle plastic bags (the bane of many!) until you are well outside of the sleeping quarters.

It is also imperative to be kind to the *hospitaleros/as* (local volunteers serving pilgrims in the *albergues*) and locals who are doing everything to serve *peregrinos*. They work long days, cooking and cleaning the *albergues* and then going home to cook for their own families, and all on either a *donativo* (donation) or small fee basis, so your patience goes a long way. Even better: Ask how you can help.

Health and Safety

Overall, the Camino is safe, but visitors should keep their street smarts on, especially as the Camino is becoming more popular than ever. Water and food are high quality and at the same high standards as the rest of Europe: all water from indoor plumbing and from indoor taps is treated and drinkable. On the trail, only drink out of fountains marked *potable*.

No inoculations are required for international travelers to Spain or France, though people may want to be sure they are up to date on their **tetanus shots.**

Safety
Violence on the Camino is nearly unheard of; however, tragedies have occasionally occurred. Most recently, in 2015, a female pilgrim was lured (via fake yellow arrows painted on the trail) to a remote farm, where she was murdered. The perpetrator is now serving the highest jail sentence possible in Spain. Since the murder, locals and municipalities have increased their regular monitoring of Camino trail markers, some installing official signs instead of hand-painted marks, and the local police and the rural police (who have always been vigilant about monitoring the trail) have increased their efforts.

Buen Camino

Many locals are proud to live on and serve the Camino, and many offer passing *peregrinos* a sincere *buen Camino,* "good way/path" the mantra of the road. There actually are nuances to the phrase *buen Camino.* Many *peregrinos* use it often with each other to mean a range of "hello," "bye," "have a good trip," "blessings," "I don't know what else to say," and "please give me space."

But when locals who live on and serve the Camino utter *"buen Camino,"* they are more often both giving a welcoming greeting and also participating in a long chain of manna and grace. This *buen Camino* is a wish and a promise, binding the two of you to the path and asking that you carry their prayers with you to Santiago and deliver them there, enriching them with blessings from your journey.

When I realized this deeper layer to the *buen Camino,* I took it more seriously and endeavored not to let it become something rote or uttered without meaning. I also realized how many people's hopes I carried by the time I reached the high altar in Santiago de Compostela's cathedral to give Saint James the ritual hug: They were all there with me.

There are a few parts of the Camino where you will be near the road or will need to cross it; at these times, take extra care to watch for quickly appearing and moving cars.

Medical and Emergency Assistance
For serious emergencies requiring either medical or police intervention, dial **112.** Many emergency operators can work out your concern, even if you do not speak a lot of Spanish. To report minor crimes that are not immediate emergencies, the Spanish police also have a hotline for visitors—**902-102-112**—with operators on

hand who speak English, French, Italian, and German. You can also ask a *hospitalero* to help you contact the right authorities and make a report.

Hospitals and Pharmacies

The Camino has a strong network of medical clinics (*centros de salud*) and pharmacies all along the trail, in towns large and small. For minor issues (such as tendonitis, bed bugs, or digestive discomforts) seek out a pharmacist. You will identify a pharmacy (*una farmacía*) with the green cross sign over the entrance.

For more serious issues, the Camino has many excellent hospitals, which locals (*hospitaleros,* pharmacists, and inn keepers) will readily help you to get to. Some major hospitals include:

Pamplona: Hospital de Navarra (Calle de Irunlarrea, 3; 848-422-222), near the university and 2.7 kilometers (1.7 miles) southwest of the historic center.

Logroño: Hospital San Pedro (Calle Piqueras, 98; 941-298-000), 3 kilometers (1.9 miles) southeast of the cathedral.

Burgos: Hospital Universitario de Burgos (Avenida Islas Baleares, 3; 947-281-800), 3 kilometers (1.9 miles) northeast of Burgos's cathedral.

León: Hospital Universitario de León (Altos de Navas, s/n; 987-237-400), 2.7 kilometers (1.7 miles) due north of the cathedral.

Sarria: (Centro de Salud): Centro de Salud de Sarria (Rúa Toleiro, 14D; 981-506-176 and 982-532-111), a 7-minute, 650-meter (2,133-foot) walk from the Iglesia de Santa Mariña to the east side of the river Sarria.

Santiago de Compostela: Hospital Clínico Universitario de Santiago (Rúa da Choupana, s/n; 981-950-000), 2.2 kilometers (1.4 miles) southwest of the cathedral.

Staying Healthy
Sun Protection and Staying Hydrated

It is strongly advised to have at least 1.5 liters (0.5 gallon) of water (more in summer) on you at all times as you hike the Camino. At the same time, if it is hot and you are sweating a lot, it is also a good idea to replenish lost salt. (Some travelers even carry a little travel-size salt shaker.)

In warm weather, protect yourself from heat stroke and exhaustion by getting an early start, right before or as the sun rises, and stop early in the day. Use sunscreen, a hat, and protective clothing, and drink ample water.

Bed Bugs

Bed bugs do not transmit any known diseases, but their bites can cause uncomfortable bumps and welts. Your best defense is to learn to identify the signs that they may be in a room, and to quickly check for these signs before setting your pack down and settling in. Bedbugs are oval and somewhat flat (when not gorged with blood) and about the size of a small lentil. They become more pea-shaped when full of blood. They also leave trails of excrement, so if you see little brown or black dots in a row on a mattress or sheet, you may be dealing with bedbugs. They like to hide by day in mattress creases or wall cracks, and then come out at night to feed. Report any signs or sightings and show them to the albergue *hospitalero* or hotel manager right away, and then find yourself somewhere else to stay. If you already paid, you can and should get your money back.

The Camino has had its share of *chinches* (bed bugs), but the vast majority of accommodations are on top of the matter, both to prevent and contain infestations. Still, if you're worried about bed bugs, consider traveling with permethrin-treated sleeping bag liners or sleeping sheets.

Ticks

Ticks are rarely discussed on the Camino, but they do exist, and in both southwestern France and northern Spain some can carry Lyme disease. Some *peregrinos* have picked up ticks when they wander off the trail for a bathroom break in the tall grasses (another reason to avoid relieving yourself on the side of the trail!). In rainy warm seasons, especially spring, they are a greater issue. If you get a tick and don't know the proper way to remove it, seek the assistance of a *hospitalero*, pharmacist, or medical clinic. Remove it immediately and disinfect the area.

Blister Prevention and Foot Care
Blisters can usually be prevented if you make sure that your hiking shoes fit you perfectly before leaving home. Test them with a few 10-15 mile (16-24 kilometer) walks at home to be certain that they don't begin to chafe when your feet get warm and swell. It's also smart to wear socks specifically woven for blister prevention. Also, make sure your pack weight is within or under the advised 10-15 percent of your body weight. As you walk, get in the habit of stopping every 5-6 kilometers (3-4 miles) to rest, take off your shoes and socks, and let them and your feet air dry before putting them back on. On rainy days when this is not possible, I like to have that extra pair—that third pair that is not drying from washing or already on my feet—of dry socks to pull from my pack and put on.

If you do get blisters, wash your feet well and let them dry, then see what the extent of the blister(s) is. If mild, some swear by Compeed or other form of second skin as a good protective barrier, but inquire with a pharmacist and see what they may offer or advise. If the blister is more extensive, seek the aid of an experienced *hospitalero* or pharmacist to help treat it, often with a sterilized needle to puncture and drain it. You will want to keep the blister free of infection and minimize any further irritation so that it will heal quickly.

Stretching
Many leg, knee, ankle, and back injuries on the Camino can be prevented

by a daily habit of stretching, especially when you have finished the day and want to collapse after a hot shower. Be sure to fit in 5-10 minutes of stretching and you should be able to prevent the vast majority of muscle and joint ailments that can plague pilgrims.

Festivals and Events

Public Holidays
On public national holidays in Spain (listed below), some places may be closed:

- **New Year's Day:** January 1

- **Epiphany** (Three Kings' Day): January 6

- **Carnival:** A few days, and especially the Tuesday, before Ash Wednesday and the start of Lent usually within February or March

- **Semana Santa:** the week leading up to Easter Sunday

- **Worker's Day:** May 1

- **Saint John's Night:** June 23, **Saint John's Day:** June 24

- **Assumption of Mary:** August 15

- **Spanish National Day:** October 12

- **All Saints' Day:** November 1

- **Constitution Day:** December 6

- **Immaculate Conception:** December 8

- **Christmas Day:** December 25

Festivals
January

- **Festival of the San Ildefonso** (Jan. 23,

Festivals During Easter

- **Semana Santa** (week leading up to and including Easter Sunday): León is one of the best places on the Camino in which to experience Semana Santa (Holy Week). The town erupts with processions and floats, and locals feast and stay up all night.

- **Os Ancares Cheese Festival** (week leading up to and including Easter Sunday): Festival of local cheese held in one of three locations near O Cebreiro. Sample cheese, sausage, and other local products, and partake in song, folkloric dance, and a midday festive meal.

- **San Guillermo's Feast Day** (Thurs. before Easter, Obanos): Blessing of San Guillermo, with religious rituals accompanied by wine.

- **Festival del Aguardiente** (Easter weekend, Portomarín): Festival of the local spirit *orujo*, with traditional dances and music, and plenty of opportunities to taste *orujo* and experience the *queimada* ritual.

Camponaraya): Mid-winter festival of the village patron saint.

- **San Tirso's Festival** (Jan. 28, Palas de Rei): Celebration of the town's patron saint.

- **Fiesta del Cocido del Porco Celta** (last weekend in Jan., Sarria): Celtic pork festival, celebrating dishes made from the native Galician pig.

March

- **Cheese Festival** (early Mar., Arzúa)

April

- **Feira do Queixo** (late Apr., Palas de Rei): Cheese festival celebrating the region's *queso de Ulloa*.

- **Fiestas del Santo** (late Apr.-mid May, Santo Domingo de la Calzada): Feast days of patron saint Santo Domingo de la Calzada, with a lot of eating and evening processions throughout town.

- **Romería de la Virgen del Puente** (Apr., Sahagún): Celebration of the produce of the land and of spring, unofficially called the *romería del pan y queso* (bread and cheese pilgrimage).

May

- **Fiesta de Melindres** (mid May, Melide): Two-day festival of the anise-laced local cookies.

- **Las Fiestas del Calle del Laurel** (last week of May, Logroño): *Pintxos/pinchos* and wine celebration on a pub-packed street.

June

- **Festividad de San Bernabó** (June 11, Logroño): Festival honoring Logroño's patron saint, Bernabó, with a communal feast of stew, bread, and wine for the city's poorest members.

- **Fiesta de San Juan de Sahagún** (June 12-13, Sahagún): Celebration of the town's patron saint.

- **Fiesta de San Juan** (June 21-25, Sarria): Five-day celebration of Saint John, with music, dance, folkloric and religious processions, and bullfights.

- **Fiesta de San Juan** (June 24, Castrojeriz): Saint John's Festival, celebrating both the summer solstice and Saint John the Baptist's feast day.

- **Medieval Festival** (June, Hospital de Órbigo): Reenactment of a famous jousting tournament with jousting, food, drink, and fanfare.

July

- **Fiesta de la Virgen de la Peregrina,** (July 2, Sahagún): Processions, traditional folkloric groups, bonfires, and festive foods.

- **Fiesta de los Sanfermines** (July 6-14, Pamplona) The famed running of the bulls, originally in honor of the town's patron saint, San Fermín. It's a massive party.

- **Festival de Santiago** (July 15-31, Santiago de Compostela): Saint James's feast day, July 25, is so big it's celebrated over a couple weeks, with music, art exhibits, and theater productions.

- **Fiesta de Ajo** (mid-July, Castrojeriz): Garlic festival.

- **Feria del Queso** (third week in July, Fromista): Cheese fair where you can taste the artisanal cheeses and meats produced in the region.

- **Fiesta de Nuestra Señora del Carmen** (July 21, Melide): Animated festivities of music, dance, processions, and foods.

- **Fiesta de la Magdalena** (July 22, Castrillo de los Polvazares): Mary Magdalene's feast day. Locals dress in traditional Maragato attire, and there are processions with the icon of Mary Magdalene, along with music, song, dance, and festive foods.

- **Festa da Praia** (last weekend in July, Finisterre): Beach festival, with food, song, and festivities.

- **Fiesta del Carmen** (last Sun. in July,

Muxía): Maritime procession from Muxía across the estuary to the village of Camariñas.

- **Fería de Alfarería y Cerámica** (July, Navarette): Ceramics fare with local wares.

August

- **Fiesta de la Almeja** (early Aug., Corcubión): Clam festival, with clam tastings complimented with crisp white wines.

- **Mary's Assumption into Heaven** (Aug. 15, Santo Domingo de la Calzada): Feast day for the town's patroness.

- **Fiesta de San Roque** (Aug. 15-21, Melide): A week of animated festivities of music, dance, processions, and foods.

- **Fiesta del Fin del Camino** (third weekend in Aug., Finisterre): End of the Camino Festival that doubles as a festival of anchovies, with eating, drinking, dancing, and chances to sample the local delicacy.

- **El Misterio de Obanos** (late Aug., Obanos): Reenactment of a local legend, involving the whole village as the stage and its inhabitants as the cast.

September

- **Celebration of Mary's Birth** (Sept. 8, Roncesvalles): Region-wide festivities centered in one of the most important Marian sanctuaries in the Pyrenees.

- **Festival of Santa Maria das Areas** (Sept. 8, Finisterre): Honoring the town patroness with processions, song, and feasting.

- **Fiesta de Sejo** (second Sun. in Sept., Castrojeriz): Celebration of the town patroness, with processions and folk traditions in music, dance, and food.

- **Virxe da Barca Romería** (between Sept. 9 and 15., Muxía): Pilgrimage and festival honoring the Virxe da Barca, Our Lady of the Boat, that brings people from all across Galicia.

- **Santa María la Real** (Sept. 15-18, Nájera): Local celebration with processions, concerts, and food.

- **Fiesta de Gracias** (Sept. 18, Santo Domingo de la Calzada): Harvest festival of thanks, during which an image of Mary is carried in procession through town.

- **Fiestas de San Mateo and Fiesta de la Vendimia** (third weekend in Sept. and centered on Sept. 21, Logroño): Festival of the wine harvest, with copious food and wine and eruptive cheer interspersed with serious blessings and gratitude.

- **Festival of La Soledad** (third weekend in Sept., Camponaraya): Celebration of the village patroness, La Soledad. Often coincides with the wine harvest.

- **Fiesta de San Fermín Chiquito** (Sept. 25, Pamplona): Compared to the running of the bulls, a smaller, more solemn, and religious festival to honor San Fermín, with a much more intimate and local flavor (and no bull runs).

October

- **Fiesta del Pimiento Riojano** (last Sun. in Oct., Nájera) Celebrating the flavorful piquant little red pepper in Riojan cuisine.

- **Fiesta de la Castaña** (Oct., Samos): Chestnut festival, with chances to try

soups, breads, pastries, candies, and preserves made with the native nut.

- **Ecological fair** (Oct., Arzúa) Natural, local, and organic products and services.

December

- **Ferias de la Concepción** (typically around the 6th to the 9th of Dec., Santo Domingo de la Calzada): Celebration with an atmospheric medieval market and Camino market highlighting thousand-year-old arts, crafts, foods, music, dance, and theater.

Practical Details

Language

Spanish is the primary language (and French, for those flying into France or starting in Saint-Jean-Pied-de-Port). **Basque** is a main language with **French** and Spanish in Basque Country and in Navarra. **Gallego** is the most-spoken language in Galicia, a language closer to Portuguese than Spanish. But everywhere, Spanish is understood.

Though the Spanish largely do not speak English, except in the upper-scale hotels and restaurants, this is changing more and more. The Spanish are remarkably helpful and willing to go above and beyond to help visitors, even those visitors lacking a lot of language skills themselves. Still, learn a little Spanish and it will deepen your experience.

Money

Be sure to alert your bank and your credit card company before you depart; let them know the days of your trip so that your cards will not be blocked from use once you land.

Cash and ATMs

The Camino is pretty much a **cash economy,** and it's smart to have an average of **€200** in your pocket, an amount you can replenish with a debit card at ATMs along the way in major cities, large and small towns, and some large villages. I also like to draw money from the ATM during open bank hours, and from a machine on the premises of the bank office —some also have machines inside in a more sheltered area of their entrance or lobby. That way, if there is an issue, I can get help right away.

You can withdraw a maximum of €300 per day from Spanish ATMs; this should last 10-12 days for those with modest budgets of €25-30/day, and 6-7 days for those with budgets of €40-50/day. Some banks may charge a fee; if so, they will always post what it is as you are about to withdraw, so that you can choose to continue or to cancel the transaction. Your home bank may also charge fees for ATM withdrawals, which is a good thing to look into before leaving. Remember also to inform your bank and your credit card company about the dates and countries you'll visit, so that they will not block the card when you begin to use it abroad.

ATM keypads in Europe are numerical, with no letters, so if your PIN code is something you remember using four letters, be sure to look at a keypad before leaving so you can translate the letters to their corresponding numbers on the same keys.

Credit Cards

It is smart to have an emergency **credit card** tucked in a safe place, or to use on a splurge such as, say, staying in a five-star establishment where credit cards are certainly accepted. The chip-and-pin card is the most common card style in use in France and Spain, but if you have a chip-and-signature or magnetic strip-style card, this should not pose a problem as long as the transaction is with a vendor who can enter the number manually to complete a transaction. It may pose a problem at self-service vending machines with no human attendants, such as gas pumps and train ticket kiosks. **Visa,** followed by **MasterCard,** are the two most widely used and accepted credit cards. While *albergues,* most rural and family-run pensions and *hostales,* and many bars and cafés only accept cash, credit cards are more accepted in urban and upscale restaurants and hotels, at tourist sights, and in tourist shops.

Exchange Rates

Though exchange rates fluctuate, approximate exchange rates are:

- **USA:** €1= $1.17 (USD, €0.85/$1)

- **Canada:** €1= $1.54 (CAN, €0.65/$1)

- **United Kingdom:** €1= £0.89 (GBP, €1.12/£1)

- **Australia:** €1= $1.58 (AUD, €0.63/$1)

- **New Zealand:** €1= $1.72 (NZD, €0.58/$1)

- **South Africa:** €1= R0.58 (ZAR/Rand, €0.58/R1)

Budget Per Day

A minimum budget of **€25-30 per day** will cover staying in *albergues* and enjoying a mix of meals, from purchasing groceries and cooking your own to also enjoying a communal meal at the albergue or *menú del peregrino* for dinner each day.

A royal budget of **€100 per day** will let you stay in all ranges of accommodations, except for the most opulent, and eat anywhere you desire. But if you stayed in *albergues* some days and modest pensiones and *hostales* on others, this budget will help you cover a night per week in a parador or other luxury hotel.

And best, in the middle, an average budget of **€40-50 per day** for food and lodging allows for mixing it up and staying in all the types of accommodations available, and also enjoying some of the best restaurants on the Camino. Some days you may want to stay in an albergue but splurge on a special meal, and other days you may stay in a nice hotel but then go for the budget-minded *menú del peregrino.*

Communications
WiFi

Wifi is becoming ubiquitous all along the Camino. (Meanwhile, public computers and internet cafés are on the decline.) And while some locals (especially some *albergues* in Saint-Jean-Pied-de-Port and the refuge in Orisson) believe pilgrims should disconnect, most *albergues,* especially the privately run ones, have succumbed to pilgrim demand for wifi, although the signal isn't necessarily always very strong. WiFi, when available, is free to paying customers in cafes and bars and to guests in *albergues* and other accommodations.

Cell Phones

If you want to bring your phone, check with your service provider to see if you can use your phone abroad and what the fees will be. If your phone is unlocked, you can purchase a Spanish SIM card with a Spanish phone number after arriving (such as at Orange, Movistar, and Vodafone) to use for the duration of your trip, paying as you go with top up-minutes that you can purchase at the mobile network stores along the way. In the more modern *albergues,* dorm beds, more and more, each have their own personal plug so that you can recharge your device overnight.

Mobile phone reception is nearly ubiquitous all along the Camino, and strongest near settlements. At times there may be brief patches of no service in the more remote stretches through less populated areas, such as when crossing the Pyrenees from Orisson to Roncesvalles, a patch here and there in the valley from Roncesvalles to Pamplona, parts of crossing León's mountains from the Cruz de Ferro to El Acebo, and on small sections of the Camino Finisterre trail toward the coast after leaving Santiago de Compostela.

Phone Calls

If calling from within the country (France or Spain), you should not need to dial the international country code (+33 for France, and +34 for Spain) before dialing the 9-digit number. In Spain, the first three digits of the nine-digit phone numbers are the regional or area code. If it begins with a "9" it is a landline, and if it begins with a "6" or "7" it is a cell phone.

Note that you can dial the emergency number, **112,** from any phone.

Travel Advice

Solo Trekkers and Women Trekkers

Spain and the Camino are generally quite safe for female and solo trekkers, but it's important to remain vigilant, as you would anywhere in the world.

Harassment, verbal or otherwise, is also rare, though with the increasing popularity of the route, some women have reported receiving unwanted advances, such as groping, and (on much rarer occasions) assault. Authorities take such incidents seriously and ask that you report them right away by dialing **112**. You can also go directly to the local police (and *hospitaleros* can help you or take you there). The Spanish police also have a non-emergency hotline for visitors—**902-102-112**—with operators speaking several languages, including English.

If you want an extra measure of security, you can ask to join **Camigas,** an all-women's network (a closed group on Facebook) of female pilgrims. Through the network, you can ask advice, or even find other women to walk with.

LGBTQ+ Travelers

The Spanish in general, and the Camino culture in particular, is open minded and tolerant, and celebrates diversity. Spain was the fourth nation in the world to legalize gay marriage, in 2005, and legalized adoption by same-sex couples in 2006. LGBTQ+ travelers will probably find more tolerance and ease here than back home. Pilgrims are a diverse mix (hailing from more than 140 countries) but overall the community is open and tolerant.

At the same time, whether heterosexual or not, people do not show too much romantic affection in public, not even kissing lightly on the lips, so all couples may want to practice discretion.

While *albergues* offer little privacy, same-sex couples will not have a problem getting a private room together, and few Spanish innkeepers will have an issue with it. There is no specific Camino network for LGBTQ+ travelers, but the all-inclusive and very supportive Camino Forum (www.caminodesantiago.me) is a good place to read other pilgrims' experiences, ask any questions that concern you, and get a balanced response.

Travelers of Color

Spain is an open and tolerant culture, and most of its citizens are very welcoming to people of all ethnicities and nationalities. Travelers may be surprised to hear Spaniards refer to someone by physical or national attribute, and anything is game: *la morena* (the brown one), *la gorda* (the fat one), *el rubio* (the blond one), *la negra* (the black one), *el Americano* (the American), *el chino* (the Chinese), *la chica* (the girl), la guapa/el guapo (the pretty/handsome one) and the like. However, no harm is meant by this. The Camino is also riotously diverse, and there are many people from all around the world, especially Europe, Asia, and Latin America, walking it. Within the local and international community of the Camino, people of color will most likely experience total ease and welcome, though there may be the rare occasion where you are seen by a villager or other pilgrim as "exotic," especially if you are of African descent.

The Camino Forum (www.caminodesantiago.me) is also a good community of pilgrims to read other pilgrims' experiences and ask any questions that concern you about walking the Camino. A good Camino memoir that shares the experience of walking the Camino as African Americans is *No Complaints . . . Shut Up and Walk*, by Emmett and Jasmyne Williams.

The Camino with Children

Walking the Camino may be one of the best things a family can do together. The Spanish culture is oriented toward children and family, and Spaniards love it when they see a multi-generational tribe on the trail. Almost everywhere you go on the Camino, you and your children will probably receive a lot of attention, cheer, and help, both from Spaniards and from other *peregrinos*. All accommodations, including *albergues,* are open to children.

Depending on the age of your children, you will want to think about the distance to walk each day. Be sure to take breaks and have snacks and water for rest stops in between cafés.

A good view into the experience of walking as a family with children is from World Towning, a nomadic family of four who walked the Camino in 2018 and beautifully documented their day-to-day trek on several YouTube videos (www.worldtowning.com; start with Episode 68, "Ready to Begin: Camino de Santiago Vlog").

Senior Travelers

The Camino is becoming as much a rite of passage for reflecting on life and deciding the next chapter for older people as it is a "gap year" for younger people. On average, 24 percent of pilgrims are 60 and older.

One of the splendors of staying in *albergues* is meeting people of all ages, from toddlers as young as two to seniors nearing 90. Additionally, Spanish culture shows a lot of respect toward older people, and help is always available should you desire it.

While the Camino is demanding, it is also well supported. It's a long-distance test of persistence, pacing, and patience, more than it is a test of sheer physical strength or speed. The stretches that challenge younger people, such as the first day of crossing the Pyrenees and the area around O Cebreiro, will also be the stretches where senior pilgrims will want to take extra care. Be sure to prepare physically in advance of your trip, and continue a regimen of daily stretching throughout.

Disability Access on the Camino

While it requires serious planning, many persons with mobility restrictions, whether cane, crutch, or wheelchair, have done the Camino. Not all sections are passable or advisable, but large sections are, including the last 100 kilometers (62 miles). While not all facilities are accessible to those in wheelchairs, awareness and support for handicapped *peregrinos* is increasing. Some services offer special planning points (as well as route planning and pack transfer) for those doing the Camino with a wheelchair, such as the Santiago de Compostela-based **Pilgrim** (www.pilgrim.es). The UK pilgrims' association, **Confraternity of Saint James**, offers good considerations for those with disabilities in planning and doing the Camino, including links to lists of *albergues* with accessibility, route maps, and other important planning tools (https://www.csj.org.uk/question/pilgrimage-for-people-with-disabilities/).

Ambitious pilgrims using canes, crutches, or wheelchairs can traverse the full Camino with appropriate training and protection. You may want to bridge difficult sections—the Pyrenees and the mountains of León, for instance—with a taxi or bus. Those doing the Camino in a wheelchair will, about half the time, like cyclists, follow the roads when the trail is too rocky or narrow, or when it's an uneven foot path, though this prospect is more treacherous in a wheelchair than on a bike, as drivers are less likely to expect or see a wheelchair. (Many who opt to do the whole Camino in a wheelchair do it in sections and/or have friends and family accompany them.) Like many pilgrims in general, most pilgrims with mobility issues begin in Sarria and make the final 115-kilometer (71-mile) trek into Santiago de Compostela, which is the most accommodating section of the Camino, and the one where you will likely not need a taxi or bus unless you feel like it. Moreover, pilgrims are a very helpful group and many will be on hand to offer assistance in a pinch.

Resources

Pilgrim Associations

Nearly every country has its own pilgrim association that is a community of information and support, both before and after walking the Camino. Many also have an official pilgrim's credential that they can send you for a small fee. The two core associations are those in **France** (La Société Française des Amis de Saint Jacques de Compostelle, www.compostell.asso.fr) and **Spain** (Federación Española de Asociaciones de Amigos del Camino de Santiago, www.caminosantiago.org). In English-speaking nations, some of the largest pilgrim associations are:

• In the **USA**: American Pilgrims on the Camino, www.americanpilgrims.org

- In **Canada**: The Canadian Company of Pilgrims, www.santiago.ca/contact-us/

- In the **UK**: The Confraternity of Saint James (CSJ), www.csj.org.uk

- In **Ireland**: Camino Society Ireland, www.caminosociety.com

- In **Australia** and **New Zealand**: Australian Friends of the Camino, www.afotc.org

- In **South Africa**: Confraternity of St. James South Africa, www.csjofsa.za.org

- In the **Netherlands**: Genootschap van Sant Jacob, www.santiago.nl/english/intro

Lists of Accommodations

In all, there are over 800 places to stay on the Camino, and more are opening each year. If you begin your Camino in Saint-Jean-Pied-de-Port, the **Pilgrim's Welcome Office** hands out a free complete listing of all *albergues* on the Camino from there to Santiago de Compostela, efficiently condensed into a three-page (front and back) document. **Camino Forum** (www.caminodesantiago.me/community/resources) also offers a free, current and nearly complete listing of *albergues* online (look for the regularly updated PDF titled "All Albergues on the Camino Francés").

Three free and basic online guides offering interactive maps and altitudes of the Camino also strive to keep current lists of accommodations, some with direct links to maps, websites, and for some, direct bookings on Booking.com. These are:

Eroski Consumer (www.caminodesantiago.consumer.es/los-caminos-de-santiago/frances)
Gronze (www.gronze.com/camino-frances)
Forwalk (www.santiago.forwalk.org)

Pack Transfer Services

There are many transfer services that will pick up your pack from the place you stayed and deliver it to the next stopping point if you have reservations and know where you are staying each day. Many accommodations work with the transfer services and have their bag tags there for you to use. These services let you reserve online ahead of time, or as you go; fees can range from €4-10 per daily transfer. Two of most common ones are **Jacotrans** (www.jacotrans.es/en; €7/daily transfer) and the Spanish postal service, **Los Correos** (www.elcaminoconcorreos.com/en; €4/daily transfer). The Los Correos website also has a lot of great tips for walking the Camino from postal workers who have done the pilgrimage themselves.

Trekking Supply Stores

The large sporting goods store **Decathlon** (www.decathlon.com) has locations in France and Spain, including in **Pamplona**, **Estella**, **Logroño**, **Burgos**, and **Santiago de Compostela**.

In **Saint-Jean-Pied-de-Port**, right in the heart of the medieval town next to many of the *albergues*, the **Boutique du Pelerin** (32 Rue de la Citadelle; 559-379-852; www.boutique-du-pelerin.com) can supply anything you may have forgotten or offer good advice about what you really need.

In **Pamplona** is the excellent **Caminoteca** (Calle Curia, 15; 948-210-316; www.caminoteca.com), 50 meters (164 feet) off the Camino in the old town near the cathedral. They carry gear and supplies tailored to pilgrim needs and also offer loads of advice at this early stage to help you fine-tune and adjust your Camino.

The Camino-oriented trekking store **Planeta Agua** (www.planeta-agua.com) has stores in **Zubiri, Viana, Logroño,** and **Santo Domingo de la Calzada;** all are on or near the Camino as it passes through these towns.

Near the train station, **K2 Planet** (Avenida Doctor Fleming, 20; 987-804-196; www.k2planet.com) in **León** has been outfitting people for the Camino since 1989 and is great for equipment as well as advice.

In **Sarria**, **Peregrinoteca** (Calle Benigno Quiroga, 16; 982-530-190; www.peregrinoteca.com) carries the latest trekking gear and is right on the Camino as you enter the town.

Maps

For paper maps, **Michelin Camino de Santiago** (Map 160) creates a light map book detailing day-to-day stages of the Camino, with the trail marked out on a detailed topographical map. John Brierley also puts out a light maps and accommodations listings-only book, **Camino de Santiago—Maps**. For digital maps, **Eroski Consumer** (www.caminodesantiago.consumer.es/los-caminos-de-santiago/frances), **Gronze** (www.gronze.com/camino-frances), and **Forwalk** (www.santiago.forwalk.org) offer digital maps for use on an internet browser or app format for any tablet device.

Glossary

Unless otherwise noted, terms are in Spanish.

A

abajo: down, below
abierto: open
aduana: customs
aeropuerto: airport
albergue: pilgrim's hostel
aldea: hamlet
alimento: food
almuerzo: lunch
alrededores: outskirts
alto: hill or height
arriba: up, above
arroya: stream
aseo: toilet (public bathrooms in bars, cafes, restaurants, and stations; can also be *servicios*)
auberge (French): pilgrim's hostel
autobús: bus
autopista: highway
ayuda: assistance

B

banco: bank
baño: bathroom (of a hotel/*hostal* room or private home)
barrio: neighborhood
bastón: walking stick/pole
bebida: soft drink
bien: good, well

billete: ticket, banknote
bocadillo: sandwich
bolsa: bag (shopping), purse
bolso: pocket, purse
bosque: forest
botillo: smoked pork sausage from El Bierzo
buen, bueno, buena: good

C

cajero: cashier
cajero automático: ATM
calcetines: socks
Caldeirada: bouillabaisse-like fish stew from Galicia and Portugal
caldo: broth
caldo Gallego: Galician soup made of beans, pork, and leafy greens
caliente: hot
calle: street
cama: bed
camarero: waiter
cambio: change, exchange
capilla: chapel
carnet de pèlerin (French): see *credencial del peregrino*
carretera: road, highway
casco antiguo: historic center
castillo: castle
castro: round hilltop fortress
catedral: cathedral
cena: dinner
cerca: near

cerrado: closed
chinches: bed bugs
Chi-Rho: an early symbol of Christ, formed by overlapping the first two letters of Christ's name in Greek
ciudad: city or large town
coche: car
cocido: stew
Codex Calixtinus: 12th-century guide to the Camino
col: mountain pass (in the romance language of Occitan)
comida: meal
Compostela: certificate completing the pilgrimage, collected at the church in Santiago de Compostela
concha: shell
conductor: driver
consulado: consulate
convento: convent
correos: post office
correspondencia: connection (train, bus, plane)
corto: short glass of beer
costa: coast
credencial del peregrino: pilgrim's passport; the document that allows trekkers to stay in albergues and collect a Compostela at the end of their journey (if they gather enough stamps)
crucero or **cruceiro:** roadside cross
cuajada: yogurt-like custard
cuarto: room
cuenta: bill, check, tab
cueva: cave

DE

dentro: inside, in
derecha: right (direction)
derecho: straight, law
desayuno: breakfast
descuento: discount
destino: destination (also destiny)
dinero: money
donativo: donation
dormitorio: dormitory
edificio: building
église (French): church
embajada: embassy
entrada: entrance

entrée (French): entrance
ermita: hermitage
estacionamiento: parking
estación: station
estación de autobus: bus station
estación de tren/ferrocaril: train station
Euskadi (Basque): Basque Country
euskara (Basque): the Basque language
excursión: excursion

FG

farmacía: pharmacy
fermé (French): closed
ferrocaril: railway, railroad
flecha: arrow
frio: cold
fuente: fountain
fuera: outside, out
gracias: thank you
gratuito: free (cost)
granja: farm
guía: guide

HI

habitación: room
horario: timetable, schedule
horreo: stone granary on stilts; common in Galicia
hospitalero/hospitalera: albergue staff (male/female)
hostal: family-run inn
iglesia: church
izquierda: left (direction)

LMN

lejos: far
lesker (Basque): you're welcome
libre: free (unoccupied)
librería: bookshop
llegada: arrival
maleta: suitcase
manta: blanket
mapa: map, plan
meiga: traditional herbalist/healer from León and Galicia
menú del peregrino: pilgrim's menu; a basic three-course meal offered in local restaurants and albergues
meseta: plateau
mercado: market

merci (French): thank you
milsker (Basque): thank you
misa: Mass
mochila: backpack
monasterio: monastery (can also refer to a convent)
moneda: cash, money, coin
monja: nun
monje: monk
monumento: monument
mozárabe: Islamic architectural style by Iberian Christians from the south in Christian Spain
mudéjar: Islamic architectural style by Iberian Muslim builders in Christian Spain
museo: museum
noticias: news

OPQR

océano: ocean
orujo: after-dinner drink
ouvert (French): open
palloza: traditional Galician round stone house with a thatched roof
panadería: bakery
parada: bus stop/subway stop/taxi stop
paradores: historic former monasteries that have been converted into state-run hotels
parque: park
pasaporte: passport
paseo: walk
pastelería: pastry shop
pèlerin/pèlerine (French): pilgrim (male/female)
peligro: danger
peregrino/peregrina: pilgrim (male/female)
periódico: newspaper
pimientos de Padrón: Little green peppers sautéed in olive oil and served with a dash of salt. In an order, about one in ten is hot and the rest are sweet.
pincho: appetizer, snack
pintxos: Basque spelling of pinchos
piquillos: stuffed roasted peppers
playa: beach
policía: police
potable: drinkable (agua potable: drinkable water)
praia (Gallego): beach

precio: price, cost
pueblo: village or small town, a people (as in el pueblo Español: the Spanish people)
puente: bridge
puerta: door or gate
puerto: pass or port
pulpo: octopus
pulpo á feira: boiled octopus seasoned with Spanish paprika, olive oil, and sea salt
queimada: ritual drink made from *orujo*, lemon and orange peel, coffee beans, and sugar, and lit before drinking
queso: cheese
refuge (French): shelter, albergue
refugio: shelter, albergue
río: river
romanico: Romanesque
romano: Roman
romería: local pilgrimage
ropa: clothes
ruinas: ruins

ST

sábana: bed sheet
sacerdote: priest
salida: departure, exit
santo/santa: saint
santuario: sanctuary
sello: stamp (both a pilgrim's credential stamp and a postage stamp)
semáforo: traffic light
Semana Santa: Holy Week/Easter Week
servicios: toilets (public toilets in bars, cafes, restaurants, and stations; can also be called aseos)
signo: sign
sin alcohol: nonalcoholic
¡socorro!: help!
sopa: soup
sortie (French): exit
taquilla: ticket office
tarjeta: card
tarjeta de crédito: credit card
tienda: shop
toalla: towel
toilettes (French): toilets
torre: tower
tortilla Española: onion-and-potato omelet
tren: train
turismo: tourist office/information

VZ
vendimia: grape (wine) harvest

viña or viñedo: vineyard
vino: wine
zapatos: shoes

Spanish Phrasebook

Common Phrases

Hello. *Good day. Hola. Buenos días.*
Good afternoon. *Buenas tardes.*
Good evening (early evening). *Buenas tardes.*
Good evening (late evening). *Buenas noches.*
Mr./Mrs./Miss. *Señor/Señora/Señorita.*
Please. *Por favor.*
Thank you. *Gracias.*
Goodbye. *Adiós.*
Until later. *Hasta luego.*
Yes. *Sí.*
No. *No.*
How much is . . . *¿Cuantos se cuesta . . . ?*
Please, where is the toilet? (asked in bars, restaurants, and cafés) *¿Por favor donde esta el servicio?*
Please, can you tell me where is . . . *Por favor, puede decirme dónde está . . .*
I need . . . *Necesito . . .*
How are you? *¿Cómo está usted?*
What is your name? *¿Cómo se llama?*
My name is . . . *Me llamo . . .*
I am [a permanent quality, such as English, married, single] . . . *Soy [Inglés, casada/o, soltera/o] . . .*
I am [a temporary state such as lost] . . . *Estoy [perdida/o] . . .*
I don't understand. *No entiendo.*
It's okay/It's not important. *No importa.*
You are very kind. *Usted es muy amable.*
I am tired. *Estoy cansada/o.*
I am hungry. *Tengo hambre.*
I am thirsty. *Tengo sed.*
Do you speak English? *¿Habla usted inglés?*
Please, where can I find . . . *Por favor, dónde puedo encontrar . . .*
To the left. *A la izquierda.*
To the right. *A la derecha.*
Straight ahead. *Todo derecho.*
The time. *La hora* (the hour, as in ¿Que hora es? [What time is it?]) or *el tiempo* (the time, as in *el tiempo del los romanos* [the time of the Romans] or *quiero llegar a tiempo* [I hope to arrive on time]).
The weather. *El tiempo.* (*Hace buen tiempo.* [The weather is good.])
The morning. *La mañana.*
The afternoon and early evening. *La tarde.*
The evening/night. *La noche.*

Transport

I need to go to... *Tengo que irme a...*
Can you please call me a taxi? *¿Puede usted por favor llamame un taxi?*
The bus. *El autobus.*
The train. *El tren.*
The airport. *El aeropuerto.*
The plane. *El avión.*
A taxi. *Un taxi.*
A car. *Un coche.*
The schedule. *El horario.*
A ticket. *Un billete.*
A map. *Un mapa.*

Days and Months

Day/week/month *Día/semana/mes*
Monday *Lunes*
Tuesday *Martes*
Wednesday *Miercoles*
Thursday *Jueves*
Friday *Viernes*
Saturday *Sabado*
Sunday *Domingo*
January *Enero*
February *Febrero*
March *Marzo*
April *Abril*
May *Mayo*
June *Junio*
July *Julio*
August *Agosto*
September *Septiembre*
October *Octubre*
November *Noviembre*

December *Diciembre*

Lodging and Places

Please, I need a bed/a room. Is there one available? *¿Por favor, necesito una cama/ un cuarto. Hay una/uno disponible?*

For one (person) *Para uno.*

For two (people) *Para dos.*

With a private bath *Con baño privado.*

A/the bed *Una/la cama.*

A/the sheet *Una/la sábana.*

A/the towel *Una/la toalla.*

Some toilet paper *Algo de papel higiénico.*

The street *La calle.*

The village/town/city *La aldea/el pueblo/ la ciudad.*

The square *La plaza.*

The church *La iglesia.*

The cathedral *La catedral.*

The monastery/convent *El monasterio/ el convento.*

The intersection. *La intersección.*

The Trail

The path *El camino.*

The yellow arrow *La flecha amarilla.*

A water fountain with drinkable water. *Una fuente con agua potable.*

Food and Drink

I/We would like the menú/combined plate/[dish listed on the menu]. *Me/ Nosotros gustaría el menú (del día, del peregrino)/plato combinado/[dish listed on the menu].*

I would like . . . *Me gustaría . . .*

Water *Agua.*

A mineral water (flat). *Un agua mineral.*

Carbonated mineral water. *Un agua mineral con gas.*

Juice *Zumo.*

Orange juice *Zumo de naranja.*

A beer *Una cerveza.*

A glass of red wine. *Una copa de vino tinto.*

A glass of white wine. *Una copa de vino blanco.*

A glass *Un vaso.*

A bottle *Una botella.*

The dish *El plato.*

The [fixed price] menu *El menú.*

A fork *Un tenedor.*

A spoon *Una cuchara.*

A knife *Un cuchillo.*

Some bread *Algo de pan.*

The soup *La sopa.*

Vegetables *Verduras, and also legumbres.*

Meat *Carne.*

Fish *Pescado.*

Shellfish *Mariscos.*

Vegetarian *Vegetariana/o.*

Vegan *Vegana/o.*

Gluten free *Sin gluten.*

Breakfast *El desayuno.*

Lunch *El almuerzo.*

Dinner *La cena.*

A snack *Un pincho.*

The check, please. *La cuenta por favor.*

Emergency and Assistance

Excuse me. I need help . . . *Disculpame. Necesito ayuda . . .*

Help! *¡Socorro!*

This is an emergency. *Ésto es una emergencía.*

Please call the police/an ambulance. *Por favor llama a la policía/una ambulancía.*

A doctor *Un médico.*

A pharmacy *Una farmacia.*

I don't feel well *No me siento bien.*

Blister *Ampolla.*

Dehydration *Deshidración.*

Fever *Fiebre.*

Cold *Resfriado.*

Flu *Gripe.*

Foot *Pie.*

Knee *Rodilla.*

Ankle *Tobillo.*

Leg *Pierna.*

Back *Espalda.*

Arm *Brazo.*

Wrist *Muñeca.*

Hand *Mano.*

Shoulder *Hombro.*

Neck *Cuello.*

A

A Balsa: 347
accommodations: 486–488, 489, 492; gear to take 478–479; lists and guides 501; *see also* specific places
Agès: 188
Aguiada: 346, 349
Airexe: 376–377
air travel: 477–480
Akerreta: 87–88
Albergue de Santa María (Carrión de los Condes): 15, 196, 233
albergues: general discussion 486–487, 492; etiquette 490–491; gear to take 478–479; list of 58, 501; and pilgrim's credential 485
Alfarería Naharro: 166
Alicornio (unicorn): 262
All Saints Day: 123–124, 379
Almanzor: 468
Alto Altar Mayor: 41, 302
Alto de Erro: 83
Alto del Perdón: 41, 95, 97, 116
Alto de Matagrande: 189
Alto de Mostelares: 41, 222
Alto de San Antón: 166, 168
Alto de Valbuena: 186
Alto do Mar de Ovellas: 434, 436
Alto do Poio: 341
Alto San Roque: 340
Ambasmestas: 330
Amenal: 391, 392–393
Amis du Chemin Saint-Jacques: 58
Amular: 57
Ara Solis (Sun altar): 449, 451
Arca: 391–392
Arcahueja: 251
archaeological ruins and sites: Camino de Santiago 466–467; Castile and León 15, 148, 188, 208–209, 250–251, 466; at Catedral de Santiago de Compostela 406; Galicia 374–375, 382, 384; La Rioja and Castile 148, 179, 188; León and Galicia 268, 296, 310, 318; Pamplona 101; of pilgrimages 412
Arco de San Benito: 241
Arco de Santa Maria: 206
Arleta: 91
Arnéguy: 68
Arroyo de Sanbol: 215
Arzúa: 30, 388–390
Astorga: 284–293; map 285
"Astorga/Camino Way" and "Astorga by Highway": 281–282

Atanasio: 407, 409
Atapuerca archaeological site: 15, 148, 188, 208–209, 466
Atapuerca village: 188, 189, 209
ATMs: 496–497
Augapesada: 436
axis mundi: 301, 376
Ayuntamiento: 287
Azofra: 172–174
Azqueta: 136

B

baggage to take: 476, 478–479
Baixo: 379
Barbadelo: 365–367
Barrio Húmedo ("wet quarter") of León: 12, 256, 271–272
Basajuan and Basandere: 73
Basílica de la Virgen del Camino: 256, 275–276
Basílica del Puy (Basílica de Nuestra Señora del Puy): 132, 133
Basílica de Nuestra Señora de la Encina: 309–310
Basílica de San Isidoro: 256, 268–269
Basque Country and Navarra: 47–91; general discussion 50–54; food and wine 52–53; itineraries 27–29, 51–52; maps 3, 48; overnight stops 50; transportation 54–55; *see also* Navarra
bathrooms on trail: 490
bed bugs: 492
Belorado: 181–182
Benedictine order of Cluny: 469
Bercianos del Real Camino: 244, 245–246
Biblioteca Pública (Burgos): 204
Biduedo: 342–343
biking. Burgos to León 203; Camino by bike 484–485, 490; Pamplona 113; Sarria to Santiago de Compostela 357; Villafranca 326
birds/bird-watching: 143, 176
Biskarreta (Viscarreta): 83, 85
black color: 122, 133
Black Madonnas: 121, 132, 133, 138, 215
Blanca Madonna, La (La Virgen Blanca or Santa María la Blanca): 228–229
blessing of the stones: 298
Boadilla del Camino: 223
bodegas: 197, 228
Bodegas Irache Wine Fountain: 13, 25, 95, 134–135
Boente: 387–388
Boneta Lopetegui, Carmelo: 130

botafumeiro (swinging incense burner): 407–408, 418
Bronze Age: 466
budget per day: 497–498
buen Camino: 491
Burgos: 191, 196, 201–213; accommodation 212; food 210–211; map 202; markets 198, 209–210; sights 203–209; transportation 203, 213
Burguete: 74, 80–82
bus travel: 480–481

C

Cabo Finisterre (Finisterre cape): 21, 41, 444, 447–451, 452, 454
Cacabelos: 318–320
Café Iruña: 103, 104
caldeirada: 432
Calvor: 349
Calzada del Coto: 245
Calzada Romana. *see* Via Romana
Calzadilla de la Cueza: 234–235
Calzadilla de los Hermanillos: 245
Cama del Santo: 451
Camigas: 498
Camino Aragonés: 120
camino de la Virgen, el: 321
Camino de Santiago: general discussion 8–9; car travel 482–484; cultural designation 472; end of 461, 463; experiences on 23; history 466–473; maps by section 2–3, 48, 94, 146, 194–195, 254–255, 352, 430; maps to take 502; markings on trail 485; modern Camino 472, 474; museum to 289; popularity 472, 474; rituals 393, 443, 449; starting points 54, 59, 199, 477; symbolism on 160–161; timeline 473; trail conditions 485
Camino Finisterre: 24, 429–463; general discussion 432–434; food and drink 432; itineraries 44–45, 432–433; maps 2, 430; overnight stops 433; tours from Santiago de Compostela 434; transportation 434
Camino Forum: 499, 501
Camino Francés: 120, 284, 336, 470, 477
Camino Primitivo: 468
Camino Real: 244, 245
Camponaraya: 34, 317–318
Canal de Castilla: 223
Canal de Pisuerga: 223
Canal de Villadangos: 278
Cantigas sculpture: 229–230
Capela a Magdalena: 375
Capela a Virxe do Espino: 454–455
Capela de Nosa Señora das Neves: 439–440
Capela de Nosa Señora do Bo Suceso: 447
Capela de San Mauro: 437

Capela de San Pedro Mártir: 440
Capilla de Condestable: 206
Capilla de la Asunción: 209
Capilla de la Corticela: 399, 408
Capilla de la Virgen del Camino: 102
Capilla del Ciprés: 346
Capilla del Espíritu Santo: 75, 77–78
Capilla del Salvador: 346
Capilla de Morgade: 368
Capilla de San Fermín: 102–103
Capilla de San Marcos: 394–395
Capilla de San Roque (Cacabelos): 318, 319
Capilla de San Roque (Melide): 383
Capilla de Santiago (Burgos): 209
Capilla de Santiago (Roncesvalles): 75, 77
Cardeñuela Riopico: 189, 191
CAREX Experimental Archaeology Center: 209
car rentals: 481
Carrión de los Condes: 231–235; map 232
Carta Perigrina (halfway certificate): 238, 242, 486
car travel: 481–484
Cartuja de Santa María de Miraflores: 191, 203
Casa Botines: 266–268
Casa Consistorial: 101, 106
Casa de Cangas y Pambley: 306
Casa de Onat: 117
Casa Felisa: 143
Casa Museo de Furelos: 381
casas rurales (rural bed and breakfasts): 488
Casco Antiguo de Pamplona: 100–104, 106
Castañares: 191
Castelo: 436
Castildelgado: 180–181
Castile and León: 193–251; general discussion 197–201; food and wine 200–201; itineraries 32–37, 198; maps 2–3, 194–195; overnight stops 197; transportation 199–201; *see also* La Rioja and Castile; León and Galicia
Castillo de Burgos: 205
Castillo de Castrojeriz: 219–220
Castillo de los Templarios: 18–19, 256, 308–309
Castillo de Monjardín: 137
Castillo de Sarracín: 256, 330–331
Castillo de Villafranca: 324
castles: Burgos 205; Castrojeriz 219–220; Ponferrada 18–19, 256, 308–309; Vega de Valcarce 256, 330–331; Villafranca del Bierzo 324; Villamayor de Monjardín 137
Castrexe: 462
Castrillo de los Polvazares: 34, 287, 294–296
Castro Bergidum/Bergida: 319, 321
Castro de Castromaior: 20, 353, 374–375, 467
Castro de Castromiñan: 462
Castro de Santa Susana: 414, 467

Castrojeriz: 30, 34, 217–222; map 218
Castromaior: 373–375
castros: 354, 374, 415, 462, 467
Castro Ventosa: 319, 321
Catedral de Santa María (Astorga): 289
Catedral de Santa María (Burgos): 196, 205–206
Catedral de Santa María de la Redonda: 154–155
Catedral de Santa María de León: 16, 256, 264–265
Catedral de Santa María la Real: 95, 100–101
Catedral de Santiago de Compostela: 20, 399, 404, 406–409; construction and tomb of Saint James 403, 404, 406, 468, 469
Catedral de Santo Domingo de la Calzada: 147, 176–177
cedar tree: 457
Cee: 440–441
cell phones: 498
Celtic-Speakers and Celtiberians: 466–467
Centro de Interpretación Templaria Medieval: 301
certificate of completion. *see* Compostela
Cesar Borgia tomb: 141
chapels: Basque Country and Navarra 75, 77–78; Castile and León 206, 209; Finisterre and Muxía 437, 439–440, 447, 454–455; Galicia 368, 375, 383, 394, 395; León and Galicia 318, 319, 346; Navarra 102–103; Santiago de Compostela 399, 408; *see also* specific chapels
Charlemagne (Charles the Great): 68, 74, 77, 78, 468
Charlemagne's chessboard: 77
cheese: Basque Country and Navarra 52; Castile and León 30, 200, 242; festivals 30, 225, 338, 378, 389, 494; Galicia 30, 358, 378, 388–389; La Rioja and Castile 154; León and Galicia 266–267, 330, 338, 494; Santiago de Compostela 358, 406, 421–422
chestnut forest: 256, 327
children, traveling with: 499
Chi-Rho symbol: 114, 115, 125, 130, 268–269, 409
chocolate and cacao: 288, 291
churches: Basque Country and Navarra 49, 57, 59, 68, 70, 76, 81, 85, 86, 87, 88–89, 91; Castile and León 196, 203–205, 206, 214, 215, 216, 218–219, 220, 223, 225, 227, 228–230, 231–232, 235, 236, 237, 239–240, 241, 245–246, 249, 250; Finisterre and Muxía 431, 435, 438–439, 440, 441–442, 447–448, 454, 456–457, 459, 462, 463; Galicia 353, 358–359, 365–366, 368, 370–372, 373, 377–378, 379, 381–382, 383–384, 386–387, 389, 391; La Rioja and Castile 14, 147, 151, 153–154, 156–158, 165, 167, 172–173, 174, 179, 180, 181, 182, 183, 187–188, 189; León and Galicia 260, 264, 269, 282, 289–290, 293, 295, 296, 298, 302, 305, 310–312, 317, 318, 319, 321, 322–324, 330, 333, 336, 339–340, 341, 344, 347, 348; Navarra 13, 95, 101–104, 114, 115, 116, 117, 119–120, 121–122, 123, 125, 126, 127, 128–132, 133, 137, 138, 139–140, 141–142, 311; Santiago de Compostela 399, 413–416, 426–427; *see also* basilicas; catedrals; chapels; specific churches
Cirauqui: 124–125
Cirueña: 174
Citadelle, La: 41, 49, 57–58
Ciudadela, La: 104–105
Cize Pass: 64
Cizur Menor: 114–115
clean-up of Camino: 236
Codex Calixtinus: at Catedral de Santiago de Compostela 406, 470; description and history 470; places referred to 72, 124, 135, 176, 297, 343, 365; and 13 stages 484
Col de Bentartea: 67
Col de Lepoeder: 12, 41, 49, 51, 67
Colegiata de Santa María: 324
Colegio de San Jerónimo: 411
Columbrianos: 316
Compostela (certificate of completion): earning of 23, 24, 357, 486; Fisterra and Muxía 417, 432, 444, 457, 486; halfway certificate 238, 242, 486; in Santiago de Compostela 402, 407, 409, 417, 485; stamps 357, 486; *see also* credentials
Compostilla: 315–316
Convento de las Concepcionistas: 310
Convento de San Marcos: 269
Convento de San Nicolás: 324
Convento de Santa Clara: 221
corbels: 225, 312, 381, 411
Corcubión: 30, 441–443
Corticela capilla, La: 399, 408
Costa da Morte: 443, 444, 447
Cova Eirós: 343
credentials (*credencial do/del peregrino* or pilgrim passport): 24, 58, 417, 444, 485–486; *see also* Compostela
credit cards: 497
crowds on Camino: 356, 357
Cruceiro de Armada: 439, 440
Cruceiro de Lameiros: 376
Cruceiro do Melide: 383
Crucero/Cruceiro de Santo Toribio: 281, 283
Crucero del Santo Cristo: 306
Cruz Blanca, La (Roland's Cross): 80
Cruz de Ferro: 299–301; leaving a stone 17, 25, 256, 257, 300–301
Cruz de Thibault: 67
Cuesta de Matamulos: 41, 214

cuisine: *see* food
curanderas and curanderos: 380
cypress tree: 346

D

Dia de Todos los Santos (All Saints Day): 123–124, 379
Díaz, Jimena: 204, 205
disabilities, travelers with: 500
Ditch Pigs clean-up: 236
dolmens: 466
Domus Roman Villa Ruins: 286
Don Suero: 280, 281
drinking water: 488, 491
duende: 219
Dugium: 462
Dumbría: 454–455

E

earth goddesses: 74, 184
Easter Sunday and festivals: 270, 338, 494
ecological fair of Arzúa: 389
Église de l'Assomption: 68
Église de Notre Dame du Bout du Pont: 57, 59
Eirexe: 376–377
El Acebo: 302–303
El Burgo Ranero: 246, 248
El Cid (Rodrigo Díaz de Vivar): 204, 205, 206, 468
El Ganso: 297
emergency assistance: 491–492, 498
emigration monument: 444
*el encierro (*running of the bulls): 34, 101, 105, 106–107
equinoxes: 187, 188
equipment and pack: 476, 478–479, 501–502
Ermita de Ecce Homo: 293–294
Ermita de la Plaza: 177
Ermita de la Virgen de Gracía: 248–249
Ermita de la Virgen del Puente: 237–238
Ermita de la Virgen del Río: 228
Ermita de la Virgen del Socorro: 227
Ermita del Divino Cristo: 316–317
Ermita de Nuestra Señora de la Plaza: 175–176
Ermita de Nuestra Señora de Perales: 244–245
Ermita de San Blas y San Roque: 316
Ermita de San Esteban: 137
Ermita de San Miguel (near Villatuerta): 127
Ermita de San Miguel (Población de Campos): 227
Ermita de San Nicolás (Puente de Itero): 196, 222–223
Ermita de San Salvador (Obanos): 120
Ermita de San Salvador (Puerto de Ibañeta): 72, 74
Ermita de San Sebastian: 303
Ermita de Santa María del Campo: 180

Ermita de Santiaguiño: 427
Ermita Nuestra Señora de Oca: 184
Ermita San Guillerme: 449, 450–451
Ermita Santa María de Compostilla: 315–316
Ermita Virgen de la Peña: 183
Espinal: 82–83
Espinosa: 183
Estella: 127–134; map 129
etiquette: 490–491
exchange rates: 497

F

façades of Catedral de Santiago de Compostela: 408–409
faro (lighthouse) at Finisterre: 21, 431, 448–449
fauna: 322
Feira do Queixo: 30, 378
Fería de Alfarería y Cerámica: 166
Feria del Queso: 225
Ferias de la Concepción: 30, 178
Ferreiros: 368
ferry transport: 481
Festa da Praia: 30, 451
Festival del Aguardiente: 30, 372, 494
Festival de Santiago (Saint James's feast day): 34, 401, 418
festival in honor of Saint John: 360
festivals and events: annual list 493–496; *see also* specific festivals
Festividad de San Bernabó: 30, 158–159
Fiesta de Ajo: 30, 221
Fiesta de Gracias: 177
Fiesta de la Almeja: 30, 441
Fiesta de la Castaña: 345
Fiesta de la Magdalena: 34
Fiesta de la Soledad: 34
Fiesta de la Vendimia: 30, 147, 158
Fiesta de la Virgen de la Peregrina: 34, 242
Fiesta del Carmen: 34, 459
Fiesta del Cocido del Porco Celta: 30, 360
Fiesta del Fin del Camino: 30, 451
Fiesta de los Sanfermines: 105
Fiesta del Pimiento Riojano: 30, 170
Fiesta de Melindres: 30, 384
Fiesta de Nuestra Señora del Carmen: 384
Fiesta de Queso: 30, 389
Fiesta de San Fermín Chiquito: 105
Fiesta de San Juan (Castrojeriz): 34, 221
Fiesta de San Juan de Sahagún: 34, 242
Fiesta de San Roque: 384
Fiesta de San Xoán: 34
Fiesta de Sejo: 34, 221
Fiestas del Calle del Laurel: 159
Fiestas del Santo: 30, 176
Fiestas de San Mateo: 30, 147, 158

Fillobal: 343

Finca da Rocha: 416

Finisterre: 30, 432, 435, 443–454; cape and lighthouse 21, 41, 431, 444, 447–451, 452, 454; closure ritual 443, 449; kilometer 0 435, 444, 448; map 446; swimming 443, 447

Finisterre, from Hospital: 439–443

Finisterre, to Muxía: 431, 432, 435, 461, 462–463

fish auction: 431, 444

Fisterana: 432, 444, 486

folklore: Basque Country and Navarra 57, 73; Castile and León 219, 225; Finisterre and Muxía 440; Galicia 366, 380; La Rioja and Castile 184; León and Galicia 262

Foncebadón: 299–300

Fonfría: 341–342

Fontaine de Roland: 67

Fonte de Saleta: 388

Fonte do Carme: 427

fonte sagrada (healing fountain): 455–456

food: 488–490; festivals 30; Basque and Navarran specialties 52–53; Castilian specialties 200–201; Galician specialties 358–359; León specialties 266–267; menú del peregrino 375–376, 488–489; Riojan 154–155; see also specific place

foot care and gear: 476, 478, 493

fountain for pilgrims: 157

fountain of Santa Irene: 391

Franco: 472

Fray Bernardino de Sahagún statue: 240

Frixe: 463

Frómista: 223–227

Fuente del Gallo: 215

Fuente de los Moros: 136

Fuentes de Oca: 184

Fuentes Nuevas: 316–317

Furela: 345

Furelos: 381–382

G

Galicia: 351–395; general discussion 354–357; food and wine 358–359, 377; itineraries 40, 42–43, 354–355; maps 2, 352; overnight stops 354; transportation 356–357; see also León and Galicia

Game of the Goose: 121, 156–157, 180, 184, 225, 387, 412

Gañecoleta: 71–72

Gaudí, Antonio: 266, 267–268, 288–289

gear to take: 476, 478–479

Gelmírez, Diego: 411, 415

geography: Basque Country and Navarra 52–53; Castile and León 198–199; Finisterre and Muxía 433; Galicia 355; La Rioja and Castile

149; León and Galicia 258; Navarra 97

glossary and phrasebook: 502–506

Gonzar: 373

goose and goose lore: 160–161, 183, 184, 297; see also Game of the Goose

Grañón: 179–180

Guenduláin church: 115

Guillermo (William, duke of Aquitaine): 117, 119, 120

H

halfway certificate (Carta Perigrina): 238, 242, 486

Hartza: 73

healing fountain (fonte sagrada): 455–456

health and safety: 491–493

Hemingway, Ernest: 80, 103, 104

hermitages: Basque Country and Navarra 72, 74; Castile and León 196, 222–223, 227, 228, 237–238, 244–245, 248–249; Finisterre and Muxia 449, 450–451; La Rioja and Castile 175–176, 177, 180, 183, 184; León and Galicia 293–294, 303, 315–317; Navarra 120, 127, 137; Santiago de Compostela 427; see also specific hermitages

history of the Camino 466–473

Hontanas: 215–216

Honto: 65–66

Hornillos del Camino: 214–215

horreos (granaries): 366, 438

Hospital: 439; to Finisterre 439–443; to Muxía 439, 454–457; from Santiago de Compostela 434, 436–439

Hospital de la Condesa: 340–341

Hospital de la Reina (Hospital de Peregrinos San Antón Abad): 184

Hospital de Órbigo: 34, 276, 279, 280–282

Hospital de San Juan de Acre: 165

Hospital de San Juan ruins: 299

hospitals: 492

Hostal de los Reyes Católicos: 409, 411

hostales: 487

hoteles: 488

Huéspeda de Ánimas ("procession of souls"): 262

human fossils: 208

I

Iglesia and Convento de Santo Domingo: 129–130

Iglesia Colegiata de Nuestra Señora del Manzano: 218–219

Iglesia de la Asunción (Navarete): 165

Iglesia de la Asunción (Rabanal del Camino): 298

Iglesia de la Asunción (Villatuerta): 127

Iglesia de la Colegiata de Santa María: 49, 76

INDEX

Iglesia de la Immaculada Concepción: 216
Iglesia de la Magdalena: 330
Iglesia de la Quinta Angustía: 305
Iglesia de la Transfiguración: 87
Iglesia de la Virgen de la Calle: 180
Iglesia del Crucifijo: 121
Iglesia del Salvador: 245–246
Iglesia del Santo Sepulcro (Estella): 128–129
Iglesia del Santo Sepulcro (Torres del Río): 95, 139–140
Iglesia de Nuestra Señora de la Asunción: 181
Iglesia de Nuestra Señora de la Soledad: 317
Iglesia de Nuestra Señora de los Ángeles: 172–173
Iglesia de San Andrés (Cirueña): 174
Iglesia de San Andrés (La Faba): 333
Iglesia de San Andrés (Villamayor de Monjardín): 137
Iglesia de San Andrés (Zariquiegui): 115
Iglesia de San Bartolomé: 153–154
Iglesia de San Cernin: 101–102
Iglesia de Sancti Spiritus: 383–384
Iglesia de San Esteban (Burgos): 205
Iglesia de San Esteban (Calzada del Coto): 245
Iglesia de San Esteban (Tosantos): 183
Iglesia de San Esteban (Zabaldika): 88–89
Iglesia de San Esteban (Zubiri): 85
Iglesia de San Esteve de Lires: 462
Iglesia de San Francisco: 324
Iglesia de San Juan Bautista (Grañon): 179
Iglesia de San Juan Bautista (La Portela de Valcarce): 330
Iglesia de San Juan Bautista (Obanos): 119–120
Iglesia de San Juan de los Caballeros: 220
Iglesia de San Juan (Fonfría): 341
Iglesia de San Juan (Portomarín): 370–371
Iglesia de San Juan (Sahagún): 239
Iglesia de San Lesmes: 203–204
Iglesia de San Lorenzo (Pamplona): 102–103
Iglesia de San Lorenzo (Sahagún): 239–240
Iglesia de San Marcos and museum (León): 269
Iglesia de San Marcos de Cadeira: 441–442
Iglesia de San Martín (Atapuerca village): 189
Iglesia de San Martín de Tours: 225, 321
Iglesia de San Martín (Frómista): 133, 196
Iglesia de San Martín (Villarmentero de Campos): 228
Iglesia de San Miguel (Cizur Menor): 114, 115
Iglesia de San Miguel (El Acebo): 302
Iglesia de San Miguel (Estella): 131–132
Iglesia de San Nicolas de Bari (Burgos): 204–205
Iglesia de San Nicolás de Bari (Burguete): 81
Iglesia de San Nicolás de Barí (Larrasoaña): 86
Iglesia de San Nicolás de Barí (Molinaseca): 305

Iglesia de San Nicolás de Barí (San Juan de la Ortega): 14, 147, 187–188
Iglesia de San Nicolas la Real: 324
Iglesia de San Nicolás (Pamplona): 104
Iglesia de San Nicolás (Portomarín): 370–371
Iglesia de San Oxan: 340
Iglesia de San Pedro (Belorado): 182
Iglesia de San Pedro de la Rúa (Estella): 95, 130–131, 139–140
Iglesia de San Pedro de Rectiva: 289–290, 293
Iglesia de San Pedro (Frómista): 225
Iglesia de San Pedro (Melide): 383
Iglesia de San Pedro (Portomarín): 371–372
Iglesia de San Pedro (Puente la Reina): 123, 133
Iglesia de San Pedro (Terradillos de los Templarios): 235
Iglesia de San Román: 125
Iglesia de San Salvador (Lorca): 126
Iglesia de San Salvador (Sarria): 359
Iglesia de San Saturnino (Pamplona): 101–102
Iglesia de San Saturnino (Ventosa): 167
Iglesia de Santa Águeda: 206
Iglesia de Santa Ana: 260
Iglesia de Santa Catalina: 125
Iglesia de Santa Eulalia (Cardeñuela Riopico): 189
Iglesia de Santa Eulalia (Dumbría): 454
Iglesia de Santa María (Belorado): 182
Iglesia de Santa María (Cacabelos): 318, 319
Iglesia de Santa María de Arenas: 447–448
Iglesia de Santa María de la Asunción: 317
Iglesia de Santa María del Camino (Carrión de los Condes): 231
Iglesia de Santa María del Camino (or Iglesia de Santa María del Mercado) (León): 264
Iglesia de Santa María del Castillo: 225
Iglesia de Santa María de los Arcos: 133, 138
Iglesia de Santa María del Palacio: 151, 153
Iglesia de Santa María del Sar: 399, 415–416
Iglesia de Santa María de Maroñas: 438
Iglesia de Santa María de Montán: 348
Iglesia de Santa María de Muxía: 459
Iglesia de Santa María de Salomé: 413–414
Iglesia de Santa María de Vizbayo: 312
Iglesia de Santa María de Xunquiera: 440, 441
Iglesia de Santa María (Ferreiros): 368
Iglesia de Santa María la Blanca: 196, 228–230
Iglesia de Santa María la Magdalena (Población de Campos): 227
Iglesia de Santa María la Real: 336
Iglesia de Santa María (Leboreiro): 353, 381
Iglesia de Santa María Magdalena (Castrillo de los Polvazares): 295
Iglesia de Santa María (Mansilla de las Mulas): 249
Iglesia de Santa María (Melide): 353, 386–387

Iglesia de Santa María (Santa Catalina de Somoza): 296
Iglesia de Santa María (Viana): 141
Iglesia de Santa Marina (Rabé de las Calzadas): 214
Iglesia de Santa Marina (Sarria): 358–359
Iglesia de Santa Susana: 414
Iglesia de Santiago (Arzúa): 389
Iglesia de Santiago (Barbadelo): 353, 365–366
Iglesia de Santiago (Carrión de los Condes): 231–232
Iglesia de Santiago de Olveiroa: 438–439
Iglesia de Santiago (Ledigos): 235
Iglesia de Santiago (Padrón): 426–427
Iglesia de Santiago (Puente la Reina): 121–122
Iglesia de Santiago Real: 156–158
Iglesia de Santiago (Triacastela): 344
Iglesia de Santiago (Valcarlos): 70
Iglesia de Santiago (Villafranca del Bierzo): 322–324
Iglesia de San Tirso: 241, 377–378
Iglesia de Santo Tomás: 236
Iglesia de Santo Tomás de las Ollas: 310–312
Iglesia de San Xil: 347
Iglesia de San Xoán: 381–382
Iglesia de San Xulián: 379
Iglesia San Julián de Moraime: 431, 435, 456–457
Iglesia Santa Gadea: 206
Igrexa de Castromaior: 373
Igrexia de Santa María das Areas: 447–448
Illaratz: 86
immigrants monument: 444
insurance: 477
Itero de la Vega: 222
itineraries: 27—45; Basque Country and Navarra 27–29, 51–52; by bike 484; Castile and León 32–37, 198; driving/road trip 483; Finisterre and Muxía 44–45, 432–433; Galicia 40, 42–43, 354–355; La Rioja and Castile 31–32, 148; León and Galicia 37–40, 257–258; Navarra 29–31, 96–97; Santiago de Compostela 44, 401

JKL

Jardín de la Sinagoga: 287
jet-stone jewelry: 409, 416–417
jousting tournament: 280, 281
kilometer 0: at Finisterre 435, 444, 448; in Santiago de Compostela 398, 402, 404
La Casa de los Dioses: 282–283
La Colegiata de Roncesvalles: 75
Ladera del Castillo: 309
La Faba mountain: 41, 256
La Faba village: 332–333
Laguardia: 159–160, 466
Laguna de Castilla: 333

lamiñaks: 73, 380
Lancía archaeological site: 250–251
language: 496
La Perla hotel: 103
La Portela de Valcarce: 329–330
La Rioja and Castile: 145–191; general discussion 148–151; food 154–155; itineraries 31–32, 148; maps 3, 146; overnight stops 148; transportation 149, 151; wine 147, 148, 153, 155, 158, 159–160; see also Castile and León
Larrasoaña: 86
Las Ánimas: 219
Las Herrerías: 332
Lastires: 345
La Tejada (Roman villa): 234
Lavacolla: 392, 393–394
Leboreiro: 380–381
Ledigos: 235
León and Galicia: 253–349; general discussion 257–260; itineraries 37–40, 257–258; maps 2, 254–255; overnight stops 257, 318; transportation 258–260; see also Castile and León; Galicia
León (city): 251, 260–275; accommodation 272–273; festivals 34, 270, 494; food and wine 266–267; map 261; markets 258, 264, 270; nightlife 12, 256, 271–272; sights 260–270; transportation 203, 273–274
LGBTQ+ travelers: 499
light and rebirth: 187, 456
Ligonde: 376
Liñares: 339–340
Lires: 462–463
Lires de San Esteve: 462
Little Fox House: 461
Logroño: 143, 151–165; accommodation 163; festivals and events 30, 158–159; map 152; markets 149, 155, 158, 159; sights 151–158; transportation 164; wine and food 12, 147, 154–155, 158, 159–162
Lonxa de Fisterra: 431, 444
Lorca: 126–127
Los Ancares: 322
Los Arcos: 97, 138–139
Lowe, Arthur: 347

M

Maestro Mateo: 406, 408, 409, 415
Maide: 73
Maindi: 73
Maju (or Sugaar): 73
mamoas: 382
Mañeru: 123
Manjarín: 301–302
Mansilla de las Mulas: 245, 248–250

Maragatería and Maragatos: 284–285, 287, 294
Mari: 73, 74, 380
markets: Basque Country and Navarra 54; Castile and León 196, 198, 209–210, 231, 248; Finisterre and Muxía 434, 435, 438, 441, 451, 459; Galicia 355, 360, 384–385, 389; La Rioja and Castile 30, 149, 155, 158, 159, 166, 170, 177, 178, 182; León and Galicia 258, 262, 285, 308, 319, 322; Navarra 98, 101, 121, 128, 138, 141; Santiago de Compostela 399, 402, 411, 420, 426; *see also* specific markets/*mercados*
Martel, Charles: 468
Martinez de Paz, Tomás: 301
Martín Sarmiento: 451
mass: Basque Country and Navarra 59, 67, 76, 81, 85, 91; Castile and León 203, 221, 233, 239, 241, 249; Finisterre and Muxía 441; Galicia 371, 391; La Rioja and Castile 154, 158, 188; León and Galicia 264, 265, 298, 302, 310, 336, 344, 345; Navarra 100, 102, 103, 122, 123, 131, 132, 138, 141; Santiago de Compostela 418; *see also* Vespers
Medel, Felisa Rodríguez, and Maria: 143
medical assistance: 491–492
Medieval era: 467–470
Medieval festival: 34
meigas: 380
Melide: 30, 353, 382–387; map 382
menú del peregrino: 375–376, 488–489
Mercado de Abastos del Conde Luna: 264
Mercado de Abastos (Logroño): 155
Mercado de Abastos (Santiago de Compostela): 399, 411, 420
Mercado de San Blas: 155
Mercado de Santo Domingo: 101
Mercadoiro: 368–369
meseta: 197, 199, 221, 222
messenger spirits (souls of the dead): 262
Milky Way viewing: 21, 160, 189, 222, 296, 302
milladoiros: 391
Misterio de Obanos, El: 34, 120
Modern era: 471–472
Molinaseca: 303, 305–307; map 306
Monasterio de Irache: 134, 135–136
Monasterio de las Huelgas: 208–209
Monasterío de San Facundo y San Primitivo: 241, 242
Monasterio de San Felices de Oca: 183
Monasterio de San Juan: 203–204
Monasterio de San Julián de Samos: 345–346
Monasterio de San Martín Pinario: 409
Monasterio de Santa Clara: 231
Monasterio de Santa Cruz: 241
Monasterio de Santa María la Real de las Huelgas: 208–209

Monasterio de Santa María la Real (Nájera): 147, 169–170
Monasterio de Santa María Magdalena: 360
Monasterio de Santo Domingo de Bonaval: 412–413
Monasterio de San Zoilo: 232
Monasterio de Suso: 172, 173
Monasterio de Yuso: 172–173
money: 496–498
Montán: 348–349
Monte Corpiño: 459
Monte del Gozo: 41, 394–395, 472
Monte Facho de Lourido: 461, 462, 463
Monte Facho (Finisterre): 449, 450, 451
Monte Irago: 17, 41, 299–300
Monte Pindo: 449, 451
Monte San Guillerme: 449, 451
Monte Santiaguiño: 427
Montes de Oca: 180
Monte Teleno: 294, 296–297
Monumento al Peregrino: 116
Monumento de los Caídos: 186
Monumento Peregrino: 306
Moraime: 456–457
moras: 219
Moratinos: 236–237
Morgade: 368
Morpeguite: 461
Morquintián: 463
Moses ben Sem Tov de León: 260
mother goddess: 160, 184, 440
mountain views: 41, 137, 333
moura: 380
Mozárabe style: 469
Mudéjar architecture: 469; Castile and León 196, 205, 206, 209, 220, 228, 232, 235, 237, 241, 242, 324; La Rioja and Castile 182; León and Galicia 260; Navarra 121, 125, 130, 132; Santiago de Compostela 411
Murias de Rechivaldo: 294
Muruzábal: 116
MUSAC (Museo de Arte Contemporaneo de Castilla y León): 269–270
Museo Arqueológico: 319
Museo Catedral (Santiago de Compostela): 408
Museo de Burgos: 208
Museo de Catedral (Astorga): 289
Museo de Chocolate: 288
Museo de la Colegiata de Santa María: 76–77
Museo de la Evolución Humana (Museum of Human Evolution): 188, 196, 206–208, 209
Museo de la Plaza de Toros: 104
Museo del Arte Sacro: 232
Museo de las Peregrinaciones y de Santiago: 399, 412, 413

Museo del Bierzo: 310
Museo del Catedral (Pamplona): 100–101
Museo de León: 268
Museo del Mar: 444, 447
Museo de los Caminos: 289
Museo de Navarra: 102
Museo de Santa Clara: 231
Museo de Santa Cruz: 241
Museo Diocesano: 265
Museo do Pobo Galego: 412–413, 437
Museo Etnográfico Provincial de León: 249
Museo-Panteón de San Isidoro: 269
Museo Romano: 285, 286–287
Museo Terra de Melide: 382, 384
music: 423–424
Muxía: 34, 432, 435, 457–461; to Finisterre 431,
    432, 435, 461, 462–463; from Hospital 439,
    454–457
Muxiana: 432, 457, 486

N

Nájera: 30, 168–172; map 169
Navarete/Navarrete: 165–166
Navarra: 93–143; general discussion 96–97;
    itineraries 29–31, 96–97; maps 3, 94; markets
    98; overnight stops 96; transportation 98; see
    also Basque Country and Navarra
Negreira: 437–438
Neolithic: 466
Neptune's pillar: 426–427
1993 Holy Year Monument: 394
noche de los difuntos (night of the dead): 262
Nuestra Señora de la Leche (Santiago de
    Compostela): 414
Nuestra Señora de la Leche (Santo Domingo de
    la Calzada): 176
Nuestra Señora de la Misercordia: 102
Nuestra Señora de la Plaza: 174, 176, 177
Nuestra Señora del Ebro: 153
Nuestra Señora del Perdón: 116
Nuestra Señora del Poyo: 140
Nuestra Señora del Puy: 122–123, 132
Nuestra Señora de Oca: 184
Nuestra Señora de Perales: 245
Nuestra Señora de Roncesvalles: 74, 76

O

oak trees: 297, 376
Obanos: 34, 117, 119–120
O Cebreiro: 41, 333–339; map 334; sunset and
    sunrise 18–19, 256, 334, 336
O Empalme: 390–391
Oficina Acogida al Peregrino (Pilgrims'
    Reception Office): 402, 407, 417
O Logoso: 439

Olveiroa: 438–439
Ondarolle: 68
O Pedrouzo: 391–392
original icon of Mary: 381
Orisson: 65, 66
orujo: 267, 359, 372, 387
Os Ancares cheese festival: 338, 494
Our Lady of Puy: 132
Our Lady of the Snows (las Nieves): 347
overnight stops: Basque Country and Navarra
    50; Castile and León 197; Finisterre and Muxía
    433; Galicia 354; La Rioja and Castile 148; León
    and Galicia 257, 318; Navarra 96

P

packing tips: 476, 478–479
pack transfer services: 501
Padornelo: 340–341
Padrón: 425–427
pagan symbols and rituals: 133, 187, 220, 300,
    366, 376, 398, 413, 427, 456
Palacio de Gelmírez: 404, 411
Palacio de los Reyes de Navarra: 130
Palacio Episcopal: 288
Palas de Rei: 30, 377–379
Paleolithic Era: 466
palloza: 336–337
Pamplona: 91, 98–114; festivals 105; map
    99; markets 98, 101; sights 100–105;
    transportation 112–113
panhandling: 354, 365
Pantano de la Cañas: 143
paradores: 488
Parque de Espolón: 158
Parque de la Alameda: 322
Parque de la Taconera: 114
Parque Grajera: 165
paseo: 490
Paseo Marítimo: 440, 441
passport for pilgrims. see credentials
patxaran: 53, 83
Pazo de Cotón de Mauro: 437
pedra dos cadrís ("kidney rock"): 458–459
pedra dos namorados (lovers' stone): 458
pedra do temón (rudder stone): 458
pedras de abalar (oscillating stones): 450,
    458, 459
Pedras Sagradas: 214
Pelayo: 403, 415, 468
pensiones: 487
Peregrina, La (statue): 242
peregrinos: see pilgrims
Pereje: 327
Peruscallo: 367
petroglifo de Castriño de Conxo: 399, 415, 416, 466

pharmacies: 492
phones and calls: 498
phrasebook: 505–506
Picaud, Aimery: 72, 470
Pic D'Orisson: 65, 66
Pico Sacro: 394
Pidre: 377
piedras sagradas/santas (sacred stones): 403, 449–450
Pieros: 320–322
Pilgrim Memorial Grove: 293
Pilgrim's Guide to Santiago de Compostela, The: 470, 472
pilgrims' hostel/dorms. see albergues
pilgrims (peregrino): archaeological artifacts 412; associations 500–501; beginnings on Camino 404; blessing 76, 371; credentials 24, 58, 417, 444, 485–486; diversity 474; etiquette 490–491; experience on Camino 9; menu 375–376, 488–489; monument to 116; supply stores 501–502
Pilgrims' Reception Office (Oficina Acogida al Peregrino): 402, 407, 417
Pilgrims' Welcome Office (Accueil des Pèlerins): 25, 27, 58, 59, 61, 501
pintxos/pinchos: 12, 78, 110
planning tips: general discussion 22–26, 476–477, 478–479, 491, 496–498; Basque Country and Navarra 50–51; Burgos to León 197–198; Finisterre and Muxía 432–433; Galicia 354–356; La Rioja and Castile 148; León and Galicia 257–258; Navarra 96–97; Santiago de Compostela 401
plateros (silversmiths): 408
Playa de Concha: 440
Plaza Consistorial (Pamplona): 101, 106
Plaza de España (Astorga): 287
Plaza de las Platerías (Santiago de Compostela): 409
Plaza del Castillo (Pamplona): 103, 104
Plaza del Grano (León): 264
Plaza de Obradoiro (Praza do Obradoiro): 398, 401, 402, 404, 409, 411, 418
Plaza de Santiago (Logroño): 156–157
Plaza de Toros (Pamplona): 103, 104, 106, 107
Plaza Virgen de la Encina (Ponferrada): 309, 310
Población de Campos: 227
police: 498
Ponferrada: 307–315, 469; map 308
Pons Ferrada bridge: 315
Ponte Aspera: 365
Pontemaceira: 436–437
Ponte Maceira: 436–437
Ponte Olveira: 438
Pope John Paul II: 394, 472

Portal de Castilla: 139
Portal de Francia/Franca: 91, 100
Porte de France: 57
Porte de l'Echaugette: 58
Porte de Notre Dame: 59
Porte de Saint Jacques (Saint James's Gate): 58
Porte d'Espagne: 59–60
Pórtico de la Gloria: 406–407
Portomarín: 30, 353, 369–373; map 370
Posadas del Camino association: 87–88, 488
Poyo de Roldán: 168
pozo de Indalecio, el (well of Indalecio): 184
Praia da Langosteira: 431, 443
Praia de Mar de Fóra: 447
Praia do Rostro: 462
Praia (Playa) de Santa Isabel: 441
Praza do Obradoiro (Plaza de Obradoiro): 398, 401, 402, 404, 409, 411, 418
public fountains: 488
public holidays: 493
Puente Canto (Agès): 188
Puente Canto (Sahagún): 239
Puente de Itero: 222
Puente de la Rabia: 85
Puente de los Peregrinos: 305
Puente del Paso Honroso: 17, 256, 280
Puente de Piedra: 151
Puente de San Pablo: 204
Puente de San Xoán: 381
Puente la Reina: 121–124; map 122
Puente Magdalena: 91, 98
Puente Villarente: 250, 251
Puerta de la Azabachería (north): 409
Puerta de las Platerías (south): 408–409
Puerta del Perdón (León): 268
Puerta del Perdón (Villafranca del Bierzo): 322–323
Puerta de Obradoiro (west): 404, 406
Puerta de Perdón (east): 409
Puerta de San Juan: 204
Puerta de San Martin: 206
Puerta Moneda: 260, 262
Puerto de Ibañeta: 12, 41, 49, 67, 72, 74
pulperías in Melide: 353, 382, 385

QR

queimada ritual: 20, 387
Quintáns: 456
Rabanal del Camino: 297–299
Rabé de las Calzadas: 214
Ramil de Triacastela: 343
rebirth and light: 187, 456
Redecilla del Camino: 180
redemption of sins: 323

Reina de los Pirineos, La (Nuestra Señora de Roncesvalles): 74, 76
Reliegos: 245, 248
Reñubero: 219
restaurants: see food, specific place
restrooms on trail: 490
Ribadiso da Baixo: 388
Riego de Ambros: 303, 305
Rioja. see La Rioja and Castile
Rioja Like a Native: 159
Rioja Wine Culture Centre: 159
rituals on Camino de Santiago: 393, 443, 449
Roble del Peregrino: 297
Roland: 67, 72, 78, 130
Roland's Cross (La Cruz Blanca): 80
Rollo de Boadilla: 223
Roman road and bridge: 13, 95, 125–126, 467
Roman ruins, remains, and architecture: 138, 234, 250, 262, 268, 285–286, 436, 437, 467
Romería de la Virgen del Puente pilgrimage (romería del pan y queso): 30, 242
romería honoring the Virxe da Barca: 459
Roncesvalles: 54, 65, 74–80; map 75
Rosa del Camino de Santiago: 113, 114, 143
rose window: 442
Route Napoleon: 51–53, 64–67
Route Valcarlos: 51–53, 54, 64, 67–74
Rue de la Citadelle: 11, 49, 59
Ruinas Iglesia de San Pedro: 141–142
running of the bulls (el encierro): 34, 101, 105, 106–107

S
sacred numbers: 117, 119, 311
sacred trees: 343
safety on trail: 491–493, 498
Sahagún: 30, 34, 196, 198, 238–245; map 239
Saint Anthony's Fire: 217
Saint James (Santiago): in Catedral de Santiago de Compostela 403, 404, 406, 468, 469; image 121–122, 158, 316; life and history 403, 468; magical boat 403, 425, 426; mural 316; sculpture 157–158, 306, 340; tomb 403, 404, 407, 468
Saint James's feast day (Festival de Santiago): 34, 401, 418
Saint-Jean-Pied-de-Port: 25, 55–64; accommodation 61–62; as departure point 27, 50, 54, 58; food 60–61; map 64; market 54; sights 56–60; transportation 62–64, 79
Saint John the Baptist: 187, 456
Saint Sernin (San Saturnino): 102, 106
Salceda: 390
Sambol: 215
Samos: 345–346

Sampedro, Elías Valiño: 472
San Antón Abad hospital: 184
San Antón (Abad) Monastery Ruins: 15, 196, 217
San Bartolome church: 245
San Baudillo monastery: 215
San Cristovo/Cristobo do Real: 345
Sanctuario de Nuestra Señora de Fatima: 287
San Esteban church: 339–340
San Fermín cult and festivals: 102–103, 105, 106, 107
Sanfermines, Los: 34, 101, 105, 106–107
San Guillerme (Saint William): 451
San Guillermo: 119, 120
San Guillermo's feast day: 120, 494
San Juan de la Ortega (engineer): 186, 187, 188
San Juan de la Ortega (village): 186–188
San Justo de la Vega: 283–284
San Lázaro neighborhood: 395
San Mamede del Camino: 349
San Martín del Camino: 279
San Martiño de Duio: 462
San Miguel de Escalada church: 250
San Millán de la Cogolla: 172–173
San Nicolás de Bari church (San Nicolás del Camino Real): 237
San Paio: 392
San Pedro church: 180
San Román church: 215
San Roque shrine: 245
San Roque village: 443
San Salvador hamlet: 462
San Saturnino (Saint Sernin): 102, 106
Sansol: 139
Santa Campaña: 380
Santa Catalina de Somoza: 294, 296–297
Santa Eulalia de Arca church: 391
Santa Irene church: 391
Santa Irene village: 391
Santa María church (Boadilla del Camino): 223
Santa María church (Morquintián): 463
Santa Maria das Areas: 448
Santa María das Areas festival: 451
Santa María de Eunate ("Church of 100 Doors"): 13, 95, 116, 117, 119, 139, 311
Santa María de las Huertas: 121
Santa María la Real festival: 170
Santa Marina church (Arleta): 91
Santa Mariña (village): 438
Santiago. see Saint James
Santiago de Compostela: 395, 397–427, 436; general discussion 398, 401–402; accommodation 417, 424–425; day trips 425–427, 434; festivals and events 34, 401, 418; food 418–422; history and etymology 415; to Hospital 434, 436–439; itineraries 44,

401; kilometer 0 398, 402, 404; maps 398, 400; markets 402, 411, 426; nightlife 422–424; services to pilgrims 417; shopping 416–418; sights 402–416; transportation 401–402
Santiago Matamoros (Saint James the Moorslayer): 157
Santiago's Altar: 407
Santiago's Relics Crypt: 407–408
Santibanez de Valdeiglesias: 282
San Tirso's festival: 378
Santo Cristo da Barba Dourada: 447–448
Santo Domingo de la Calzada (engineer): 174, 175, 176, 177, 181
Santo Domingo de la Calzada (town): 30, 174–179; map 175
Santuario da Virxe da Barca: 21, 41, 431, 435, 458–459
Santuario Virgen de la Peregrina: 196, 241–242
San Xil: 345, 347–348
San Xulián do Camino: 379–380
San Zoilo: 139
Sardiñeiro: 443
Sarela de Abaixo: 436
Sarria: 349, 357–365; accommodation 362–363; festivals and events 30, 34, 360, 362; map 360; market 355, 360, 362; sights 357–360; transportation 363, 365
scallop shells: 25, 58, 161, 404
scams: 365
Semana Santa (Holy Week): 34, 270, 494
senior travelers: 499–500
shuttle: 55, 63, 79, 80, 98, 112
Sierra de Atapuerca: 148, 188, 189, 208
siesta: 490
Sima del Elefante (Elephant Pit): 208
singing nuns of Santa María: 15, 196, 231, 233
solar alignment: 187, 188
solo trekkers: 498
Soul Garden: 299
spa: 292
Spanish Civil War: 472
Spanish glossary and phrasebook: 502–506
stamps for certificate of completion: 357, 486
starting points for Camino: 54, 59, 199, 477
stonemasons: 119, 404
stones at Cruz de Ferro: 17, 25, 256, 257, 300–301
stones at Finisterre and Muxía: 403, 449–450, 458–459
strategic advice for walking the Camino: see planning tips; see also specific region
Sugaar (or Maju): 73
Sun altar (Ara Solis): 449, 451
sunset and sunrise: Finisterre and Muxía 449, 457, 459; O Cebreiro 18–19, 256, 334, 336
supply stores for trekkers: 501–502
swimming, in Finisterre: 443, 447

T
tapas: 12; see also food
tapita: 271
Tardajos: 213–214
Tau cross: 161, 217
taxi: 481
Teiguin: 346
Templar Knights: 229, 235, 301, 308–309, 387, 469
Teodoro: 407, 409
Terradillos de los Templarios: 235–236
tetilla cheese: 358, 406, 421–422
tetraskele: 413
Theodomir (bishop): 403
thistle: 57
ticks: 492–493
tipping: 489–490
toilets (on trail): 490
top experiences: 10–21
Torre del Reloj (clock tower): 310
Torres del Río: 139–140
Tosantos: 182, 183
Trabadelo: 327, 329
Trabadelo's Ancient Chestnut Forest: 256, 327
trail conditions: 485
train: 480
training for trek: 476–477
transportation: general discussion 477–485; Basque Country and Navarra 54–55; Castile and León 199–201; Finisterre and Muxía 434; Galicia 356–357; La Rioja and Castile 149, 151; León and Galicia 258–260; Navarra 98; Santiago de Compostela 401–402; see also specific places
Trasgos: 380
trasgo/trasgu: 219
Trasufre: 455
travelers of color: 499
travel insurance: 477
Tree of Jesse: 406
trekking equipment and pack: 476, 478–479, 501–502
Triacastela: 342, 343–345
Trinidad de Arre: 91
Turpin Chronicle: 470
tympanums: 359, 365–366, 371, 381, 456

UV
Uterga: 116
Vaca Blanca, La: 262
Valcarlos: 68, 70–71
Valiña Sampedro, Elías: 336
Valtuille de Arriba: 321
Valverde de la Virgen: 276, 277–278
Varela, Maria: 377
Vega de Valcarce: 330–332

Ventas de Narón: 375
Ventas shopping complex: 68
Ventosa (Galicia): 436
Ventosa (La Rioja): 166–168
vermouth: 201
Vespers: Castile and León 221, 233, 241, 249; Finisterre and Muxía 441; La Rioja and Castile 178; León and Galicia 298, 305, 345; Navarra 119
Via de la Plata: 283–284
Viana: 140–143
Via Romana (or Via Traiana/Trajana or Calzada Romana): 64, 198, 244, 245, 248
Vidal, David: 283
Vierge de Biakorri (Vierge d'Orisson): 65, 66–67
Vieux Pont des Pèlerins (Old Pilgrims' Bridge): 59
Vigo de Sarria: 349
Vilachá: 369
Vilar: 443
Villadangos del Páramo: 278–279
Villafranca del Bierzo: 322–327; map 323
Villafranca de Oca: 184
Villafranca Montes de Oca: 183–186
Villafria: 191
Villalcázar de Sirga: 228–230
Villamayor del Río: 181
Villamayor de Monjardín: 136–138
Villambistia: 183
Villamoros de Mansilla: 250
Villaoreja monastery: 236
Villar de Mazarife: 276–277
Villares de Órbigo: 282
Villarmentero de Campos: 227–228
Villatuerta: 127
Villavante: 277
Viloria de Rioja: 181
Virgen Blanca, La (La Blanca Madonna or Santa María la Blanca): 228–229
Virgen de Junquera: 441
Virgen de la Acogida, La: 225
Virgen del Camino, La: 275–276

Virgen del Camino statue: 102
Virgen del Milagro, La: 336
Virgen del Sagrario: 100
Virgen del Txori, La: 123
Virgen de Socorro: 447
Virgen de Valvanera, La: 158
Virxe da Barca festival: 34, 459
visas: 477
Viscarreta (Biskarreta): 83, 85
volunteering: 236
Vuelta del Castillo park: 105

WXYZ

walking distances and time: general discussion 26, 27, 476; Basque Country and Navarra 50; Castile and León 197–198; Finisterre and Muxía 432; Galicia 354; La Rioja and Castile 148; León and Galicia 257; Navarra 96
Way, The (movie): 62, 79, 87, 105, 115, 269, 472
weather: Basque Country and Navarra 53–54; Castile and León 199; Finisterre and Muxía 434; Galicia 355–356; León and Galicia 258; Navarra 97
wifi: 50, 58, 498
wildlife-watching: 197
wine/wineries: Basque Country and Navarra 53; Castile and León 200–201; festivals 30; Galicia 359; La Rioja and Castile 147, 148, 153, 155, 158, 159–160; León and Galicia 267, 317, 318, 320, 321–322; wine fountain 13, 25, 95, 134–135
women trekkers: 498
World Tree (axis mundi): 301, 376
xanas: 380
Xan López Palloza-Museo: 337
Yacimiento Arqueológico de Lancia: 250–251
Yacimientos de Atapuerca: 208–209
Zabaldika: 88–89
Zaragoza: 403
Zariquiegui: 115–116
Zubiri: 85–86

LIST OF MAPS

Front Map
Camino de Santiago: 2-3

Basque Country and Navarra
Basque Country and Navarra: 48
Saint-Jean-Pied-de-Port: 56
Roncesvalles: 75

Navarra
Navarra: 94
Pamplona: 99
Puente la Reina: 122
Estella: 129

La Rioja and Castile
La Rioja and Castile: 146
Logroño: 152
Nájera: 169
Santo Domingo de la Calzada: 175

Castile and León
Burgos to Carrión de los Condes: 194
Carrión de los Condes to León: 195
Burgos: 202
Castrojeriz: 218
Carrion de los Condes: 232
Sahagún: 239

León and Galicia
León to Ponferrada: 254
Ponferrada to Sarria: 255
León: 261
Astorga: 285
Molinaseca: 306
Ponferrada: 308
Villafranca del Bierzo: 323
O Cebreiro: 334

Galicia
Sarria to Santiago de Compostela: 352
Sarria: 360
Portomarín: 370
Melide: 382

Santiago de Compostela
Santiago de Compostela: 398
Santiago de Composela (Center): 400

Camino Finisterre
Camino Finisterre: 430
Finisterre: 446

PHOTO CREDITS

MAP SYMBOLS

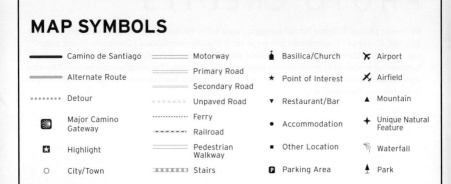

▬▬ Camino de Santiago	═══ Motorway	⌂ Basilica/Church	✈ Airport
▬▬ Alternate Route	═══ Primary Road	★ Point of Interest	✈ Airfield
	═══ Secondary Road		
••••••• Detour	------- Unpaved Road	▼ Restaurant/Bar	▲ Mountain
Major Camino Gateway	•••••••• Ferry	• Accommodation	✦ Unique Natural Feature
Highlight	▬▬▬ Railroad	■ Other Location	Waterfall
	═══ Pedestrian Walkway		
○ City/Town	▭▭▭▭ Stairs	P Parking Area	▲ Park

CONVERSION TABLES

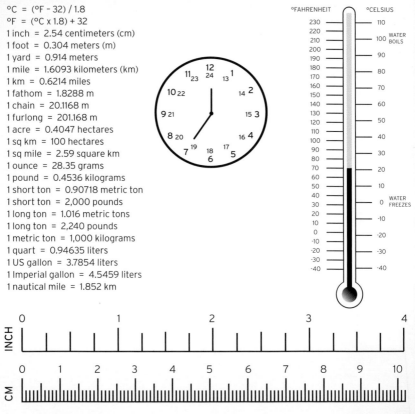

°C = (°F - 32) / 1.8
°F = (°C x 1.8) + 32
1 inch = 2.54 centimeters (cm)
1 foot = 0.304 meters (m)
1 yard = 0.914 meters
1 mile = 1.6093 kilometers (km)
1 km = 0.6214 miles
1 fathom = 1.8288 m
1 chain = 20.1168 m
1 furlong = 201.168 m
1 acre = 0.4047 hectares
1 sq km = 100 hectares
1 sq mile = 2.59 square km
1 ounce = 28.35 grams
1 pound = 0.4536 kilograms
1 short ton = 0.90718 metric ton
1 short ton = 2,000 pounds
1 long ton = 1.016 metric tons
1 long ton = 2,240 pounds
1 metric ton = 1,000 kilograms
1 quart = 0.94635 liters
1 US gallon = 3.7854 liters
1 Imperial gallon = 4.5459 liters
1 nautical mile = 1.852 km

Stunning Sights Around the World

Guides for Urban Adventure

MOON
NEW ENGLAND
Road Trip

BOSTON, ACADIA NATIONAL PARK, WHITE
MOUNTAINS, BERKSHIRES, NEWPORT, AND CAPE COD

JEN ROSE SMITH

MOON
PACIFIC NORTHWEST
Road Trip

SEATTLE, VANCOUVER, VICTORIA,
THE OLYMPIC PENINSULA, PORTLAND,
THE OREGON COAST & MOUNT RAINIER

ALLISON WILLIAMS

MOON
ROUTE 66
Road Trip

JESSICA DUNHAM

MOON
SOUTH FLORIDA & THE KEYS
Road Trip

WITH MIAMI, WALT DISNEY WORLD, TAMPA &
THE EVERGLADES

JASON FERGUSON

MOON
SOUTHWEST
Road Trip

LAS VEGAS, ZION & BRYCE, MONUMENT VALLEY,
SANTA FE & TAOS, AND THE GRAND CANYON

TIM HULL

MOON
VANCOUVER & CANADIAN ROCKIES
Road Trip

VICTORIA, BANFF, JASPER, CALGARY,
THE OKANAGAN, WHISTLER &
THE SEA-TO-SKY HIGHWAY

CAROLYN B. HELLER

Road Trip USA

Covering more than 35,000 miles of
blacktop stretching from east to west
and north to south, *Road Trip USA* takes
you deep into the heart of America.

This colorful guide covers the top road
trips including historic Route 66 and is
packed with maps, photos, illustrations,
mile-by-mile highlights, and more!

MOON NATIONAL PARKS

ACADIA NATIONAL PARK
HILARY NANGLE

ARCHES & CANYONLANDS NATIONAL PARKS
W. C. McRAE JUDY JEWELL

BANFF NATIONAL PARK
ANDREW HEMPSTEAD

DEATH VALLEY NATIONAL PARK
JENNA BLOUGH

GLACIER NATIONAL PARK
BECKY LOMAX

GRAND CANYON
KATHLEEN BRYANT

GREAT SMOKY MOUNTAINS NATIONAL PARK
JASON FRYE

MOUNT RUSHMORE & THE BLACK HILLS
including the Badlands
LAURAL A. BIDWELL

ROCKY MOUNTAIN NATIONAL PARK
ERIN ENGLISH

In these books:

- Full coverage of gateway cities and towns
- Itineraries from one day to multiple weeks
- Advice on where to stay (or camp) in and around the parks

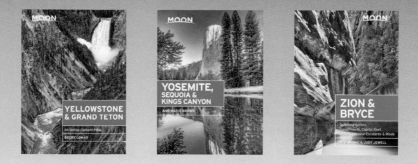

MOON CAMINO DE SANTIAGO
Avalon Travel
Hachette Book Group
1700 Fourth Street
Berkeley, CA 94710, USA
www.moon.com

Editor: Nikki Ioakimedes
Copy Editor: Chris Dumas
Graphics and Production Coordinator: Lucie Ericksen
Cover Design: Erin Seaward-Hiatt
Interior Design: Darren Alessi, Lucie Ericksen
Moon Logo: Tim McGrath
Map Editor: Kat Bennett
Cartographers: Lohnes + Wright, Kat Bennett
Indexer: François Trahan

ISBN-13: 978-1-64049-328-5

Printing History
1st Edition — April 2019
5 4 3 2 1